THE AUSTRALIAN ADVENTURE

ALLAN MOULT

Copyright © Australian Adventure Publications Pty Ltd 1987
First published 1987
Second Edition 1988

ISBN 0 7316 1991 9

Printed in Singapore by Tien Wah Press (Pte) Ltd.
Typeset by The Typeshop Pty. Limited, Sydney
Colour separations by Scanforce, Sydney

Australian Adventure Publications Pty Ltd
39 East Esplanade
Manly NSW 2095 Australia
Tel: (02) 977 3377
Tlx: AA 74473 IMR
Fax: (02) 977 5157

THE AUSTRALIAN ADVENTURE

The Explorer's Guide to the Island Continent

PHILLIP QUIRK

ADVENTURE
PUBLICATIONS

THE AUSTRALIAN ADVENTURE

Publishers and Editorial Directors:
Stephen Smith and John Keeney
Editor-in-Chief:
Oliver Freeman
Executive Editors:
Tim Griggs and John Sexton
Associate Publishers:
**Michael Z. Soker, John Wilson
and Mark Fallon**
Product Development:
Prospect Publishing, Sydney
Design and Art Director:
Ken Gilroy
Art:
Sue Edmonds
Photographic Editor:
Allan Moult
Senior Research Editor:
Anne Matthews
Researchers:
Isobel King, Patsy Irwin and Petra Playfair
Editor and Production Manager:
Robyn Flemming
Production Co-ordinator:
David McGonigal
Production Consultant:
Noel Searle
Staff Writers and Editors:
**Saturday Brander, Simone Clarke,
Catherine Clifford, Nigel Dique,
Andrew Fisher, Oliver Freeman, Tim Griggs,
Gill Hewitt, Joy Jobbins, Isobel King,
Stephanie Lewis, Nick Lush, Anne Matthews,
Marc Rosenberg, Natalie Scott
and Stephen Smith**

Contributing Writers:
Geoff Atkinson, Captain Peter Cook, Noni Farwell,
Andrew Fisher, Lincoln Hall, Leigh Hemmings,
Peter Horrobin, Jennifer Isaacs,
Owen Johnstone-Donnet, John Keeney,
Christopher Leonard, Mungo MacCallum,
Craig McGregor, John McNally, Robert Mayne,
Allan Moult, Jan Oldham, Petra Playfair,
Wendy Richards, Natalie Scott, Vincent Serventy
and Peter Stone
Circulation Director:
Patrick Maloney

Special Assistants to the Publishers:
Megan Whitfield, Lisa Cara and Kerrie Lindsay
Assistants to the Editor-in-Chief:
Tessa Johnson, Katie White, Damian Archer
and Charlotte Steer
Assistants to the Executive Editors:
Gail Clarke, Denise Dodd and Jenny Hislop
Market Research:
Jeanne Strachan
Marketing Consultant:
John Singleton Advertising

Special Thanks:
Lima Foxtrot Delta, Jill Mullens, Diane Cilento,
Foxtrot Hotel, Peter Cook, Brian A. Beh, Alex Searle,
Pauline Clayton, Richard Beeman, Elizabeth Smith,
OPK and Marguerite, Audrey and Adam,
Michael Fallon, Tony Bracey, Susie Brew,
Mary Ann Szeps, Art Krieger, Chris Grosser,
John King, Roger Hook, Anthony Hill,
Annabel Birch, Kok Weng Chin, Judy Pyne,
Steve Colman, Tim Macartney-Snape, Agnes and Jason,
Nick Kilvington, Ric Williams, Warwick Deacock
Andrew Hunter and Espie
Maps:
Sue Edmonds, Otto & Chris
Photographic Consultants:
Horizon International
Wildlight Photo Agency
Photographers:
Philip Quirk, Trevern Dawes, Oliver Strewe,
Milton Wordley, David Simmonds, Douglass Baglin,
David McGonigal, Grenville Turner, Heidi Ecker,
Penny Tweedie, Bruce Usher, Barbara Hemmings,
Carleen Carroll, Carolyn Johns, Craig Marshall,
David Mahoney, Dennis Schultz, Gilbert Rossi,
Gunther Deichman, Jean-Paul Ferrerro,
Jennifer Isaacs, John McNally, John Everingham,
Julia Court, Kate Wimble, Kathy Shears, Ken Ross,
Kevin Diletti, Lance Nelson, Lee Pearce,
Leo Duyckers, Leigh Hemmings, Malcolm Holmes,
Margaret Olah, Mark Hanlon, Mark Steven,
Andrew Fisher, Michael Jensen, Michael Rayner,
Michael Langford, Mick Turner, Nick Brokensha,
Paul Simcock, Pat Manly, Pauline Clayton,
Peter Horrobin, Rob Rowe, Rob Walls,
Simon Cowling, Steve Liddell, Steve Lovegrove
and Stuart Fox

Publishers' Introduction

Of all the inhabitants of the planet, only mankind endures hardship and danger for the thrill of it. And the reason for this is man's sense of adventure. Our willingness to push beyond the known frontiers is what sets us apart.

For some, that frontier is a physical one, requiring ice-axe and piton to rise to the challenge posed by the physical landscape. For others, the adventure is cerebral, requiring a journey of the mind or the senses. In all cases, it involves striving, learning and experiencing, for their own sake.

This spirit of adventure has brought us a long way. And one place it has brought us to is Australia.

Australia is an adventurer's country. A vast continent still barely explored, it stretches from close to the equator almost to the Antarctic. It straddles several climatic zones and an extraordinary range of terrain: alpine snow country, tropical rainforest and harsh red desert. Its wildlife is bizarre and fascinating. And best of all, it is almost empty, which is good news for the outdoor adventurer.

Virtually all of the population lives in the six largest cities, making Australia one of the most urbanised societies on earth. And that means that there is much to offer the cerebral adventurer, too: architecture, botanic gardens, museums, galleries, the arts and a myriad of festivals.

The Australian Adventure suggests thousands of ways in which the adventurer can enjoy Australia. We have researched and selected Australia's finest adventures, and the book is designed to take you easily to the adventures or activities that interest you. A good number of these adventures are within a two-hour drive of the major towns and cities. Others are further afield along the coast and into the interior of this giant southern island.

The book contains over 500 photographs and more than 300,000 words of text written by Australia's finest writers and most ambitious travellers and explorers. We invite you to join them!

John Keeney & Stephen Smith

Contents

147
Features
Our editors travelled tens of thousands of kilometres to discover some remarkable people and places, and the grandeur of the land.

Contents

Contents

Contents

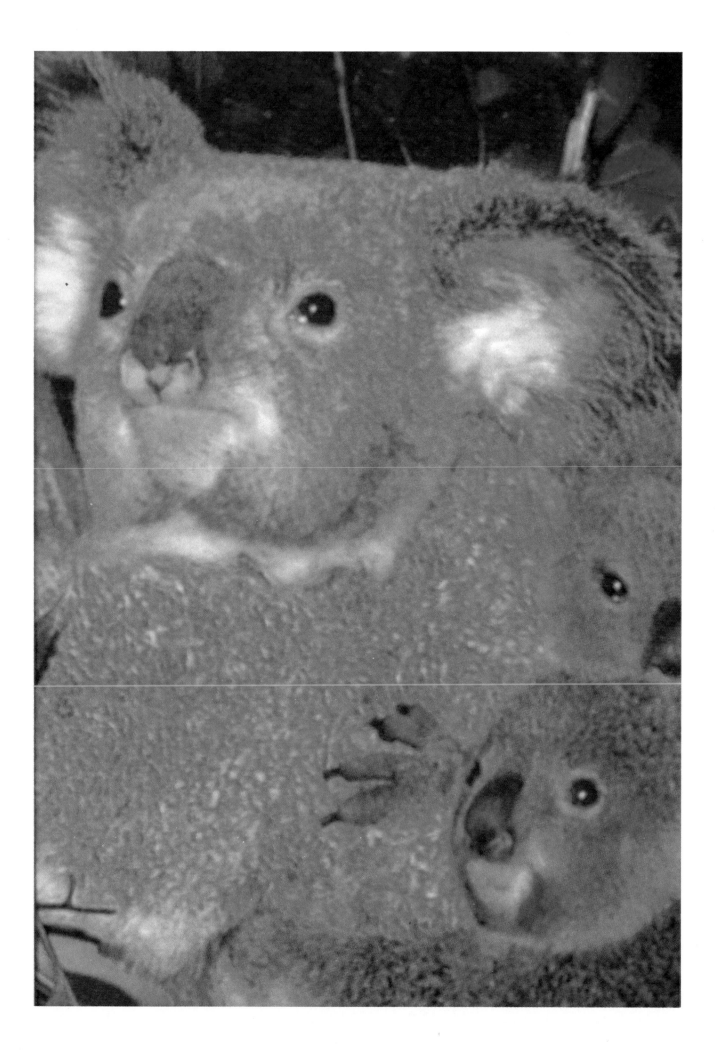

VISIONS
of AUSTRALIA

Soft plumes of smoke echo the stately white trunks of ghost gums in the wake of a fast-moving grass fire at Pine Creek, Northern Territory

The timeless landscape of Australia, legacy of aeons of geologi

nult and erosion, lives on in elegant natural splendour ...

TREVERN DAWES

JOHN MCNALLY

Rainbow Valley, left, lives up to its name as the late afternoon sun reflects off its cliffs. The Simpson Desert's rich hue, above, aptly indicates the origins of the fabled Red Centre

... ageless, but vibrant ...

Millions of years of erosion have left little of the original mountains which once dominated the Kings Canyon area, left, near Alice Springs. The mighty Olgas, above, which lie west of Ayers Rock, have better stood the test of time

... the Red Centre glows with history ...

ALLAN MOULT

*With broad wings outspread, a
spoonbill rides the endless thermals of
the desert country of the Gulf of
Carpentaria*

... wind, rain, floods, fire and volcanic eruptions - all have help

ALLAN MOULT

Huge sand dunes dominate large sections of the coastal plains of the Fitzgerald River National Park in southern Western Australia

ulpt the varied landscapes of this ancient island continent ...

Gum trees freckle the Snowy Mountains to provide a uniquely Australian winter landscape

... and winter brings its own bleak wilderness to the Sno

ALLAN MOULT

*Rugged terrain over thousands of square kilometres lures
many hundreds of cross country skiers to the Snowy
Mountains each winter*

ALLAN MOULT

ALLAN MOULT

ountains where a mantle of snow disguises a unique area ...

Lush vines carpet a clearing in a northern New South Wales rainforest

... diversity persists in the richest land-based ecosystems - t

A young fern slowly unfolds in the early stages of growth

eatened rainforests ...

The Australian Adventure

Far left, top to bottom: A rainbow lorikeet pauses for a drink; a Goulds island goanna holds his ground; grey kangaroos engage in a round of fisticuffs; and the ubiquitous galahs gather on a branch to plan their next feeding sortie. Left: A dingo, the native Australian wild dog surveys his domain at sunrise. Near left: A friendly possum stares out of the bush. Below: The gregarious Australian pelican certainly lives up to its scientific description - Pelecanus conspicullatus

PENNY TWEEDIE

JULIA COURT

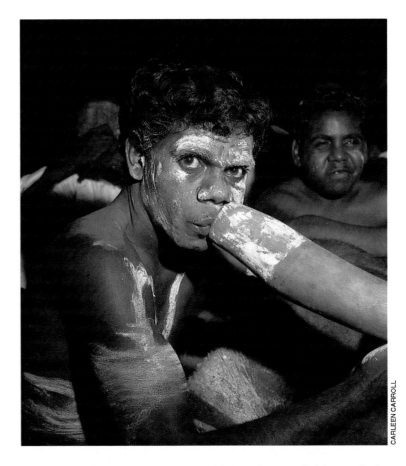

CARLEEN CARROLL

A young Aborigine plays the traditional didgeridoo - a primitive musical instrument not unlike a hollow pipe which provides an eerie, haunting tone that is never forgotten, especially when heard in the vast open spaces of the Outback

... a timeless land with a timeless people - the Aboriginals s

CARLEEN CARROLL

A young Aborigine paints himself with ochre in preparation for a traditional corroboree - a tribal meeting - which is often followed by a series of dances which enact tribal histories and episodes out of their fascinating Dreamtime legends

...in their remarkable traditional heritage of The Dreamtime ...

Elcho Island women proudly display their woven mats

DOUGLASS BAGLIN

... a link between the past and the present is reflected in the art

Australian Aboriginal art is keenly sought after by collectors worldwide. A painting by Binyinuwuy, left, is typical of recent art being produced in the Northern Territory, and Njiminuma children, above, show off classic bark paintings

Aboriginal peoples and the traditional motifs that dominate their work

Australia is a land of contrasts, and has since the beginning of time presented a harsh challenge which has always been met with gusto, a cheerful sense of adventure, and an ability to adapt. A hard life in the Outback is reflected in camel expert Noel Fullerton's face, opposite, while a Sydney teenager, above, breathes a sigh of relief after her first hardhat dive

... young and old alike share a spirit of adventure ....

PHILIP QUIRK

While dominated by a inhospitable interior, this vast island continent can often evoke poetic vistas as shown at the base of Ayers Rock, in the Northern Territory, right, in the mallee landscape of western Victoria, top, and the Brindabella Range, New South Wales, below

OLIVER STREWE

... between the arid interior and the coast lies a mellow

OLIVER STREWE

dscape which has been slowly tamed by settlement ...

A service helicopter takes off from a mammoth oil rig, above, sited in the wild waters of Bass Strait, south of Victoria. The setting sun also highlights the rugged Kiama coast south of Sydney, top right, the equally dramatic coastline of the Port Campbell National Park, centre right, and rock fishermen engaged in their timeless rituals ...

ROB ROWE

TREVERN DAWES

TREVERN DAWES

KEN ROSS

... and energetic pursuits ...

Visions of Australia

35

The remnants of an Outback pioneer's brave attempt to settle the arid interior slowly return to dust

A remarkable breed of pioneers tackled the harsh environment fr

PHILIP QUIRK

earliest days - some survived and prospered, many did not ...

DAVID SIMMONDS

*A cheerful Jillaroo (station hand), above, and a tired horse wrangler
heading home, right, typify the contrasts of Australian station life*

Station life reflects the diversity of the Australian landscape a

...ies from sublime temperate areas to bleak Outback spreads ...

Brumbies, above, head off at full gallop in a mountain roundup in northern Victoria, while two Hopeton, Victoria, wheat farmers, below, take life a bit easier

Life on the land. A hard, vigorous life of immense importance

LEE PEARCE

*A stockman, above, churns up the dust as he works cattle in the yard, and a
shearer, below, works on a sheep at Keri Keri Station, south-west New South Wales*

CAROLYN JOHNS

economy of this big country. Wild horses and wild men

Magnificent examples of colonial homesteads can be found through the country, such as the one near the Rous River in north east New South Wales, above.

Australia's small towns and villages abound in a timeless collection of quaint architectural styles borrowed from diverse and historical influences as shown, right.

Too young to have established an architectural style, Austra

A stockman, above, churns up the dust as he works cattle in the yard, and a
shearer, below, works on a sheep at Keri Keri Station, south-west New South Wales

economy of this big country. Wild horses and wild men

Magnificent examples of colonial homesteads can be found through the country, such as the one near the Rous River in north east New South Wales, above.

Australia's small towns and villages abound in a timeless collection of quaint architectural styles borrowed from diverse and historical influences as shown, right.

Too young to have established an architectural style, Austra

PHILIP QUIRK

PHILIP QUIRK

ALLAN MOULT

OLIVER STREWE

ALLAN MOULT

OLIVER STREWE

PHILIP QUIRK

ALLAN MOULT

...netheless hints at eclectic and exciting elements in the wings ...

TREVERN DAWES

Australia shares the world's business pulse - and equally its hu

*Australia's capital cities are vibrant
and exciting places - full of keen
energy for the thrust of business, and
the pursuit of fame and power*

bustle, wheeling and dealing, and general excitement about the future

GILBERT ROSSI

PHILIP QUIRK

*Sun, sea, surf and sand - the
Australian recipe for outdoor
hedonism unequalled anywhere else in
the world*

... and heads for the beach

Bushwalking

Activity Lodges & Centres

Historic Houses & Inns

Farm & Station Holidays

Executive & Country Retreats

Casinos

Air Tours

Boating Cruises

Boat Charter & Hire

Bicycling

Ballooning

Wine Country

Railway Journeys

National Trust

National Parks

Islands

Camel Trekking

Canoeing, Kayaking & Rafting

Diving & Snorkelling

Fishing

Golf

Horseriding

Motoring — Campervans

Motoring — Four-wheel-drives

Rockclimbing, Abseiling & Mountaineering

Skiing

AUSTRALIA - THE ISLAND CONTINENT

Australia, the smallest, flattest and driest continent on earth, has an area of over 768.2 million hectares, and a coastline of just under 20,000 kilometres. Located in the southern hemisphere, between the latitudes of 10 and 43 degrees south and longitudes of 113 and 153 degrees east, Australia is bounded by three Oceans - the Pacific, Southern and Indian - as well as the Timor and Arafura Seas to the north.

It is a remarkably flat land. Mount Kosciusko at 2228 metres is the highest point - a mere mound in comparison with the peaks of Asia, the Americas or Europe. All other continents have at least one peak over 5000 metres. Australia is also, geologically, very old - the land as we see it today came about over the past 250 million years. Unlike other continents which have been shaped by relatively recent glacial activity, the island continent's smootheddown appearance is a result of many processes of erosion over a long period of time.

Australia experiences a wide range of climatic conditions. One third of the continent is north of the Tropic of Capricorn, and this region is subject to the summer 'wet' season. The southern areas, however, receive most of their rainfall in the winter months and are located in the temperate zone with the highlands of New South Wales, Victoria and Tasmania receiving substantial snowfalls in winter - a fact which often surprises the overseas visitor. By contrast, the continent's hottest spot is Marble Bar in Western Australia which often has an average daily temperature of 38 degrees Centigrade. The highest-ever recorded temperature was in Queensland in 1889 when it reached 51.1 degrees.

Approximately one third of Australia is desert and semi-desert unsuitable for human settlement. Australia's 16 million plus population is crowded into coastal fringe cities and towns that make up a minute 0.13 % of the land area yet contain the great majority of the population. In contrast with over 40,000 years of aboriginal occupation, the mere 200 years of white settlement has been brief indeed.

Australia today is divided into six states and two territories with Sydney, Melbourne, and Brisbane the largest cities. Canberra, in the Australian Capital Territory, is the seat of the Federal Government.

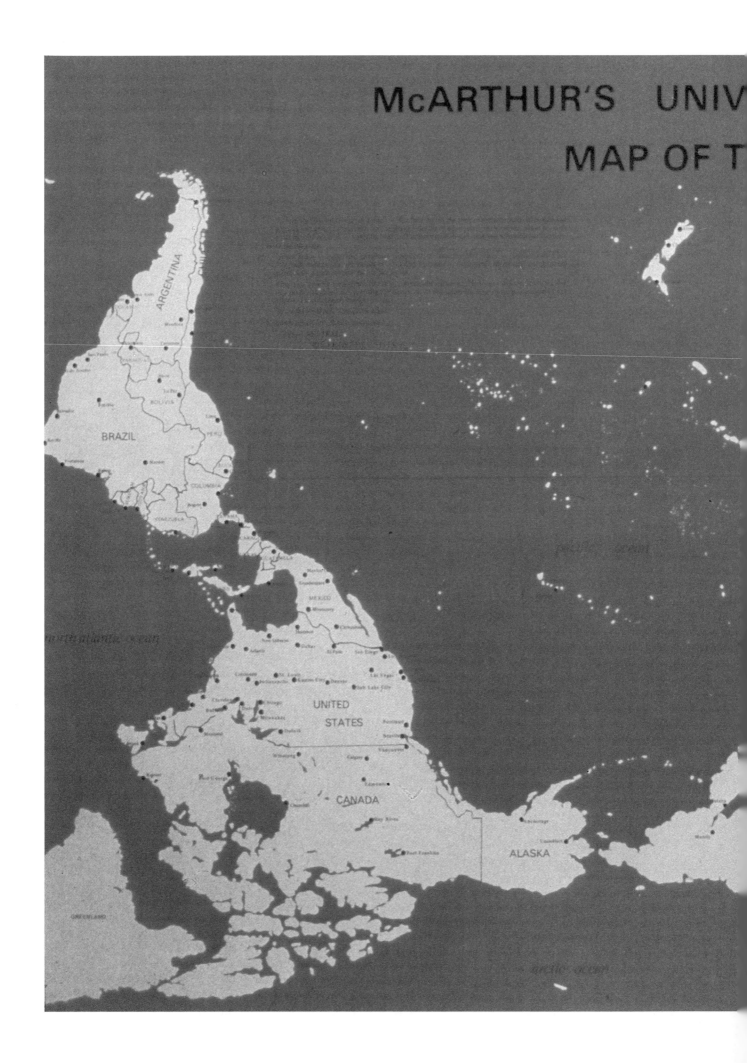

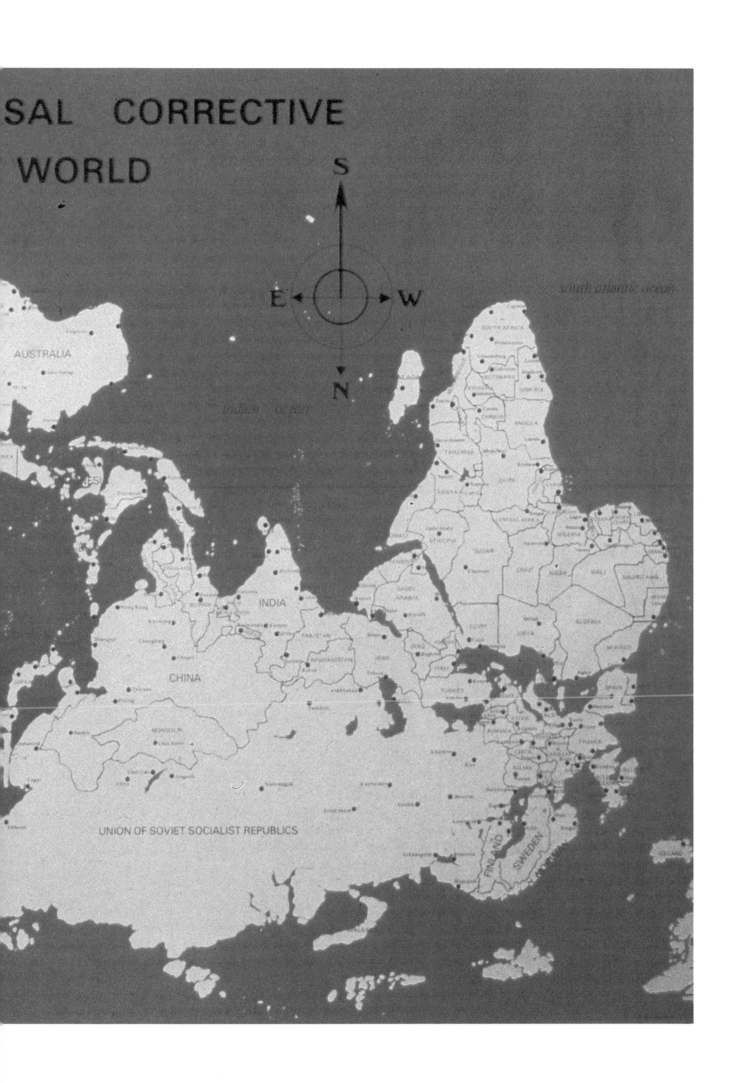

SAL CORRECTIVE

WORLD

PORTRAITS OF THE
CITIES & STATES

DAVID SIMMONDS

Introduction

Paris, 1531. French map-maker Oronce Fine places an imaginary continent in the southern part of his map of the world. Carefully, in his finest calligraphy, he inks in its name: 'Terra Australis' — the southern land.

But it was not until 1817, some 30 years after the First Fleet had entered Botany Bay, that Governor Macquarie took a lead from Matthew Flinders' *Voyage to Terra Australis* and officially recommended that 'Australia' be used to name this vast empty continent. Australia was now a fact in both deed and word. In Western eyes, that is, because the gentle Aborigines had colonised their land of dreams about 40,000 years before.

Extremes and contrasts are at the heart of Australia. They daunt and surprise whether you are visiting the country for the first time, are a frequent in-bound traveller, or are one of the 16 million inhabitants surfacing from the magnetic city life that holds most of them in its sway.

Let us look first at its size. Australia's land mass occupies 7,686,884 square kilometres. Its coastline is 36,735 kilometres in length. A journey across the continent at its widest points would cover around 4,000 kilometres between east and west and 3,200 kilometres between north and south.

These distances, however, are no tyranny. Australians, you see, are a strangely parochial people. We counter the serious size of the country by staying put in our cities and suburbs. We are, as a result, one of the most urbanised countries in the world. You'll find us crowding into the half dozen or so major conurbations and leaving the rest of the place to the birds. In Sydney or Melbourne, you have no sense of the vast empty deserts, mountain ranges, and bushland that stretch for mile upon mile to the north and west. For

many, it is only the work of painters, writers and film-makers that communicates an experience we may never have had.

The next surprise for the traveller, particularly one from Europe, is the contrast between age and youth. Age, that is, of the place. Away from the cities, the terrain has an old worn-down feel. It is as if the millenia of fierce heat, gusting winds, and drought have created a sense of resignation in everything on the land's surface to the vicissitudes of the climate. There are no people involved in this drama. Indeed, you are struck by the impassiveness of the rock and stones and trees, often feeling like an intruder, and most unlikely to find traces of people who have been there before you. Australia, in this sense, is a country without a human history.

This aged anonymity is in counterpoint to the youthfulness of the cities. 'Old' in Sydney, Perth or Melbourne means less than a century. While the 19th-century civic and domestic architecture is lovingly restored, often with great panache, the overwhelming sense is of the new. High-rise buildings in city centres and sprawling suburbs of red-roofed red-brick homes have been built so quickly in the last 20 years that the cities have been transformed.

This threat for development is not a phenomenon of the cities alone. Coastal land is being claimed and resorts are mushrooming. The Queensland coast from the Gold Coast in the south to far north Queensland is booming and in Port Douglas, the latest mega tourist development is opening its doors.

If we have identified a lack of moderation in distances, climate and the development of the cities and tourism, we may pick up the thread once more in the culture and the people of Australia.

The truly indigenous people, the Aborigines, have been swamped by two centuries of largely white colonisation — by people who have little sensibility for a stone-age culture that had been preserved in a timeless world. These Caucasian newcomers were, at the beginning, outcasts from their countries of origin and, even today, new migrants such as the Vietnamese and the Cambodians are displaced people from other lands.

This combination of refugees, exiles and poor people looking for a fresh start infuses Australia's culture. Together, they create attitudes that are central to any understanding of the place. Here is the source of the anti-intellectual, hedonistic, love-for-the-underdog and the give-it-a-go mentality that is special to Australia. These attitudes are both frustrating and rewarding. They induce a lack of concern for the environment, but also an enthusiasm and honesty which really makes you believe that anything is possible.

Australians are used to disparaging remarks being made about them. Years ago, they might have felt somewhat defensive on these matters. Today, there is a growing confidence — despite the irreverence of flash capitalists, the greed of entrepreneur-developers, and the parochial concerns of political debate — that we have a few things going for us. We view the parlous state of England, still sticking to its outmoded class structure and putting people out of work in order to preserve it, the patent self-deception of the United States' approach to the rest of the world, and we reckon this just might be a better place to live.

Whether you live here or not, as a tourist in Australia you are doing the 'in' thing. For Australia is one of the most sought-after destinations, where tourism is growing by 30% each year. The attractions are both stupendous and singular. Every visitor 'does' the Sydney Opera House and the Harbour Bridge, the Great Barrier Reef and the Red Centre — man-made and natural wonders. Koala, platypus, kangaroo, shark, crocodile, cocky, snake and spider are sought out in both natural and controlled environments. A journey north along the eastern seaboard takes you from the temperate south to the snows of the Great Dividing Range, through bush and outback to the tropical country of Cape York.

The Australian Adventure seeks to capture the extremes and contrasts of Australia and to show how diverse are the things that the country has to offer enthusiastic tourists.

New meets old. The adventure begins.

NOEL LEVY

Sydney, from Tall Ships to Tall Poppies

On 13 May 1787, Captain Arthur Phillip set sail in HMS *Sirius* from Portsmouth Harbour. His tender ship, HMS *Supply,* was close at hand. They made their way through the choppy waters of the Solent with their charge — six transport ships carrying 756 convicts. The First Fleet was heading south. The male contingent of 450 crew members and necessary civil and military personnel were accompanied by 28 wives and 30 children. Eight months later, on a hot summer Friday, Phillip sailed into Botany Bay. One week later, he hoisted the British flag in Sydney Cove, now Circular Quay.

The following May, two Aborigines were killed by white settlers in Rushcutters Bay. On 22 September, the first white baby, Rebecca Small, was born. The white colonisation of the 'lucky country' had begun.

It is fitting that the first white settlers in Sydney were delivered from the sea. Above all else, Sydney is a maritime city. Its natural harbour is unsurpassed in beauty. Houses crowd to the land's edge to seek a water view, the newer brick and timber constructions competing with those built from natural pale golden sandstone. Sheer rocky cliffs and preserved bushland interrupt the red, white, gold and green of developed residential land. And in the very heart of the harbour, the high-rise business districts of the City and North Sydney, clad in glass, concrete and neon, stand sentry to the Harbour Bridge and the Opera House, its white shell-like ears cocked forward as if listening for the music of the waters on which it stands.

Water *is* the music of Sydney. The arrangement of the score is so diverse that whether your love is for classical, jazz or rock and roll, you will find plenty to your liking. The natural contrasts are striking. The waters of the main harbour are smooth and deep. The tides reveal neither muddy banks nor large sandy beaches, for this is one of the greatest natural marinas in the world. When it comes alive, it bustles with motor cruisers, ferries, sail boats, fishing boats, tankers, submarines, large yachts, racing skiffs, destroyers, aircraft carriers and pleasure boats pursuing business, defence or entertainment. Yet at other times, such as early on a winter morning, the harbour is empty except for a ferry cutting its way through the grey-green water or a fishing boat puttering slowly home.

Middle Harbour shares many of the main harbour's qualities. It has, however, the best harbour beach — Balmoral, near Mosman — which is frequented by families and those who prefer a sheltered haven to the ocean beaches such as Bondi and Manly.

Sydney Harbour empties into the Tasman Sea through the Heads — North Head near Manly and South Head near Watson's Bay. The huge swell that rolls in through the Heads warns of the sea-change beyond. Here, the coastline is oceanic. Yellow sands beneath sandstone cliffs are subjected to the relentless pounding of the surf. Barren rocks and cliffs splinter crashing waves into coarse spume and fine mist. And the boats of the inner harbour give way to people congregating on the beach. People of all ages: young surfers, windsurfing yuppies, topless sunbathers, lifeguards, joggers, families picnicking by the sea, and older people walking quietly along the shore, contemplating their lives. The beaches, among the best in the world, are as integral a part of Sydney's waterscape as the harbour.

The northern ocean beaches are particularly fine. Excellent surfing conditions prevail, and the little towns which have grown up along this stretch of coast are favoured places in which to live. Manly, Harbord, and Newport are seaside towns — holiday and weekend venues as well as suburbs of the city.

At the apex of the northern peninsula is fashionable Palm Beach. Here, where the land comes to a point at Barrenjoey Lighthouse, is perhaps the best place to see Sydney's watery contrasts. From its high, wooded ridge (site of some of Sydney's most sought-after real estate), the panorama encompasses the Pacific Ocean, the huge estuary of the Hawkesbury River and the calms of Pittwater. This is what Sydney is about. A meeting of the waves.

But Sydney has expanded well beyond the harbour reaches. In 1900, the city had a population of half a million. Almost a century later, it has grown seven-fold. The size and pace of growth have pushed the city into the hinterland in search of usable building land. Today, it occupies 12,000 square kilometres and comprises seven separately administered cities (Sydney, Parramatta, Liverpool, Penrith, Campbelltown, Blacktown and Bankstown), four shires (Baulkham Hills, Hornsby, Sutherland and Warringah) and 33 municipalities. Sydney's land space is greater than that of New York City or London. As in those cities, urbanisation has encroached upon distinct local communities, filling in the spaces between them with new developments. The visitor will find that the oldest of these villages, and the most interesting, are close to the city centre.

Sydney's oldest village is The Rocks area, at the southern foot of the Harbour Bridge. It was here that the first settlers made their home. From its very beginning, The Rocks had a reputation for low life. Straggling stone cottages, numerous pubs, dark alleys and light fingers made it a place for the down-and-out and the larrikin. Henry Lawson captured the menace of the gangs which roamed the place in his description of 'The Captain of the Push', whose

> *whistle loud and piercing, woke the echo*
> *of the Rocks.*
> *And a dozen ghouls came sloping round the*
> *corners of the blocks.*

Those days are long gone. Many of the dilapidated buildings were demolished following an outbreak of bubonic plague at the turn of the century. Since then, the building of the Harbour Bridge and renovation of the old housing stock have turned The Rocks into one of the prettiest areas in the inner city.

Sydney's oldest house — Cadman's Cottage, built in 1816 — is to be found here, as well as the city's oldest hotel, The Hero of Waterloo, in Lower Fort Street. The area abounds with seafood restaurants and souvenir shops (one of which is stacked with shells and ephemera from the sea). Ken Done, whose paintings have done so much to capture the spirit of Sydney, has a splendid gift gallery here.

The harbourside villages of the Eastern Suburbs are among the most sought-after residential areas in Sydney. The shoreline from Darling Point to Watson's Bay boasts vast harbourside mansions and apartments, and yachts and cruising boats compete for mooring space. Its public face is best seen in Double Bay. Banjo Paterson lived here long before the chic restaurants and exclusive shops became the drawcard. Take a seat at one of the pavement cafes in Knox Street and become part of a 24-hour cocktail party. Rolls', Porsches and Mercs move slowly along the kerb, their occupants admiring and being admired. All that glitters *is* gold.

There is much more, of course, to this coastal strip than boats, houses, shops and cars. Two of Sydney's prettiest historic houses are here. In Elizabeth Bay, named after the wife of Governor Macquarie, is Elizabeth Bay House. Built in 1832 for the Colonial Secretary Alexander Macleay, it was designed by John Verge and overlooks the harbour. Its sophisticated gentility is in contrast to Vaucluse House, which is much more of a country home in the English style, set in pleasant gardens further up the harbour.

Elizabeth Bay is also home to one of Sydney's most popular hotels, the Sebel Town House, A small hotel, it is favoured by visiting stars of stage, screen and pop music.

Rose Bay, beyond Double Bay, is the windsurfing centre of the inner city suburbs and also the home of the Royal Sydney Golf Club. The long sweeping bay ends at the base of a hilly climb through Vaucluse and on to Watson's Bay. Watson's Bay has a very special atmosphere and enchanting views across the harbour back towards the city. There are few nicer ways of

Portraits of the Cities & States

spending an afternoon than a lazy lunch with oysters and champagne at Doyles on the Beach, followed by a walk round to South Head and back to the Gap, infamous for shipwrecks and suicides.

The ocean suburbs are less glamorous than their harbourside cousins. Perhaps the fierce southerly winds ruffle even the most carefully secured hairstyle. Bondi Beach, the 'place of breaking waters', is nevertheless very special. It deserves its world renown, for here is a splendid beach which attracts a true cross-section of Sydney folk. The smart and the less so rub shoulders on the broad stretch of sand and in the delightful cafes and restaurants along the main drag — Campbell Parade.

Between the coast and the harbour are two of the prettiest villages of all, Woollahra and Paddington. Here, young trendies have bought and renovated the picturesque terraces and sandstone houses that line the narrow streets. The iron lacework which decorates many of these old workers' cottages was originally ballast in the great sailing ships which plied their hazardous way to the colony last century. Pale pastels and deep olive green are the colours of today. Clusters of shops, restaurants, art galleries and cafes meet the needs of a community which lives on its streets. Paddo's Oxford Street market, held each Saturday in the grounds of a local church, is a colourful event. Here you can buy anything from fashionable hand-knitted sweaters, jewellery and bric-a-brac to jars of honey and healthy takeaway food.

To the south of Oxford Street lies Centennial Park, a huge area of ponds and picnic spots, woods and playing fields. Its central cinder track is a favourite place for horse-riding and in the summer it becomes a throng of children, cyclists, extremely extended families enjoying long picnic lunches and flannelled fools hitting little red balls with their bats. Flannel is worn more seriously at the Sydney Cricket Ground nearby. Renovations and new stands have made it one of the best Test Cricket grounds in the world and only its famous Hill is a reminder of yesteryear.

On the other side of the park, Randwick boasts the University of New South Wales and the famous Royal Randwick racecourse. Each Easter, the city celebrates its devotion to the turf with an autumn carnival of racing. The Rosehill races, near Parramatta, are the venue for the state's glittering prize, the Golden Slipper. The famous Inglis Yearling sales are held at Randwick at this time, too.

The feeling of the country in the city is no more evident than at the Royal Easter Show. For ten days, men and women from the bush take over the city from their city cousins, bringing with them a whiff of eucalyptus gum and reminders of Australia's great agricultural wealth.

To the west of the city lie the villages of Glebe and Balmain. Glebe's long main street, Glebe Point Road, has a concentration of some of the city's best eating haunts. Lebanese, Thai, Indian and Italian restaurants ply their trade in competition with neat little cafes,

The great ferry race is an annual summer event on Sydney Harbour

takeaway food outlets and more upmarket eateries. The area has a large student population, derived from the nearby University of Sydney.

By contrast, Balmain — in many ways Sydney's premier village — has a more settled population. Balmain is both arty and artful. Beautiful stone houses and little terraces have been constructed cheek-by-jowl with a rich variety of architecture in what was one of the earliest settled parts of the city. Residents make do with the tiny aprons that pass as gardens in order to live in a pleasant, self-contained community which attracts upwardly mobile writers, painters and publishers. And they, with their friends, enjoy the antique markets and little cafes, the pubs and hotels which are so important to the bohemian and literary set.

North across the Harbour Bridge lie the villages of the Lower North Shore, which stretches from Hunters Hill in the west to Mosman in the east. The housing stock here is very different from that in the Eastern Suburbs. Hunters Hill, with its wide tree-lined streets, has some of the city's oldest and most beautiful residential sandstone buildings. The place has a quiet grandeur and some of the best waterfrontage on the harbour. Longueville and Greenwich, Waverton and Wollstonecraft share this feeling of open space until they come into collision with the city's second business centre, North Sydney, which has developed at the northern end of the Harbour Bridge.

East of the bridge, the busy shopping areas of Neutral Bay and Cremorne give way to quiet and secluded streets running down to little bays of the harbour. Kirribilli is the home of the Royal Yacht Squadron and the Prime Minister, when in town, lives at Kirribilli House.

Further east, Sydney's Taronga Park Zoo in Mosman scales the hills above the harbour, and there are some excellent harbourside walks and picnic spots at Bradley's Head and Clifton Gardens. This is an excellent spot from which to watch the racing yachts in summer. The famous 18-footer skiffs boom down the harbour each Saturday, their bright spinnakers catching the brisk easterly winds. And on Boxing Day, there is no more thrilling sight than the start of the Sydney to Hobart Yacht Race. Maxi yachts dwarf their smaller rivals as they make their way up the harbour for the start which may bring line honours in Tasmania six or so days away.

Like the downtown areas of many recently developed cities, Sydney's city centre is quite small. Its early civic architecture has been all but smothered by high-rise office blocks, and the city's streets are continually being refurbished and redirected. Though small, the centre has much to offer. The major hotels, though hard-pressed to cope with the burgeoning numbers of business and holiday visitors, are of a standard comparable with the best in the world. The Sebel Town House, the Regent, the Intercontinental, the Sheraton, the Hyatt and the Holiday Inn are justly proud of their achievements. A new visitor on leaving the Regent said to this writer, 'Are all Australians as well mannered as the staff here?'

The visitor also enjoys busy shopping areas in the heart of the city. Here are to be found not only the best of the local stores, such as David Jones and Percy Marks, but also the cream from around the world, including duty-free stores, Cartier, Dunhill, Gucci, Louis Vuitton and Hardy Brothers. One of the most spectacular shopping complexes is the Queen Victoria Building, near the Town Hall, whose lofty internal colonnade and tiled walkways have been meticulously restored. The Victorian Strand Arcade, where the master jeweller Robert Clerc works, producing among other things a range of refined Australian-inspired jewellery, has many boutiques and cafes. Other complexes in this shopping paradise include Centrepoint and the modern centres in and around Martin Place.

In the middle of town is the Centrepoint Tower, which stands 104.8 metres high — the tallest building in the southern hemisphere. Lunch or dinner at its revolving restaurant offers an unparalleled view of the city beneath and miles beyond.

The international flavour of the city centre is complemented by those things which are so specifically 'Sydney'. The majestic colonial buildings of Macquarie Street include the Hyde Park Barracks with its museum and excellent cafe, the State Parliament building, and the Mint, now a decorative arts museum. Macquarie Street is also the gateway to the Domain, a grassy area where at weekends soap-box orators pontificate, and to the fine Botanic Gardens, a verdant haven that runs down to Farm Cove. Beyond The Domain lies the handsome Art Gallery of New South Wales, whose ponderous neo-classic walls house a comprehensive collection of Australian paintings and sculpture.

The development of the city centre has occurred in stages, and the noise of steam drills and jack hammers tells you that you are witnessing the latest of these. Pitt Street pedestrians are being mollified with a vehicle-free mall. Space is being cleared for new office blocks seeking perhaps to match the splendour of the State Bank of New South Wales in Martin Place. And where the harbour nudges the city to the west — Darling Harbour — the most ambitious plan of all is being carried out. A 50-hectare site has been cleared to make way for a 3,500-seat convention centre, a 25,000-square-metre exhibition centre, and a 12,000-seat entertainment complex as well as a two-hectare Chinese garden to which over 30 specialists from China have contributed. Shops, cafes and restaurants, walkways and a monorail to the city will support these major developments. The National Maritime Museum and Aquarium, and the Powerhouse Museum are also to be found here.

Two existing features of this part of town must not be

overlooked. At Pyrmont, the daily Fish Market is a riot of wet fish, prawns, oysters, crabs, mussels and other marine delights. Some of this harvest from the sea finds its way to Chinatown, which lies to the east of the existing Entertainment Centre and extends to George Street, north of Central Station. Sydney's Chinatown is a wonderful place to sample the best cuisine from mainland China, Hong Kong, Singapore and Malaysia. Dixon Street is its main thoroughfare and there are many shops selling clothes and keenly priced groceries.

ALLAN MOULT

The Pyrmont Fish Markets have become a popular shopping destination for Sydney's growing Japanese population

The specialisation of Chinatown is of quite a different sort from that of Kings Cross, Sydney's version of Pigalle or Soho. Yet among the sleazy sex shops, nightclubs and bordellos are some excellent restaurants and brasseries and the place has a slightly quaint, unthreatening air.

Sydney's restaurants are a treat in themselves. There was a time when traditional European and Chinese cuisine accounted for most of the city's eating places, but in recent years a proliferation of ethnic restaurants — Thai, Japanese, Indonesian, Lebanese, Italian, Vietnamese — has made selection difficult. The best areas for searching out new places to eat are Crown and Oxford Streets around Taylor Square in Darlinghurst, Campbell Parade and Bondi Road in Bondi, Glebe Point Road, and Norton Street in 'Italian' Leichhardt.

Tall poppies? A profile of Sydney would be incomplete without its people. If Australians have a

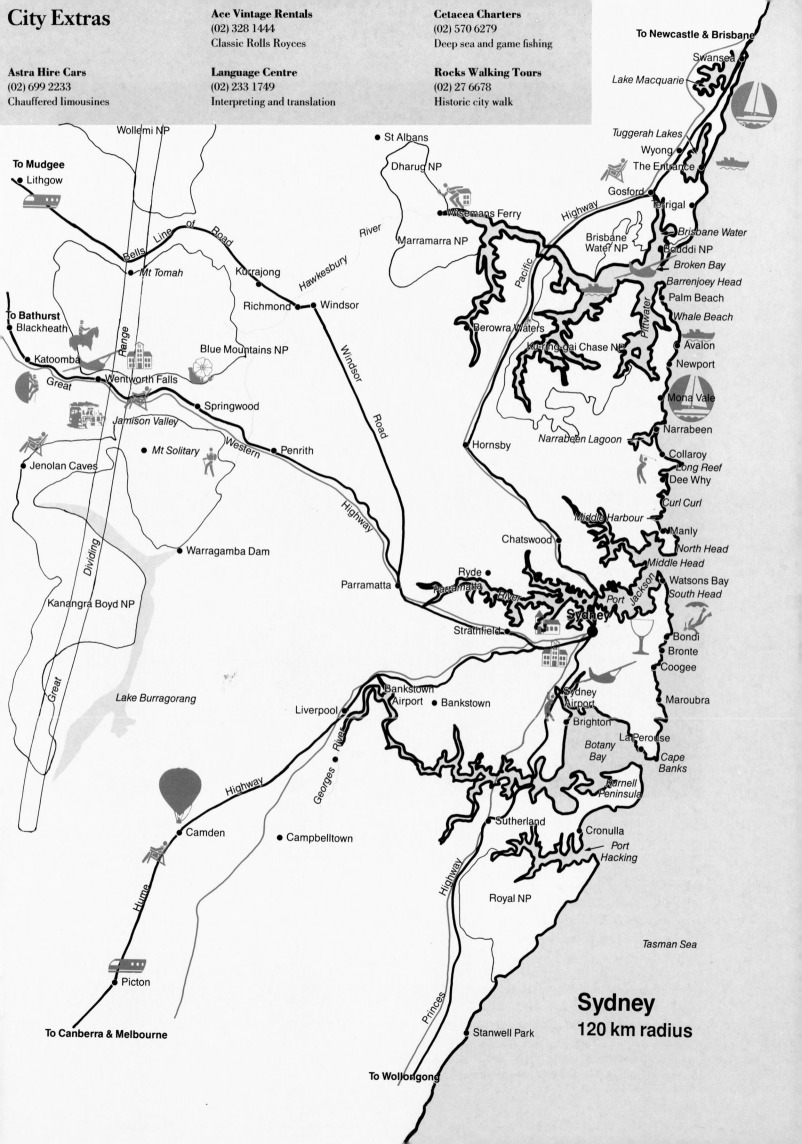

City Extras

Astra Hire Cars
(02) 699 2233
Chauffered limousines

Ace Vintage Rentals
(02) 328 1444
Classic Rolls Royces

Language Centre
(02) 233 1749
Interpreting and translation

Cetacea Charters
(02) 570 6279
Deep sea and game fishing

Rocks Walking Tours
(02) 27 6678
Historic city walk

To Newcastle & Brisbane
Swansea
Lake Macquarie
Tuggerah Lakes
Wyong
The Entrance
Gosford
Terrigal
Brisbane Water
Bouddi NP
Broken Bay
Barrenjoey Head
Palm Beach
Whale Beach
Avalon
Newport
Mona Vale
Narrabeen
Collaroy
Long Reef
Dee Why
Curl Curl
Middle Harbour
Manly
North Head
Middle Head
Watsons Bay
South Head
Bondi
Bronte
Coogee
Maroubra
La Perouse
Cape Banks
Botany Bay
Kurnell Peninsula
Cronulla
Port Hacking

Wollemi NP
To Mudgee
Lithgow
St Albans
Dharug NP
Marramarra NP
Bells Line of Road
Mt Tomah
Kurrajong
Richmond
Windsor
Hawkesbury River
Pacific Highway
Brisbane Water NP
Wisemans Ferry
Berowra Waters
Ku-ring-gai Chase NP
Pittwater
To Bathurst
Blackheath
Katoomba
Wentworth Falls
Great Range
Blue Mountains NP
Windsor Road
Springwood
Jamison Valley
Mt Solitary
Western Highway
Penrith
Hornsby
Narrabeen Lagoon
Jenolan Caves
Warragamba Dam
Chatswood
Ryde
Parramatta
Parramatta River
Port Jackson
Sydney
Strathfield
Kanangra Boyd NP
Great Dividing Range
Lake Burragorang
Bankstown Airport
Bankstown
Sydney Airport
Brighton
Liverpool
Georges River
Hume Highway
Camden
Campbelltown
Sutherland
Royal NP
Princes Highway
Picton
Tasman Sea
To Canberra & Melbourne
Stanwell Park

Sydney
120 km radius

To Wollongong

Manly is a mecca for bathers, surfers and sailboarders alike ...

reputation overseas for being insecure, then Sydney-siders love to prove them wrong. Confidence shines from the faces of its hard-working, pleasure-loving people. A good life is about having the best, and the best is what Sydney has in spades. The best climate, the best beaches, the best harbour in the world. The best of everything. No wonder the citizens of Australia's commercial and international centre are a bit brash, a bit flash, and love their cash. And it shows. But this is no tinsel town. Sydneysiders care about the arts and culture. They support private galleries and top designers of all kinds. They buy thousands of books and movie tickets and warm to the offerings of a busy theatrical life in dance, opera, ballet and drama.

The best tribute to the place is that those visitors who have chosen not to live here have Sydney as number two on their list.

Let us leave the final word to James Hingston, a writer for the Melbourne *Argus*. Writing in 1879, he describes his first visit to Sydney Town. Of this 'Venus risen from the sea,' he concludes, 'we think, as we look about us, that nothing but a forcible exportation would make anyone wish to leave the place.'

Tall poppies? Yes, and proud of it!

Oliver Freeman

MARTIN COLEMAN

New South Wales

There was a time when New South Wales *was* Australia — when the colony stretched from the Cape York Peninsula to Van Diemen's Land, now Tasmania, from the east coast to a line almost as far west as the boundary of Western Australia.

Between 1825 and Federation in 1901, parts of New South Wales were removed as state after state was created. It ended up as a territory of 802,000 square kilometres, with a coastline of 1,900 kilometres.

Of all the states, New South Wales has the greatest variety of climate and environment. In contrast, South Australia, Western Australia, the Northern Territory and western Queensland are dominated by vast tracts of dry, near-desert landscape — once the exclusive province of the original Australians, the Aborigines, whose presence there was the lightest and most sensitive of all occupations.

New South Wales, too, has its share of great stretches of dry, flat land, some of it agricultural and some of it desert. It is also significantly blessed with the tablelands, a great farming region that falls away east from the Great Dividing Range, the mountain chain that lines the east coast of Australia from Cape York to the Bass Strait.

To the north, pushing up against the lush subtropical and tropical expanse of south-eastern Queensland, the climate along the coast is hot, often steamy in summer and balmy in winter. Further south, the coast becomes an ideal holiday playground with steady temperatures and gentle winters. The central coast and southern coast from Sydney to the Victorian border are very warm in summer, tending to quite cold and wet in winter.

All that being said, it must be remembered that Sydney is the same distance from the Equator as Casablanca. North of Sydney, Australians live in a distinctly non-European climate where the temperature can rise to well over 40°C.

In northern New South Wales, the inland areas can be cold at night and freezing in the winter, due to the extra altitude of the tablelands. Armidale and the New England area have brisk climates and the plains to the west of Sydney around the towns of Orange and Bathurst are by turns icy and hot.

It was the plains of Bathurst that saved the colony of New South Wales. The mountains around the central region were impenetrable until, in 1813, the explorers Blaxland, Lawson and Wentworth found a route and opened farmlands that sustained cattle and sheep, wheat and vegetable produce. In this way, a colony that had proved a headache to its masters in Westminster became an asset.

The Great Dividing Range offers travellers some very special experiences. The central section, the Blue Mountains, has resorts and towns that are the starting place for visiting the area's spectacular scenery. Further south, in the Snowy Mountains region, is Mt Kosciusko, Australia's highest mountain, and the snowfields that stretch down into Victoria. To the north are rainforests in the foothills of the range and the university town of Armidale.

Squeezed between the Great Dividing Range and the sea is a narrow coastal strip averaging around 150 kilometres in width. It is here that most of the population of the country's most populous state lives. The strip is green and fertile as a result of the moisture-laden winds that blow in from the Pacific Ocean.

The dairy farms of the north and south coasts, the sugarcane and tropical fruit plantations of the north, and the market gardens, farms and cattle stations celebrate their harvests at the annual Royal Easter Show in Sydney and at a string of smaller shows in the state's main districts.

The transport and communications systems reflect the origins and central importance of Sydney as the birthplace of an English colony. The 1,600-kilometre Pacific Highway runs the length of the coastal strip from Queensland to the Victorian border. And the Hume Highway from Sydney to Melbourne is dual carriageway for nearly all of its length.

Radiating out from Sydney are many highways. Due west, across the Blue Mountains, they pass through Bathurst, Orange, Parkes and beyond. The New England Highway takes travellers to Queensland from Newcastle, north of Sydney, following a route north-west away from the coast.

The Sturt Highway in the south-west travels along one of the state's great rivers, the Murrumbidgee. The Riverina Highway further south follows the banks of the Murray River, Australia's largest, which rises in New South Wales and flows to South Australia, forming on its way the boundary between New South Wales and Victoria.

Rivers in Australia are generally unreliable and may fill up or run dry from one season to another. The dry continent lacks the vast expanses of well-watered damp earth that countries like Canada and Brazil possess.

New South Wales, however, possesses some of the continent's biggest and most reliable rivers. Close to Sydney is the Hawkesbury River, one of the most beautiful of all and comparable in parts to the northern stretches of the Hudson River as it flows through New York state.

South of Sydney, the Murray and its tributaries include the Darling, a river that flows up over north-western New South Wales and by another name into Queensland, forming a river system of over 600,000 square kilometres. The system is the basis of vital irrigation systems, including the Murrumbidgee Irrigation Area and the Riverina.

Further up the coast from the Hawkesbury is the Hunter River, which flows into the sea at Newcastle. Between Newcastle and the river lies the Hunter Valley, a basin containing some of Australia's finest vineyards and said to be the last place in Australia to dry up in times of drought.

The Northern Rivers district includes the Manning, Macleay and Hastings rivers. Above them are the Clarence and Richmond rivers, which are subject to dramatic flooding, although the state's worst floods have been those of the Hunter River near Newcastle. One of Australia's most successful feature films, *Newsfront*, featured graphic archive footage blended with new material to recreate one of the worst floods of all time at Maitland. An idiosyncracy of early Australian radio was the daily broadcast of river heights, a monotonous list of the height of every river worthy of the name in New South Wales.

The state's railway network mirrors the radial nature of the road system. Central Station in Sydney is housed in an attractive sandstone building in the style of London's main line termini. Its restored glory attracts great affection from Sydneysiders who periodically hold balls in its main hall.

Trains leave Central for the north coast and Brisbane. A fast and comfortable express service to this neighbouring capital has well-designed individual travelling and sleeping compartments. A similar service operates to Melbourne, though the line is inland from the coast.

Other trains run to the south-west and west across the plains to Broken Hill. To the north-west, the line runs out at Bourke and the expression 'Back of Bourke' is used to mean the beginning of the outback.

The most romantic of Australia's trains, the 'Indian Pacific', leaves Central and travels west through Broken Hill on its long journey to Perth.

When the Australian states came together in a Federation in 1901, arguments were bitter and urgent about the location of the Commonwealth's capital. Victorians wanted Melbourne to be the capital; New South Welshmen wanted Sydney. A compromise was finally reached, and Canberra, a city more or less equidistant from Brisbane, Melbourne and Adelaide, was plonked down in empty farming country in New South Wales.

Travelling north from Sydney in an anti-clockwise direction, the main regions of New South Wales are as follows:

The Central Coast

The Central Coast of New South Wales is a great playground for Sydneysiders. It extends from the Hawkesbury River in the south, some 35 kilometres north of Sydney, to just above Lake Munmorah and Budgewoi in the north. To the west, it takes in Mangrove Mountain and Wiseman's Ferry.

There was a time when access to the Central Coast was mainly by steam train. Smoky carriages left from Central or Hornsby station and stopped at places such as Gosford, Wyong and Woy Woy from where buses took passengers to Tuggerah Lakes, Avoca, Ettalong, Norah Head and Long Jetty. An expressway has now been built north of Berowra which traverses the central coast area, making travelling time from Sydney around one and a half hours.

The Hawkesbury River and Broken Bay, where it enters the sea, are the beginning of the Central Coast. The northern part of Broken Bay enters Brisbane Water, a network of bays and stretches of water which produces the pleasant environs of many of the Central Coast towns. At the northern entrance to the bay is a spit of land which has ocean beaches and frontages to the estuaries. The main beaches include McMasters, Avoca and Terrigal. Avoca and Terrigal beaches each

NEW SOUTH WALES

To Brisbane

Queensland

Border Ranges NP
Tweed Heads

Murwillumbah

Sturt NP
Tibooburra

Lismore

Byron Bay

Lightning Ridge •

Moree •

Nymboida & Clarence Rivers

Inverell •

Grafton

Bourke

Mt Kaputar NP

Glen Innes

White Cliffs •

Darling River

Mitchell Highway

Narrabri •

Coffs Harbour

Armidale •

Macleay River

Dorrigo & New England NPs

Gunnedah •   Tamworth •

Hastings River

Warrumbungle NP   • Coonabarabran

Pacific Highway

Wilcannia

Barrier   Highway

New England Highway

Port Macquarie

Broken Hill

Range

Gloucester

To Adelaide

Menindee Lakes System

Outback

Dubbo •

Muswellbrook •

Myall Lakes NP

Hunter Valley

Menindee •

Blue Mountains & Wollemi NPs

Maitland   Port Stephens

Kincheega NP

Ivanhoe •   *Indian   Pacific*

Parkes •

Blue Mountains

Newcastle

Tuggerah Lakes

Willandra NP

Orange •

Gosford

Broken Bay

Bathurst •

Ku-ring-gai Chase NP

Katoomba •

Mungo NP

Kanangra-Boyd NP

Sydney

Port Jackson

Mildura

River

Griffith •

Berrima

Botany Bay

Murrumbidgee

Royal NP

South Pacific Ocean

Cootamundra •

Wollongong

Narrandera •

Sturt Highway

Gundagai •

Goulburn

XPT Express

Deniliquin •

Wagga Wagga •

Canberra

Jervis Bay

Melbourne & Sydney Expresses

Hume Highway

Great

Princes Highway

Batemans Bay

Murray River

Albury

Snowy Mountains!

• Cooma

Dividing

Merimbula

To Melbourne

Mt Kosciusko   • Jindabyne

Eden

Tasman Sea

Kosciusko NP

Victoria

100 km

have lagoons. They are popular for fishing and bushwalking and Avoca has two old-fashioned beach cinemas with an amazing variety of films.

Further north is The Entrance at Tuggerah Lakes, perhaps the best known of all the New South Wales coastal playgrounds. You can hire old-fashioned wooden boats to go prawning and fishing.

Inland from the Central Coast is the town of Gosford, a thriving commercial town; further inland are the beautiful valleys of Dooralong and Yarramalong. The area around Mangrove Mountain has a number of country retreats, including some ashrams.

Wiseman's Ferry has a lovely old pub and a quaint car ferry. Along the Hawkesbury River are settlements where generations have lived and died and the churches and graveyards indicate the close-knit ties between kith and kin, a little like the Appalachians in the United States. The Central Coast is well worth a visit from Sydney.

The Hunter Valley and Coast

The Hunter Valley, two hours north of Sydney, is a large area of lowland which has a wealth of natural resources. Some of the historic homesteads and grand mansions in the Hunter Valley date back to the early days of the colony. It is the site of the first vineyards in Australia, and these still produce some of Australia's finest wines.

Newcastle itself is one of the largest cities in Australia and the second largest in New South Wales. It is a wealthy and energetic city, with much to recommend it, including drama festivals, art galleries and fine old houses. It was to the north of Newcastle that the colony spread even before a way had been discovered through the Blue Mountains into the western Tablelands area.

Newcastle and its environs offer excellent fishing, particularly in places such as Myall Lakes and Port Stephens, as well as other holiday attractions.

The Holiday Coast

The Holiday Coast stretches north from Port Macquarie, 400 kilometres north of Sydney, to Tweed Heads on the Queensland border. The coastal road passes through a landscape so captivating that many families have left the cities and settled here in recent years. Life here is paced to a different drum.

Behind the beaches of Crescent Head, Nambucca Heads, Coffs Harbour, Yamba, Evans Head, Ballina and Tweed Heads, with their surfing, sailing, fishing and scuba diving, is a verdant hinterland with hills, valleys and rainforests. The subtropical climate along this coast boosts plantlife, be it wild or cultivated. Avocados, bananas, mangoes, pawpaws and macadamia and pecan nuts flourish along with other tropical fruits in lush profusion. The locals say that even a wooden leg would grow if planted here.

The estuary at Sawtell, near Coffs Harbour, northern New South Wales

The 'hippie' settlements of Nimbin and Mullumbimby, with their creed for simple living, form compatible rural communities with local farming families. Many settlements in the area have market days for the selling of homemade crafts, foods and clothes. The best known is the Channon market, held every second Sunday, at Terania Creek near Lismore.

Many of these localities have been the site of campaigns where environmentalists have fought to save the rainforests from timber and logging interests. These forests are areas of glorious scenery, with rich and varied vegetation and rare bird and animal life.

The Holiday Coast also offers activities as diverse as hang-gliding in the thermals above the cliff-tops, and gambling. Coffs Harbour has splendid surf and a safe harbour and marina for yachts. Byron Bay's Cape Byron Walking Trail leads to the most easterly point of the continent. South-west Rocks and Angourie are surfing paradises. Ballina has one of the state's biggest boat anchorages, while Evans Head is surrounded by the coastal national parks of Broadwater and Bundjalung. The list of attractions goes on and on.

Accommodation in the region ranges from budget to luxury, and restaurants range from health bars to those offering *haute cuisine*. And entertainment varies

New South Wales contains diverse geography, ranging from rain forest to desert and outback, and as shown above, extensive rich grazing lands.

The sun sets behind wild brumbies on the western plains of New South Wales.

from local musicians performing in village pubs to luxury clubs offering world-class entertainment.

It's a coast where the fish bite, and where, in the main, the pace of life is slower.

North-west Country

The North-west Country is a vast and diverse tourist region, with many assets and attractions to explore and enjoy. Its agricultural areas are rich in grain crops, wheat and cotton, and a huge pastoral area supports cattle and sheep. Mineral wealth also abounds. The opal country of Lightning Ridge owes its origins to the discovery there of surface opal in 1902. Prized since the time of the Pharaohs, no two opals are identical. They range from subtle pastels to rich, deep colours, and their value is determined not only by size and colour but also by their brightness, pattern and shape. Quality black opals are prized above all and this is the only area in the world where they are found.

The major centres in this extensive region include Bourke, Brewarrina, Cobar, Coonabarabran, Coonamble, Gilgandra, Gunnedah, Lightning Ridge, Moree, Narrabri, Nyngan, Tamworth, Walgett and Warren. Fishing enthusiasts are drawn to the Namoi, Barwon, Castlereagh, Macquarie and Narran rivers as well as the Darling, which yields good catches of perch, bream, catfish and cod. Freshwater crayfish (yabbies) can also be caught in many streams, dams and bore drains. A delight to eat, yabbies are the curse of farmers as they bore holes in the sides of dams.

Aquatic playgrounds are to be found at the water storage dams of Keepit, Chaffey and Copeton lakes; while unique to the north-west are the heated subterranean waters which provide Moree with spa baths and Lightning Ridge and Burren Junction with bore baths.

The region also boasts three national parks. The Warrumbungles, discovered by Surveyor General Evans in 1818, present nature at its most breathtaking. Forested ridges, barren spires and deep gorges once fed and sheltered the Kamilaroi tribe, evidence of whose occupation has been found in the park. Often described as the point where east meets west, the Warrumbungles support plant and animal species of both the dry western plains and the moist east coast.

At Warrabah National Park, on the upper waters of the Namoi River, huge granite boulders balance like sculptures above gorges, quiet pools and bubbling rapids. Fishing, swimming and rockclimbing are excellent and canoeists are in their element. Inquisitive bushwalkers and campers may be rewarded with sightings of a variety of wildlife. Mount Kaputar National Park is also ideal for bushwalkers, rockclimbers, geologists and nature lovers in general.

Many festivals are staged throughout the year in this region of New South Wales. Tamworth, situated at the junction of two major highways, the New England and the Oxley, hosts the Country Music Festival each January. Up to 30,000 enthusiasts converge on the city, which in 1888 was the first in the southern hemisphere to have electricity light the streets.

North-west Country is an historian's delight. It is strewn with the names of the great explorers, Evans, Sturt, Oxley, Mitchell and Cunningham, and the exploits of early expeditions and discoveries are well documented and proudly remembered.

The Warrumbungles mountain range, near Coonabarabran, borders outback New South Wales

New England

The high tablelands of the New England area with its plateaux, deep gorges, spectacular waterfalls, rivers and streams, and vast pastoral holdings in an invigorating alpine climate contrast with the coastal region, a short drive away on the other side of the Great Divide.

At the heart of this region is the university city of Armidale, with its historic buildings including "Booloominbah", built between 1883 and 1888. One of its huge stained-glass windows depicts General Gordon's stand at Khartoum and is classified by the National Trust. Fallow deer imported from Indonesia in the 1890s roam alongside wallabies and kangaroos in the Deer Park nearby. The Museum of Antiquities houses Cypriot and Greek pottery, and the imposing modern building of the Dixon Library houses a large collection of books.

The towns of Glen Innes, Inverell, Tenterfield, Walcha, Uralla and Guyra are scattered across coun-

ALLAN MOULT

The Australian Alps

Although the Australian Alps are not high by world standards (with the highest peak, Mount Kosciusko, standing a mere 2,228 metres), blizzards are liable to burst suddenly across the mountains at any time of the year. So exposed are these mountains that many an incautious skier and summer walker has been caught by the almost unpredictable changes in the weather.

In the winter, thousands of skiers crowd into the resorts. In the summer, the Alps attract an even larger number of visitors interested in fishing, bushwalking or simply admiring the wildflowers that cover the mountainsides.

The Alps were first sighted and named in 1824 by the explorers Hume and Hovell during their cross-country expedition between Sydney and Port Phillip (Melbourne). The Alps were first climbed officially in 1840 by the Polish explorer Strzelecki. He named the mountain he climbed — which he believed to be the highest — Mount Kosciusko, because he said that it resembled the tumulus of the tomb of the Polish patriot Tadeusz Kosciuszko. It is possible that he in fact climbed the nearby Mount Townsend, whose summit is surmounted by a tumulus (unlike Mount Kosciusko) and which is just 18 metres short of the tallest mountain.

Strzelecki was probably not the first white man to penetrate these mountains. Settlers had been moving into the area for some years looking for new land. Although they were not officially sanctioned by the administration in Sydney, the settlers took advantage of the high country in the summer with its lush grass and plentiful water and drove their stock into the mountains as soon as the snow began to melt. The high country was used for summer grazing until the 1950s when much of the area was declared a national park.

The Kosciusko National Park is the largest national park in the country, covering 625,810 hectares. It has been somewhat embattled from time to time by graziers resentful of the loss of summer grazing and by the Hydro-electric Scheme established in 1949, which was to dot the mountains with dams and power stations.

Before Strzelecki and the settlers, however, the various Aboriginal tribes in the area had long regarded the mountains with awe. In summer, the tribes went into the mountains to feast on the large white Bogong moth. They believed that the Bogong moth was transformed in the cold weather into flakes of snow, thus turning the high country white for several months of the year.

This is, of course, also the country of 'The Man from Snowy River'. A. B. ('Banjo') Paterson is said to have composed the ballad in a small slab hut that once stood by the Snowy River not far from Jindabyne. The hut is now beneath the waters of Lake Jindabyne, a long way from the location used for the film loosely based on Patterson's poem. The 'wild bush horses', called brumbies, still course through parts of the mountains where men rarely go. I can remember as a child being taken out on horseback by my parents and seeing the herds of brumbies streaming across distant slopes and ridges. With the greater numbers of people now coming to the mountains, the brumbies have withdrawn into the more inaccessible regions.

Skiing has become one of Australia's fastest growing participation sports. From the Queen's Birthday weekend in June until Labour Day weekend in October, the roads are full of cars crowned with ski racks making their way to the mountain ski resorts. The fastest growing mountain sport is cross-country skiing, for which these mountains, lacking the long steep pistes of Europe and America, are particularly suitable. Cross-country races of up to 30 kilometres attract thousands of entrants. The most popular of these, the Kosciusko Alpine Club's race, had 535 entrants in 1986. This same club, founded in 1909, claims to be one of the world's oldest ski clubs.

Skiing began in Australia at the time of the goldrush in the 19th century when 'diggers' strapped planks to their feet and hurtled down the slopes near the mining town of Kiandra. This once-busy town is now just a few buildings. Over the years, winter sports became increasingly popular and in the 50s and 60s a number of resorts were opened, beginning the boom that continues to this day.

The mountains and their climate contrast with the rest of Australia, the flattest and lowest continent in the world.

Christopher Leonard

STUART FOX

The dingo fence covers 5,765 kilometres along the borders of South Australia, New South Wales and Queensland. This barrier is vital in stopping the flow of dingoes into the rich grazing lands of New South Wales and Queensland

try where giant granite formations known as Devil's Marbles, some 225 million years old, loom up out of paddocks and the bush in the stunningly beautiful wilderness parks. Not to be missed is the awesome Bald Rock near Tenterfield. Rising up 200 metres, with a solid dome 750 metres long and 500 metres wide, this exposed monolith is said to be the second largest in the world, Ayers Rock being the largest. Rafting, riding, trout fishing and swimming are popular, as is the collecting of local paintings and craft. Fine examples of early Australiana can be found in these long-settled districts, while sapphires, topaz and tourmalines can still be found at Reddestone Creek.

The National Parks and Wildlife Service has organised interesting guided walks in the area and on Friday nights rangers will organise both twilight and spotlight strolls in order to observe what happens when the sun goes down. Bushwalkers and backpackers can follow marked trails through the towering trees to observe a proliferation of birdlife.

New England, where the bushranger Thunderbolt robbed the unwary, provides many reminders of the goldrush and earlier times with its folk museums and historic grazing properties.

It also provides today's traveller with excellent and varied motel, hotel, town and farm accommodation, colourful pubs and restaurants, magnificent scenery, plus a counterpoint of cultural life centred around the university in an invigorating rural environment.

The Outback

Balranald, Wilcannia, White Cliffs, Warri Gate, Menindee — what do they have in common? If travelling by road, each will be reached after hundreds and hundreds of dusty kilometres, and each is set in a pitiless landscape which some call lunar.

This is the outback of New South Wales, where it meets Queensland and South Australia, where the struggle to live decently is waged continuously against heat, dust, distance and drought. Yet there is to be found here a stark beauty which is brutal, powerful and awe-inspiring. Somewhat unsettling to many an international traveller as well as to Australians from suburbia or gentler districts, it would be impossible to claim a rounded view of our vast southern continent without a brief visit to this distinct and remote region. Its plains extend endlessly to the far horizons and the tyranny of distance here is all too real.

A jumping-off base from which to gain some insight into the outback is Broken Hill. Accessible from the major capitals by air and road, 'The Silver City Comet' and the 'Indian Pacific' railways also service this city where current production from the major operating mines amounts to approximately 2.5 million tonnes each year.

Once aboard these trains, passengers enjoying the luxury of good meals and berths may well find themselves speculating on travel in earlier times when travellers in the outback could, and did, die of thirst. Now, lounge bars are available for drinks.

Broken Hill is a place of dry heat and immense, intensely blue skies where low verandahs provide shade. Once here, take an underground mine tour, sit in on a session of the famed School of the Air, or visit the Flying Doctor Service which supplies a unique health scheme to isolated stations. Naturally, the more energetic pursuits of golf, bowling, swimming and so on are available, and the marvellous old pubs and their patrons are a pub-crawler's delight.

Broken Hill has many art galleries exhibiting Aboriginal work and the work of the bushmen of the bush — independent outback artists whose paintings may well prove aesthetically rewarding and perhaps a sound investment.

Some 28 kilometres north-west of Broken Hill is Silverton, a ghost town rediscovered by both local and overseas film producers, whose population is regularly boosted by actors and film crews.

Further afield are three magnificent national parks. Kinchega, dominated by the Darling River and the overflow system of lakes, small basins and channels, has extensive red plains. Here, too, the Kinchega Woolshed can be visited. Constructed from local timber, it was used when Kinchega station ran 143,000 sheep.

Sturt National Park, named for the explorer Charles Sturt, preserves the habitat of the unique flora and fauna of this arid region as well as some history of European settlement.

Mungo National Park is dominated by spectacular white sand dunes, and the dry bed of Lake Mungo, the site of the earliest Aboriginal occupation in Australia. The fascination of the outback is limitless. From ochre-red sand and grey-green saltbush, to the pockmarked landscape of White Cliffs which marks the remains of 50,000 opal-mining shafts, to the Birdsville Races in nearby south-western Queensland, to the grave of the camel-keeper from the Burke and Wills expedition, it can well justify its claim to fame, and its claim to a traveller's time.

Murray-Riverina

The Murray-Riverina, in common with other regions of New South Wales, presents a pleasant problem: how to have enough time to take in everything there is to offer. The area is today a far cry from the 'barren

An abandoned homestead in southern New South Wales

desolation, a howling wilderness' described by John Oxley when he first discovered it in 1817.

Some 170 years later, Oxley has been proved very wrong. The region embraces not only the major inland cities of Albury-Wodonga and Wagga Wagga, the two mighty rivers of the Murray and the Murrumbidgee (Aboriginal for 'never-failing water supply'), but also the staggeringly rich Murrumbidgee Irrigation Area. This irrigation giant has transformed an arid semi-desert into a fertile patchwork of fields and paddocks where food and wine for millions of Australians is produced. Fruit and vegetables, rice, fat lambs and prime cattle thrive here.

Bushrangers Ned Kelly, Ben Hall, Captain Moonlight and Mad Dog Morgan made these districts their stamping ground and preyed on the wealth created by the goldfields. Reminders of the abandoned goldfields and diggings still exist.

There are countless echoes of history and myth here. For example, the idea of Federation was conceived at the town of Corowa. Jack Riley, the real Man from Snowy River, is buried in the region. At Gundagai, there is the famed Dog on the Tucker Box.

Cobb & Co. coaches were constructed in the town of Hay. And in more recent times, Walter Burley Griffin, who planned Canberra, used the national capital's same radial design for Griffith and Leeton, and Sir Donald Bradman learned to wield a cricket bat at Cootamundra. However, the Murray-Riverina is not all history and agricultural enterprise, though the latter makes possible guided tours and happy wine tasting at 18 wineries in the Griffith-Leeton district.

This is also an important area for the production of the culinary specialities of the Italians, who have so successfully used the oasis created by the irrigation scheme. Local salamis, olives, artichokes, smoked trout and more whet the traveller's appetite, and every second Easter, Griffith indulges in a Vintage Festival, a supreme food festa. There are also traditional woolshed meals to be sampled and enjoyed, should the traveller wish to search out the food that sustained the early settlers.

Motels, hotels and farms provide accommodation within range of the local sports centres and activities such as ballooning and gliding. Learn to throw a boomerang in the afternoon, then disco the night away.

Towns such as Junee, Narrandera, Cootamundra and Deniliquin have art galleries, pioneer museums, garden centres and antiques, plus some surprising festivals. One such festival is the Golden Fashion Award, held in Wagga Wagga in May, when top designers from Australian capitals trundle their wares into the inland. Another is saloon car racing in Albury, and, surprisingly, a surf carnival in bottomless boats on the dry riverbed of Hay.

A further aspect of the Murray-Riverina region is its enormous variety of water activities. Rafting and canoeing, trout fishing, water-skiing and windsurfing can all be enjoyed on the immense inland lakes and dams. Hatcheries keep the fish biting for the angler (the famed Murray cod has been known to weigh in at 50 kilograms).

Henry Lawson wrote of the Murray-Riverina in 1916: 'The area is a spread of green, all chequered off, with little homes and trees and clear green fringed canals and channels, just like English brooks, set in the midst of a bare scorching dusty red and parched yellow dead land that's a lot older than Egypt.'

The Snowy Mountains

The Snowies, the roof of Australia, provides strongly contrasting seasonal delights. In winter on this range, which stretches for 160 kilometres and which culminates in Mount Kosciusko at 2,228 metres, are to be found slopes ideally suited to both the beginner and expert skier. Low by world standards, which means that snow cannot always be guaranteed, these mountains nevertheless provide superb skiing in an area which has developed rapidly during the last three

Memorable sunsets are a year-round feature of the Snowy Mountains landscape

decades since the Snowy Mountains Hydro-electric Scheme provided electricity and irrigation projects in the area.

It was in 1840 that Paul de Strzelecki climbed and named Mount Kosciusko. And Australians pioneered skiing as a sport as early as 1860 when miners on the goldfields of Kiandra strapped fence palings to their feet with the express purpose of gaining easier mobility. From this has resulted the Kiandra Snow Shoe Club, one of whose early office bearers was 'Banjo' Patterson, famed creator of 'The Man from Snowy River'.

With half a million skiers today heading for the snowfields each year, the resorts of Perisher Valley and Thredbo provide excellent hotel and lodge accommodation, lifts and ski hire, plus the après-ski delights of good food and wine.

Summer in the Snowy Mountains is also a time of beauty. With the melting of the snows come not only more accessibility, but a superb abundance of alpine wildflowers. Snow daisies, buttercups and 101 other delights for the botanist carpet acre upon acre of the 6,200 square kilometres of the Kosciusko National Park. In this harshly beautiful terrain, with distant snow drifts as a backdrop, short and easy treks can be enjoyed, as well as more taxing trails for the more hardy. Climb or take the chairlift up Crackenback Mountain and then head for the summit. Or walk the 10 kilometres from Dead Horse Gap down to the Thredbo River and along the valley floor.

Rangers in the park will lead parties or provide route maps. Naturally, it is advisable to take a map and compass on any long or unmarked walk on the main range.

Ski, hike, fish, sail or raft in awesomely beautiful country. Or ride in summer and sleep under the stars. The Snowy Mountains are a world away from smog and car fumes.

The South Coast

The South Coast of New South Wales is that area of coastline between the Illawarra region and the Victorian border. The region is easily accessible by road or plane from Melbourne, Canberra and Sydney, making it a popular holiday destination.

The town of Merimbula is the key to the area. It has a fine airport, many motels, a pretty lake and excellent tourist facilities for diving, riding and water sports. In Eden, a famous old fishing port, visitors can see the remnants of the coastal steamer trade in the town's deep-water wharfs. At one time, transport around the Australian coast was largely undertaken by steamships. Eden is also a centre for oil exploration and oil-rig servicing.

The south coast's many national parks and towns such as Bermagui and Bateman's Bay have much to offer the traveller. From Bateman's Bay, at the inlet of a river, one can strike inland to delightful valleys and fields that are reminiscent of Europe. The wildlife of the south coast area is also quite extraordinary, as are the subtropical rainforests and deserted beaches between Bateman's Bay and Durras.

All along the south coast, fishing boats and small boats can be hired and taken inland to explore the mangroves and oyster beds where a great variety of fish are found.

Along most of the south coast, the farming land fronts the ocean. And the kangaroos here are very tame and will eat out of your hand.

Illawarra

The Illawarra region, just south of Sydney, is a truly magical blend of mountains and the sea. Its narrow coastal plains and beaches rise to an escarpment of great beauty.

Easily accessible by rail from Sydney, the train follows one of the world's most scenic routes where mountains literally fall into the sea. It was in this area that D. H. Lawrence wrote his novel *Kangaroo*. The bushlands of the Royal National Park burst onto the ocean at Stanwell Park and surround all beaches south.

Surfing, scuba diving, fishing and hang-gliding are popular. The wings of gliders hover like multicoloured hawks against cliff and sky where the pioneer aviator Lawrence Hargrave once tested box kites. Other jump-off spots are to be found at Mt Keira, Port Kembla and Saddleback Mountain above Kiama.

At Kiama, a blow-hole was discovered by explorer George Bass in 1797. Rough seas spout water up to 60 metres like a mammoth rock-bound whale. Settled early, the area originally had only sea transport to Sydney.

The old dairy centres of Berry and Kangaroo Valley are set in extraordinarily lovely country. And though the great escarpment divides the coast from the highlands, several picturesque towns and the Morton National Park lie between.

The Illawarra Escarpment can be seen when sailing on Lake Illawarra behind Port Kembla or as far away as Bowral's rich pastoral properties, frequently planted with a profusion of English trees.

Fitzroy Dam and Fitzroy Falls, which plunge over sandstone cliffs before falling further to the valley floor, are well worth visiting, as are the Wombeyan Caves. Five of the caves are open to the public. Studded with stalagmites and stalactites, they present a vision of rock tapestries and frozen cascades.

Moss Vale, Bundanoon, Exeter, Sutton Forest, Robertson, Bowral and Mittagong in the highlands beyond the escarpment offer excellent accommodation. The invigorating climate, which lures holiday-makers onto the many attractive walking trails in the area, can seem more like parts of Scotland than the Australian bush when the mists roll down in autumn.

Berrima, an early settled village, has at least 50 historic buildings, including the Berrima Gaol, which

are an important part of Australia's national heritage. Here is the oldest continuously licensed inn still trading within its original walls. The town has good restaurants, galleries, antique and craft shops, and some charming nurseries.

'Find yourself or lose yourself in the Illawarra' is a slogan of the local tourist commission. It's a suggestion with which many locals and visitors will readily concur.

The Blue Mountains

The Blue Mountains, a little more than 100 kilometres from Sydney, can be reached by fast, airconditioned train from Sydney, or after a drive of around two hours.

Traditionally a weekend retreat from the city, the towns and villages of the Blue Mountains provide relief from the summer heat (at a maximum altitude of around 1,000 metres) and an experience of snowy conditions in winter.

A number of romantic hotels were built, including the Hydro Majestic in the spa town of Medlow Bath, and the Carrington at Blackheath, now being renovated. A variety of elegant boarding houses were also built at Mt Victoria and Blackheath. Most are still operating and Glenella and Cleopatra at Blackheath provide luxury accommodation and *haute cuisine*.

Katoomba is the main tourist centre of the area, with a scenic railway, cable cars, the Three Sisters (one of Australia's best-known rock formations) and views over the lush Megalong Valley.

The area is also famed for its gardens. In spring many towns open private gardens to the public, and spectacular displays of rhododendrons and cold-climate flowers are a delight for visitors.

The Blue Mountains are a breath of fresh air, a place of calm and an expanse of beautiful bush and rugged landscape.

Andrew Fisher and Natalie Scott

The Blue Mountains - a traditional escape for Sydneysiders at the height of summer

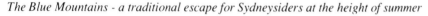

Melbourne, Pride & Tradition

Melbourne has always enjoyed an alluringly ambiguous reputation, even from its earliest days as a struggling riverside settlement. Its champions were proud of its situation and booming economy; its detractors scoffed at its pretensions to grandeur and its wide, empty, 'ruled-off' streets. But Melbourne's inhabitants have never doubted its importance. In the early 1840s, the grand city centre was planned and laid out in straight, wide avenues, even though not enough money was available to clear those impressive boulevards of tree stumps.

More than any other Australian city, Melbourne is enormously diverse. Not only is its population drawn from the most varied cultural backgrounds — a phenomenon reflected in the vast range of ethnic restaurants, markets and clubs scattered throughout the city — but its weather is surely the most changeable of any city in the world — a single day in Melbourne can display climatic extremes that other cities need 12 months to produce. It is this variety, this intriguing mixture, that gives Melbourne its special character and charm. It is a city that resists any superficial label, but which rewards even the most cursory attempt to explore it. It may be a difficult city to enjoy as a spectator, but it is surely among the easiest and most welcoming to enjoy as a participant.

And what better way to participate in the life of the city than to start exploring it on the famous Melbourne trams? Arm yourself with a day ticket and off you go! Although some of the older trams will look like museum pieces, do not be discouraged. If they are on the tracks, they are in use and fair game, and you will be surprised at just how user-friendly the public transport of this city can be. Take a short ride within the city just to accustom yourself to the whole idea, to get your

'tram-legs' — a ride to the top of Collins Street, perhaps, getting off in front of the Treasury Buildings.

This end of Collins Street was once known as the 'Paris end', because of its elegant buildings and tree-lined pavements. It has been pretty thoroughly vandalised since then, and many of the finest buldings have been pulled down, but a stroll back down to the city centre will reveal glimpses of its former glory.

While the 'Paris end' of Collins Street may have gone, Melbourne retains some of the world's most impressive examples of Victorian architecture. And the beauty of Melbourne's architectural heritage is that it is not just the large public buildings (such as the Royal Exhibition Buildings in Carlton) that have been saved; the Victorian domestic architecture remains in the rows of terraced houses and streets of timber workers' cottages in the inner suburbs — the greatest concentration of Victorian architecture anywhere in the world. Walk along Drummond Street in Carlton, or Gipps or Powlett Street in East Melbourne.

Most of Melbourne's finest buildings are a legacy of the goldrush. Gold provided not just the economic wherewithal to plan the splendid new mansions and civic buildings, but also the necessary mood of aggressive optimism to carry out their construction. The discovery of gold was not an unmixed blessing, however. At the time, there seemed a real danger of Melbourne disappearing altogether! Whole suburbs of the city were deserted, crime was rife, and to make matters worse, within six months of the news of the first strike, 38 of Melbourne's 40-strong police force had resigned. For a time, Geelong became the favoured port of the colony because it was closer to the diggings, and the merchants of Melbourne resorted to the underhanded ploy of printing false maps of the gold-

MILTON WORDLEY

*Home of the Melbourne Cup, Australia's premier multi-million dollar horse race, the southern city retains a
year-round interest in track events*

fields showing them snuggled up close to Melbourne and relocating Geelong on the other side of Port Phillip Bay. They need not have worried. Lucky diggers instinctively returned to Melbourne to spend their money, and as the gold petered out many of the not so lucky ones came looking for work in the new industries that had developed in the city.

Many important buildings are now maintained by the National Trust. These include La Trobe's Cottage in The Domain, South Yarra, our first Government House, and the Melbourne Maritime Museum in South Melbourne, which features the restored barque *Polly Woodside*, and a collection of nautical bits and pieces. A visit to the gardens of 'Como' in South Yarra or 'Rippon Lea' in Elsternwick is also highly recommended. As an antidote to the airy light and grace of those properties, a visit to the Old Melbourne Gaol should prove effective. Still in use during the Second

World War as a military prison, the remaining cell block has now been preserved by the National Trust as a penal museum. This building has seen more than 100 hangings, including that of the notorious bushranger Ned Kelly, and it houses an appropriately grisly collection.

Every bit as prison-like in appearance — it even has a moat — the National Gallery of Victoria is home to the state's impressive art collection. Despite its forbidding appearance, it is surprisingly easy to get in and out of, as was demonstrated in 1986 when a group of disaffected Melbourne artists walked out with the gallery's recently acquired Picasso, 'Weeping Woman'. No one noticed until the group sent a letter to the Minister for the Arts, explaining the action as a protest against almost everything connected with the arts in Victoria. The painting was subsequently returned, security was tightened, and the gallery resumed normal activities. Normal activities at this innovative and imaginatively administered gallery include music recitals, public lectures and discussions, and special exhibitions from its own and other collections.

The Victorian Arts Centre, of which the National Gallery is a part, is situated on the Yarra River opposite the Queen Victoria Gardens. The theatres and Concert Hall are worth exploring, not least for the paintings and other artworks in the foyers. You can't miss the complex, one of whose buildings has a very large inverted ice-cream cone on the top. Government publicists insist that this has become a prominent Melbourne landmark and to prove that Melbourne really is the home of Australian humour, the spire is illuminated at night.

Melbourne has always supported a large and lively artistic colony, which has consistently found itself at loggerheads with the city's more respectable citizens. This bohemian community, perhaps the city's hardiest ethnic group and certainly the least likely to be assimilated, is much in evidence today and still has a style all its own. Neither as precious as Adelaide nor as flash as Sydney, the art of Melbourne is characteristically robust, irreverent, wry and accessible. Such work is to be found in the small galleries and theatres of the inner city and a careful reading of the What's On section of the press will always turn up something of interest.

Live theatre is very much a Melbourne speciality and as often as not the key note is humour. Many of the small theatres are unprepossessing affairs (rug up in winter!), but much of the best Australian drama passes through these venues before the playwrights win acclaim, move to Sydney, and begin appearing on daytime television instead of writing.

No review of the culture of Melbourne would be complete without mention of the passion for sport. Unlike cities which segregate art and sport, in Melbourne the two have always been comfortably intertwined. The city's most famous sporting arena, the Melbourne Cricket Ground, needs only an illuminated spire for the similarities between it and the buildings of the Arts Centre to become apparent. This connection between the arts and sport has long been noted. In 1886, Fergus Hume wrote, 'If there is one thing which the Melbourne folk love more than another, it is music, their fondness for which is only equalled by their admiration for horse-racing.'

The admiration for horse-racing is alive and well. Every November, the whole of Australia stops what it is doing for the running of the Melbourne Cup, the showpiece of the Spring Racing Carnival. Throughout the Carnival, Flemington Racecourse is a sea of morning suits and millinery in the Members' Stand as the toffs compete in the fashion stakes and are mercilessly lampooned in the public enclosure.

Flemington is only one of the four racetracks in

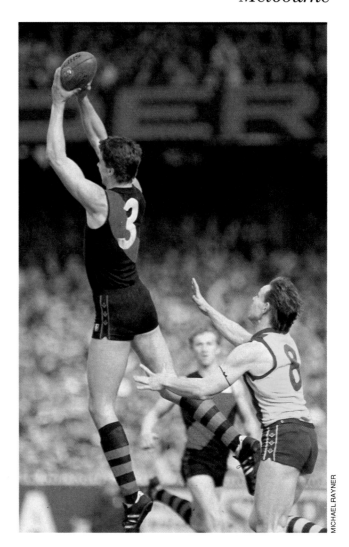

'Footie' is another sporting tradition in Melbourne - a game that dominates all other outdoor activities

MICHAEL RAYNER

Melbourne; the others are Sandown, Caulfield and Moonee Valley. All have their feature races, of course, but for something a little different, consider spending a Saturday night at 'the trots' at Moonee Valley. The spectator areas are enclosed and air-conditioned and are fully equipped with betting facilities and restaurants. Take to the dance floor or watch the races — either way, you could end up with more in your wallet than you started with. How many other restaurants tip their customers?

Horse-racing is only one of Melbourne's passions, however. At various times of the year, the city becomes equally excited about the tennis, the golf and the cricket. But never quite as excited as it does in September when the Grand Final of the football takes place. Australian Rules Football, of course. An opportunity to attend a finals match in Melbourne should not be missed. Experience the excitement and the spectacle of 100,000 crazed, but essentially good-natured, football fans. There is nothing quite like it.

Like most Australian cities, Melbourne sprawls over an enormous area and it is not surprising that there are many centres of commercial activity. Melbourne people are fond of the city's local markets which bustle with activity and offer a baffling variety of goods for sale. When buying from the stalls, the emphasis seems to be on enjoyment — there is plenty of banter, community information is exchanged, and regulars are greeted as friends. There are markets all over Melbourne, each with its own special character, but the busiest and most frantic is the Queen Victoria Markets.

A visit to the Queen Victoria Markets on a weekend is an education in the variety of the Melbourne population. People of every nation, shade and persuasion mill around the stalls, steering their shopping jeeps through the crowds, and arranging small children and shopping baskets on their arms. The air is thick with the smells of fresh bread, fragrant cheeses and spicy sausages.

A more genteel buying frenzy can be observed in the swish shopping centre of South Yarra. From the corner of Punt Road and Toorak Road, boutiques, bookshops, galleries and restaurants are concentrated along Toorak Road and down Chapel Street. Other notable shopping streets, particularly for designer clothing, include Lygon Street in Carlton, High Street in Armadale, and Bridge Road in Richmond.

Melbourne is also handsomely endowed with parks and gardens in which to relax. Again, the most distinctive feature of the city's parks is their variety. You can walk along the river and enjoy the quiet bushland setting of the Yarra Bend Park, or along the foreshore of St Kilda; you can enjoy the expanse of the Treasury and Fitzroy Gardens and visit Captain Cook's Cottage, or stroll around the more formal King's Domain and watch the eights rowing on the river or visit the Shrine of Remembrance.

Whatever you do, do not miss the Royal Botanic Gardens in South Yarra. One of the finest landscaped gardens in the world, it puts the botanic gardens of other cities to shame. A network of pathways traces its way through massive oaks and towering river red gums, around lakes and ponds, and through ferny dells of recreated rainforest. It is truly remarkable and has a special place in the hearts of Melburnians. Regular visitors have their favourite views and picnic spots. The thick screen of trees that surrounds the Botanic Gardens seems to filter out the noise and bustle of the city. The air itself seems cleaner here and the world a little saner.

One of the supreme joys of living in Melbourne is dining out. No other Australian city is as richly stud-

An eight-man racing skiff sets out along the Yarra River for a training run

City Extras

Astra Chauffeured Hire Cars

Ph. (03) 489 7777
Chauffeur-driven tours

Budget Chauffeur Drive

Ph. (03) 320 6161
Tours, secretarial services and interpreters

Hughes Chauffeured Limousines

Ph. (03) 646 4333
Sight-seeing, shopping trips and picnics

Luxury Chauffeur Drive

Ph. (03) 478 8788
Sight-seeing and interpreters

Melbourne Out and About

Ph. (03) 241 1085
Heritage walking tours of Melbourne

Receptive Oceania

Ph. (03) 699 6810
Multi-lingual guide service

Vintage Fun Hire Cars

Ph. (03) 754 7670
Chauffeur-driven tours and picnics using authentic vintage cars

LANCE NELSON

ded with restaurants, and because of the diversity of the population it is unlikely that there is a single cuisine that is not represented. The choice is so bewildering that it may be necessary to buy or borrow an up-to-date restaurant guide — any bookshop or hotel will be able to recommend one. Take your time looking through it and be adventurous! Melbourne is a harbour city, with some of the finest seafood in the country. Some of the smaller ethnic restaurants pay more attention to the quality and authenticity of the food than to the niceties of decor, but they usually represent extremely good value for money. On the other hand, there is no shortage of elegant, first-class restaurants if that is your preference.

Melbourne is not a city to be enjoyed passively. Its character can never be caught on postcards; it has to be experienced. Much has been written and said about the 'rivalry' between the two great eastern cities, Sydney and Melbourne. There is nothing to it. No-one in Melbourne can see where Sydney even approaches their city. It certainly cannot rival it. Take the time to explore and exploit Melbourne and you will agree with the conventional wisdom: Sydney is beautiful, but Melbourne is authentic.

Howard Firkin

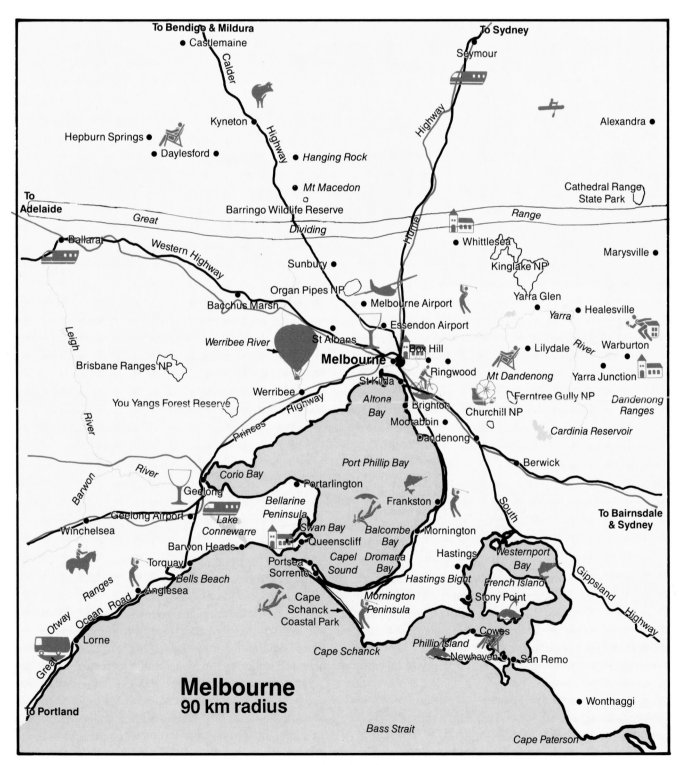

Melbourne
90 km radius

Victoria

All the variety Australia has to offer — natural, artificial and social — is on show in Victoria. Rugged coastline and rolling pasture, alpine ski resorts and spectacular surf beaches, hillside vineyards and harsh scrubby deserts are all to be found in a state that makes up only 3% of the whole country. That means less travelling and more arriving!

Variety and contrast are the key words in any description of Victoria. The smallest of all the mainland states, it is the most densely populated, producing around one-third of the gross national product. It is home to some of the country's oldest and best-established families, and yet it was the site of the country's only armed uprising. Its geographical and climatic diversity is such that it has some of the last of the world's temperate rainforest and some of the most inhospitable desert. And, as might be expected of such a place, its history has been one of boom and bust.

European settlement of Victoria got off to a shaky start. In 1803, 400 convicts, soldiers, free women and children left England to found a settlement on the Mornington Peninsula at Sorrento. It was an adventure characterised by a lack of enthusiasm on the part of almost everyone involved. The sole purpose of the settlement was to keep out the French who were looking around the southern coast of the continent and exhibiting an interest in the area. The English could not understand their interest, but were sure that it was unacceptable. This first settlement lasted only seven unpleasant months, being ultimately defeated by lacklustre leadership and the difficulty of farming the poor, sandy soil.

A second attempt to settle the region was not made until almost 25 years later. Again, it was French interest in the area that prompted the move, but although the land around the site chosen on the shores of Westernport was a little more rewarding, this second expedition fared no better than the first. Its pioneers barely had time to celebrate the first anniversary of the camp before the huts were abandoned and the cattle turned loose. It seemed to cool the French ardour for the place, anyway.

However, Victoria was not entirely without European inhabitants. While there was no permanent settlement, all along the coast small gangs of men worked as sealers and whalers. A rough and independent breed, there was no official record of their number. Many were escaped convicts who eked out a precarious life in lonely makeshift huts by trading oil and seal-skins when sailing ships anchored nearby.

The business of the whalers was with the sea, yet they were in some part responsible for Victoria's first permanent settlements at Portland and Melbourne. The Tasmanian schooners that traded for kegs of oil and seal-skins took back with them the whalers' stories of vast sweeping pastures, ideal for grazing sheep and cattle. Such stories found ready listeners in the older colony of Tasmania where most of the best sheep country was already occupied and whose thriving pastoralists were eager to find new, cheap land. The European settlement of Victoria can thus be traced back to three expeditions from the then tiny Tasmanian township of Launceston.

The first Tasmanians to cross Bass Strait and settle in Victoria were the Henty brothers. They chose Portland Bay for their camp and soon established a whaling station on the coast and sheep runs extending inland for some 100 kilometres. Expeditions organised by John Batman and John Pascoe Fawkner soon followed to Port Phillip Bay. A settlement began at a 'delightful spot' near the mouth of the Yarra River, where William Street now runs down to the river.

Within months, hundreds of sheep were being unloaded and the push into Victoria's interior began in earnest.

All three expeditions were in defiance of the law. The official policy of the British government was to 'confine settlement' in the interests of maintaining effective administrative control. It was fighting a losing battle. The squatters and their sheep spread out over the land until Victoria was little more than a huge, unfenced sheep run, dotted with homesteads and shepherds' huts. The squatters were eventually granted permission to graze the land, but it was little more than a concession to the inevitable.

The squatters who established their flocks in the rich grazing lands of Victoria's west were originally political rebels. They defied the government in settling the region and were the loudest voices in calling for an independent colony of Victoria. Once they were accorded legitimate status, however, and had acquired freehold to their vast sheep runs, they became the colony's 'society' and the western districts quickly formed their own 'squattocracy'. Their power was not simply economic. They dominated the Legislative Council of the colony and made it one of the most fiercely conservative houses of parliament in the English-speaking world.

The speed of the expansion of the pastoral industry in Victoria was remarkable enough, but it was the discovery of gold in 1851 that really set things humming. Actually, gold was 'discovered' in Victoria many times before 1851, and there are dozens of incidents recorded of shepherds coming to Melbourne to sell nuggets they had picked up. In 1847, for example, a particularly down-at-heel shepherd walked into a Collins Street jeweller and pulled out a nugget 'as big as an apple'. He claimed not to have bothered with 'any of the smaller ones'. The Governor of the day, Joseph La Trobe, was well aware of the existence of gold in Victoria, and Earl Grey, the Colonial Secretary, told the president of the Royal Geographical Society that he would not 'facilitate its discovery, but would rather send someone to hide it'. This led to the situation in 1849 when the news of the Californian goldrush reached Melbourne of men leaving to hazard the long overseas journey to California when one of the richest goldfields in the world was literally at their feet.

When word of the enormous riches of the Victorian goldfields did get out, the whole world seemed to be fighting for a share of the prize. Crews deserted their ships, husbands deserted their families, sanity deserted everyone. In the decade that followed the discovery of gold, the population of the state increased seven-fold. Tales of huge nuggets just inches below the surface, of creek beds glistening with gold powder, of hotels that washed down their floors every night to recover the gold dust the miners' boots left scattered about, of the fabulous wealth to be had brought men in their thousands to the tiny colony. The diggings were a sea of canvas tents and rude slab huts. Towns sprang up overnight and fortunes made on the diggings were left mostly in these towns, in the sly-grog shops and gambling schools, and in the opium dens and brothels.

The goldrush ended in the 1860s, but its effect was permanent. Not only had the state become instantly populated — a population that now supplied the manpower to work the new industries that grew up everywhere — but the capital, Melbourne, had become the financial and commercial capital of the country and wore its status proudly. In 1890, Melbourne's first sky-scraper was built. At a staggering 12 storeys, the 'Australian Building' was taller than anything in New York. The large population and the concentration of wealth set the scene for Victoria's continued growth, and they have ensured that the state remains a major industrial and manufacturing power

and that its importance nationally continues to grow out of all proportion to its physical size.

Physically, Victoria is dominated by the end of the Great Dividing Range, the 'backbone' of Australia's eastern states. These mountains sweep across most of the eastern half of the state in a broad horizontal band. They break just north of Melbourne to accommodate the Hume Highway — the major escape route from Sydney — and reappear in the gentle hills and mountains of the Central Highlands district. Then, just as it seems set to fizzle out into a series of scattered volcanic hills, the Great Dividing Range concludes in a burst of beauty in the spectacular Grampians.

There are enormous differences between the different sections of the Great Dividing Range in Victoria. The Grampians in the west, for example, are not-ed for their sheer cliff faces and rock caves, many of which are decorated with ancient Aboriginal paint-ings. The mountains of the Central Highlands district are less spectacular, but are famous for their abundant mineral springs. And the mountains in the east, the highest in Victoria, are the site of the state's booming ski industry.

Victoria has some of the best-developed snow-fields in the country for both downhill and cross-country skiing. Downhill skiers are well catered for at all the major resorts, where networks of ski tows and lifts provide the kinetic energy necessary for their sport, and hotels, clubs and discos absorb any excess energy in the evenings. Cross-country skiers are also well looked after and their numbers continue to increase. Traditionally, cross-country skiers were 'a breed apart'. If they deigned to use a ski resort at all, it was only as a hub of their explorations of the moun-tains, a place to leave the car and to return to for a wash and a meal after a few days' camping out in the

Captain Cook's cottage in Melbourne, above, has been faithfully restored, as has Puffing Billy, left, which cruises along on regular schedules in the nearby Dandenong hills

snow. And if the downhill skiers thought them slightly comical in their knickerbockers, jumpers and knapsacks, striding out like clockwork toys, the cross-country skiers were openly contemptuous of the flashily dressed 'yo-yo's' (moving senselessly up and down) and concentrated on 'serious skiing'. There appears to be more understanding now between these rival alpine cultures, and most resorts now have properly marked and maintained nordic ski trails and offer tuition in the mysteries of the art. It is even quite acceptable for skiers to admit to enjoying both types of skiing, although some nordic purists, shivering in their tiny alpine tents, view the sudden popularity of their sport with a great deal of misgiving.

The alpine region is also slowly being developed as a summer tourist destination. The Bogong High Plains in the very heart of the Victorian Alps, for example, have some of the most beautiful mountain scenery in the country and are a delight for bushwalkers and campers. In spring and early summer, the mountains are covered with wildflowers and the streams and lakes are well stocked with trout which feed hungrily on both insects and fishing lures. The whole area is oversupplied with tourist beds in summer, and it is possible to spend an inexpensive and relaxing holiday exploring the quiet beauty of the mountains. It need not be without adventure, of course. Members of the lunatic fringe of the fitness movement might like to tackle the Alpine Walking Track which will take them from the beautiful mining town of Walhalla in the south of Victoria through 400 kilometres of the Victorian Alps to the Kosciusko National Park in New South Wales.

North of the Alps are the richest river plains of the Murray. This region supports a large sheep and cattle grazing industry, but is best known for its fruit, particularly peaches, pears and apricots. These are great eating, without doubt, but watching fruit ripen is a pretty uninspiring tourist spectacle. There is, however, another fruit grown extensively in the region: grapes.

West of Albury/Wodonga is Rutherglen, Victoria's premier wine town. The area surrounding the town is dotted with vineyards, many of venerable ancestry, all of which welcome visitors thirsty for knowledge of the region's robust, full-bodied wines. There are many ways of visiting the wineries. Driving yourself by car would seem the obvious choice, but it does restrict the time that can be spent on serious appreciation of the wines, given Victoria's particularly harsh drink/driving laws. For this reason, special tours are organised by rail and coach, but an increasingly popular way of getting around is to take part in a group bicycle tour. This may sound like another commando exercise designed to appeal to those hairy-chested masochists who tackle the Alpine Walking Track and similar jaunts, but these 'Winery Wobbles' are conducted in a far more civilised spirit. The cycling is generally fairly leisurely, speed being sacrificed to the necessities of

sight-seeing, and the grace and bearing of the riders usually decreases markedly in direct proportion to the number of wineries visited. A support vehicle is on hand to cart around any purchases and to encourage and assist stragglers.

There is also much of historical interest in the area, some of it unconnected with wine. The township of Beechworth, for example, is a perfectly preserved goldfields town. Every second town in rural Australia is labelled 'historic', but Beechworth is the genuine article. Over 30 of its buildings are classified by the National Trust. It was originally built to serve as the administrative capital for north-eastern Victoria, and no expense was spared in building a permanent town in the beautiful honey-toned granite of the area. Most impressive of all the Beechworth sights is the group of

From cross-country skiing to drifting down a river - it's all possible on any one winter's day in Victoria

government buildings, comprising the Court House, the Lands Office, the Police Station, the Gold Warden's Offices and the Gaol. Other notable attractions include the Powder Magazine, the Murray Breweries, the Mental Hospital and the Coach and Carriage Museum. The countryside around Beechworth is also very beautiful and visitors should plan a picnic at one of the sites along the Forest Drive which winds its way through the hills to the south-east.

Still in the eastern half of the state but south of the mountains is the region known as Gippsland. In West Gippsland, around Korumburra and Leongatha, the land is characterised by steep rolling hills of lush pasture. Further east, the country is more rugged. The early settlers took two and three generations to clear these mountains, the Strzelecki Ranges, of most of their original vegetation before discovering that the land was far to steep to farm successfully. Fortunately, the mountains of the Bulga National Park were never cleared and it is today one of the very few examples of temperate rainforest anywhere in the world. The mighty Mountain Ash and thick scrub found here once covered most of Gippsland. Travelling along the Grand Ridge Road which twists tortuously through the mountains leaves an undying impression of the heroic proportions of the blunder made when trying to clear this land for farming: a rural Charge of the Light Brigade. A sad reminder of past times and attitudes is the small plaque marking the site of the world's tallest tree. Legend insists it was cut down in order to measure it accurately.

West of the Strzelecki Ranges are the beautiful

ALLAN MOULT

saltwater lakes that make up Australia's largest system of inland waterways. The Gippsland Lakes are renowned for their quiet beauty and they attract thousands of visitors each summer who come to fish, swim, cruise, sail, surf and, if they have time with over 400 square kilometres of waterways to explore, relax. Lakes Entrance is the centre of activity; a sleepy town in the off-season, it becomes frantic in the summer months.

Without doubt, the jewel of this region of Victoria is one of Australia's favourite national parks, Wilson's Promontory (or, to give its local name, 'The Prom'). A much-loved holiday destination, it has spectacular views, fascinating animal and plantlife, and an intriguing geological diversity. One of its most telling advantages is its accommodation facilities, which include

self-contained flats and lodges as well as the more usual camping sites. This makes it very popular with comfort-conscious nature lovers. The Prom offers all the usual coastal attractions — walking tracks, beautiful beaches, stunning ocean vistas, mosquitoes, and so on — but it is also a great favourite with the scuba diving fraternity who explore the dozens and dozens of shipwrecks in the area.

Nearer to Melbourne is the resort of Phillip Island. Something of a last resort, in a way. The cheap fibro holiday shacks that abound on the island are so tacky they are almost appealing. And yet the beaches of Phillip Island are very beautiful, ranging from quiet, often empty, sandy coves to long, open surf beaches. The island is also home to thousands of fairy penguins, the smallest species of penguin, and on summer evenings they can be observed struggling up from the sea to their nests in the sand dunes.

To the west of Phillip Island is the Mornington Peninsula, the long arm of land that curls around and encloses the waters of Port Phillip Bay. It has long been the most popular summer destination of the citizens of Melbourne, and the towns on both sides of the peninsula are well equipped to cater for tourists. Portsea and Sorrento are two of the most popular towns. Both are famed for their beaches: the bayside beaches favoured by the socialites, and the 'back beaches', the surf beaches, where people occasionally go so far as to get wet. Despite its popularity, Sorrento is a picturesque seaside town, with old buildings of local limestone. It is of historic interest, being the site of the first European settlement of the state. Portsea has its own claim to fame. Not only was the first shot of the First World War fired from Point Nepean, but it led to the first prisoners of war being taken. Ask a local if you don't believe it.

The other side of Port Phillip Bay is the Bellarine Peninsula. Snuggled at its base is Victoria's second largest city, Geelong. Geelong once rivalled Melbourne in importance — in the eyes of most of its inhabitants it still does — but the superior harbour of Melbourne eventually ensured its dominance. However, it was a pretty close run, especially during the goldrush when Geelong was the favoured port for diggers as it was closer to the goldfields. The effects of the goldrush on Geelong can still be seen in its fine civic buildings and private mansions. Of special interest in Geelong is the Memorial Art Gallery, which has a fine collection of colonial paintings, the Botanic Gardens, one of the earliest gardens established in Victoria, and Barwon Grange, an especially fine homestead overlooking the Barwon River. Two prefabricated homes are also of interest: Corio Villa, a cast-iron home manufactured in Scotland, and The Heights, a weatherboard prefab from Germany that makes today's designs look totally inadequate. It has 14 rooms, a dovecot, stables and lookout tower. Geelong is also home of one of the most loyally supported football teams in the Victorian Football League, and visiting teams dread the fiercely parochial barracking dished out at Kardinia Park. It is generally agreed that the Geelong football supporters are so one-eyed they would boo Santa Claus. So far, he hasn't been game to show up.

The seaside towns of the Bellarine Peninsula have escaped the uncontained expansion that has disfigured some of the once-pretty towns on the Mornington Peninsula, and especially in the cooler months they have an enchantingly dreamy air. This is particularly true of Queenscliff, with its many pretty Victorian cottages, grand hotels, and the rather quaint (though it must surely have once seemed redoubtable) Fort Queenscliff standing guard over all.

This part of Victoria's coast has some of the country's best surf beaches, including Bell's Beach and Jan Juc Beach. The surf here, unlike the picture postcard stuff found further north, has the reputation of providing some of the most testing and exhilarating surfing to be found anywhere in the world. The Easter Surfing Carnival held at Bell's Beach is a major event on the international surfing calendar and attracts a large and colourful crowd.

Lorne marks the beginning of one of the most spectacular drives in the country. The Great Ocean Road winds around the rugged coastline and sheer cliffs of the area, offering breathtaking views. The section between Princetown and Peterborough, where the fierce winds and violent seas have left the limestone cliffs along the coast studded with strange formations, is unforgettable. Arches, shelves, blow-holes, and massive sculptured figures rise out of the sea. The Loch Ard Gorge, the Grotto, London Bridge and the Twelve Apostles are some of the features to be seen. The whole of Victoria's south-western coastline is treacherous for ships, and none more so than this stretch.

Not to be missed, also, are the coastal towns of Port Fairy and Portland. Port Fairy is one of the prettiest, most charming villages in Australia, with much of interest in the town itself and in the surrounding countryside. Portland has some fine architecture as well as the natural beauty of its environs, particularly Cape Bridgewater and the Great South-west Walk.

Away from the coastline, Victoria's west becomes increasingly dry. The great volcanic plains of the Western District still enjoy sufficient rainfall to support a huge pastoral industry, but as you progress further north, the vegetation begins to thin out, the land supports fewer people, and the signs of successful farming become fewer. As you might expect, the nearer you get to South Australia, the bleaker things become. By the time you reach Sunset Country in the north-west corner of the state, the country has given way to rolling sand-dunes and scantily grassed flat plains. There are several areas of desert and semi-desert wilderness areas in the north-west, including Wyperfeld National

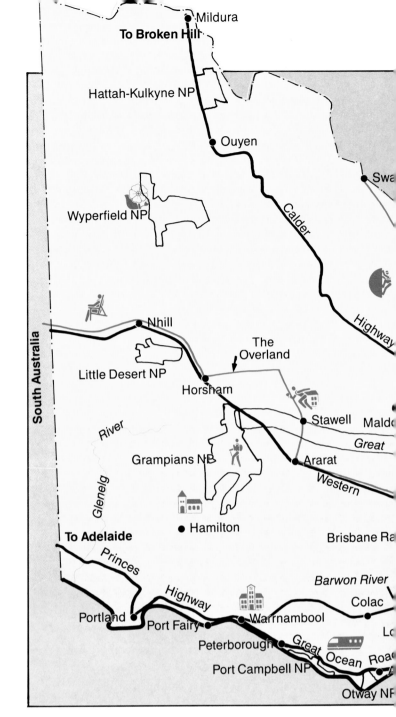

Park and Pink Lakes State Park. Although the country seems harsh and forbidding, a surprising variety of wildlife is found here. The birdlife is especially diverse.

In the far north of the state, the situation changes again, thanks largely to the irrigation waters of the Murray River. The area around Mildura and Swan Hill produces much of Australia's dried fruit as well as citrus and stone fruit. But, in the north, the real attraction is the river itself. People come to fish, swim and boat. Many different river cruises are available. You can take a trip on a restored old paddle-steamer, or hire a luxury houseboat and explore the river at your own pace. Perhaps the most interesting town on the Murray is Echuca. Once the largest inland port in Australia, Echuca possess a massive red gum wharf, recalling the days of the river trade. If you cruise up the river towards Cobram, you will find beautiful sandy beaches in the bends of the river.

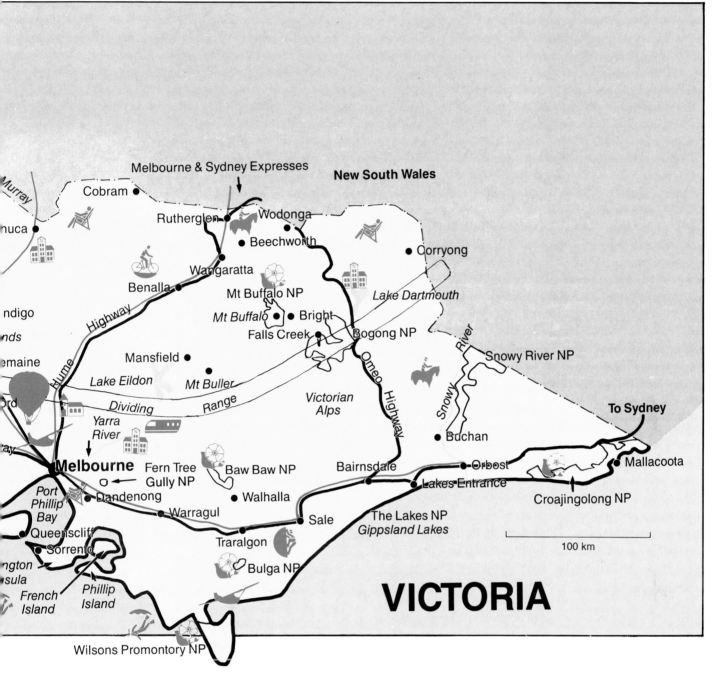

Melbourne & Sydney Expresses
New South Wales
Cobram
Murray
huca
Rutherglen
Wodonga
Beechworth
Corryong
Wangaratta
Benalla
Mt Buffalo NP
Lake Dartmouth
ndigo
Mt Buffalo
Bright
nds
Falls Creek
Bogong NP
maine
Mansfield
Omeo Highway
Snowy River
Snowy River NP
Lake Eildon
Mt Buller
Victorian Alps
To Sydney
rd
Dividing Range
Yarra River
Buchan
Melbourne
Fern Tree Gully NP
Baw Baw NP
Bairnsdale
Orbost
Mallacoota
Port Phillip Bay
Dandenong
Walhalla
Lakes Entrance
Croajingolong NP
ay
Warragul
Sale
Queenscliff
Traralgon
The Lakes NP
Gippsland Lakes
100 km
Sorrento
ngton sula
Bulga NP
French Island
Phillip Island
VICTORIA
Wilsons Promontory NP

The Central Highlands district of Victoria is one of the richest areas of tourist interest. In the north of this district is Bendigo, the third largest city in regional Victoria. Bendigo grew up surrounded by one of the richest goldfields in the world. The enormous wealth created by the goldrush allowed the burghers of Bendigo to construct buildings in any style they fancied. It seems that their taste ran mostly to the ornate. Certainly Bendigo now has an impressive legacy of the sometimes florid architecture of the times, notably the Shamrock Hotel. But more important than any single building are the old streetscapes, and a walking tour around the town will more than repay the effort. Other points of interest are the Central Deborah Mine, the idiosyncratic mansion 'Fortuna', the Bendigo Art Gallery, and the Chinese Joss House. The Bendigo Pottery is a famous attraction, and there cannot be many tourists who have left Bendigo without at least one small piece of its distinctive ceramicware.

The other main city of the Central Highlands is Ballarat. Between Bendigo and Ballarat, however, are several places of interest. Maldon is a town so well preserved and restored that it seems more like a recreation than a living town. Castlemaine has an incongruously classical market and fine Art Gallery. Daylesford and Hepburn Springs are famous for their mineral springs. Clunes is a sleepy gold town, largely unspoiled. And Creswick, home of the Lindsay family, has a very fine collection of local art in the Historical Museum in the Town Hall. If that weren't enough, the drive to Ballarat passes through lush forests and farmlands.

Ballarat, with a population of well over 60,000, is the state's most important inland city, and the most famous of Victoria's many gold towns. It was the setting, not only for some of the biggest gold strikes, but also for the famous Eureka Uprising when thousands of rebellious miners burned their gold licences and proclaimed themselves independent of the harsh mining laws and of the brutal methods used to enforce them.

By 1854, much of the easily accessible gold had been won and most miners were finding barely enough gold to keep body and soul together. They were still required, however, to find 30 shillings a month to pay for their licence fee. Discontentment with the fee was rife all over the diggings, but it was more concentrated in Ballarat because much of the gold there was found in deep underground leads which took many months of hard work to reach — if it could be found at all! The catalyst for the miners' rebellion was the murder of James Scobie, a popular digger, by the suitably unpopular publican of Bentley's Hotel. Bentley was acquitted of the crime by the magistrate, a personal friend, and the enraged miners saw this as one more powerful example of the attitude of the authorities to the miners in general. They rioted at Bentley's pub and burned it to the ground.

On 29 November, the miners gathered on Bakery Hill and made a bonfire of their licences, calling for an end to the licence fee and for the right to vote. 'No taxation without representation!' was the cry. The government of the 'squattocracy' responded by ordering a licence hunt, and the miners gathered behind the hastily built Eureka Stockade and hoisted their flag, still preserved in the Ballarat Fine Art Gallery. Poorly armed and never really expecting an attack, the miners were quickly overcome when soldiers and troopers opened fire. The rebellion was over in less than 15 minutes. Thirty miners were killed and the stockade was razed. The site is marked by a memorial diorama and a mock stockade nearby.

Ballarat has much to interest the casual day-tripper as well as the more dedicated tourist. Perhaps the best-known and most popular attraction is Sovereign Hill, a recreated goldmining town which displays the processes of gold-digging (puddling, cradling and panning, as well as shaft and lead mining) and the secondary commercial life that so quickly sprang up around the goldfields: bakeries, stables, blacksmiths, and so on. There are restaurants and cafes, and visitor accommodation is available.

Ballarat also boasts an important regional art gallery, containing many Australian paintings and the Lindsay Gallery — a recreation of the sitting room of the Creswick home of this famous artistic family.

Ballarat's botanic gardens are especially fine and are dotted with sculpture, much of it donated last century by mining magnates. A feature of the gardens is Prime Ministers' Avenue, which displays the busts of every prime minister since Federation. Visitors come from all over Australia just to say a couple of words, usually very brief, to these august figures of our past and present. The gardens also contain Adam Lindsay Gordon's Cottage, where this flamboyant and ill-starred poet lived in 1867–8.

Life is mostly froth and bubble,
Two things stand like stone,
Kindness in another's trouble,
Courage in your own.

He committed suicide in 1870.

There is much more to Ballarat, including the Hymettus Cottage Garden, the Ballarat Wildlife and Reptile Park, the Gold Museum, Montrose Cottage and the Old Curiosity Shop. It also has some of the best restaurants outside of Melbourne.

Because Victoria is so compact and, for Australia, densely populated, it is well serviced by public transport and the rail and coach tours are many and varied. But the best way to explore the state is still by car. Victorian roads are well maintained and clearly marked, and Victour, the government tourist authority, produces an excellent booklet of suggested tours to make by car. The whole state is studded with hotels, motels, campsites, and every sort of accommodation in between. Driving is itself a pleasure in Victoria.

The best thing about motor touring in Victoria is that you do not find yourself halfway between two isolated towns in the middle of the night with four hours' driving still ahead of you. Wherever you are in Victoria, you are not far from a town, and chances are that it will be a recognised tourist destination. By all means have a look at other states if you have time, but if you only have a year or two, spend your time in Victoria.

Howard Firkin

Melbourne, one of the world's most intact Victorian cities, also contains many imaginative new buildings amongst the old.

The Murray River Queen takes passengers up the 2300 km. Murray River system which includes the Murrumbidgee and Darling Rivers and is one of the longest river systems in the world.

PAULINE CLAYTON

Brisbane, the Sunshine Capital

Blame it on the climate, or on the city's proximity to umpteen seaside, island, bush and mountain resorts, but Brisbane is quite unlike any other Australian city.

If you find the city laid back, remember that's how Brisbane folk want it, but don't be deluded. Beneath that country town charm is a big city vitality.

Brisbane is officially the capital of Queensland. Unlike its sister states, however, Queensland is highly decentralised, and other cities like Toowoomba, Rockhampton and Townsville tend to shoulder capital status in their various regions.

This does not diminish Brisbane's importance. It is, after all, the state's historic and cultural capital, seat of government and a major port. But the visitor should be aware that at the state level, the party that governs is the National Party, historically a 'country' party which still derives the majority of its support from the rural areas.

The city of Brisbane is virtually a state unto itself. Administered by an elected council — the Brisbane City Council — it was for many years dominated by Labor. But now it is firmly in the hands of the Liberals, with former journalist and mother of six, Sallyanne Atkinson, at the helm as Lord Mayor.

The election of a new administration has reflected to a large extent the changes that are transforming the city. Once a relatively prosaic 'dormitory' city, which people lived in but played outside of, Brisbane can now boast a cultural and social sophistication equal in quality if not in size to that of the large cities to the south.

If it seems paradoxical that Brisbane can be both casual and sophisticated, there is another element of its character to confuse the issue totally — a conservatism which thoroughly respects law and order, tends to undermine the power of trade unions,

and encourages the developer-entrepreneur to pursue profits with relatively little constraint. This has drawn the criticism of anti-intellectualism, but before making a judgment on this, it is worth briefly recounting some history.

In September 1822, the British government requested the Governor of New South Wales, Sir Thomas Brisbane, to report on the capacity of Port Bowen, Port Curtis and Moreton Bay 'for the purposes of convict settlement'.

The following year, John Oxley set sail on his voyage of discovery and reached Moreton Bay in November. His first encounter was with three convicts — Richard Parsons, John Finnegan and Thomas Pamphlett — who had been taken out to sea by a storm when on a wood-collecting mission from Sydney and shipwrecked on Moreton Island. They had made their way to the mainland in a native canoe and they escorted Oxley to their major find, the Brisbane River.

The next year, the sailing ship *Amity* sailed from Sydney. Governor Brisbane wished the voyage God-speed with these words to Oxley: 'The *Amity* is placed under your orders for the purpose of crowning your late discovery of a large river flowing into Moreton Bay with the formation of a new settlement in its vicinity. The spot which you select must contain three hundred acres of land, and be in the neighbourhood of fresh water. It should lay in the direct course to the mouth of the river, be easily seen from the offing of ready access. To difficulty of attack by the natives, it ought to join difficulty of escape for the convicts.'

Oxley, Lieutenant Henry Miller (commandant of the new settlement), surgeon and storekeeper Walter Scott, Allan Cunningham (botanist), Oxley's assistant, Robert Hoddle, 29 convicts, and 14 soldiers set sail on 1 September 1824. They founded the convict settlement, which, isolated from Sydney, could only survive by developing a fierce self-reliance and independence. These characteristics remain and no doubt partially explain the desire of Queenslanders to do things 'their way', in matters political and economic. This inward-looking resourcefulness is well expressed by the sovereign-status accorded to Premier Joh Bjelke-Petersen.

Brisbane was destined to become one of the bright stars of Australia's colonisation and today, with a population of more than one million, it is the third largest of Australia's cities. The climate is semitropical, so when Sydneysiders and Melbournites are rugging up for winter, Brisbane folk are on the beach or swimming in garden pools, visiting the parks and gardens, enjoying barbecues and the healthy outdoors.

Brisbane's planners have landscaped it with flame trees, jacarandas, bougainvilleas, frangipanis, oleander, coral trees, tulip trees, flowers and shrubs. The 50-hectare Botanic Gardens are a riot of colour and fragrances and there is little to match an early-morning walk along the Brisbane River as it meanders through the gardens in the centre of the city.

Brisbane has the look of a city that has recently grown up. In fact, the shock of the new is over-whelming. Tourism, business and property develop-ment have encouraged the inner-city construction of high-rise buildings and a necklace of lights over the city bridge invites participation to its coming out party — World Expo '88.

Much of the old and unsightly has been bulldozed and replaced with glittering glass and concrete towers, hotels and paved shopping malls. Unfortunately, some of the old that was possibly worth keeping also went. But many valuable early buildings were lost in the great fire of 1864. One of the surviving settlement buildings is the Old Observatory and Windmill in Wickham Terrace, just west of the railway station. The irony with this building is that the windmill technology never worked, so grain grinding was done by a treadmill.

Other early buildings of note are the Old Government House (1862), the early part of the State Parliament (1868) with its eyecatching copper roof — both in George Street — and St John's Cathedral in Ann Street. It is odd that the Cathedral is still under construction (work began in 1901) when all that is new seems to flash up in five minutes. The Deanery of the Cathedral was built in 1853 and was the first Government House.

The streets of the inner city are narrow, their direction dictated by the sweep of the river, and the city still holds much of the magic of a small town lazing in the noon-day sun. Pretty weatherboard houses with broad slatted verandas nudge the edges of the centre. Many of these cottages have been restored and converted into attractive offices, guesthouses and

Brisbane's Chinatown is a popular shopping area

restaurants, providing an interesting, if precarious, co-existence of old and new.

The new Cultural Centre on the south bank of the Brisbane River, designed by the highly respected local architect Robin Gibson, is testimony to the city's desire to be ranked with the world's more progressive cities in preserving culture and providing enter-tainment for the people.

Although some have commented that it has a rather 'blockish' exterior, it is set among attractive subtropical landscaped gardens, sculptures and water malls. It now holds the Queensland Museum and State Library, three large theatres, several restaurants, including the notable Fountain Room, and the Queensland Art Gallery. The Museum has Aboriginal art displays, and freeze-dried flora and fauna from all over the state. The theatres comprise a major opera house, a concert hall, and a small theatre, achieving a functional balance which the builders of Sydney's Opera House lost along the way. Lawns extend down to the river and ancient trees provide shade from the Queensland sun.

Next door to the Cultural Centre, where a fountain leaps 50 metres above the river, is the site of Expo '88 which opens in April 1988. Another important public

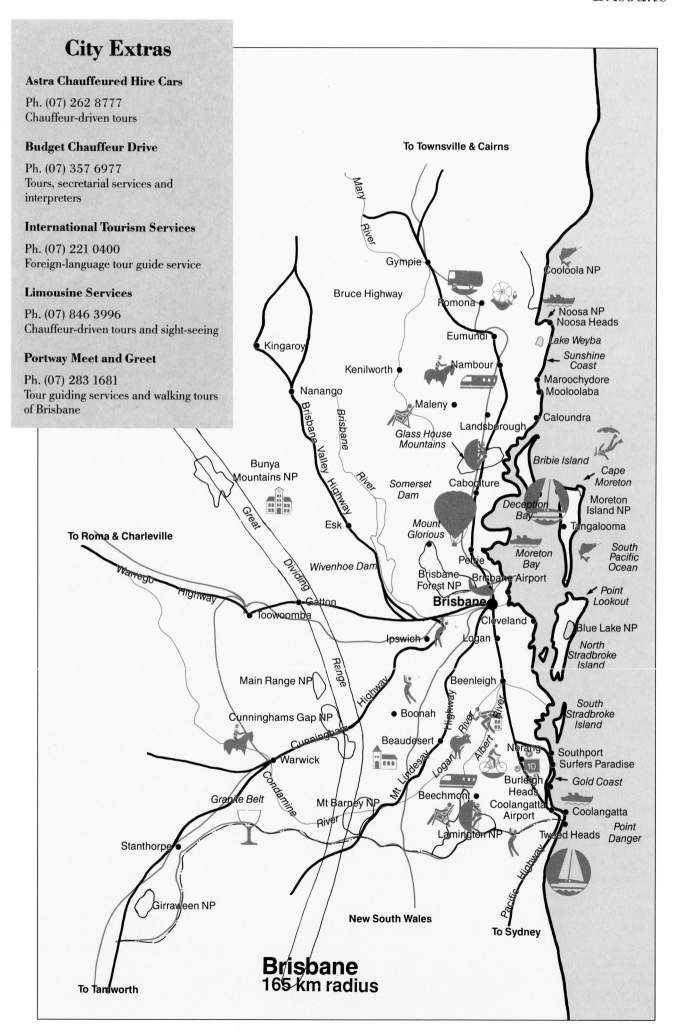

City Extras

Astra Chauffeured Hire Cars

Ph. (07) 262 8777
Chauffeur-driven tours

Budget Chauffeur Drive

Ph. (07) 357 6977
Tours, secretarial services and
interpreters

International Tourism Services

Ph. (07) 221 0400
Foreign-language tour guide service

Limousine Services

Ph. (07) 846 3996
Chauffeur-driven tours and sight-seeing

Portway Meet and Greet

Ph. (07) 283 1681
Tour guiding services and walking tours
of Brisbane

To Townsville & Cairns

Mary River

Gympie
Cooloola NP
Bruce Highway
Pomona
Noosa NP
Noosa Heads
Eumundi
Lake Weyba
Kingaroy
Kenilworth
Nambour
Sunshine Coast
Maroochydore
Mooloolaba
Nanango
Maleny
Landsborough
Caloundra
Glass House Mountains
Bribie Island
Cape Moreton
Bunya Mountains NP
Somerset Dam
Caboolture
Deception Bay
Moreton Island NP
Brisbane Valley Highway
Brisbane River
Tangalooma
Esk
Mount Glorious
Moreton Bay
South Pacific Ocean
Great Dividing Range
Wivenhoe Dam
Petrie
To Roma & Charleville
Warrego Highway
Brisbane Forest NP
Brisbane Airport
Point Lookout
Brisbane
Blue Lake NP
Gatton
Cleveland
Toowoomba
North Stradbroke Island
Ipswich
Logan
Main Range NP
Beenleigh
South Stradbroke Island
Cunninghams Gap NP
Boonah
Cunningham Highway
Nerang
Southport
Surfers Paradise
Warwick
Beaudesert
Beechmont
Burleigh Heads
Gold Coast
Granite Belt
Mt Barney NP
Condamine River
Coolangatta Airport
Coolangatta
Point Danger
Stanthorpe
Lamington NP
Tweed Heads
Girraween NP
Pacific Highway
New South Wales
To Sydney

Brisbane
165 km radius

To Tamworth

building is the large entertainment complex at Boondall, on the edge of the city, where a theatre-in-the-round seats 13,000 and international performances are staged.

The Queen Elizabeth (QE II) sporting stadium, built for the 1982 Commonwealth Games, attracts athletes from all over the world.

But back to the outdoors. Brisbane boasts some of the finest horse racing facilities in the country, thanks to keen racing man Russ Hinze, Queensland's Minister for Racing, Main Roads and Local Government.

There are two main tracks, Eagle Farm and Doomben, both a 15-minute car or bus ride from the heart of the city. Doomben boasts a magnificent $7 million public grandstand with all modern facilities and a perfect view across the course. Eagle Farm is older and more established, but has a large glassed walled bar at the top of a grandstand, excellent facilities throughout the grounds, and well-laid gardens and easy parking.

During the winter months, champagne racing features the cream of Australasia's thoroughbreds. The Gold Coast Turf Club holds races every Saturday at the picturesque Southport track, a 45-minute drive from Brisbane. Although a provincial club, it boasts the fourth million-dollar race to be held in Australia, which is run in January.

Rugby League enjoys a strong following at Lang Park during the cooler months, reaching fever pitch during the State of Origin series when teams from Queensland and New South Wales battle for the honours in a best-of-three match series.

That great game of the south, Aussie Rules, recently migrated north to Carrara on the Gold Coast, where the Brisbane Bears host the best teams from the south and west.

If you like dining out, you'll enjoy sampling cuisine from every corner of the globe — Brisbane has a great number and a great variety of restaurants. Try Queensland beef. Many would argue that nothing compares with a steak washed down with a glass of Queensland's own beer tapped from a wooden keg at the famous Breakfast ('Brekkie') Creek Hotel. It's also worth a visit to the Penthouse Restaurant at the top of the Sheraton Hotel, which has wonderful 360° views of the city below.

Like many cities, Brisbane has a Chinatown, but the curb-to-curb restaurants in Brisbane's Fortitude Valley ('the Valley') area feature not only Chinese with Sunday yum cha, but Indian, Vietnamese, Malaysian, Thai and Italian cuisine.

Visitors can view the city in comfort from the paddlesteamer *Kookaburra Queen*, which sails up the river daily for luncheon and again in the evening for a candlelit dinner. You might pass a Chinese junk sailing majestically in the opposite direction or the Golden Mile Ferry, which runs to Moreton Bay, 50 kilometres downstream, each Sunday.

JON GOLDEN

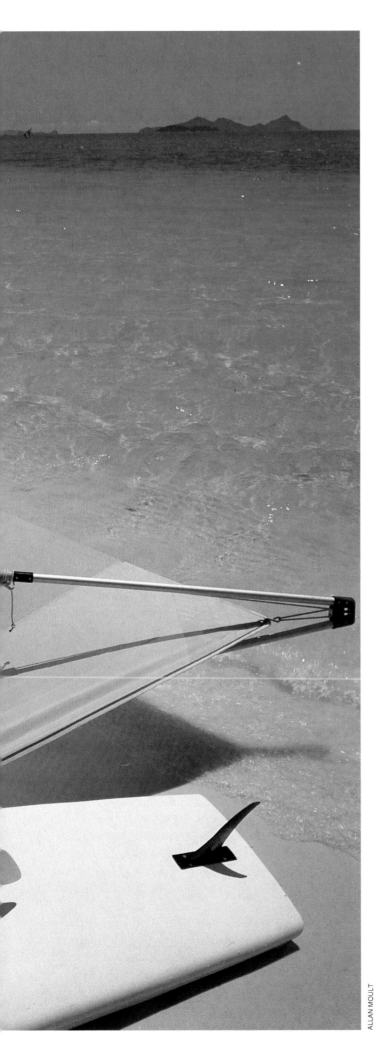

ALLAN MOULT

Brisbane's sunny climate lends itself to outdoor pursuits - in sports, and the arts. Sailboarding on the nearby beaches, athletics at the QEII Jubilee Sports Centre, above, and browsing around the grounds of the Brisbane Art Gallery, below, are popular weekend activities

COVELL PUBLICATIONS

Brisbane's business centre has literally 'grown up' during the past decade as investment capital has poured in

Another cruise takes visitors upriver to the Lone Pine Sanctuary, which houses more than 100 koalas as well as tame kangaroos, wallabies, emus and frilled-neck lizards in its large walk-though reserve.

An unusual start to the day, and an excellent way to see Brisbane, is a hot-air balloon flight over the city at dawn, followed by Roger Meadmore's breakfast of croissants and fresh tropical juices mixed with champagne.

Brisbane offers a wide range of accommodation, including the luxury Sheraton and Hilton, the popular Mayfair Crest and Park Royal Hotels, and guesthouses in the European style as well as backpackers' hotels in the New Farm area.

Shopping in Brisbane ranges from elegant modern stores to open markets. At the new Riverside Centre on Sundays, high-quality craft items made locally are on sale, including exquisite hand-blown glass and hand-made candles. At Samford, just out of Brisbane, is a well-established 'hippie-style' open market. And a large antique market operates seven days a week at Clayfield.

Local people and visitors have a wide choice of entertainment. Theatre is flourishing and local companies include the Queensland Lyric Opera Company, the Brisbane Light Opera Company, the Queensland Ballet Company and the Royal Queensland Theatre Company. The excellent venues

have attracted top overseas performers, from Whitney Houston to the Royal Philharmonic Orchestra.

City pubs, like the Caxton Hotel on Saturdays and the Post Office Hotel on Sundays, offer jazz and other popular music forms in informal surroundings.

But, as the locals will tell you, what you get in Brisbane is a lot more than what you see. Four-lane highways connect Brisbane with the fabulous Gold Coast to the south and the Sunshine Coast to the north, neither more than one hour's drive away and both possessing surfing beaches with no peer anywhere in the world. And within easy reach of these areas are breathtaking national parks, mountain rainforests and scenic picnic spots.

Nearby Moreton Bay has more than 300 islands, the chief ones being North Stradbroke Island, 34 kilometres long and largely unspoiled, but offering excellent accommodation, South Stradbroke Island, Moreton Island, whose Tangalooma Island Resort has replaced an old whaling station, Coochiemudlo Island, St Helena Island and Bribie Island.

All these islands are part of the Greater Brisbane Region and offer excellent fishing and, depending on their position and layout, skiing, surfing, sailing and cycling.

So what's the hurry? The visitor to Brisbane soon settles into the pace of the place and finds that a floppy cloth hat, shorts and thongs are *de rigueur.*

STEVE LIDDELL

Queensland

The Queensland adventure began many years ago. Before the white man came, hundreds of tribes of Aborigines had settled throughout the region. Perhaps half of the country's 250,000 dreamtime people were living here in self-contained communities — some as small as 50, others over 1,500 strong. For thousands of years they successfully adapted to an environment that is at times forbidding and severe. These survival skills were not uniform throughout the area. In its geography, climate, flora, fauna and natural resources, Queensland is the most diverse of Australia's states — a diversity that is reflected in its history, people and culture.

Queensland is the country's second largest state. It has a resident population of two and a half million people and a land mass of just under one and three-quarter million square kilometres. The Tropic of Capricorn bisects the state 650 kilometres north of Brisbane at Rockhampton while, from south to north, the Great Dividing Range continues the journey it started in Victoria until it peters out in Cape York Peninsula.

Over 60% of in-bound tourists to Australia have Queensland as their primary destination. If tourism is booming in Australia, then it is Queensland that leads the way. From the Gold Coast in the south to Cape York in the north, over 60 international hotels and resorts are being developed or constructed to accommodate holiday visitors. And a dozen marinas are underway to service the increasing number of private yachts, cruisers and charter boats that explore the Great Barrier Reef, the Whitsundays, and the other resort islands of Queensland's coral sea. Parks, sports and entertainment centres, motels, restaurants, and the ancillary businesses required by both developers and tourists are flourishing in this mad

dash to capitalise on the natural wonders of the Sunshine State.

The Great Barrier Reef

The most famous of Queensland's holiday destinations is, without doubt, the Great Barrier Reef. In our feature article on the Reef, Wendy Richards — a marine biologist — provides a fascinating insight into the way a scientist views this maritime marvel. Yet science is not the only source of inspiration. Scuba divers and snorkellers, fishermen and sailors, photographers, artists, writers and tourists all find something different in the Reef.

It is fitting that the Reef now belongs to the world. As a World Heritage listing, its protection against the ravages of pollution and unbridled development is more secure than at any time in recent years. Even so, vigilance is necessary. The ecological balance of 2,000 individual reefs that make up the world's largest organic structure is delicate. And tourism could threaten this fragile equilibrium. As we enter this enchanted world, we must remember our responsibilities to give as well as take. The Reef is the only life-form visible from the moon. And what a life-form it is. Naturalists estimate that a simple reef composed of millions of tiny coral creatures may act as a shelter for over 500 fish species, more than are to be found in the Atlantic Ocean.

The Reef is enormous. Its northernmost point is in the Gulf of Papua and it extends south to the Tropic of Capricorn along 2,300 kilometres of coastline and covering an area of 230,000 square kilometres. The reef coast is dotted with hundreds of islands which have their own fringing reefs and it is these that most visitors see. The outer reef moves closer to the coast at certain points along its length. In the Flinders group of islands, it is only 20 kilometres or so from the shore at Cape Melville. At Mackay, further south, it is over 200 kilometres away.

There are many ways to experience the Reef. For the tourist on the move who is experiencing the diversity of Queensland's attractions, an organised trip to the outer reef is an excellent way of sampling this coral paradise. The most popular venues are reached from Cairns and Port Douglas where the Reef is about two hours from the coast. High-speed cruisers take visitors to permanent pontoons from where the rich marine life can be seen. A visit to one of the continental islands offers a more leisurely way of seeing the Reef. Many of these islands offer holiday packages that include boat, snorkelling and scuba diving trips, or you can visit an island and set off from there on a two or three-day tour of the Reef.

Queensland's islands are famous for the wealth of adventures they offer. Along the Reef, they fall broadly into two categories. The larger islands, like those that make up the fabulous Whitsundays, are the peaks of submarine mountains. They provide some of the most luxurious island holidays you could want to experience. The names of these continental islands — Orpheus, Lindeman, Dunk, Lizard, Daydream, Hayman — conjure up a world of romance where you can take yourself away from the pressures of daily toil and relax in your new-found haven. Then there are the islands of the Reef itself, or of coral cay, such as Green Island near Cairns and tiny Heron Island off Gladstone which is popular with scuba enthusiasts.

South of the Reef along the coast are other wonderful islands. The biggest of these, and the largest sand island in the world, is Fraser Island, off the coast of Maryborough. Closer to Brisbane are Stradbroke, Moreton and Bribie Islands.

The Gold Coast

Between Southport and the southern border at Coolangatta is Queensland's most populous tourist area — the Gold Coast, including Surfers Paradise. Over three million visitors come to the Gold Coast each year to enjoy its 35 kilometres of sun-drenched golden beaches and a vast tourist infrastructure hell-bent on providing leisure, entertainment and relaxation. Travellers who know Florida, the French Riviera or Spain's Costa Brava will not be surprised by the style of development here. Yet for Australia, this is an atypical resort. Our beach life usually consists of small pockets of commercialisation set in the midst of vast stretches of deserted coastline where the wind and the seas play to an empty theatre. The Gold Coast is for the gregarious. If the developers have created an artificial, perhaps alien, environment with their high-rises crowding the coastal strip, even cheating the sands of the late afternoon sun, the beaches themselves are excellent.

Surfers Paradise is at the centre of this urban adventure. It is, of course, no longer the hideaway that the builders of the Surfers Paradise Hotel envisaged in 1936. You may find it excessive, but there is much to recommend a pampered getaway from more strenuous activities. Jupiters Casino at the Conrad Hilton is one of the main attractions. Here you can combine swimming and golf with the excitement of gambling at the tables. The Gold Coast is a wonderful place for children, too, with marine displays at Southport's Sea World and the Disney-like Dreamworld entertainment park at Coomera.

The Sunshine Coast

North of Brisbane, the Sunshine Coast stretches from Caloundra in the south to Double Island Point in Cooloola National Park in the north. The character of the Sunshine Coast is very different from that of the Gold Coast. It's a much more proprietorial place. This is where the residents of Brisbane take their holidays and build retirement homes. The pace of life is less frantic, and attitudes are more considered. Of course, tourist development cannot be denied. The beaches and the coastal streams draining into the sea through great headlands are of great beauty. Sun-seekers love the year-round warmth that bathes the coast. There are many hotels, motels and restaurants, but the feel of the place is in sharp contrast to its southern neighbour.

One of the main reasons for this difference is that the obsession with being slap-bang on the coast has been diluted by development inland. In growth terms, the region has expanded at a phenomenal rate. The resident population rises by between 10% and 15% per annum here, but the people are not all involved in service industries. Tropical fruit plantations provide

Night view across the Gold Coast's Nerang River

KATHY SHEARS

some 100,000 tonnes of pineapple for Brisbane's canning industry. Macadamia nuts are another important crop, and there are cottage industries of arts and crafts. And it is perhaps worth noting that the main highway, unlike the Gold Coast highway, winds its way north at a respectful distance from the coast.

Where the Noosa River empties into the sea above a headland covered with forest and below a beautiful national park is the resort town of Noosa. It really does offer the best of everything — sublime surfing beaches and safe, still waters suitable for children in the river's estuary. It is a great spot, too, for fishing. The resort at Noosa Heads has all the facilities you could need. And excellent camping and picnic facilities are available in the nearby protected parklands. The area also has rainforests and a spectacular long stretch of sand at Rainbow Beach.

The coast between Maryborough and Bundaberg is sometimes known as the Sugar Coast. The brilliant green fields of sugarcane stretch from here more than 1,000 kilometres north past Cairns. Fraser Island is the main tourist attraction of the area, while Lady Elliot Island, off the coast from Bundaberg, is the most southerly coral cay of the Great Barrier Reef.

Capricornia

Further north around Gladstone and Rockhampton, the impact of tourism gives way to the more conventional impact of commerce. Once a small port used for shipping coal, Gladstone has developed into the world's largest centre for aluminium processing and a significant port for shipping coke and steaming coal. Like the sugarcane towns throughout Queensland, Gladstone has suffered from a dramatic fall in world prices for energy and natural resources, but no doubt the gently cyclical trend in these things will bring prosperity and growth in the future. Gladstone is also the embarkation point for Heron Island.

Rockhampton is Australia's beef capital. The farmland of the region supports an astonishing number of cattle and is remarkable for breeds like the Brahman which can tolerate the tropical climate. Rockhampton has interesting colonial architecture and is significant, too, as the marker for what locals call Capricornia. The eponymous tropic has been the focus for a separatist movement since the middle of the 19th century, but today the political zeal has waned as internationalism has become the major source of economic development.

Tropical Queensland

A third of Queensland lies north of the Tropic of Capricorn. The more temperate climate of the south, which attracts tourists year round, gives way here to a tropical climate. Selecting your holiday dates is more hazardous. Not only must you contest with high

A windsurfer at sunset in the Whitsundays

temperatures and wet seasons, but you must also take into account the more exotic exigencies of flora and fauna. As a rule, Queensland's tropics are best visited in the winter months — and the further north you go the more this is so. Shark attacks, though rare, are more likely in waters above 21°C, while the infamous box jellyfish is to be found in the muddied coastal waters of a tropical summer. Crocodiles are present year round, but they are less easily spotted in the swollen rivers of summer. Some corals are poisonous and special precautions should be taken to avoid skin contact.

Tropical Queensland is dominated by two major cities, Townsville and Cairns. Unlike the other states, Queensland is no one-city place. Of course, Brisbane is important to the state as a whole, but when you visit Cairns or Townsville you are not entering satellite towns of a state capital but autonomous regional centres.

The Big Pineapple on the Sunshine Coast

Cairns and Far North Queensland

Cairns is buzzing. Queensland's most northerly city, some 1,766 kilometres from Brisbane, it is the tourist gateway to far north Queensland with its fertile southern tableland, Great Barrier Reef resorts and wonderful rainforests.

Blessed with an international airport, the 60,000 or so inhabitants of Cairns are host to one of the largest tourist developments in Australia. The city of Cairns has grown around Trinity Bay. It started life as a port handling tin and gold from inland mines and the oldest parts of the city are found around the harbour area, along the Esplanade and Wharf Street. Here, the many old buildings have wide verandas to provide shade from the hot sun. The harbour itself is famous as the base for the local fishing industry. And what an industry it is. Above all else, Cairns is a marlin fishing centre, attracting game-fishermen from all over the world. Marlin feed about 50 kilometres offshore and

are prized for their fighting qualities. Crowds gather at Marlin Jetty during the season to watch the boats returning from their sport, hoping to see a huge black marlin of 500 kilograms or more being brought ashore. Tuna, shark, barracuda and sailfish are also caught in these waters. Fish and coral are also to be seen at the Cairns Reef World, just behind the jetty, and at the Windows on the Reef show at nearby Green Island Wharf.

Cairns is a tropical city. Brightly coloured birds, exotic palms, fig trees and brilliant displays of flowers are in evidence everywhere. The visitor can enjoy this paradise aboard a horse-drawn wagon or take an inland tour on a paddleboat through the port and on to Admiralty Island to the south.

On foot, a place to look out for is the recently opened Cairns Museum which is in the School of Arts building at the corner of Shield and Lake Streets. The Museum holds early Aboriginal artefacts and materials, and there are displays on goldmining in the region and on the building of the Kuranda railway.

Beaches are not Cairns' strong suit. Most visitors use Cairns as a base for exploring further afield, travelling north along the coast to find other beaches or taking day trips to Green Island, a coral cay, where they can swim and snorkel. More exclusive island holidays are available at Lizard, Orpheus and Dunk Islands which can be reached by air, or at Fitzroy Island which is under an hour from Cairns by boat.

Inland from Cairns, the Atherton Tableland — part of the Great Dividing Range — forms the barrier between the tropics and outback Queensland to the west. The scenic railway, built 100 years ago from Cairns to Kuranda, is the most popular first stage in reaching the tablelands from Cairns. The one and a half hour journey winds through deep gorges and sugarcane fields to the base of the Macalister Range and then climbs steeply through tunnels to Kuranda at the top. The panoramic views are spectacular. You can see the coast around Cairns and the ocean stretching out to the Reef, huge rocky escarpments, and water-falls at Stony Creek and in the wet season at Barron Falls. The tablelands beyond Kuranda are a rich green, for this is some of Australia's most fertile arable farmland. It supports a large tobacco industry, crops of potatoes and onions, and for travellers, pleasant walks along the shores of volcanic lakes, by pic-turesque waterfalls and in the Chillagoe limestone caves.

The Cook Highway from Cairns to Mossman, 80 kilometres north, is the last stretch of a sealed road that begins in Brisbane 2,000 kilometres to the south. It is a coastal road with marvellous beaches in the east and sweeping fields of cane to the west. Port Douglas, born in Queensland's goldrush, is an hour or so from Cairns and is one of the prettiest spots in the area. Famous for its excellent restaurants and long golden beaches, it is also a major departure point for trips to the outer reef and the coral cays of the Low Isles. Here is the home of one of the biggest resort developments in Australia. The Sheraton-Mirage to the south of the town provides luxury five-star holidays, with its main features being a modern marina, a championship golf course, and the biggest swimming pool you have ever seen.

Mossman, further north, is a sugar-growing centre. A small town, just south of the Mossman River, it is built on a plain covered with cane. In sharp contrast, however, is Mossman Gorge, about eight kilometres west. It is cool and wild, with picnic spots and excellent walks. This is the southernmost part of the Daintree Rainforest which forms a huge national park. The rainforest is spectacular and covers over 50,000 hectares. Here is wilderness Australia at its most beautiful. Mountains and valleys are covered in a lush green tropical growth which supports an exotic array of wildlife. Rivers and streams cut through the dense vegetation on their way to the sea, and the forest extends to the very edge of the Pacific. It is so dense that access for tourists is limited.

When you cross the Daintree River by ferry, notices indicate that only four-wheel-drive vehicles can be used on the dirt road north to Cape Tribulation. Cape Trib, as it is fondly called, was named by Captain Cook. No doubt he was contemplating the troubles caused by running his ship aground on Endeavour Reef. His tale of woe also took into its ambit Mt Sorrow, which rises behind the Cape. It is a wonderful place of rainforest and secluded beaches.

Cape Tribulation is in the south of the north-eastern triangle of Australia bounded by the Gulf of Carpentaria in the west, Torres Strait, and the Pacific Ocean in the east. Cape York is a huge, sparsely populated area that has had little land-based economy since the goldrush ended on the Palmer River. Bauxite at Weipa and cattle are the only activities of any note. But plans for a space satellite station near Weipa will undoubtedly have enormous impact on the region. Travel is difficult and only advisable in late winter and early spring. For the moment, however, there are excellent adventures to be had by four-wheel-drive and by air charter.

Townsville

Australia's largest tropical city is 374 kilometres south of Cairns. The people here regard their city as being the capital of northern Queensland. If universities were a measure of such things, they would be right for Queensland's second university is sited here. The commercial success of Townsville is based on its port which acts as a conduit for mining and agriculture from the vast hinterland. Indeed, Robert Towns — its founder — saw the need for a port for the beef industry and dairy products of the great inland cattle stations. However, like the rest of Queensland, tourism is the business focus of today. The Sheraton Breakwater Casino has already opened and further hotels and marinas are under construction.

Perhaps the most ambitious project is the Great Barrier Reef Wonderland which has just opened on the coast at Flinders East. This Bicentennial commemorative project sits on 10,000 square metres of land backing onto the wharf at Ross Creek. Three major components form one of Australia's most exciting new attractions. The live coral reef aquarium, the largest in the world, has been stocked with the fish, algae, sponges and marine life of the Reef in a carefully balanced ecosystem. Visitors experience the reef in a 20-metre viewing tunnel. Sensations of a different kind are projected at the Omnimax Theatre where a huge dome-shaped screen and a sophisticated sound system provide an audio-visual feast which parallels for the Reef what planetariums have done for the sky. The complex also houses a

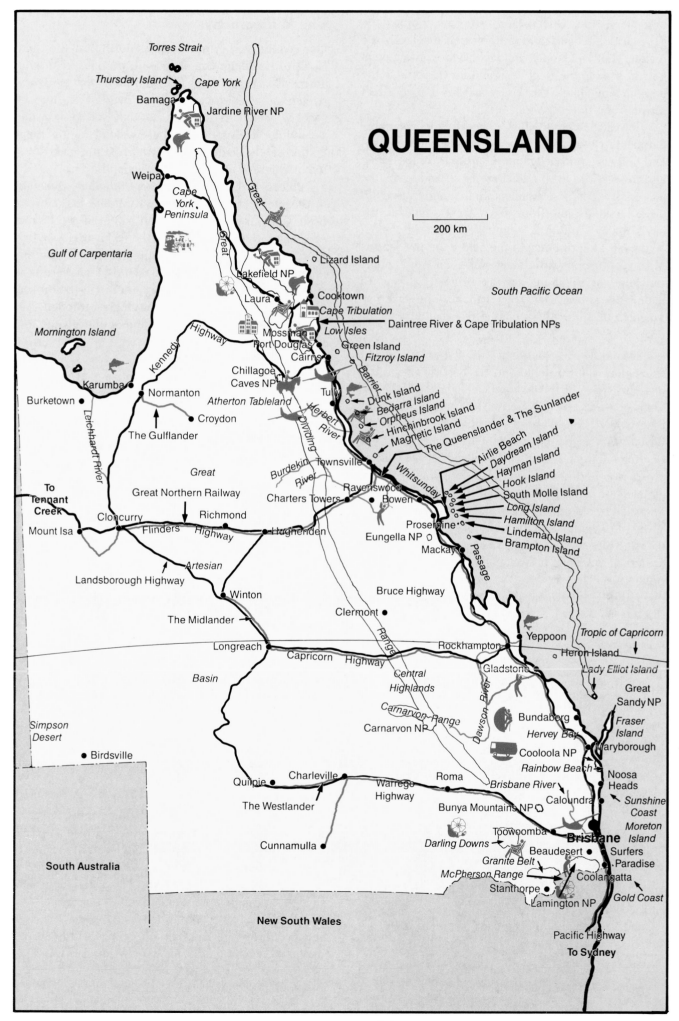

QUEENSLAND

Torres Strait

Thursday Island Cape York

Bamaga Jardine River NP

Weipa

Cape York Peninsula

Gulf of Carpentaria

Mornington Island

Lizard Island

Lakefield NP

Laura Cooktown

Cape Tribulation

Daintree River & Cape Tribulation NPs

Mossman *Low Isles*

Port Douglas Green Island

Cairns *Fitzroy Island*

Chillagoe Caves NP

South Pacific Ocean

Karumba

Burketown

Normanton

Atherton Tableland

Croydon

The Gulflander

Tully Dunk Island

Bedarra Island

Orpheus Island

Hinchinbrook Island

Magnetic Island

The Queenslander & The Sunlander

Airlie Beach

Daydream Island

Hayman Island

Hook Island

South Molle Island

Long Island

Hamilton Island

Lindeman Island

Brampton Island

Great

Great Northern Railway

Great

Basin

Burdekin Townsville

River

Charters Towers Ravenswood

Bowen

Eungella NP

Proserpine

Mackay

To Tennant Creek

Mount Isa Cloncurry

Flinders Highway

Richmond

Hughenden

Landsborough Highway

Winton

Clermont

The Midlander

Bruce Highway

Longreach

Capricorn Highway

Rockhampton

Yeppoon

Tropic of Capricorn

Heron Island

Gladstone

Central Highlands

Lady Elliot Island

Simpson Desert

Birdsville

Carnarvon Range

Carnarvon NP

Dawson River

Bundaberg

Hervey Bay

Great Sandy NP

Fraser Island

Maryborough

Quilpie Charleville

Roma

Cooloola NP

Rainbow Beach

Noosa Heads

The Westlander

Warrego Highway

Brisbane River

Caloundra *Sunshine Coast*

Bunya Mountains NP

Toowoomba

Moreton Island

Brisbane

Cunnamulla

Darling Downs

Beaudesert Surfers Paradise

Granite Belt

McPherson Range

Coolangatta

Stanthorpe Lamington NP

Gold Coast

South Australia

New South Wales

Pacific Highway

To Sydney

200 km

Northern Territory

Portraits of the Cities & States

branch of the Queensland Museum devoted to geological, biological and technological displays of the region. The Reef Wonderland is also the starting point for day trips to the Reef itself and for transfers to the new floating hotel, the Four Seasons Barrier Reef Resort.

Townsville's city mall is a cheerful place running parallel to Ross Creek. Giant games of chess, snakes and ladders and backgammon are part of the scene and people love to wander here or sit and watch the passers-by. The best architecture is found in the port area. Looking back from the water, Castle Hill, the city's major landmark, dominates the town below. Within striking distance of the centre are the Jezzine Military Museum, rainforest walks and an animal sanctuary at Billabong on the Bruce Highway, 15 kilometres south. Day trips can also be taken to Magnetic Island with its coastal resorts and national park.

Townsville lies between two major sugarcane fields along the Burdekin and Herbert Rivers. To the west are some of the major Queensland goldfields, some of which are still active. Charters Towers and Ravenswood were born during the goldrush. Ravenswood is now a ghost of its former self, but Charters Towers has retained some of its earlier prosperity. Both towns are notable for their colonial architecture and lovers of old buildings are well rewarded by a round trip of some 300 kilometres from Townsville. Inland, too, the tranquil summer waters of the rivers are swollen during the wet season and there are great waterfalls at Wallaman, Stoney Creek and Little Crystal Creek.

Whitsunday beach scene

ALLAN MOULT

The Whitsundays

Our coastal journey has taken us north from the Gold Coast to Rockhampton and south from Cape York to Townsville. A glance at a map will reveal that there is a stretch of coast between. The major city here is Mackay, which shares with Townsville access to the beautiful Whitsundays. These islands with their golden sands, sheltered bays and fringing reefs are a major centre of tourism in Queensland.

Access to the Whitsundays is from Shute Harbour to the north of Mount Conway National Park. From here, you can join an organised trip or, if you prefer, charter your own boat. But the Whitsundays offer more than the delights of boating. Bushwalks can be taken on Hayman and Long Islands and there is a superb underwater observatory ten metres below sea level on Hook Island. Scenic flights through Air Whitsunday cover the region and scuba diving and fishing are very popular.

West of the Great Divide

Let us turn our backs on these coastal splendours and stand at some lofty point on the Great Dividing Range. The fierce red sun sets in the distance and our panorama from north to south encompasses a different world. Here is most of Queensland. Close to the Divide, and particularly in the Darling Downs in the south, the land is fertile. Great plains of richly patterned fields have made Toowoomba the grain capital of the state. Queensland's garden city is a simple, honest place catering for the needs of farmers and graziers. They celebrate their rural wealth each spring at the Carnival of Flowers, when thousands of visitors come to town to add human colour to the floral festivities.

These rolling downs soon give way to the red earth of the heart of Australia. Arable farming is now replaced by sheep and cattle stations, each commanding larger and larger territories as we journey into the great beyond. In his feature article in this book, Christopher Leonard takes us on a trip through some of these outback towns — small patches of civilisation painted on a huge canvas which sits firmly on Mother Nature's easel.

This part of Australia, and up to the Gulf of Carpentaria, offers some of the most rugged adventures for the ambitious traveller. Private aircraft and four-wheel-drives are the main forms of transport. Great holidays are available on cattle stations where a working holiday in the form of jackarooing and jillarooing can be a most exhilarating experience.

Stunning river landscapes following the wet season, vestiges of Aboriginal culture from a bygone age, and ancient landforms like the granite hills near Mount Isa are a constant reminder of how recent a phenomenon our civilisation is.

Oliver Freeman

Australia contains many distinct and arid regions, each with their own special beauty such as the channel country of Queensland, near Boulia.

The Adelaide Grand Prix, which runs in the month of November, attracts visitors from all over the world.

Adelaide, a City of Light

What's surprising about Adelaide is the fact that it is so surprising. It should be the quiet and staid capital of a southern state. Instead, the people of South Australia have created a city with a world-class arts festival and a Formula One Grand Prix race, near an important wine-growing region. When the people of Adelaide do something well, everyone sits up and takes notice.

For all that, one can still enjoy its leisured pace and easy access to the country. High-rise development is frowned upon by civic fathers, so there are no concrete canyons for the wind to whistle through, to blot out the sun or to crowd the skyline.

Thanks to its imaginative founder, Colonel William Light, Adelaide is a well-planned city, bordered by the Mount Lofty Ranges to the east and by gulf waters and long sandy beaches to the west.

Colonel Light, who still points an imperious finger at the city below from his pedestal on Montefiore Hill in North Adelaide, designed the inner business district as a one-mile square and then encircled it with 700 hectares of parkland.

Because it is so compact and flat, Adelaide is a city best explored on foot. King William Street — the main artery — houses some handsome civic buildings, including the Town Hall and the Renaissance-style Edmund Wright House which doubles as a marriage registry and chamber music concert venue. In the chandelier-lit foyer of the Town Hall is a life-size sculpture of Queen Adelaide, after whom the city was named, and a collection of royal memorabilia is displayed in one of the reception rooms.

Conventional sight-seeing is made easy in tree-lined North Terrace, the city's so-called culture belt. Side by side are the Museum, with its unique collection of Toas (Aboriginal signposts), the Public Library,

the Art Gallery with its notable local artworks and an unrivalled collection of South-east Asian ceramics dating from 3000 BC, the Conservatorium of Music, and the faculty buildings of the University of Adelaide. Also located along this broad boulevard are Government House, the Casino and Parliament House, behind which is the Adelaide Festival Centre on the banks of the Torrens River.

The Festival Centre, with its three performance areas, is the main venue for the city's much-acclaimed biennial Festival of the Arts, a two-to-three-weeks international banquet of music, drama and opera, and the occasion for spirited meetings of writers and artists from many parts of the world.

An international event of a decidedly different character is the Australian Formula One Grand Prix, held each October. City streets are cordoned off for the motor race, which has been lauded as one of the best grand prix circuits in the world.

At the centre of the city is fountain-sprayed Victoria Square, and from there it's an easy stroll west to the cosmopolitan Central Markets. Its 74 open stalls sell a wide range of local foodstuffs and crafts. In this area, too, with its inexpensive ethnic cafes and restaurants serving delicious local whiting and quail, the South Australian Opera Company operates out of the refurbished Opera Theatre, presenting some six productions a year.

Victoria Square is the departure point for the city's only tram, which winds its way through suburbs of red-brick, sandstone and bluestone cottages to the seaside suburb of Glenelg where the colony was proclaimed in 1836.

Back towards North Terrace is Rundle Mall, where most of the retail stores are located, while the city's nightlife is concentrated just across King William

Street in Hindley Street.

Shopping for antiques still makes sense in Adelaide, and genuine bargains can be found. South Australian opals are an obvious buy, and bush clobber, in the form of moleskin trousers, shirts and leather boots, can be found at any of the famed R. M. Williams outlets.

Adelaide's Jam Factory, which provides studio space for craftsmen, is well worth a visit, as is Carrick Hill, a property bequeathed to the state in the affluent suburb of Springfield. Set in English-style gardens surrounded by bushland, the estate's mansion houses one of the finest private collections of art and Jacobean oak furniture in Australia. An impressive sculpture park features works by Epstein.

Adelaide's usually calm traffic flow makes it an easy city to get in and out of. Short day trips are a hassle-free experience. The Adelaide Hills with their stately homes, workmen's cottages, orchards and giant gumtrees growing alongside English elms, poplars and birches are only 20 minutes from the city.

The best-known of the small Hills towns is Hahndorf, which was founded by German settlers escaping religious persecution in Europe. In its restaurants, shops, galleries and museum, Hahndorf draws heavily on its German heritage for its share of the tourist trade.

A little over an hour's drive to the north-east of Adelaide, the huge wineries of the Barossa Valley also bear proud German names and the Germanic influence is clearly reflected in the valley's buildings, its neat and tidy towns, its high-steepled churches, festivals and band music. The Barossa's oom-pah-pah bands are a must at most festive gatherings.

South of Adelaide, another wine area — Southern Vales — is part of the Fleurieu Peninsula tourist region which includes such scenic attractions as the historic port of Goolwa and the establishment beach resort of Victor Harbour.

McLaren Vale, the heart of the Southern Vale district, is only 40 minutes from Adelaide. It is seen at its best during the spring months when the almond blossoms, particularly at nearby Willunga, are at their peak.

Noni Farwell

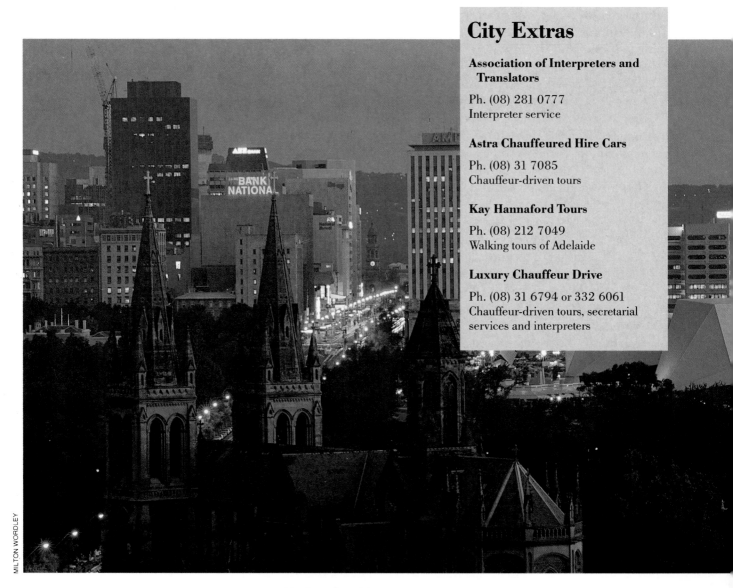

MILTON WORDLEY

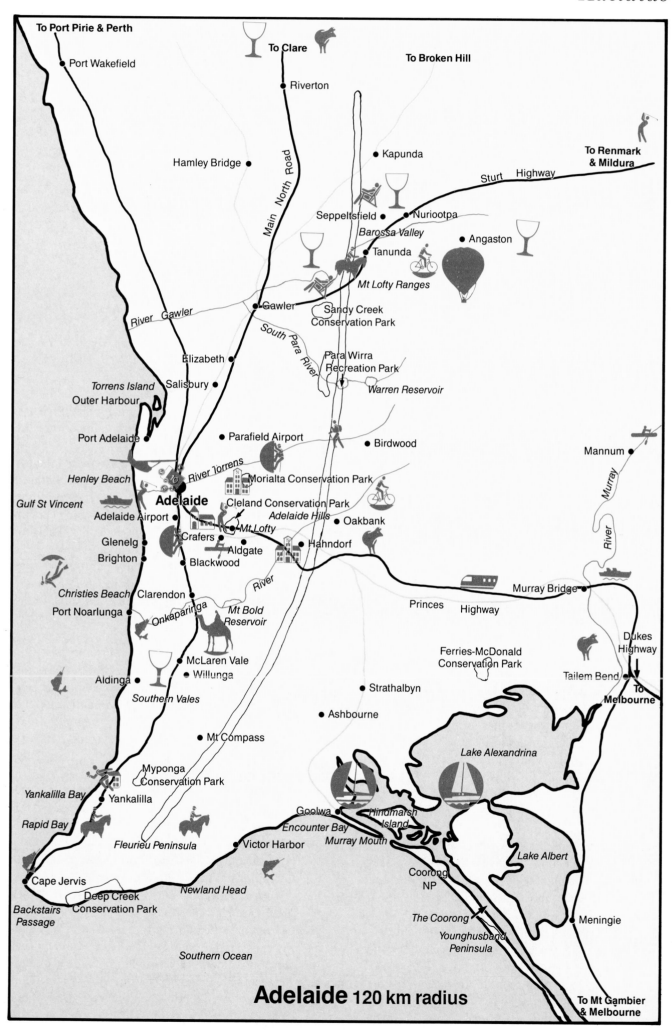

Adelaide 120 km radius

HENNA

South Australia

South Australia is wine, crayfish and opals, gibber deserts, sandhills and lush green pastures, and is home to the hairy-nosed wombat, the yellow-footed rock wallaby and the white pointer shark. It takes up 12.81% of Australia's land mass, covers an area of 380,000 square kilometres and has 3,700 kilometres of coastline.

The driest state in the driest continent in the world, South Australia surprises the visitor with its areas reminiscent of the gentle English countryside and its gracious, century-old mansions.

It alone shares boundaries with all the other mainland states, but it stands aloof from their common and often violent heritage of convict settlement. Only free men and women came from England to the colony. They purchased Crown land instead of gaining tracts free, and brought out labourers to help them work it. They, in turn, toiled diligently to acquire the money to set up farms of their own. Fortunately, they saw no evil in the grape, and planted vines along with their cereal crops. South Australia is now the largest producer of wine in Australia.

The early settlers were thrifty, setting value on hard work rather than the licentious habits and intrigues of their eastern state compatriots. This attitude was evidently supported by the then Savings Bank of South Australia, now the State Bank. It proclaimed that its establishment in 1848 was 'for the encouragement of frugality and that persons possessing small sums of money beyond what they require for the supply of their immediate wants should be afforded an opportunity of depositing the same on good security to accumulate at interest'.

Something of that attitude towards an overt display of wealth still prevails. Extravagant, highly publicised parties on the lavish scale found in Sydney, Melbourne and Perth are not considered quite the form in Adelaide, the state's capital, named after the consort of King William IV.

Hard work was also a virtue esteemed by early Lutheran peasants escaping religious persecution in their native Prussia. They arrived under the protection of leading colonialist George Fife Angas two years after the proclamation of the colony in 1836. Their influence on the state's eating and drinking habits, on its architecture and music, particularly band music, was not inconsiderable and is still very much in evidence today in regions such as the Adelaide Hills and in the Barossa Valley, South Australia's best-known wine-producing area.

South Australia also differs from other states in the absence, until recently, of a long-time Asian population. Chinese coolies were smuggled ashore last century at Robe, on the coast south of Adelaide, but their sights were set firmly on the rich gold diggings of Ballarat and Bendigo. They made hazardous journeys overland to avoid the £10 poll tax then required at the well-policed Victorian ports.

More colourful in the state's early history were the Afghan camel train drivers who ferried supplies to the northern outback stations and helped to build the telegraph line from Adelaide to Darwin.

For a state with a conservative image, South Australia continues to throw up a remarkable number of firsts, especially where women are concerned. It was the first Australian state to give women the vote, to appoint a woman to the police force, and to admit women as university undergraduate students. Another first was its appointment of a woman to an Australian Supreme Court bench and as a university chancellor. Headlines also were made when the state government initiated another controversial reform — the

TREVERN DAWES

decriminalisation of homosexuality between consenting adults.

With its generally mild Mediterranean climate and pollution-free skies, South Australia has become a favoured locale for the production of local films, notably *Breaker Morant* and *Sunday Too Far Away*, and for the filming of scenes for *Gallipoli, Picnic at Hanging Rock* and *Mad Max 3*.

The climate, particularly in spring and autumn, favours the bushwalker and the nature lover. Some 7% of the state's land is given over to national parks, game reserves and recreation and conservation parks.

Tour operators have the state well and truly covered. The adventurer can cross the Simpson Desert in the far north-east in a camel caravan, or join another safari around the Cooper's Creek area made famous in the ill-fated Burke and Wills expedition. Four-wheel-drive tours in the cooler months will take the traveller in search of solitude to the most remote areas in the state, while a weekend air safari promises prolific birdlife around Lake Eyre, the world's largest salt lake.

One of South Australia's most productive pastoral regions, referred to simply as the south-east, is fabled for its crayfish and Coonawarra wines, particularly its reds which are remarkable for their depth and fullness. The area is centred on robust Mount Gambier. Of volcanic origin, it is encircled by man-made pine forests and is the home of the famous Blue Lake. Many stories circulate about the reason for the changing colour of the lake, which becomes a brownish grey each March and does not resume its brilliant blue colour until November. At the height of its intensity, the blue is maintained whether conditions are clear or overcast.

Easily accessible by air, rail or road, the southeast, with its pedigree stock and comfortable homesteads, is a pleasant four or five-hour drive from Adelaide. For the committed ornithologist, one of the most rewarding routes south is via the Coorong.

Named Kurangh (long neck of water) by the Aborigines, who lived there for more than 300 generations before the arrival of white settlers, the Coorong is a saline lagoon more than 100 kilometres long and up to 41 kilometres wide. It is separated from the ocean by the sand dunes of the Younghusband Peninsula.

Lying adjacent to the mouth of the Murray River, the Coorong is a sanctuary in times of drought for many species of Australian waterbirds and home to vast numbers of migratory waders. It is a major breeding ground for terns and silver gulls, and for the Australian pelican. With its remains of former Aboriginal habitations, including campsites, cooking ovens, middens and burial sites, it is also one of the most significant archaeological sites in Australia.

Tourists from all over the world come to the Coorong in the season starting early October and con-

tinuing until January. Other summer visitors include the red-necked stilt and the sharp-tailed sandpiper, which breed in the tundras of Siberia.

Further to the south is the town of Kingston, whose claim to fame is made clear by a huge sign depicting a giant lobster. The lobster season runs from the beginning of October to the end of April. The best place to stay overnight in the area is the charming seaport of Robe, the nearest equivalent Australia has to a Mediterranean-type fishing village. Many of its historic buildings and cottages of the 1840s still stand. One of Robe's best-known hotels, the Caledonian Inn, was built with materials salvaged from ships wrecked on its coast.

To the south-east of Robe, nearly midway between Mount Gambier and the flourishing country town of Naracoorte with its famous caves, is the Coonawarra wine district. Coonawarra (Aboriginal for wild honeysuckle) produces some of the country's great reds in small family and large company wineries. Vigneron Max Lake, of Hunter Valley fame, in his book *Classic Wines of Australia*, says, 'When climate

The Arid Beauty of the Flinders Ranges is blessed by creeks and pockets of White Gum

TREVERN DAWES

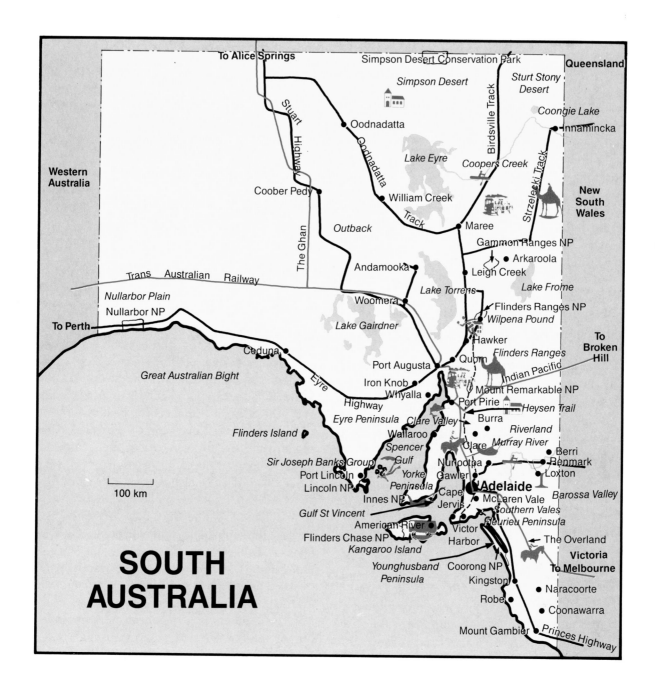

SOUTH AUSTRALIA

and making combine to produce a good wine in Coonawarra, it is truly great, leaving one stranded trying to do justice to its incomparable attractions, best tasted rather than talked about.'

Some fine old hotels and converted homesteads offer luxury accommodation in the south-east, but the Tantanoola Hotel rates a special mention for its stuffed tiger, which has glared with glassy eyes at generations of beer drinkers. Many tales have been told of the Tantanoola Tiger, said to have been an escaped Assyrian wolf that killed many of the district's sheep late last century before an intrepid grazier shot it.

Closer to Adelaide, in the east, is the district known as the Riverland. The best way to see Australia's largest river, the Murray, is by paddlesteamer, luxury cruiser, self-skippered houseboat, or by canoe through a myriad of creeks, lagoons and billabongs.

The neat little Riverland towns are noted for their

wines, dried fruits, and citrus fruits and juices. Most have historic links with the once-thriving Australian river traffic. Morgan, for example, was at one time one of the nation's busiest river ports, with a railway line from Adelaide to the paddlesteamer traffic on the Murray/Darling River systems.

Perhaps the best known of the towns is Renmark, Australia's oldest irrigation settlement, which was founded in 1887 with a joint agreement between the state government and the Chaffey brothers, formerly of Canada. Renmark also pioneered the establishment of Riverland community hotels, which are run by a board elected by the people. Profits are used for community improvements.

One of the state's best-kept secrets for many years, the now rapidly expanding tourist resort of Kangaroo Island is 113 kilometres south-west of Adelaide across the Backstairs Passage from Cape Jervis. Discovered by English explorer Matthew Flinders on his epic circumnavigation of Australia in 1802, the island gained its name because the kangaroo was the first fresh meat his sailors had eaten in months. Shortly afterwards, French commander Nicolas Baudin dropped anchor in one of the island's many bays, and he was followed in turn by American sealers and whalers.

Kangaroo Island was the initial choice for a settlement site in South Australia, but its lack of fresh water swung the balance to the area around the Torrens River where Adelaide now stands.

The island, which can be reached either by air or ferry services, has a long-established farming community, but it comes alive in the major tourist months of spring, summer and autumn. A large part of it consists of the Flinders Chase National Park, which has a thriving colony of koalas, kangaroos and wallabies. Around 10% of the world's sea lion population is found in the island's Seal Bay Conservation Park.

More than 40 ships — one with the intriguing name of You Yangs — have been wrecked off the rugged coastline of Kangaroo Island since 1847.

Back on the mainland, the affluent region known as the mid-north is about two hours by road from Adelaide. Set in its gentle, undulating hills are spacious old homesteads such as Martindale Hall (used for location scenes in *Picnic at Hanging Rock)*, merino sheep studs, reminders of the former days of copper mining glory, and some of the best white wine-producers in the country.

Clare, the heart of the Clare Valley wine-producing area, is also one of the most attractive towns in the state. Over Easter in even-numbered years, it holds a vintage wine festival and many wine-lovers return in mid-May for a gourmet weekend spent sampling food prepared by top restaurateurs at the valley's wineries.

One of the most picturesque wineries in the valley, just south of Clare, is Sevenhill Cellars, run by members of the Jesuit Order. One of the most impressive wineries, Queltaller Wines, is further south at Watervale. The Sevenhill Cellars, designed originally for the production of altar wines, is in a quiet bush setting, and in the crypt beneath the sandstone church rest well-remembered wine-makers of bygone years.

To the east of Clare, via a side road that winds through sheep-grazing country, is the handsome town of Burra. Once the centre of a copper-mining boom, it was more recently the setting for the Banjo Paterson/Boer War Australian film, *Breaker Morant.* Although the copper boom lasted only 29 years following its discovery in 1845, it helped to lift the young colony out of a state of near bankruptcy. Today, tourists can rent accommodation in restored miners' cottages while they explore the town and district with its colonial buildings and other physical reminders of its mining background.

Across the Gulf of St Vincent, on a decidedly masculine leg-shaped Yorke Peninsula, the towns of Kadina, Moonta and Wallaroo have also preserved their mining heritage buildings and diggings. As in Burra, Cornish miners came to the area to work the rich ore, first discovered in 1859. Biennally, in May, the towns combine to stage a Kernewek Lowender or Cornish Festival. In Little Cornwall, as it's called, it is almost obligatory to eat the delectable Cornish pasty, which is to South Australians what the meat pie is to the rest of the nation.

Further west, across Spencer Gulf, is Eyre Peninsula. It was named after the explorer Edward John Eyre, who made three journeys into the interior, overlanded cattle from Sydney to Adelaide, and explored the route to Western Australia.

West Coast Country, as it is known, has model wheat and barley farms and is encircled by magnificent beaches, some of which have rollers coming in from the Southern Ocean. The steelworks town of Whyalla, at the top of the gulf, is its largest town, and Port Lincoln is its tourist centre. Fishing for tuna and the state's gourmet King George whiting lures many visitors, while the big game fishermen come for the rightly feared white pointer shark. Port Lincoln's Tunarama Festival is also a major attraction.

The leap from the golden beaches, green and straw-coloured fields, and tidy, tree-lined country towns of the south to the arid, sometimes desolate outback can come as a shock, but the astonishingly beautiful Flinders Ranges cushion the transition for the traveller, especially in early spring when the wildflowers are out in riotous colour.

The Flinders is a region of ever-changing blue, purple and red serrated ridges thrusting skyward, of steeply plunging ochre gorges, sandy, boulder-strewn creek beds lined with ancient red river gumtrees, and screeching flocks of white cockatoos and pink-breasted galahs.

Painters, in particular South Australia's most celebrated artist, the late Sir Hans Heysen, are addicted to the area. Nowhere else in Australia does the red gum seem to come into its own in the way it does in the Flinders, and many of Heysen's best works glorify them. The painter has also given his name to the 1,000-kilometre Heysen Trail, one of the world's classic long-distance bushwalking trails. It begins at Cape Jervis on the rugged coast south of Adelaide and meanders through pasture land, the Mt Lofty Ranges and the Barossa Valley, ending at Mt Hopeless in the northern Flinders Ranges. Due to fire restrictions in the hot summer months, the trail is closed from 1 November to 30 April. Hikers on all South Australian bush trails are advised never to walk alone and always to carry water.

Camping out in a swag under the stars is regarded by many Flinders fanatics as the only way to go, but more orthodox accommodation is available, notably at

The Murray River is Australia's mightiest river, which runs from the raging white waters of the Murray gates in the Snowy Mountains of New South Wales, through the gently flowing lower reaches of Victoria before finally entering the sea in South Australia. Lush vegetation along its banks provides home to some of the most splendid birdlife in Australia.

The Southern Vales, south of Adelaide, where rich farm land noted for its superb wine production, meets the sea.

Ruins of a long ago settlement near the expansive dry Lake Eyre.

Giant gum trees at Moralana frame the distant Flinders Ranges

Wilpena Pound, a vast natural amphitheatre dominated by St Mary's Peak. The Pound, and the surrounding former sheep station, is now part of the Flinders Ranges National Park where the curiously gaited emu runs freely with many other wildlife species.

The landscape is even more rugged and dramatic in the northern Flinders, which also at one time had its share of copper mines. Arkaroola, a 61,000-hectare wildlife sanctuary, is its centre and a mecca for geologists.

It is where these northern ranges peter out that the real outback begins — the stony deserts, sandhills and dry lake beds. There are constant reminders of the harshness of the environment in the bleached bones of cattle and sheep, and in the ruins of homesteads deserted by settlers who battled the country and the droughts, and lost.

This is not country to be treated lightly by the inexperienced traveller, who may well feel safer on the Stuart Highway from Port Augusta to the Northern Territory border. This newly opened road, labelled Australia's adventure highway, passes through Woomera (site of the Weapons Testing Range) and the opal towns of Andamooka and Coober Pedy.

Some 1,000 kilometres north-west of Adelaide, Coober Pedy, Australia's oldest and biggest opal-mining town dating from 1915, supplies a large part of the world's opal. Miners come from many countries to take their chance at striking it lucky, at making that one big find in the bizarre, lunar-like landscapes. They dig underground. And to escape the dust and the heat, they live underground, sometimes in surprisingly sumptuous conditions. Even the churches are in dugouts. Travellers with a permit can dig for opals, or they can simply buy them at source.

There are more arduous ways to go north, through country once travelled by explorers such as Sturt, McKinley, Burke and Wills, and by pastoralists seeking new lands to claim and to tame. Among the better-known routes are the Strzelecki and Oodnadatta tracks, both of which cross the dingo fence. The world's longest protecting wire fence, it extends more than 3,000 kilometres across the centre of Australia to keep dingoes from crossing into the pastoral zones of the south.

Above all, there is the legendary Birdsville Track. Books have been written about the track, immortalising its pioneers, mailmen, police patrols, camel trains and epic cattle drives south from western Queensland.

On either side of the track, which stretches from Marree to Birdsville in south-western Queensland, are huge stock runs such as Muloorina, Mirra Mitta, Cowarie, Etadunna, Dulkaninna and Clifton Hill. Unlike their forebears, the station people today live in some style, but their children's early education is still by courtesy of the School of the Air and their urgent medical needs are dependent upon the Flying Doctor Service, both of which are run from Port Augusta at the head of Spencer Gulf.

If the Birdsville Track can ever be said to have a steady trickle of traffic, it is in September when the Birdsville Races are held. These days, though, race-goers are more likely to fly into the dusty outback town in light aircraft.

For hot and thirsty overlanders, the Birdsville Hotel, happily, is not just another of the mirages they have seen along the track.

Noni Farwell

JIRI LOCHMAN

Perth, a Golden Oasis

For a city known as the hive of millionaires, a place of energetic growth and vigorous youth, Perth had a less than auspicious start.

Captain James Stirling, who established Western Australia on the banks of the Swan River where Perth now stands, reported in his original survey that the climate, soil and water supply were excellent for a colony. He was wrong, but the band of settlers, workers, officials and soldiers he led there in 1829 did not realise it.

They dreamed of establishing a colony free of convicts, close to the gold and spices of the East, which would soon be wealthy in trade and agriculture. Those dreams were shattered by their failure to understand the country and they spent the first 20 years in a bitter battle to survive. Even the arrival of convicts in the 1840s did little to make Perth more than a struggling colonial outpost. By 1861, the population of all Western Australia was only 15,000.

The wealth, when it did come, came from inland and underground. Gold was discovered at Murchison in the 1890s. It and vast quantities of iron ore contribute most to the wealth of Perth and Western Australia today.

Nowadays, the ultramodern city of Perth nestles by a kilometre-wide expanse of the Swan River, which spreads out like a lake or harbour, edged by expensive suburbs and white sand beaches. A million people call it home and if you asked them why, the last thing they would say is because it is the gateway to the riches of the East.

Many locals live for the sun and the surf, riding the waves in the Indian Ocean or bobbing about in boats on protected river waters. Perth is the sunniest of all Australian cities, averaging eight hours of sunshine a day, and boasting a superb climate, with the average summer temperature of 29°C and a mild 18°C in winter.

The climate helps to give Perth a casual atmosphere, open and welcoming to everyone. It's a thriving city that has retained its intimacy and friendliness. It's young, beautiful, bright and breezy, with a spirited youth and vitality. People have the energy and courage to 'give it a go', and ideas are given time to develop and grow.

There's still a pioneering feeling in Perth. People here have proven that almost anything *is* possible. The city breeds entrepreneurs like rabbits and there are more millionaires per square kilometre than anywhere else in Australia; their modern wealth has as much to do with sharemarkets as with goldmines.

The city's people express themselves in many ways, not only in the business and mining world. There are talented people in all the creative arts — live theatre, the young and vital film industry, and the painters, potters, jewellers and other craftspeople are world class. Prime Ministers John Curtin and Bob Hawke were Perth natives.

Perth is not only a beautiful city, but also a well planned one. Its modern, efficient freeway is unique in that it was designed also as a park. Pedestrians can wander over lawns, under leafy trees, feed ducks and black swans and meander over little wooden bridges into a bushland grotto, complete with gushing waterfall — all within metres of the city's traffic.

But then, native bushland, gumtrees and wildflowers are an integral part of Perth's design. Within walking distance of the city, King's Park commands magnificent views of the city and the Swan River. Its 400 hectares of bush are a green and beautiful proof of the wisdom of the city's founding rathers. Gazetted by early governors as a park for the

Not the America's Cup but a Sunday afternoon's sailing on Perth's picturesque Swan River.

*Perth's Royal Arcade boasts many carefully restored
colonial buildings in an atmosphere of old and new.*

people, most of it is still in its natural state of wilderness, remaining a cool and peaceful escape for city workers. Many a civic battle has been fought to keep it that way.

The people of Perth are proud of their heritage and have fought long and hard to preserve the city's historic landmarks. The small archway at the end of St George's Terrace caused a furore that almost brought down a government in the long battle for its preservation. The arch is made of mellow, chequered, hand-crafted bricks whose warm glowing colours are arranged in geometric patterns over the walls.

This form of brickwork is typical of the historic buildings of early Perth, and the architectural style can be seen in several other superb examples — the old Town Hall, on the corner of Barrack and Hay Streets, Government House in its romantic gardens, and the Cloisters, snuggling in front of a towering office block at the end of Mill Street — a perfect example of the integration of old and new.

The old and the new merge in grand style and harmony across the railway line in Northbridge, too, where the Art Centre complex (consisting of the modern, streamlined Art Gallery and Alexander Library, a paved mall, striking statues and cooling plane trees) is in happy association with the old Perth Boys' School and the stately old museum.

When the sun sets, the Northbridge area comes alive as the tempting aroma of spicy food wafts into the streets. This cosmopolitan suburb is renowned for its restaurants, with Chinese and Italian its particular specialities.

The city's one million people have more than 1,500 restaurants to choose from, offering everything from Lebanese to Yugoslavian, Mongolian and Malaysian cuisines. Most of the five-star hotels also boast world-class restaurants. Nightclubs and discos can be found in the big hotels, too, such as Clouds at the Sheraton and Juliana's at the Hilton. The Ansett International Hotel is particularly noted for its splendid business facilities and pleasant, welcoming staff.

Much of the action for night-owls can be found at the new casino at Burswood Island, which is much more than simply a place to try your luck against the dice. The complex also boasts a five-star hotel, a golf course and many restaurants.

Perth is a city where the car reigns supreme, and discovering the best that the city and its suburbs have to offer really needs to be done by car or bus.

A tour of Perth is best begun from King's Park, on the hill at the end of St George's Terrace, with its view over the city, the river and to the distant foothills of the Darling Range. From King's Park, make your way through the bush to Nedlands, site of the University of Western Australia, Perth's grand old lady of education. It's a magnificently planned campus with buildings made from golden sandstone and terracotta tiles,

giving a superb unity to its overall design.

Wander around this serene place of learning, under the neo-Spanish colonnade of Winthrop Hall, with its 100-metre-high clock tower. Rest in the leafy gardens, and pause to gaze in the reflecting pool before searching for the Sunken Gardens and the Somerville Auditorium, hidden among the foliage.

The annual Festival of Perth is held at the university each January. World-famous musicians and performers appear in this breathtakingly beautiful venue, performing out of doors in the warm nights as well as in the theatres and halls.

From the university, move along Jutland Parade and Victoria Avenue past the palatial mansions of millionaire's row. Hiding behind stone walls and set in manicured gardens are masterpieces of modern domestic architecture. Royal Perth Yacht Club is here, home of the America's Cup during its short stay in Australia.

Pause for a break at Nedlands Park Hotel, affectionately called 'Steve's' by the locals, where university students rub shoulders with salt-encrusted sailors and successful barristers sipping cooling ales in the beer-garden and around the bar. Some of the most spectacular riverfront restaurants are located in this area. Upstairs in the hotel is Stephanie's, which combines old-world charm with elegant eating. Tables on the veranda overlook the river and foreshore and another restaurant, Jo-Jo's, built right out over the water on a jetty. Another superbly situated eatery, the Matilda Restaurant, is beside the Royal Perth Yacht Club, right on the river's edge. It has stunning views and equally stunning food.

From Nedlands, follow the curved riverside route to Claremont. This is the Knightsbridge, Rodeo Drive, Double Bay or Toorak area of Perth, with designer boutiques, bistros, wine bars and everything in between. Sip coffee, a cocktail or an al fresco aperitif at Kim's pavement cafe while you check out the trendies sauntering past.

Claremont has more to offer than exclusive apparel, however. The Claremont Fresh Markets are the best in the state, with the widest array of exotic fruits and vegetables imaginable. Feathery herbs and sweet Chinese melons are colourfully displayed alongside all the basics like tomatoes and potatoes. The markets also stock exotic smoked meats and poultry and a huge array of cheeses and breads, staying open seven days a week until 7 pm.

From Claremont, move back to the river and the old-established and exclusive suburb of Peppermint Grove. Here, elegant mansions with commanding views and opulent style clamber down the cliff-face to the river's edge.

On the ocean side is North Cottesloe Beach, made famous by Prince Charles who swims here when he is visiting Perth. On his most recent visit, he was unceremoniously dumped by a wave, and on a previous occasion he was kissed here by a shapely local girl.

Perth isn't just millionaires and mega-bucks — it's a playground for everyone to enjoy. On the river, tiny sailboards flit amongst the yachts like brilliantly coloured dragonflies. Small dinghies jostle for position with the big floating gin palaces, and small motor boats zip past luxury launches and streamlined ketches. Tourist boats chug from Perth down to the ocean port of Fremantle or up-river through old settlements and vineyards, calling at places of interest along the way, to the accompaniment of popping corks and gourmet food.

Perth is a place for everyone who enjoys the wind in their hair and the salty sea-breeze, especially the Fremantle Doctor, so-named because it is a life-saving blast of cool air which regularly refreshes on scorching summer afternoons.

Perth is one of the few places in Australia where you can see the sun set over the ocean. The summer sky is often daubed with a fiery palette, while the sea is set alight with spectacular sunsets of brilliant pink, gold, orange and red.

Sunbaking is a pastime pursued by most Western Australians. The metropolitan area is blessed with no fewer than 19 beaches which stretch along the coast from South Fremantle to Mullaloo in the north. The gleaming white sands are all within easy reach of the city and there's something for everyone, including those who do things au naturel. Bare bronzed bottoms are the mode at Swanbourne Beach. The long stretches of sand offer good surfing spots as well as safe family areas.

The coast is ideal for joggers and walkers in the cooler months and, for the more energetic, a bicycle track fringes the coast all the way from Cottesloe to the port of Fremantle, a thriving, bustling port, full of charm and history. But that's another story.

Jan Oldham

City Extras

Annie's Walking Tours

Ph. (09) 341 7378
Guided walks around Perth

Astra Chauffeured Hire Cars

Ph. (09) 328 6939
Chauffeur-driven tours

Away for a Day

Ph. (09) 227 8538
Exclusive personalised tours in and around Perth

Budget Chauffeur Drive

Ph. (09) 322 1100
Tours, secretarial services and interpreters

Deluxe Chauffeured Limousines

Ph. (09) 325 2817
Chauffeur-driven city and country tours

Fremantle Walking Tours

Ph. (09) 335 8417
Walking tours of historic Fremantle

Interpreters International

Ph. (09) 481 0880
Bi-lingual and multi-lingual tour guides

Tour Guide Agency and Tours

Ph. (09) 274 1502
Personalised shopping or sight-seeing tours in and around Perth

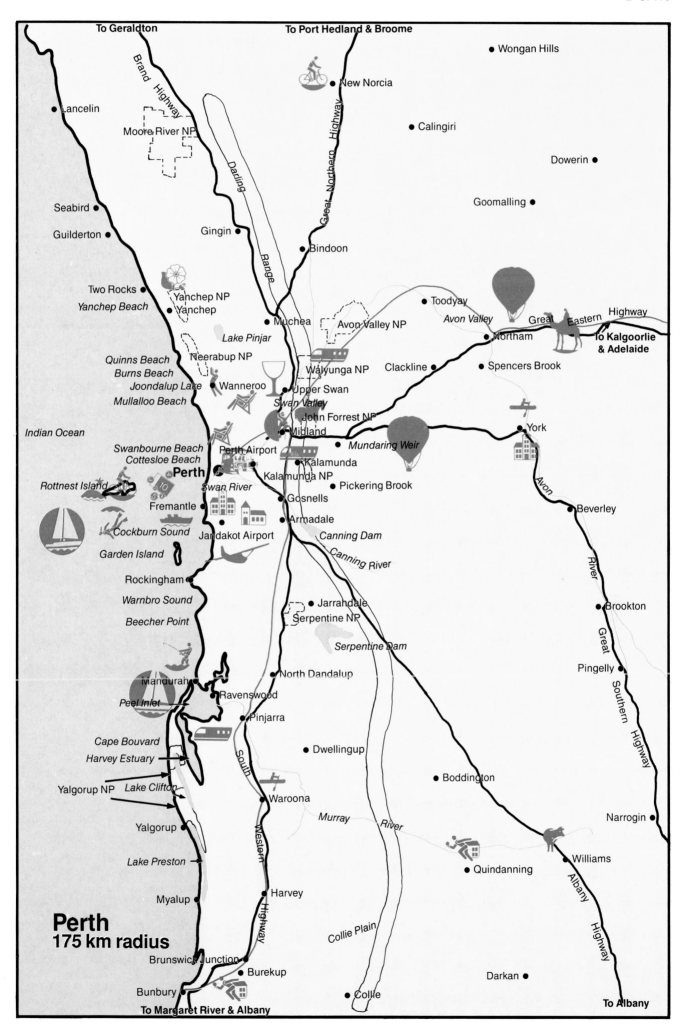

Perth
175 km radius

Fremantle

Fremantle is a working, living port — a city of the past and the present, alive with history and action.

The city recently basked in the spotlight of the America's Cup, its 19th-century charm spruced up and gleaming with newly decorated splendour.

While in other cities developers have bulldozed in the name of progress, replacing the past with monstrosities of steel and cement, Fremantle has kept her historic beauty, aided and abetted by three generations of mayors from the same family. It was Sir Frederick Sampson who fought for and passed a civic law preventing the building of structures higher than three storeys.

Fremantle moves at a leisurely pace. The atmosphere is cosmopolitan. Fremantle was one of the first cities in Australia to allow pavement cafes. Now families wander slowly along the streets, pausing to chat to friends sitting under gaily fluttering umbrellas at Papa Luigi's or Gino's in South Terrace.

Take a seat and a drink a cup of coffee and watch the world move past. The locals come for breakfast, to read the paper; they drop in after work, or in the wee-small hours after a night on the town.

The port city is best seen on foot. Wander through the meandering one-way streets and discover the delightful old-fashioned pubs, newly resplendant and renovated with a lick of paint and a filigree of iron lace. The Sail and Anchor, the first of the boutique breweries, has a huge choice of local and imported beers and their own made-on-the-spot brews— lagers, ales and the famous Dog Bolter, which really packs a wallop.

Play it by ear when you explore Fremantle, especially when it comes to music — stop, listen and follow the sounds of the throbbing rhythm of the jazz pubs. Pubs not to miss are the Norfolk, the Sail and Anchor, the Newport and the Commercial.

For elegant old-world charm, relax over a cup of tea or a Gin Sling cocktail in the Esplanade Plaza Hotel, where the historic past is combined with modern streamlined convenience. The magnificent colonial facade gives way to another world inside, where a huge glass atrium four storeys high and towering majestic palm trees reach for the skies.

Historic buildings are a part of the living design of Fremantle. The Round House, originally a 12-sided limestone prison, is the oldest building in the state. Perched high on a hill, it overlooks the sea and the new Challenge Harbour.

The Fremantle Maritime Museum, with its Cape Dutch architecture, was built last century as an asylum. It is now a grand group of renovated stone buildings, housing a comprehensive and fascinating record of our history — a barnacle-encrusted treasure trove with cannon, pieces of eight and other artefacts from the 17th century buccaneering days when Dutch ships were wrecked off the Western Australian coast.

As with most of Fremantle, there is nothing superficial or pretentious about the Fremantle Markets. They are a real marketplace, where the locals shop for the cheapest fruit and vegetables. The market building has always been a marketplace, being built for the purpose in 1896.

You can indulge in all the senses as you mingle with the bustling crowds on Fridays, Saturdays and Sundays. The sound of jazz music competes with the raspy country singing busker; the perfume of freshly ground coffee combines with the tempting aroma of freshly baked bread. You can sip a cooling ale or a healthy, freshly squeezed fruit juice, or put your feet up and take a breather in the delightful old-fashioned tearooms.

Part of Western Australia's living history can be experienced in the Aboriginal Gallery in High Street, where bark paintings and other artefacts are displayed for visitors to admire and purchase.

Fremantle expresses its colourful, multi-cultural tradition in the Blessing of the Fleet. This custom, which originated in the Mediterranean, was revived by the Italian migrants who moved to Australia. The

fishermen and their families, dressed in the colourful costumes of their homeland provinces, join in a winding procession behind a statue of the Virgin Mary through the streets to the water's edge and the fishing boats, which are decorated with fluttering flags for this special event.

A visit to Fremantle must include the waterfront at Fishing Boat Harbour, where the America's Cup Defence headquarters were located and where all the action began when the 12-metre boats were racing. Fremantle Sailing Club now has one of the largest marinas in Australia.

Sit by the docks with your fish and chips, while you enjoy the atmosphere of the fishing boats and the port, and throw out a chip or two for the squawking gulls swooping overhead.

Jan Oldham

A benign year-round climate encourages the outdoor social life, above, in Fremantle - a classic fishing and trading port which also boasts elegant architecture, opposite

GILBERT ROSSI

Western Australia

Take a deep breath before visiting Western Australia, and take plenty of time. It's a big chunk of land, occupying one-third of the Australian continent, or nearly four times the area of the US state of Texas.

Be prepared to be awed by size, be it the 12,500-kilometre coastline extending from the tropical north to the Southern Ocean, or the homes of Australia's richest men revealed in all their brash magnificence as you cruise the Swan River.

Big in landscape, big in history and big in the way it has developed its industries, Western Australia presents plenty of challenge for those who would wish to know her better.

Perth, the capital, is superbly situated on the Swan River, so-named when Dutch navigators of the 17th century first saw black swans, previously believed to be mythical birds. Black swans can still be seen today in quiet reaches of the river.

Ease into your Western Australian adventure at the nearby port of Fremantle, home of Australia's America's Cup Defence. Set the historical perspective with a visit to Fremantle Museum were you can relive the experiences of Dutch and other seafarers who sighted the great land mass only to come to grief on reefs that are now a graveyard for some 700 vessels.

Just 19 kilometres from Perth is the island of Rottnest, so-named by the Dutch navigator Vlaming because of its inhabitants, unique and endearing nocturnal marsupials called quokkas which he thought were strange rats.

Travel there by air or ferry and visit its numerous limestone cliffs sheltering white beaches where, close to shore, the water is crystal clear and sparkling, and further out it is turquoise green, blue and purple. Here, the mode of dress is bathing costume and hat and bicycles are the mode of transport — no cars are allowed. The main settlement at Thomson Bay, which

dates back to the 1840s, is reminiscent of the Mediterranean, with simple stone cottages in a unified lime-wash of warm yellow ochre. The Governor's former summer residence is now the hotel. You can swim at any of the little bays, fish from the encircling reefs or from boats in the open sea, play golf or tennis, or just go for walks on the sandhills.

Perth is blessed with nearby swimming and surfing beaches similar to those found along the entire coastline. But it's not all sun and sand. A short drive takes you to the Darling Range and its pretty hills and valleys, orchards and townships, national parks and spring wildflowers. At Armadale you can step back into history in an authentic re-creation of a pioneer village, where 19th-century arts and crafts are carried on by the people living there. A village blacksmith makes hand-wrought ironwork; a wheelwright and carriage-builder restore dilapidated buggies and carriages; and a metal-spinner hand-shapes copper kettles. There's a goldsmith, a bookbinder, a carver of boomerangs and an apothecary's shop where you can buy herbal remedies.

Other attractions within easy reach of Perth are Cohunu Wildlife Park, where native animals and plants can be seen in their natural style, and El Caballo Blanco, 96 kilometres east of the city at Wooroloo, where dancing Andalusian horses strut their stuff in a Spanish hacienda. Southwards is the small timber town of Jarradale on the way to the man-made Serpentine Dam, beautifully integrated with the bushland, where a family can spend a whole day picnicking, bushwalking or dining in ease at open-air restaurant terraces.

You can dally in the Perth hinterland, but it is time to move on. Go up the Great Northern Highway and you will pass through sheep and wheat farms to New Norcia, a Benedictine Monastery established by

The Pinnacles rock formations in the New Norcia region of Western Australia

Spanish monks in 1846 as a mission for Aborigines. Its buildings include a library of rare books, an art gallery of European masters, a chapel and guest rooms. Nearer the coast are the Greenough Flats, once the state's chief wheat-growing district. Three great flour mills close to Dongara township have been restored as local museums.

The sunny port of Geraldton is the target for holidaymakers in winter and you can take a boat to the legendary Abrolhos Islands, named by the Dutch navigator Houtman and scene of many wrecks during the 17th and 18th centuries. Spanish coins, pottery and other artefacts have been recovered by divers and are housed in Geraldton, Perth and Fremantle museums.

The journey north approaches the Tropic of Capricorn at Shark Bay, where pearls were found 300 years ago by the English buccaneer and navigator, William Dampier, who reported that the country was 'dry, barren and useless'. Today, at Monkey Mia, friendly dolphins make daily visits to be fed. Here also at Hamelin Pool are the strange stromatolites, an ancient life-form and relic of the world's remote past.

The West Coast Highway leads on past North West Cape and the US Space Tracking Station. In this region are Exmouth Gulf, popular with deep-sea fishermen, the old port of Onslow and the new coastal town of Dampier, created to export iron ore and nickel from the rich mines nearby. Other new mineral towns include Tom Price, Newman, Paraburdoo and Goldsworthy.

Set on a coast vast in scale, primeval in character and even today, practically uninhabitated, Cossack was once the chief pearling port with a population of several thousand where lugger crews sheltered during the months of the cyclone or 'blow'. After the pearling beds were worked out, the luggers moved eastward and Broome became the centre of the pearling industry, leaving the old harbour to silt up and Cossack to become a ghost town. However, the former magnificence of Cossack can be seen in the large public buildings, designed and built by WA government architect George Temple-Poole, that have survived more than half a century of neglect. The

Court House has been restored by the government and the Customs House is maintained by Wittenoom's asbestos millionaire, Lang Hancock.

And now Western Australia's grandeur begins to unfold: a few miles inland, the Pilbara, first settled in the 1860s by pastoralists who took up huge leases, often of 400,000 hectares and more, and Roebourne, which from 1865 was the administrative centre.

After the sheep came a mild goldrush, but the present-day mineral wealth of the region has resulted in the creation of new towns such as Dampier, Port Samson and Port Hedland, resulting in the decline in importance of the original centre. The asbestos-mining town of Wittenoom is a favourite for those who wish to see the beautiful and dramatic gorges of the Hamersley Range — gorges which carry cascading waterfalls after the rains, and which drop sheer for hundreds of metres, the cliffs changing colour and shadows playing over the fiery red, orange, purple, brown and gold of stone, terminating far below in tranquil, ice-cold pools.

Further east, the pearling town of Broome provides the gateway to the rugged Kimberleys. Broome recalls romantic days of pearling fleets, a once-busy Chinatown, and Japanese divers whose remains are buried in a Japanese cemetery with natural stone graves. Little pearling is done by luggers these days, the market for pearl shells having been destroyed by plastic manufacture. But cultured pearls are a vital industry at Kuri Bay further north.

With a winter temperature of between 16° and 24°C, many people contrive to escape the cold and rain of southern Australia and spend the months between May and October here. Attractions are swimming at mile-long Cable Beach and viewing the primeval coast with its huge rocks flung around as though frozen at a moment when the world was being created. Indeed, this impression is not far from the truth, for embedded in the rocks at Gantheaume Point are footprints of a dinosaur, made in the soft mud 130 million years ago.

Near Derby is the famous Prison Boab Tree, in whose bulbous trunk natives were held; the longest cattle trough in the southern hemisphere, at Myall's Bore; and Aboriginal settlements with their own store, where paintings and carvings are sold. And all the best northern fish are found splashing in the water around Broome, including Spanish mackerel, tuna and shark. Fish for them at the town jetty.

Further east are some of the most fascinating parts of the Kimberleys. The modern town of Kununurra was created to serve construction of the great Ord River Dam, which holds eight times as much water as Sydney Harbour. At Kununurra, the historic homestead of the pioneering Duracks of Argyle Station has been lovingly rebuilt, the original location lying beneath the waters of the dam. From Kununurra, launches travel daily to beautiful Lake Argyle where tropical birds and wildlife abound — a popular area year round for water sports.

Further north is Wyndham, the port of the East Kimberley, with five rivers flowing into Cambridge Gulf and man-eating saltwater crocodiles sunning themselves around the banks. Dramatic, panoramic landscapes reveal themselves, including that of the recently-opened vertical mountain formations at Bungle-Bungle — eerie, gaunt, twisted shapes that could be relics of science fiction. Nearby, and not far from the Northern Territory border, is the Argyle diamond mine, claimed to be the biggest in the world.

On the highway linking the East and West Kimberleys is old Halls Creek where the first payable gold in Western Australia was discovered in 1855. A modern town has been built in a more suitable location a few miles away, but interesting ruins of the old township remain.

On the Fitzroy River is Fitzroy Crossing, noted for flooding. From this town, launch tours travel upriver to spectacular gorges like Geikie Gorge, Windjana National Park and many others. As the boat approaches, crocodiles slide noiselessly from the bank into the water.

Modern transport by air and road has opened the area up to tourists, and modern towns provide all the amenities. There are guided camping safaris for the adventurous — this is not a region to treat lightly. The fantastic coastlines (where the tides make incredible patterns like abstract paintings), great rivers, rough mountain ranges and tropical wildlife all make for a memorable experience.

Where the north is raw, bleached and harsh, Western Australia's south is soft and gentle, with cool rains and mild summers. Travel south from Perth along the coast and discover Mandurah, a fishing paradise providing much of the seafood, including superb blue-swimmer crabs and school prawns, for the metropolis. Further south, Bunbury has modern hotels, motels and restaurants, a fine harbour and beautiful ocean beaches.

Enjoy spectacular scenery at Wellington Dam, which offers picnic spots, barbecues and gentle bush walking. On the route south, Ludlow Forest preserves the majestic tuart trees with an under-storey of weeping peppermint trees and banksias, and annual seasonal groundcover of exotic white aram lily.

Busselton has many historic homesteads of the first pioneers. Several are owned by the National Trust and are open to the public — discover part of our cultural history in literature, drama, local music and song at Cattle Chosen and Fairlawn.

At Busselton, take a stroll on the longest working jetty in the world. Striding 1,753 metres out on black, spidery legs into the Indian Ocean, the Busselton jetty is surpassed only by the 2,145-metre long amusement pier at Southend in England, which is not a working jetty. The original jetty was built in the 1860s.

One of Australia's most eerie natural wonders, the Bungle Bungles is a true wilderness area some 2000 km from Perth. The range covers 700 square kms. These extraordinary shapes reflect a process of erosion by wind and water from a sandstone that is extremely brittle and which crumbles underfoot, thus requiring careful environmental protection.

The vast remote Kimberley region has been visited by very few people. It is a region of gorges, canyons and rivers, as seen above at Windjana Gorge.

Yallingup, on the coast, has long been renowned for its magical caves and wonderful surfing beach. The delicate Lake Cave and Mammoth Cave, with its colourful stalactites and stalagmites, are beautifully lit and accessible by daily guided tours. Now the region is the centre of a new and exciting wine-growing district, which is already producing some of Australia's finest award-winning table wines. Take a guided tour to the vineyards and taste the wines. Each year, thousands flock to the famous Leeuwin Estate, where millionaire-owner Denis Horgan brings one of the world's acclaimed orchestras to participate in the Festival of Perth.

The London Philharmonic, the Berlin State and the Danish Symphony Orchestras have all performed here, under the stars, with a majestic natural amphitheatre of huge karri trees forming a towering backdrop in silhouette against the midsummer sky.

Drive down over Alexander Bridge on the Blackwood River and into the great karri forests where the spectacular trees, ferns and tall bushes of the green and rusty-pink kangaroo paw are all indigenous to the area. The karri trees, slender columns dappled silver-grey and pale gold, are among the tallest in the world, rising to more than 120 metres. On the ground below, the hovea, crowea and other delicate wildflowers are lit up by the sunlight which penetrates the canopies.

Manjimup is the chief town of the karri industry. The other timber town is Pemberton, renowned for its trout hatcheries, from which young trout constantly replenish the creeks and dams of the south-west to provide sport and delight to fishermen and gourmets.

Further south is Albany, with a harbour that vies with Rio de Janeiro as the most beautiful in the southern hemisphere. Albany was the state's main port during the whole of the last century, until the brilliant engineer C. Y. O'Connor created Fremantle Harbour, enabling big ships to enter the mouth of the Swan. Although Albany's importance waned, much produce is still exported from the port.

Guided tours enable visitors to explore the rugged coast, including the Natural Bridge, granite cliffs and blow-holes, pounded by the huge swells of the Southern Ocean. Visit Dog Rock and Strawberry Hill Farm, then take a short trip inland to the spectacular Stirling Range and the smaller Porongorups, rising almost vertically from the coastal plain.

Further east lies the pleasant port of Esperance and the cluster of islands that make up the Archipelago of the Recherche, names that recall the French navigators of the last century. Large wheat, sheep and cattle properties now extend east of Esperance, beyond which are extensive national parks preserving the area's fragile flora and fauna.

Esperance was the starting point in the 1890s for the thousands of men who arrived by ship from the eastern states to make their way to the rich gold discoveries at Coolgardie, Kalgoorlie, Norseman and elsewhere in the north and north-east.

Gold was discovered at Coolgardie in 1892, and by 1896 it had grown to be the third largest town in the state, with a population of 15,000 and 10,000 living in surrounding centres. It boasted 26 hotels (16 in the main street), three breweries, four clubs (including a Japanese club), seven newspapers (including three dailies), two stock exchanges and 25 stockbrokers.

Coolgardie today has only relics of its former glory in the impressive public buildings that line the wide streets. These are today maintained as museums

MILTON WORDLEY

The Cassidy mine shaft at Kalgoorlie, Western Australia

to tell of the first mineral boom that brought prosperity and people to the state. Most goldmining sites are now ghost towns with no inhabitants, or only a few old prospectors fossicking for specks of the elusive metal. The exception is Kalgoorlie, which is still a busy, thriving city.

From Kalgoorlie, the Great Northern Highway runs through former goldfields and pastoral properties, the towns of Mount Magnet, Cue and Meekatharra to link up with the old goldmining towns of the Pilbara, Naullagine and Marble Bar, the hottest town in Australia. Finally, you are joined by the North West Coastal Highway at Port Hedland.

So, if you do decide to visit Western Australia, take plenty of time. The place demands attention, and a lot of respect.

Jan Oldham

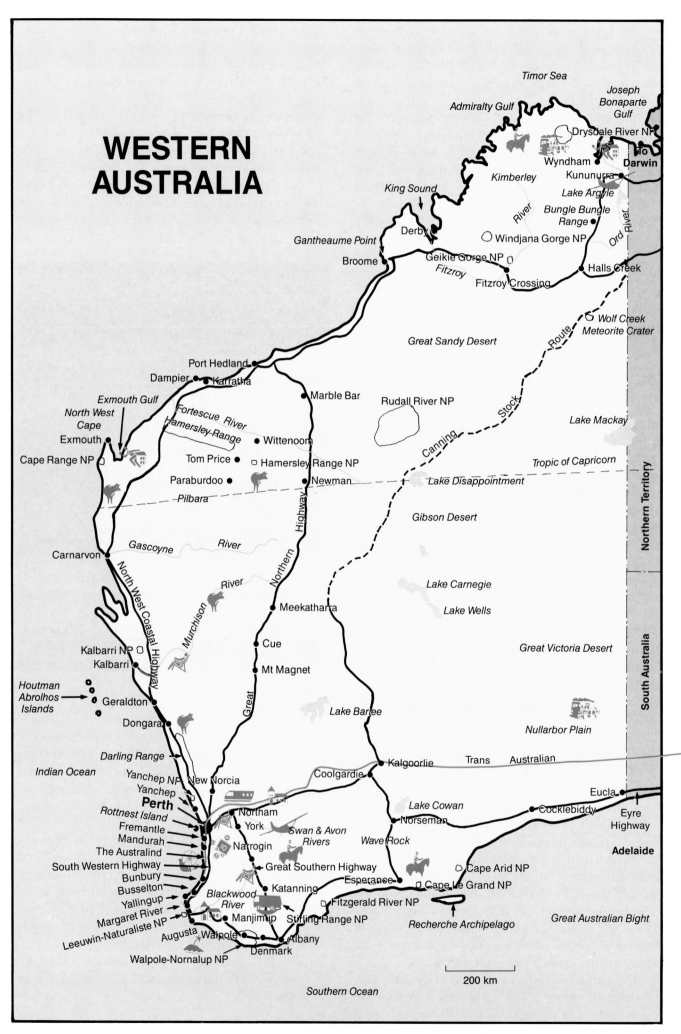

WESTERN AUSTRALIA

Timor Sea

Admiralty Gulf

Joseph Bonaparte Gulf

Drysdale River NP

Wyndham

Kimberley

Darwin

Kununurra

Lake Argyle

King Sound

River

Bungle Bungle Range

Derby

Windjana Gorge NP

Gantheaume Point

Geikie Gorge NP

Broome

Ord River

Halls Creek

Fitzroy Crossing

Fitzroy

Wolf Creek Meteorite Crater

Great Sandy Desert

Stock Route

Port Hedland

Dampier

Karratha

Marble Bar

Rudall River NP

Lake Mackay

Exmouth Gulf

North West Cape

Fortescue River

Hamersley Range

Wittenoom

Canning

Exmouth

Tom Price

Hamersley Range NP

Tropic of Capricorn

Cape Range NP

Paraburdoo

Newman

Lake Disappointment

Pilbara

Gibson Desert

Gascoyne

River

Northern Highway

Carnarvon

Lake Carnegie

Murchison

River

Lake Wells

Meekatharra

Great Victoria Desert

Kalbarri NP

Kalbarri

Cue

Houtman Abrolhos Islands

Geraldton

Mt Magnet

Great

Lake Barlee

Dongara

Nullarbor Plain

Darling Range

Indian Ocean

Yanchep NP

New Norcia

Kalgoorlie

Trans Australian

Yanchep

Coolgardie

Perth

Eucla

Rottnest Island

Northam

Lake Cowan

Cocklebiddy

Fremantle

York

Norseman

Mandurah

Swan & Avon Rivers

Eyre Highway

The Australind

Narrogin

Wave Rock

South Western Highway

Adelaide

Bunbury

Great Southern Highway

Cape Arid NP

Busselton

Esperance

Cape Le Grand NP

Yallingup

Katanning

Blackwood River

Margaret River

Fitzgerald River NP

Leeuwin-Naturaliste NP

Manjimup

Stirling Range NP

Recherche Archipelago

Great Australian Bight

Augusta

Walpole

Albany

Denmark

Walpole-Nornalup NP

Northern Territory

South Australia

200 km

Southern Ocean

Gold fossicking is an ancient pursuit that still attracts hopeful diggers to their small mining leases in the wake of the big mining companies

Gold!

The Australian goldrush began seriously in 1851 when gold was discovered at Ophir in New South Wales by Edward Hargraves. Within months, 10,000 prospectors, or 'diggers' as they became known, were at the New South Wales' goldfields. Attention was switched quickly, however, to impressive finds at Bendigo, making Victoria the prime source. Mining also began in Queensland, but the major discoveries were to be made in Western Australia at Kalgoorlie and Coolgardie in the 1880s and 90s.

By the turn of the century, gold accounted for 75% of the dollar value of Australia's mineral production and its importance has been a crucial factor in the country's development and in the development of Western Australia in particular.

Today, Western Australia accounts for 70% of Australia's gold output. And Australia is the world's fastest growing gold-producing country. In 1980, the output was 17 tonnes; in 1987, it reached 100 tonnes. It is fitting, therefore, that in 1986, Gold Corp Australia was established to undertake an international gold programme. And its first major activity has been the launch of the new gold bullion coins, the Australian Nugget.

The coins come in four sizes: one-tenth ounce, one-quarter ounce, one half ounce, and one ounce. They are the first gold coins to feature gold as the subject of their design. 'Little Hero', 'Golden Eagle', 'Hand of Faith' and 'Welcome Stranger' are the four famous nuggets featured in the design of the coins.

From the diggers of last century to the sophisticated gold industry of today, we can trace an exciting story in the life of Australia. Perhaps the final word should be left to Henry Lawson, who captured in his poem *'Eureka'* the sense of adventure that drove the early miners in their quest:

> *All gleaming white amid the shafts o'er gully,*
> *hill and flat*
> *Again I see the tents that form the camp*
> *at Ballarat.*
> *I hear the shovels and the picks, and all the*
> *air is rife*
> *With the rattle of the cradles and the sounds of*
> *digger-life.*

Hobart, Jewel of the South

From the crest of Mt Wellington, Hobart — Australia's smallest capital — sprawls far below with all the cheerful arrogance of Sydney and San Francisco, two cities it is easily, and often, compared to in physical terms. There the comparison must rest, for Hobart has an unhurried charm, elegance and insouciant lifestyle that neither of the others can match. It is a marriage of town and country. With a population of perhaps 180,000 in the Greater Hobart area, sprawled over 3,340 square kilometres, it is not exactly crowded, and that is one of the most delightful benefits of this gracious city — a sense of spaciousness.

Viewed from the mountain's crest — a 20-minute drive from the city centre — the city's buildings and suburbs nestle round the hills that demarcate the fingers of river valleys and twisting estuaries which fan out everywhere.

Hobart is blessed with a verdant urban landscape that wraps itself gracefully around a magnificent deep-water harbour on a wide river estuary. Its intricate waterfront consists of sandy beaches, weather-worn sandstone coves, shallow estuaries and swampy bird havens. There are cliffs and reefs and coastal parks.

The friendly hulk of 'the mountain' protects Hobart from the excesses of the wild weather flung at Tasmania's western shores. It has been known to snow on Christmas Day on Mt Wellington, while the city below basks in the sun!

A home without a water view in Hobart is not easy to find, and the city's business centre itself embraces Sullivan's Cove, one of Australia's most intact — if threatened — older waterfronts.

In real estate terms, Hobart can be schizophrenic, and in many areas there is an often discordant intermingling of aged elegance and brassy modern. This mingling of styles is finely illustrated in Sullivan's Cove, with its elegant architecture of nearly two centuries of waterfront activity. Two fingers of older buildings flank the cove. The northern arm has some stunning examples of early architecture, as well as the vibrant restoration and revamp given the old IXL jam factory, which has been converted into the new Tasmanian School of Art.

Opposite is Salamanca Place, a timeless row of sandstone warehouses. At least, it looks as if most of the buildings have been here for at least a century, but the truth is that there have been some very sympathetic additions. The most recent is the Galleria — a four-storey complex of small shops and businesses grouped around an imposing courtyard. It is linked internally with a sister project on the corner of Salamanca Place and Knopwood's Retreat. Both are built of modern materials, but are clad in a sandstone rendering which blends chameleon-like into the neighbourhood.

This civic spirit by private enterprise has not always been reflected in the public buildings along this unique Australian waterfront, but the citizens of Hobart are quick to react to any intrusions on the 'waterfront'. They learned their fighting tactics in the battle to save the Franklin River from being dammed, and refined them to fight the monolithic form of a proposed new international hotel. This basic brick structure, with the architectural lines of a power station, created an absolute furore, and the indignant residents nearly succeeded in getting the project abandoned. They were finally forced to accept an eight-storey compromise in place of the original proposal for an 18-storey glass tower.

Hobart is also the setting for an interesting real es-

ALLAN MOULT

Wrest Point Casino, Australia's first casino, dominates Sandy Bay

tate revival, not unlike those that have transformed Sydney's Paddington and Melbourne's Carlton. While not in the major leagues in terms of turnover and prices, this renovation revival is keeping the Tasmanian market buoyant.

The mini-boom in Hobart is basically being fuelled by newcomers from interstate who suddenly find that they have bought a new home in Hobart, twice the size of their former home in Melbourne or Sydney, for half the price. These new residents have obviously been spreading the word and there has been a distinct if gradual increase in the number of mainland migrants to Tasmania.

Many such migrants have cashed in their superannuation and, faced with a too-early retirement, are pumping their energies instead into their new homes. Others have simply opted for the lifestyle — the easy pace of living, the realistic real estate prices, the almost non-existent crime and drug problem, and Australia's ideal environment for raising children.

Still, the real revival of Hobart is being carried out in the suburbs, particularly in the residential areas adjoining the city. There's Battery Point, North and South Hobart, inner Sandy Bay, and the current market leader — West Hobart. West Hobart sits midway up the slopes of Mt Knocklofty and has some of the best views in Tasmania. Most homes enjoy a sweeping view of the Derwent and the broad waters of the bay.

Although Hobart is tiny by comparison with the mainland capitals, it nevertheless offers most attractions of a big city — in smaller, more accessible doses. It also offers the dedicated night owl and bon vivant the rare pleasure of attending all first nights at theatres and galleries. For gourmets, there is a reasonable sprinkling of outstanding restaurants —

ALLAN MOULT

Hobart, and Tasmania's, 'colonial' accommodation is a welcome alternative to hotels and motels

Dear Friends, Beards, Siscos, Mures — and a host of others dotted throughout the city and suburbs that thrive on a regular clientele.

It is a busy creative city during the week. Then, on Saturdays, the waters of the harbour are freckled white with hundreds of sails as the yachties vie for club race honours, and many others simply cruise. Elsewhere, sportsgrounds are buzzing with activity, often with few spectators in evidence — they are all on the grounds, having a go!

For others, depending on the season, Hobart offers ocean surfing, cross-country skiing, world-class trout-fishing, bushwalking, wild-water rafting, kayaking, flatwater canoeing, horse-trail riding, scuba diving — all within an hour of the GPO.

At Salamanca Place, the weekly market is underway. The local townspeople promenade and mix with their country cousins, the organic gardeners. the Mom and Pop secondhand dealers and the Huon hippies. The atmosphere is relaxed and friendly, with teasing banter between shopper and merchant. It's a market in the old sense — a weekly gathering at a social level, and tourists can't believe the soft sell.

Hobart is like that, too — a genuine soft sell.

Allan Moult

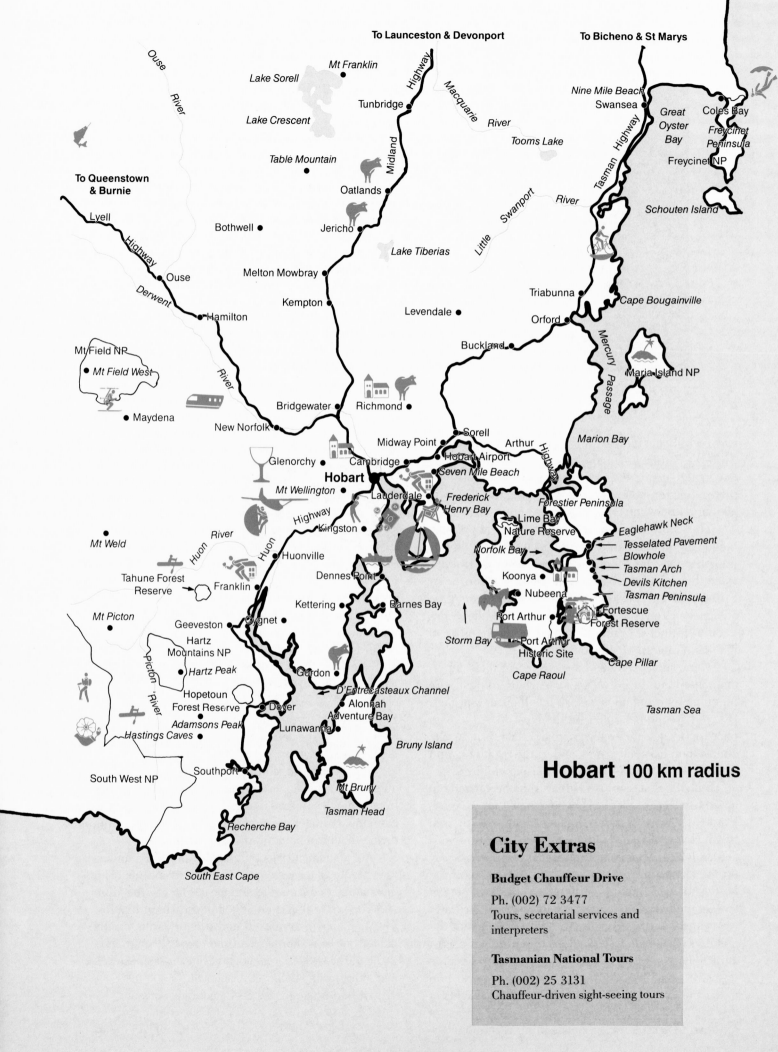

To Launceston & Devonport

To Bicheno & St Marys

Ouse *River*

Mt Franklin

Lake Sorell

Tunbridge

Macquarie

River

Lake Crescent

Tooms Lake

Nine Mile Beach

Swansea

Great Oyster Bay

Coles Bay

Freycinet Peninsula

Table Mountain

Midland

Highway

Oatlands

Freycinet NP

Tasman Highway

To Queenstown & Burnie

Lyell

River

Little *Swanport*

Schouten Island

Bothwell

Jericho

Highway

Lake Tiberias

Triabunna

Cape Bougainville

Melton Mowbray

Derwent

Ouse

Kempton

Levendale

Orford

Mercury *Passage*

Hamilton

Buckland

Marion Bay

Mt Field NP

Maria Island NP

Mt Field West

River

Maydena

Bridgewater

Richmond

New Norfolk

Sorell

Midway Point

Arthur

Highway

Glenorchy

Cambridge

Hobart Airport

Hobart

Mt Wellington

Seven Mile Beach

Lauderdale

Frederick Henry Bay

Forestier Peninsula

Highway

Kingston

Lime Bay Nature Reserve

Eaglehawk Neck

Huon River

Norfolk Bay

Tesselated Pavement

Mt Weld

Huon

Huonville

Blowhole

Tasman Arch

Tahune Forest Reserve

Franklin

Koonya

Devils Kitchen

Dennes Point

Nubeena

Tasman Peninsula

Mt Picton

Kettering

Barnes Bay

Fortescue Forest Reserve

Port Arthur

Geeveston

Cygnet

Storm Bay

Port Arthur Historic Site

Hartz Mountains NP

Gordon

Cape Pillar

Hartz Peak

Picton *River*

Cape Raoul

Hopetoun Forest Reserve

D'Entrecasteaux Channel

Alonnah

Adamsons Peak

Dover

Adventure Bay

Tasman Sea

Hastings Caves

Lunawanna

South West NP

Southport

Bruny Island

Mt Bruny

Hobart 100 km radius

Recherche Bay

Tasman Head

South East Cape

Tasmania

South! To the bleak southern seas, the tumultuous storms of the Roaring Fifties, the last wilderness, and the wild waters of Bass Strait which were once teeming with sea elephants, fur seals, fairy penguins and muttonbirds. And undisturbed home for them just 200 years ago was the protected east coast of King Island.

King Island is just one of 14 major islands — totalling nearly 4,000 square kilometres in area — that necklace the island state of Tasmania, and is typically marked by stark physical contrasts and a vibrant, often violent, history of settlement. It is flat and basically featureless; the highest point on its 1,099-square-kilometre land mass is barely 100 metres above sea level. The pilot switches on the intercom and his metallic voice reverberates around the small cabin: 'It will be a bit bumpy, so fasten your seatbelts — and hang on to your suitcase when you walk across the tarmac.'

He meant it. The wind gusted merrily, and suitcases and briefcases floated as if levitated. Sanctuary in the tiny airport terminus brought an ominous comment from a departing passenger. 'Be careful when the wind stops,' she said. 'The locals fall over.'

Conversation is drowned by the wind during the short ride into Currie, the unkempt capital of the island, and headquarters for one of the world's most unusual industries — kelp harvesting — and its ubiquitous end-product: alginate. And it is the wind that makes the industry feasible — strong gale-force winds which tear the giant bull kelp off the seabed and toss it on to the serrated rocks of the wild west coast. Here it is collected and taken to the factory to be dried, shredded and pelleted.

The end-product, basically a tasteless gelatin-like substance, has an amazing role to play in the world's industries. Its remarkable qualities are particularly sought after by the food industry who use it to help stabilise, thicken, suspend and gel all kinds of food products and pharmaceuticals, including ice-cream, frozen foods, juice drinks, toppings, salad dressing, pet foods, toothpaste and milkshakes. And, yes, it is used to create two Australian staples — beer and meat pies. In the amber fluid it is used to keep a longer head of foam, and in the humble floater, its presence thickens the sauce, suspends the meagre meat in a jelly, and stabilises the shell for longer shelf life.

Today, King Island is a placid, if windswept, rural haven which among other things produces Australia's finest cheeses. Its beginnings were more violent and tragic, for this western guardian of Bass Strait has a sad and lengthy record of shipwrecks, including the largest loss of life in a civil disaster in the country. The wreck of the *Cataraqui* on the night of 4 August 1845 caused the loss of 399 lives out of a total of 408 on board.

Flinders Island to the east is another storm-lashed mass which used to be a whaler's haven. Today it houses an independent rural community whose annual high point is the short muttonbird season. It is separated from the Tasmanian mainland by Cape Barren Island and Clarke Island, two rugged deep-water stepping stones.

And there is Macquarie Island — halfway to Antarctica — a haven (no doubt purely through isolation and the international decline in whaling) for a host of penguins, seals, sea elephants and sea birds who thrive on the abundance of pelagic fish cruising its waters.

Elsewhere there are islands such as Bruny — a long sliver of low-lying land that hangs off the south-east of Tasmania and is home for fat cows and sheep. The mountainous hulk of Maria Island, off the east coast, was once an infamous isolation prison for convicts. Today it is a national park.

For the visitor, perhaps the ideal way to see Tasmania is from the air. Almost any commercial airstrip offers scenic flights, and at Strahan seaplane flights are available. And it is from the air that Tasmania's isolation becomes apparent. Indeed, isolation made Tasmania and its islands an ideal site for the infamous penal settlements that freckled the young Australia.

First discovered in 1642 by Abel Tasman, it was not settled until 1803 when 49 people under the command of Lieutenant John Bowen came ashore at Risdon Cove to establish what later became Hobart.

Tasmania itself lies just a short distance to the south of King Island. It's a 15-minute flight to the north-west corner — site of one of the biggest farms in this island state — Woolnorth. It is still owned by the Van Diemen's Land Company, which received its original Royal Charter in 1825 from King George IV.

Further east lies the triangular hulk of Robbins Island, scene of one of Australia's most unusual cattle drives. Here, the Hammond family — father Gene, and sons John, Keith and Chauncey — take on the tricky waters of the Montagu Passage when they need to get cattle to the mainland markets. It can only be undertaken during exceptionally low tides and critical timing is required to swim the cattle across when the tide racing through the passage is at its weakest.

This haven for man and beast is in stark contrast to the battered west coast — home of bleak landscapes and strong men and women. Here, the island state bears the brunt of the storms born in the tumult of the Roaring Forties — the ceaseless trade winds that circle the globe in a broad belt centred on latitude 40° south.

Strahan is the gateway to the magnificent, if unpredictable, waters of Macquarie Harbour, site of one of the most ill-famed convict outposts in the Empire. It is also the gateway to the lower reaches of the Gordon River which drains the waters of the Franklin and Olga Rivers among others. For many years, it was the only way out for the copper ores from Mt Lyell Mine at Queenstown. It has been said that on the evening of the official opening of the road into Queenstown from Hobart there were only three sober men in town, and they would not have been sober had not the town's supply of beer given out. But, as author E. T. Emmett said, 'One cannot blame the coasters for getting excited, for were they not imprisoned for over a hundred years?'

As he explained in his delightful book, *Tasmania by Road and Track*, the west coast was the first part of Tasmania to be seen by European eyes and it has been the last to be opened up by road.

'For many years the richest copper mine in the British Commonwealth had no outlet by land, and four goodly-sized towns in the Mount Lyell district

. . . were unconnected by road not only with the rest of Tasmania, but with each other.

Each of those towns had motor cars, but they were leg-roped as effectively as the cows whose milk they distributed.'

That rich copper mine, now in its final death throes, has the dubious distinction of being described 40 years ago by a visiting journalist as 'Hell — with the fires out'. Visitors today would not be disappointed in the gaunt vista that surrounds them as they drive through Linda Valley on the final approach to Queenstown. Here they come across hills and mountains sheared to the nub of all living plants. Where once giant blackwood, huon, celery top and myrtle trees thrived, there is today a bare and barren undulation poisoned by fumes from the mine's wood-fired furnaces, and barely able to support even the toughest weed.

Logging to supply wood fuel for the copper smelters started the dramatic decline; bushfires wiped

out the little growth remaining; and the ceaseless soot and fumes from the smelter finished the job.

In recent years, the decline in mining activity has enabled some pioneering plants to make a bold comeback on the fringes of this man-made moonscape, but their battle to survive has only just begun.

The Queenstown Council has decided that the bizarre landscape is a tourist attraction and they feel justified in killing off the cheeky new growth. However, simple economics might foil their plans. When the mine finally closes, there might not be the funds to weed their man-made desert, despite a recent $3 million grant from the government to create a mining museum at Mt Lyell. However, Queenstown will always linger on the Tasmanian tourist map as the gateway to the splendours of the wild west coast and the picturesque coastal port of Strahan, the only town on this forbidding coastline.

Strahan was originally a Huon pine timber milling town, and its growth was boosted by the copper boom at Mt Lyell Mine. Today, it handles the freight to and from Queenstown and is used by crayfish, abalone and shark fishermen, but the use of the harbour is limited by the formidable bar at Hell's Gates, the mouth of the harbour.

The town also became the unwitting headquarters for the battle to save the Franklin River from being dammed. This single event has possibly done more to centre attention on the diminishing wilderness and sheer natural beauty of the rest of the island than any tourist campaign run by the government at any time.

Now, a steady stream of migrants from the Australian mainland and all parts of the globe are filtering into Tasmania and slowly, but inevitably, altering the whole character of this renowned backwater.

An earlier battle was fought — and lost — to prevent Lake Pedder from being flooded. Today, it is a gigantic haven for record-breaking trout, weekend fishermen, and tourists. The old lake with its unique

Tasmania's south-west coastline, left, is one of the world's unique wilderness areas - a pristine natural sanctuary. A mellow contrast is offered, above, at Nubeena, a small fishing village on the Tasman Peninsula to the south-east

ALLAN MOULT

ROB WALLS

quartz beach — a white sliver of pristine sand wind-swept and washed by waves into a gentle pattern of diamond-shaped dune valleys — lies under many metres of water welled up by a Hydro Electricity Commission dam.

Before its premature flooding, the beach was renowned for its rich intertidal fauna, and the beach and lake itself harboured at least 18 endemic species of aquatic plants and animals. UNESCO was moved to describe the flooding as 'the greatest ecological tragedy since European settlement in Tasmania.'

The south-west coastline is a typical drowned landscape — of a natural kind. The offshore islands would have been headlands when the sea level was about 120 metres lower during the ice ages. The magnificent Bathurst Harbour and Port Davey were once river valleys. Behind the coastline lie three classic walking trails — the Port Davey, South Coast and South West tracks. Each route has its own special attraction and, come summer, dozens of bushwalking devotees tackle them with a zest not unlike that of a puppy tackling a dinosaur thigh bone.

The most popular route is the South Coast Track which, like all Tasmanian walks, features a great diversity of geographic features. It traverses the south coast of Tasmania from Cockle Creek in the east to Melaleuca in the west, where it links up with the Port Davey Track which follows most of the original track cut in 1898 as an escape route for shipwrecked sailors. The third route — the South West Track — is an in-and-out hike across some of the most exposed coastal terrain in the state.

These hikes are for experienced groups only. The unpredictable weather, the exposed countryside and the real logistic problems created by the distance from aid in this, the last wilderness, call for self-sufficiency of a high order.

This is not to deny the beauty of the Tasmanian wilderness to those not able to spend the time to explore, or not physically capable of coping with the extended stress of long walks in the wild. At either end of most routes there are often a number of well-marked trails for half-day or day walks. And Tassie, being Tassie, offers spectacular scenery at every turn and over every crest.

Tasmania's south-east is mellow, and with the exception of Greater Hobart, fairly sparsely inhabited, consisting mostly of small villages centred on fruit orchards, forestry or dairy farming.

Using Hobart as a base, there are many delightful drives to be made into the picturesque countryside. There are many nooks and crannies to be explored, first-class craft workshops and studios, museums galore and, always, the friendly locals.

Accommodation varies from luxury hotels in Hobart and Launceston to renovated colonial cottages and mansions offering bed and breakfast. Colonial accommodation is found everywhere — from tiny histor-

ALLAN MOULT

The start of the famed Cradle Mountain/Lake St Clair walking track

ic villages such as Ross and Richmond, to city backstreets and abandoned farms way off the beaten track.

People make the island state. They have a mañana attitude to haste and hype, and they are passionate about their perceived paradise. They're relaxed about life, and it's easy to understand when you explore the island at a leisurely pace.

Browse slowly through the magnificent sandstone warehouses that front Hobart's fine harbour at Salamanca Place and discover a beehive of creative energy — craftsmen of fine calibre, woodworkers, metalsmiths, leatherworkers, glassblowers and jewellers all work here. Their workshops and studios are interspersed among antique shops, fine old-fashioned pubs, restaurants and outlets for finely crafted Tasmanian furniture.

TASMANIA

Ramble through history in magnificent settings such as Port Arthur and Saltwater River. Meander lazily through restored villages such as Evandale and Richmond. Wander through working ports like Swansea, Bicheno and Stanley. Strike up a conversation and score a fresh fish for dinner.

There's much to do and see — slowly.

Tasmania is often compared with Ireland, which at 82,500 square kilometres is only a fifth bigger. But Ireland with its population of over three million is comparatively crowded! It is also often likened to the state of Vermont, which shares a similar population base, but is less than half the size.

All three share a tourist paradise of diverse scenery — a blend of rugged wilderness and rural tranquillity. And they all offer much to the visitor who meanders lazily.

Tasmania's small population of about 450,000 is spread widely across the state. They're basically friendly and straightforward people, but not too many are employed in the tourist industry. They've got a living to make, and they get on with it. They will, however, embrace the genuine traveller with overwhelming hospitality. Generally a laconic group, Tasmanians have a finely honed sense of humour and the visitor is well advised to seek them out.

There are many journeys to be taken in Tasmania. There are rivers to be rafted, highways to be driven, mountains to be climbed, suburban gardens to be explored, beaches to be combed, ferries to be boarded. . . . The isolation of the island state ensures unique journeys and many great escapes.

Allan Moult

Tasmania boasts landscapes unlike those found elsewhere in Australia, such as the serenely rugged landscape of the Western Arthurs in the South West National Park wilderness area.

STEVE LOVEGROVE

Darwin, East Meets West

Darwin is all that a great frontier town should be. Brash, fabulously rich, yet unpretentious, it is a place of happy contradictions. Isolated atop Australia's sun-bleached north where the Outback meets the Arafura Sea, Darwin is the country's fastest growing capital. It is a marriage of slick city architecture and an ancient, rugged land.

For many overseas visitors and the majority of Australians in the teeming cities of the south, Darwin remains a foreign, almost alien, place on the edge of a 'Never-never' land — a place where beer-swilling cowboys perform heroic deeds straight out of *Crocodile Dundee*. And, in part, this is true. Darwin still ranks high among the world's beer-drinking capitals. Ringers and jackaroos from the inland cattle stations hold up the bar in local pubs, while crocodile steaks and 'Dundee Burgers' sell for the price of half a dozen beers in many swank city restaurants.

But Darwin is much more than this. As the gateway to Asia, it was here, in 1942, that Australia was invaded for the first time. More than 300 people died in the 60 Japanese air raids. Natural disasters have also struck, with equally devastating effect. On Christmas Eve 1974, Cyclone Tracy all but destroyed the town. More than 100 people died, and many more were missing. And during the three months that followed, the population fell from 47,000 to 25,000 as a result of the country's biggest peacetime evacuation.

The old Darwin died that Christmas Eve — the sounds and smells of Chinatown, the birds, the dream homes, and every leaf on every tree.

Slowly, a new breed appeared in the devastated town: caravans of young men and women escaping the life of the south, fortune hunters and construction workers. Their mission — backed by the federal government — was to rebuild a bigger and better Darwin.

The new Darwin is just such a place, with luxury hotels, schools by the dozen, and a booming manufacturing industry which boasts Australia's only duty-free Trade Development Zone. Yet it remains isolated from the rest of Australia. Adelaide, the closest capital city, is 3,620 kilometres south down the Stuart Highway — known locally as the Track — and the long-promised rail link is still to materialise.

Darwin is most accessible from the air, and the best time to visit is in the dry season between May and October when the rest of the country rugs up for winter. By southern standards, it's hot. Depending on the time of day, it will be anything between 18 and 33ºC. Discard any preconceived notions about Darwin along with your coat; head for the nearest car rental outfit and then head for town, about five kilometres from the airport.

Accommodation in Darwin is plentiful, offering a choice of cut-rate cheapies through to the ridiculously opulent. The Old Darwin Hotel, the Travelodge, the ritzy Beaufort and the guesthouses along the Esplanade have spectacular harbour views and are within walking distance of town. In the heart of the city is the five-star Sheraton Hotel and the suburbs abound with motels.

The people of Darwin are gregarious and, given half a chance, charmingly disarming. They are a multi-racial mix of Chinese, Caucasian, Aboriginal, Greek, Italian, Timorese, Spanish, Indonesian and Scandinavian, to mention a few. Standard dress around town is shorts, lightweight cotton tops, and thongs (open rubber sandals), or the more formal Bermuda shorts, long walk socks and open-necked shirts favoured by the city's public servants.

The Old Victoria Hotel in the Mall (home of the City Circle Traders) is worth a visit after walking about the town. Built from locally quarried stone in 1891, the pub's palm gardens and lunchtime entertainment attract a throng of visitors. Gone are the days, though, when drinkers spilled happily out into the street. The consumption of alcohol anywhere within two kilometres of a liquor outlet is now prohibited by law.

Crocodile Corner, opposite the Post Office at the bottom of the Mall, is where the 'long-grass' people — Darwin's homeless — warm up after a night spent on park benches or in the bush. It is so-called because they 'put the bite on' the passersby. From here, head down to Cavanagh Street. Sue Wah Chin's, a 19th-century clothes shop and warehouse, is all that remains of the paper-lanterned cafes, backyard opium dens and high-stake gambling halls of the old Chinatown born in the wake of the goldrush boom of the 1870s. Inside the quarried stone walls disguised by four generations of flaking paint, an old Chinese woman watches the new Darwin from behind barred windows.

The Chinese still own vast portions of the town, but the central business district, like most of the population, moved to the northern suburbs following Cyclone Tracy. The period since has been one of unprecedented growth. In 1986, the population reached 73,939.

What makes Darwin unique among Australia's capital cities is the astonishing blend of races and ideas which not only survive in harmony but thrive because of the differences. Aborigines comprise more than 25% of the population of the Northern Territory, and one in three non-Aboriginal territorians is born overseas. Take a drive down to the night market on Mindil Beach and look into the face of Asia. Have a foot massage, or your fortune told by a gypsy, or eat at one of the food stalls selling anything from Vietnamese, Lebanese or Thai food to steak sandwiches or ice-cream crushed from frozen fresh fruit.

It's an easy walk from the night market to the Diamond Beach Casino which attracts high-rollers from Asia, in town for a week with a minimum bank of $20,000. Have a flutter yourself, but save some cash and join the punters on a Saturday at Fannie Bay Racecourse where perhaps only four or five horses chase a small purse. The biggest meet of the year is the Darwin Cup, held over three days in August, where interstate horses and jockeys vie for big prizes.

Darwin is also renowned for its wackier style of entertainment. The Beer Can Regatta is a fun event for spectators who watch from the sand as boats constructed from empty beer cans race across the calm waters off Mindil Beach. Or drive down to the Humpty Doo Hotel, just off the Arnhem Highway past the satellite city of Palmerston. With luck, Norman the beer-drinking Brahman bull will be putting in an appearance. Norman can down a two-litre Darwin stubbie of beer — one of the Northern Territory's best-known tourist exports — in 44 seconds. His closest rival, a regular patron of the hotel, has managed only 1 minute 55 seconds. Even more bizarre, two one-armed thrill-seekers can be seen dancing barefoot at the Beachfront Hotel amid the snapping claws of cantankerous mud crabs at the August World Mud Crab Tying Championships. For the last six years, the event has been won by local buffalo shooter, Bill Lowry. Eight months before the 1986 title, he broke his pelvis and both legs . . . and still won, earning him the name 'Territory tough'.

Darwin has a number of popular beaches, though crocodiles still haunt the quieter spots and deadly sea-wasps arrive in the monsoon months between October and May. From town, drive out to the East Point past the Museum, the Ski Club, Sailing Club, Trailer Boat Club and the corrugated-iron walls of the old Fannie Bay Jail. The jail is now a museum where the old hangman's noose sways in the breeze as catamarans, jet-skis and sailboards dart between the colourful flotilla in front of the Sailing Club just below the cliffs.

From here, continue down to East Point Reserve, the Pony Club and the War Museum, with its wreckage of fighter planes, heavy artillery, old transport trucks and the empty shells of gun turrets and machine-gun nests.

Down by the last of the City Council barbecues, where the wallabies feed near the old golf course, rests the remains of the Darwin Rock Sitters' Club — a twisted flagpole amid some rubble off the beach. The rock sitters used to perch on the platform to watch the giant tides roll in until the flagpole acted as a lightning rod and the rock was blown to smithereens.

One of the world's best free light shows occurs in Darwin during the build up to the wet season — a testing time of soaring temperatures and high humidity known locally as the 'suicide season'. On such nights, as flying foxes swoop and squeal between heavily laden fruit trees, storms brew over the horizon. Sheet lightning electrifies the sky and thunder clouds hurl long white daggers to the ground. More lightning flashes are recorded at Darwin Airport than anywhere else in the world. Between October and December, some 40,000 flashes are usual, compared with about 11,500 in Brisbane and 30,000 in the Florida Keys.

This is the time when fishermen take to the harbour's saltwater arms in tiny aluminium boats in search of the silver barramundi — a splendid table and game fish that grows to more than 30 kilograms.

Many of Darwin's Aborigines still look to the harbour and the bush to supplement their diet. Such families provide a fascinating insight into the traditional way of life in the area and a history that has been largely unrecorded.

These same families dominate the sporting arena in Darwin. As in most Australian towns, Darwin's heroes are born on the playing fields. And just about every sport imaginable, from underwater hockey to rugby union, draws a big following. But it is in Aus-

Darwin's Government House.

Darwin, a great modern frontier town, much of it in new form since its near total destruction by Cyclone Tracy on Christmas Eve, 1974.

*A Darwin sunset looking north onto Beagle Gulf, an inlet
of the Timor Sea.*

City Extras

James Luxury Tours

Ph. (089) 27 9526
Chauffeured limousine tours of Darwin
and the surrounding area

Kay Rooney Private Car Hire

Ph. (089) 81 2000
Chauffeur-driven tours

Keetleys Tours

Ph. (089) 81 4422
Limousine services — tours and
transfers

**To Katherine
& Alice Springs**

tralian Rules football, introduced around the turn of the century, that Darwin has made its mark, with wins against Victorian Football League premiers, Essendon, and the multi-million dollar New South Wales club, the Sydney Swans. Both teams were walloped by local teams of virtual unknowns in front of crowds of more than 12,000 on the palmed edges of the Botanic Gardens.

But the role of giant killer rests uneasily on the shoulders of what has become Australia's fashionable frontier. Progress has arrived like the crack of a gun and the restful pace of the outback is fast being drowned in a sea of traffic lights, hotels and multi-

million dollar investment. But beneath it all, the old Darwin survives. Look for it in the nooks and crannies of the inner city, or in the trendy suburb of Fannie Bay where for more than 30 years George Maritos has kept a crocodile in his backyard. Or find it in the eyes of the hunter as he crosses a mangrove swamp with a throw net draped across his shoulder.

Come to Darwin with an open mind, but heed its warning. Australia's north pole has a magnetic charm, and like many others, you could become a permanent statistic — something the locals are proud to call a Darwinite.

Geoff Atkinson

ALLAN MOULT

Northern Territory

Take a glimpse at Australia's past, a timeworn land of contrast where the Aboriginal Dreamtime has awakened to the warning cries of sulphur-crested cockatoos and the steady hum of progress.

This is the Northern Territory, twice the size of Texas and four times the size of Italy. It is remote, but growing fast, faster than any other state in the nation.

There are surprises aplenty, from the capital city, Darwin, holding tight to the coat-tails of the northern seaboard, to Australia's Red Centre.

Toss a swag under the pale arms of a ghostgum or experience the outback in luxury at the Yulara Resort — a $160-million oasis rising incongruously from the desert floor only 20 kilometres from Ayers Rock.

The territory is big — about 1.35 million square kilometres. Though it is an unforgiving land, the Aborigines have survived here for more than 40,000 years, and their heritage has been preserved in rock art and the word-of-mouth legends of the Dreamtime.

About 150,000 people call the Northern Territory home. They live in Darwin, Katherine, Alice Springs and the tiny bush towns tracing the path of the overland telegraph line down the Stuart Highway. Others work the mining camps and cattle stations. Many Aborigines have retained close ties with the land, remaining near their birth sites, sacred ground to which they will return to die.

Despite early European contact, the vast distances and the cow-poke rhythm of the interior made for agonisingly slow settlement. Dutchman Jan Carstensz arrived in 1623 in his boat the *Arnhem*, a tiny wooden vessel which gave its name to Arnhem Land. But long before this, Malay seafarers hunted trepang, a sea-slug still prized on Asian dinner tables, along more than 1,500 kilometres of the territory's coast, parts of which remain uncharted to this day.

The social impact of these fishermen can still be seen in the faces and customs of the coastal Aboriginal communities, in their Dreamtime tales and in their art. Pepper-haired Roy Harika, a tribal leader from the old Methodist Mission at Yirrkala on the Gove Peninsula, still smokes a Makassan-styled pipe about 25 centimetres long.

Permission to visit Aboriginal communities must be obtained from the Land Council offices in Darwin, Alice Springs or the Tiwi Islands.

European links with the territory remained tenuous until the 19th century when Matthew Flinders charted sections of the coast on his 1803 circumnavigation of Australia. The colonials behaved with all the social grace and flair for violence of the latter-day Spanish conquistadors. Aboriginal men were killed, the women were raped and children were scared off into the bush in a chapter of Australian history largely forgotten in social studies classes. French interference and the rapid spread of Dutch trade hastened the first attempt at permanent British settlement. Captain Gordon Bremer took possession for Britain (as a part of the colony of New South Wales) of that part of the country between 135° and 129° longitude, still the Northern Territory's western boundary. But the settlement of Port Essington, launched on 20 September 1824, was shortlived. After three days, it was moved to Fort Dundas on Melville Island. Failure turned to farce as this settlement was also scrapped, along with the following attempt at settlement at Raffles Bay.

No further attempt was made until Bremer and Captain Owen Stanley selected a site at Port Essington and named it Victoria. Like its predecessors, the new settlement languished and was finally abandoned in 1849.

Palm Valley is a surprising garden of Eden in the centre of vast deserts, near Alice Springs.

The first camels were imported to the Australian interior in 1840 to open up new supply routes. There are many wild herds of camels that are rounded up for training and which ultimately provide a great deal of sport, such as in the annual Camel Cup race near Alice Springs.

Ludwig Leichhardt was the first of the overland explorers. In 1844, he set out from Brisbane and trekked around the Gulf of Carpentaria in search of an overland route to Port Essington — a journey which covered more than 5,000 kilometres and lasted more than 14 months.

But it was John MacDouall Stuart who opened up the territory in the 1840s and 50s. By 1862, he had conquered the continent from north to south. In so doing, Stuart and the pastoralists paved the way for South Australia's claim over the land, which at this stage was still part of New South Wales.

In 1863, the British gave the land to South Australia. The territory's first government resident, Colonel Boyle Travers Finniss, was appointed in 1864 and sent to establish a northern gateway at the mouth of the Adelaide River. This attempt was abandoned two years later and it was not until Surveyor General George Goyder arrived in 1869 that a successful site was established at Palmerston in Port Darwin. Palmerston survived, and under the federal government which took control in 1811, it became Darwin, the territory's capital, now with a population of 73,000.

The Northern Territory attained self-government on 1 July 1978, and since then a new wave of hope has embraced this savage environment. Mining and tourism are now riding high on the crest of an economic boom.

Allow plenty of time to see the territory. It covers about one-sixth of the continent, but has less than 1% of the population. About 80% of the total land mass lies in the torrid zone above the Tropic of Capricorn. From south to north it is split by the Stuart Highway which loosely follows Stuart's epic journey across the continent, as does the Overland Telegraph Line completed in 1872.

It was during the building of this communications line that gold fever struck the territory. In his book *The Front Door — Darwin 1869-1969*, journalist Douglas Lockwood talks of the mad rush. 'Thousands of ounces of gold were produced, much of it in circumstances that led to the scandalous waste and loss of immense sums by innocent investors. Upon this picture was superimposed a few thousand Chinese tramping and haggling their way to the fields, deserting their jobs to do so, pockmarking the countryside with shafts and costeans that are visible today. They carried essentials on sticks across their shoulders. Those who struck it rich, and many did, were able to retire to lives of ease in China.'

But for every one who made a fortune there were many who failed. The Chinese influence from the goldrush days is still apparent around Pine Creek and Adelaide River. Fossick through the ruins and visit the new goldmine at Pine Creek — the latest in the country — about 200 kilometres south of Darwin.

Most of the territory is less than 450 metres above

From the air, the Northern Territory's Simpson Desert looks bleak and barren, an image totally reinforced at ground level

sea level, forming part of Central Australia's lowlands. From the crocodile-infested coastline with its backing of mudflats and flooded swamps, a range of hills rises to a plateau. Up to 320 kilometres wide, this range divides the coastal river drainage system from the inland drainage system. The land rises gradually to the south, reaching more than 600 metres above sea level in Central Australia, where it is crossed by the MacDonnell Ranges which stretch from the east across the Tropic of Capricorn. These climb to more than 1,200 metres.

The spectacular folds and colours of the MacDonnell Ranges were captured on canvas by Aboriginal artist Albert Namatjira, copies of whose works once appeared on the walls of almost every home in Australia.

At the Top End, as locals call the coastal fringe, temperatures vary from 16°C to 34°C depending on the season. Up here, there are only two seasons 'the wet' and 'the dry'. The wet season lasts from October to May, and heavy tropical fruit drops to rot on the ground. Flying in a light aircraft over the Top End during 'the wet' is a unique experience. From a few hundred feet, you can see spooked cattle chased by lightning across swollen floodplains, waterfalls racing down the face of the Arnhem Land escarpment, and flocks of waterbirds fishing in endless swamplands. Sit horrified as the pilot plays chicken with wild bush horses called brumbies, which monopolise the isolated bush airstrips in their search for high ground. Don't always expect balmy nights in the Northern Territory. Down in the Red Centre, night temperatures can drop below freezing.

The territory is best visited in the dry season. Sit back with the sun-seekers, drink beer from almost anywhere in the world, and pick up a tan. It is a country of fun. Look for it in the Darwin and Alice Springs casinos, the outback bars, or the tour boats of Katherine Gorge.

But remember, it is also a land prone to violence. A number of people have died in the jaws of crocodiles over the last few years; some people have died of thirst in the desert; and others have suffered after being stung by deadly sea-wasps which abound in the ocean waters in the wet season. A dozen or so people have also died climbing Ayers Rock.

In the wake of the *Crocodile Dundee* movie and a couple of gruesome deaths, the crocodile has recently been unofficially adopted as a tourist mascot in the territory. Conservation Commission rangers have stuck up signs all over the place showing a crocodile with its mouth open, and carrying a simple but grim warning — crocodiles inhabit these waters. The Aborigines have survived with the crocodile for thousands of years. Gumatj clan leader and former Australian of the year, Galarrwuy Yunupingu, claims a sacred attachment to the reptile. 'We have never considered the crocodile an evil thing. We believe we

came as the crocodile and we believe that all the tribal land we own from our forefathers was created and given to us once by a crocodile. Everything I have comes from the crocodile.'

The Aborigines are a people of two times. They have accepted some of the ways of the 20th century while retaining a unique and ancient culture. It is generally accepted that the first Aborigines arrived in Australia about 40,000 years ago, though some researchers argue that the first arrivals could have crossed from Asia about 120,000 years ago. Since 1829, when the British declared Australia 'an unoccupied waste', the number of Aborigines has declined dramatically.

Their traditional lifeline was severed by the encroaching pastoral industry, early massacres and an abysmal standard of living. Women were bought and sold for alcohol and opium and the family unit was destroyed when the government of the day decided to

split up mixed families. Between the 1880s and 1950s, thousands of half-caste and part-Aborigines were taken from their parents to be trained in missions, compounds and special schools.

In 1962, all Aborigines received the right to vote. In 1964, they became full Australian citizens and restrictions on alcohol consumption and cohabitation were removed. In the same year, the Pastoral Award stipulated that all Aborigines should receive equal pay by 1968. This led to mass unemployment as hundreds of Aboriginal stockmen were sacked. The Aboriginal Land Rights (Northern Territory) Act recognised in 1976 the traditional ownership of Aboriginal reserves and the right of Aborigines to apply for title over freehold Crown land. Today, about 50% of the Northern Territory is either owned by Aborigines or subject to Aboriginal land claims.

There are two ways to approach the territory: through Darwin or Alice Springs. From Darwin there are day trips to Kakadu National Park, joy flights to Bathurst and Melville Islands, and there are many things to see close to town. Bathurst and Melville Islands are only 80 kilometres from the coast. Perched on the edge of the Apsley Strait, Nguiu is home for about 1,000 Tiwi Aborigines.

Across the narrow bottleneck of water is Melville Island — Australia's second largest island and home for another 1,000 Aborigines. Wander among colourfully decorated iron-wood totem poles and pottery displays, and buy some Tiwi Island fabric, printed in their own workshop. Stay long enough for a spot of fishing and dig into a sunset feast of mangrove worms, turtle eggs and dugong — a giant sea-cow thought to be responsible for the legend of the mermaid.

Back on the mainland, cruise down the Stuart Highway, the main route to the outback and known up here as 'the Track'. All the main tourist routes are

The area south of Alice Springs boasts a dramatic diversity of scenery - like the Gosses Bluff area, left, and the eerie forms of the Olgas, above

sealed and the biggest road dangers are fatigue, wandering stock and mechanical breakdown. Always carry plenty of spares: tyres, oil, fan belts and water — lots of water.

The Arnhem Highway is only 30 kilometres from Darwin. Get up early and drive down to Corroboree Billabong, on the edge of the Mary River system. It's the next best thing to Kakadu. Flat-bottomed boats meander through delicate paths of waterlilies and a patchwork blanket of waterfowl. Try your hand at catching a barramundi — the famed fighting fish of the north. It's nowhere near as hard as the fishing gurus would have you believe. Just tie a lure to the end of a line and troll it behind the boat. If the fish are biting, you're in business. If they're not, buy a feed at the Bark Hut Inn back on the Arnhem Highway.

There are plenty of sidetracks on the way to Kakadu and most are worth exploring. Follow the tributaries and count the crocodiles on the banks of the Mary River. Slip into Kakadu National Park and photograph the rock paintings at Nourlangie or Obiri Rocks, eat barramundi and buffalo at ritzy restaurants, or swim in the safe waterfalls. The park consists of six regions, varying from spectacular escarpment to tidal mudflats and undulating forests rich in birdlife and history. Stage 1 of the park has been nominated for World Heritage listing.

If you find Kakadu a little tame, take a trip off the tourist route. Head for Gurig National Park on the Cobourg Peninsula. The park is rich in Aboriginal culture, and isolated areas contain relics of the Makassan trading era and the lonely remnants of early white settlement. Entry to the park is by permit only, using private boats or four-wheel-drive vehicles along a beaten road from the uranium mining town of Jabiru. Enterprising architects have come up with the ultimate in tourist kitsch by designing a huge hotel-motel in the shape of a crocodile, to be built on Aboriginal land close to Jabiru.

Litchfield Park, just a couple of hundred kilometres from Darwin, has three-metre-high magnetic hills dotting the plains like miniature castles, as well as hot springs, waterfalls and rainforest. It is due to be opened in late 1987. Within a day's travel from Darwin, you'll find darkened gorges, waterfalls, freshwater springs and wildlife parks. Daly River Nature Park and Waterfall Creek — a large waterhole used in the filming of *Crocodile Dundee* — complete with snappy freshwater crocodiles are also well worth a visit.

The wild little town of Katherine sits astride the Stuart Highway, 330 kilometres from Darwin. Katherine is undergoing dramatic changes as the town prepares to be invaded by the Australian Air Force. Hundreds of homes, new schools, hospitals and playing fields are springing from the red dust on the edge of town. Visit Kirby's Hotel on Friday afternoon. Bush poets, construction workers, outback Aborigin-es, cow-cockies, town-camp drunks and office workers swap tall tales, fight in the beer-garden and chase whatever girls are in town. There aren't many. Katherine is a man's town.

Escape to Katherine Gorge, 32 kilometres away, with its steep-sided ravines, flowing waterways and Aboriginal art. In the dry season it is a peaceful haven where you can watch freshwater crocodiles — not usually dangerous to man — glide silently through pools shaded by flowering wattle trees alive with parrots. In the wet season, the quiet gorge becomes a steep mountain track of rapids throwing themselves off the cliff faces and diving into ravines masked by fog and fallen logs.

If you are in the Top End during the Anzac weekend in April, drive down to the Barunga Sports and Cultural Festival on the edge of Beswick Aboriginal Reserve, 80 kilometres south-east of Katherine. It's everything a territory bush bash is

When it comes time for the annual cattle muster, all station hands - including the women, and some children - get in on the act

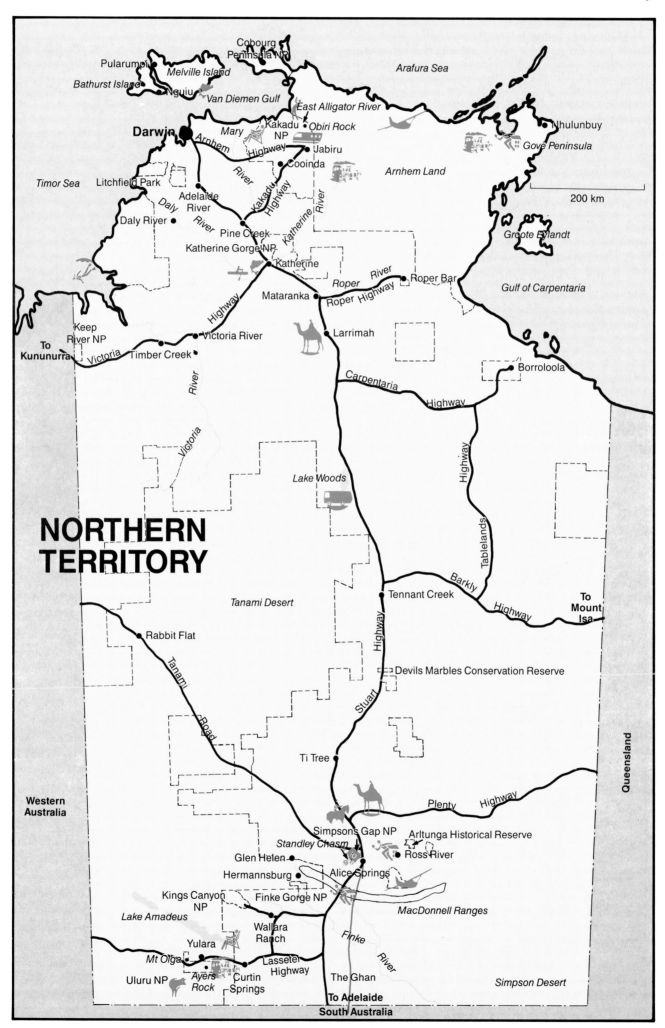

NORTHERN TERRITORY

meant to be: multi-racial, fun and often loud. Here amid the dust, dogs and camera-clicking tourists, Aboriginal clans from almost every corner of the territory rage and play in the sun. Old Johnny Coniston came all the way from Ti Tree, 800 kilometres to the south, in the back of a cattle truck. He remembers beatings at the hands of cruel cattle barons when he was paid in tobacco and sugar. He claims his first clothes were made from a hessian bag with holes cut out for his arms and head. With his cowboy hat covering failing eyes, he is a pensioner and says he has never been better off. Robert Tipungwuti, from Milikapiti on Melville Island, arrived by car and light plane to watch the football. He was in for a shock. His island home is warmed by the Arafura Sea, whereas Barunga, 400 kilometres to the south on the road to the Roper River, was hot by day and bitterly cold at night.

Sit among the Aborigines in makeshift bush huts, eat bush tucker and immerse yourself in their customs.

The various Aboriginal clans have very little in common. Phylis Wynjorroc, the queen of the Jawyon clan which has a land claim over Katherine Gorge and strong ties to the Beswick region, wanted nothing to do with the festival. We found her fishing deep in the bush. Phylis still lives in the traditional way. The men of her tribe stalk wallabies, kangaroos and goannas, while the women gather fruits and nuts. But times are changing. Now the Barunga Store sells white-fella tucker and an endless variety of knick-knacks. The children walk about with ghetto-blasters held to their ears listening to loud rock music.

Local traditional artist Paddy Fordham has made a comfortable living through his paintings on sacred bark. He covers his head with feathers and teaches the young a corroboree — an Aboriginal folkdance passed down from the Dreamtime. As he jumps in the air, imitating a bird or a dingo, his leopard-skin jockettes flash under a bright red lap-lap.

Stop at some of the cattle stations along the road to Alice Springs. If you're lucky, the boss cow-cocky will let you drink lemonade on the wide open homestead veranda as black cockatoos and pink and grey galahs feed in the dry paddocks. This is the land of the cattle baron and a few of the huge grazing properties are bigger than some European countries.

Alice Springs is at Australia's Red Centre. Also in this part of the territory are Ayers Rock, the MacDonnell Ranges, King's Canyon and the Finke Gorge, a tiny oasis sprouting palms seen nowhere else in the world. Sitting close to the edge of the Simpson Desert, Alice Springs was forged in gold, cattle and thirst. Much of the early building materials came from the land, but equipment for the goldmines, luxury items and essential food supplies were ferried north on camels. Hundreds of these animals still roam the centre. The train connecting Alice Springs with South

A big hat is this young child's answer to keeping cool at the local rodeo

Australia was named 'the Ghan' after the Afghans who led the camel caravans.

Visit Virginia Camel Farm, 80 kilometres south of Alice Springs. Camel herder Noel Fullerton, with his flowing white beard pushed back in the wind, prepares for a safari. He takes visitors to places few white men have seen and only a handful of Aborigines remember. 'We can trek for 40 kilometres a day and get into places where four-wheel-drives just don't have a chance', he says. His domain is the desert, hills and hidden springs shaped by the red sands of time. He'll take you to Palm Valley, Deception Creek or Wild Eagle Plain, and he'll tell you tales of the outback, a land forgotten by time.

There are places that demand attention in the Northern Territory. Ayers Rock, and the Olgas towering above the desert floor, the MacDonnell Ranges and Katherine Gorge. There is far too much to see in one trip. Follow the trails of the drovers, 1,000 kilometres of bush track connecting the territory to the southern marketplace. Or sit by a waterfall with a quiet beer. The outback has been compiling its tourist itinerary for millions of years, but the process of discovery has only just begun.

Geoff Atkinson

KEN ROSS

Canberra & the Australian Capital Territory

Canberra and the surrounding 2,360 square kilometres that make up the Australian Capital Territory have the enormous advantage that they can be visited and enjoyed in just a few days without any sense, on leaving, of unfinished business.

There are things to be seen and done that are unique and richly rewarding in this city that some might think of pairing with other created cities such as Brasilia or Chandigarh. Canberra has features that no other place in Australia — and very few in the world — has going for it.

For starters, it is a highly educated city, which means that it demands a fair level of sophistication in its daily (and nightly) life, for which its comparatively wealthy community can afford to pay.

Canberra is also a very comfortable city; the services are all there, but there is no feeling of mad rush. (Although it must be said that Canberra has now developed an evening rush hour, as public servants make their way home after finishing work at precisely 4.51 pm each day. The rush hour lasts exactly seven and a half minutes.) A common line about Canberra is that it has all the advantages of living in a country town, and very few of the disadvantages.

The challenge for the visitor is not that there is nothing to do, see or buy, but tracking it down. The town is generally planned in such a way as to conceal things like hotels, shops, restaurants and a number of tourist attractions as far as possible from the public view. If you have a native guide, preferably with a car, to show you around, you will have no problems. If not, your first stop should be the tourist bureau, or one of its increasingly numerous offshoots, to pick up a reasonable map of the place and a general guidebook.

Canberrans are proud of their town. They are happy to convince visitors that it has a lot going for it,

and will go out of their way to show sceptics that taxpayers really are getting something for the money that has been invested over the years. So don't hesitate to ask, particularly if you have lost your way. Due to the planned nature of the city, this still happens frequently — even to long-term residents.

The name 'Canberra' is said to be derived from the Aboriginal word 'canberry', meaning a meeting place. Appropriately, any tour of Canberra should start with Parliament House, the meeting place of politicians. Canberra is, after all, a political town, run by politicians for politicians, and they have finally done themselves proud. But it was not always thus, and to understand why there is so much interest in the building that was planned to be opened in about the winter of 1988, it is necessary to go back over a bit of history.

In the second half of the 19th century, settlement of the Canberra region was a contest between squatters and selectors who got the opportunity to take up small holdings after the passing of the Free Selection Act of 1861. (The Aborigines had been well and truly displaced by this time.)

It was only after Australia became a nation in 1901 that the region was seriously considered as a site for the national capital. The issue was marked by bitter rivalry between the states, and particularly between Sydney and Melbourne. Sydney was unquestionably the senior partner. But in the intervening years, Melbourne had consistently grown in importance, becoming the political heart of Australia. In the first years after 1901, the national Parliament sat in Melbourne.

The argument between the two cities was fierce and unremitting, but eventually they compromised; the capital could be in New South Wales, but it had to be at least 100 miles from Sydney. That decision gave birth to Canberra. To obtain the best design for the city, a world-wide competition was launched in 1911. Boycotted by British architects who objected to this form of adjudication, it drew 137 design entrants and was won by Walter Burley Griffin, a 35-year-old landscape architect from Chicago, whose efforts earned him a prize of 1,750 pounds sterling. Griffin liked the present site, partly because of the symmetrical arrangement of hills around the valley, and partly because there was a river flowing through the middle, which meant he could plan for an artificial lake. The fact that it was at the time a windswept sheep station in the middle of nowhere did not discourage him.

As can be imagined, the logistics of putting together a permanent city in these circumstances were mind-boggling; in parts of Canberra today there can still be seen the remnants of temporary structures which were being used while the real building was going on. And by far the most celebrated of these is the old Parliament House, a rather charming white building near the south side of the lake, opened in 1927 purely as a stop-gap, and still determinedly in use 50 years later.

It has been enlarged several times, but it has been hopelessly inadequate for years. No real politician, let alone public servant, would put up with the conditions for a moment if there were any choice. It took the politicians a long time to decide where the permanent substitute was to go, and to summon the nerve to tell the people they were going to spend several hundred million dollars putting it together. (In fact, the final cost will be somewhere over a billion dollars.) But once the decision was made, except for a couple of political hiccups, they stuck to their guns. It won't be quite as lavish as the architects planned, but by Australian standards it will be immense. It will be the only building in the country which can be mentioned in the same breath as the Sydney Opera House.

But when you're looking around Canberra, have a look at the old one, too. Notice the cramped corridors, the pokey offices, the little lobbies, the nooks and crannies (ideal for setting up a conspiracy). The old Parliament House was like a politician's mind; the new one will be like his ego, even down to the vastly priapic flagpole on top of it. Inquire about tours of the House and there will be opportunities to sit in the visitors' gallery when Parliament is sitting.

A monument that has always fascinated visitors is the National War Museum. It is a vast area with an extraordinary number of exhibits illustrating Australia's part in wars since the country first sent a contingent to New Zealand to help fight the Maoris.

For those conscious of their heritage, it is a deeply moving place, not at all war-like, but compassionate, emotional and proud in the way it chronicles, more often than not, the tragedies that seem to have marked the country's rise to nationhood. Collections of the artefacts of war, the ordinary possessions of ordinary people caught up in desperate events, and dioramas of far away scenes of conflict are set up with great skill and sensitivity.

Two interesting monumental buildings on the other side of Lake Burley Griffin are the National Library and the High Court. The National Library, with its fluted columns and white marble, contains every book published in Australia. It has fine reading spaces and is set in an open space of green grass.

The High Court now sits in a building that must be unique in the catalogue of legal architecture. Built with the strong support and encouragement of the former Attorney General and Chief Justic, Sir Garfield Bárwick, it is breathtaking in its use of space and in the design not just of the courtrooms but of the staircases and landings in which are hung photos and paintings depicting much of Australia's constitutional history since Federation. Watching the court in session is also something that could be fascinating for many.

The National Gallery, opened to the public in

The Carillon at Lake Burley Griffin

PHILLIP QUIRK

1982, is by world standards a small collection, but it contains some masterpieces, including Jackson Pollock's 'Blue Poles', purchased for $1.3 million, well before the building was completed.

Much of the interest is in a very good selection of white Australian art, and perhaps more importantly, a first-rate collection of Aboriginal art, which is well worth a look for anyone who is thinking of buying a bark painting or a sculpture to take home. (Incidentally, the gallery shop is an excellent place for souvenirs.)

The entire upper floor is devoted to the full history of Australian art spanning 200 years. Works range from those of the early settlers to the important 20th-century painters and include such names as Tom Roberts, Arthur Streeton, Sir Sidney Nolan (whose Ned Kelly series, begun in 1946, occupies a special place in the gallery) and Margaret Preston. They cover sculptures, decorative arts, illustrated books, prints, drawings, watercolours, photographs and mural decorations. There is also Asian and European art, including a small collection of French Impressionists.

And while we are on the subject of aesthetics, one place absolutely not to miss in Canberra is the National Botanic Garden. This is unique in that it consists entirely of Australian native species, brought from all over the country and somehow persuaded not only to survive, but also to flourish in the city's climate of extremes (blistering dry heat in summer, and below-zero nights in winter; by far the best times to visit are the mild spring and autumn months). The garden covers almost one whole side of a mountain, and is constantly expanding. There are always interesting things in flower and it is packed with native birdlife.

It is by far the best crash course on Australian nature available in the country, and is well worth at least half a day — especially as it also runs a pleasant, if simple, outdoor restaurant (bring your own alcohol).

In general, eating out in Canberra, as in most Australian cities, offers a very wide choice of ethnic restaurants, as well as traditional western cooking. There are bush-type restaurants, which often also feature bush bands, on the outskirts of Canberra and

The federal capital has evolved from a bush setting into a tree-lined pattern of boulevards

TREVERN DAWES

in the many country towns within about an hour's drive. Most have slightly odd opening hours, so it is best to check with the tourist bureau. There are also comfortable bus tours (package or otherwise), which take in Canberra's still rural surroundings.

For the more adventurous, Canberra also has horseback trail rides, or holidays on still-operating sheep and cattle stations. Unlike the bigger cities, Canberra is still very much in touch with its origins.

The Australian National University has a campus that is well worth visiting. And when the weather warms up, there is swimming and sailing on Lake Burley Griffin. Close to the city, a marvellous experience is swimming off sandy beaches in the Murrumbidgee River.

There are plenty of other occasional attractions in the city itself: hot-air ballooning, a festival of arts, entertainment, and food and drink of a good standard. Canberra is also a useful jumping-off point for other parts of Australia. A two-hour drive south gets you into the heart of the Snowy Mountains for winter skiing or graded summer bushwalks. And two hours east takes you to the south coast, and some of the nicest unspoiled beaches in the country, from which you can often see dolphins and, if you are in real luck, whales.

About an hour from Canberra through beautiful country is Lanyon Homestead, with its important display of paintings by Sir Sidney Nolan. Just out of Canberra are preserved colonial villages such as Bungendore, and the Brindabella Mountains with good restaurants and craft museums.

Walter Burley Griffin's brief was to design a city for a population of 25,000. His conception was not implemented with any real conviction until the establishment of the national Capital Development Commission in 1957 and by then the population had swelled to 39,000. Today it stands at 250,000.

As the national capital has grown, so have not only the local facilities (restaurants, theatre, music, and so on) but also access to and from the city. Canberra is truly no longer a place in the country. It's a city with a rich and varied cultural life well served by touring and local productions and events including ABC concerts.

When the trees undergo a spectacular change in colour in autumn, and forest log fires appear in the restaurants, it is hard not to feel that Canberra is a good place in which to live, a city that represents Australia's future.

Mungo MacCallum

City Extras

Budget Chauffeur Drive

Ph. (062) 58 9494
Tours, secretarial services and interpreters

Canberra Hire Cars

Ph. (062) 49 7844
Chauffeur-driven tours

Hire-a-Guide

Ph. (062) 49 7978
Personalised guide/host service of Canberra and environs

Lyons Hire Cars

Ph. (062) 48 0051
Chauffeur-driven limousine tours

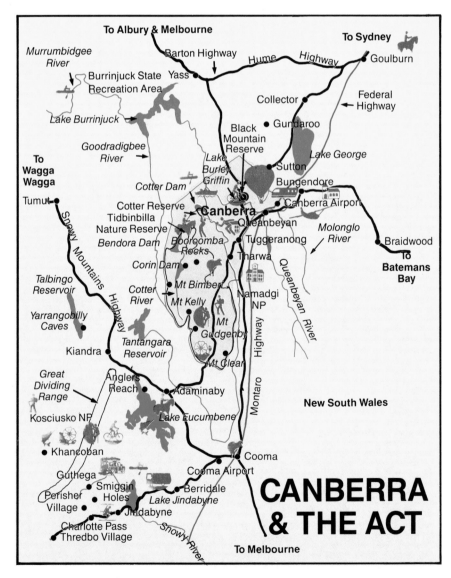

CANBERRA & THE ACT

Canberra is situated midway between Melbourne and Sydney, the result of a rivalry for its placement dating back to the early part of the century. It is among the world's most successful, totally planned cities with the present population in excess of 270,000.

FEATURES

In Kakadu, the Dreamtime Goes on

Craig McGregor

Up here, nothing lasts for long. It's the Tahiti of Australia, a tropical fast-turnover environment stricken each year by drought ('the dry') and flooding ('the wet'), by violent thunderstorms that flatten trees and the three-metre-high speargrass during the season the Aborigines call *bang-gereng* ('knock-'em-down season'), and by fires which have swept through for thousands of years — a land of such extremes that it supports only 2,000 people in the area the same size as Bali, which has a million.

ROBBI NEWMAN

Yet these same people are the exception to Kakadu's high-energy recycling of everything in it. The Aborigines have lived in Kakadu for more than 25,000 years and have created amid the red-ochre bluffs and gorges and crocodile wetlands and savannah woodlands the oldest continuing culture in the history of the human race.

In the caves and rock shelters of Kakadu National Park are Aboriginal rock paintings which were done before the ice age and which probably predate the famous paintings at Lascaux and elsewhere in Europe. Tourists can see paintings of the striped thylacine (Tasmanian tiger), which died out on the mainland of Australia thousands of years ago. In one campfire-blackened shelter near Obiri, archaeologists have found the oldest edge-ground stone axes in the world; at another, there is a continuous tradition of human art which stretches from before the ice age to 1964, when an Aboriginal artist known as Barramundi Charlie painted an extraordinary series of x-ray paintings using, probably, Reckitts washing blue as well as the old rock-ground pigments.

Indeed, when the park was added to the World Heritage list of treasures a couple of years ago, it achieved its ranking on two grounds: because it is one of the most precious and spectacular land formations in the world; and because it is, in the words of Danny Gillespie, 'a unique cultural treasure' — over 5,000 art and archaeological sites which, together with the landscapes, brought almost a quarter of a million visitors to the park in 1987.

Danny should know. A tall, bearded, laconic man of 41 with an irreverent sense of humour, he has lived and worked with Aboriginal people in the Northern Territory for 15 years and is now Assistant Director of the National Parks and Wildlife Service, which means in effect that he is responsible for Kakadu and Uluru (Ayers Rock).

A few years ago, he was dropped regularly by helicopter into remote parts of the park where he camped for some weeks in one of the Aboriginal shelters while he documented its art. When he 'ran out of tucker' on one occasion, he trekked to the nearest settlement but found that it had been temporarily abandoned and had to return to his camp. 'I lived on half a can of spaghetti a day. Lost a lot of weight!' he says, laughing.

Danny is one of the many Australians who, over the years, have become entranced by Kakadu. He has spent the last nine years involved in the park and has gained an understanding of some of the Aboriginal clans who still own most of the park and who lease it to the Service. (Kakadu is a corruption of 'Gagudju', the name of one of the Aboriginal languages.) He has also come to understand, in part at least, the culture they have created out of this ever-changing environment.

So what's so special about Kakadu? Why should it have become, in the last few years, one of the most fa-

mous wilderness areas in the world?

'I think it's because of this stunning juxtaposition of different landscapes — everything from estuaries to floodplains to tropical bushland to the Arnhem Land escarpment all crammed up together in one place,' he says. 'It's amazing. I mean, that's spinifex there' —

This graphic message is clearly stated

pointing to a graceful plant on a rock ledge — 'that's a desert plant, and yet just four paces over the edge and we're in one of the major wetlands of Australia!'

He is standing on top of a high rocky 'outlier', as it's called, of the massive escarpment that runs along the eastern boundary of the park and separates it from Arnhem Land. In fact, if you look south, you can see hundreds of kilometres of tree-and-speargrass bush land which is typical of this territory and then the rocky, serrated edge of the escarpment itself, its high cliffs looking like the gnarled faces of banksia men. By simply turning around to the north, however, you are suddenly staring down at the immense floodplain of the East Alligator River — a lush green expanse of grass and swamp which looks almost mown, complete with a tongue of English-shaped trees, and a flat grey lake of river overflow, and in the distance a series of bluffs and outcrops, which could be an ancient, eroded seashore.

'I love the floodplains. They're so powerful,' says Danny. 'For the Aborigines, they're like a savings bank, a storehouse of food that's easy to harvest: turtles, water chestnuts, water birds like the magpie geese that come here in the thousands, shellfish down by the coast. Back here in the woodland, there are marsupials to hunt, rats, possums, honey from the wild bee,

edible fruits like wild plums and apples. It's a real border zone. Aw, and crocodiles.' He lapses into Kriol (Aboriginal-modified English). 'Full of bloody 'gators. Too many!'

As the virtual flak-catcher of the park, the crocodiles are something of a problem for him. Since they are no longer hunted, the crocodiles have multiplied and become 'cheekier', which means more dangerous. The tourists have multiplied, too, and most of them want to see the stars of *Crocodile Dundee* — if not Paul Hogan, at least the crocs. There are signs at all the likely swimming holes along the East, South and West Alligator Rivers warning people not to swim there and to keep children and dogs away from the water's edge ('crocs are supposed to love dogs', says Danny), but only recently a man was taken by a crocodile while walking across a causeway and a woman researcher from Sydney University was attacked and only just managed to escape.

'The saltwater crocodiles are the most dangerous, but we warn people not to go swimming anywhere,

whether they think there are only freshwater crocs around or none at all,' he says. 'In the end, people have to be responsible for their own safety.'

Sometimes the croc problem has a funny side to it. One large local croc is known as Tony, and the day before we caught up with Danny Gillespie some of the locals had come across Tony sunning himself on a causeway. They decided to have a bit of fun with him and gave him a nudge with their four-wheel-drive vehicle. Tony reacted violently and the vehicle ended up in the river. Tony then laid his chin on the bonnet, eyeballing them, while the frightened locals waited on the truck roof to be rescued! Score: Croc 1, Humanoids 0.

Eden?

Apart from the crocodiles, however, it slowly becomes clear why Kakadu has been the site of human life and human culture for such a uniquely continuous time. In many ways, Kakadu is an antipodean Eden, a lush,

Nourlangie Rock, left, is a sacred Aboriginal site and home of many cave and rock paintings like the one shown above

fertile, tropical garden with an inexhaustible supply of food and sunshine and animal life, no predators, and a climate which for all its extremes allowed the Aboriginal hunter-gatherers to move from sea coast to estuary to lowlands to plateau shelters as they wished, working for perhaps the first three or four cool hours of the day only and then spending the rest of the time in leisure and intellectual pursuits: eating, swimming, making love, sleeping, gossiping, holding ritual ceremonies and corroborees, painting, thinking, and creating the myths and legends which have been spun down to our time about how this magical world was created.

If the Israelites had Eden, the Aborigines had Kakadu. It is much more luxuriant and less hostile than one would expect — some 20,000 square kilometres of park land within two hours' drive of Darwin, in the top end of the Australian continent, with a major bitumen road system going through the heart of it, plus thousands of kilometres of dirt roads, tracks and walking trails which are safe even for inexperienced four-wheel-drivers and bushwalkers. (The

croc, the only 'serpent in the garden', can be avoided by keeping out of the water.)

It's been a national park for only eight years. Before that, its rugged, isolated nature protected it to such an extent that many of its wildlife species are still undescribed by European science. However, it's known to have over 1,500 different plants, and 10,000 insect, 75 reptile, 45 fish, 51 mammal and over 250 bird varieties — a third of all Australia's bird species are found here.

The park has a dozen or more serviced campsites, and high-standard tourist centres at the South Alligator River, Jabiru and Cooinda, complete with hotel/motels and swimming-pools, and a ready supply of four-wheel-drive tours and boat trips around the vast internal series of billabongs (waterways) that are so characteristic of Kakadu.

At Yellow Waters, near Cooinda, I went on a two-hour cruise in a flat-bottomed boat through kilometre after kilometre of inland lakes and channels surrounded by green swamplands of waterlilies and drowned palms and paperbarks of which the only likely equivalent I know in the world are the bayous of Louisiana and Florida in the United States. It was late afternoon, an unreal world of islands, plains and hundreds of water birds (sacred ibis, sea eagles, jacana and pelicans) feeding and crying out on the banks, a fringe of trees in the distance, and plantations of giant red waterlilies called nelumbo (lotus lilies) with leaves as big as elephant ears waving in the breeze.

Wild geese and ducks flew ahead of us, and water buffalo grazed a long way off. On a muddy bank, I came across the first saltwater crocodile I had seen in the park: an enormous 17-foot monster, its jaws propped open so that you could see its pink mouth and reptilian teeth, as motionless as if it were stuffed. Most surprising of all was its massive body bulk, like a bullock lying on its side. Crocodiles sometimes blunder into boats that get in their way when they are trying to escape. The Kakadu rule is, don't go too close or you might find a croc in the boat with you!

The Edenic nature of Kakadu came through most powerfully when, after a three-hour drive over a rough track through bushland blackened by fires, we reached the gorge country at Jim Jim (Djim Djim) Falls, at the foot of the Arnhem Land escarpment. This is the most dramatic and perhaps symbolic landscape of the Kakadu region. Enormous towering red-ochre bluffs and cliff faces are topped by a dreaming silhouette of trees; the sun beats down even in early winter, creating a sense of heat and distance and an ancient, uncaring landscape — the totemic vision of Central Australia. It's a long way from anywhere here, in the arid heartland of the outback, and it feels like it.

Yet, after a short walk into the gorge, we suddenly came across a large, limpid, rock-bottomed lake, languid with dragon-flies and zephyrs, fringed with pandanus palms and water gums and white sand beaches, like a paradisical oasis in the middle of Arnhem Land. It's incredibly tropical, almost like a Barrier Reef island, with the slash and wind roar of the distant falls sounding like surf breaking on a lagoon reef.

We swam and rock-hopped our way up the lake to another even more idyllic lagoon, the gorge cliffs closing in around us, until at the very end we came to the plunge pool into which the twin falls drop from hundreds of metres above. And here the nature of the place changed. A vast semicircular bowl which the sun rarely penetrates, the water here is icy and forbiddingly dark; the sheer rock face is blackened by centuries of water spray; and to get to the base of the falls, one has to swim across a waterhole that looks as if it could have swallowed the *Titanic,* or even the black omphalos of the universe, without trace. If ever there was a place where the bunyip dwells, or some other legendary evil spirit, this is it.

Yet only 12 kilometres away is Twin Falls, where the water cascades down an open red rock face and sandy beachlets hang in beneath the Namatjira escarpment. On the way back, we stopped at the edge of the descent to the Alligator floodplains. It was absolutely peaceful: no wind, no sound except the distant distorted cry of a crow, the escarpment turning purple as the sun sank behind the coastal flat land. Soon this place would return to its Aboriginal blackness, and not even the stars would wake it. We switched on the headlights of the four-wheel-drive and set out on the arduous drive back to Cooinda.

The Aborigines

This is the land the Aboriginal people came to, according to archaeologists, some 40,000 years ago via the land bridge that then linked the Australian continent with what are now the islands of South-east Asia. They settled here, and today some 200 or more of their descendants still live here. They have special hunting rights, negotiated with the National Parks and Wildlife Service. They run Cooinda. Some are park rangers and others live in outstations in the bush. Between them, they have set up the Gagadju (Kakadu) Association to co-operate with the Service about how the park develops.

' For Aborigines, the truth is eternally manifest in the shape of the environment, in the crevices and outcrops and caves which the creation heroes made. '

Says Toby Gangale, president of the Association, who has worked in the Alligator Rivers region as buffalo hunter, crocodile shooter, safari guide and park worker:

'We are very happy to have this national park here. Tourists can come and enjoy themselves — have a good look at the birdlife, go to Jim Jim Falls, look at cave paintings, but they can't go to ceremony places. They've got a lot of places to go, but they can't go to sacred sites, dreaming places and burial places.

'The other thing is that we've still got to have our country. Us blokes have still got our culture hanging on — we got to keep it. In some ways the old days are gone, but we are still living on the land — we've still got tribal law, ceremony, funeral. We never give it away, us blokes. We still get bandicoot, waterlily, sugar bag, porcupine, barramundi, possum, duck — everything. We never give it away, that one.'

When they took over this land, the hunter-gatherers created myths about the creation heroes of the Dreamtime who gave the place its shape and iden-

Nature's greatness in places like Twin Falls in Kakadu are the source of intricate Aboriginal Dreamtime myths.

One third of all of Australia's·bird species can be found within Kakadu, such as the Jabiru Bird, which lives here in profusion.

tity, and they painted these myths on the rock faces where they sheltered. These are the paintings, and the legendary figures, we can see today:

Namarrgon, the Lightning Man, is drawn with stone axes at his head, elbows and knees. He used these to produce lightning and thunder by striking them against the ground.

Namandjolg, the Dangerous Spirit, was seduced by his sister on the rock outcrop known as Nourlangie. She plucked a feather from his head-dress and placed it on the rock escarpment (where the mark can still be seen) to signal her deed to the world. Namandjolg then killed her, whereupon she turned into the Rainbow Serpent.

Burrung-gui is the area through which two white-shouldered rock wallabies travelled in the creation era. As they passed, they cut two deep crevices in the rock. Still common there at dawn and dusk, wallabies were easy game for Aboriginal hunters.

Mimi figures are tall, thin spirits who live in rock crevices. A long time ago, they taught the Aborigines how to hunt. Usually drawn as stick figures, no living Aborigine has seen one. They are friendly, but mischievous, and disappear into rocks when people approach.

Says Danny Gillespie, 'This country is alive with the truths of how it was made. For Aborigines, the truth is eternally manifest in the shape of the environment, in the crevices and outcrops and caves which the creation heroes made. Their earth-building activities are finished, but they are still here; they can still control the way people and the elements behave.'

One archaeologist was interested in exploring the theory that the strange circular grinding holes in rock surfaces at Kakadu — generally ascribed to the grinding of foods such as wild rice — might have been used to grind the edge-ground stone axes which predate such axes found anywhere else in the world. In order to try to discover more, he took one of the oldest women in a local clan to look at them and to recount what lore had been handed down to her about them.

'We used to fill 'em up with water to give the dogs a drink,' was her pragmatic reply.

Near Obiri, with its paintings of a warrior frieze and a Tasmanian tiger, is a rock overhang that has deliberately been kept off the tourist track. It is believed to be the site of the oldest continuous human habitation in the world. Dating back almost 40,000 years to the time of the ancient settlement at Lake Mungo in New South Wales, it was still being used by Aborigines a few years ago. A stark, somewhat desolate place, unmarked even by rock paintings, it is utterly dry in the wet season, and cool in the fierce heat of the dry season.

'Too smart, that black fella,' says Danny Gillespie laconically, parodying 'pidgin' English. 'The technology they developed for trapping geese is amazing; given time, they'd have invented the helicopter!'

When he was camping out at Obiri and documenting its paintings, Danny developed a method of protecting the paintings with silicon drip lines. This method is now used throughout Kakadu; the drip lines are almost unnoticeable, but they prevent water from eroding the paintings. Native wasps also build their nests on the paintings, and wasp control methods are being investigated.

Tourists walk along timber platforms that allow them to get close to the rock art without interfering with it. Danny has also relocated the car-parks so that, instead of there being 'a sea of shining Holden rooftops' around the sites, the cars are hidden away in the surrounding trees and speargrass.

The Future

Is tourism a threat to Kakadu National Park?

'We've spent $4.5 million on capital works in the park. There are 60 rangers and others in the National Parks and Wildlife Service here, and we have a new Visitors' Information Centre. The number of visitors jumps every year.

'But we're not worried about tourists, as long as we can manage the park properly. That means money.'

A different threat to Kakadu is uranium mining. Already, the Ranger mine is in operation at Jabiru, and there is the possibility of further mining if the large uranium corporations get their way. There is also an argument going on about a proposal by the Ranger mine to release stored water, which it says is only slightly contaminated, into the park's water systems. The Aborigines' reply is: if it's so safe, why not release it into Jabiru's town water supply?

Australian public opinion, spurred on by the conservation movement, seems firmly against further uranium mining and so may protect the park. Its listing as a World Heritage treasure will help. So too, perhaps, will increasing public awareness of Kakadu's unique Aboriginal value.

'Kakadu is important, just as Uluru (Ayers Rock) is,' explains Danny Gillespie. 'It makes people realise that you can't just keep bashing the environment; you have to help preserve it.

'The Aboriginal people want to share Kakadu with white people and get information across in a dignified and positive way.

Eden? The Dreaming Time? They were all the same once. If Toynbee is right and the history of civilisation is a response to challenge, the Eden-dwellers got expelled and started on their long trek through the cultures to the nuclear bomb, while the Dreamtime-dwellers stayed where they were. In Kakadu, they and their land remain intact. Almost.

Craig McGregor, an Australian writer and journalist, has written and edited several books on Australia and the Australian landscape.

A Revolution in Food Paradise

J. M. F. Keeney

A friend of mine, a great French chef, once explained his achievements thus: 'Cooking is 70% shopping'. His idea of a good bedtime read is the works of such titans as Careme and Escoffier. And his travels are confined almost exclusively to local markets where he gets what he wants or raises six kinds of hell.

Oasis Seros' poussin baked in lotus leaves, ginger and pastry crust. From the top, left to right, the four stages of · presentation

Were he to visit Australia, the smile he uses once or twice a week to commemorate perfection might appear more often — he would be dazzled by Australian products. And being something of a social historian on the subject of food, he would no doubt perceive the stirrings of a culinary revolution Down Under.

Treasures from the Sea and Land

Apart from being a chef's drawing board, a market functions as a showcase of a nation's bounty. This continent has the world's longest national coastline (which would stretch half way around the planet if straightened out and 2,400 kilometres further if the Barrier Reef were included), remarkably fertile coastal soils enjoying high rainfall, a strong farming tradition, temperate, mediterranean and tropical climates, and increasingly diverse ethnic communities who fish, farm or manufacture an enormous wealth of superb products. Chefs who migrate here feel blessed by their good fortune.

Washed by two oceans and several seas, each with distinct ecosystems, the coast yields many delectable if occasionally peculiar species in abundance. A by no means comprehensive list would include orange roughy (sea perch), barramundi, King George Sound whiting, abalone (both green and black-lipped), mussels, swordfish, skate, flathead, flounder, John Dory, schnapper, baby octopus no bigger than a thumb, blue fin tuna, yellow fin tuna, big eye tuna, babounia (red mullet), sea trout, squid, morwong, ling, bream, garfish, angel shark, carpet shark, saw-dog shark, gummy shark, snapper shark, black-tip shark, mud crab, spanner crab, lobster, Western Australian scampi, prawns, Tasmanian scallops, and the splendid (if misnamed) coral trout from the reef.

Unique to these waters are yabbies, a small burrowing crustacean related to crayfish, and bugs, a broad-backed, richer tasting cousin to the lobster — called Balmain bugs in the south, and Moreton Bay bugs in Queensland where they are larger, and sometimes referred to as the shovel nose bug. The marron, indigenous to Western Australia, is like an American freshwater crayfish but is two or three times larger and black.

The Pyrmont wholesale fish market in Sydney — the biggest in Australia — is a very merry place to visit. George Costi, son of Greek immigrants, runs one of the larger stores at the market. 'I have American and European tourists here who can't believe the variety. On a given day, we have over 100 different items on display.' His favourite fish to cook whole is the large sand whiting, and in filletted form, the orange roughy. 'I'll tell you,' he says, 'you can't find this many kinds of fish in fresh form anywhere in the world — not in Italy or Greece or America or Japan. I've looked.'

Even more dramatic specimens can be seen at any of the wholesale markets situated by the sea. The opa (or sun-fish), for example, is a giant oval disk, three feet across and only inches wide, with an enormous eye and a bright orange teflon-like skin. Despite its weird appearance, it commands a high

The Grand Dining Room of Mietta's Restaurant, Melbourne

DAVID SIMMONDS

price for its rich flavour.

Another rarity has recently reappeared in Melbourne after an absence of 60 years. Called the moon fish, it lives very deep, coming toward the surface only during the full moon when it can be found swimming with seals. A Melbourne chef describes it as 'the best fish to serve raw I've ever found. It's like a cross between salmon and tuna, and is also excellent when baked.'

Seeking advice on shark, I contacted Malcolm Dadd, chef at Manly Pier Restaurant in Sydney. An avid sports fisherman, he spends half his time camped on deserted beaches in far north tropical Queensland, indulging in his hobby. 'Shark is one of the better fish in Australia — not the best, but good. The problem with it is that it's at the head of the food chain, so the big ones can have a fair bit of mercury. Best to get 'em small. The baby green sharks you can catch at the mouth of the Shoalhaven River in New South Wales are great. Two nice fillets and no bones.'

'A lot of people don't know this,' he continues, 'but shark is one of the most eaten fish in Australia — tonnes of it. Just about all the fish and chips in Melbourne are made from shark.' When asked the best way to cook it he doesn't even pause. 'It's a dry fish, so it needs a heavy beer batter to completely cover it. Then when you cook it in hot oil, the inside is like it's been steamed.' So what is his favourite fish? 'Without a doubt, the king of fish is the barramundi cod, which has nothing to do with barramundi — totally different. Problem is, you can't buy it. You have to catch it yourself up north. But then, mate, until you've landed one of these and cooked it on the spot, you haven't lived anyway, so go for it!'

Bill Irons, executive chef of the Reef House in Cairns, offers a definitive three-word comment on crocodile, which is served by about a dozen restaurants in that city. 'It's a gimmick.' When asked to explain further, he adds, 'It just doesn't have any taste. Tourists like to try it, which is fine, and if only a small percentage of them do order it, there still won't be enough to go around.' Croc meat is taken from the tail, legs, back and jaw of the animal and is sold in frozen blocks.

Bill's lack of enthusiasm for this prehistoric monster notwithstanding, he suggests that it is best prepared by pan-frying it in butter with a rich red ginger sauce. What he does get excited about is the Maori wrasse. 'A beautiful fish. I wish I could get it more often. They usually come in around 80 or 100 pounds, and have an unusual green flesh which turns white when cooked.'

A great number of small specialty farms have mushroomed all over the country in recent years. There's not a good chef in Australia who isn't now collaborating with, or at least buying direct from, one or more of these farms.

As market demand has increased for exotic fruits,

game birds, milk-fed veal, blueberries, leaner strains of beef like limousin, venison, market garden specialities such as raddichio, small-leaf watercress, the French bitter lettuce mache, and various types of mushrooms, so have many enterprising people started farms either as a hobby or a full-time business.

For hundreds of kilometres along the north Queensland coast, tropical fruits are grown in the rich coastal soils. Over the past couple of decades, farmers have imported and cultivated a number of exotic fruits and plants, including the abu fruit (like a giant lychee), the pepino (a yellow and purple melon-like fruit), macadamia, cashew and pecan nuts, and custard apples from South-east Asia.

Andre Perez, executive chef of Hayman Island resort, extols the range of fruits grown in the region. 'Tropical fruits here are amazing. We have jackfruit, star fruit, the bamako (a hybrid of pawpaw and banana), rambutan, lychee and beautiful guavas.'

The story of Australia's cuisine begins with the extraordinary bounty of products available to the chef

Apart from the ambitious wine industry, innovation is being applied nowhere better than in Australia's burgeoning cheese industry. A brief tour of the country reveals quality cheese production in every state, and the world's only tropical cheese factory, situated in Millaa Millaa, inland from Cairns. A number of Australian cheese styles, though modelled after European types, are nevertheless unique in taste or texture, such as the excellent emmental-like St Claire and Gippsland blue. A variety of product names suggest the mix of nationalities involved in cheese manufacture: gbejna, pecorino, kefalotyri, Bjelke blue (named after the Premier of Queensland), camembert and monterey.

Vienna-born Australian, Josef Vondra, claims in his definitive book, *A Guide to Cheese in Australia,* 'The average Australian shopping at a Sydney or Melbourne cheese shop would have a greater selection of both local and overseas varieties than someone in Vienna, Paris, London and New York. Our food industry, whether on the manufacturing side or the restaurant level, has been subject to the influence of almost every nation: for the cheese-lover, the available selection is probably the best in the world.'

Beautiful Basics

It would be easy in summing up Australia's superb food products to pass over some of the more common, yet no less spectacular, items: bread, pasta and beer.

The mixture of nationalities in Australia today makes it possible to find quality breads of almost every description in any of the major cities. Some of those available include perfectly authentic Italian pane, a rather good French baguette, a huge variety of English-style whole-wheat loaves, a full range of German-style ryes, pumpernickels and caraway seed breads, and Swedish crispbreads.

The same is true of pasta, both in variety and quality. It is nearly impossible today to walk more than two blocks in any major Australian city without encountering freshly made pasta in a myriad of forms, whether in a deli, small factory, supermarket or restaurant.

The mass-produced beers with well-known names like Fosters, Victoria Bitter and XXXX stand up very well against similar brews produced on a large scale overseas. Each state has its favourite beers, and these are still a source of rivalry.

There has also been an upsurge of new, small breweries turning out excellent beers and stouts in small quantities. The Anchor Brewing Company of Perth has gained national distribution, and Anchor beer is now available in a few pubs on draught. Anchor produces a superlative small family of pilseners, stouts and bitters, demonstrating a fine bit of one-upmanship against their British progenitors in both taste and packaging. The miniscule Balmain Brewery in Sydney has produced a remarkable and delicious beer, called simply Bock. It can only be found locally.

In the small-to-medium size range, between the giants and the boutique breweries, is the time-honoured South Australian firm of Coopers which has produced Australia's only ale for over 135 years. Produced by a process similar to that used in the manufacture of champagne, Coopers Ale is distributed nationally and is now available on draught in a handful of the more distinguished city pubs. An excellent and original product, it has been regarded over many decades as the ale for connoisseurs. Its fermentation process gives it a very sturdy effervescence, one that permits it to be served with shaved ice, a little-known but very sensible Australian style of drinking beer on a hot day. Coopers also produce a light lager and a very good stout, a little lighter than Guinness.

FOJO

Much more could be written about this country's fine ingredients and produce. So, before we turn to a discussion of the Australian art of food preparation, let us give the Australian cornucopia a last good shake and see what comes out: edible flowers, zucchini and nasturtium; a mass of different honeys, culled from a galaxy of unique wildflowers, among the best being leatherwood; the Aboriginal 'potato', a glorious bulb of the wild swamp orchid and available to Top End bush foragers only; water buffalo, an excellent lean meat; wild pheasant from King Island, whose pheasant season lasts only four days; sea urchins, periwinkles and *bêche-de-mer* (sea slug); superb Dijon and Meaux-type mustards, using local seeds, vinegars and herbs; ultra-sweet Victorian baby carrots; Queensland pineapples; sorrel, tarragon, chives and basil; Chinese vegetables including chrysanthemum and kan kun (the hollow Chinese plant grown like rice in paddies); the best beef and lamb in the world, barbecued over eucalyptus leaves for seasoning; really exceptional asparagus, thin, fat, green or white, and tender young okra, the mucilaginous wonder ingredient of Cajun and Indian food; the strange kwanido, a horned orange, hand-grenade of a fruit; pomegranates, lemons, tangelos, and strawberries of a surprising size and taste; bananas and Bundaberg Rum; and a small avalanche of bottles — a sample of the many cleansing local mineral waters!

Modern Australian Cooking

Michael Symons, author of the ultimate book on Australian food, *One Continuous Picnic*, is a chef and owner of the Aristologist restaurant in Adelaide (named after Australia's first cookbook).

Like any superior book on food, *One Continuous Picnic* reaches well beyond food into history, social life, politics and economics. It provides us with some enjoyable bits of trivia — including the surprising fact that Fosters beer was introduced to Australia by an American — and the complete story on all-Australian Vegemite, the sticky brown paste used in sauces and sandwiches. Symons also provides the most complete assessment yet of the pavlova — a meringue and passionfruit cake, the invention of which has been hotly claimed by both Australia and New Zealand. The jury is still out, but Symons favours Australia.

The book is built, though, on more substantial foundations than these. Symons spent two and a half years living in Tuscan villages, researching, cooking and, part of the time, running a restaurant. He was greatly influenced by the Italian peasants he met and lived with, and by their gardens, cottage farms, fresh ingredients and beautiful, simple food.

As Symons knows, Australia will never have, nor would it want to possess, a peasant population, which he sees as the basis for any great cuisine. But all may not be lost.

Australia's cheese industry has grown to include a variety of superb cottage industry goat cheeses

ANTHONY BLAKE

Here's another way of looking at Australian food in the past, present and future. First, if we insist on drawing conclusions about the future of this nation's cuisine from its past, we should focus almost exclusively on the last 10 or 15 years. If we go back any further, the only fair comparison we can make is with America in the early 19th century, when that country had been settled for well over 200 years, contained a predominantly Anglo-Saxon population roughly similar in size to Australia's today, and had a basic English-derived cuisine which was scorned by the Europeans.

Secondly, concerning the present day, let's have a look at the recently published *Australian Cookbook*. It is a bestseller, moving quickly into its second printing, and is aimed squarely at the middle of the market.

This large collection of recipes provides the most accurate single measure available at present of the nation's tastes. Here we find a revealing mixture of menu suggestions, including traditional Australian ones (jumbuck stew — lamb ribs and yams in an iron pot), and a worldly collection of others: cauliflower and prawn stir fry, goulash, fennel with mushrooms, Chinese watercress salad, lamb and pawpaw curry, paupiettes, Spanish-style fish and rice, chicken tacos, Siamese fried rice, Cuban beans and rice, vegeroni con tonno, lamb shogayaki, filo pastry with silverbeet green, nasi goreng, Old English pudding, and kofta. A rather international selection, to say the least.

Thirdly, we have the future, and in fact, it's probably already begun. We have arrived at a point where there is sufficient creativity and energy to claim the existence of what I call modern Australian cooking.

If *One Continuous Picnic* is now less than a decade old, it is to its author's — and a few other chefs' — credit that the culinary scene in Australia has reached such heights in so short a time. If this new form of Australian cooking is not widespread, its broader impact will soon be seen in the influence of our great restaurants.

Along with Symons' peasant-cooking-as-the-source theory, a 'trickle down effect' has worked throughout history: the impact of the Chinese and European courts and, later, the grand restaurants of Europe cannot be discounted as important in the creation of national cuisines. And, as the *Australian Cookbook* shows, the tastes of the nation are changing, creating in the process new demands.

Apart from the impact of a great rush of immigration from all corners of the world, modern Australian cooking has been the result of several phenomena occurring over the past two decades. These have included a greatly increased propensity to travel widely, and a younger generation of travellers who during the 1960s and 70s went nearly everywhere, and at length, returning home with new ideas and desires; revolutions in French cooking which, for the first time in history, were promoted globally through widely available books and other media; and a growth in the number and quality of Chinese and other Asian restaurants, and the 'average' Australian's new-found appreciation for this food.

The eclecticism of modern Australian cooking - Philip Searle's warm salad

Modern Australian cuisine is generally light. It features a huge variety of fresh local products; it is strong on fish and game, experimental with the uses of pasta, and reflects the influence of French, Chinese, Japanese, Thai and Italian cuisines among others.

There are those who would argue that this is not Australian cooking at all, but a mixture of foreign influences, thereby missing the point that the whole history of food preparation and national styles is one of exchange, evolution, refinement — and borrowed influences. The important aspect is whether the borrowing results in something regionally distinct, better or freshly original, and these three criteria are admirably met by our best chefs.

Vivarois, a three-star Michelin restaurant in Paris to which I am severely addicted, is famous for, among other things, a splendid hors-d'oeuvre of delicately curried, large oysters (Portugaises) baked in the shell. If anyone insisted that this dish was Indian-like rather than French, owing to the curry, they would be scorned as a bad-tempered, hair-splitting swine, and would probably be horse-whipped into the bargain. Cannot Australia also be allowed to create new dishes (from our own original products) without having them kidnapped in broad daylight by older, larger national cuisines?

The Australian coast yields an abundance of seafood delicacies

The sabre-tongued American man of letters, and chronicler of the foods of Baltimore, H.L. Mencken, reports appropriately, if with typical exaggeration, that not until the 18th century did the French 'pull cooking out of the stable and put it in the dining room'. Indeed, it was the arrival of Catherine de Medici from Italy, who married Henry II, that gave the French court its first taste of refinement. She introduced a number of Italian dishes which have since become famous as French: quenelles, sweetbreads, aspics, and truffles among many others.

When entrepreneur-chef, Paul Bocuse returned to France after several months in South-east Asia during the 1960s, he carried in a number of notebooks the ideas — and influences — which would become the foundation of *la nouvelle cuisine*.

It is well known that Bocuse and his immediate peers produced masterpieces in this new style of cooking, while other less able practitioners gave new meaning to the word 'quackery', creating an expensive form of gastronomic charlatanism. These issues

THE AUSTRALIAN ADVENTURE

The Windows Restaurant
Burswood Island Resort, Perth
Chef: Peter Foster

Cold terrine of jewfish with wild mushrooms, served with warm yabbies and a garnish salad of raddichio and watercress, lightly tossed with vinaigrette

*

A dry rosé such as Houghton Cabernet Rosé or Orlando R.F. Chardonnay

Oasis Seros, Sydney
Chef: Philip Searle

Cream of abalone and pena mushroom soup, the abalone essence having been created through an intense Chinese steaming process, and with the mushrooms sliced paper thin, combined with a light chicken stock and egg yolk and cream

*

A high-quality fino sherry Seppelt D.P. 117 flor fino or Lindeman's Hunter River Chablis

Stephanie's Restaurant, Melbourne
Chef: Stephanie Alexander

Tasmanian scallops with basil noodles

*

Petaluma Rhine Riesling

Butler's Restaurant, Sydney
Chef: Mogens Bay-Esbensen

Balmain bugs in champagne, with a julienne of leeks, carrots, celery and hijiki seaweed

*

Wolf Blass Chardonnay Cuvee Champagne or Wolf Blass Classic Dry White

Reef House, Cairns
Chef: Bill Irons

Maori wrasse fillet wrapped in a blanched lettuce leaf, steamed, served with a light veloute sauce, flavoured with red capsicum

*

McWilliams Elizabeth Riesling or, if available, Robinsons Family Chardonnay

Mietta's, Melbourne
Chef: Jacques Raymond

Tasmanian-grown Atlantic salmon fillet on a bed of mache (wild bitter lettuce) tossed in a vinaigrette made with butter, served with steamed potatoes

*

Wyndham Estate Chablis Superior

Neddy's, Adelaide
Chef: Cheng Liew

King squab rare roasted in a rich sauce made by pressing the carcass to create a salmis, served with prawn ravioli

*

Rosemount Roxburgh Chardonnay or Rosemount Show Chardonnay

Mistress Augustine, Adelaide
Chef: Ann Oliver

Pheasant breast stuffed with pigeon breast, which holds a quail breast, seasoned then roasted, served pink with a black grape glaze

*

Peter Lehmann Barossa Valley Pinot Noir or St Huberts Pinot Noir

Chez Oz, Sydney
Chef: Andrew Blake

Veal fillet bundles stuffed with bocconcini cheese, tomatoes and anchovies, pan fried, sauced with veal stock, butter and port, served on spinach and egg tappadelles

*

Chateau Reynella Coonawarra Cabernet Sauvignon

Max's Restaurant
Hyatt, Melbourne
Chef: Patrick Murray

Fillet of beef with wild Australian oak mushrooms, served with a duxelle of cêpes and oak mushrooms

*

Penfolds Koonunga Claret, Penfolds Bin 389 or Penfolds St Henri Claret

Oasis Seros, Sydney
Chef: Philip Searle

A lightly cooked hot salad of Chinese vegetables, oysters and wood fungus, with a sauce of oyster juice, rice wine, tamarind, lime leaves, and many other Asian spices

*

Yalumba Pewsey Vale Rhine Riesling or Yalumba Heggles Rhine Riesling

Hayman Island Resort
Chef: Andre Perez

Tropical fruit plate of guava, rambutan, starfruit, with a puree of bamako

*

Hardy's Beerenauslese botrytised riesling

Dear Friends, Hobart
Chef: David Brian

Wild mountain berries in an almond biscuit basket served on a creme anglaise

*

A sweet white such as Evans family or Rothbury Estate botrytised riesling or a lighter-styled fortified wine such as Mick Morris Tokay

comprise the most tired debate in food-land, but I recall Bocuse to illustrate another, very different, point.

Curiosity, energy, openness to new ideas, and a willingness to experiment sensibly from an established base of knowledge are the cornerstones of any period of rapid culinary advance. These conditions existed to a great degree in France during the 1960s and 70s and are very much present, though in smaller quantity, in Australia today.

Manhattan's excellent restaurant, Arcadia, proclaims a new American cuisine to such an extent that it is, apart from being a very good dining spot, a sort of living tribute to a new creativity with roots in a feeling of confident nationalism.

If there are no restaurants in Australia which speak as loudly (Australians are not as brash as their North American cousins) as Arcadia does about its national identity, there are several dozen very good chefs contributing — deliberately or not — to the growing wealth of modern Australian cuisine. Of these several dozen, there are perhaps six or eight leading the way with world-class levels of creativity and skill.

Great Chefs and Restaurants

Among the best of the modern Australian chefs is certainly Philip Searle, now presiding over his and partner Barry Ross' stunning new Sydney restaurant, Oasis Seros. But, as he says, 'At the vanguard of new Australian cooking are two women, Gay Bilson and Stephanie Alexander. Any consideration of what is going on in food in this country wouldn't make sense without first referring to them.'

It is interesting and instructive to note that Gay and Stephanie are both former librarians and self-taught chefs. They each came independently to the simple realisation (a little like Isaac Newton watching the apple fall) that cooking in this country should reflect our climate and acknowledge our position as being a part of Asia, an obvious idea only now that they have put it into practice, shaking off in the process a yoke with the weight of two centuries.

In the early 1970s, Gay and Tony Bilson opened Le Bon Gout restaurant in Sydney, offering very good traditional French cooking. It became very popular, attracting among others a number of Labor Party officials of the Whitlam government then in power. This was the first time in Australian political history that the Labor leaders had openly endorsed the pleasures of great food and wine, treating it as a regular part of the enjoyment of life rather than as a patrician frivolity, at odds with honest political pursuits.

Someone once asked Tony during these early days how a socialist could drink champagne, and he responded, no doubt putting the question to bed for good, 'You should see how the French and Italian socialists live.'

Stephanie's Restaurant, Melbourne - a superb restaurant in a remarkable building

Later, Gay and Tony opened the Berowra Waters Inn, a beautifully positioned restaurant on a tree-lined waterway, just outside Sydney. Year after year, it has been regarded as the best kitchen, bar none, in Sydney. The menu, which changes daily with availability of products, has offered many brilliant adaptations of French-based cooking, and numerous original creations. Some show Asian influences, like the light and refined fish consommé with prawn wontons. This is a *cuisine bien recherché*, the product of a highly talented chef who is also a voracious reader of books. A provincial French or Italian *plat du jour* nearly impossible to find on short notice in either of those countries, such as stuffed pig's ear, appears on her menus in a new and yet 'authentic' form — such is the work of a master practitioner. One finds pheasant, hare, venison or skate on her menus and all are treated with originality and care.

Some of Gay's, Stephanie's and Philip Searle's dishes point to a noteworthy and perhaps unique tendency in modern Australian cooking: a reflection of a variety of Mediterranean cuisines and an interest in provincial and peasant cooking.

It is true that Paul Bocuse, having incited a major movement with *la nouvelle cuisine*, abruptly changed paths, like many a good painter, and declared himself interested in returning to the solid basics of *la cuisine bourgeoise*, and so urged another, if quieter, movement in cooking. But what he didn't do, being unshakeably French, was to extend this 'return to basics' to include the provincial cuisines of other European countries. There is no such thing, a Parisian girlfriend once taught me, as being part French.

But the young chefs of Australia, not being French at all, can be and are 'part French'. They grew up regarding the cooking of France as the *sine qua non*, and their first culinary inspirations came from Paris, Bourgogne, Landes, Auvergne or Provence. But by the time they had matured, and perhaps lived in or visited France, they became fascinated by all the cuisines of the Mediterranean as well as those of Asia. The practical result is the sort of menus Australia's chefs are likely to create, menus such as Gay Bilson's which show a willingness to derive from a variety of sources.

Stephanie was greatly motivated by three years spent in France, working as a teacher and au pair. She and her first husband, a Jamaican, returned to Melbourne and opened a small restaurant called Jamaica House. The marriage ended and she returned to librarianship. She cooked incessantly and passionately for friends for five years, and then with her second husband — a disenchanted barrister who had returned from several years in Hong Kong — opened the first Stephanie's. This was an immediate success, and soon led to their acquiring one of the great National Trust-classified stately homes in Melbourne, where they now both live and work. This building is worth a visit for its own merits, even apart from the superior cuisine.

Stephanie's repertoire is large, based on four seasonal menus. She is a great lover of game birds, artichokes, the freshest fish, and is very strong on the sweet finish to a meal. The lamington, a traditional Australian cake, which in this country is either laughed at (comedian Barry Humphries mocks it regularly) or taken very seriously, has been updated brilliantly at her restaurant.

One very impressive plate is a friture of red mullet and prawns (French) and vegetables (Japanese tempura-like) with Mediterranean tomato sauce, and a salsa verde (Mexican) on the side, served with Queensland-grown limes. In this dish, the resulting whole is infinitely greater than the sum of its parts. This friture is unique to, inspired by, and available only in Australia.

The executive chef of Burswood Island Resort in Perth, Peter Foster, a food philosopher, offers this observation about the present state of Australian cooking: 'There are some great chef-owners in this country. They're not just great cooks, but very able entrepreneurs. Australia is a good place to be an entrepreneur in any business; the mood is right. It's easy to forget that restaurants are businesses too.'

At Oasis Seros we can also witness some genius in the kitchen. The food being produced by this new restaurant is eclectic, inspired and damned good.

The menu changes with the ebb and flow of the seasons. Consider, in this case, winter: pheasant consommé with pheasant ravioli and pork wontons; spicy crab, coconut and noodle soup; steamed prawn cakes; stir-fried basil noodles, squid and clams; a salad of artichokes and buckwheat tagliatelle and roquette lettuce; stir-fried oyster and pancetta salad. This partial list of entrees is followed by such main

courses as grilled tuna steak and pesto, tomato and saffron; deep-fried red cooked squab served with goose liver and polenta; pheasant breast with pheasant sausages, celeriac and chestnut puree; *pot-au-feu* with brisket, oxtail, tongue, pork and preserved goose; venison escalopes with horseradish porridge (wow!); and, extraordinary in every way, a poussin baked in lotus leaf, pine mushrooms and ginger,

The Rock Pool - created by Stephanie - one great dish from the wide range of modern Australian cooking

served in a dense pastry crust cut off at the table to reveal a Chinese wrap of lotus leaves and a perfectly baked whole bird.

Philip Searle grew up in the small inland New South Wales town of Dubbo, Self-taught, he has lived for the past few years in the relative isolation of Adelaide. If this isn't Australian cooking (albeit modern Australian), I don't know what is. Most of the

dishes are of his own invention, and those traditional ones like *pot-au-feu* bear his inimitable stamp. He describes his influences as being 'provincial Mediterranean cooking, and all of Asia'.

It is clear that along the way he has not missed the classic lessons provided by Brillat-Savarin in his seminal work, *The Physiology of Taste*. There is not a silly or misguided recipe to be found here — nor a flaky one — except for pastry crust, which is as light as a butterfly's eyelash. A forthright but modest fellow who prefers boosting his peers to talking about himself, Searle has said as much as he will and sends me packing to visit a friend of his in Adelaide.

Here on a quiet street in the city of churches sits Neddy's, an unprepossessing small restaurant located in a former shopfront. The chef-owner, Yew Cheong Liew, is a Chinese Malaysian who grew up in his family's restaurant business and has resided in Australia for nearly 20 years. His is an ambitious style of cooking, European with strong Chinese influences and elements of other oriental cuisines.

On a given day (except on Mondays when Neddy's does a full-out traditional Chinese menu), Cheong Liew might offer a fillet of King George Sound whiting deep-fried with a salt and Indian coriander seed 'dip'; a boned-out quail stuffed with rabbit and pork lightly braised and served in a shark-fin and ham fricasse; steamed cucumber and lamb brains with spicy red sauce; zucchini flowers stuffed with a puree of goat cheese lightly battered and fried; a warm salad of grilled Moreton Bay bugs with Chinese toasted salt fish on a bed of snow peas with avocado puree; or a marinated kangaroo steak which has been sealed on the grill then roasted. Kangaroo, which is legally available only in South Australia, was brought back into fashion at Neddy's which first served it over ten years ago.

Cheong Liew regards King George Sound whiting as 'the best fish in the world' for its delicacy, and personally likes to eat it accompanied by a salad made of lettuce garnished with salt fish in oil, bean sprouts, sunflower seeds and lemon juice.

When not in the kitchen, he can be found touring the surrounding farms. At one particular farm he has been a prime collaborator in developing a cross-breed of king squab. The squab are killed Chinese-style, by suffocation, so as to retain the blood which Cheong Liew describes as 'very important for the ultimate flavour, and a sort of return to the idea of game hunted in the wild.'

Another Adelaide restaurant, with both a seductive name and menu, is Mistress Augustine, owned by the chef, Ann Oliver. Here we find updated Australian food, and a beguiling mixture of European and Asian cookery. She serves kangaroo fillets with a French oyster sauce, and a pea and ham soup with a kangaroo pie floater — a refined adaptation of the colonial dish.

A meal here might start with a puree of rockmelon

soup with champagne and strawberries, followed by one of Ann's eclectic inventions like her pouch of duck. In this dish, duck skin is stuffed with pink roasted breast meat and black rice, served with a raw peanut and chilli sauce.

Some 4,000 kilometres to the north-east, where the tropical rainforest and big river country sweeps into the sea, Mogens Bay-Esbensen has created a restaurant called Nautilus, certainly the best in tiny Port Douglas and outstanding when judged on a national basis. Formerly of Sydney, where he founded — and still owns — Butler's restaurant, this Danish-born chef lived for years in Bangkok and authored a book on Thai cuisine before emigrating here. 'Local products?' he muses, before responding with considerable pleasure, 'Green peppercorns grow wild and beautifully in the forests in this area. Okay, here's a recipe. Take Moreton Bay bugs and plunge them into strongly boiling water and remove them instantly. They are not cooked in this way but the flesh is firmed. Then marinate them for 24 hours in lime juice and coconut milk, both produced locally, and of course, add the whole green peppercorns which give a fine subtle flavour.'

It would be foolish to ignore the contributions made by a handful of other great, if more traditional restaurants, to the overall culinary scene in Australia. Indeed, the lines between classical cooking and modern Australian cuisine are perhaps not always so rigidly fixed. Robert Molines, chef of the Pokolbin Cellar Restaurant at Hungerford Hill, offers dishes inspired by South-east Asia (such as his curried stuffed leg of chicken), though his reputation has been built on superb French provincial cooking.

And Stephanie acknowledges her debt to Damien Pignolet, chef and owner of the very superior Claude's restaurant of Sydney, for teaching her a number of techniques. Reflections, located in the far north of Sydney near Palm Beach, also runs an admirable French kitchen which is well worth visiting.

In the opinion of a good number of knowledgeable souls, the best restaurant in the country is Mietta's in Melbourne. My view is that if her restaurant were to be magically transported to France — lock, stock and barrel — it would quickly earn a two-star Michelin rating. This is due to owner Mietta O'Donnell's constant attention to detail in supervising what has become Australia's grandest restaurant in the classical style, complete with several dining rooms, exquisite furnishings and a sommelier who knows his trade, Ken Johns. Contained within his excellent wine list we find what is, without question, the best collection of French red and white burgundies in the country.

The chef de cuisine, Jacques Raymond, has worked in two legendary French kitchens: as saucier in Les Baux's three-star Oustau de Baumaniere, and as sous-chef in the two-star Jacques Cagna in Paris. He produces a well-balanced range of French dishes,

is masterful with all manner of forcemeats, terrines and galantines, sparing but effective with *nouvelle cuisine* accents, and is among the very few chefs in Australia with the good sense to offer simple home-cooking-style dishes like *petit salé au lentilles* (a pork and lentil stew). His fish soup, saddle of rabbit and *coq au vin* are magnificent.

Jacques is remarkably forthright in praising Australian products: 'The baby vegetables we buy from the Mornington Peninsula are clearly superior to anything available in France, and so is the King Island crab. Gippsland blue cheese is outstanding, a bit more moist than roquefort.'

He is delighted by his clientele's curiosity about cooking, commenting that 'Australians are very interested in the background and preparation of a dish, far more so than I would have thought before coming here, and more interested in these things, I have found, than most Americans.'

The strong trends of creativity and invention in modern Australian cooking are not, in my opinion, a flash in the pan. We can expect far more, rather than less, excellence of the kind here described in the future. This is only the beginning of what may become — who knows? why not? — one of the world's most vigorous and ambitious cuisines over the next 50 or 100 years.

We've learned the history, reviewed the wealth of products, and met the farmers and chefs. Now let us listen to Patrick Murray, a French-trained Dubliner who is the head chef at Max's restaurant at the Melbourne Hyatt Hotel, and who loves his new country: 'I'm feeling good here. I'm looking around, seeing new things, feeling creative. I want to change, grow, in my cooking, my career. Australia's open and free, the products are great, and the customers are willing to try things.

One Great Dish

Now here is a difficult task — to nominate one single Australian dish that is somehow representative of all that has been said about this modern Australian cuisine. I am sure that most of the chefs mentioned could provide alternatives, but the dish I have selected is: The Rock Pool, prepared by Stephanie's Restaurant.

This is not only a world-class dish, it is world-leading. It is so good that it should be placed on a giant silver platter on which is engraved 'This is modern Australian cuisine, and ain't it surprising!' and then paraded through the great kitchens of the world. It is a modern Australian dish in which 'influences' have been so perfectly assimilated that they disappear entirely to become something altogether new. It is a dish so perfect to look at, it should be painted as well as photographed.

The name itself is very Australian — understated, laconic, wry. The artfulness of the dish, which reflects

Australia's place in Asia, proves conclusively that this country is not short on great culinary ideas. Served cold, it suits our warmer climate admirably. It is also a visual and taste celebration of some of our finest sea products.

The dish consists of a shallow bowl in which is placed a lightly jellied consommé made with shellfish. The making of this consommé is a major and separate operation in its own right, one requiring very considerable light-handedness. Into this consommé are arranged baby squid, prawns, oysters, periwinkles cooked and replaced in their shells, caviar, crayfish, sea lettuce, soaked and sauteed Chinese tree fungus, and many other compatible items as available. The Rock Pool changes! Each one is an individual arrangement, an edible food 'sculpture'. The dish relies, however, on the purity and flavour of the lightly jellied consommé.

The preceding Australian Adventure Menu is not designed, as it were, for consumption. Not even Louis XIV, the Sun King, could have consumed such quantities! It is meant as a showcase for some of the many Australian products, chefs, restaurants and preparations. Its style of explanation is uniquely Australian. The dishes are presented at some length, but unlike American menus, they are not 'sold' or promoted through the description — the Australian rendition is meant to explain the preparation clearly. If French or Italian menus are less explanatory, it is because their clientele enjoy a bigger, indeed historical, base of knowledge.

Perhaps this menu style can be attributed to Gloria Staley, who owns a trio of fine restaurants — Fanny's and Glo Glo's in Melbourne and Chez Oz in Sydney — all of which have influenced modern Australian cooking. Robert Mayne, our wine editor and a prolific taster, has matched these dishes with suggested Australian wines.

Our review of the rarefied and noble levels of modern Australian cooking excludes a great number of very good restaurants of all kinds, which complete the culinary picture of Australia today. First-time visitors to Australia often expect small, provincial cities and are pleased to discover how worldly this country's capitals have become. Chinese food — at all price levels — can be found in abundance in Sydney and Melbourne, and to a lesser extent in other cities. Some really first-rate Chinese kitchens can, through special arrangement, produce multi-course banquets of staggering variety and finesse. In Sydney, two such restaurants are the Marigold and the East Ocean.

Italian, Greek and Lebanese restaurants are found everywhere, having become as typical as the traditional Australian milk bar. More recently, Thai, Indian, Vietnamese and Malaysian restaurants have been increasing in number on an almost daily basis. There are many Japanese restaurants and sushi bars. Very good Spanish, African, Polish, Russian and other ethnic restaurants can be found in smaller numbers. In Sydney, Melbourne and Perth, one of the most worthwhile small investments to be made is a copy of the excellent *Cheap Eats* guide, which lists hundreds of small and interesting eateries in the low and medium price range.

Most of these restaurants extend 'BYO' (Bring Your Own) privileges, entitling the diner to bring his or her own wine or beer. This Australian custom is very worthwhile, enabling the restaurant customer to pick and enjoy some excellent vintages at reasonable prices, free of the large mark-up normally charged by licensed premises.

Let us close on a pair of recipes and a small act of thievery. The first comes from Serge Dansereau, executive chef of Kables restaurant at the Regent Hotel in Sydney. This dish needs to be cooked on the beach in sand, and we have more of that than any country on earth! Serge explains, 'My father taught me a special way to cook beans. You dig a hole in the sand and light a fire in it. After the fire dies down, remove the ash, place a big crockery pot in the hole, fill the pot with white beans, bayleaf, molasses, tomato ketchup, dry mustard and chicken stock. Cover the pot with the lid and sand and go to bed. It will still be simmering in the morning.'

Here now is my recipe for how to enjoy this lovely pot of beans.

Take one bright autumn day on the coast of Tasmania and go abalone diving. Catch your limit, and play around like a seal for a while. When you get out, your teeth will be chattering, but your brain will be singing. With a nylon rope from your dive-bag, tie the neck of a bottle of that incomparably fine Tasmanian wine, Heemskerk Chardonnay, and let it sit in the water for about 15 minutes until it is cool but not cold.

Uncover beans. Uncork wine. Drink straight from bottle. Eat noisily. Lean back.

Take in the view!

John Keeney credits his father, 'A man of Einsteinian curiosity and the digestion of a shark' with introducing him to food. During his years in Europe, the author contributed food articles to the Paris Metro *magazine, and hiked and ate his way through over 70 French Départements. With his wife Audrey, he is developing a farm devoted to artichokes and other niceties for the table. The book he would like to write is tentatively titled,* Commies in the Kitchen: A History of the Marxist Onslaught against Cuisine, Restaurants and Specialty Farms.

Tasmanians, a Tough but Generous Breed

Allan Moult

Tasmania — Australia's island state — is a land of powerful physical contrasts thanks to a dramatic landscape which juts into the belly of the Roaring Forties, the tumultuous belt of rain-laden trade winds which circle the globe's lower latitudes. The island's western mountains push the winds skyward, forcing them to drop their welcome cargo on one of Australia's lushest landscapes. The west takes the brunt of the storms that develop; the eastern half basks in the gentle overflow. It's a landscape that produces a tough, but generous, breed of people.

To the despair of the Tasmanian Department of Tourism, while Australia's mainland states have seen their tourist arrival figures boom — 10-25% in most cases — Tasmania's tourist figures are actually declining. Yet key tourist destinations like Cradle Mountain Lodge are actually enjoying full houses most of the year. It appears that the beds are being kept full by Tasmanians — and they must be on to something special if you follow the advice of jaded international travel writers. Their universal credo is always to get off the beaten track, and do as the natives do.

Well, the Tasmanian natives are out there enjoying the countryside. They are revelling in one of the world's most benign paradises: a land of physical contrast, temperate climate, and fertility.

The wild west coast offers dramatic scenery for some of the world's classic bushwalking trails — the South Coast Track, the Port Davey Track, and others as rigorous. There are mountains to be climbed, rivers to be rafted and giant waves to be surfed. Further inland, rivers and lakes abound in waters rich in trout — iridescent lively rainbows and bulkier browns.

A fine example of a native doing what has to be done is Jason Garrett and London Lakes. Here, in a wide shallow valley just south of the Central Plateau, Tasmanian-born Jason, a former surveyor in New Guinea, has built two huge lakes — Lake Big Jim and Lake Samuel. His single-minded passion is trout fishing, and sharing the pleasures of this magnificent obsession.

A large luxury lodge has been built of native timbers and stone. Catering for a maximum of ten guests at any one time, it's just five minutes by road to Dee Lagoon (another famed fishing location) and five minutes by helicopter to the wilderness waters of the 'Land of Three Thousand Lakes'. Among his regular guests are American businessmen who fly to Australia just for a week at London Lakes.

Consuming passions are, it seems, a Tasmanian trait. West of London Lakes lies rich mining territory. It is home for characters like Ernie 'Iron Man' Coleman, the hermit of Zeehan, who at the age of nearly 80 still seeks his Eldorado as he prospects in the rugged hills and valleys of this wild coastal area. Even today, Ernie could hold his own with young men a quarter of his age. His barrel chest is the by-product of having run the equivalent of nearly 300 marathons between his work at Mt Lyell Mine and home in Zeehan.

As Ernie explains, 'I wasn't running any races in the beginning. It was simply the quickest way to get home each weekend. The train from Queenstown to Zeehan took eight hours or more. I could run it in less than three hours.'

Naturally word got out about his weekly 24-mile runs and soon Ernie was being coaxed into charity runs and quite a few gambles. 'I was a sucker for a two bob bet,' he says wryly.

Among the bets was a classic run from Queenstown to Strahan and back — a return trip of nearly 90 kilometres along one of the windiest and steepest roads in the state. About 3,000 people lined the streets of Queenstown to see 'Iron Man' finish. 'I lost that one — it took me eight hours and 13 minutes, which was just 13 minutes too long.'

Men like Ernie Coleman have inspired many writers, poets and artists to capture the unique lifestyles of the hardy pioneers of the west coast. Hobart painter Peter Stephenson has become obsessed with the larger-than-life characters of the area — the axemen, the miners and the fishermen who people this forbidding landscape. As he says, 'All

A group of Tasmanians enjoy a yarn over a beer

Tasmania's legends, past and present, have emerged from the exploits of men such as these. They are heroic figures — flawed, but impressive. My paintings try to interpret their involved rituals of mateship by illustrating their instinctive body language. Their communication was earthy and superficial, but there were many unwritten codes of honour inherent in their basically masculine society.'

Stephenson has a strong affinity with the men he paints. 'I was in the Australian Navy for nine years, and I spent a lot of time as a deckie for abalone divers up the west — that's where Tasmania's fishermen, axemen and miners congregate. They're a great lot. Late at night their stories might be embellished, but the core — the myth or fable, if you like — remains sacred.'

There's a creative edge in Tasmania that has nurtured much talent in recent years. It includes potters like Les Blakeborough and Derek Smith, woodworkers like Kevin Perkins and Merv Gray, artists like Stephenson and Archibald Prize-winner Keith Looby, and sculptors like Gay Hawkes and Peter Taylor. They are all equally passionate about their art, and reap the benefit of national attention for their work.

Tasmanians take pride in what they do — work and play — and they do it with a zest that would exhaust a 'north islander' (their affectionate term for mainland Australians).

Tasman Peninsula farmer and road-building contractor Hayden Nichols is typical. A big man with a rolling gait, Hayden enjoys an enviable reputation as a master earthmover, a farm dam-builder and road constructor, and he leads a tough team of men and heavy earth-moving equipment for the task — a seven-day-a-week job at the best of times. In between, he runs his two farms and somehow finds time to practise his hobby — woodchopping.

Now in his 50s, Hayden decided a year ago to take up again the sport that he had enjoyed as a much younger man, and immediately chopped his way to become the state's veterans champion.

Other Tasmanian passions are more staid. It's time to meet the East Coast Strollers on a Sunday morning early in June. The late-autumn sky is crisp and the horizon clearly defined by the low sun.

The Strollers are an eclectic group of locals ranging in age from 4 to 80, and a number of dogs, including three-legged Billie. Among them are farmers, a retired school headmaster, a nurseryman, two youth hostel managers, and a photographer. Once a month they meet for a few hours' walking and a picnic lunch. The walk is a local tradition which was instigated by Helen Gee and Bob Graham, who farm at nearby Stonehurst.

'Everybody's welcome', says Helen. 'The walks started when we moved to live in the area. We had small children, and we couldn't do much of the long-distance wilderness travel we were both used to. We also wanted to get to know the area. We formed a Wilderness Society branch, but because of the politics of this rural area, that wasn't much of a success. However, on the walks, people come together, talk and chat, and I guess we achieve the same purpose. We get to know people and talk informally, which is what the Wilderness Society is all about anyway. We've simply dispensed with all the formalities and our meetings take place along a beach.'

Once the walks became established, Helen and Bob encouraged the participants to seek out new walks to explore and share. Says Helen, 'There's so much obvious delight when the day's leader knows his or her walk is being enjoyed. They walk them during the week, try them out, and revel in seeking out local knowledge from friends, farmers and storekeepers in the area. The community generally enjoys what we are doing.'

Another Sunday, and a typical early November day in Tasmania. A cloudless sky, barely a breath of wind, cool on the coastal plains, but a touch temperate in the sclerophyll valleys. It's the first Sunday of the month, and the East Coast Strollers are on the march again. This time their destination is Hallam Cave — a small low-slung incision in a shallow cliff wall

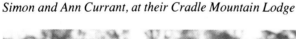

Simon and Ann Currant, at their Cradle Mountain Lodge

ALLAN MOULT

sheltering Hallam Cave Creek. The nomenclature of the area reflects either a sense of humour with tongue in cheek, or early explorers with not much imagination. Within just a few kilometres there are hills called Big Bedding, Gravelley, Flatrock, Big Peppermint, Dead Dog, Brown, Goat Rock, Pigeonwood and Gentle Annie, a cuddly curve on the southern horizon.

Today attention is focused on the terrain underfoot — the wild orchids are in bloom, and the Strollers are easily distracted by the search, and by the cooling waters of the nearby creek. Hours pass easily in conversation; drinks and snacks do the rounds; someone barbecues a few sausages; kids and dogs splash in the rocky pools; and quite a few species of orchids are discovered by various search parties. Today's distance covered by the hikers is minimal, but the long journeys traversed in comradeship cannot be measured.

The relaxed air of the Strollers is also reflected on Saturday mornings at Hobart's Salamanca market. It's a promenade — an old-time celebration, a weekly festival. And where else would you find a federal Senator selling stoves? Norm Sanders, Democrat Senator and fly in the establishment political ointment, is often to be seen cheerfully hawking his popular Hot Prospect slow-combustion heater to a discerning audience. Tasmanians enjoy being comfortable during their long, and often wet winter, and Norm's stoves fill a welcome niche.

The stoves began as a hobby and now employ a small group of friends and family. Says Norm, 'My wife Jill turns the blackwood knobs. I make the patterns for casting and do the fitting and turning. The doors are cast by a small foundry in Derwent Park. The welder is a former instrument technician, from New South Wales. He had taken a welding course, liked it, came to Tasmania, liked it — and liked trout fishing. He also liked the Georgian house he found at Oatlands, and he's happy.'

Norm Sanders, like so many 'new' Tasmanians, came here first for a short visit. 'I came here originally on a Fulbright scholarship to study the Tasmanian coastline for a PhD in geomorphology. When I finally got here, I fell in love with it. This place is a jewel. This kind of place is rare in the modern world. Why, we've got dinosaur fodder here — trees that were around when Tasmania was part of the supercontinent, Gondwanaland.

It has a scale you can absorb. You can come to grips with Tasmania, and it's an understandable entity. The thing that is most noticeable about Tasmania is that it has survived many of the excesses of 20th-century man and progress. Still, we have to be honest and say that was purely because there was not that much development. The isolation of the place saved it.

And that isolation is the best-kept secret in the world of tourism.'

Allan Moult is a full-time freelance writer/photographer based at Nubeena on Tasmania's Tasman Peninsula. Here, at Summerhill Farm — a five-hectare bush retreat overlooking the ocean — he writes up his travels and adventures.

Federal Senator, and stove salesman, Norm Sanders

The World's Longest Mail Run

Andrew Fisher

In the drizzle of an autumn evening in South Australia, Captain Peter Docking looks sufficiently the part to quieten the most nervous passenger. Gold bars and a cap braided with a tasteful minimum of gold spaghetti show him to be the master of the Rockwell Aero Commander sitting outside the main terminal at Adelaide Airport.

GRENVILLE TURNER

Inside the six-seater aircraft, the passengers — a man and two women — break out their food packs and pour themselves wine grown in vineyards less than 40 kilometres away. The Captain does his duty, 'Welcome aboard Augusta Airways Flight 07 to . . . er, where are we going?' The three passengers laugh and sip their riesling. Jokes are part of the service, especially on Friday evenings.

Augusta Airways, owned by husband-and-wife team Tony and Christine Kingham, runs a commuter route on week days between Adelaide and the dour industrial town of Port Augusta, some 300 kilometres to the north-west. At weekends, the company's comfortable Aero Commander becomes a bush plane flown by bush pilot Peter Docking, servicing communities up north through the heart of Australia along one of the world's most remote and celebrated roads, the Birdsville Track. Usually there is a spare seat or two for paying passengers.

North of Adelaide the land spreads like an English chequerboard landscape of neat fields squared by trees until it runs against the dark basalt savagery of the Flinders Ranges. Smoke streams out from the paddocks, carried by the prevailing westerly wind, a wind that has blown across the Roaring Forties to become the poor land-ridden cousin of its former turbulent self.

Flight BH 07 is still aloft when night falls, leaving glints in distant clouds to echo the passing day. Suddenly the smoke streams are lost to sight and the fires that farmers have set to clear stubble are visible red teeth devouring the harvested wheat fields.

The Laurie Wallis Airport, named after some Labor Party worthy, consists of a sealed runway set amongst salt bush and drainage channels well outside Port Augusta (or, as the locals have it, Port a Gutter). Just off the apron, Augusta Airways maintains a small terminal building and a cat. Next door is a flying club and across the way are three big hangars for medically equipped aircraft. This is the main southern base for the Flying Doctor Service.

The passengers pick up luggage that Peter takes out of a hatch at the rear of the plane. He gives the cat some milk in the terminal office and turns out the runway lights.

The closest accommodation to the airport is the Standpipe Motel. At the entrance to its dining-room is a hatstand and on it are six Akubra hats. The hats mark the beginning of serious country. It will be really serious country when the men wear hats while sitting down to eat.

The Standpipe Motel is on the site of the last bore water outlet before the desert. That same outlet, a standpipe, nurtured camel and bullock trains in the last century. Mr Singh, the owner, says that there is a ghost in the lovely old building that houses the kitchens and the restaurant. 'From time to time the cook hears the voice of a barman who hanged himself

there.' On the nights when the ghost speaks the cooking is apparently a bit patchy.

Next morning, Peter and the cat are checking out the plane and paying particular attention to the inside of the engine cowlings. In the desert at night, small finches seek out warm engines and build nests on them. This means nasty surprises in the morning for pilot and birds.

The Channel Run to Boulia via Birdsville is subsidised by a variety of mail contracts and rural subsidies from government bodies. Today's run is vital to farmers and people of the outback, providing them with weekly mail, contact, School of the Air material for children, urgent supplies, fast travel and general assistance.

Peter, now in dark green working clothes, loads mail, cardboard boxes and emergency rations. In the boxes are 30 kilos of vegetables, newspapers, 40 loaves of bread, tractor parts, and shirts and moleskins from R. M. Williams.

The single booked passenger, a ringer going back to his sheep station, hasn't turned up. 'Probably enjoyed himself too much last night,' says Peter. 'I had an Aboriginal stockman once who turned up to go back to work, his bag packed and ticket in his hand. At the last minute he wouldn't go. Said it was too lonely out there.'

Peter and the other pilots of the Channel Run are the latest in a line of mailmen who for more than 100 years have brought the mail to outback stations along the Birdsville Track.

At 8.40 am, Flight BH 001 takes off into the murk and turns north toward the next stop, the coal-mining town of Leigh Creek. The cloud cover envelops the cockpit and Peter tunes a high-frequency radio to the Flying Doctor channel to find out if there are any messages waiting for him and to check whether any landing strips are out because of the rains.

Just before Leigh Creek the plane breaks out of cloud and flies alongside a spur of the Flinders Ranges that looks like a line of giant supper bowls edge to edge in a drying rack. Leigh Creek comes into view in a pocket of the hills, a small town surrounded by the sinister black scars of open-cut coal-mining. Peter puts the Aero Commander into a descending turn and drops it on to the runway of the neat commercial airport. 'The controllers give me a mark out of ten for each landing,' he says, taxiing in. 'That was seven.'

Inside the terminal the men of air traffic control wear shorts and official shirts in front of a large console. Pilots radio in as they cross the skies of the flight region — now a local flight, now a transoceanic Qantas 747, now a military Caribou. Peter gets weather reports and notices for airmen, exchanges gossip, makes coffee and picks up more mail. Outside, the plane is topped up with fuel and a flock of wedge-tailed eagles spirals above the parked aircraft.

Although I grew up in Australia, most of my 20 years of adult life have been spent in England. Strapped into the right-hand seat of the Aero Commander, I'm now about to experience something that will in some way complete my return to the land of my birth. I'm in the hands of Augusta Airways and Peter Docking, apprehensive but fascinated.

Thirty minutes after it arrived, Flight 001 climbs out north, scattering the eagles. Our largest bird of prey, with wingspans averaging two metres, they pair for life and build their nests in commanding positions from sticks and branches. Why they should flap around airports like huge black pigeons is something for which Peter has no explanation.

Peter Docking is a fair-haired, wiry 28-year-old. He has been a pilot for ten and a half years, holds a senior commercial licence and has six and a half thousand hours' flying time. By rights he should be flying for an airline that takes 747s across the world, but he can't stay away from the outback. 'I enjoy the run, but at times I curse it. Each time I start out it seems a huge task, but once I'm off it opens up. I don't known when I'll ever get away. I'm happy here, there's nothing like it.'

To the right is a huge crater. Inside it are the rocky tiers of a vast blown-out Roman Colosseum. Ahead, great slabs of rocky crust rear out of the desert floor and fold back on themselves. Flight 001 is passing over the oldest geological formations on earth, heading in the direction of one of the hottest places in Australia, a town once called Government Gums and now called Maree.

Nearby is the site of the town of Farina (Latin for flour), named in honour of the local wheat. The problem was no-one ever wanted to live at Farina, and it's still just a name on the map.

Mesas that could have been imported from Death Valley in California slide past the window as the plane descends toward Moolawatana station.

A brace of kangaroos put their heads up as we run along the dirt strip. Peter calls Broken Hill flight control. 'Cancel Sarwatch.' Sarwatch is the search and rescue service that will swing into action if we are ever more than five minutes late reporting in from our destination.

At the end of the strip, Mrs Sheahan, wife of the station manager, is waiting in a four-wheel-drive jeep. 'It means a lot, the mail. We get letters from the children at school, Christmas parcels. Even junk mail. We don't mind that because it keeps us up to date.' In the distance is a hazy blue Mt Babbage. 'Babbage was an explorer with Eyre, but he was so meticulous the others got sick to death of him and sent him off,' Mrs Sheahan laughs. 'He called it Mt Hopeful, but when he got there he called it Mt Hopeless. Now it's named after him.'

Peter asks Mrs Sheahan about dingoes. 'Don't get me wrong, dogs are lovely, but in their place,' she says.

'We caught nine dogs last Christmas and we lost a thousand sheep to them. They've got through the fence and they're breeding in the hills.' Nearby is the dingo fence, the longest fence in the world, over 3,000 kilometres from start to finish. It's an attempt to keep the animals out of southern grazing areas. 'The bounty is $2.50 a scalp, but we'll pay $20.'

Peter lines up the Aero Commander and the howling Lycoming engines push the plane off the rough strip into a milky blue sky. Peter's schedule reads like a litany of the great names in outback mythology. Next is Merty Merty station on the way to the Cooper Basin. Cooper's Creek, known to the old-timers as the Barcoo, stretches across the horizon in the distance.

The plane's course converges on the Strzelecki Track. Dotted around are the microwave repeater towers which carry essential communications for the outback. Long straight lines appear across the landscape as though a cosmic draughtsman has been scribing the earth in drawing exercises. These lines are cut by bulldozers with automatic direction-keeping electronics. The terrain is overlaid with a grid. Explosive charges are set off, and the results are recorded by seismographs. It is the methodology of modern oil and gas exploration and it has led to finds such as the Moomba Gas Field further north.

'There's a welcoming committee of swaggering desperadoes, with moustaches, sunglasses and pointed hats, and Aboriginal stockmen in chaps and waistcoats.'

To the left are the salt plains of Lake Blanche and, nearby, the dregs of Lake Harry where an experiment in growing date palms was frustrated by the desert conditions and by the inability of the palm to fertilise itself without a certain small North African insect.

The Aero Commander Model AC500F that Augusta Airways has chosen for outback flying is perfectly suited to the job. Its high wing conformation means that stones and sticks thrown up from dirt runways are kept away from the propellers. It's a strong plane and the twin 290 hp Lycoming IO 540 engines don't have the uncertain temperament of high-powered turbocharged power plants. The engines, according to Peter, have never failed to bring the plane home.

Peter flies a curved approach to Merty Merty. Drover Malcolm Scott comes out to meet us in his utility. This station is one million hectares, the size of a small European country. In the distance, the iron head of an oil well nods steadily. It is morning and the temperature has risen to over 30°C.

As the desert heats up, the air at 2,000 feet gets a little bumpy. Along the Strzelecki Track, a plume of dust rises from a fast-travelling car.

*In the late afternoon, Captain Peter Docking prepares to
land at an outback sheep station to deliver the mail.*

One of the bleaker vistas available to the air passenger over outback Australia. Pinpoint navigation skills are essential when traversing such harsh and uncompromising country.

Cooper's Creek — discovered by Captain Sturt in 1845 — is approximately 25 kilometres west of Innamincka. The explorer Burke died under a spreading coolabah tree on the banks of the Innamincka water-hole in 1861. Over Innamincka, the plane circles a cluster of tin-roof buildings and glides onto a rough red strip. This is Innamincka station, once the second largest rural property in the world: 4,144 square kilometres in all.

Two Toyota four-wheel-drive utilities are waiting and Peter unloads the bulk of his cargo. Mrs Mary McSporan is the wife of the manager of Innamincka station and they have been there for 18 months. This vast holding is run by six ringers and six boys. A ringer is a qualified stationhand and a boy is a trainee. It takes four years for a boy to become a ringer. Mrs McSporan enjoys the life. 'We even get television via satellite now, although it's just the ABC.'

Ron Duffy manages the hotel at Innamincka and is a little bemused as to why he is there at all. 'I'm in partnership with two friends and we wanted to buy a hotel. We saw this one advertised and someone suggested that we buy it and run it. I didn't even know where it was.' Ron is pleased nevertheless. 'We get Americans, Europeans, Japanese and one weekend we had some Canadians and Dutch. They can see Burke's grave, Aboriginal carvings, we take them camping and there's a good bar at the hotel.' The population of Innamincka? 'Sixteen. No, 17 — one lady has gone off to have a baby and they'll both be back soon,' says Mrs McSporan.

A lattice of creek beds is marked from the air by dark green lines of trees and yellow water as the plane heads toward Durham Downs station. 'The trick here is to actually find Durham,' says Peter, peering into the distance. He finds an old airstrip 'that points right at Durham' and relaxes.

A black and white herd of goats scatters as Flight 001 turns tightly into the huge dirt landing strip. Wayne Degamore is a ringer on this 1,350-square-kilometre station. He looks a romantic figure out of the wild west, wearing a pointed US military hat, a torn blue shirt and brown trousers. He talks about the rapidly receding wet. Wayne's accent is a soft burr, a hair's breadth away from an English west country accent.

Back in the air, Peter tells the next station, Arrabury, to expect us in 15 minutes. The country is now flat, with red ridges of sand like great healed wounds. A grass fire, started by lightning, which swept across the land two years previously shows its traces in a light green sweep of regenerated growth.

On the ground at Arrabury, the temperature in the early afternoon is around 36°C and rising. There's a welcoming committee of swaggering desperadoes, with moustaches, sunglasses and pointed hats, and Aboriginal stockmen in chaps and waistcoats. Peter tells them that one of their two landing strips has been closed by the Department of Aviation because the sand is a bit soft. 'That inspector said nothing to us when he was here. No point in grading the bloody strip; it just stirs up the surface and the sand's back soon enough,' says Bob, the senior stockman.

With vegetables safely delivered to the Arrabury posse, the plane leaps into the air heading for Birdsville at 6,500 feet. In the distance, the Diamantina shows itself, the river that passes through Birdsville.

Here the animals of the desert have adapted to survive the blistering hot summer days and the harsh winter nights. Some of the oldest species on earth live near Birdsville: monotremes, like the ant-eating, egg-laying echidna; planigales, minute insect-eating marsupials with flat heads; and dunnarts, mouse-sized, sharp-nosed insectivorious marsupials. Kangaroos include the red kangaroo, whose adult male stands as high as a man, the western grey kangaroo and the euro kangaroo. There are rodents such as the pseudo mouse and the wonderful hopping mouse. Hopping mice walk on all fours when moving slowly, but when in a hurry they hop on hind legs like tiny kangaroos.

Peter flies a full circle above the houses of Birdsville 'to alert the policeman so he'll come out and meet us'.

Birdsville has a substantial airport with a sealed runway for big jets. The terminal is a standard-issue outback public shed. People are waiting. Angus and Anne Marie McDonnell are nurses running the town's small cottage hospital. In their soft-spoken, dedicated way they talk about their regular clinical rounds which extend 5,000 kilometres by road. The hospital has two beds and two cots and sees mainly general complaints and road accidents.

Richard Stein is a relieving policeman. 'This is a quiet town, no trouble here. My main job is to win back the hotel for the publican when he looks like losing it at pool.'

David Agiss is the publican of the famous Birdsville Hotel. Behind the hotel is a string of cosy new rooms.

On the first Friday and Saturday in September, the Birdsville Races are held. 'This town of 150 has a weekend population of 5,000. People camp everywhere. There are 200 planes at the airport, with people sleeping under the wings,' says David. 'And the police population rises to 30,' adds Richard.

Peter Bailey is the town's schoolteacher. He also has a part-time job pumping gas for Augusta Airways. The 21 pupils of all grades in his one-room school include quite a few Afghani children, descendants of the Afghans who came to the centre of Australia to run the camel trains. 'They are a typical bunch of kids, and I'm proud of them one day and spit chips the next. I volunteered to come here for one year and after the year I couldn't bear to leave. It was a moment of madness. I think we're all like that — once we're here, we can't leave.'

Peter Barnes is the town mechanic. His utility is parked by the terminal. It has a sign on the back, 'Peter Barnes Motor Vehicle Repairs: we may be rough, but at least we're expensive.'

Wedge-tailed eagles circle when half an hour later the plane takes off, on the last leg of the day, for Boulia. Peter takes out a magazine and reads. The channel country is covered with delta formations made up of creek beds lined with growth. As the route penetrates higher into Queensland, the climate gets wetter and the colours of the surface become greener.

The local agent, Brian Whittaker, meets the flight at Boulia Airport and takes us to the Australian Hotel. Out here, everyone wants to shake a visitor's hand and the men of the outback apply very powerful grips.

Brian has a charter plane service called Diamantina Aviation. Years of flying in the hot sun have given him a laconic manner and a protective squint. 'How is it down in funnyland?' he asks Peter.

In the main street of Boulia is a sign which says, 'For the next 120 kilometres towards Winton you are in the land of the Min Min light. This unsolved modern mystery is a light that at times follows travellers for long distances. It has been approached but never identified. Erected by Boulia Shire Council in the interests of tourism.'

Overnight accommodation at Boulia is basic. Four motel rooms come in fibro packages with a dining-room that is attached to a hotel that serves amiable conversation, cool beer and hearty food, all maintained and run by the local council.

Next morning, driving to the airport, there's another sign above a lump of wood. It says, 'This is the red stump. It marks the fact that if you go any further out you will come out the other side. To the west of Boulia is the vast Simpson Desert. Travellers are advised to carry ample food, water and fuel.'

By the airport, a sculptor has erected a fibreglass ball on a tower surrounded by ultraviolet lights. It looks extraterrestrial, but it's actually a tribute to the Min Min light.

Sunday morning, the plane is surrounded by small trees and shrubs. Peter is to take the beginnings of a nursery to a market gardener in Birdsville. Peter and Brian load the plane and check the engines for the cheeping of small birds. Overnight cobwebs cover the propellers.

Flight 002, now a flying greenhouse, doglegs back to Birdsville, calling in at Sandringham station. The land is a marbled red ochre and green lining the margin of the Simpson Desert. Sand ridges like wormsign on the planet Dune run north and south providing navigational clues.

At Bedourie, Mrs Jean Smith is the postmistress and landlady of the pub. She brings out on her shoulders a heavy sack of mail. 'I like tourists if they don't treat us like animals in the zoo. You can't stop some of them stickybeaking. They go through doors marked private, upset my cocky, annoy the dogs and get the chooks worried.'

There's a passenger for the plane, Derek, a 16-year-old returning to school at Port Augusta. He climbs gingerly into the second row, nursing a mass of plastic bags.

At Glengyle station, Mrs Diane Clark, wife of the manager, is waiting, 'There's a demarcation line between sheep people and cattle people. This station is all cattle,' she says proudly.

Back in Birdsville, an anxious nurseryman unloads a lot of drooping plants and there is time for lunch in the hotel. Inside, a party of ladies at one end of the bar eat a sponge cake. The barman wears a hat, two Aborigines at the bar wear hats, a retired cattleman wears an ancient hat. This is very serious country indeed.

Behind the bar is a great stack of beer coolers, polystyrene jackets that keep a bottle or can of beer cool while you drink it. It's so hot that anything out of the refrigerator warms up fast. Each cooler has the name of the owner written on it. You could guess the town's population by counting the beer coolers.

David Agiss and Peter Bailey have a complaint they want taken to the city. 'We've got one single telephone line out of Birdsville and that's a radio line. Boulia is on the automatic exchange, but only one person at a time can talk here. Why can't we have a proper phone service?'

Peter lines up for take-off and cockatoos covering the trees along the Diamantina screech. The course is now down the Birdsville Track. On the left will be Sturt's Stony Desert, a great red wasteland covered with small, hard shiny stones called gibbers. The plane lands at station after station whose runways are paved with gibbers. They are marvellous to pick up and hold, and wonderful souvenirs.

On the right of the flight path is the Simpson Desert, extending across half of Australia. Crossing the Diamantina, flocks of pelicans float by in the distance.

More stations follow: Pandie Pandie, Alton Downs, Clifton Hills. If a strip is deserted, there is always a mailbox with mail bags inside. The boxes are an art form in their own right — some are disused refrigerators, others are old oil drums in a forked stump.

At Cowarie station, Mrs Oldfield lives with her three sons on a station of 650 square kilometres. 'We're outside the dog fence, so we only have cattle. We're just recovering from a grasshopper plague.' As we take off, insects bombard the windscreen.

Landing at Mungerannie, a kangaroo charges toward the plane and veers off at the last minute. Ten minutes earlier Derek had thrown up. 'Was up a bit late last night,' he apologises. Peter has seen it all before. 'Don't worry, I've got just the thing.' Peter cleans up and Derek gets a pill and falls asleep.

Two station hands carry the mail bags back to the terminal

'The barman wears a hat, two Aborigines at the bar wear hats, a retired cattleman wears an ancient hat. This is very serious country indeed.'

At Mulka station, Mrs Overton orders flowers from Peter. Next Sunday is Mother's Day and she is having a gathering of friends, so Peter will fly in fresh flowers from Adelaide. Her children proudly demonstrate the station's thermal exchange power station, driven by hot bore water. It's the first in the country.

Etadunna (pronounced eathadinner) station is one of the great cattle stations, and the people who live in them are part of a small number of outback dynasties with names such as Scobie, Clark, Morton, Oldfield and Crombie.

Twenty-three landings after Flight 001 left on Saturday morning, we approach Port Augusta in the dark. Peter keys a sequence on the airport frequency. The runway lights blaze in the distance and the plane drifts in across the bay at 6.40 pm on Sunday evening.

Thirty-four hours after that first departure, I knew that things would never seem the same again. Astonishingly, in that short time I had been in direct contact with a huge cross-section of Australia. I now understood something about my land and its people that moved me and left me exultant. I was truly home.

The cat is waiting for its evening meal and is relieved to see the plane again. Peter starts cleaning the fuselage, rubbing off oil and dirt from where commuters might brush their suited shoulders.

Tomorrow, Captain Peter Docking will take them to Adelaide.

Andrew Fisher was one of a generation of Australians who went to live in London in the 60s. He returned to live in Sydney in 1984 where he now edits and writes and contributes to travel books and magazines.

The Coral Empire, Earth's Greatest Reef

Wendy Richards

**The Great Barrier Reef is the world's largest living structure
with more varieties of life per square inch than are found in
any other living system. A first encounter with it assaults the
senses. Active profusion, intense colour and vigorous life
abound no matter how closely the reef and its inhabitants
are scrutinised.**

The barrier it makes is not a single wall. It stretches along 2,300 kilometres of the Queensland continental shelf and is composed of over 2,100 individual reefs, each with its particular character and form. Some are massive structures stretching over tens of square kilometres; others rise like pinnacles from the ocean depths and can be swum around in minutes.

The reef is young as reefs go, a mere two million years old, little enough when the world's first reefs appeared 450 million years ago. It began to form when the sea was about 100 metres below its present level. At that time, you could walk to the edge of the continental shelf amongst scattered hills and mountains, but as the land subsided, or an ice age passed, the sea began to rise and the mountains were drowned. Because Queensland's coast was in warm latitudes, corals settled and grew on the firm, newly submerged hilltops. They could make no home on the sand and mud between because they were smothered by sediment. The sea continued to rise. Corals kept growing towards the surface on the skeletons of old corals, making the reefs we see today. They are a true reflection of the early continental shelf.

The sea has risen and fallen many times in the last two million years. When it fell low, during the ice ages for example, the entire reef was left high and dry and eroded away for thousands of years at a time. During the subsequent rise, corals recolonised old reef structures, building new reefs on the old. As recently as 15,000 years ago, the continental shelf was dry and only in the last 8,000 years has the extravagant beauty we see in the reefs today emerged.

Although the whole reef system was formed simultaneously, there is great variation in reef types from south to north, reflecting the original terrain. On the southern limits of the reef (east of Gladstone), known as the Capricorn-Bunker group, are roughly circular platform reefs, often with sand cays sitting on top of their shallow reef flats. The well-known resort of Heron Island is one example. These reefs lie fairly close to the coast, often surrounded by beautiful clear water because of the prevailing currents and their proximity to deep ocean waters.

In the central section of the reef, the continental shelf widens and the sea is not quite so deep. The reefs lie generally more than 160 kilometres from the coast and because of this inaccessibility, they are not regularly visited. These huge platform reefs, known as the Swains-Pompey complex, have been greatly eroded during past low sea levels to form spectacular caves, 'blue holes' and channels.

Lying closer to the coast on this central section are several groups of spectacular and easily accessible islands of which the Whitsundays are the best known. Called continental islands, they are hilltops and mountains of mainland rock rather than cays of fine coral sand. Coral reefs grow round their submerged edges, but because of their proximity to the coast water visibility is often reduced and coral diversity is not as high as on the outlying reefs.

Between Townsville and Cairns, the shelf narrows and isolated platform reefs lie scattered from 50 to 160 kilometres from shore. North from Cairns, the shelf narrows even more and its outer edge is bordered by special reefs known as 'Ribbons'. These reefs first grew along the continental shelf edge and retained their linear shape as their seaward growth was restricted by the plumetting depths of the Coral Sea Trench. There is very little influence from land-based sediments here and the sea is reliably clear since the ocean waters that bathe these reef oases are remarkably sterile and desert-like.

Extraordinary as the wall of reefs may be, the tiny corals which make them are more so. These reef builders, whose skeletons accumulating over millions of years have created this great living structure, produce an environment which supports more diversity of species than even the moist tropical rainforests of Queensland's coast. Yet their hard or stony corals are very simple animals, only 1-10 millimetres across, consisting of a mouth and stomach surrounded by a ring of stinging tentacles. This soft part of the coral, called the polyp, is housed in its own limestone cup into which the tentacles can be withdrawn in daylight or when danger threatens at night.

Most of the corals grow as colonies in which a single polyp buds off clones of itself, each with its own limestone cup connected to others in the colony. The huge variety of coral shapes — staghorns, plates, brains, honeycombs and cabbages among others — are all the result of the way in which these polyps arrange themselves in a colony.

The corals' greatest secret, however, in fact the reason behind their enormous success, lies in their relationship with tiny plants called *zooxanthellae*. Reefs, like rainforests, are very productive ecosystems. On land, an abundance of plantlife, using the sun's energy to make food, feeds the many forest animals. On a coral reef, equally abundant but microscopic plants live inside the translucent coral tissues. These single-celled plants — *zooxanthellae* — absorb the sun's energy to make food which they leak back directly to their coral host. In fact, the coral receives 95% of the food these plants make, and in return, the *zooxanthellae* receive protection and are fertilised by the coral's waste products. As landlords go, the coral is doing well.

The *zooxanthellae's* contribution doesn't stop there, however. They also greatly increase the rate at which the coral's skeleton can form. Altogether, this neat arrangement allows corals to grow around ten times faster than they could on their own. It also explains why reefs only grow in warm waters less than 30 metres deep where enough light penetrates to keep these plants alive.

Even in death, corals depend on plants to help cement their reef-building work. As soon as these hard corals die and their skeletons become bleached and white, cementing algae bind them together like mortar, securing the colony and building up the reef.

Although corals may be the foundation of reef life, they are by no means its limit. Once present, they provide homes and food for the countless other organisms that cohabit on a coral reef. In daylight hours, the reef vibrates with the hues, stripes and shimmerings of innumerable fish — 1,600 species in all — breathtaking and even confusing in their variety.

Juveniles of one species grow up to wear completely different colours as adults, and males may have no resemblance to their corresponding females. All this makes for a kaleidoscope of contradiction, but not without purpose. The fish have colour vision, and in the crowd of reef inhabitants they wave their colours like an identification badge so that no mistakes are made in territorial disputes or breeding. Some use colour combinations to indicate that they taste bad (a combination of yellow, black and white is one example). Others use disruptive patterns to break up their body shape and deceive predators.

At dusk, a dramatic change occurs as long sinister shadows pervade the twilight sea. The familiar, brightly coloured fish of the day move down amongst the coral branches where their colours fade to avoid detection as they sleep. Under cover of darkness, the beautiful cowries, volutes and cones, starfish, urchins, worms, shrimps and crabs emerge from their daytime hiding places. Many of them graze on the algal turf, but some hunt with the deadly efficiency required for survival.

It is at night, too, that the delicate coral polyps with their ring of stinging tentacles emerge from their protective limestone cups to form a sea of waiting mouths. Not only is there an absence of fish predators, but the transparent waters of daylight have been transformed into a soup of minute darting shrimps, worms and other planktonic creatures. Should one of these hapless animals touch the tentacle of a coral polyp, it will be harpooned with a tiny poison dart and then passed by the tentacles to the central mouth. The coral, by day a passive feeder on the *zooxanthellae*, becomes a ruthless carnivore at night.

In the relentless struggle to survive and breed amongst such a huge crowd of reef inhabitants, many

'Reproduction in reef animals is an extravagant but often confusing affair.'

These colourful daytime fish consume a variety of foods. Some are quite specific in their requirements and others are opportunists. The beautiful butterfly fish feeds on coral polyps and the mucous they secrete as well as other encrusting organisms. Beaked parrot fish scrape the living coral to obtain algae and other organic matter and excrete the crushed coral skeleton as a fine sediment. Large schools of grazing surgeon fish forage like ambling cows for the fine turf algae that grows on the dead coral surfaces, and always the larger predators such as coral trout haunt the shadows ready to pounce on unwary stragglers.

Because there are so many fish searching for food by day, it is not surprising that the slow-moving, soft-bodied animals have strong defences to protect them. The sea cucumbers, sometimes called *bêche-de-mer*, that lie about the reef by day contain fish poisons in their skins. These save them from fish, but not from man. Man has taken a liking to these creatures, believing them to be an aphrodisiac. He has found that boiling neutralises the poisons, so that they can be eaten.

Invertebrates, such as the beautiful Christmas tree worm and burrowing clams, build their homes within the coral, and speedily withdraw inside when threatened. The gaudy nudibranchs absorb poisons from the sponges and ascidians on which they feed, and advertise this fact with their brilliant colours. Many invertebrates simply don't show themselves by day when there is extra risk of being eaten.

species have evolved special relationships with others. The coral and the *zooxanthellae* have the most important bond, but a better-known example is that between sea anemones and the small fish who swim amongst their tentacles. These cheeky little anemone fish will stare you squarely in the face until you pass your hand as if to grab them. Suddenly, they snuggle down amongst the tentacles, knowing that no predator will follow. They achieve immunity by gradually coating their skin with the mucous on the anemones' tentacles, thus preventing the tentacles from firing their poisonous barbs. Anemone fish also probably protect the tentacles from larger fish wanting a free meal.

One of the reef's most enthralling experiences is observing the little cleaner wrasse serving his fellow fish. With the help of a few brethren, he sets up a kind of doctor's surgery or cleaning station near a prominent coral outcrop where other fish regularly wait their turn for his vivacious attention. The cleaner removes parasites, fungal growths and dead skin, thereby obtaining a meal for himself and keeping his host healthy. He is never eaten by the fish he cleans because evolution has shown that cleaners are essential to the survival of most fish species.

Reproduction in reef animals is an extravagant but often confusing affair. Most release millions of eggs or sperm directly into the water and let them take their chances as they come. Although corals commonly bud once a year to reproduce themselves, they do it in just this way. Indeed, the most spectacular event on

'A single visit to the reef is enough to make even the most casual observer aware of the need to conserve its rich beauty.'

the yearly calendar of a coral reef is the night of sexual reproduction of the corals. Usually on the fourth or fifth night after the full moon in early spring, about one hour after dark, most of the hard corals on the reef spawn simultaneously. A diver can be immersed in the liquid blackness of reef waters, with only the night plankton buzzing around like annoying flies, when suddenly the corals begin to erupt. The water becomes clouded with tiny pink egg bundles and milky sperm as each coral mouth ejects its own contribution to this great orgy. Within minutes, the water surface is thick and stinking with this vast reproductive effort. The tiny larva produced from fertilisation floats in the sea for up to a month, after which it sinks to the bottom, secreting its own limestone cup and cementing itself to the reef surface. Now, the process of budding will produce asexually a new coral colony.

Sex in the reef fish is not such a simple affair. For a start, most change sex as they mature. Take the bicolour angel fish. It lives in a family group of from four to seven, with just one dominant male, the remainder being females. The male constantly patrols his territory and prevents any of his harem from being stolen by neighbouring males. Should he die, however (or be removed by a cunning scientist), the largest remaining female will begin to take over his role within a few hours of his removal. In only a few days, her tissues will have changed to male and 'she' can breed with the remaining females in the group. What sexual deviates these reef fish are!

A single visit to the reef is enough to make even the most casual observer aware of the need to conserve its rich beauty. In 1983, the Great Barrier Reef became the world's largest marine park. It is controlled by an Australian government-funded body called the Great Barrier Reef Marine Park Authority. Its major role has been to divide the individual reefs into zones which allow various categories of activities from commercial fishing, shell collecting, leisure fishing, boating and snorkelling to scientific research and total preservation. This means that all reasonable uses of the reef's resources can be accommodated without destroying our natural heritage through overuse.

There have been many debates in the past over threats to the reef. Oil was once seen as a resource it might provide, but drilling has now been banned forever. Sometimes changes in the reef have been blamed on man's intrusion into the environment. Over the last 20 years, there has been a rising tide of documentation and debate on the crown of thorns starfish. This carnivore drapes its stomach over living coral and digests it externally, leaving only the

MICK TURNER

Divers swim through the spectacular Piccaninny Ponds at Mount Gambier, South Australia

bleached white skeleton behind. Aggregations of these starfish can be very destructive to specific reefs.

As yet, there is insufficient evidence to indicate whether these plagues are caused by man. It has been suggested that an increased flow of fertilisers from agricultural runoff into the seas has increased phytoplankton production, thereby providing more food for the juvenile starfish and increasing their survival rate.

The varied formation of the Great Barrier Reef plays host to a
complex ecology of life forms, and in total, is the world's
largest living organism.

The reef contains hundreds of islands, lush tropical paradises of all sizes, many of them isolated and uninhabited by man.

PAT MANLY

A diver pauses to stroke a giant potato cod.

Without doubt, man has been responsible for some unfavourable changes in the reef environment. Agricultural activity along the adjacent coast has increased the sediment and nutrient load of rivers. Trawling for prawns on soft bottoms around inshore reefs has resulted in physical and ecological destabilisation of these communities. These two factors together have resulted in increased siltation of many inshore reefs, with a subsequent decline in hard corals

and an increase in soft corals and algae.

Although the reef's creatures exist in a finely balanced equilibrium with each other and their environment, change has always been a natural part of the reef's existence. For example, widespread 'bleaching' of corals in some years could be associated with lowered sea levels caused by worldwide climatic events. Seasonal increases in algal growth are probably associated with higher water temperatures and nutrient levels. Cyclones can do a tremendous amount of damage; the energy produced by such natural efforts could never be matched by man's puny attempts at destruction. If you consider that only 15,000 years ago every reef we see today was left high and dry, you will realise that these dynamic reef systems are capable of incredible growth and repair. Even as little as 15 years after being ravaged by crown of thorns starfish, a reef can establish a very high coral cover.

Research has an important role to play in helping us answer the management problems posed by such questions. In Townsville, there are two major centres for tropical marine research. James Cook University has become prominent in coral reef fauna studies, while the Australian Institute of Marine Science examines the overall ecology of the reef.

Education is another essential investment in the reef's future. Reef Biosearch is a unique organisation built on the three-point foundation of tourism, education and research. Some of the group of eight marine biologists visit one of the northern outer reefs daily to

An aerial view of Hook and Hardy reefs - part of the necklace of reefs that make up the Great Barrier Reef

A chartered adventu

Superlatives. That's what the Whitsundays is all about. It is home to our best-known resorts. There are islands everywhere you look. It's in the tropics, and the unbelievably blue water teems with exotic marine life.

Technically, there is no such place as the Whitsundays. It is an amalgamation of the Cumberland and Sir James Smith groups of islands and the Anchor and Repulse islands. Today, all 74 islands are collectively known as the Whitsundays. This name is derived from the Whitsunday Passage, the shipping channel which runs through the middle of them, named by James Cook R.N. on his epic voyage of discovery in 1770.

Quite apart from the area's incredible beauty, it is also a dream for trivia buffs. There is the wreck of a supposed Spanish galleon, said to have met its fate a couple of centuries before Cook's arrival. Cannibalistic Aborigines once inhabited the islands and did unspeakable things to early explorers. During the Second World War, the entire US Pacific Fleet anchored unobserved by the enemy in one of the deepwater inlets. But what caught our imagination was a remark made by David Gemmell from one of the local yacht charter companies. Dave produced a map of the area and marked an 'X' just off one of the islands. 'Check that out. It's the Australian headquarters of the CIA.'

Six of us were about to take off for a week's cruising in the Whitsundays using a chartered bareboat for accommodation, something none of us had done before. The term 'bareboat' means that you supply the crew. Apart from that, your boat will be anything but bare.

All the charter companies in the Whitsundays are totally professional and greet you on arrival with that legendary North Queensland hospitality. You are given a complete briefing on the area before you board your boat. A company boathandler then gives you a hands-on run through of its operation, just cruising around until you are totally at ease. For an extra charge, he will come along for a day or so if you are really rusty and, if you prefer, he will skipper the entire charter. The extra cost involved in doing this can be worth every cent because these locals know the area intimately. All boats have two-way radios, as do the island resorts and the charter companies' mainland bases. The latter are on standby 24 hours a day and can reach any charter boat in the Whitsundays very quickly. All good reassuring stuff when it's your first time.

Naturally on your charter you'll need to eat and will probably partake of the odd cleansing ale. For inbound tourists, partaking of the cleansing ale is a great Australian tradition and the Whitsundays is one of the best places you'll find to practise it. But be warned. As with your food, leave its purchase to your charter company. Tell them what you require and everything will be waiting on board ready for your departure. The

FOLIO

show visitors what makes the Great Barrier Reef worth preserving. This 'hands on' guided naturalist tour is a way of sharing some of the reef's wonderful secrets. The research programme puts something back into the reef directly by monitoring the short- and long-term changes that occur by recording population fluctuations in about 60 species of fish.

The future of the reef looks very bright. We have entered an age where natural resources and their conservation have a high priority. More importantly, with affluence and ease of travel, more people can see first hand just how remarkable this reef system is. Tourism is the greatest impetus to reef conservation that has ever occurred because it makes the reef economically important and motivates government and industry to devote funds to its preservation.

Wendy Richards, a marine biologist, operates Reef Biosearch aboard Quicksilver Connections from Port Douglas, North Queensland. She has spent the last 15 years in the area observing the Great Barrier Reef.

the Whitsundays

cost will be around supermarket and hotel prices and the quality of provisions is first class. Be warned? Yes. There are no corner stores in the Whitsundays. Should your thirst get the best of your supplies and you choose to purchase takeaway alcohol from an island resort, your credit card could suffer meltdown.

Now to our yacht. We'd chosen a Ben Lexcen-designed Whitsunday 42, which is the most popular among sailors in the area. It has three double cabins, two toilets, a saloon big enough to hold a party in, and some real magic when it comes to performance. All up, there are about 120 bareboats for charter in the Whitsundays, both sail and motor cruiser. The price varies, but when split between a group, it is excellent value. Our cruise was a magical experience. Turtles, dolphins, oysters, coral gardens, deserted beaches, island resorts, spectacular scenery — an experience that none of us will ever forget.

The attractions are endless, and to really see everything takes much longer than a week. This is nature's Theme Park, and unlike the man-made variety it is ever-changing.

Nara Inlet, for example, on the southern side of Hook Island, is a magnificent anchorage. Like a fjord, it is surrounded by mountains which plunge straight into the sea. But there is more to Nara Inlet than just its natural beauty. In the upper reaches, there is graffiti on the rock walls. Now there are two schools of thought surrounding graffiti. One holds that it is vandalism;

the other holds that it is of historical significance. Nara has both. Visiting sailors have for years been leaving their mark, and while the more recent notations are frowned upon, those left by the US sailors during the Second World War are not. Up on the mountains, in the caves where Aborigines once lived, are much earlier examples. Art? Graffiti? History? Vandalism? That's for the individual to decide.

Whitehaven Beach, on the eastern side of Whitsunday Island, is another example — a stunning geological freak. It's sand is pure white silica, a leftover from millenniums past. And it's a great place for barbecues though they tend to attract scavengers — ants if you're in the bush, seagulls if you're near the water. Our barbecue on Whitehaven was different: it attracted goannas. Chewing on a chop while four big lizards, each measuring a good two metres in length, are greedily eyeing it is an unusual experience. But while they look menacing, they're not. A barbecue is for sharing, which is what we did.

And yes, we did check out the CIA's headquarters. It's a brain coral of unbelievable dimension — umpteen billion tiny polyps going about their day-to-day life while fish of kaleidoscopic colours dart around it in water that from above looks so blue that it is unnatural. Unless, of course, you are cruising through the Whitsundays.

John McNally

Outback Australia, the Permanent Frontier

Christopher Leonard

**Flying westward from the coast, the naked red earth appears
through the tufts of vegetation below. This is the Australia
that lurks far beyond the east coast's Great Dividing Range,
the Australia that may never fundamentally change — the
permanent frontier.**

ALLAN MOULT

This was the image of Australians created by bush balladeers and film crews. The women of the outback were sun-scorched, its men were wiry, and everyone spoke at a quarter of the pace of city folk.

'Not true!' countered 90% of Australians with an embarrassed moan. 'We're not like that! We're not all "g'day, mate" and "where's ya billy?" '

However, things have changed. Now, the bush hat, the stockman's raincoat called a 'dry-as-a-bone' and elastic-sided riding boots are all the rage. This image is at least recognisably our own.

I set out to discover again what I already knew: Australia is inventing its own image, just as America manufactured the cowboy from the real thing. The truth is that 80% of Australians (a conservative estimate) have never sat on a horse, and the nearest they've been to a kangaroo, koala or wombat is in one of the metropolitan zoos.

Various towns claim to be the gateway to the outback, and it is true that its boundaries are not clearly defined. It stretches westward beyond the foothills of the Great Dividing Range across the rest of the continent. Its edge can be taken as a slow arc that begins in the Flinders Ranges, north of Adelaide, then curves up through New South Wales along the Darling River, and then up through Queensland by way of Charleville, Longreach and Winton to the Gulf of Carpentaria.

Our re-exploration of the outback began at the town of Charleville in south-western Queensland and passed north-westward through land that is full of childhood images derived from the verses of A. B. 'Banjo' Paterson. It was in this area that Paterson wrote the words for what is now Australia's most popular national song, 'Waltzing Matilda'. It is also the region he was thinking of when he wrote of the letter he had sent to his friend, Clancy of the Overflow. The reply he received looked as if it had been 'written with a thumb-nail dipped in tar', and said that Clancy had gone to Queensland droving.

> *And the bush has friends to meet him, and their*
> *kindly voices greet him*
> *In the murmur of the breezes and the river on*
> *its bars,*
> *And he sees the vision splendid of the sunlit*
> *plains extended*
> *And at night the wondrous glory of the*
> *everlasting stars.*

Paterson goes on to contrast his 'dingy little office' and the 'weedy' townsfolk with the healthy, robust life in the bush, and concludes by saying, 'I somehow rather fancy that I'd like to change with Clancy'. This sentiment still draws young men and women to work on the stations of the outback, and it is not all that surprising that many jackaroos and stockmen were born and raised in the cities.

On an Anzac Day evening in a pub called the 'Clancy of the Overflow' at Isisford, I heard a Queensland's ex-Agent General to London whipping up a table of outback landed gentry into a fury of applause when he said that the people of the outback have the sort of friendships that city people wouldn't know about. He went on in this vein to the adoring gaze of middle-aged wives, while the husbands tossed back a few more tumblers of whatever their poison may have been. At the end of this speech, someone slurred, 'That was good, Wally. Just the same as last year.' Ah, irony is sweet, and it prevented us from hurling the remains of our steak and chips in his direction.

View past an outcrop to the Bungle Bungle Ranges

The necessity for mutual support in the outback has led to the development of some remarkable institutions. One is the Royal Flying Doctor Service and the other is the School of the Air. The Royal Flying Doctor Service was established at Cloncurry in 1928 by Rev. John Flynn of the Australian Inland Mission. In Queensland alone it serves over 33,000 patients. The School of the Air uses the radio to educate children in the outback. They use the radio to speak to their teacher and to each other, and lesson notes are provided for use between radio sessions.

Because of the importance of air transport in these parts, it is not surprising that the Queensland and Northern Territory Aerial Service, now known more succinctly as QANTAS, was established in Longreach in 1921. In its first days it had only to cope with galahs on the runway and goats chewing the planes. They must seem like halcyon days when compared with the problems of running a major airline today.

Coming from the city, Charleville — our first outback town — was a bit of a shock. It was like suddenly applying the brakes in a fast-moving car. I regaled myself in an Akubra hat and elastic-sided boots, and turned my mind to what lay ahead. Here we saw thousands of sheep being loaded into huge road-trains where once the railway would have taken them to their destination. And before the railway, it would have taken weeks on horseback to reach the coast. We sat in a pub, with the television chattering about the arts in Sydney, while some drunken soldiers told us we'd have to stay out here for years before we could really know it. More like a lifetime.

It was here that Judy Moody reminded us of the danger of wildlife and stock on the roads. Early one morning as she was heading off for Brisbane, a kangaroo leapt in front of the car, jumped through the windscreen, and sat dazed on her lap. She was just as dazed as the kangaroo. They sat there looking at each other calmly while wound in each other's arms as if they were long-lost relatives.

Then began the first leg of a long drive of 1,200 kilometres that was to take us north to Mt Isa. We passed through tough mulga scrub with the ubiquitous eucalyptus and a variety of scraggly native pines and through towns with magic names like Augathella until we reached Blackall with its bottle trees and water that rises hot from the ground. On the night we arrived, there was the smell of an overflowing septic tank in the air. I didn't like to comment until I was told that it was the smell given off by the gidgee tree when it is about to rain. Sure enough, that night it rained.

Blackall is where the original Black Stump once stood. 'The Black Stump' has passed into the Australian vernacular to mean the edge of civilisation. Though the stump has long since disappeared (it was used by early surveyors), you soon realise the accuracy of the term: there is no other town of any size west for nearly 1,600 kilometres.

Stockmen and others who profess to know the outback rattle off town names like a litany. It becomes a way of testifying to your knowledge of the outback. You can often hold a conversation simply by reciting such names as Augathella, Windorah, Longreach, Kynuna and Julia Creek. Of course, it helps if you've had a couple of rounds of amber liquid to begin with.

Every town, no matter how small, has at least one pub. The more important the town, the more pubs line its main street. And they are about as unchanged as the towns. In many cases, they are the largest buildings in town, with a veranda on the first floor where the bedrooms are. The veranda used to serve another purpose beside providing shade: in towns such as Winton it is still possible to see numbers on the pub's veranda allocating sleep-out positions.

It is in the pubs, which are still the domain of men, that one hears the stories of the district. In this area you won't find signs saying 'Women welcome', as I saw in the Snowy Mountains tourist town of Jindabyne. In many things, change comes slowly to the outback. In spite of the arrival of television, the good yarn is still valued. Here is one I heard in the pub shown in the

Wild horses (known as "brumbies") thresh their way through a shallow pool (called a "billabong" in Australia) to escape a pursuing helicopter

legendary *Crocodile Dundee*. Helicopters had been in the area laying down satellite communications dishes. These helicopters have large scoops attached to their front. Someone spotted one of these helicopters and called the police, saying that there were some pretty clever sheep duffers working the area. The police rushed the landing place. With guns drawn, they surrounded the helicopters and demanded of the non-plussed Telecom workers the whereabouts of the stolen sheep.

The stealing of stock is not unknown. After all, a careless poacher was among the characters celebrated in 'Waltzing Matilda'. Most Australians are unaware that the story of the swagman has its foundation in the 1895 Shearers' Strike. A swagman is

an intinerant worker who takes his name from his swag, the rolled blanket which contains his few personal belongings. In 1895 there was a shearers' strike and talk of proclaiming an independent republic in this part of Queensland. It is the unrest and conflict between the bosses and the workers that is reflected in the song. A little way west of the tiny town of Kynuna is the Combo Waterhole which is said to be the site of the original billabong where the unfortunate swagman was supposed to have drowned himself.

You can still hear versions of the well-known stories in the pubs if you ask the right garrulous character. Few stories can match the one about Harry Redford who drove some cattle 1,500 kilometres over unmapped territory. The feat was all the more noteworthy because the cattle were stolen. Harry Redford was also known as Captain Starlight, whose story has been fictionalised in the novel *Robbery under Arms*. And there are stories of fierce shearing competitions and incredible numbers of sheep being shorn in one day. Jackie Howe, the king of shearers, held the record until quite recently with 365.

The bravery (or foolhardiness) of the men and women who settled this area is still remarkable. They learned quickly the signs of the bush which could help them find their way through this vast land. White ants, for instance, construct their huge anthills so that they lean to the west. This keeps their cities as cool as possible.

Recognition of the stockman as a prototypical Australian character has been paid in the building of the Stockman's Hall of Fame, a few kilometres south of Longreach. At the cost of $12.5 million, the museum displays the stockman's bush crafts, such as plaiting leather, as well as informing the public of his knowledge of the bush. Stockmen knew the land well enough, for example, to pull the spiky spinifex from the ground, turn it over, and make a mattress of it.

The stockman and his feats on the old stock routes are being celebrated in the Bicentennial year with an event called Droving Australia. A cattle drive of 1,200 cattle will leave Newcastle Waters in the Northern Territory in May 1988 and arrive some four months and 2,000 kilometres later at Longreach. There will also be 16 Drovers' Camps for 15-18 year olds in the Northern Territory. Each camp will cover about 200 kilometres and will follow the old stock routes. Horsemanship is still tested each year with a 250-kilometre race from Winton to Longreach. It is sometimes covered in as little as 13 hours.

The arrival of the white man in the outback was quickly followed by that of the Chinese, few of whom are still to be seen except in the Chinese restaurants to be found in many country towns — often the only place a visitor can get a meal outside the pubs. Willy Mar has lived in Winton since he arrived as a young man one day out of the blue from Hong Kong to help his father. He lives in a corrugated-iron house next to a corrugated-iron shed from which he sells fruit and vegetables. He has no electricity, and although he is well liked, his contact with the locals is minimal for he still speaks little English. He is one of the last of the Chinese cooks and greengrocers who were once to be found throughout the outback.

There is also little sign of the Afghans who were brought to Australia with their camels to travel through otherwise impassable territory. Wild camels can still be seen, and there are now a number of camel farms which breed them, reputedly for export back to the Middle East.

Technology has caught up with this part of the outback and mustering these days is done on

ALLAN MOULT

motorbikes or even with helicopters. Stations that once used many stockmen now use very few. May Downs, a property of 2,600 square kilometres not far from Mt Isa, is largely run by the friendly young couple, James and Marjory Lord, who own it. More than in most places, the horse is still king at May Downs.

The place has been a station for only 16 years; before that it was just wild territory with only a few wild horses and stray cattle. Even now it's on the frontier — the edge of the workable land. I rediscovered my old love of horses as I watched James round up a herd and saw them come with a beat of hooves and a plume of red dust into the yards. It was here also as we sat in the late afternoon and looked at the plains and the distant Selwyn Range that stories began to flow, and I learned that the blue cattle dog at my feet had been bought at a secondhand market. These people's lives may be solitary but they are not lonely, and they literally glow with health and well-being. I felt a little of what 'Banjo' Paterson felt about his Clancy.

Most of the towns have changed very little over the last 30 or 40 years. The larger ones such as Longreach and Charleville have been graced with the occasional new building. Other towns such as Winton, Blackall and Isisford seem to have changed hardly at all, becoming in the process almost living museums. Steele Rudd's stories of native bush life, written at the turn of the century, could easily take place in and around these towns today.

Long before the Europeans settled this area there were tribes of Aborigines. At Blacks' Palace, 140 kilometres west of Blackall, we saw Aboriginal paintings and carvings on one of the few rock faces in the whole of these plains. The site was connected with fertility rites as well as being a burial site. High up on the cliffs are small caves in which the dead were placed.

The Aborigines did not give up their land without a fight. The last major confrontation was between the Kalkadoon tribe and troopers at Battle Mountain near Cloncurry in 1884. The Kalkadoons were conquered,

Outback images etched in the sands of the Simpson Desert

as were the other tribes before them, and today, except for the occasional rock painting, little remains to be seen of the life the Aborigines once led.

Before man, other creatures inhabited this country. At the Dinosaur's Trackway, 170 kilometres south-west of Winton on the edge of the eroded Tully Range, tracks in country covered by spinifex tell a story of a giant dinosaur hunting smaller prey by the shores of a muddy lake some 100 million years ago.

It is said that these tracks were discovered by some locals fossicking for opals, flakes of which are still to be found in the quarries and disturbed ground in the area. We found one or two poor specimens within a few minutes, a reminder of the mineral wealth that lies below much of this country.

More than anything else, it is the extreme age of this land that is so impressive and at times almost overpowering. It is the sheer emptiness you feel at first, and then there is the sense that every rock and every worn range of hills shows the earth's face at its very oldest. Even the animals of Australia testify to its age, its unchanging character. Kangaroos and the rest of the marsupial family were regarded by scientists as virtually extinct until they were discovered thriving in Australia.

You are continually reminded of the toughness of the white men who first explored and settled this country. Many of the early explorers came from gentler landscapes, and many died in their attempt to know this land. Burke and Wills, the famous explorers who crossed the continent from south to north, returned to their base camp to find that the rest of their party had left only hours before. The tragedy of Burke and Wills' death was made more poignant by the fact that it was a good season and the Aborigines were living well off the meagre fruit of the land.

One mystery of this district has defied explanation — the Min Min Light. The light has been seen by travellers in the area near Boulia, and is said to be as bright as a car's headlight and about the same size. It seems to follow travellers. It was first reported by a

stockman who had passed by the place where the Min Min Hotel had stood before it was destroyed by fire. From a little graveyard behind the hotel the stockman saw a light rising, which followed him most of the way to Boulia. It might have been dismissed as the ravings of a drunken stockman if thousands of sightings of the Min Min Light had not been reported since.

Evidence of the sheep boom is seen in the largest shearing shed in the world at Isisford Downs. At the same huge station, the old shearers' quarters stand rather forlornly with its fly-netting flapping in the warm breeze and its floors ringing hollowly as if in mockery of the rowdy times that once were. In Blackall is the disused wool scouring shed. The ancient machinery is covered with cobwebs and the only people there now are a 'few old-timers' tanning sheep skins. They still reminisce about the days when thousands of bails of wool passed through the shed.

The days of the great homesteads are not over, though some are now owned by city-based companies. Lorraine Station, near Winton on the Longreach Road, maintains the life of a large station with its many workers by admitting tourists who sleep in cabins, are shown the workings of a sheep station, and go their way having seen a little of the outback life. Here we felt that the squatter still reclines in his squatter's chair with its folding out planks to support his weary feet after a hard day in the saddle.

The outback's fascination is its vastness and its harshness, the very things that make it resistant to change. The American frontier was overcome because of its fertility. Yet here, man will never have the impact he has had in the gentler areas near the coast. Without mining, it is unlikely that the population will increase by much, and without a miracle of some kind it is unlikely that the land will support more stock. For these reasons, the outback will be a remote and challenging frontier for a very long time.

Christopher Leonard is a writer and poet who has travelled extensively within Australia and overseas.

Crocodiles

Vincent Serventy

**About 20 years ago, an Australian survey showed
that the word causing the most powerful response, from a list
that included death, fire, poison, murder and rape, was
'shark'! In a similar survey today, 'crocodile'
might oust 'shark'!**

Surprisingly fast reactions and powerful jaws allow for numerous tea time snacks along the water's edge.

The fresh water crocodile is smaller and has a longer, tapered snout than its salt water cousin and it differs also in being unthreatening to humans.

The last hundred years in Australia have seen 55 recorded attacks by crocodiles, 30 of them fatal. Of the 55 attacks, 20 have occurred in the last six years, and eight were fatal.

Much earlier in our history, the Australian Aborigines looked on crocodiles as an article of food, an enemy to be feared, and a creature to be venerated. Anthropologist W. R. Roth described how Queensland Aborigines hunted the saltwater crocodile early this century. Sometimes a group of men would drive a crocodile into a pool and slip a noose over its snout. This technique is still used because while the jaws can close with great power, the opening muscles are much weaker.

Another method was for a 20-metre-long wooden screen to be so placed in tidal waters that a gap would allow crocodiles to enter with the incoming tide. Their return would be blocked and the victims snared.

Nooses from overhanging branches were also used and a crocodile could also be killed at close quarters by a spear thrown into a vulnerable spot, usually just under the forearm.

In *Wanderings in Wild Australia*, the famous anthropologist Baldwin Spencer commented that a party travelled in single file 'and put an old woman in the rear, because, so they believe, the crocodile always seized the last person, and the loss of an old woman does not matter much'.

An animal that was important in the hunt was usually important in Dreamtime mythology. Anthropologist Herbert Basedow described a crocodile ceremony in the Cambridge Gulf region. The person representing the animal ancestor wriggled along the ground between the legs of the rest of the clan. Once out of the human file, he stood erect 'opens his mouth and emits a harsh booming note resembling that of a crocodile'.

Aboriginal rock art of Arnhem Land often features these reptiles. Many are painted in the x-ray style, where not only the outside shape but also some of the internal organs are shown.

Australia is not the only country where crocodiles are hunted, feared or venerated. Drawings and carvings in ancient Egypt show the crocodile god, Sebek, as either a man with a crocodile head, or as the animal itself. Lewis Carroll wrote of the Nile crocodile:

> *How cheerfully he seems to grin,*
> *How neatly spreads his claws,*
> *And welcomes little fishes in,*
> *With gently smiling jaws.*

The reptile can hardly be blamed for the fact that it appears to be smiling when the jaws are closed. Paradoxically, the same smiling mouth shape in the dolphin earns our affection.

There are many fascinating aspects of crocodilian history and habits. We are all familiar with the dinosaurs of hundreds of millions of years ago. Yet, in our crocodiles, we have a reptile group that thrived even before the dinosaurs, and which has continued to the present day. A lineage of 200 million years is impressive. Fossil crocodiles 20 metres in length have been discovered.

There is some argument as to which is the world's largest species of crocodilian. The African Nile crocodile and the Australian saltwater species vie for this honour. Early records give lengths of nine metres for our species and it is possible that animals of seven metres still lurk in our tropical waters. The Interna-

The awesome Australian

tional Union for Conservation of Nature, in its authoritative *Red Data Book*, gives 6.2 metres as the record published length. Weight is even more difficult to measure accurately, but zoo specimens reach at least a tonne.

The saltwater crocodile is often called the Australian crocodile, but we share it with a number of other countries. It ranges from Sri Lanka, the eastern Indian coast and north as far as Bangladesh, through south-west Asia to the Philippines and south to our northern Australian coasts, estuaries and, in some places, freshwater rivers and lakes.

An accurate range in Australian waters is hard to give, but it is considered to be from the Fitzroy River in the west, around the northern waters to the Tropic of Capricorn in the east. Because of the animal's ability to take long sea-going voyages, individuals may occasionally be found further south.

The crocodile has a powerful armoury of physical features. Large size, of course, is a protection for any animal. The nostrils open to the surface from a lump on the tip of the snout. The eyes also protrude above the general line, as do the ears which lie just behind the eyes.

Such a profile — nostrils, eyes and ears above the water line — is common to water creatures such as the frog and the hippopotamus. It enables the animal to breathe, see and hear while most of the body is hidden.

The huge tail, flattened from side to side, makes up about half the total body length. Used for swimming, it is also a massive weapon. The back legs have webbed claws, which are useful in climbing mud banks. The huge teeth offer a firm grip on struggling prey.

Each ear has a flap that closes when the animal is diving so that water cannot enter; valves on the nostrils serve the same purpose. In the back of the mouth, another valve stops water from rushing into the stomach when the crocodile is holding a victim. Even more interesting, and also found in mammals, a bone shelf separates mouth and nose so that the animal can breathe even when the mouth is full of food.

What kind of food do these jaws, teeth and powerful tail serve to catch? As is true of many hunting animals, what is caught depends on the size of the hunter. Young crocodiles eat insects, shrimps, crabs and small fish. A two-metre one has been seen to use a neat hunting technique. The crocodile curled its tail inwards as it swam along the bank so that the frightened fish swam forward towards the waiting jaws. The tail is also used to sweep an animal from the edge into the water.

Anything a large crocodile sees in the water or on land is regarded as food, so its diet ranges from insects to kangaroos, cattle or people. Naturalist Eric Worrell examined the stomach contents of 300 large crocodiles killed many years ago for the skin trade. He found their diet to be as varied as turtles and their eggs, smaller crocodiles, snakes and wallabies. Animals in captivity need fresh food, but in the wild he saw them eating decaying flesh, including that of other crocodiles that had been dead a fortnight.

The teeth are not suited to chewing, so a crocodile either eats the prey whole, or shakes the body vigorously until some of the flesh breaks away.

While the saltwater crocodile is the species usually in the news, it has a close relative, the smaller freshwater crocodile. This species has a much slenderer snout, and the teeth are needle sharp, rather than strong conical pegs. With these, it hunts fish, frogs, other reptiles, water birds and smaller mammals. Even creatures as small as insects and crustaceans can serve as food.

More tourists are now visiting northern Australia and attacks are becoming more frequent. Between 1934 and 1985, only six people were killed, but there have been seven fatalities during the last two years.

Most of these unfortunate victims were killed while swimming or wading in shallow waters. One man

OLIVER STREWE

Saltwater crocodiles lurk together on sandbanks in a tropical river estuary

was taken while sleeping on a river bank. A zoo keeper lost an arm while feeding his pet crocodile, and there has been at least one fatal attack by a zoo animal.

A person may not be safe even while travelling in a small boat. According to a press report, when the body of one victim was being brought in, a large crocodile leapt 1.5 metres out of the water to bite at the corpse, which was wrapped in plastic.

Public solutions to these problems vary. For a few people, the only good crocodile is a dead one. Others feel that humans intruding into the reptile's domain must accept the risk of attack. Shark attacks on popular ocean beaches have been prevented by nets laid to reduce the total number of sharks. The same method could be used in tropical waters where many tourists swim. The present practice is to remove problem animals to a crocodile farm or national park. In the Northern Territory, more than 500 crocodiles have been removed in this way.

National parks are fragments of the wild, where nature remains unchanged and management ensures the integrity of the region, so a visitor must accept the risks involved. Notices warning against swimming in, or camping near, waters containing crocodiles should be sufficient. Sleeping near the water's edge is foolhardy, and standing in shallow water is equally risky. The stealing of warning signs by vandals is a criminal offence.

By the end of the 60s, the two species were threatened with extinction and governments became alarmed. Western Australia brought in legal protection in 1971, followed by the Northern Territory in 1972. As Queensland refused to join in the ban, illegal shooters had a selling outlet in this state and the killings continued.

Ironically, the cattle station owners who had welcomed shooters in the early days now regarded them as more of a pest than the crocodiles. Not only did hunters leave the bodies of victims to rot and foul waterholes, but they also shot cattle for food or bait. Shooters also broke through fences to get to good hunting spots. So, with the pressure from conservationists and station owners, in 1973 the Australian government imposed an export ban which destroyed the skin market. Queensland imposed a ban in 1975, so closing the local markets.

International attention led to the saltwater crocodile being placed on the list of threatened species This meant that in the more civilised countries there was no trade in skins.

What does such protection mean to the average tourist? I went to Kakadu in 1965, long before it became a national park. My guide was a former crocodile shooter who had turned to farming tourists as a more lucrative occupation. He offered to show me a crocodile. We crept towards a clump of paperbarks. Four hundred metres away, I saw a crocodile about four metres in length. As I came out into the open to take a photograph with a telephoto lens, it disappeared into the water as though by magic, showing how terrified these animals were of people.

In 1986, I went to the same place in Kakadu National Park. Crocodiles had become so tame that I could have leaned out of the boat and touched a four-metre specimen. I resisted the temptation!

What is the present conservation position? In 1984, the IUCN removed this species from the Appendix I list, where it was totally protected, and placed it on the Appendix II list, where harvesting can be carried out under strict guidelines. Egg harvests will be restricted to flood-prone sites and the taking of live crocodiles will be in accordance with management plans. A number of crocodile farms have already been organised to provide skins for the trade.

The position today is still clouded with argument. Dr Graham Webb, the Northern Territory government expert, claims that the population today is around 30 to 50% of what it was when commercial harvesting began in 1945–6. At that time, it was considered that there were 100,000 individuals. He points out that the present animals may not be quite as large, but that there are at least some that are seven metres in length

and that weigh over a tonne. In the territory, their conservation position is safe.

But there is another side. Professor Harry Messel, with a dedicated group of helpers, studied crocodile numbers, not only in the territory but over the whole of northern Australia. The survey took ten years and covered 70,000 kilometres. Professor Messel and G. C. Vorlicek point out that buffalo and cattle are not the only problem. Fishermen's nets drown hundreds of the bigger animals and such nets are still being set in Kakadu National Park, though steps are being taken to phase out this activity.

The comparatively innocuous Australian freshwater crocodile

CAROLYN JOHNS

The authors of the survey also say that more national parks are needed. If culling in the wild must take place, it should be concentrated on the one-to-two-metre animals, since the majority of these die from other causes. Crocodile farming should be encouraged and eggs taken only from nests that are flooded during the summer wet. The survey ends with the following sobering comment:

> We now end this paper with our own view on the long-term future of *C. porosus* outside of national parks in Australia: considering the present greedy nature of society, IT HASN'T ANY. . .! And even in the rivers of national parks, unless net fishing is prohibited in them, the future for *C. porosus* is grim.

Since that was written, most of the buffalo have been removed from Kakadu National Park, and net fishing is being phased out, so the conservation position does look more satisfactory.

Throughout most of the world, it is taken for granted that it is in national parks that wildlife has the best chance to survive. The saltwater crocodile is one of the splendid sights of our northern parks. We can never see live dinosaurs, the huge reptiles that shook the earth a hundred million years ago, but at least we *can* see, with a mixture of admiration, awe and fear, the one-tonne crocodile whose ancestors shared the ancient world.

Vincent Serventy, President of the Wildlife Preservation Society of Australia, is a prolific and well-known author and documentary film-maker on wildlife and conservation subjects. He is the recipient of the Order of Australia and many other awards.

The Red Centre, a Timeless Dream

Christopher Leonard

**The Centre — the extraordinary Red Centre of Australia —
brings to mind images of the earth as glowing coals under a
breathlessly blue sky. Photographs cannot capture its
vastness, its colour and its variety. Everything is bigger,
more delicate and more extravagant in hue than
one is prepared for.**

A place of grand silences and natural beauty, it has for millenia been the home of several tribes of Aborigines who have adapted to and become part of the land in a way that has made it possible for them not only to survive but also to thrive in this land where the rain rarely falls. And for 100 years it has supported cattle stations and the growing town of Alice Springs.

At the centre of the Centre, Alice Springs has changed from being an outback town of heavy-drinking rugged inhabitants. There is now a casino, a shopping mall, and boutiques selling everything from boomerangs to Louis Vuitton luggage. Don't expect to be welcome in some pubs if you are wearing jeans, no matter what their label or cut. What may be acceptable in New York, London or Paris is now strictly forbidden in certain bars of the Todd River Tavern. Such chic!

A little way out past Heavitree Gap on the Ross Highway is a camel farm run by Nick and Michelle Smail. At the farm I met Greg Warburton leading a pack of donkeys along the dry Todd River, and learned that he was training them for a trip he and his girlfriend planned to make from Kununurra in the far north-east corner of Western Australia to the almost inaccessible Bungle Bungle Range. The coincidence did not strike me at first, but a Colonel Peter Warburton led a camel expedition into the western deserts from Alice Springs in 1873.

Nick Smail arranges camel treks along the dry bed of the Todd River to Chateau Hornsby Winery. You can sample the vintage of this improbable vineyard where Ted Egan, a professional 'character', beats rhythmically on a beer carton while telling stories about the 'characters' of the bush. To be called a character here is a sort of accolade, an acceptance of eccentricity. Looking around at the busload of American tourists listening to Ted Egan, I saw that their faces betrayed a bemused well-what's-the-joke look as they reached for another beaker of Chateau Hornsby red.

Camels were introduced into this area as a means of exploration and transport, and in the last century camel trainers and drivers were brought out from Afghanistan. Men such as Nick Smail who work with the camels are fond of the beasts and defend them against their reputation for being cantankerous. 'They're like all of us — we respond well if we're treated well', he said, saddling up one of his favourites. 'They require patience — a camel takes six months before it's suitable for riding.'

One morning before dawn, we were dragged full of sleep by a bouncing Ken Watts to see his hot-air balloon. Wishing that I was still in bed, I helped raise the balloon, and then looked around. The morning star gleamed like a beacon in the perfectly clear and silent sky. We headed back towards the MacDonnell Ranges and landed at the airport. The precise landing was a first, since the only means of navigating is to manoeuvre the balloon using air currents. We picnicked in the fresh early morning air on champagne and chicken and I felt that I had had a full day's experience, though it was only just after nine.

Alice Springs was originally a supply dump for the Overland Telegraph. It then became a centre of the cattle industry. It has now been transformed into one of Australia's major tourist centres. It has its own well-publicised festivals such as the Camel Cup and the Bangtail Muster, which are both held in May, and the Henley-on-Todd Regatta which is held in the dry riverbed of the Todd. These events have a particularly harum-scarum quality, enlivened by huge quantities of beer, as if to remind everyone that 'the Alice' as it is called has not given up its wild old ways.

The George Gill Range at King's Canyon

At the Alice Springs Cup, ladies teetering on high-heeled shoes and sporting gloves and hats pick their way elegantly over bodies overcome by spiritous liquors. It's a long way from Royal Randwick or Flemington. Or is it?

'The Alice' is set in the midst of the steep Mac-Donnell Ranges which are in view from most parts of the town, a reminder that the desert is 'just out there'. You do not have to go very far from Alice Springs to get on to dirt roads where you can drive for days without sighting another vehicle.

The immensity of the Centre seems to swallow up even the swelling number of tourists. Of course, Ayers Rock, some 460 kilometres from Alice Springs, attracts thousands of people. It is an unnerving experience to have been alone all day and then arrive at Ayers Rock. As the sun begins to set, people appear as if they have sprung from the earth. Hundreds and hundreds of people jostle for room on the best vantage points, with the sun to their backs. Some, unable to tolerate the stillness of the Rock, carry radios; others carry more camera equipment than a Cecil B. de Mille film crew. A dozen buses disgorge people from all over the world wearing that special costume adopted by many people when travelling, a costume of old shorts, thongs, and a silly hat saying Ayers Rock, Coolangatta or Disneyland. The contrast with the silence and magic of the Centre can be a shock to the strongest system.

The explorers Eyre and Sturt penetrated into these areas and in 1860 and 1861, John McDouall Stuart opened up the Centre. Ernest Giles made several journeys and named many places in the Centre. Giles was the first man to sight and name Ayers Rock and the Olgas. In 1870, Charles Todd, South Australia's Postmaster General, supervised the construction of the Overland Telegraph Line from Adelaide to Darwin. Alice Springs was named after Todd's wife. By August 1872, the repeater station was in operation and was the only reason for the existence of the small settlement.

Nearby, at least in Central Australian terms, was once a more populous settlement called Arltunga. Some 97 kilometres from Alice Springs, Gary Bohning and his wife Elaine are its only inhabitants today. 'It's not that far really into the Alice — only as long as it takes to drink four cans of beer,' says Gary. Gold was discovered there in 1887 and for the next ten years it was a thriving goldfield and Central Australia's first township. Droughts made it too difficult to continue mining, and starving horse teams became too weak to cart the ore. In 1901, the government boiler burst at the cyanide works and ore could not be crushed for seven months, and that meant in effect the end of the town. Attempts have been made over the years to mine the area, but to no avail. Even as late as 1905, a town was being surveyed, but it was finally abandoned when surface gold became hard to find. It is thought that that consummate spinner of yarns, Harold Lasseter (who claimed to have found a vast reef of gold out towards the Western Australian border) once passed through here. Nothing remains of Arltunga but a ghost town whose sturdily built stone houses are gradually being reconstructed. The Bohnings run the pub near Arltunga and a sign outside says, 'If the pub is unattended, please sound your car horn.' Gary and Elaine Bohning found Alice Springs too noisy, and so moved out to this area several years ago.

'Someone says the Sheraton has five stars,' Elaine said as she looked up at the sky, 'but we've got a million stars.'

The Bohnings made a big find on Christmas Day 1980 when they unearthed a nugget weighing 1.109

kilograms. They are still fossicking, but it seems certain that the wealth still to be found here will have to be mined using modern technology.

Alice Springs was slow to grow mainly because transport into the area was by camel train until the railway from Darwin was finally opened in 1929. It was named 'the Ghan', in recognition of the Afghan camel drivers. In 1939, Connellan Airlines established the first flights to the outlying cattle stations and at the same time the Royal Flying Doctor Service began operation.

A misconception about the centre is that it is useless, barren land. For thousands of years, however, it has supported several tribes of Aborigines who developed a culture we still have much to learn about. At Hermannsburg Mission, 120 kilometres west of Alice Springs, Albert Namatjira came into contact with the Melbourne artist Rex Betterby who helped him to learn the techniques of watercolour. Namatjira became an immediate success and his watercolours were sold out at his first Melbourne exhibition. He was offered and accepted full citizenship in 1951. However, tribal law meant that he shared all he earned

Rainbow Valley's multi-hued sandstone cliffs are mirrored in a pool of

with his family. Citizenship also gave him the right to buy alcohol, which he also shared with his family. The supplying of alcohol to Aborigines was at that time against the law and Namatjira spent some time in prison for this offence. He died in 1959, alcohol being one of the contributory causes of his death.

In the Centre, certain tribes such as the Papunya have drawn public attention to their 'dot-paintings', which are now eagerly sought by collectors and galleries. An adaptation of traditional sand-painting, 'dot-painting' uses European art materials on portable and durable canvas.

Ayers Rock is still the most popular tourist destination in the Centre. The Rock has become one of the symbols of Australia that is recognised everywhere in the world. And most Australians would recognise a photograph of it as easily as one of their mother. Nothing, however, can give a sense of its size except standing beneath the towering 348-metre wall of rock. To give some idea of its size, a tourist coach beside it looks like a Dinky Toy bus against the walls of a house. It is necessary to be with the Rock for some time to appreciate fully not only its size but also the way it ap-

the valley floor after a rare rainstorm

GUNTHER DEICHMAN

pears continually to change. From one angle, it looks almost like a huge box; from another, it sprawls elegantly across the plain like some giant beast. Depending on the time of the day and the weather conditions, it can be black or purple or sandy-coloured, or bright red, and when it rains it turns blue-black with ribbons of silver cascading water.

'The tall walls of the crater stand on the plain like a barbican guarding some sort of secret.'

For the Pitjantjatajara and Yankuntjatjara tribes, Ayers Rock (or Uluru) was the centre of their lives and there are many legends about it. They tell that long ago the Kuniya, or carpet-snakes, journeyed from a waterhole near the tabletop Mount Conner to Uluru where life was good for them. At that stage they believed that Uluru had been a giant sandhill and was changed at the end of the Creation Period into its present form. The women of the Kuniya were changed into the large boulders in Tjukiki Gorge and the men, who liked to sleep in the sandhill's shadow, were turned into the boulders on the plain.

There is also the story of the Mala who came to Ayers Rock to perform the ceremonies to make boys into men. The ceremonies took place in a cave which was absolutely forbidden to women; they were not even permitted to look in that direction as they passed by. While the ceremonies were in progress, the Mulga-seed men from the Petermann Ranges sent a message to invite the Mala to a ceremony and asked that they bring decorations with them. The Mala were angered by this invitation and sent a curt reply. The Mulga-seed people were in turn angered and asked their medicine men to seek revenge. They created the giant dingo, Kurpannga, who went to Ayers Rock and after killing two men caused the Mala people to scatter.

Today, the traditional owners of the Rock are concerned about the influx of tourists whom they believe will desecrate the site. If this occurs, they believe that there will be no spiritual future for them.

Near Ayers Rock are the equally impressive Olgas, named by Ernest Giles after the patron of the sciences, Grand Duchess Olga of Russia and wife of the king of Greece. To the Aborigines, the area is known as Katatjuta, which means literally 'the place of many heads'. The Olgas are a collection of huge rock domes, about 30 of which can be climbed. Mount Olga itself is half as high again as Ayers Rock.

As with Ayers Rock, there are many stories associated with the Olgas. Here is the home of Wanambi, the giant serpent who lives in the wet season in the waterholes on top of the mountain and in the dry season in one of the waterholes in the gorges. If the waterholes dry up, Wanambi enters the rock itself. His anger is shown by the gusts of wind that blow through the gorge and it is said that if a fire is lit or someone drinks at the waterhole, Wanambi will rise into the air as a rainbow and kill those who dare to enter his domain.

There are many other important sites in the Centre. We spent several teeth-jolting days in a four-wheel-drive to reach some of them. One is King's Canyon, a gorge rising 200 metres — again coloured a startling red. Here also is the 'Garden of Eden', an unexpected oasis of lush vegetation. The red is repeated everywhere: in the sandhills, in the rocks, and in the glowing cliffs overhanging the Finke River, named after one of Stuart's backers, which is said to be the oldest river in the world. Palm Valley, which branches off the Finke, contains palms that have survived from a time when large areas of the Centre were damp. Now the palms survive on the seepage from the cliffs to the solid basic rock which prevents the water from draining away.

West of Palm Valley, the Finke River and Hermannsburg, the land becomes undulating. Driving along the dirt road, turned to sticky mud by recent rain, we glimpsed what appeared to be a range of blueish hills. As we approached, the hills became sheer cliffs rising abruptly out of the earth. This is Gosse's Bluff, a crater formed when a comet collided with the earth some 131 million years ago. The impact shattered the earth for 19 kilometres around, and the energy released was so great that it melted quartz, the melting point of which is 1,732°C. The crater is five kilometres in diameter, with cliffs rising up to 274 metres over the surrounding plain. And this is just the crater's remains!

The tall walls of the crater stand on the plain like a barbican guarding some sort of secret. As we approached them, bumping around in the four-wheel-drive so much that I thought my jaw would part company with my head, their massiveness became even more overpowering. Passing through the entrance to these walls was like passing through the gates of some legendary castle, and I had a sense of incipient discovery. I didn't know what I would find — maybe something like King Solomon's Mines. There is a story that the history of the Aborigine is contained in crystals hidden in one of the caves of Gosse's Bluff. The silence inside the crater is even more powerful than in the rest of the desert. Apart from the occasional wallaby, there is only the awesome red cliffs and the silence.

Still stunned by Gosse's Bluff, we passed through rounded hills that seemed as green and gentle as the Surrey Downs. The green comes, however, from the spinifex and beneath that is the ever-present red earth. Haast's Bluff, which is precisely on the Tropic of Capricorn, is in the heart of Aboriginal land. A precipitous upward thrust of rock, it was frequently depicted by Namatjira and other Aranda artists.

ALLAN MOULT

Two faces of the Red Centre - patterns in the sands of the Simpson Desert, above, and the serene smile on the face of a stockman, right

Behind us were the running purple cliffs of the Mareenie Bluff; in front, beyond the mountains and the Bluff, was nothing but endless space barely touched by anything but the caress of the indigenous Australians. I began to feel that I had come to another land, another Australia that I knew nothing of.

On the way back to Alice Springs from Haast's Bluff we again entered the MacDonnell Ranges and passed by the better known sites of the Centre: the gorges and gaps which cut through the range. Near the old station of Glenn Helen, now a hotel, is Ormiston Gorge with its permanent water reflecting the tall cliffs behind it. At Glenn Helen Gorge, the rush-lined river passes through tall cliffs so formed by nature that it does not seem fanciful to imagine that they were sculpted by some unknown race. They are a reminder that the art of the Aborigines arose out of the natural forms around them.

As we sat on the terrace at Glenn Helen having an early breakfast and watching the effect of the light on the colours and shapes of the cliffs, I didn't want to leave.

Nowhere in the world have I seen such light. The essence of the centre is light: its purity and the sharp clarity of everything, a clarity that is deceptive. Nothing is stable, the effect of the light being such that from moment to moment, from day to day, nothing ever looks quite the same.

Christopher Leonard is a writer and poet who has travelled extensively within Australia and overseas.

STUART FOX

The Australian Wilderness

Leigh Hemmings

The word 'wilderness' first appeared in a 1500s translation of the Bible from Latin to English. Then, a wilderness was a place of evil and of desolation, a cursed land where God sent people as punishment. If they were to survive, the wilderness must be transformed to make it 'blossom like a rose'.

Crater Lake in Tasmania's Cradle Mountain region

Magpie Geese skim across the water in Kakadu

Exiled in Australia as punishment, our first European settlers believed that the bush and its inhabitants were enemies to be fought and conquered. They set out to do just that, using every means at their disposal. They altered and degraded vast tracts of land, making extinct a range of animal species and producing short and long-term ecological disasters for which we are still paying.

Defining a wilderness today is a tough task. For some people, just venturing beyond the city skyline out into the bush is an exciting encounter with the wild. For them, the abundant wildlife, sparkling rivers, rolling hills, secluded forests and vast flat landscapes are all undoubtedly wilderness. Others take a harder line. They look at the same areas and see diminished wilderness values: roads, tracks, dams, burning, feral animals, weeds, logging, mining, frequent overflying aircraft, developments and sometimes just the results of unsympathetic national parks service management.

A wilderness in the true sense should have a minimum core of 25,000 hectares, and preferably a surrounding buffer zone of at least the same size.

But it is more than that. Well-known conservationist Dr Bob Brown views wilderness as 'an area of natural country substantially free from the impact of modern man. It is a large tract of country where a person can stand with his senses entirely steeped in nature and free of the distractions of modern technology. Wilderness is like a rainbow. The closer you approach it by motor car, the further it recedes.' Viewed in this manner, wilderness is a rare, non-renewable resource now found in only a very small part of Australia.

With so much of Australia no longer a wilderness, the need to preserve the little that remains would seem to be obvious. Yet, in some parts of the country, the original biblical attitudes towards wilderness still exist. A good example is the hysterical reaction against the NSW government's proposed Wilderness Act, which sought to preserve a mere 4% of the state. Other state governments show their attitude to wilderness by encouraging mining and mineral extraction and hut and road construction in the wilderness cores of national parks. Some even oppose World Heritage listing.

In the 1900s, when vast tracts of the country were untouched, some visionaries recognised the need to preserve wild places. In America, Henry David Thoreau saw 'in wilderness. . .the preservation of the world'. John Muir told townsfolk to 'climb the mountains and get their good tidings. Nature's peace will flow into you as sunshine flows into trees'. George Catlin wanted 'A nation's park, containing man and beast, in all the wild and freshness of the nature's beauty'. His call was soon answered in Australia with the declaration of the world's second national park, the Royal National Park, south of Sydney. Many more parks eventually followed in each state.

Regrettably, the declaration of national parks proved not enough to preserve wilderness. Often through poor management, the wilderness qualities were diminished and in some cases lost. National parks were seen as places to be modified. Exotic deer were released in Royal National Park, and in other parks a desire for easier access created a network of high-speed tarred roads. Some parks never had a chance to retain wilderness qualities. So-called national parks the size of pocket handkerchiefs were declared where it is now impossible to escape the cacophony of urban development.

The desirability of something more was realised in the 1930s by the Australian father of wilderness, Myles Dunphy, who wrote of people's need

'. . . for really "primitive" areas — great portions of national parks wherein no roads may be constructed, no buildings erected and no fences or other "improvements" are allowed. To lose themselves for a while in such roadless, primitive areas, to "go bush" in the mountains, is the great endeavour of countless thousands of human beings. . .

More and more, the people want back again the forested and mountainous wilderness which has been lost. The movement is not merely a

passing phase. The more complicated existence becomes, the more necessary it is to have this wonderful palliative handy to preserve the natural balance of minds and perfect healthy physique; also to preserve for the human race that connection with things natural and wholesome which now is more than ever necessary, because of our remarkable artificial city and town environment.'
(*Myles Dunphy*, edited by Patrick Thompson, Ballagarin Press, 1986.)

In Australia, this concept was enshrined for the first time in the 1960s in the declaration of a wilderness zone in Kosciusko National Park. The Australian Conservation Foundation, formed in 1965, adopted its first wilderness policy in the 1970s. The value of preserving wilderness developed a great public consciousness in the unsuccessful campaign to save Tasmania's Lake Pedder from inundation, in the formation of the predecessor of the Wilderness Society, and in the successful battle for preservation of an undammed Franklin River in Tasmania.

In Australia, the Commonwealth government is examining proposals for a national wilderness preservation programme. The task of choosing the top Australian wilderness areas is one that borders on the impossible, requiring a balanced combination of criteria: remoteness from access and settlement, and aesthetic and biophysical naturalness. Different weightings of any of these qualities would give differing opinions as to which places should be included in the list.

In the purest sense of wilderness, arguments could be put forward for scrapping some on the list and adding another 10 or 20. Most of these chosen wilderness areas are within the relatively safe boundary of a national park. Past experience has shown that publicising unprotected wilderness areas can lead to their degradation through deliberate vandalism. As consultant to the Department of Arts, Heritage and the Environment, John Sinclair points out that 'A simple process such as bulldozing a track through a wilderness area can eliminate a very large section of land as wilderness, or indeed eliminate the wilderness values of the whole wilderness area.'

This discussion of the politics of wilderness preservation in Australia has outlined difficulties which face advanced economies throughout the world. We should not forget that compared with the United States, for example, Australia is rich in wilderness areas.

Wollemi, Blue Mountains and Kanangra Boyd National Parks

From Sydney on a clear day you can see a range of mountains which took the first settlers 30 years to cross. Today, the Blue Mountains and the nearby Jenolan Caves are meccas for tourists, yet within sight of the popular mountain towns are vast areas of untouched forests accessible only to experienced bushwalkers. The Blue Mountains National Park is in the centre of a chain of national parks which includes to the south, Kanangra Boyd, containing the superb Kanangra Walls, and to the north, Wollemi National Park, containing the huge, virtually roadless wilderness of the Colo-Hunter.

Wollemi comprises just less than 500,000 hectares, and contains the largest tract of wilderness in New South Wales. This is an outstanding region, with rainforests, high peaks, deep sandstone gorges (including the longest sandstone gorge in New South Wales), and wild rivers, including the Colo, Capertree, Wolgan and Wollemi. There are rare species of gliders and wallabies, bush turkeys, and a large range of fruit pigeons and other migrating birds. Those tireless lobbyists for wilderness, the Colo Committee, list more than 160 birds, 36 mammals, 14 fish, 16 amphibians and 601 plants in the region.

Up until recently, the Colo-Hunter wilderness was virtually left alone, even by bushwalkers. This is amazing considering that it is only 70 kilometres from Australia's largest city. The reasons for its sanctity lie in its being too rough for development, and lacking in good grazing country. In short, it is a truly wild place. In the Sydney Bushwalkers club magazine, Alex Colley wrote (referring to a 1930s trip when he stood on the summit of Mt Uraterer), 'In the foreground there was a maze of wooded gullies and cliffs and crags. It was a scene of great wilderness rather than beauty; it would make a master bushman shudder.'

The Australian Alps

The Australian Alps, spanning the NSW and Victorian border, is a vast region overlaid by a mantle of snow every winter and enriched by a carpet of wildflowers every summer. It is made up primarily of about 650,000 hectares of Kosciusko National Park in New South Wales but in Victoria it is still fought over by a gaggle of self-interested groups.

In winter, the greatest cross-country skiing wilderness experience in the Australian Alps is to tour the main range from the old goldmining fields of Kiandra to the highest peak in Australia, Mt Kosciusko. Kiandra was the birthplace of snow-skiing in Australia. Miners on the diggings first skied using palings from the local cemetery fence and formed the second ski club in the world.

Australia's ancient, weathered landscape makes for lower overall altitudes (Kosciusko is only 2,228 metres), and less likelihood of avalanches.

Summer trekkers can choose a good range of tracks where sightings of gliders, rock wallabies and wombats are not uncommon. A furtunate few will glimpse the rare, delicate mountain pigmy possum. Lower slopes are clustered with a variety of beautiful

Australia's great wilderness areas remain a haven for wildlife such as these Brolgas in flight, which can be found in flocks of thousands.

gumtrees, including yellow box, much favoured by apiarists for the clear light honey that bees produce from its blossom. Higher up are some of the straightest, tallest trees in the world, alpine ash and mountain gum. Above 1,830 metres, where the snowgums cease, the alpine herb fields dominate. In the short period between the snowmelt and the onslaught of winter, you will find masses of wildflowers, both in alpine and sub-alpine areas.

Willandra Lakes Region

The Willandra Lakes region is perhaps the least known of the World Heritage sites in Australia. Yet it takes its place on a list that includes the Grand Canyon in the United States, Tanzania's Serengeti Plains, the Pyramid Fields of Egypt and Sagarmatha in Nepal. What makes this region covering 6,000 square kilometres in far western New South Wales so special?

A remarkable tale of archaeological discovery holds the key. The lakes were once part of an ancient drainage system which dried up around 15,000 years ago as the ice age drew to a close. Then followed a dramatic period of natural erosion which carved out deeply etched gullies whose sand has been whipped up into huge crescent-shaped dunes, sometimes known as lunettes. The creation of this wonderful eerie landscape has revealed the most spellbinding archaeological finds. We know today that some 40,000 years ago the region was home to some of the earliest inhabitants of Australia. Human remains, stone tools, and old fireplaces with evidence of the culture of the people who lived here have been revealed to give us an insight into an ancient lifestyle. Fossilised remains of prehistoric marsupials have also been discovered.

As you walk and marvel at the dramatic dune configuration called the Walls of China on Lake Mungo, you may be reminded of the words, 'Tread softly, because you tread on my dreams'.

Access to the region is difficult. Your best starting points are from the south at Mildura, Pooncarie or Balranald. The round trip from Mildura is well over 200 kilometres and visitors should note that there are no sources of food or petrol in or near the region.

Wilson's Promontory

Victorians have loved Wilson's Promontory almost since George Bass happened upon it in 1797. Known as 'the Prom', this rugged coastal knob is the most southerly section of mainland Australia, with 130 kilometres of wave-pounded beaches, rocky headlands and more than 80 kilometres of walking trails. For early seafarers, 'the Prom' had a feared reputation, thanks to craggy promontories and unheralded storms. Many ships foundered. But still the sealers and whalers thrived, along with rapacious timber felling and quarrying until it was declared a national park in 1905. Today, the only hunting permitted is by rod and reel.

The Prom's present popularity is due to preservation of the natural environment. Within the park boundaries are dense forests, fern-cluttered gullies, lonely granite headlands, unpeopled white sand beaches and heathlands lit by wildflowers. Sadly, the park is fire prone, so no open fires are allowed between November and May.

Explore the Prom via a network of established tracks. The track to a beach called Squeaky (which does squeak between your toes) is covered by tea-tree canopies containing big twig nests crafted by ringtail possums. By slinging a swag and tramping over the isthmus you reach a wilderness section of the park. You can ascend Mt Oberon, blow over Windy Saddle and slip-slide down the narrow track through Fern Glade. After having your energy renewed by the paperbarks, fish-bone ferns and soft tree-ferns, you emerge at Sealer's Cove. Equipped with a national park bush camping permit, a strong backpack, bivvy and sleeping bag, and food and water, this can be the start of a week's wilderness walking.

Cradle Mountain-Lake St Clair

We all owe great thanks to those people who had the foresight to fight for the protection of wild places. An Austrian, Gustav Weindorfer, was the driving force, when Tasmania was being logged, for preservation of Cradle Mountain-Lake St Clair before vast tracts were systematically degraded. Gustav Weindorfer died in 1932 near his beloved forest home, Waldheim, and most trekkers begin their Overland Track odyssey nearby. First completed in 1935, the Overland Track meanders south from Cradle Mountain, ending at Lake St Clair. It takes anything from eight to 18 days, depending on how many detours you make along the way. The 85-kilometre track grew from a cluster of tracks blazed by prospectors and hunters eager to exploit the land's bounty, and the leftovers from their failures can be seen along the way.

The Overland Track traverses a region of prodigious annual rainfall. Ever-present water and thousands of trekkers each year combine to create long mud-strewn, sloshy and bottomless sections, but the rainfall engenders the lushest of mosses, lichens and rainforests, along with enthusiastic leeches. Park nomenclature utilises not only the usual collection of pioneers, literary and scientific figures, but also Greek mythological characters. Given the blessing from these gods, under a clear sky you trek into the wilderness finding places where your eyes sweep 360° to absorb a full complement of glacier-carved valleys, alpine lakes and tarns, and stark mountain peaks all unaltered, undeveloped and unscarred. There are many peaks to top on the trek, with few requiring technical rockclimbing skills.

The Australian outback varies in colour with the sun and the seasons as with Mount O'Connor in the MacDonnell Ranges near Alice Springs.

Travelling on an overland track from Alice through the red hot desert, one is relieved to at least reach the western edge of the Kimberleys at Halls Creek. From here, it is another 400 kms north west as the crow flies to the Indian Ocean, navigable only by air or by those intrepid enough to walk it.

Campsites along the way can be memorable. Lake Windermere, for example, is a tree-fringed alpine lake set in a broad valley backed by a semicircle of rugged mountains. Late afternoon's warm light gives the whole scene a quality reminiscent of a Rembrandt painting, and at night the blackness is punctuated by sparkling diamonds as numerous as grains of beach sand.

Franklin River

To raft the Franklin is to explore one of Australia's last truly wild rivers. Rhythmic paddling in quiet sections is combined with churning through white water, and each day you travel on a one-way trip deeper into the Tasmanian wilderness.

In a way, rafting a river is like living a story. The introduction is gently flowing water which lulls you into absorbing the beauty of the surroundings. Ominous characters are introduced as the sides of the river come closer, then turn into steep gorges. Tension builds as roaring water approaches, and sparkles dance on the surface as the climax builds.

Thundering rapids give the Franklin story its complex plot and multiple endings. You have some clue of what lies ahead, but it all becomes hypothetical after the raft glides into a smooth patch of water. Then things move at adrenalin-pumping speed. Cumbersome rafts dance, swoop, swirl and bounce under and through fast-moving water. You race to the conclusion of another chapter of the Franklin story, sometimes still in the raft, sometimes not, but always keen to know what's ahead.

You live the river, camping beside it in places like Angel Rain Cavern. A gossamer mist plays on the entrance to the cave and it's like being nestled in behind a delicate waterfall. Caves, caverns, gorges and waterfalls are important on the Franklin. The most famous cave is Kutikina, where radio-carbon dating indicates human occupation began about 20,000 years ago. It is the southernmost occupation point of ice-age man on Earth. Tragic to think that, if some politicians had had their way, it would have been drowned under dammed waters for an unnecessary hydro-electric scheme.

The Nullarbor Caves

The Nullarbor Plain stretches across the border of Western Australia and South Australia. As you get closer to it, the world seems to become flatter and flatter, then so vast that you imagine you can see the curvature of the earth. A surveyor, Dellisser, named the Nullarbor from the Latin 'null arbor', meaning no trees. There are in fact a few trees to be seen from the Eyre Highway. Off the highway, you enter a region unseen by the great majority of travellers. It is devoid of signposts or landmarks, though criss-crossed by a maze of tracks. Beneath the ground is Nullarbor wilderness, a myriad of caves created when the sea

receded and rainwaters etched through what had been the limestone sea bed. Locating the sunken entrances (called dolines) to Nullarbor caves takes good navigation skills.

Exploring the depths of these caves is dirty work and it can be physically demanding, but it offers an extraordinary wilderness escapade. Caving is very warm work. Although the Nullarbor is known for its extremes of temperature, the caves are a pleasant 19°C. In order to see in the dark, each caver needs a miner's light and wet-cell battery pack, a waterproof torch and, as an emergency precaution, candles.

Although there are more than 200 caves in the Nullarbor network, each is individual and unique. In Cocklebiddy and Weebubbie caves, both snorkelling gear and inflatable boats can be used to explore gigantic subterranean lakes. The ultra-clear water has a gentle green colour and swimming on the surface is like space walking.

Some Nullarbor caves are so tiny you must squirm and twist to enter. Others are huge. Mullamullang Cave, more than 12 kilometres long, is one of the largest in Australia. Only a small part can be explored during a full day. After descending the doline, you walk beside a sandy stream bed, then clamber over huge boulders heaped up into 50-metre hills. After squeezing through a narrow section where a wind blows constantly, you encounter an amazing sight — an underground sand dune!

A quiet stretch of the often wild Franklin River

Bungle Bungle Range

The Bungle Bungles, as they are affectionately called, are only now becoming imprinted on the minds of travellers who seek in Australia adventures into the unknown. Here is a true wilderness area, 2,000 kilometres from Perth and several hundred kilometres south of the nearest town, Kununurra, in the Kimberley region of north-west Western Australia.

The Bungle Bungles is a magical region. The range covers 700 square kilometres and has to be a close contender for the eighth wonder of the world.

The range is a spectacular formation of beehive or bell-shaped crinolated sandstone. The geological striation of the rocks creates wonderful contrasts of reds, yellows, blacks and greys which together generate mauves and burnt siena. These majestic piles rise from the black soil plains and are interspersed with massive gorges, cliffs and valleys spiked with palm trees and stony river beds.

It is, however, a fragile paradise. The extraordinary shapes reflect a process of erosion by wind and water of a sandstone that is extremely brittle and which crumbles underfoot. The violent swings in climate from monsoon wet to fierce dry heat also make it a difficult environment for mankind, flora and fauna. These harsh and unstable conditions create problems for the development of the Bungle Bungles as a tourist destination.

Kakadu National Park

Kakadu, east of Darwin in the Northern Territory, is one of Australia's five World Heritage properties. It was accepted on the register because of its landform and variety of fauna and flora and its legacy of Aboriginal art and occupation sites. Stages 1 and 2 comprise more than 12,000 square kilometres of harsh landscape, the product of 2,000 million years of weathering, erosion and sedimentation. It is a tough place. Summer is hot and wet, the time of spectacular waterfalls, but also the time when massive flooding covers much of the land through tropical cyclones, onshore winds and high tides. Winter is hot and dry, but a much surer time to travel.

Even in the dry seaon there are extensive wetlands with large numbers of waterbirds. The whole park is believed to contain about one-third of all Australia's bird species. A bird-lover's delight is to go gliding quietly aboard a punt on Yellow Waters Lagoon in the late afternoon, when the tropical sunset turns the waters blood red. Swimming in the lagoon may have the same effect, as it is home to man-eating saltwater crocodiles. There are, however, many safe places to swim in the park.

Kakadu National Park is now owned by the Aborigines and is leased back to the government. It is an appropriate situation since the Aboriginal presence in Kakadu dates back to the ice age. The explorer Leichhardt made the first record of Aboriginal rock paintings in 1845, but there are more than 1,000 known art sites. Of the paintings, the x-ray, barramundi and Tasmanian tiger images are outstanding, with Obiri Rock being one of the most spectacular galleries.

The Great Barrier Reef

Queensland's prized possession is statistically incredible: 2,000 kilometres long, it covers 35 million hectares. It is the largest coral reef system in the world, with more than 1,500 species of fish, 400 species of coral, 4,000 species of molluscs, 240 species of birds and a staggering array of other marine life. Statistics are one thing, but to appreciate a coral cay on the Great Barrier Reef you have to wake on board a charter vessel to a vibrant morning with the air crisp and salty. You gaze across pale turquoise water to a minute strip of sand with low scrubby vegetation. Stepping ashore is similar to entering a new world. The coral sand is so white it hurts your eyes.

There are resorts on some cays, but staying on a wild uninhabited coral cay isn't simple. There will be no fresh water or shelter, and everything must be brought with you. There are camping permits to organise and boats to charter. Camping equipment, diving gear, first-aid kits and water containers can be hired, but they need to be organised well in advance.

To call the cays uninhabited is an injustice to the natural residents. Muttonbirds (shearwaters) fish out to sea all day, returning to burrows on the cays at dusk. Night spotlighting is the way to discover these bumbling seabirds sharing your refuge. Tread carefully, for their burrows honeycomb the sandy ground. Turtles are also frequent cohabitors of the cays. During the mating season, they lumber precariously up the coral beaches to scoop out nesting places for their eggs. Back in the water, they are light and graceful.

At the lowest level, to experience the delights of a living tropical coral reef you need only the ability to float and breathe through a snorkel. At high tide, the inner reef (the one you can walk on at low tide) is covered by less than two metres of water, perfect for floating on the surface, while gazing down through some of the clearest, warmest water in the world and watching the inhabitants — from the tiniest molluscs and corals to the largest clams and fish — all going about their lives.

Hinchinbrook Island

From Cardwell-by-the-Sea, 100 kilometres or so north of Townsville in Queensland, the largest national park island in Australia appears as a large, brooding mountainous mass just across the Hinchinbrook Channel. The channel you gaze across is actually a drowned river valley, for Hinchinbrook is a continental island complete with jagged peaks, deep gorges, and valleys.

Much of Hinchinbrook National Park's 39,350 hectares is a seldom-visited wilderness. Not that Hinchinbrook is difficult to reach. There is a launch service to the resort at Cape Richards. From here you can trek to a national parks camping area at Macushla, or canoe further around into Missionary Bay. Growing out into the bay, like huge green fingers, are mangrove swamps. Using a national park map, a little luck and a lot of paddling, a boardwalk through one of the mangrove forests can be found in this maze of channels. Once back on land, the track leads across a series of sand dunes to the eastern shore.

The park has established walking tracks which radiate from the Macushla camping area. You can trek through dense rainforest, open eucalypt scrub and along golden sandy beaches. The beach on Ramsay Bay is a favourite with beachcombers and it provides magnificent views of Mt Bowen. This towering mountain peak, covered in dense vegetation on its lower slopes, is often lost in the clouds. Venturing in requires excellent map-reading skills and the ability to be completely self-sufficient.

The Great Sandy Region

The Great Sandy Region, east of Maryborough in Queensland, contains the largest sand island in the world, more than 200 Aboriginal shell middens, an entire undisturbed river catchment, and an internationally significant bird migration area. It covers 350,000 hectares. It is not included on the World Heritage list and the name doesn't apear on official maps. Instead, reference is made to Cooloola, Fraser Island and the Great Sandy Strait.

You can explore the region for weeks, beginning in the pristine Upper Noosa River system where the reflections off tannin-stained water are mirror perfect, then travel until the river becomes a series of water-holes and opens out into vast wallum plains country which is alive with wildflowers. At dusk on the edge of the Noosa Plain, the high-pitched call of the rare glass parrot penetrates the still air. And at dawn, the coloured sand cliffs towering above a seemingly endless beach are lit up by the sun.

Taking to a boat, you can meander through a myriad of waterways called the Great Sandy Strait. It is a flyway for migratory waders from northern Asia and Alaska and the sheltered waters support several species of marine turtles, dolphins and dugong (an endangered species).

Adjacent to the strait is Fraser Island. Almost all sand except for three rock outcrops, this incredible island contains vast dunes, more than 40 freshwater lakes, an uncounted number of freshwater streams and an ecosystem which climaxes in dense notophyll vineforest growing out of pure sand. Trekking the island from south to north along silent tracks is an outstanding wilderness experience.

Leigh Hemmings is one of Australia's most prolific adventure travel photo-journalists. His articles and photographs appear regularly in a variety of travel and adventure publications.

A gorge within the fabulous Bungle Bungle Range

DAVID MCGONIGAL

Aboriginal Art

Jennifer Isaacs

Australia has an enormous diversity of styles of Aboriginal art. Each of the dynamic traditions, though varying in form from region to region, is united by common religious themes expressing the relationship between people, their land, and the ancestral beings. Aboriginal art is one way that people mediate with the ever-present Dreaming ancestors; it is one of the great religious arts of the world.

Aboriginal people have probably lived across Australia for up to 100,000 years. Small groups of people, very often just the immediate family of husband, wives and children, moved over their lands with the seasons and available food supply, supporting themselves by hunting, fishing and food gathering. They evolved a technology and way of life which remained in perfect harmony with their environment.

They believe that in the time before man inhabited the land, the ancestral spirits wandered the earth in both human and animal form. They created in their epic struggles many features in the landscape such as rivers, hills, waterholes and special rock formations, and gave to their descendants all the sacred arts. The main forms of Aboriginal art are body painting, rock painting or carving, bark painting, wood carving and painting fibre arts and ground painting transferred to spectacular modern acrylics on canvas.

Aboriginal artists utilised natural earth pigments in all their work — red iron ochre, yellow ochre, charcoal and kaolin or white pipe clay. For special effects, feathers and down were incorporated in the designs with human blood used as an adhesive. Occasionally, also, particularly in ground painting, plants and seeds gave height and texture to the design.

Traditionally, paintings were done on a wide variety of surfaces, including rock surfaces and cave interiors, bark shelters and bark strips, the bodies of dancers, and the surfaces of carvings and mortuary sculpture.

Body painting can only be seen in the ceremonial context, but throughout Australia there are many beautiful and complex paintings on the interior surfaces of caves. Hunting scenes as well as 'mimi' or spirit figures, love magic and sorcery themes are depicted. The origins of 'X-ray' art appear in caves in western Arnhem Land and contemporary bark paintings from this region show similarities in style. In eastern Arnhem Land, highly decorative and complex designs depicting mythical events are painted. Bark paintings are now well known, and their richness and variety justly appreciated.

Bark paintings are a very old Aboriginal art form. Once practised on the inside surface of bark shelters, they are now found throughout Arnhem Land. A suitable section of bark is removed from the stringy bark tree, usually during the wet season, and the rough outer layer is hacked off with a sharp tool or axe. The bark is then thinned by removing more outer layers until only the smooth inner section remains. This is placed over a fire to uncurl and is weighted with stones to completely flatten it. After removal of the charred sections, the bark is painted using natural clays and rocks — yellow ochre, red iron ochre, white pipe clay and black manganese.

Traditional brushes vary. The finest lines, particularly those in the cross hatching, are executed with fine long human hair brushes or palm leaf fibre. For applying background colour, broad brushes and chewed twigs are used. European brushes are favoured for some types of painting.

Using similar techniques, the same designs that appear on bark are also painted on many carvings,

particularly bone containers, and eastern Arnhem Land carved animals. Ritual participants paint beautiful detailed patterns on their bodies and sometimes add other features such as bird down, feather head-dresses, armbands and string girdles.

In Central Australia, elaborate and very large ground paintings were made for ceremonies and these not only utilised ochres but also any other material that would give the necessary colour and texture, including blood, feather, down, twigs and seeds. Over the last 15 years, these designs have been transferred to hardboard and are painted in acrylics. However, they still retain their complex symbolic meanings and religious significance.

The Tiwi, from Bathurst and Melville Islands, produced the largest carvings in their elaborately painted 'Pukamani' poles, erected on graves for burial ceremonies. The spectacular Tiwi carved poles are now made for ceremony and for sale through the traditional art company on Bathurst Island, Tiwi Pima. The painted surfaces of the poles are similar to the designs that the Tiwi place on bark baskets, sculptures of birds, usually pelicans, or ancestral figures from the 'Purukapali' myth.

Tiwi art is completely abstract and vigorous, even rough in appearance. The broad, strong linear patterns are augmented by masses of dots, applied with a Tiwi invention, a multi-pronged comb.

Elsewhere, Aboriginal skills with wood included ceremonial figures, birds, animals and fish. The surface of carved objects might then be fluted, or incised again with meaningful symbols or designs based on segments of myths.

The richest and most varied collections of Aboriginal art are painted in cave galleries and carved on rock outcrops at numerous sites throughout Australia. The galleries are of such antiquity, so beautiful, and of such magnificent variety that it has been suggested by many archaeologists that Australia may well house the largest and most important collection of Palaeolithic art in the world.

The art spans a period from at least 20,000 years ago to the present. Ancient rock grooves in the dark recesses of Koonalda Cave in South Australia are the earliest known art of the ancestors of modern Aborigines, and a variety of styles of rock carvings or engravings are found ranging in age throughout the continent. Vast galleries of paintings occur in Arnhem Land, the Kimberleys and Cape York, and paintings are also found in Central Australia, Queensland and New South Wales.

Rock engraving and cave paintings were practised by Aborigines for many reasons. Some caves and rock sites were obviously of great importance and housed the image and spirit of great ancestral beings of the Dreaming. In addition, during the wet in the steamy north, small groups gathered in sandstone caves and painted the rock surfaces with designs of fish, animals and other totemic creatures and by the very act ensured a successful hunt. Sorcery was common and painting the image of a victim upside down or of a malevolent sorcery spirit figure, accompanied by the appropriate chant, would ensure that harm befell the victim. Love magic and fertility magic were also common themes.

Many Aboriginal communities, seeking to maintain their traditional life in remote areas, have turned to a fuller utilisation of their creative skills to provide a means of economic survival for their people, making many traditional works for sale to galleries in the major cities.

Young Aboriginal artists are also exploring new techniques and subject matter reflecting their changing responses to their role as Aborigines in larger Australian society. Some of this art examines important social issues — from the dispossession of their ancestors from their land to the alienation of Aborigines in the cities. Others express religion and mythology in contemporary paintings or prints.

A most remarkable Aboriginal art movement has grown up in the Australian desert: modern acrylic paintings inspired by traditional ground constructions have been hailed as the most important development in contemporary Australian art of the last ten years.

The movement began at Papunya in the early 1970s from a children's mural on the school wall using geometric shapes and symbols such as circles and zigzags. Intrigued, some of the older men came closer, and upon encouragement, took over the task, completing a traditional design over the whole wall. The interest and fervour of the men to paint their Dreamings grew until up to 20 artists were using available scraps of masonite and board, and grinding ochres or obtaining paint, producing many paintings in completely traditional symbols.

The paintings that have flowed since those early years have developed to the point where major galleries and collections now show well-articulated large abstract canvasses. Federal grants cover the services of an adviser in Papunya who acts as agent, organiser and intermediary between these artists, their co-operative company Papunya-Tula, galleries and the public. Over 100 artists, both men and women, now paint wonderful works on canvas in locations hundreds of kilometres apart, though most are at Kintore, a settlement 300 kilometres due west of Papunya in the Kintore Ranges, not far from the Western Australian border.

Despite stylistic variations, the central theme of all paintings, as of ground designs and ceremonies, is the events of the Dreaming. Each painting is about a place, frequently the birthplace of the artist or of his Dreaming ancestors. Each painting represents not only the site but also the events that took place there in the Dreaming. Sites may be specific rocks, waterholes, special trees, mountains and many others. The creation ancestors, which can be honey ants, bush onions, wild kangaroos, sweet potatoes or budgerigars, are thought to be at rest at these places, but their power and force become one with the dancers during ceremonies.

PENNY TWEEDIE

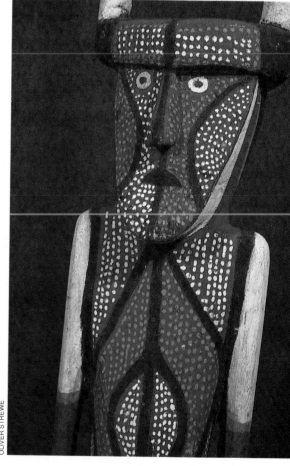

OLIVER STREWE

Dancers kick up the desert dust during a corroboree dance in Arnhem Land, source of much of Australia's Aboriginal art, including bark paintings

Australian Aboriginal traditional arts are unique. The paintings, designs and carvings produced today are a direct continuation of a rich tradition which has existed since man's earliest origins on this continent.

In the Sydney and Hawkesbury River areas of New South Wales, there are large engraved linear ground figures of ancestral beings, animals, birds and fish. These Aboriginal engravings also include a wide range of hunting compositions illustrating the spearing of kangaroos and fish and the use of boomerangs as weapons. Dotted throughout the valleys from Berowra to the Colo River are many isolated figures, including paintings of stencilled hands.

The National Parks and Wildlife Service rangers at Ku-ring-gai Chase National Park will direct people to easily accessible engravings.

The task of protecting this art heritage is immense and in the long term is almost impossible. Although a large proportion of the important sites are within park boundaries and cared for by rangers, and although it is illegal to deface or damage artworks, the remoteness of sites outside parks and reserves does not allow any control. It is too easy for trail-bike riders or holiday-makers to find a site and yield to the impulse of leaving their own mark on history. One magnificent large ancestor hero on Wheelbarrow Ridge Road is defaced with the wheel marks of motorbikes and many others have initials carved into the rock surface. At Maroota, two giant ancestor figures straddle the sides of a rock platform and between them is another series of engravings, including rows of pits, seven kangaroos, a snake and an emu with eggs.

Across the wild sandstone escarpment area of the Kakadu National Park in the Northern Territory are numerous precipitous rock faces and caves and it is here that some of the most famous Aboriginal art galleries are to be found. The X-ray bark paintings are derived from the same tradition and indeed are identical to many X-ray paintings on rocks in western Arnhem Land. Fish are common subjects, along with animals like the emu, kangaroo, wallaby, lizard, possum and other prey of the hunter. Immense figures of ancestral heroes of the Dreamtime, like the Lightning Spirit, also occur, as do numerous ancient monochrome linear paintings of the fragile mimi spirits. The two main galleries are Nourlangie and Obiri Rocks. Both are open to visitors, who can travel there in the comfort of coaches or cars.

Many of the great rock art sites, no longer maintained by present-day Aborigines, are under threat of extinction from a variety of agents. Weathering in particular, with the action of rainwater, humidity and rock flaking, causes untold damage to the delicate images in unfixed ochres. Plant matter such as algae, fungi and mosses, as well as insect and animal activity, are also destructive, but the most widespread damage has been caused by careless visitors and vandalism. Mining and development plans have frequently threatened rock art sites, though in recent years many mining companies have been more aware of their responsibilities in safeguarding these sites.

The traveller who visits Darwin has the unique opportunity of taking a tour to the Bathurst and Melville Islands. (See the Islands section for tour details.) On Bathurst Island, the Tiwi run a small shop which markets their traditional carvings, paintings and a range of ceremonial body decorations. Visitors may also be shown a group of Pukumani poles in situ, left to rot after the burial ceremony.

Two important modern Aboriginal enterprises may also be seen — the print workshop, where young designers hand-print Tiwi fabrics for sale to galleries and the fashion industry, and the pottery. This is a stoneware-producing Aboriginal pottery which was begun in the early 1970s. Darwin and Bathurst Island are the only places where the pots may be seen, as most are snapped up after each firing.

This is the only Aboriginal settlement or community which may freely be visited by tourists, but access is strictly controlled. Tours over several days, with camping arrangements, can be organised through operators in Darwin. These combine access to art with bush food, a beautiful environment and a unique experience of Aboriginal culture.

The Cape York escarpment district near the small towns of Laura and Cooktown, north-west of Cairns, houses the most extensive galleries of cave or rock painting discovered within the last 20 years. The first sighting of a European with a horse is recorded here. The animal is immense, reflecting the awe of the artist. These galleries house all manner of paintings of animals, reptiles and birds, as well as malevolent sorcery figures, images painted for love magic purposes, and other long-striking stick-like figures known as Quinkans. Local legends tell that these are night marauders who attack the unwary with the stone axes they have on their elbows and knees.

The Giant Horse Gallery has an extraordinary series of images that obviously post-date European settlement, or at least record the first sightings of explorers with horses. There are three shelters in which large horses appear, dwarfing and superimposing on other images. In one shelter about 18 metres long, a white and yellow horse 3.35 metres long by 1.83 metres high is shown with red reins extending forward over the head to the hand of a red horizontal image of a man who appears to have been thrown from the horse. A pig is also shown. Pigs were first released in Cape York in 1770 by Captain Cook, who hoped they would multiply to provide food for shipwrecked sailors.

The most distinctive figures of the Quinkan Gallery are human-shaped images of spirits with various names, but most are frequently termed Quinkans. They wear a variety of head-dresses and

A famous bark painter, Gabargu and his family in the Northern Territory.

often have some non-human features with distortions of body, limbs, head or genitals. One important gallery may have been a sacred cave. Large male figures are shown with rayed head-dresses; other figures depict dingoes, kangaroos and emus.

Art Collections

For those interested in the history of Aboriginal art and the many forms it takes, major collections are displayed in museums and art galleries around the country. Displays change, however, and researchers may need to ask curators to see stored items of particular interest.

Aboriginal Arts Australia

This national company was established by the Australian government to market Aboriginal art and craft through a comprehensive network of galleries in Sydney, Melbourne, Perth, Darwin and Alice Springs. Each gallery offers bark paintings, weaving, carving, desert acrylics on canvas, boomerangs, shields and modern fabrics, books, records and cassettes.

The galleries in Alice Springs and Darwin are more regionally specialised; the Darwin gallery is close to the rich bark paintings of Arnhem Land and therefore exhibits much of this work.

Alice Springs is the closest town to the desert communities, and artists from Papunya, Haasts Bluff and other areas often gather here. These paintings are visually exciting, with every feature of their narrative expressed in symbols, particularly circles, U shapes, wavy lines and dotted patterns.

The Australian Museum

This museum, centrally sited in Sydney, is particularly interesting because of its permanent Aboriginal Culture Gallery which traces religion, customs and the relationship of people to their land from ancient times to the present. The display includes cave art, regional displays of art and artefacts, a complete 'dig' showing archaeology at work deciphering Australian Aboriginal prehistory, modern videos of urban social programmes and a changing gallery for photographs and art. The Museum collections are extensive but most are stored. The strong point is the northern Queensland collection put together by a surveyor named Roth at the turn of the century. The Museum shop has a particularly good stock of Aboriginal art and craft and a wide range of books on the subject.

Australian National Gallery

The premier Australian art gallery, located in Canberra, has a permanent display of Aboriginal paintings, and due to its policy of purchasing major artists' best works, the collection is outstanding. In particular, the complete works of Yirawala and Wandjuk Marika are held. Both bark painters epitomise the best in style of their respective traditions — the Gunwinggu of western Arnhem Land and the Riratjingu of eastern Arnhem Land.

In addition, the Gallery's central Arnhem Land bark paintings include impressive works by Milpurru, Bulun Bulun, Malangi, Dhatangu and many others. Huge acrylics on canvas from the central desert are usually on view — spectacular abstracts of dots and lines, great religious works and a major Australian contribution to international contemporary art.

Northern Territory Museum and Art Gallery

In Darwin, the Northern Territory Museum and Art Gallery, although a relatively new institution, has strong regional interests. It has amassed a marvellous collection of Aboriginal art with particular emphasis on the bark paintings of the coastal Northern Territory. It also houses the spectacular bold abstract paintings and huge hardwood painted carvings of the Tiwi people, who live on Bathurst and Melville Islands, off the coast of Darwin.

Mititjulu Arts and Crafts

One of the least-known venues for seeing Aboriginal art and craft is the Mititjulu Arts and Crafts Gallery right at the base of Ayers Rock, run by the Aboriginal traditional owners themselves. Tucked away in the bushes, it is not on the usual tourist runs, but is a delight to visit.

The Pitjantjatjara and Yankuntjatjara people mainly carve wood and make superbly crafted weapons, particularly spears, womerahs, shields and boomerangs. Two local woods are used — 'mulga', a type of wattle, and the roots of the river red gum. Desert artists reveal an uncannily accurate observation of nature in their carved snakes, lizards, perentie, wild cats and small marsupials. Aboriginal artists frequently visit the centre, and sometimes demonstrate spear-throwing or weapon-making.

Jennifer Isaacs has lived and worked with Aboriginal people for many years. In the early 1970s, she pioneered programmes in the Australia Council to encourage Aboriginal culture and to promote Aboriginal arts nationally and internationally.

The close ties she developed with the Aboriginal community led to her adoption by the Rirratjingu of eastern Arnhem Land and the Thanaquith of Cape York. Her husband and children are also part of this extended Aboriginal family.

She has curated international touring exhibitions and has written many articles, catalogues and books on Aboriginal art, including Australian Dreaming — 40,000 Years of Aboriginal History.

*One of the ancient Aboriginal cave paintings to be seen at
Kakadu National Park.*

ADVENTURES

A group of riders fords a stream - a welcome respite from the dusty trail

Adventures

CRAIG MARSHALL

Activity Lodges & Centres

Australians take their leisure seriously, and sport and open-air recreation play a large part in the Australian way of life. Indeed, for some they are almost a religion. That owes something to an innate Australian competitiveness and sense of adventure, as well as to a sympathetic environment.

Australians are certainly world-class in a wide range of sports. They have excelled in tennis and golf, hockey and netball, and as surfers, flyers, swimmers, cyclists and runners. Australians recently climbed Mt Everest, while others have performed well internationally in such diverse sports as hang-gliding, canoeing and yachting.

Every country throws up a champion from time to time. But what makes Australia and Australians distinctive is that participation in these activities is considered the norm, and not the preserve of the elite.

Comparative wealth, a reasonable degree of leisure and a general 'give-it-a-go' spirit have all contributed to this. But more than anything else, the reason has to be the ready accessibility of the space and terrain to indulge in these pursuits.

A new breed of 'resort' has recently sprung up across Australia — holiday locations designed to cater for an enormous variety of activity both strenuous and sedate. Sometimes these are brand-new and custom-built. Sometimes they are converted homesteads or farms, offering their guests a glimpse of an older Australia as they pursue their chosen pastime. Always the range of choice is staggering, and the range of budgets catered for almost as wide.

We have christened these places 'activity lodges and centres'. Such a centre in the high country of New South Wales or Victoria, for example, may well offer to the energetic activities as diverse as cross-country skiing in the Snowy Mountains, horse riding on mountain trails, and four-wheel driving over rough country. The more leisurely will usually find golf courses and tennis courts nearby, and those with a taste for the good life are rarely far from vineyards or even locations for ballooning trips complete with champagne reception.

In Tasmania, the attractions might be white-water rafting or trout fishing. In South Australia, Western Australia and the Northern Territory, trips to the true outback, camel-riding, birdwatching and wildlife studies will be among the options.

In Queensland — with its tropical climate and superb beaches and reefs — water sports will almost certainly be high on the visitor's agenda. In fact, it is hard to find anywhere within reach of the sea in Australia where aquatic pastimes are not prominent on the list. With the longest coastline of any country on earth, and much of it empty, it is not surprising that surfing, water-skiing, sailboarding and all manner of boating activities are hugely popular. Generally warm waters and the world's most spectacular reefs — complete with wrecks — mean that diving is also growing in popularity by the year.

Fishing is popular wherever there is water — salt or fresh — in Australia. The majority of the activity centres we have selected will point the angler in the right direction for some sort of catch — whether it be the fighting barramundi in Queensland or the wily trout of the south-east's upland rivers.

Bushwalking is in the same league of popularity, and every guesthouse and hotel will suggest walks for the visitor through the locality. And walking in Australia can mean more than a quiet stroll: treks that last days on end are available to the real enthusiast.

Once again, variety is the keynote, with tropical and temperate rainforest, snowbound mountains, semi-desert and vast tracts of eucalypt forest within easy range of major cities.

Locations

New South Wales

1 **Midginbil Hill**, located near the border of Queensland and New South Wales in the Tweed Valley, is particularly popular for its horse riding facilities.

Guests can either stay in family rooms at the lodge, or camp beside the creek near Nightcap Range.

The sheer cliff face of the Nightcap National Park forms an imposing backdrop to the Midginbil Hill Holiday Farm. Orienteering courses are marked through the property and maps are distributed to interested guests. The farm has a dairy and chickens, donkeys, horses and sheep. A tennis court and swimming pool keep energetic guests entertained.

The owners, John and Annette Flower, often pack lunches for guests taking trail rides or embarking on expeditions to Mount Warning. Rides leave at different times during the day, and evening bushwalks, escorted by John, afford the opportunity to catch glimpses of the region's indigenous fauna in their natural habitat.

Clarrie Hall Dam, nine kilometres away, is a popular spot for canoeing and swimming.

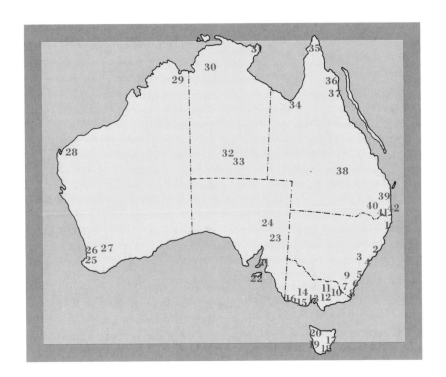

2 **Mt Seaview Resort** is located just 55 kilometres from Wauchope on the Oxley Highway. The resort is set in a picturesque valley on the banks of the Hastings River.

The activities offered include horse riding, swimming in an eight-kilometre stretch of the Hastings River, bushwalking, canoeing, gold panning, fishing and wilderness journeys. These journeys range from half-day explorations to three-day camping safaris. Mt Seaview also has modern four-wheel-drive vehicles available for the camping trips.

A nine-day golf holiday package is offered and includes twin-share accommodation, golf tuition, green fees, safaris and horse riding.

Four-wheel-drive safaris can also be arranged for journeys through other regions of Australia. One takes 26 days, travelling through central Australia to Kakadu

National Park, Darwin and returning through Queensland. The vehicles supplied are airconditioned and fully equipped, and the driver/guide is selected for his extensive knowledge of Australia, and for driving skills in all conditions.

3 In the foothills of the Barrington Tops, just north of Dungog and a three and a half hour drive from Sydney is **Bellbird Valley Country Retreat** — a 100-hectare property with its own mountain streams and rainforests.

Birds and wildlife abound, and the quiet observer may be lucky enough to spot an elusive lyrebird or koala. In summer, visitors cool off in a deep pool beneath overhanging tree ferns, and the winter alternative is a brisk walk along crisp, frost-covered paths, returning to a huge open log fire.

The individual lodges are luxuriously appointed

with all modern conveniences. Each one is built of logs and lined throughout with pine. They have two bedrooms and a fully equipped kitchen and bathroom, as well as a lounge room and private veranda. Guests can choose to cater for themselves, or eat all meals in the comfortable licensed restaurant. Emphasis is on country-style cooking. After the meal, visitors can relax with a drink beside the roaring log fire, or — in warm weather — in the cool, shady courtyard surrounded by flowering shrubs.

Horse riding is very popular and there are horses and ponies to suit all ages and capabilities. All-weather floodlit tennis courts are just a two-minute drive away. The famous vineyards of the Hunter Valley are also within easy reach.

4 **Legges Camp** is situated in the heart of the scenic Myall Lakes National Park. The camp provides accommodation in tents and caravan sites with all amenities available.

Many outdoor recreational activities are available, such as swimming, canoeing, boating and guided bushwalks through the natural rainforests. There is a comprehensive range of boats, canoes, sailboards (including children's sizes), catamarans, tents and camping equipment for hire.

The park lessee, Doug Honeyman, and his wife Carol, offer canoe and camping tours around the lakes for both school and family groups.

5 **Ferndale Lodge**, owned by Jim and Jean Lorraine, is a one and a half hour drive from Sydney. It is a delightful old colonial house, beautifully situated above the Hawkesbury River.

Ferndale offers accommodation in comfortable one or two-bedroom log cabins in a bush setting with magnificent views of the Hawkesbury. Appetising meals prepared from locally grown vegetables are a speciality at Ferndale. Log fires provide a marvellously warm atmosphere during the winter months.

Activities include trail riding, canoeing, water-skiing, tennis, swimming and horse riding.

6 Just two hours' drive from Sydney, on the south coast of New South Wales, is an activity centre where swimming, bushwalking, golf, boating and horse riding are all popular.

Coolangatta Historic Village is the site of the first settlement on the the south coast of New South Wales, and its buildings are situated on a 120-hectare property overlooking Shoalhaven Heads.

Its current owners, the Bishop family, were born and raised on the property, and they have restored and redecorated the old convict buildings to their present state. All guest rooms have ensuites, and the property has a nine-hole golf course, tennis and volleyball courts, push bikes, a swimming pool and a recreation and games room with billiard table and darts.

Close by are country bushwalking tracks, horse riding schools, museums, art galleries, the Old Coolangatta Pottery and waterslides for the children. Seven Mile Beach and Shoalhaven River are ideal for swimming, boating and fishing. Water-skiing and windsurfing are popular, too. A four-wheel-drive trip to the summit of Mount Coolangatta is arranged for interested guests.

An old community hall has been restored and a garden restaurant added. The Great Hall is the venue for banquet evenings on Saturdays, when a traditional dance is held.

7 **Thredbo Alpine Village** is one of Australia's leading ski resorts, located right in the heart of Kosciusko National Park. It has over 100 kilometres of skiing trails, and a chairlift that operates all year round. There are good spots for beginner, intermediate and advanced skiers. The ski school is internationally competitive, with professional tuition available from instructors. From early spring until as late as November, cross-country skiing is popular.

The Alpine Village itself is always a bustling centre of activity during winter, with its 15 restaurants, quaint shops and a comprehensive choice of accommodation.

Although winter is obviously the peak tourist season, various other activities are available at different times of the year. There is a horse riding school in the village, a golf course, six day tennis courts and two evening ones, and many bushwalking trails around the adjacent national park.

At Lake Jindabyne, a half hour's drive from Thredbo, sailboards can be hired, and swimming is safe both here and at Friday Flats. Canoeing, paddleboating and water-skiing are also available at Lake Jindabyne.

Fishing is also popular in the lakes and streams in Kosciusko National Park. For the less adventurous, there are the Thredbo Valley Trout Springs and Deer Park, and the Garden Trout Hatchery in Jindabyne. Gear, tackle and boats can be hired locally.

Thredbo Alpine Village is approximately seven hours' drive from both Melbourne and Sydney.

8 **The Oaks Holiday Ranch** is situated at Mossy Point on the NSW south coast. It is a popular base for horse riding, canoeing, fishing, tennis, swimming, bushwalking, croquet and volleyball. There is also a games room and a golf driving range, while the beach is only two kilometres away. Bob Fineman is a Californian and the home he and Margot have established is reminiscent of the Spanish hacienda style popular in the southern United States.

The Oaks was 18 years in the planning and it shows. It now has a thriving farm, with Hereford cattle, donkeys, pigs and sheep and with its own Welsh mountain pony stud. Wildlife is abundant nearby, particulary kangaroos, wallabies and wild birds. The Oaks caters for three-day minimum stays and also takes weekend bookings.

MARK STEVEN

Adventures

223

Australian Capital Territory

9 **Canberra Motor Village** is an accommodation resort located just three kilometres from Canberra and set in four hectares of landscaped grounds overlooking the beautiful Black Mountain Nature Reserve.

Facilities at the village include a licensed restaurant and mini-market, a swimming pool, tennis courts, a barbecue area and a community kitchen. Bicycles are available for cycling around Canberra, and the village is in a perfect location for bushwalking excursions into the nature reserve.

Accommodation includes caravans, mobile homes and self-contained motel units, as well as camping facilities. The village is a 'Life! Be In It' property and was a 1986 National Tourism Award nominee.

Victoria

10 Lake Dartmouth in the Victorian Alps is the highest earth-filled dam in Australia, forming a lake as big as Sydney Harbour. Here, at the **Lake Dartmouth Resort,** guests can avail themselves of excellent recreational facilities.

Accommodation exists in the form of a group lodge, which caters for up to 22 people, self-contained lodge units, and a caravan park. There is also a recently completed motel with 30 rooms.

The resort boasts an international-standard restaurant, and plenty of barbecue areas.

Whilst staying at the resort, guests can play tennis, go canoeing, fishing, swimming, pan for that elusive gold nugget, take a bush walk, or saddle a horse and spend several hours familiarising themselves with the territory. Four championship golf courses are each a little over an hour away, and for the children, there is a BMX bike track with bikes for hire. Archery, pony rides and trampolining are also available.

11 Celebrating 75 years of mountaintop hospitality, **Mt Buffalo Chalet** has been described as an 'island in the sky'. Mt Buffalo is off the Ovens Highway, 330 kilometres north-east of Melbourne and 130 kilometres south of Albury. It is easy to reach by car, even in the depths of winter, with a sealed road right to the chalet and the snowline. Alternatively, visitors can take the train to Wangaratta where they will be collected by bus.

At the chalet, guests find all the charm of the old world with starched table linen, gleaming silverware, log fires, a croquet lawn and old English-style hospitality. There is also central heating, a bottle shop, colour television, washing and drying machines, a coffee shop, in-house movies, dancing, carpet bowls and bingo.

Mt Buffalo was one of Australia's first ski resorts, and in winter all the necessary equipment is available for hire. The chalet ski school provides professional instruction during the winter months to cater to every need, from beginners through to advanced skiers.

In summer, guests can swim in the chalet pool or in nearby Lake Catani. The lake is also suitable for fishing, canoeing and kayaking. Tennis is popular at any time of the year when snow isn't covering the courts, and the less energetic can play billiards, pool and snooker in the games room. There are also alpine ponies for hire by the hour, half day or day.

12 In the foothills of the Bogong National Park in north-east Victoria is the **Mountain Creek Centre.** It is set amidst pines and open bushland and is bounded by state forest and some 60 hectares of farmland. In winter, its close proximity to the ski resort of Falls Creek makes it an ideal location for skiing enthusiasts.

The area abounds with a rich variety of animal, bird and plant life, and staff can arrange special-interest tours for those guests wishing to enjoy the spectacular scenery and observe the wildlife in its natural habitat. Horse riding is a particularly popular activity, especially on warm summer evenings. Horses can be hired locally and are brought to the centre for groups to use. Both horse-riding and skiing packages can be organised in advance.

Accommodation is in two pine log cabins, catering for a maximum of 60 guests. Each bedroom sleeps four people in pine bunks with mattresses, doonas and pillows provided. The centre has a

Kooralbyn Valley, Queensland

Previous page: Thredbo Alpine Village is situated in the heart of the best downhill skiing area in the country

spacious, centrally heated dining room and kitchen, with a glass wall to take full advantage of the views.

13 'Arrabri' is an Aboriginal word meaning a camp near a large mountain, and this accurately describes the **Arrabri Lodge** — a holiday camp and guesthouse in a magnificent mountain setting at East Warburton, close to Melbourne.

There is accommodation here for school camps, social clubs and families, with carpeted cabins equipped with pine bunks and bedding. Also available is a group leader's lounge with open fire and easy chairs, and a licensed dining room which also welcomes BYO. The lodge is centrally heated.

The five-hectare complex has recreational facilities for tennis, trampolining and volleyball, and there is a fenced in-ground pool. Nature, fitness and orienteering courses are conducted through the bush and there are numerous hikes along Forestry Commission tracks.

Resident owners Stephen and Roslyn Brown and Peter and Barbara Bond, all experienced youth leaders, can assist in putting together programmes, hikes and tour arrangements. Indoor activities include billiards, table tennis, darts, cards, carpet bowls, dancing and film nights. Television and video are also available.

14 **Jinda Park** is a 4,300-hectare property located at the foot of the Otways in Victoria, surrounded by magnificent state forest on all fronts. It is only minutes away from some of the best beaches in Australia, and a day trip from most Victorian tourist attractions.

Each of its log cabins is widely separated from the others to ensure complete privacy, and contains three bedrooms to sleep about six people. All cabins have their own log fires.

Visitors use Jinda Park as a base for expeditions into the surrounding forest on foot, or even on

motorbike. Horse-riding facilities are also available.

Owner Neil Moore regards himself as a farmer first and he welcomes guests' participation in all farming activities.

The park also caters for disabled visitors. One cabin is specially fitted out, with access to a sauna and spa room.

15 **Beacon Point** is set in the Otway Ranges at Apollo Bay, just 170 kilometres from Melbourne. Each lodge accommodates up to five persons and each has its own living area and kitchen, open log fires, two bedrooms, and individual outdoor barbecues. All blankets and pillows are supplied, but guests must bring their own linen.

Various activities are available. There is a choice of river or rock fishing, while the many lovely bushwalks through Otway National Park will keep naturalists enthralled for hours. Boating and yachting are popular pastimes and for the more energetically inclined, squash courts and a golf course are only minutes away.

16 On the Great Ocean Road, 222 kilometres west of Melbourne and 35 kilometres from Apollo Bay in the southern region of Victoria, **Glen Aire Log Cabins** offer a breathtaking panorama of the Otway Ranges, The Aire Valley and the Southern Ocean.

Set in 44 hectares of natural bush and farmland,

Many bushwalking trips allow participants to get fairly close to the native fauna

the spacious cabins offer every comfort. Each has a log fire, barbecue, carpeted bedrooms and living area.

Glen Aire has been the site of some very exciting archaeological finds and every summer scientists return and continue their search for dinosaur fossils. Recent finds have led to the naming of Dinosaur Cove, access to which is opposite the cabins and takes visitors into the Otway National Park.

Three main camping areas are available in the park — at Johanna, Aire River and Blanket Bay. The park offers opportunities for walking, fishing, surfing, sightseeing and nature study. Fine views can be obtained along the Great Ocean Road, while walking tracks and beaches allow for both short and extended walks. The Cape Otway Lighthouse, adjacent to the park, can be visited on Tuesdays and Thursdays and is a must for viewing the huge sea swells and ferocious gales of the Southern Ocean.

Tasmania

17 Situated opposite Seven Mile Beach, Hobart's most popular surfing beach, is the **Pines Resort**. Though close to the city, The Pines still retains a true holiday atmosphere.

It boasts a Wimbledon-type grass tennis court, pool, sauna and spa. Registered members of a golf club will be welcomed at the Royal Hobart Golf Club; sailboards and surfboards are available at the beach, and there is a fully licensed restaurant.

The two-bedroom apartments are designed for family comfort and are fully self-contained.

This conveniently located beachside resort is set among stately pine trees in seven and a half hectares of grounds.

18 The Huon Valley is a famous apple-growing district just south of Hobart and is home of Tasmania's Huon pine. On the hills above is situated **Balfe's Hill Farm,** a small dairy and sheep farm overlooking the Huon and Cygnet Valleys.

The hostel has comfortable twin-room accommodation and share facilities, and farm-fresh food is always available.

While staying at the farm, visitors can take one or two-day rafting and canoeing trips on the Huon and Picton Rivers, or set off on a two-day walk along the edge of the south-west wilderness, just 50 kilometres west of Hobart.

Balfe's Hill Farm itself is a family business, but four guides are employed to conduct comprehensive tours of the region through rainforests, eucalyptus woodland and alpine areas.

19 Recently $5 million has been spent upgrading **Cradle Mountain Lodge,** located on the edge of Tasmania's Cradle Mountain in Lake St Clair National Park. The project included 60 new accommodation units and upmarket suites, two trout lakes, a covered tennis court and skating rink, and facilities for cross-

country skiers, hikers, canoeists and trout fishermen.

The 126,000-hectare estate embraces mountain peaks, wild open moorland, gorges, forested valleys, lakes and tarns. The whole scene is dominated by Cradle Mountain with Dove Lake at its foot. Listed by the World Heritage Committee in 1982, this wilderness is joined by only 130 sites around the world in an exclusive catalogue of the world's most precious places.

With only nine guest rooms, the atmosphere is casual and friendly at the lodge, particularly in the comfortable guest lounge with its open fire, and in the licensed dining room. Self-contained cabin accommodation is also available with linen, towels, doonas and blankets provided. All cabins have well stocked wood fires. Each evening, animals from the surrounding forests come down to the lodge to feed, providing another special attraction.

The area offers many kilometres of bushwalking tracks for walkers of all levels of experience. The streams and lakes are well stocked with Tasmanian trout, and the Cradle Plateau is excellent terrain for cross-country skiing.

The patient observer might well be rewarded by a glimpse of Australia's famous platypus in rivers in the district.

20 **Mountain Valley** is an ideal base from which to explore the spectacular Leven Canyon in Tasmania. Guests stay in log cabins in river valley surroundings, ringed by mountains and forests.

Mountain Valley activities include trips to glow

Typical Tasmanian alpine country, famous for superior brown and rainbow trout fishing

worm caves, river fishing and swimming, horse riding, mountain walks to Alpine Lake and track walks through rough country to Cradle Mountain National Park. This wilderness of 126,000 hectares of peaks, moors, gorges, valleys and lakes is dominated by Cradle Mountain, with Dove Lake at its foot.

South Australia

21 **Wirrina** is a 522-hectare resort, 90 kilometres south of Adelaide on the Fleurieu Peninsula. It is close to the wineries of Langhorne Creek, Reynella and McLaren Vale, with access to fishing along the peninsula.

The resort is often used by travellers on their way to Kangaroo Island, and has its own 18-hole golf course, all-weather tennis courts, outdoor pool, solarium, sauna and spa. Various hikes around the cliffs and beach areas are well worth the investment for unparalleled ocean views, and horses can be hired, complete with lessons from experienced instructors, for a leisurely ride around Wirrina.

There is a health and fitness centre on the premises, as well as a licensed restaurant and bar, a conference centre and luxury accommodation.

22 Located on the shores of the American River inlet on Kangaroo Island is **Linnett's Island Club.** The club has a swimming pool and spa, tennis courts, horse riding, table tennis, scenic walks and facilities for catamaran sailing, scuba diving, and fishing from the club's 16-metre launch.

Bowling greens and golf courses are close by and sightseeing tours are conducted by coach and launch.

In the motel-style units and in the club's four self-contained flats there are en-suite facilities, fridges, colour TVs and airconditioning. The club has a fully licensed restaurant and two cocktail bars, and a barbecue and dining area overlooking the pool.

23 One of South Australia's best-known outback venues is the **Wilpena Pound Resort.** In the Flinders Ranges, it is a vast area covering some 76,000 hectares and is situated 40 kilometres from the settlement of Wilpena.

Accommodation is provided in motel units, or for those who prefer to 'rough it' there are hundreds of informal camping sites alongside Wilpena Creek under red gums and native pines. Amenity blocks, a general store and petrol pumps service these sites.

There are scenic tours from the resort by four-wheel drives and mini-bus, excellent walking tracks in the vicinity, and also scenic flights departing from the resort's air strip.

Guests can see Aboriginal paintings at Ackaroo Rock and carvings at Sacred Canyon.

24 **Arkaroola Sanctuary** — the Dreamtime land of Aboriginal myths and legends — lies 600 kilometres north of Adelaide. Some 61,000 hectares in area, it includes all the spectacular granite mountain country of the Flinders Ranges of South Australia.

The country is rough, with towering granite peaks, razor-backed quartzite ridges slashed by precipitous gorges, and creeks with cool, deep waterholes framed

Wilpena Pound Resort is on the fringe of the Flinders Ranges National Park

by stately gums. Rare wallabies and many other marsupials make the region their home, as well as more than 160 species of native birds and a fascinating variety of native plants.

Accommodation in the Arkaroola Village is comfortable and reasonably priced. The Greenwood Lodge has twin-bedded and family suites, with double beds and two bunks. Mawson Lodge has spacious attractive suites, each with a double bed and two single beds. There are also two bunkhouses, each with 18 bunks, situated in the caravan park. These are suitable for low-cost school and club excursions.

Visitors can explore copper mines worked 100 years ago, or enjoy the thrills of flying through the mountains on a scenic flight. Nearby are Paralana Hot Springs, the last vestige of volcanic activity in Australia, with near-boiling water flowing from the rocks.

Western Australia

25 **Merribrook** is a natural holiday haven on 70 hectares of bush and well-timbered farmland alongside the Leeuwin-Naturaliste National Park, 15 kilometres from Margaret River.

Richard and Lorraine Firth have combined the challenges of outdoor adventure with all the comforts of home. Guests can chance their luck at the exhilarating sport of abseiling from a granite outcrop, or try picking the pinot noir and cabernet sauvignon grape varieties at the local vineyard.

There are miles of tracks to explore on the property, plus rocks to climb, diving and fishing. Meals of fresh local produce are taken in the central lodge, where visitors relax around a fire and talk over the day's adventures with fellow guests.

Individual chalets have been designed and sited for maximum privacy, offering uninterrupted views of the lake and bush from sheltered verandas. Each chalet contains a queen-sized bed with continental quilt, shower and toilet, double bunks for family accommodation, and plenty of hot water.

Merribrook offers bushwalking, vineyard tours, canoeing, climbing on the Willyabrup Cliffs and abseiling, as well as caving, snorkelling and bicycling.

Richard Firth is the adventure host. A qualified outdoor instructor, he is an expert rockclimber, canoeist, caver and group leader.

26 **Evedon Park Bush Resort** is situated just off the South West Highway, two and a half hours' drive south of Perth, in the foothills of the Darling Range at Burekup. It is a bush retreat offering luxury accommodation in two-bedroom, self-contained cabins, built with local timber. The cabins have gas, hot water and stoves, with an open log fire in the lounge. All cabins overlook the lake and give views to Bunbury and the blue ocean beyond.

Evedon Park is situated in 300 hectares of

Lake Argyle Tourist Village has a spectacular location overlooking the Ord Dam

undulating bush adjoining the unspoiled Collie River jarrah forest, with the rugged Bibbulmun Trail along its eastern boundary.

27 **Quindanning** describes itself as an olde English Inne, and it offers an escape and uninterrupted solitude. Built in 1924, this quaint inn is just over two hours' drive from Perth, and a short distance from the Albany Highway.

There are two adjacent tennis courts, a new golf course at nearby Baddington, bushwalks around the area, and air rifle target shooting. Fishing is also possible at selected locations in the area. A dinner dance on Saturday nights is a highlight for guests.

The inn has 18 bedrooms, including four bridal chambers, and an additional annexe which accommodates another 20 guests.

There is a dining saloon and public lounge, and Quindanning's gardens and lake setting are reported to be among the best in the state.

28 **Norcape Lodge** is located in Exmouth, one of the world's great fishing spots, and the lodge resort offers accommodation in a natural, tropical setting. It features a pool, sauna and spa, and there are also caravan park facilities.

Operating all year round, it has been established for 25 years and is very popular. Even royalty has been entertained here, a testimony to the quality of its service and accommodation.

Personalised holiday packages are its speciality

DAVID McGONIGAL

and it can cater for the fisherman, the diver and the bushwalker.

29 Kununurra could be called the centre of the real north-east of Western Australia, and it has developed a character and appeal all of its own. It is near the banks of the mighty Ord River, a favourite haunt for fishermen seeking to hook the big barramundi. It is a fine spot for bird lovers, too. The graceful brolga and many other colourful birds live on the banks of the Ord.

The irrigated farms around the Ord River Diversion Dam are worth visiting and a visit to Hidden Valley is a step into the Aboriginal Dreamtime. Aboriginal paintings date from an era when man was still new to this land.

The Hotel Kununurra in the **Lake Argyle Tourist Village** maintains a high standard of accommodation at two levels, while the Overland Motor Inn also has extensive conference facilities. The VIP, double and single suites are comfortably furnished and there is a licensed restaurant.

Tours can be arranged to Lake Argyle, Australia's largest inland sea, to Keep River National Park in the Northern Territory, and to the Argyle Homestead Museum, containing equipment, artefacts and photographs from Patsy Durack's homestead built in 1894.

Accommodation is also available at the Lake Argyle Tourist Village itself, which is idyllically located in the mountainous outback overlooking the Ord

Dam. The village, although isolated, is self-contained, with a hotel offering enjoyable meals and a choice of motel units or caravan and camping facilities.

Northern Territory

30 One of the most enjoyable stops in the Northern Territory is **Mataranka Homestead,** situated one kilometre south of Mataranka on the Roper River, seven kilometres east of the Stuart Highway.

Mataranka Homestead was established in 1916 as an experimental cattle station by the Northern Territory's then Administrator, Dr Griffith. The homestead has since become a major tourist attraction, mainly because of the nearby thermal pool in its tropical rainforest setting. The waters here maintain a temperature of 34°C.

Today, Mataranka Homestead has modern facilities and a well-stocked kiosk to cater for all travelling needs. The managers also have hire boats and canoes and run scenic tours which capture the beauty of the surrounding Roper River area.

The friendly atmosphere at Mataranka Homestead makes it the ideal place to spend a few days relaxing and enjoying this part of the territory. Accommodation includes a motel, a youth hostel and camping grounds.

Mataranka also offers a Homestead Wagon Safari, a Bushman's Breakfast by the Roper River, and a daily Roper River Adventure Tour with Brolga Tours. This trip includes a trip to the replica of 'Elsey' station, constructed in 1982 for the film *We of the Never Never.*

31 The **Hideaway Safari Lodge,** near Nhulunbuy on the Gove Peninsula, must be one of Australia's most isolated lodges. Located around 650 kilometres from Darwin, Nhulunbuy is the commercial centre of the area and was established in 1969 as a bauxite mining town. Today, the population numbers almost 4,000 and the township is served by regular flights from Darwin and Cairns.

The lodge provides accommodation for visitors in ten air conditioned rooms and it offers full-board service. Facilities include a tennis court and swimming pool for cooling off in the Northern Territory heat. Manager Tony McMichael offers a programme of tours with Arnhemland Adventure Safaris into areas that are normally not open to tourists, using the Hideaway Safari Lodge as a base.

Safaris are conducted by Aboriginal tour guide Terry Yumbulul, also a talented artist, and fellow Aborigines such as Richard Bathuman. Groups are limited to four or six members. The tour guides discuss their heritage and explain the spiritual relationship of their people to both the sea and the land. They demonstrate the gathering of bush tucker, and take groups on cruises of Melville Bay as well as on fishing excursions in the Arafura Sea. There are also scenic helicopter flights available and a chance to see turtles, huge stingrays and the crocodiles which abound in these waters.

32 Situated on Gap Road, Alice Springs, is **Toddy's Holiday Accommodation.** Bunkhouses, cabins, family deluxe rooms and holiday flats are available and the facilities include two large community kitchens, a barbecue patio and swimming pool, and two laundries.

Toddy's offers a variety of camping safaris and bushwalking tours, ranging from two to five days. The lodge also arranges early morning hot-air balloon flights over Simpson's Gap National Park.

The two-day Palm Valley Safari visits Hermannsburg Aboriginal Settlement, Gosses Bluff and Redbank Gorge, while the King's Canyon Bushwalking Tour visits Henbury Meteorite Craters, The Lost City and the Garden of Eden. The two-day Arltunga Safari includes walks through the gorges and sections of the old Arltunga townsite, boomerang throwing, and horse and camel riding. In addition, five-day safaris tour the Olgas, Ayers Rock and King's Canyon. Accommodation and camping facilities, meals, and transport by coach or four-wheel-drive vehicles are included in all the safari packages.

33 An old cattle homestead established in 1898, the **Ross River Homestead** is located 80 kilometres east of Alice Springs (one hour's drive). The homestead offers airconditioned red gum cabins with private facilities, as well as bunk-style accommodation and camping sites.

A variety of unusual adventure tours can be arranged into the Ross River Cattle King country, including camel sunset dinner tours, overnight camel safaris, Ross River day tours and overnight trail rides.

The Camel Sunset Dinner Tour takes visitors to the 'Old Loves Creek Homestead', once used as a depot for the camel trains bringing supplies for the goldfields at Arltunga. At the end of the ride, a hearty outback-style meal is served in the homestead dining room.

The Ross River Cattle King Country one and a half day tour in a comfortable airconditioned coach allows visitors to try their hand at boomerang throwing and to travel the eastern MacDonnell Ranges to the heart of Cattle King country. In the N'Dhala Gorge, they see traditional Aboriginal rock carvings that have remained undisturbed for thousands of years.

Queensland

34 Escott Station is 18 kilometres south-west of Burketown, in the Gulf of Carpentaria. First established in 1864, today it runs approximately 8,000 head of Brahman Cross cattle.

Barramundi Lodge Escott Resort is a 225-square-kilometre resort situated within the boundaries of Escott Station on the original homestead site and it is run in conjunction with the cattle station.

There are 320 kilometres of waterways, and numerous waterholes and lagoons for swimming.

Accommodation is available at the lodge or at Coolibah Camp on the Gin Arm River. There is a swimming pool and a barbecue area. Campers are also welcome in the caravan park or at allocated river spots.

Guests are welcome to join in with the daily activities involved in running the station. Other activities include barramundi fishing, two to four-day horse trail rides, a visit to the crocodile hole (home of the abnormally large Johnson river crocs), joy flights, wild pig hunts, swimming and safaris.

The resort also offers a two and three-day four-wheel-drive safari. The tour heads out towards the Northern Territory border into some of the continent's most lonely and beautiful country.

35 **Cape York Wilderness Lodge,** 400 metres from the tip of Cape York, was established as a fishing and wildlife lodge to allow visitors to experience the wilderness in comfort and safety.

A new bush camp has been built for overnight camping trips. These trips afford travellers the chance to marvel at the wildlife in this remote Australian environment where crocodiles, turtles, exotic waterbirds and schools of brightly emblazoned reef fish are abundant.

The staff includes a naturalist and three professional fishing guides to lead fishing expeditions.

There are over 150 species of birds in the area and an abundance of frogs, reptiles, mammals and marsupials, as well as dozens of different palms and giant oaks. Birdwatching parties venture out in the early morning and evening.

Fishing in this area is first rate. Trevally, Spanish mackerel, barracuda, and queenfish teem in the waters of the Torres Strait Islands, while the Jardine River and Jacky Jacky Creek are best for barramundi, saratoga and cod. Most forms of blue-water fishing are catered for.

36 Tropical cabins in the rainforest of the Greater Daintree National Park at Cape Tribulation provide the setting for **Rainforest Retreat** in far north Queensland.

The Great Barrier Reef lies just kilometres away, offering a variety of fishing and snorkelling opportunities. Drives along scenic routes in this north Queensland wonderland take in panoramic views of coastline, cliffs and virgin rainforest. Bush tracks must be used to reach the Rainforest Retreat. Each cabin is fully self-contained and secluded. A fully equipped shop stocking all necessary commodities is nearby.

At night, groups can go spotlighting for nocturnal creatures — especially crocodiles — and during the day there are boat trips around the various waterways of the area, such as the Daintree and Bloomfield Rivers. There are also four-wheel-drive safaris along the infamous Bloomfield Track, and expertly guided bushwalks through untouched rainforest.

Packages to the Rainforest Retreat must be organised through Going Places Travel in Cairns.

37 Six freestanding cabins line a cliff face above the Mossman River in far north Queensland, representing the only piece of freehold land at the border of the Mossman Gorge National Park. This is the **Silky Oaks Colonial Lodge,** operated by Moss and Therese Hunt, just 82 kilometres north of Cairns International Airport.

The cabins are built of cherry, rosewood and local silky oak, and each sleeps up to four persons. Each has its own private bathroom, kitchenette, queen-size bed and bunks, and a spacious veranda overlooking the nearby billabongs and rainforest islands.

With Silky Oaks as home base, four-wheel-drive safari trips edge their way into the wilderness areas of Daintree, Cape Tribulation, Roaring Meg, Cooktown and Laura, with qualified and experienced guides leading the expeditions.

Hiking into the higher reaches of the Gorge Mountains is another popular activity. In addition, canoeing, freshwater swimming, archery and bicycling are available to the energetic holiday-maker.

38 **Carnarvon Gorge Oasis Lodge,** founded in 1968, was first established for guests wishing to explore the Carnarvon area with its wealth of fauna, flora and Aboriginal artefacts.

Over the years, the lodge has hosted thousands of visitors, both local and from overseas, and has developed along lines that create minimum impact on the environment. Surrounded by cool green lawns, shaded by ancient macrozamia palms and tall gums, and set under a deep blue sky, the lodge is a true oasis around which countless birds and animals congregate.

The choice of accommodation includes cabins located close to the main lodge building. All cabins are carpeted and feature hand-made timber furniture.

Safari tents offer a comfortable alternative, located around the well-maintained grounds amongst eucalypts and palms.

Activities include early morning bush breakfasts, guided walks, spotlighting at night, and five and eight-day organised tours. These include explorations of Carnarvon Gorge, Ward's Canyon, Alifon Falls and visits to the Aboriginal paintings at Cathedral Cave.

39 A drive of only 75 kilometres from Brisbane, or minutes from the Gold Coast, will bring the traveller to **Yarramalong Recreation Centre** — a 70-hectare property in a valley of great scenic beauty.

Horse riding is the speciality of this outdoor recreation centre, both for the experienced rider and the beginner. Riders travel through the spectacular scenery, from semi-rainforest creek banks to wide open spaces.

There are any number of other outdoor activities, including canoeing, archery, water-skiing, camping,

and just relaxing by the campfire at night or sunbaking by day.

Canoeing on Reynold's Creek is great fun and the larger waterholes are excellent for swimming and fishing. Archery is also available, and so is volleyball, orienteering, bushwalking, exploring and bird-watching.

There are camping facilities in an idyllic setting in the Gorge of Mt Edwards where emphasis is placed on personal privacy, and where overcrowding is never a problem. Tents can be hired or guests can stay in a six-berth caravan.

40 Barely an hour's drive inland from the Queensland capital of Brisbane and from the Gold Coast's hectic pleasure palaces lies **Kooralbyn Valley,** set in a cleft in the foothills of the MacPherson Ranges.

Kooralbyn offers country villa and motel lodge accommodation — and a 4,000-hectare backyard. It has its own tennis village, with ten all-weather day-and-night courts.

The Kooralbyn championship golf course is rated number one among Australian resort courses, and coaching clinics are available with resident professionals.

Horse-riding excursions take visitors up into the surrounding hills, and a network of bushwalks fans out from Kooralbyn for guests who prefer to do their exploring on two legs.

But relaxation is the name of the most popular game at Kooralbyn Valley. There are four swimming pools, three bars, and restaurants with dancing into the night.

41 Founded by an adventurer named Bernard O'Reilly, the **Green Mountain Retreat** overlooks the Lamington National Park, some 35 kilometres inland from the Gold Coast. A beautiful green sweep of lawns, complete with small local wallabies called pademelons, surrounds the guesthouse, attracting birdlife. Albert lyrebirds, satin bowerbirds and gold and black Regent bowerbirds are just a few. Some 140 kilometres of signposted walking tracks weave through this woodland retreat. A four-wheel-drive mini-bus for the less energetic follows the rainforest tracks to different mountain lookouts each day of the week. There is plenty of rockclimbing to be done and long hikes into some of the more remote areas can be arranged.

Guesthouse and motel-style accommodation are both available. Some of the units are specially designed to cater to the needs of the physically handicapped.

O'Reilly trekked through the national park in 1937 to rescue survivors of a crashed Stinson airplane after previous search parties had given up hope of finding them. The remains of that plane still lie in the park.

42 **Binna Burra Mountain Resort** is also situated amidst the magnificent scenery of the Lamington

National Park. The park's well-graded walking tracks lead to deep gorges, lookouts, rainforest areas, waterfalls and creeks.

The Binna Burra Lodge is perched on top of Mt Roberts, 790 metres above sea level, and offers a great range of holiday activities. Guests can choose to participate in activities organised each day by the lodge staff, or do their own thing. The daily programme includes guided walks, adventure hikes through rugged terrain, abseiling and scenic bus tours. At night, there are movies, bush dances, night walks, and the opportunity to reflect on the day's activities at the camp's open fire. There are also special events, and particular weeks are set aside for arts, abseiling, photography and gardening courses.

The lodge was founded in 1933. Accommodation is cabin style, and packages include meals and selected activities.

Activity Lodges & Centres Contacts

Operators

New South Wales

1 **Midginbil Hill**

Uki
via Murwillumbah NSW 2484
Ph. (066) 79 7158

2 **Mt Seaview Resort**

via Wauchope NSW 2446
Ph. (065) 87 7133 or 87 7155

3 **Bellbird Valley Country Retreat**

Bellbird Valley
Chichester Dam
Dungog NSW 2420
Ph. (049) 95 9266

4 **Legges Camp**

Myall Lakes National Park
Bombah Point
via Bulahdelah NSW 2423
Ph. (049) 97 4495

5 **Ferndale Lodge**

River Road
Lower Portland NSW 2756
Ph. (045) 75 5223

6 **Coolangatta Historic Village Resort**

Coolangatta
via Berry NSW 2535
Ph. (044) 48 7131

7 **Thredbo Alpine Village**

C/- Thredbo Centre
Level 2
49 Market Street
Sydney NSW 2000
Ph. (02) 268 2681

8 **The Oaks Holiday Ranch**

Old Mossy Point Road
Mossy Point NSW 2536
Ph. (044) 71 7403

Australian Capital Territory

9 **Canberra Motor Village**

Kunzea Street
O'Connor
Canberra ACT 2601
Ph. (062) 47 5466

Victoria

10 **Lake Dartmouth Resort**

PO Box 1
Dartmouth VIC 3701
Ph. (060) 72 4511

11 **Mt Buffalo Chalet**

PO Box 76
Porepunkah VIC 3740
Ph. (057) 55 1500

12 **Mountain Creek Centre**

Mountain Creek Road
Tawonga VIC 3697
Ph. (057) 57 2257

13 **Arrabri Lodge Holiday Camp & Guest House**

Woods Point Road
East Warburton VIC 3799
Ph. (059) 66 2202 or (03) 531 8834

14 **Jinda Park**

Airyes Inlet Road
Bambra VIC 3241
Ph. (052) 88 7204

15 **Beacon Point**

PO Box 67
Apollo Bay VIC 3233
Ph. (052) 37 6218

16 **Glen Aire Log Cabins**

Glen Aire Park
Great Ocean Road
Glen Aire VIC 3238
Ph. (052) 37 9231

Tasmania

17 **The Pines Resort**

Surf Road
Seven Mile Beach
Hobart TAS 7170
Ph. (002) 48 6222

18 **Balfe's Hill Farm**

RSD Criterion Street
Hobart TAS 7000
Ph. (002) 95 1551

19 Cradle Mountain Lodge

Box 153
Sheffield TAS 7306
Ph. (003) 63 5164

20 Mountain Valley

RSD 255
Loongana TAS 7315
Ph. (004) 29 1394

South Australia

21 Wirrina Holiday Resort

PO Box 63
Yankalilla SA 5203
Ph. (085) 59 4001

22 Linnett's Island Club

American River
Kangaroo Island SA 5221
Ph. (0848) 33 053

23 Wilpena Pound Holiday Resort

C/- 32 Whitmore Square
Adelaide SA 5000
Ph. (08) 212 6386 or (086) 48 0004

24 Arkaroola Tourist Resort & Wildlife Sanctuary

Arkaroola Travel Centre
Suite 1, Ground Floor
Wales Building
50 Pirie Street
Adelaide SA 5000
Ph. (08) 212 1366

Western Australia

25 Merribrook

PO Box 27
Cowaramup WA 6284
Ph. (097) 55 5490

26 Evedon Park Bush Resort

Burekup WA 6227
Ph. (097) 26 3012

27 Quindanning Hotel Holiday Resort

Quindanning WA 6391
Ph. (098) 85 7053

28 Norcape Lodge Resort

Trustcott Crescent
Exmouth WA 6707
Ph. (099) 49 1334

29 Lake Argyle Tourist Village

Western Resorts Corporation
PO Box 111
Kununurra WA 6743
Ph. (091) 68 1064

Northern Territory

30 Mataranka Homestead

Travel North
C/- BP Roadhouse
Katherine NT 5780
Ph. (089) 75 4544

31 Hideaway Safari Lodge

Prospect
via Nhulunbuy NT 5797
Ph. (089) 87 1833

32 Toddy's Holiday Accommodation

41 Gap Road
Alice Springs NT 5750
Ph. (089) 52 5999 or 52 1322

33 Ross River Homestead

PO Box 84
Alice Springs NT 5750
Ph. (089) 52 7611

Queensland

34 Escott Lodge

Escott Station
Burketown QLD 4830
Ph. (011) Burketown 45 5108

35 Cape York Wilderness Lodge

C/- 62 Abbott Street
Cairns QLD 4870
Ph. (070) 50 4305

36 The Rainforest Retreat

C/- Going Places Travel
26 Abbott Street
Cairns QLD 4870
Ph. (070) 51 4055

37 Silky Oaks Colonial Lodge

PO Box 396
Mossman QLD 4873
Ph. (070) 98 1666

38 Carnarvon Gorge Oasis Lodge

Carnarvon National Park
via Rolleston QLD 4702
Ph. (079) 84 4503

39 Yarramalong Recreation Centre

Lake Moogerah Road
Kalbar QLD 4309
Ph. (075) 63 7369

40 Kooralbyn Valley

PO Box 216
Beaudesert QLD 4285
Ph. (075) 44 6100 or 44 6222

41 O'Reilly's Green Mountain Retreat

Canungra QLD 4275
Ph. (075) 45 1611

42 Binna Burra Mountain Resort

Beechmont
via Nerang QLD 4211
Ph. (075) 33 3622 or 33 3566

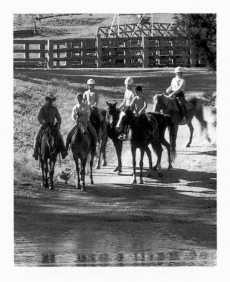

JEAN-PAUL FERRERO

ALLAN MOULT

Air Tours

Australia opens up to aeroplanes as an exotic flower unfolds to the morning sun. Only from the air can a traveller appreciate the vastness of the rich canvas colour that is this ancient continent.

Passengers in high-flying jets will see, in the centre, the north and the west, tracts of land criss-crossed with mysterious survey lines looking like the markings of a lost South American civilisation. Mountain ranges thrown up in an early geological age and marking the boundaries of remote deserts swim into view. In the south and the east, they can discern the fenced boundaries of huge cattle and sheep stations, antipodean principalities ruled by generations of farming men and women whose souls belong to the land.

On the continental margins, they will find the great wheat lands, coloured according to season, and then the blue-green mountain ranges furred with eucalypts. And at the very edge, cities, dairy farms, rainforests, crescent beaches, sandstone cliffs, estuaries, and lines of white-capped waves. Passengers in low-flying propeller craft can make out far more detail than this as they pass over a variety of undulating land and seascapes.

Air touring has increased in popularity in the last few years in Australia and more people than ever before are now experiencing the very real adventure of this specialised form of travel.

The simplest way to see the country from the air is to book a seat on a Fokker Friendship flying one of the domestic routes. These comfortable, high-wing prop jets provide excellent viewing, weather permitting, since they fly at half the height of their pure jet cousins. Most large country towns are serviced by Fokker Friendships and many inter-city runs are operated by airlines like East-West which use fleets of

Friendships. A variety of smaller piston-engined and prop jets fly lower still, providing excellent views of this landscape of contrasts.

There are now some major luxury-class air tours available. These tours in specially converted planes take passengers on a conducted itinerary of several days' duration to some of the most spectacular areas Australia has to offer, such as Western Tasmania, Broken Bay in New South Wales, around Cairns and the Whitsundays, and along the coast of Western Australia.

In many of these regions, short joy flights and charter hire are available in seaplanes. Few activities are more exciting or romantic than taking a seaplane flight to a remote lake or river, spending a few hours fishing, exploring, picnicking and then returning to catch the sun falling on to the becalmed, light-reflecting waters at dusk.

Land planes, too, are available for charter and there are many operators who will help travellers organise trips to areas of great interest and beauty. Sleeping under the wing of a small plane in the Australian outback is just one of the many unique experiences travellers can look forward to.

For those with a taste for some of life's finer pleasures, there exists a handful of charter companies in Australia whose hangars are full of sleek jets such as Lears, Cessna Citations, British Aerospace HS 125s and Dassault Falcon 20s which provide the ultimate in air travel luxury. Although the rates for chartering these aircraft average about $2,000 an hour, they guarantee passengers less waiting time before flight departures and access to small airstrips that larger aircraft could never contemplate. These craft are exceedingly comfortable. Passengers can walk about the plush cabins without stooping; they have access to video-screens and hi-fi sets; and they are served the ultimate in *haute cuisine* as well as the finest champagne and tropical fruits.

Not quite as decadent as these luxury air tours, but rapidly increasing in popularity, are helicopter flights. This unique mode of transport affords passengers a viewing capacity and mobility unequalled by any other aircraft. Australia's vast distances and sometimes inhospitable terrain readily embrace the helicopter as a quick, convenient and pleasant mode of aerial transport.

Helicopters are coming into their own as an integral part of organised tours to remote areas. Bushwalkers, canoeists and visitors to wilderness lodges and resorts can be collected and taken with ease to where their adventure begins. Alice Springs, for example, is home base to a number of imaginative helicopter operators. Passengers who have disembarked at the foot of Australia's greatest monolith,

Ayers Rock, or landed on sheer cliffs that drop to a swelling ocean, or stepped into an open clearing just metres away from rows of grapevines in the picturesque Hunter Valley marvel at the flexibility and freedom they can enjoy in an aircraft where totally unimpeded vision is the outstanding feature.

The most popular helicopter used for scenic flights is the Bell 206 Jet-ranger which accommodates the pilot and four passengers. However, most helicopter organisations have aircraft varying in size from the 24-passenger Sikorsky S61 to the diminutive Robinson R22 which accommodates just one passenger. The majority of tour operators are more than happy to work around passengers' plans and schedules to provide the utmost in versatility in an air tour of this kind.

Travellers who are themselves pilots will find a network of aero clubs with reciprocal membership rights. This makes the renting of planes and the

At dawn, this scene is underway at many outback airstrips

JOHN EVERINGHAM

planning of flights pleasant and practical. At the more remote airports there are country charter operators flying small planes who are quite willing to hire their craft out for several days at a time. In these localities, the aerial workhorses are usually the Cessna 172, followed by the Piper Cherokee and the Piper Warrior. Passengers are able to appreciate the remoteness of these areas when they see the large drums of gasoline necessary for refuelling left unceremoniously at airfields by semitrailer hauliers.

Because of the vast distances involved, the requirements for navigation and cross-country flying experience are quite demanding. There is a network of beacons and VHF Omni Ranges (VORs) — radio-operated navigational aids — around the coast and populated areas, but further away they become few and far between. Sarwatch, the search and rescue network, keeps a close eye on flights away from the main population areas.

Whatever way it's done, flying in Australia is a very special and rewarding experience.

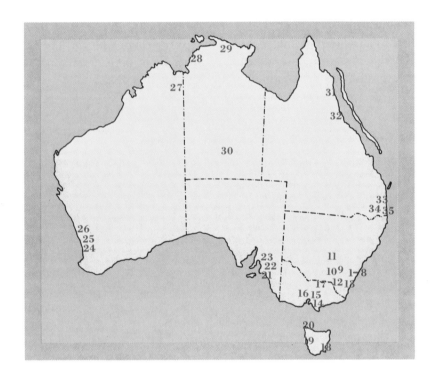

Locations

New South Wales

1 Headed by Australia's travel expert, Bill Peach, **Air Cruising Australia** offers excellent air tours to some of the best parts of Australia in a 40-seat Fokker Friendship.

One tour flies to the Red Centre via Coober Pedy, Ayers Rock and Alice Springs; an alternative is to take the same route, but to include a visit to an outback sheep station as well as Cairns in north Queensland. Other itineraries take in a flight over Thursday Island, off the tip of Cape York, and return via Mount Isa; or a flight to the northern centres of Darwin and Kununurra, Broome and Mount Newman — the world's largest open-cut mine.

A special-interest flight — 'The Wandering Gourmet' — allows passengers the opportunity to sample Australian cuisine, vineyards, restaurants and pubs throughout the country.

2 **Air NSW**, one of Australia's largest domestic airlines, offers an enormous range of flights to selected destinations throughout the country. Based at Kingsford Smith Airport, just a 20-minute drive from the heart of Sydney, Air NSW specialises in aircraft charters, holiday packages, group travel, and conference and convention planning. Their 'Escape Kit' packages provide comprehensive tours of the favoured tourist locations — the Centre, the Holiday Coast, the Outback, the Sunshine Coast, Sydney and Tasmania.

Highlights of the 'Centre' tour include stopovers at Broken Hill (christened the 'Silver City' for the enormous mine workings in the region), Ayers Rock, Alice Springs (set in the geographic centre of Australia) and Cairns, Queensland's most northerly city and capital of big-game fishing for the famous black marlin.

DAVID McGONIGAL

The Holiday Coast of New South Wales — a big producer of sugarcane — also grows such tropical fruits as bananas, pineapples, pawpaws, mangoes, avocados, peanuts and macadamia nuts. Winters are mild, dry and sunny, while summer temperatures are moderated by cool sea breezes. The north coast towns of Coffs Harbour, Ballina and Byron Bay are included in the itinerary of this tour.

Like the 'Centre' tour, Air NSW's 'Outback' flight gives visitors the opportunity to see thriving towns in the far west regions of the state. Moree, Lightning Ridge, Coonamble, Dubbo, Griffith, Narranderra, Wagga Wagga and Cooma are just some of the centres included in a tour designed to show the real Australia beyond the busy capital cities.

The 'Sunshine Coast' escape is the ultimate in sun, sea and surf holidays. Situated north of Brisbane, the Sunshine Coast stretches 140 kilometres from Deception Bay to the bottom tip of Fraser Island. There's something to appeal to everyone. Visitors can swim, sail, surf, scuba dive and fish. Journeys to the coastal hinterland reveal a checkered pattern of plantations producing bananas, pineapples, ginger, sugarcane and tropical fruits.

Air NSW also offers flights to Tasmania. Situated at the southern tip of Australia and divided from the mainland by the waters of Bass Strait, it provides surprising contrasts in such a small area. Imposing mountains, temperate rainforests and sections of unexplored wilderness as well as a fascinating history, a wide range of entertainment activities and rich flora and fauna make Australia's island state excellent for touring. Flights operate direct between Sydney and Hobart and Sydney and Devonport.

Air NSW also provides a tour package which encompasses its home base, the city of Sydney. Sydney Harbour, the Royal Botanic Gardens, Sydney Opera House, Hyde Park, Kings Cross, The Rocks, Taronga Park Zoo and Parliament House are just some of the scenic attractions included in a discovery of Australia's oldest and liveliest city.

3 The Pittwater side of the Palm Beach peninsula, some 48 kilometres from Sydney, is the base for **Aquatic Airways**. Established 12 years ago, it is the only scheduled commercial seaplane service in Sydney.

Aquatic Airways flies De Havilland Beavers and an Australian-built ten-seater Nomad on short scheduled services to and from Rose Bay in Sydney (once a thriving international flying boat base). They also run a service to Gosford in the heart of the NSW Central Coast.

Aquatic transports passengers from their yachts or the cruise boat the *Lady Hawkesbury,* or takes them to lunch at one of Sydney's splendid waterside restaurants such as the Berowra Waters Inn. A flight from Rose Bay to Palm Beach is an unparalleled way of enjoying the beauty of Sydney.

Aquatic also has scenic flights out of both Rose Bay and Palm Beach, and Hunter Valley day tours which take off from the water and land at Cessnock Airport in the Hunter Valley region.

4 **Bel Air Aviation** offers an unusual urban air tour. Their champagne flights take in the spectacular glow of Sydney against the backdrop of the night sky. Flights last approximately an hour and provide passengers with some of the most breathtaking sights of night-time Sydney, such as the Harbour Bridge and its connecting network of expressways, the neon advertisements atop the skyscrapers of the central business district, the pinnacle of Sydney Tower shining orange-red over 300 metres above street level, the sprawling flickers of suburbia with tentacles reaching as far as the bushland outskirts, and the soft reflections on the waterways.

Bel-Air uses a modern twin-engine aircraft for the flights and there is a minimum number of four passengers. Guests can drive themselves to Mascot Airport to join the flight or be chauffeur-driven in a limousine. The cost of the flight includes champagne.

5 Flying is perhaps the best way to encapsulate the outback experience and to put its vast reaches

into some sort of perspective. A company by the name of **Flight through the Spectacular Land of the Dreamtime** can fly visitors just about anywhere, from Sydney or Melbourne to Cape York and the Torres Strait, the Kimberleys in Western Australia, and the opal mines at Coober Pedy. Visitors will also see the pearl divers at Broome and crocodiles at Kakadu National Park.

These tours cover the most remote regions of the outback and embrace historical, archaeological and natural sites and sights. Accommodation varies along the way from outback homesteads to the luxury of the Yulara Sheraton at Ayers Rock and the glitter of the new casino at Darwin.

Each trip is limited to 16 passengers and includes accommodation, most meals, and all ground touring except at Alice Springs and Darwin.

6 **Navair Air Charter** is based at the Hoxton Park Aero Centre at Hoxton Park Airport and at the Navair Flying School at Bankstown Airport. Both are a short distance from Sydney and offer a range of charter facilities as well as flight training.

7 Flying in a dirigible airship is unlike any other kind of flying. Suspended only a few hundred metres above the ground, these graceful airships move slowly and deliberately across the sky, affording passengers aerial views that cannot be enjoyed from the confined spaces of a light aircraft.

Passengers on **Sydney Sky Cruise** flights can admire the delights of Sydney Harbour with its flotilla of harbour ferries and yachts with their brightly coloured spinnakers, and the sails of the Opera House rising from Bennelong Point not too far from the 'coathanger' arch of the Harbour Bridge. To the west, the blue haze of the Blue Mountains can be seen. Back in the city centre, other famous landmarks include Sydney Tower, St Mary's Cathedral ringed by the greenery of the Domain, Hyde Park, Australia Square, and the Sydney Cricket Ground with its towering light stands that turn night into day for the many sporting fixtures played at the ground.

The Sydney Skycruise company offers one and a quarter hour flights over the city of Sydney, departing from Bankstown Airport. Flights operate year round, with the exception of two days a week between July and December. Five flights operate each day. West Australian entrepreneur Alan Bond introduced the idea of conducting dirigible joy flights and they have proved an enormous success.

Nowadays, airships are perfectly safe, being lifted by inert, non-flammable gases and powered by reliable modern engines.

8 **Water Wings** operates a personalised service for two or three passengers interesting in taking an aerial expedition across the skies of Sydney and its surroundings. A typical scenic flight leaves Rose Bay, skims low out through Sydney Heads and turns along the northern beaches to Lion Island in Broken Bay. The flight then comes back over Pittwater, Middle Harbour and the Opera House before returning to Rose Bay.

Flights along the central coast include an hour-long journey to Forster, then 50 minutes to Nelson Bay, 20 minutes to Wyong and The Entrance, and a quick ten-minute excursion to Avalon and Church Point at Pittwater.

Water Wings also has flights operating south of Sydney to Wollongong, Ulladulla and Batemans Bay.

9 **Blue Mountains Air Charter** is based in the heart of one of Australia's great national parks, the Blue Mountains, just a couple of hours' drive west of Sydney. Blue Mountains Air Charter has been in operation for 20 years, offering air services, charter work and licensed passenger and cargo transport locally and interstate.

Some of the best flights offer low-level flyovers above the Blue Mountains, Kanangra-Boyd Park, the Colo River, Wollemi National Park and also to Lake Burragorang, Yerranderie Village, Hill End and Burrendong Dam. Passengers view spectacular scenery: cliffs and valleys carved out of the mountains, waterfalls and the Jenolan Caves. A landing at Yerranderie gives passengers a short break during

Previous page: Western Australia's Alligator Airways scuds along, while in Sydney, passengers aboard the Sydney Skycruise enjoy this bird's eye view of the city from the company's dirigible airship

DAVID MCGONIGAL

which time they can look around this historic settlement.

10 **Venture Out,** based in the Blue Mountains, specialises in taking passengers on tours to some of the remotest parts of the country in twin-engined eight-seater Piper Chieftains or single-engined four-seater Piper Cherokees.

The tours include accommodation on a twin or triple-share basis, and most meals are provided.

Tours are all ex-Sydney and include a seven-day loop round the Flinders Ranges, Coober Pedy, Ayers Rock, Alice Springs, Birdsville and back to Sydney. Another flies to Cairns, Flinders Island and Raine Island, with a further option being a detour to Cooktown and Lakefield in northern Queensland.

Venture Out is a relatively new organisation which prides itself on extensive knowledge of the Australian bush and its plants and animals. The trips are not only educational, but also full of adventure.

11 **Hazelton Airlines** is a commuter airline operating out of Sydney, Canberra and Cudal, with a network of routes throughout New South Wales. They have an air charter service as well as 'big country tours' to the central west and south coast of the state. These tours are relatively short excursions of one and two days' duration.

'Meet-a-Cocky', 'Rainforest Safari', 'Stroke a Kelpie', 'Outback Opalfields', 'Golf at Historic Duntryleague', 'Stub Your Toe on an Opal', 'Hit it off with the Galahs' and 'Billy Tea in the Rainforest' are some of the humorously named tours that are available.

Australian Capital Territory

12 Canberra's **Mile High Club** offers romantic night flights over Canberra, complete with champagne served in luxurious surroundings. Passengers have the option of sipping champagne while the sun sets, or of reclining comfortably after dinner with a cognac or port. Other flights available include chicken and champagne breakfasts, picnic lunches and other scenic flights.

Prices include food and drink. Arrangements can also be made for passengers to be collected and returned to their restaurant or hotel.

13 **Outback Travel** provides a variety of first-class air tours over Canberra. Passengers can savour the highlights of Australia's capital and see the extent to which this young city is so perfectly planned.

Some of the main attractions include the War Memorial, New Parliament House, Lake Burley Griffin, Black Mountain Tower, Mount Stromlo Observatory and the Tidbinbilla Tracking Station. There is much to see that attests to the great planning skills of Walter Burley Griffin, who won the international design competition for the new city with his unique and innovative layout.

Outback Travel also offers evening excursions where passengers can see the lights of Canberra and its floodlit attractions. This is a popular after-dinner flight. There are also romantic evening flights with a touch of elegance. Passengers sip champagne as they admire the stars against the velvet backdrop of a night sky.

Victoria

14 **Australian Vintage Travel,** part of Rebel Air, operates out of Melbourne and offers flights on a luxurious DC3 named 'The Spirit of Melbourne'.

'The Spirit of Melbourne' operates regular services between Melbourne, Flinders Island and Hobart in Tasmania and provides champagne flights over night-time Melbourne.

15 **Kendell Airlines Australia,** also based in Melbourne, has a network of routes through Victoria and into southern New South Wales and eastern South Australia.

They have a good selection of holiday packages and tours ex-Melbourne and Adelaide. One of their feature tours flies from Melbourne to King Island and Merimbula. There are also flights and packages to Mildura, the Coonawarra wine district and to Thredbo and the Snowy Mountains.

The Snowy Mountains Main Range presents a dramatic view from the cockpit

16 **Penair,** based at Essendon Airport in Melbourne, is an air transport charter service with a fleet of twin-engined jet-prop and piston-engined aircraft. They offer flights to all the popular tourist centres in Australia.

Passengers enjoy a relaxed and knowledgeable commentary from the pilot and the planes are staffed with a well-qualified and experienced crew.

17 **Drage Airworld** is located near Wangaratta in north-eastern Victoria, close to snowfields and wineries. After enjoying a wander around the many displays, visitors can take a joyflight in a Tiger Moth and experience the pleasure pioneering pilots felt in open-cockpit flying, a far cry from the fully aircondi-tioned, pressurised supersonic aircraft of today. For the very adventurous, aerobatic flights are also available.

For those interested in aviation history, historic aircraft, or even in bicycles and cars, Drage Airworld should not be missed.

Drage Airworld is host to a vast collection of historic aircraft, including a Westland Widgeon, B.A. Eagle, Lancashire Prospector, and Gypsy Moth (flown by Charles Kingsford-Smith), as well as a number of vintage cars, motorcycles and bicycles.

DAVID MCGONIGAL

Tasmania

Listed among 152 World Heritage areas, Tasmania's South West National Park occupies 4,422 square kilometres of virtually intact temperate wilderness: a region of steep mountain ranges, fast flowing rivers, exposed lakeland plains and solitary beaches.

18 **Par Avion** flights take passengers across this region, taking in views of the city of Cambridge before moving on to Mt Wellington and Mt Anne, guarding the shores of Lake Pedder. From there the journey continues over Crossing Plains and into Port Davey-Bathurst Harbour. A low-level flight from Melaleuca Inlet to the Maatsuyker Islands reveals something of the vast ocean waters between them and Antarctica. Civilisation reappears gradually on the return journey, with scattered and remote farmlets coming into view around the D'Entrecastreaux Channel dividing southern Tasmania from Bruny Island.

Par Avion operate two tours in this south-west wilderness region. A two-hour flight is available for a minimum of two passengers, and a day excursion leaves Port Davey at 9 am which includes a boat cruise and barbecue lunch before returning to Hobart in the late afternoon.

19 **Wilderness Air** is an exciting air service that flies seaplanes into the Tasmanian wilderness. Using Cessna float planes and Lake Buccaneers, Wilderness Air gives travellers access to the remote rivers and lakes of World Heritage wilderness areas and the national parks of Tasmania.

Home base is Strahan, a delightful fishing port.

Wilderness Air's seaplane service is something special among air tours and most people see a trip with them as the highlight of their Tasmanian visit.

20 **Tasmanian Scenic Flights** are based at Wynyard on the western side of Tasmania. Using a Cessna 172 and occasionally a Beechcraft Bonanza, they specialise in scenic flights over western Tasmania, Cradle Mountain and the south-west wilderness area.

They offer one of the best ways of appreciating the extraordinary beauty and spectacular landscape of Australia's island state.

With the smaller Cessna 172, a minimum of two passengers is required. Tours depart from Devonport, Wynyard and Queenstown. These are generally of 30 minutes' duration, offering some excellent sightseeing over Tasmania's wilderness.

South Australia

21 **Augusta Airways,** based at Adelaide Airport, cover vast distances into the centre of Australia. The company is both an airline and an air tour operator. The world's longest mail run from Adelaide to Port Augusta, Innamincka, Birdsville, Boulia and Mount Isa is one of the most extraordinary flights a passenger could ever take. Originating as a vital mail run, the company has opened it up with a few seats for passengers.

The mail run takes in views of the Flinders Ranges and Lake Torrens, makes stops to collect mail for distribution to cattle stations along the Birdsville Track, and flies over some of the most remote scenery in the world: sandhills, salt lakes, stony desert and channel country.

Augusta Airways also offer a one-day 'Glimpse of the Outback' tour which includes a visit to the Royal Flying Doctor Base and the School of the Air — an educational radio broadcast service that teaches children in Australia's remote areas by correspondence and radio.

22 Dick Lang has been operating adventure safaris within Australia for 16 years. His flying career has encompassed survey and rescue work in the arid deserts of Australia, third-level airline and charter work, long-distance offshore flying for the big fishing fleets in the Southern Ocean, as well as time spent flying in the rugged highlands of Papua-New Guinea.

His **Desert Air Safaris** utilises a fleet of twin-engined aircraft to show visitors the best of the Australian outback. The 'Opal Field Special', a weekend or two-day safari, takes in the centres of Coober Pedy, Andamooka, Alice Springs, Ayers Rock and Adelaide. This excursion allows passengers to see two of the world's wonders — the opal gem fields and Ayers Rock in the heart of Australia.

The 'Burke and Wills Safari' provides passengers with an interesting and adventure-filled weekend in Cooper's Creek in the very heart of the Australian outback. The Flinders Ranges and Lake Eyre are features of this flight which includes a landing at the Burke and Wills Dig Tree in Queensland and a four-wheel-drive excursion to Burke's grave near Innamincka.

A nine-day expedition with a bushman-pilot guide takes in Ayers Rock, the mining town of Mt Isa, Coober Pedy, tropical Cairns and the Great Barrier Reef.

23 **Skytours** is Australia's oldest and most experienced operator of outback adventure air sataris. There is 1,600 kilometres of outback country between Alice Springs and Adelaide, and passengers can start their Skytour from either of these centres. All safari tours visit Ayers Rock and Alice Springs, as well as 'off the beaten track' destinations such as Andamooka and William Creek, north-west of Adelaide.

Safari departures are limited to a maximum of ten people, and itineraries are specially designed for visitors who have limited time in which to see the outback. Tours are fully inclusive, covering airfare, a full-time guide, accommodation, ground tours, and all meals including in-flight refreshments and morning and afternoon teas.

Western Australia

24 The **Royal Aero Club of Western Australia** has an impressive facility at Jandakot Airport outside Perth. Apart from the usual range of flight training that such clubs offer they conduct sightseeing and air safari activities and operate on an air charter basis.

Pilots can become a member of the Royal Aero Club for a nominal fee. This entitles them to reciprocal membership rights with most other Australian aero clubs.

The club runs monthly flying competitions and air rallies to country centres. It also holds regular social functions for members and guests.

The club has a fleet of 30 well-maintained aircraft. Jandakot is generally excellent for flying. Cloudless clear skies, bright sunshine and little wind turbulence afford passengers the best conditions to enjoy the sights of Perth and its surrounds.

25 **Skywest Airlines** is the sister company to East-West Airlines, Australia's third domestic airline with a substantial Australian network operating out of Sydney. Skywest offers air services and some excellent tours around Perth and regional Western Australia.

Skywest specialises in short visits to some of the most spectacular parts of Australia such as the pink lakes of Esperance, the Valley of the Giants in the Walpole/Nornalup National Park, the Fitzgerald River, the Dolphins of Monkey Mia, Kalbarri and Mount Augustus, as well as Kalgoorlie and Geraldton.

26 **Travair Aerial Services**, which flies out of Perth Airport, has a motto: 'Getting there is as important as being there'. A Douglas DC3 (otherwise known as a Gooney Bird) takes passengers on

For nostalgia buffs, there are plenty of Tiger Moths suitable for hire

organised or chartered air tours.

They have a northern tour of eight days and seven nights taking in Perth, Broome, Lake Argyle, Aktabroon, Carnarvon, Joulton and back to Perth. This tour takes in the vastness of Western Australia, looks at Port Hedland, the Ord River Scheme, Fitzroy Crossing, the Pilbara Coast and the bays and sea beds of Shark Bay.

The southern tour of four days and three nights takes in on the first day Perth, Rottnest Island, the wine-producing areas of Western Australia, and Albany. On the second day, the flight continues to Esperance, flying over the Princess Royal Harbour and its islands, and then over the Pink Lake and coastal beaches. The third day features a visit to a wildflower and wildlife park and then a flight to the gold and nickel-mining area of Western Australia, flying over the natural salt pans to Kalgoorlie, followed by a visit to a 'two-up' school. On the last day, there is a visit to the ghost town of Coolgardie, a gold-panning demonstration and a visit to a goldmine before returning to Perth.

27 **Alligator Airways** gives passengers a chance to see some of Australia's remotest northern and western districts. Their home base is at Lake Kununurra in Western Australia.

Alligator Airways operate float planes and conduct a variety of short flights from Lake Argyle or Lake Kununurra as well as two-day coastal fishing charters which give travellers a chance to try their luck with barramundi, Spanish mackerel, queenfish, salmon, mangrove jack and even cod. Alligator Airways also offer five-day fishing safaris.

Access to Lake Kununurra is via Ansett WA and safaris can be combined with any Ansett Western

Australia fly-stay holiday or apex fare, and with most other special fares for travellers.

Northern Territory

28 **Air North** is the largest general aviation company in Darwin and operates throughout Australia's Top End. They fly Gooney Birds (DC3s) and twin-engined Cessnas.

Air North offers a variety of tours, including tours to Kakadu of one, two and three days' duration. Another tour visits Bathurst and the Melville Islands, which are the home of the Tiwi Aborigines with their unique culture and traditions and their traditional arts, pottery, wood carving and screen printing. A one-day tour flies to Victoria Settlement on the Cobourg Peninsula.

Air North is an easy way for passengers to acquaint themselves with *Crocodile Dundee* territory.

29 The northern region — Kakadu and Arnhem Land — has a vast and diversified landscape. The opportunity to grasp this spectacle comes only with flight. **Kakadu Air Services** runs air tours of the Northern Territory, offering views of the endless escarpments of the Arnhem Land plateau. Some 2,000 million years of erosion have left huge boulders and pillars that jut into the sky. Seasonal monsoonal rains fill the reservoirs of the plateau, and excess water plunges through the faults and down the valleys, creating many waterfalls that last well into the dry season. Below the plateau are strings of billabongs which form the major river systems. These waters eventually flow into the vast floodplains.

Kakadu Air pilots provide a qualified and interesting commentary throughout the flight over this region. Their familiarity with the area enables them to vary the route to suit seasonal variations and to follow the migration of herds of buffalo and flocks of birds.

Passengers can choose either an all-day tour from Darwin or half-hour, one-hour or day trips to Cobourg Peninsula from Jabiru.

30 **Chartair** is a Northern Territory company that offers a very unusual air excursion. A Cessna light aircraft, operating from Alice Springs Airport, is the mode of transport for the traveller seeking an adventure with a difference — an 'Outback Mailman' flight.

Passengers can join the 'Outback Mailman' for a day trip, flying to remote cattle stations and Aboriginal communities, delivering freight, mail and word-of-mouth news. In Central Australia, where distances are vast and the country is rugged, the 'Outback Mailman' flights provide regular communication and deliveries for isolated stations and communities.

Chartair also offers scenic flights from Coonallan Airport (Yulara, Ayers Rock). The grandeur of Ayers Rock and the beauty of the Olgas can only be fully appreciated from the air.

ALLAN MOULT

Queensland

31 **Air Queensland Safaris,** which fly out of Cairns, are renowned for their Gooney Bird (DC3) three-day tours.

The Gooney Bird takes travellers low over the Cape York Peninsula of Queensland. On the first day, it calls at Cooktown with its museums, then flies over the Daintree rainforest and Cape Tribulation, around Lizard Island, through the Flinders Group and across the Great Barrier Reef to Weipa on the Gulf of Carpentaria for the night.

On the second day, passengers fly up the Gulf to the northern tip of Australia and Thursday Island, with a pause for refreshments at Australia's northernmost pub and for a tour of the island.

After returning to Weipa for the evening and a morning tour of a bauxite mine, the tour continues with a barramundi barbecue at Edward River followed by a visit to a Crocodile Farm and to Aboriginal communities. The tour then returns to Cairns.

The company also offers day air tours out of Cairns to Cooktown and Lizard Island. These provide opportunities for snorkelling and experiencing the Reef as well as general exploration.

32 **Air Whitsunday** is the Great Barrier Reef airline. The largest operator of seaplanes in the southern hemisphere, it boasts an impressive fleet of Lake Buccaneers, De Havilland Beavers and two famous Grumman Mallards restored and refurbished after giving 30 years of service.

Air Whitsunday caters for a diverse range of travellers and their operation includes scheduled flights, specialised tours and charter flights in and around the Great Barrier Reef. They have twice won a state award for tourism and transportation.

Air Whitsunday operates an interesting series of air tours, including an economy tour for two adults from Cairns, covering Townsville, Whitsunday, Proserpine, Hamilton Island, Hayman Island and Mackay; a middle-market tour for two adults from Townsville; and a luxury tour for two adults from Whitsunday.

Scenic flights are also available in both helicopters and an open-cockpit Tiger Moth.

33 The brochure reads, 'Want a real thrill? Fly with **Biggles'.** Operated by Citizens Investments, Biggles is, in fact, an open-cockpit Tiger Moth that makes regular flights across the skies of Brisbane, giving adventurous passengers a ride they won't easily forget.

Passengers are transported back to a nostalgic time where they can relive the romance, experience the daring, and reflect on the heroism of those 'magnificent men in their flying machines'.

Scheduled flights last for one to one and a half hours and depart from Archerfield Airport. A limousine is provided to transport passengers to and from the airport.

34 **Gold Coast Aviation Centre** has its base at Coolangatta Airport. Captain N. A. Currey, an ex-RAAF officer and a member of the airforce for 30 years, is in charge of this experienced and professional operation.

The basic activity of the Centre is to provide flight training, which it does very thoroughly. However, planes are also available for charter flights and local scenic flights in and out of Coolangatta Airport.

35 **Seair Pacific** is based on the Gold Coast. It operates from Moreton and Stradbroke Islands, the Brisbane River, and from Lady Musgrave Island on the Great Barrier Reef.

Seair specialises in half and full-day scenic flights. They also offer overnight tours and a comprehensive charter service covering Brisbane, south-east Queensland and the Gold Coast.

Travellers will notice that the pilots on this unconventional airline are barefooted. They also take passengers on picnics to remote islands, then cook them lunch, and offer informative advice about the surrounding wilderness area.

Air Tours Contacts

Operators

New South Wales

1 Air Cruising Australia

Kyle House
27 Macquarie Place
Sydney NSW 2000
Ph. (02) 27 8742

2 Air NSW

Kingsford Smith Airport
Mascot
Sydney NSW 2020
Ph. (02) 268 1678

3 Aquatic Airways

Barrenjoey Boathouse
Governor Phillip Park
Palm Beach
Sydney NSW 2108
Ph. (02) 919 5966

4 Bel-Air Aviation

2/58 Bay Street
Rockdale
Sydney NSW 2216
Ph. (02) 597 3717

5 Flight Through the Spectacular Land of the Dreamtime

Level 59, MLC Centre
Martin Place
Sydney NSW 2000
Ph. (02) 260 0207

6 Navair Air Charter

Building 487
Avro Street
Bankstown
Sydney NSW 2200
Ph. (02) 708 1222

7 Sydney Skycruise

C/- Thomas Cook Travel
44 Market Street
Sydney NSW 2000
Ph. (02) 234 4000

8 Water Wings

9th Floor
54 High Street
North Sydney NSW 2060
Ph. (02) 92 0272

9 Blue Mountains Air Charter Company

PO Box 1666
Katoomba NSW 2780
Ph. (047) 88 1115 or 82 3046

10 Venture Out

PO Box 82
Katoomba NSW 2780
Ph. (047) 820 5022

11 Hazelton Airlines

Orange Road
Cudal NSW 2864
Ph. (063) 64 2104

The sheer joy of piloting a helicopter is captured on this pilot's face, left, while Rottnest Island, west of Perth, above, beckons the pilot

Australian Capital Territory

12 Canberra Mile High Club

PO Box 3
Mawson
Canberra ACT 2607
Ph. (062) 86 3343

13 Outback Travel

PO Box 3
Mawson
Canberra ACT 2607
Ph. (062) 86 3343

Victoria

14 Australian Vintage Travel

Level 45, Rialto
525 Collins Street
Melbourne VIC 3000
Ph. (03) 615 0040

15 Kendell Airlines Australia

431 Little Collins Street
Melbourne VIC 3000
Ph. (03) 676 2677

16 Penair

Building 92
Essendon Airport
Melbourne VIC 3041
Ph. (03) 374 2085

17 Drage Airworld

Greta Road
Wangaratta VIC 3677
Ph. (057) 21 8788

Tasmania

18 Par Avion

Cambridge Aerodrome
Tasman Highway
Cambridge
Hobart TAS 7170
Ph. (002) 48 5390

19 Wilderness Air

Strahan Jetty
Strahan TAS 7468
Ph. (004) 71 7280

20 Tasmanian Scenic Flights

PO Box 41
Wynyard TAS 7325
Ph. (004) 42 3838

Helicopters

New South Wales

Helicopter Charter

Sight-seeing and tourist flights are run by Helicopter Charter, who operate two Bell jetrangers. The capacity of the helicopters is four adult passengers and their luggage (children can sometimes sit two to a seat). The company has been in operation for five years and between them the pilots have 36 years of experience and an unblemished safety record.

Heliport Place
Mascot Airport
Sydney NSW 2020
Ph. (02) 693 1188

Helicruise

If you would like to have a good aerial view of Newcastle and the surrounding country, Helicruise can provide it. They offer a series of scenic flights over the Newcastle and Hunter region, one being a Vineyard Lunch Special, which takes you to a restaurant in wine country. The pilot will be happy to take you to see a particular point of interest during the flight.

PO Box 30
Wickham NSW 2293
Ph. (049) 62 1045

Heliflite

A variety of tours of the area around Sydney are offered by Heliflite, who fly from Mascot, not far from the centre of the city, or Castle Hill on the city's outskirts. You can select an overview of the harbour, a trip along the northern beaches, a flight to the Blue Mountains, or an excursion to the wine country of the Hunter Valley. In addition they will take you to historic Goollooinboin station, 75 air miles north-west of Sydney, which you can visit for the day or stay overnight.

RMB 44
Windsor Road
Castle Hill
Sydney NSW 2154
Ph. (02) 680 1511

Western Australia

Barrack Helicopters

Groups of from six to 20 persons can be accommodated by this company's fleet of helicopters. Charter flights and sight-seeing services are both available, and destinations include tranquil Rottnest Island, just a short distance from Perth, and a trip to the Margaret River area, 280 kilometres south of Perth. Leeuwin Estate, one of Western Australia's premier wineries, is visited on this tour which includes wine tasting and a tour of the winery. Special VIP excursions can also be arranged to the wine coast region and other areas of Western Australia.

PO Box 33
North Fremantle WA 6159
Ph. (09) 430 4126

Great Northern Helicopters

Sight-seeing charters are available to suit your interests. If you go west, you can visit the resort of Rottnest Island; in the east, you will find the vineyards of the Swan River valley; in the south are jarrah forests, orchards and the port and resort of Bunbury; and to the north is Yanchep National Park, where you can see black swans, kangaroos, koalas and an abundance of natural bush.

PO Box 653
Subiaco

Perth WA 6008
Ph. (09) 417 9895 or 387 3036

Northern Territory

Alice Heli Tours

This company operates scenic flights daily from Glen Helen Lodge over Ormiston Gorge, Mount Sonder and Palm Valley. They run a Kawasaki-Bell helicopter, piloted by John Atkinson, and carry three passengers. Specialised charter flights are also available. The flights offer spectacular views of the Western MacDonnell Ranges and the rugged scenery surrounding Alice Springs.

PO Box 701
Alice Springs NT 5750
Ph. (089) 52 7015

South Australia

21 Augusta Airways

PO Box 1756
Port Augusta SA 5700
Ph. (086) 42 3100

22 Desert Air Safaris

PO Box 80
Highbury
Adelaide SA 5089
Ph. (08) 264 7200

23 Skytours

GPO Box 2434
Adelaide SA 5001
Ph. (08) 352 3411

Western Australia

24 Royal Aero Club of Western Australia

Jandakot Airport
Jandakot WA 6164
Ph. (09) 332 7722

25 Skywest Airlines

GPO Box R1248
Perth WA 6001
Ph. (09) 321 9235

26 Travair Aerial Services

PO Box 207
South Perth WA 6151
Ph. (09) 367 7255

27 Alligator Airways

PO Box 10
Kununurra WA 6743
Ph. (091) 68 1575 or 68 1164

Northern Territory

28 Air North

PO Box 38133
Winnellie
Darwin NT 5789
Ph. (089) 81 7188

29 Kakadu Air Services

PO Box 95
Jabiru NT 5796
Ph. (089) 79 2031

30 Tillair

PO Box 87
Yulara NT 5751
Ph. (089) 56 2280

Capricorn Helicopters

A range of scenic flights around Alice Springs is offered by Capricorn Helicopters. They will take you to the Todd River and along the MacDonnell Ranges to Emily Gap, or to Mount Gillen and Simpson's Gap. Also available is a trip to the old telegraph station and the original Alice Springs township. Flights are of 35-40 minutes' duration and are conducted by pilots who will make sure you have the best views possible. The craft accommodate two passengers at a time and during the summer they fly without doors (but you will be securely strapped in with a seatbelt).

4 Bacon Street
Alice Springs NT 5750
Ph. (089) 52 4202

Central Australian Helicopters

A different angle on Ayers Rock is offered by Central Australian Helicopters who have helipads at the Yulara Resort and alongside the Park Ranger entry station. They will take four or six passengers in their Bell jet helicopters on flights around Ayers Rock and the Olgas, or further afield, on request. The company's fleet is based at Alice Springs and although they operate primarily in the Northern Territory, they will accept assignments anywhere.

101 Lackman Terrace
Alice Springs NT 5750
Ph. (089) 52 3059

Queensland

Helicopter Aviation

On their Reef Discovery trip, Helicopter Aviation will take you 75 kilometres from the Hamilton Island Resort to their heliport and luxury floating hotel on the outer part of the Great Barrier Reef. Once there, you can walk on the reef itself, view it from a glass-bottom boat, or you can go snorkelling or scuba diving. They also offer adventure flights over the Whitsunday Islands.

Hamilton Island Resort
Hamilton Island QLD 4803
Ph. (079) 46 9144

Helicorp

If you would like to see the Gold Coast and surrounding regions from the air, Helicorp has a number of half-day and full-day tours available. They operate tours to the Tweed Valley, with its avocado and tropical fruit plantations; Moreton Bay and Stradbroke Island; Currumbin Valley and Coogham National Park; Thunderbird Park where you can see fauna in natural surroundings; and the Terranora Lakes. Coach links are provided where needed, and meals are included with some of the tours.

Hangar 220
Archerfield
Brisbane QLD 4108
Ph. (008) 07 7363 (Toll free)

Captain Peter Cook of Sydney's Heliflite

Lloyd Helicopters

Lloyd Helicopters offers a number of Wings to Paradise trips, ranging from their 40-minute Reef Rhapsody tour over the reef in the Cairns region, to a 75-minute flight to the Mossman Gorge and Silky Oaks Lodge and back, flying over rainforests and mountains. This tour includes either breakfast or lunch, depending on what time you leave Cairns. Several sight-seeing trips over the reef are also offered by the company from Capricorn Iwasaki Resort at Yeppoon.

PO Box 6310
Cairns Mail Centre
Cairns QLD 4871
Ph. (070) 52 1244

Queensland

31 Air Queensland

62 Abbott Street
Cairns QLD 4870
Ph. (070) 50 4314 or (008) 77 7901

32 Air Whitsunday

PO Box 166
Airlie Beach QLD 4802
Ph. (079) 46 9133

33 Citizens Investments

21 Avebury Street
Hill End
Brisbane QLD 4101
Ph. (07) 844 6671

34 Gold Coast Aviation Centre

Building 2
Coolangatta Airport
Bilinga QLD 4224
Ph. (075) 36 7586

35 Seair Pacific

PO Box 348
Runaway Bay QLD 4216
Ph. (075) 37 2855

NICK BROKENSHA

Aircraft charter

Aircraft are available for charter from
the following companies who include
Lears, Cessna Citations, British
Aerospace HS215s and Dassault
Falcons in their fleets.

Australian Jet Charter
Ross Smith Drive East
Mascot
Sydney NSW 2020
Ph. (02) 693 2855

Pacific Aviation
Eleventh Street
Mascot
Sydney NSW 2020
Ph. (02) 669 2219

Skybird Aviation Services
PO Box 230
Niddrie
Melbourne VIC 3042
Ph. (03) 379 7300

Information Sources

The following Aero Clubs can provide
information on plane hire and charter
and flying schools, and some will
provide a trial instruction flight for
people thinking of learning to fly.

New South Wales

The Royal Aero Club of NSW
Marion Street
Bankstown Aerodrome
Sydney NSW 2200
Ph. (02) 70 0291

Australian Capital Territory

Canberra Aero Club
Canberra Airport
Fairbairn
Canberra ACT 2600
Ph. (062) 47 4841

Victoria

Royal Victorian Aero Club
Moorabbin Airport
Mentone
Melbourne VIC 3194
Ph. (03) 580 0088

Tasmania

Aero Club of South Tasmania
Tasman Highway
Cambridge
Hobart TAS 7170
Ph. (002) 48 5370

South Australia

Royal Aero Club of South Australia
Parafield Aerodrome
Parafield
Adelaide SA 5109
Ph. (08) 258 2912

Western Australia

Royal Aero Club of Western Australia
Jandakot Airport
Jandakot
Perth WA 6164
Ph. (09) 332 7722

Northern Territory

Darwin Aero Club
Darwin Airport
Darwin NT 5790
Ph. (089) 81 5402

Alice Springs Aero Club
Aerodrome
Alice Springs NT 5750
Ph. (089) 52 1250

Queensland

Royal Queensland Aero Club
Beatty Road
Archerfield
Brisbane QLD 4108
Ph. (07) 275 3244

Aero Club of North Queensland
Captain Cook Highway
Cairns QLD 4870
Ph. (070) 53 1438

Townsville Aero Club
Aerodrome
Garbutt
Townsville QLD 4814
Ph. (077) 79 2069

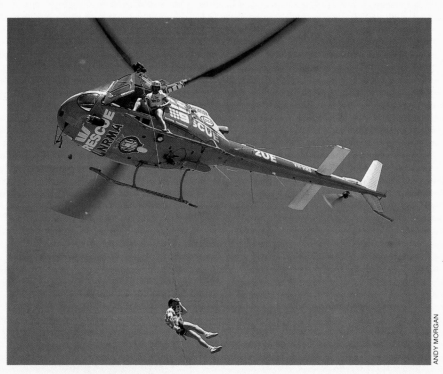

ANDY MORGAN

IAN POTTER

Casinos

Australians are inveterate gamblers. A true story: a young British zoologist was in a hotel in the outback of the Northern Territory when a friendly jackaroo, his lean face deeply etched by years in the sun, rolled towards him and placed his wristwatch on the bar. He pulled a two-bob piece from his grubby moleskins and issued the challenge. 'G'day. Like a bet? . . . Right. I'll toss you's for the ticker. Heads, I keep it, tails you's win.' The no-lose nature of the offer was obvious but this did not deter the jackaroo from launching the coin towards the ceiling. Tails. 'Good on yer, mate. Here's the watch.' And before our zoologist could object, Jack had stumbled away into the night.

A decade or so has passed since this discovery of the origins of the 'two-bob watch', but the story expresses the naivety and enthusiasm of the humble Australian punter.

Two-up is the most famous Australian betting game associated with the culture of the bush. The spinner throws two pennies into the air and the gamble is in guessing right on a double-head or double-tail drop. Betting routines in legalised casino versions vary in complexity, but the 'heads or tails' theme is the essence of this simple pastime. As the true odds of guessing right are three-to-one and you are likely to be offered even money, it is easy to see that Divine Providence rather than Lady Luck will have to intervene for a win against the house.

Horses, camels, crabs, mice, dogs, ferries, 18-footers on Sydney Harbour — whenever two or more things move in roughly the same direction, the punters will be there hoping to beat the bank or their mates.

Much of Australia's gambling has been illegal — unlicensed small casinos and clubs still proliferate — but, much like the rest of the world, the gambling scene has recently become freer with sensible regulation and it now provides a useful source of revenue for the Treasury.

In recent times, the development of casinos has been rapid. The first opened in Tasmania in 1973 at Wrest Point in Hobart, and Diamond Beach Casino opened in Darwin in 1979. In the 80s, these developments have gathered pace. Lasseters in Alice Springs and the Launceston Country Club were opened in 1981 and 1982 respectively. The Adelaide, Burswood Island in Perth, and Jupiters casinos all started business in 1985, while the Sheraton Breakwater Hotel in Townsville started spinning the wheel in 1986.

In the near future, Sydney's Darling Harbour Casino (the biggest in the world) will be completed. At that time, Victoria will be the only Australian state not to operate a casino.

Jupiters Casino and Conrad International Hotel on the Gold Coast

PETER FYFE

Casinos reflect a growing sophistication among punters in the lucky country. Management skills, legalisation and gambling practice have together created an environment that is both conducive to the local fascination for the punt and accessible to the visitor from overseas.

Australian casinos attract huge audiences. Weekly attendances of 250,000 to 300,000 are not uncommon. Jupiters on the Gold Coast, the top draw, claims nearly half that total. The casinos employ over 7,000 staff and in property development terms they represent investments of millions of dollars.

Nevertheless, great debate has attended the development of Australia's casinos. Some see it as pandering to an innate weakness in the Australian character — an irrational compulsion to gamble. Others argue that it is better to control gambling by strong regulation than to let it proliferate in illegal ways.

For the most part, however, attendance at a casino is seen as entertainment — not a way of life. During the first six months of operation of the Adelaide Casino, the average loss was only $20 per player and its managers estimate that there are only a few hundred 'high rollers' who carry more than $200,000 with which to play.

Turnover statistics for the casinos are interesting. Currently, about $280 million is earned by the casinos in gross revenue. Excluding in-bound tourists, this works out at around $18 per head of Australia's population.

Throughout the world, casinos attract tourists, and casinos here are no different in that regard. Australia's late entry into the gambling business has enabled operators to learn from the mistakes of their overseas counterparts, and visitors to any of Australia's casinos will find themselves well looked after. Service is courteous, the games are open to all customers, and security on casino premises is excellent.

All of our casinos, except Adelaide offer accommodation, so the visitor does not have far to go to bed, to dream dreams of good fortune, or to cry himself to sleep.

Locations

Tasmania

1 **Launceston Federal Country Club** is a new hotel-casino, operated by the same group who administer Wrest Point near Hobart. Unlike its sister, this is a low-rise development set in 85 hectares with an 18-hole championship golf course, a lake, stables and riding trails. Guests may also swim, play squash and tennis, and enjoy the night life of cabaret and disco, or just relax outdoors on the terrace overlooking the peaceful countryside. Unlike other casinos, this is a country retreat often used for business meetings.

The club also attracts many interstate and overseas visitors. For high-rollers, this is a very attractive setting. Private planes regularly deliver patrons to the casino for a night of serious gambling and whisk them away afterwards.

Blackjack, roulette, poker, mini-dice, two-up and keno are the most popular games with Federal Country Club guests.

2 **Wrest Point Federal Hotel-Casino,** just outside Hobart, was established in 1973. It is recognised as having set the standard for the new generation of Australian casinos. Its outstanding record is matched by the setting. The tower, which has 278 rooms, has a revolving restaurant on the 17th floor from which guests can admire panoramic views of the Derwent River estuary, Sandy Bay, Hobart and Mount Wellington.

Poker is Wrest Point's most popular gambling attraction. The casino also offers baccarat, mini-dice, keno and two-up. Both poker and blackjack can be played in regular tournaments.

The accommodation is five-star, with pleasant variations of mood in the decor. This is an excellent venue on which to base a Tasmanian holiday. There are plenty of things to do in and around the hotel, with its cabaret, disco, tennis, squash and health facilities, and good food. Wrest Point has also established a reputation as a popular centre for business conventions.

South Australia

3 **The Adelaide Casino** is housed in an historic building — the Old Railway Station Booking Hall — which was erected in 1929. By far the most stately of Australia's casinos, it is located in the heart of the city close to the Festival Centre, hotels and accommodation. The Ansett Gateway Motel opposite

the casino offers very attractive holiday packages.

The huge chandeliers, panelled walls, marble floors and Corinthian columns provide the setting for a night of good fun and, hopefully, good fortune. Poker tables have been added to the other games — keno, blackjack, roulette, craps, mini-dice, baccarat, two-up and money wheel. There is an International Room (jackets for men), which is separate from the public tables, and excellent bars and restaurants.

A Victorian 'high-roller' recently won a record $500,000 at the roulette table, which no doubt helped towards his cost of travel.

Adelaide, with its reputation for sleepy conservatism, has certainly awakened the interest of the gambling community. Three million visitors were received in the first year of the casino's operation.

Western Australia

4 **Burswood Island Resort Casino,** just a few minutes' drive from the heart of Perth, near the Causeway Bridge, is unlike its interstate rivals. While most casino licences are granted on the stipulation that the gaming venue be part of a hotel complex, at Burswood the concept has been extended to include the casino as part of a huge island resort complex.

The hotel has over 400 rooms, servicing a large exhibition centre, sports and entertainment venues, and a business convention resource with a 3,500-capacity theatre. The casino, which opened in 1985, is licensed to accommodate 142 tables for blackjack, roulette, baccarat and craps. Guests may also choose from among keno, mini-dice, money wheel (big and small), two-up and video games. The range of services provided by Burswood means that it caters for a complete cross-section of local and tourist communities and the business world.

As one would expect with a complex of this size,

MILTON WORDLEY

Heads, or tails? A 'spinner' prepares to launch a round of 'two-up' - the traditional Aussie gambling game

guests have their every whim attended to. Visitors to Burswood can also enjoy a range of health, tennis, swimming, golf and leisure facilities, as well as a wide range of restaurants and bars.

Burswood occupies a 100-hectare site on the Swan River and is the largest resort of its kind in Australia and one of the largest in the world.

Lasseters Casino, Alice Springs

Northern Territory

5   At the Top End of Australia, the **Diamond Beach Hotel-Casino** is situated in Darwin — not the likeliest of places for an international casino. Architecturally, Diamond Beach is impressive and its setting beside Mindil Beach, which looks out across the Timor Sea, is equally captivating. Visitors are assured of an excellent holiday in elegant and comfortable surroundings. It takes only a few minutes to reach Diamond Beach from the airport and many visitors use the hotel as the springboard for their visits to Kakadu National Park and other tourist attractions of the area.

Following recent refurbishment, the hotel offers two casino venues. The major casino offers all the usual games, a separate keno lounge, and a poker machine hall. Upstairs, however, is Aspinalls International, an exclusive casino where entry is by membership or invitation. The 'high-rollers' assemble here, playing for large stakes in luxurious surroundings, assured that their anonymity is preserved.

This venue is the top social meeting place in Darwin for the local population and it attracts many interstate and overseas visitors.

6   **Lasseters Casino** in Alice Springs draws over half of its visitors from overseas, many of whom use the hotel as a convenient starting point for exploring Australia's red centre. The resort faces Alice Springs across the tree-studded sandy course of the Todd River, yet is only minutes away from the city centre and 11 kilometres from Alice Springs Airport.

Tennis, swimming and golf are among the other activities offered, and there is a good range of leisure and dining facilities. It has a reputation for being very relaxed, yet this does not detract from the seriousness

of the games. A private gaming room is available on request.

Lasseters offers all the popular games — two-up, blackjack, roulette, mini-dice plus keno and poker machines. A 350-seat theatre is available for conventions. And children enjoy the animal enclosure, with its native animals and birds.

Lasseters Casino offers all the excitement — and glamour — of an international-standard casino/hotel, complete with elegant and air-conditioned accommodation and first-class restaurants and bars, in an environment which is truly unique.

Queensland

7   The **Sheraton Breakwater** in Townsville is Australia's newest hotel/casino. Completed in 1986 at a cost of $60 million, this casino caters for local people as well as the growing interstate and international tourist trade. The hotel boasts 200 rooms and guests have access to the best in luxury resort facilities. Water surrounds the hotel on three sides and it is next to the huge $20 million Marine and Wharf development. And, of course, the Sheraton's location makes it a splendid springboard for quick visits to the Great Barrier Reef, Cairns and the islands.

The tables offer blackjack, roulette, two-up, craps, mini-dice, baccarat, keno and video games. And all patrons are treated with the same friendly service — from the novice keen to enjoy a little flutter to the professional 'high-rollers' who make a living on the risky roll of the dice.

There is also a pool, sauna, gym and tennis courts at the disposal of guests.

8   **Jupiters Casino** is Australia's largest casino and it ranks with the biggest in the world. It forms part of the new Conrad International Hotel complex at Broadbeach Island on the Gold Coast, about an hour's drive from Brisbane or 30 minutes from Coolangatta. The Conrad International is connected with the Hilton Hotel Group and is Australia's largest hotel, with over 600 rooms. The resort (which opened in 1985) offers tennis, swimming (with transfers to the local beaches) and extensive dining and health facilities — not to mention a musical fantasy show called 'Galaxies'.

Dress regulations in the casino are informal and the mood invites ordinary folk as well as seasoned gamblers to test their skills in games of skill and chance.

It's a 24-hour affair, with blackjack, baccarat, roulette, craps, sic-bo, keno, bix-six and two-up, and the tables are flanked by video casino games.

The great attraction for the thousands of visitors to Jupiters is that the fanatical and the casual, cognoscenti and novices, locals and visitors all feel at home. A range of alternative activities provides a complete holiday opportunity. Jupiters also caters for business conventions.

Casinos Contacts

Operators

Ansett Holidays offer package tours to all Australia's casinos. The tours are inclusive of economy-class return airfare, accommodation and airport coach transfers.

Contact your local Ansett Travel office in Australia or, if you are inquiring from overseas, contact your preferred travel agent.

Tasmania

1 **Launceston Federal Country Club Casino**

Country Club Avenue
Launceston TAS 7250
Ph. (003) 44 8855

2 **Wrest Point Federal Hotel-Casino**

410 Sandy Bay Road
Hobart TAS 7000
Ph. (002) 25 0112

South Australia

3 **The Adelaide Casino**

North Terrace
Adelaide SA 5000
Ph. (08) 212 2811

Western Australia

4 **Burswood Island Resort Casino**

Great Eastern Highway
Victoria Park
Perth WA 6103
Ph. (09) 362 7777

Northern Territory

5 **Diamond Beach Hotel/Casino**

Gilruth Avenue
Mindil Beach
Darwin NT 5790
Ph. (089) 81 7755

6 **Lasseters Casino**

Barrett Drive
Alice Springs NT 5750
Ph. (089) 52 5066

Queensland

7 **Sheraton Breakwater Casino-Hotel**

Sir Leslie Thiess Drive
Townsville QLD 4810
Ph. (077) 72 4066

8 **Jupiters Casino**

Broadbeach Island
Gold Coast Highway QLD 4218
Ph. (075) 92 1133

The Adelaide Casino by night

The Sheraton Breakwater Casino Hotel, Townsville, at dawn

DOUGLASS BAGLIN

Executive & Country Retreats

Each person's idea of an ideal haven is different, but in most cases it entails a total escape from the hassles of everyday life. For some it is a luxurious country estate; for others, a secluded tropical paradise. Opportunities to 'get away from it all' exist everywhere in Australia. The country caters to all tastes, offering a great diversity of retreats in a wide variety of locations. These range from the simplest to the most opulent, from snowy mountaintop to tropical rainforest.

New South Wales and Victoria have some splendid country retreats, many of which are reminiscent of a more gracious bygone era.

Many of these retreats are historic homes lovingly renovated and refurbished in keeping with their period. The beautiful 121-hectare Milton Park Estate, in Bowral in New South Wales, and Burnham Beeches Country House, in Sherbrooke, Victoria (one of two Australian members of Europe's select Relais et Chateaux, the other being Mount Lofty House) are two excellent examples. Prices for this kind of venue are usually on par with a five-star hotel, but their location and facilities far surpass the offerings of their ritzier city cousins.

Queensland's terrain, clothed in some of the country's finest rainforests, stands in sharp contrast to the more pastoral surrounds of the southern states. Here in the far north, travellers can stay in a humble lodge set in a tropical wilderness and accessible only by four-wheel-drive vehicles. Or they can pass idle days swimming off uninhabited islands, diving in clear blue waters, and fishing off coral reefs.

Some retreats emphasise health and fitness, such as Warburton Health Centre in Victoria and Maleny Health Resort in Queensland. Some provide programmes aimed at stress reduction and weight loss — and will even help the visitor give up smoking.

Others use the services of masseurs and alternative practitioners of health and medicine. All encourage nutritious eating, plenty of country walks, the odd game of tennis and a few laps in the pool, tailoring their services to suit guests' needs and requirements.

For those wanting a more active escape, some retreats double as activity centres, offering a full range of outdoor experiences. In Victoria at Mt Buffalo, The Chalet provides ski lessons for winter visitors, while up north in Queensland's Cape Tribulation, guests of Bloomfield Wilderness Lodge can take advantage of boating facilities to explore and fish the wonderful offshore coral reefs.

The accommodation and service offered by these retreats varies from simple, self-contained units to deluxe suites with four-poster beds, open fireplaces and antique furnishings. Most of these have the modern additions of en suite facilities, colour TV and more often than not a spa bath. Some resorts foster interactivity between guests; others ensure complete privacy. Those that provide total service usually also offer first-rate catering and their restaurants are often a feature in themselves.

Locations

New South Wales

Attunga is Aboriginal for 'high place', and **Attunga Park** is so named because of its hilltop location, overlooking mountains, valleys, meadows and creeks in the picturesque borderland straddling the New South Wales/Queensland border.

The park stretches over almost 13 hectares of green hill country near the foot of Mt Warning in the MacPherson Range. It is less than two hours' drive south of Brisbane.

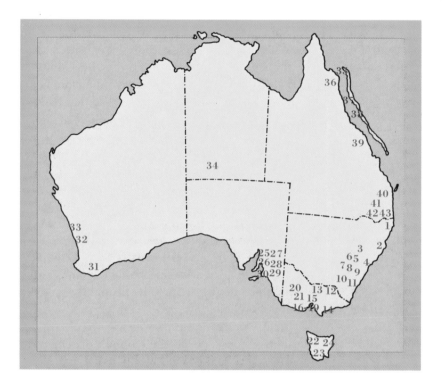

ROB WALLS

Peppers Guest House within the Pokolbin vineyard area of the Hunter Valley, NSW

The property runs cattle and horses, and there is horse riding available just 20 minutes away. Bass and perch can be caught in the creeks running along the edge of the property. Fine rainforest country is only a 20-minute drive away through areas of avocado and banana plantation, and there is an international-standard golf course nearby.

Attunga Park's owners, John and Sheila Taylor, call it a place to unwind, 'somewhere people can go to rediscover themselves'. They can accommodate up to eight guests in four secluded bungalows, each with its own garden, refrigerator, TV, video and music system, as well as a roomy spa bath. Guests have a choice of either queen-sized or twin single beds. The main house has a dining room, TV lounge and a full-sized snooker table.

Each night, guests meet for cocktails before a private dinner party.

2 Near Taree is the elegant country retreat of **Linley House**. This exclusive home accommodates just six people each weekend in twin or double rooms. Guests are guaranteed a time of total relaxation among some of the prettiest scenery in the country. Linley is set in the Manning Valley, world-famous for its dairy products and recognised as possibly the richest pastureland in Australia.

The region is also known for its timber, and there are spectacular rainforest areas nearby. Hidden among them is the highest single-drop waterfall in the southern hemisphere, Ellenborough Falls.

Fine beaches are just 30 minutes away, and also within reach is the town of Wingham, a National Trust town with an English-style common. One of the town's drawcards is Wingham Brush, the last remnant of coastal rainforest in the region, huge Moreton Bay fig trees are home to hundreds of flying foxes.

On the property of Linley itself is a golf-driving range and a swimming pool, and there is a four-wheel-drive vehicle for excursions.

A feature of a luxury weekend at Linley is the gourmet food, which can also be prepared for picnics on request. Meals are relaxed, and Linley makes the perfect retreat for an exclusive house party.

3 A visit to the wineries of the Hunter Valley can be made into a very special occasion by staying at **Peppers Guest House** in Pokolbin, about three hours' drive north of Sydney.

Set in ten hectares of bushland, commanding great views over the valley's green vineyards and rolling hills, this striking mansion offers luxury accommodation and excellent food.

Its facilities include an all-weather tennis court, indoor heated pool and spa, a gym, and a restaurant, bar and lounge. Other services include therapeutic massages, hairdressing on the premises by arrangement, and babysitting.

There are 47 double en-suite rooms, each with grand old beds, dressers, rugs and vases of fresh flowers.

Although Peppers would look to most like a restored old stone colonial mansion, it is in fact only a few years old and was built by current owners, Suzi and Mike O'Connor.

4 Set in a secluded subtropical paradise overlooking Toowoon Bay is **Kim's Resort**, just 90 minutes' drive north of Sydney.

Guests can take advantage of long walks along the beach or into the nearby Watagan Mountains. There are plenty of good surfing beaches in the region, with sailboarding hire only a five-minute drive away at Long Jetty on Tuggerah Lakes. Bicycle hire and horse riding are also available.

Kim's beachfront bungalows have recently been renovated, and were designed to blend in with the natural surroundings. All have wide verandas overlooking the sea. Some have their own heated jacuzzi set into the timber deck, while others have fireplaces or indoor spa baths.

The Beach Deluxe Bungalows vary in size and accommodate between two and five persons, while the Garden Deluxe Bungalows accommodate only two. A Family Deluxe Bungalow has space for five. All bungalows are serviced daily.

The new fully licensed dining rooms are elevated to provide a panoramic view, and there is a guest lounge and cocktail bar.

Meals are of the highest quality and often feature local seafood specialities.

5 Set in the solitude of Blackheath, in the Blue Mountains, one and half hours' drive west of Sydney, is **Glenella**. One of the better established of the small Blue Mountains' guesthouses, its delicious (mostly French) cuisine and comfortable accommodation lure many guests back for more.

With stained-glass windows, broad verandas, deep armchairs and cosy log fires, the main house incorporates 14 bedrooms, a lounge and a licensed restaurant which is open to the public. Two adjacent self-contained cottages each have three double bedrooms, a kitchen, lounge and bathroom.

An 18-hole golf course, tennis courts and a swimming pool are all close by.

Glenella does not accommodate children.

6 With only seven guest rooms, **Pegum's** is one of the smallest guesthouses in the Blue Mountains district. Pegum's is in the tiny town of Lawson, nestled on the edge of the Blue Mountains National Park.

Built in 1893, it is a timber building surrounded by wide shady verandas and carefully tended gardens. The owners, Stephen and Margot Pegum, have faithfully restored it to its early colonial style, and its ambience is intimate and friendly.

Guest rooms vary in size, but all are spacious and most open onto their own verandas.

The food at Pegum's has an excellent reputation and visitors eat in the leafy atmosphere of the dining room, its large windows overlooking the rear gardens.

Summer activities include bushwalking, tennis, golf and bicycling.

Ideal for a quiet, relaxing weekend (the guesthouse does not cater for children), Pegum's is open from Friday to Monday. Prices include dinner, bed and breakfast.

7 In the heart of the Blue Mountains lies **Fairmont Resort,** one of the newest resort developments in Australia.

8 **Jenolan Caves Guesthouse** is a unique historic guesthouse situated 199 kilometres from Sydney near the spectacular Jenolan Caves.

Accommodation is available at the guesthouse on a bed and breakfast basis, though special packages can be arranged over three days and two nights with meals included.

Located not far from the guesthouse itself, in a quiet bush setting on the fringe of the Jenolan Caves Reserve, are eight self-contained holiday cabins

Linley House - an exclusive country retreat

accommodating a maximum of six people per cabin. Each cabin has a pot-belly log fire, bathroom and fully equipped kitchen.

9 **Macarthur Lodge Country Resort** is at Mt Keira at Wilton, 90 minutes' drive from Sydney. Set in ten hectares of sloping lawns and nature reserve, the Lodge includes a winery, aviary, rockeries, and a fish pond and creek.

Guests like to potter quietly around the property, taking walks and keeping an eye open for kangaroos. Those seeking slightly more active pursuits can play tennis, or swim in the outdoor heated pool. Canoeing on the Nepean River is only five minutes away, and horse riding, hot-air ballooning and parachuting are also very close.

Each Saturday night, guests can kick up their heels at the Australian Bush Dance, held in the Lodge's restaurant.

Macarthur Lodge has 25 airconditioned luxury units, each with en-suite bathrooms.

10 The 121-hectare **Milton Park** estate was bought in 1984 by two Sydney doctors who turned it into an exclusive country estate. The house was originally built by one of Australia's great trading families, the Horderns, in 1901. It has what is regarded as one of Australia's finest and most historic gardens, featuring four hectares of formal Edwardian English-style gardens.

The original Hordern homestead has now been completely renovated and includes restaurants, a bar, a private dining room, formal lounges, and libraries. Twenty three-bedroom, fully self-contained country-side villas have recently been built adjacent to the hotel. The service is excellent, with an unusually high ratio of staff to guests.

Fitness facilities have a high priority, and there is an indoor heated swimming pool, a spa and gym, tennis courts, bicycles for hire, a cricket pitch, and various walking and jogging tracks. The food is of a high quality, and is complemented by an extensive wine selection.

Milton Park is located in the southern highlands of New South Wales, 170 kilometres south-west of Sydney.

11 Less than two hours' drive from both Canberra and Sydney, in the lush Southern Highlands, is **Mount Broughton Country Retreat**. Tucked away in blissfully quiet surrounds, it is set in ten hectares of pastoral land, with carefully manicured gardens and undulating lawns.

Built in 1926, it is constructed mainly of sandstone. Inside, the Great Hall is a magnificent sandstone walled room with a ten-metre high ceiling and wonderful full-length leadlight windows. A large fireplace operates throughout the winter. The dining room is open to the public.

There are 11 double bedrooms, some with adjoining sunrooms, and all with splendid views.

Guests can take pre-dinner drinks in the bar, and afterwards play billiards on the full-size antique table in the billiard room. There is also an all-weather tennis court and many scenic walks and drives.

Victoria

12 **Lake Dartmouth Resort** is close by the Victorian Alps in the north-east corner of Victoria. This wonderful resort enables guests to breathe high country mountain air, take in the superb views, enjoy the abundance of wildlife to be found in this subalpine region, and simply do whatever they wish whenever they want.

Guests can play tennis, fish, swim, pan for gold, bushwalk, and go canoeing and horse riding. Children can enjoy BMX bike rides, swimming, archery, pony rides and trampolining. The golfer has a choice of four championship courses all within close proximity. The accommodation includes a 30-room motel, group and individual lodges, and caravan park facilities.

Lake Dartmouth Resort boasts an international-standard restaurant which is open for all meals.

13 Perched on the very crest of Mt Buffalo in north-east Victoria, 330 kilometres from Melbourne, is **Mt Buffalo Chalet**. This rambling old guesthouse has been operating since the turn of the century, and for some it has become an institution, attracting 80% return bookings, many during the ski season.

Excellent ski slopes for beginners are only a few kilometres away, and the Chalet runs daily ski instruction. Tobogganing is also available and the cross-country skiing is very good.

In summer, the mountainous bush terrain is ideal for bushwalking and horse riding. Tennis and swimming are other popular summer pursuits.

Although the accommodation and facilities are quite modest, the Chalet's friendly and relaxed atmosphere makes it a special place to stay. There are 103 rooms (most with en-suite facilities) and a formal dining room and a coffee shop. Large comfortable chairs and huge log fireplaces in the lounge and drawing rooms are a big attraction for cold and weary guests after a hard day on the slopes. And on Thursday and Saturday nights the place comes alive with music and dancing.

14 Some 232 kilometres east of the town of Stratford, **Akoonah** nestles in 200 hectares of natural bushland on the edge of the Perry River.

The Akoonah property farms sheep and cattle, and guests who visit have the opportunity to enjoy a swim in the permanent waterholes nearby, take leisurely bushwalks, or use the cottage's canoe to explore the river and its attractive scenery. Other facilities available include horse riding, pottery crafting, table tennis and rabbit shooting.

Akoonah's open fireplace is a boon in the cold

winter months, and the books and games available at the cottage occupy guests in the warmth of a blazing fire while they enjoy the spectacular views of the Great Dividing Range.

Akoonah is close to the township of Sale, the Gippsland Lakes, and a number of wineries.

15 Located in 16 hectares of lovely bushland on the banks of the Howqua River, **Howqua Dale Gourmet Retreat** offers unrivalled gourmet food and wine as well as fine hospitality. Just three hours' drive north-east of Melbourne, it has a fast-growing reputation for being one of the best retreats of its kind in Australia.

A modern, centrally heated homestead with wide verandas, Howqua Dale accommodates up to 12 people in six double rooms; four have en-suites with private access to the garden, while two smaller rooms share a bathroom. The spacious living and lounge areas have beautiful views of the Howqua Valley.

Guests are treated to excellent cuisine in the formal dining room which is housed, along with the kitchen, in a newly designed building.

For those who wish to spend the day bushwalking, proprietors Sarah Stegley and Marieke Brugman will pack an exotic bush picnic. They also conduct cooking classes on the premises.

Howqua Dale also provides horse riding and tennis, and there is a pool for those who prefer not to swim in the river. Trout are plentiful in the creek at the foot of the property. Boating and water-skiing are only one kilometre away at Lake Eildon, and Howqua will provide all the necessary equipment.

16 The **Warburton Health Care Centre**, set in five hectares of garden amongst the forests of the Great Dividing Range, places emphasis on sound nutrition and healthy activity. Just 77 kilometres east of Melbourne, it is the perfect place to unwind and rejuvenate.

A range of courses is offered at the Centre, including weight and stress management, and executive health and fitness. There is also a course to help visitors stop smoking. Guests are able to book in advance and participate in one of these courses, or simply spend their time relaxing and taking advantage of the Centre's two fully equipped gyms, two heated swimming pools, tennis courts and hydrotherapy spa. Those with a bit more energy to burn can go on half and one-day trips to nearby Mt Victoria and Mt Donna Buang. The Centre also offers a wide range of treatments, including therapeutic massage. All meals are vegetarian.

The Centre's staff of 150 includes doctors, physiotherapists, creative activity therapists, nutritionists, health educators, physical educationalists and a pharmacist as well as nursing staff.

17 In Europe, country houses noted for their luxurious facilities and outstanding service earn membership of a select group called the Relais et Chateaux. **Burnham Beeches** in Victoria is one of only two country houses in the Pacific region to have been awarded membership of this group.

Located in the beautiful Sherbrooke region of the Dandenong Ranges near Melbourne, it represents the finest example of Art Deco in Australia today. Built over 50 years ago as a private estate, it was taken over by its current owners, John and Kenny Guy, in 1981. It is a beautifully decorated English-style country house set amidst 22 hectares of grazing paddocks and landscaped gardens paved with walkways.

A comfortable lounging area, a fully stocked bar and a well-presented dining room provide plenty of space for relaxing. There is a formal candlelit restaurant, serving outstanding à la carte dishes,

A beach scene on beautiful Orpheus Island

which has won many awards for excellence in cuisine.

Five of the 52 guest rooms are located on the upper floors of the original white stucco building, and the remainder are scattered over a two-storey connecting annexe. The Nicholas Suite, the original master bedroom, incorporates an enormous living/dining area, a private bar, a boudoir with king-sized bed and dressing alcove, a spacious private deck and two marble baths, one with a massive step-up whirlpool tub.

18 Now restored to the Victorian elegance and tranquillity enjoyed in its heyday, one of Melbourne's most gracious small hotels, **The Tilba,** has earned a reputation for pampering its guests.

Lofty ceilings, original leadlight windows, delight-

ful Victorian furnishings, as well as the added touches of wildflower soaps, Victorian shaving mirrors and the pleasures of breakfast taken in the airy glass-roofed atrium, are some of the features which create the timeless environment of The Tilba.

Situated in Toorak Road, The Tilba is ideally located to take advantage of the bustling activity of Melbourne's city centre. Guests can enjoy a leisurely stroll to the Victorian Arts Centre, or wander down St Kilda Road, the heart of the business district, or browse in this exclusive shopping area where boutiques are intermingled with a rich selection of restaurants and cosy coffee shops. Nearby, the Royal Botanic Gardens provide a relaxing environment in which to admire a host of unique flora.

19 **Narrabeen Cottage** is located on Phillip Island, at the southern edge of Westernport Bay, just out of Melbourne. Visitors can get there by ferry, by the bridge link from San Remo, or by light aircraft from Melbourne.

A quaint guesthouse with comfortable accommodation for ten and typical home-style cooking, Narrabeen Cottage was built in the 1920s. It has a spacious sitting room, a large kitchen with breakfast area, and a cosy cottage atmosphere.

A 'weekend-only' retreat, it provides a base from which to see the attractions of Phillip Island. The island abounds in wildlife, most notably the fairy penguins that come ashore nightly to feed their young. It also harbours a colony of seals, as well as a substantial koala population.

Narrabeen's owners, Christine Monk and Jane Daly, admit that it is 'nothing too exotic', but the cottage has received favourable reviews from passing critics.

Chris and Jane usually provide a barbecue lunch on Sundays, and serve breakfast outdoors whenever possible in their landscaped gardens.

Tennis courts, a golf course and one of the most protected beaches on the coast are all within easy walking distance.

20 **Boomerang Holiday Ranch** is bounded by natural forest only one hour's drive from Melbourne. Set in picturesque surroundings close to Hepburn Springs, famous for its sparkling spring water, there are many activities to keep guests entertained for the duration of their stay.

Horse riding is a speciality at the ranch. Fifty well-trained horses and ponies are at the disposal of visitors who are keen to venture along riding trails into the nearby forests. All trails and tuition are supervised by experienced staff.

Other activities at the ranch include table tennis, mini-golf, volley ball, lawn bowls, swimming, golf and fishing. For those who prefer to laze indoors, video movies, television, a games room and billiards room are also available.

Bedrooms and cabins are carpeted, and there are

open fires in the dining and games rooms. Groups of up to 80 can be adequately catered for and the home-cooked meals are delicious.

21 **Bellinzona Country House**, a large Edwardian house, was built in 1903. Its current owners, Bob and Sue Glover, have kept strictly to the original design in their renovation, while incorporating wood panelling, brass fittings and beamed ceilings.

Some 105 kilometres north-west of Melbourne, it is only five minutes from Hepburn Springs. These springs pump out around 55,000 litres of mineral water each day and are the site of Australia's only hydrotherapy treatment centre.

Situated as it is in the untouched bushland of the Wombat State Forest, there are plenty of excellent walks to be taken from two to eight hours' duration. Horse riders can take advantage of two schools just minutes away, while there are plenty of trout to be caught in the nearby streams.

Bellinzona has 22 bedrooms, all with en-suite facilities. For those with a penchant for bubbly of both kinds, the executive suites have their own private bar and spa bath. The honeymoon suite has not only the spa and bar, but also an open fireplace and full room service.

There is a large indoor heated pool, a courtyard spa tub, squash courts, an all-weather tennis court, and a fully licensed à la carte restaurant.

Tasmania

22 **Cradle Mountain Lodge** is located at the northern end of the Cradle Mountain-Lake St Clair National Park. This area is dominated by Cradle Mountain itself, with Dove Lake at its foot. Here, towering mountain peaks, wild open moorland heath, deep gorges, forested valleys and crystal lakes form an imposing back-drop to this secluded retreat.

Constructed from local timbers, each cabin provides the ultimate opportunity to get away from city congestion. Guests can cook their own food or eat delicious meals in the lodge's dining area. All cabins have well-stocked wood fires.

Each evening, wild animals from the surrounding forests come down to the lodge to feed. Tiger cats, possums, Tasmanian devils, native cats and wallabies delight guests with their antics.

There are many kilometres of prepared tracks along which to meander in the national park, as well as dozens of gorges and mountains to test the skills of the avid climber and abseiler. The streams and lakes proliferate with trout, and swimming and skiing are also available.

Other local attractions include the Mole Creek Caves, the Tasmanian Smokehouse, Lake Barrington, and the Don River Tramway.

23 **The Pines Resort** is situated opposite Seven Mile Beach, Hobart's most popular surfing beach.

Close to both the city and airport, it is ideally placed for guests who wish to enjoy sweeping beaches and the city's evening entertainment.

The resort boasts a Wimbledon grass tennis court and a pool, sauna and spa. Nearby is the Royal Hobart Golf Club for the keen golfer. At the beach, sailboards and surfboards are supplied by the resort for its guests.

The Pine Cone Restaurant is fully licensed and serves excellent meals, featuring fresh Tasmanian seafood, steaks and poultry. The menu is comple-mented by an extensive wine list. The Tavern Bar is a pleasant meeting place.

The two-bedroom apartments are designed for the ultimate in family comfort.

24 **London Lakes Resort**, situated in the Central Highlands region, is just two hours' drive from both Launceston and Hobart. The resort is primarily a fly fishing lodge with two private fishing grounds — Lake Big Jim and Lake Samuel — which cater for the trout fisherman. Professional guides will instruct the novice, or guide the experienced angler to the best fishing spots around this 1,700-hectare property.

Although the resort attracts mainly fishermen, non-angling partners are also accepted, and will enjoy the peaceful surroundings and magnificent highland scenery. London Lakes does not cater for children under the age of 16.

The Lodge accommodates only ten guests, and is constructed of hand-crafted log and stone. Panelled with Tasmanian timbers, it has ground-floor bedrooms and a lounge room, complete with log fires, with a library and boardroom on the first floor. First-class meals and excellent house wines are provided, and the angler has the opportunity to eat his or her catch of the day.

Fishing tackle and waterproof clothing are included, and chauffeur-driven limousine transfers from Launceston or Hobart can be arranged. The Lodge is open during the fishing season from September to April.

South Australia

25 Within an hour's drive of Adelaide, nestling amid the Barossa Valley's vineyards, is the **Hermitage of Marananga**, a secluded retreat in the warm surrounds of a rich alluvial floodplain which saw the birth of South Australia's wine industry almost 150 years ago.

The Hermitage is the ideal base for a stay in the beautiful Barossa. Major wineries of the region are all within easy reach, while numerous historic churches, museums, arts and crafts centres and fine restaurants await the traveller keen to explore the delights of this lovely area.

Large, homely suites offer comfortable accommo-dation and all rooms overlook the Hermitage's own

Mount Lofty House is a rural retreat yet lies only 20 minutes drive from Adelaide

vineyards. Delicious meals are served in its Barossa Dining Room, or guests may choose to dine on the sweeping veranda, sipping champagne in the morning sunshine or savouring the fresh bouquet of a fine locally produced wine over dinner.

Hot-air balloon excursions can also be arranged from the resort and a wide range of sporting activities are close at hand for the energetic.

26 A visit to South Australia's Barossa Valley can be combined with a stay in one of the region's lovely cottages. **Lawley Farm,** built in the 1850s and set amidst native bushland, is an ideal base for those wishing to explore this famous wine-growing region.

The farm's owners, Mike and Janice Nichols, operate two-day special gourmet wine tours which include visits to the valley's selected wineries, vineyards and restaurants.

Guests can stay in the privacy of either The Cottage or The Barn, which are both situated behind the farmhouse. These have been converted into self-contained suites each with a bed-sitting room and en-suite bathroom.

The farm offers a 'help yourself' style of accommodation, and fresh produce is provided each morning for a 'do it yourself' breakfast. The farm will also provide barbecue packs and picnic lunches for guests. The valley is full of excellent restaurants and, naturally, an abundance of excellent wines, so there is no problem taking a stroll to one of these for the evening meal.

27 Dreams of a peaceful cottage in the country with a cosy bedroom, a log fire, a hearty breakfast, and long walks through beautiful rural areas are the sort of delights guests can enjoy with a stay at the **Landhaus** in the Barossa Valley, just one hour's drive from Adelaide in the village of Bethany.

A former shepherd's cottage built in the 1850s, this building has been fully refurbished by Frans and Vivien Kroese, showing rough-hewn beams, an open fire and a vine-covered courtyard. This is Australia's smallest motel, accommodating just two people. It features a spa, a parlour, and a licensed restaurant seating up to 12 persons.

A master chef and baker create excellent meals, and the Landhaus is the perfect venue for luncheons or dinner by appointment.

28 The **Lodge** in South Australia's Barossa Valley only opened for guests in January 1987.

A gracious 1905 bluestone and brick country residence set in 1.2 hectares of lawn and gardens, the Lodge is ideally situated for those wishing to indulge in the valley's attractions. Guests can take in a bird's eye view of the vineyards and wineries by ballooning from across the road at Seppelt's Winery, or go exploring on the Lodge's bicycles, sampling wines en-route. Horse riding is only 15 minutes away in Tanunda, and on the property itself there is tennis and a swimming pool.

Accommodation is limited to four private en-suite rooms, ensuring total seclusion for those wishing to enjoy the fresh air and peaceful surrounds.

29 **Mount Lofty House Country Estate** in Crafers, 20 minutes from the centre of Adelaide, provides luxury accommodation within easy reach of the Barossa Valley and Southern Vale. It is the second Australian member of the select Relais et Chateaux group.

Built in 1852, using sawn freestone and local sandstone, it was all but destroyed, save for its massive hand-hewn stone walls, in the infamous Ash Wednesday bushfires of 1983. However, through the designing work of Adelaide architect Ross Sands, its burnt shell has been transformed into the lovely estate it is today.

Mt Lofty House is only about 600 metres from Mt Lofty itself, sitting on six hectares of prime hill land with beautiful views over the Piccadilly Valley. Head gardener Jane Jutner and her team of eight were responsible for clearing the piles of rubble left by the bushfires and creating a new garden. Today, the Estate boasts flower, herb and vegetable gardens, and lawns surrounding the swimming pool.

The house is not far from Mt Lofty Botanic Gardens and Cleland Wildlife Park with its koalas, kangaroos and native birds and plants.

Guests are accommodated in eight suites, each with colour TV, en-suite bathrooms, private dining areas and open fireplaces.

There are two restaurants, both of which are open to the public, and a quiet cocktail lounge.

30 The most alluring aspect of **Kondoparinga Homestead** for city dwellers is perhaps its beautiful country setting. Located in Ashbourne, about 80 kilometres south of Adelaide, the property is a peaceful retreat, with the Finnis River running through its grounds. It is surrounded by some wonderful rural views of rolling paddocks, untouched bushland and creeks.

The property is a pleasant drive from Christies Beach on the Fleurieu Peninsula, where visitors can enjoy fishing, swimming and long lazy walks.

The homestead dates to 1880 and features slate terraces, huge wisteria vines and spacious lawns. Inside, there is a library, a billiard and drawing room complete with baby grand piano, and a dining room featuring wonderful blackwood panelling. Most rooms have log fires, and all the cooking is of the best home-country style. Up to ten guests can stay in either double or twin-share rooms. Weekend packages are available which are all-inclusive.

Western Australia

31 **Mount Shadforth Lodge** is located on Western Australia's lovely south coast in the charming town of Denmark. Set amidst beautiful woodland and pastures, this Tudor-style lodge has lovely views of the Southern Ocean, Wilson's Inlet and the distant Parongunups.

Its location, close to Ocean Beach, is ideal for those who enjoy surfing and swimming. For most of the year, Wilson's Inlet is a lake enclosed by a sand bar at Ocean Beach, and here visitors can water-ski, swim, go prawning or simply lie back and enjoy the sun.

The town, established around the turn of the century, sits on the banks of the Denmark River. Its setting provides a combination of rugged coastal scenery, peaceful rivers and lush farmland. Nearby lies William Bay National Park which has sheltered swimming inside its reef, and good fishing from the beach and rocks. Parry's Beach, 28 kilometres away, can yield excellent salmon to the angler.

The Lodge's log fires, beamed ceilings and old prints create a pleasant ambience, particularly in winter. It also has a cocktail lounge for quiet relaxation over a few drinks.

Guests are accommodated in motel-style units, each with en-suite facilities and colour TV.

32 The **Burswood Island Resort and Casino,** situated on the scenic Swan River foreshore, offers the utmost in opulence and indulgence for guests looking to find a premier holiday playground.

The dazzling casino provides non-stop action for high-rolling gamblers keen to try their luck at any number of games including blackjack, roulette, baccarat, two-up, mini-dice, money wheel and keno.

In addition to the casino, there is always something happening in the immense Exhibition, Sports and Entertainment Centre to interest visitors — such as international tennis tournaments, trade shows and exhibitions, and even rock concerts.

Burswood also provides an indoor/outdoor pool, cycling paths, jogging tracks, a golf course, tennis courts and all manner of water sports facilities to keep guests busy from dawn till dusk.

Accommodation is five-star, with the best in comfort and service. All 417 rooms offer spectacular views of Perth, the Swan River and the Darling Ranges.

33 The **Joondalup Country Club** is located in undulating bush and dune land within the city of Wanneroo, 25 kilometres north-west of Perth.

The club is the centre-piece of a superb residential development, and features an 18-hole golf course, three all-weather tennis courts, and a fully licensed tavern and restaurant.

The 6,275-metre, par 72 golf course is of the highest championship standard. The club also has a fine basketball stadium, excellent spots for swimming and fishing, nature trails with lookouts along Lake Joondalup's shores and, just across the lake in Wanneroo, all manner of sporting facilities from motor racing to equestrian events and a gun club.

Northern Territory

34 Situated in the heart of the Red Centre, the **Sheraton Ayers Rock Hotel** is shaded by giant sails — a unique feature of this desert resort.

The view from the hotel's well-appointed rooms and suites is breathtaking. There are special rock view rooms affording guests the chance to marvel at the ever-changing moods of Ayers Rock as it melts into ochres, oranges, rusts and reds during the course of the desert day.

International chefs prepare Australian delicacies at the Sheraton's numerous restaurants. The elegant Kunia Room, in particular, offers superb international cuisine and the best in Australian wines. The less formal split-level brasserie, The Desert Rose, is a comfortable and relaxed spot for a rendezvous with friends over coffee.

This luxurious hotel also provides recreational facilities such as spas, saunas, tennis courts, squash courts, and, of course, an enormous swimming pool to cool off when the heat is on.

Queensland

35 **Lizard Island** has changed little since August 1770 when it was named by Captain James Cook. It is still remote, ruggedly beautiful and surrounded by some of the finest beaches and clearest waters of any Barrier Reef island.

The main lodge complex on Lizard is of Queensland colonial design, with wide verandas facing the sea. Alongside the lodge, connected by a timber walkway, is a freshwater pool and a flood-lit full-size tennis court.

Suites have a king-size bed and sofa, or twin beds and sofa. Deluxe suites have two rooms and a private veranda offering views of Anchor Bay. Both styles of accommodation have private facilities and a refrigerator stocked with wine, spirits and chocolates.

Warm sunny days on Lizard Island are spent swimming, sun-bathing, skindiving, sailing, water-skiing, hiking, playing tennis, or climbing the island's highest peak, Cook's Look. Archery and scuba diving can be easily arranged.

36 The **Bloomfield Wilderness Lodge,** the closest mainland-based resort to the outer Barrier Reef, is a secluded paradise where guests can swim on isolated islands, walk through tropical rainforests and go reef fishing.

Located at Cape Tribulation in far north Queensland near the mouth of the Bloomfield River, it is a small operation whose main clientele are keen anglers, snorkellers, divers and those simply seeking a wilderness environment in which to escape.

The beaches to its south border Cape Tribulation National Park, and white coral sand cays and jungle-clad islands are just a short boat trip away.

The pleasant weather from May to September attracts the majority of visitors, though the real fishing season is from October to the end of January, with the peak period from August to November. Spanish mackerel, wahoo, barracuda, sailfish, tuna and marlin are just a few of the hundreds of species of fish to be caught. The lodge has two reef boats operating daily and guests have full use of the lodge dinghies. All fishing gear and bait are supplied.

The lodge accommodates 30 people in eight suites and seven bedrooms. There is a central fireplace. The decked swimming pool is surrounded by shady trees overlooking blue river water.

The premises are not licensed, so guests must organise their own liquor. Suitable arrangements can be made with the proprietor. Access to the lodge is mainly by four-wheel drive and the tariff includes all accommodation, air fares and transfers, meals, boat trips, organised tours and use of the lodge's boats, vehicles and tackle.

37 Bedarra Island is a tropical paradise just seven kilometres off the north Queensland coast. The island is 1.5 kilometres long and less than a kilometre wide, with a proliferation of rainforest vegetation and white sandy beaches.

Set in this idyllic location, **Bedarra Bay Resort's** guest bungalows along the water's edge are flanked by tropical gardens of flowering trees, ferns, orchids and coconut palms. The resort's lounge/dining room/bar complex overlooks the jetty and the swimming pool.

Bedarra's atmosphere is intimate — casual, but elegant. The emphasis is on complete relaxation with a minimum of organisation. Dinghies, fishing gear, paddle skis and sailboards are provided. Bushwalking, oystering and private picnic lunches are a feature. Guests can also arrange fishing trips and reef tours if they so desire.

38 Orpheus Island is 24 kilometres off the north Queensland coast and 80 kilometres north-east of Townsville. This volcanic island is fringed with coral reefs and has more than 1,360 hectares of national park. **Orpheus Island Resort** is a secluded retreat in an idyllic tropical landscape on the south-western side of the island. Guest units, designed to blend with the environment, nestle among coconut palms and other tropical plants on the shores of Hazard Bay.

In the heart of the resort are the restaurant, bar, reception area, boutique, swimming pool and spa.

The long lazy days at Orpheus can be spent swimming, water-skiing, skin diving, bushwalking and just soaking up the sun. Catamarans, windsurfers and other water sports gear are all included in the tariff.

Accommodation is provided in studio rooms and private bungalows for 50 guests and all rooms are equipped with modern facilities.

39 The **Eungella Chalet** sits in the midst of one of Queensland's largest national parks overlooking the picturesque Pioneer Valley.

Situated in the far north of Queensland, just 85 kilometres from Mackay, Eungella is the destination for hundreds of hang-gliding enthusiasts each year as the chalet hosts the North Queensland Hang-gliding Championships.

There is no shortage of stunning scenery to explore, and guests can enjoy horse riding, as well as climbing expeditions to Mt Dalrymple, Queensland's second highest mountain.

The chalet has a swimming pool, fully licensed bars with a cabaret on Saturday night, and a restaurant serving country breakfasts, bistro lunches and à la carte dinners. Picnic lunches can be arranged for bushwalking enthusiasts.

Buses to the Chalet are available from Airlie Beach every Tuesday and Thursday, and from Mackay every Wednesday and Saturday.

40 **Maleny Health Resort,** which overlooks the Glass House Mountains, about 100 kilometres north of Brisbane, specialises in health and fitness for its guests. Visitors are provided with therapeutic massages, and can take advantage of the services of a naturopath, physiotherapist, acupuncturist and reflexologist, as well as a beautician and hairdresser.

There is a heated indoor pool, a tennis court, a billiards room, a spa, steamroom and gym. The more active can go cycling, or take guided walks through the surrounding countryside. Horse riding and golf are close by.

The resort will provide food for people on special diets (such as the Pritikin and Weight-Watchers' diets), but it also provides standard meals. There is special assistance for those wanting to give up smoking. The resort will even tutor its guests in pottery, art, the piano and the organ.

Accommodation is provided at the Maleny Hills Motel. All units are fully self-contained and include a kitchen, refrigerator, washer and dryer, colour TV, electric blankets, laundries and barbecues. Squash courts, art galleries and potteries are all nearby, as are some very good restaurants to lead astray well-intentioned health enthusiasts.

41 **Binna Burra Mountain Resort** is situated in Queensland's Lamington National Park — 21,000 hectares of rugged mountain scenery, subtropical rainforests, mountain streams and spectacular waterfalls, with vistas of the park and the blue waters of the Pacific Ocean.

The lodge, perched on Mt Roberts, is a magic spot to get away from the hustle and bustle of the city and offers a wealth of holiday activities to occupy guests during their stay.

Special events are organised, and weeks devoted especially to the arts, abseiling, photography and gardening, among other subjects, are planned on a regular basis. The resort also caters for small seminars and conventions as well as for individuals looking to relax in the peaceful seclusion of this country retreat.

42 Barely an hour's drive inland from the Queensland capital of Brisbane and from the Gold Coast's hectic pleasure palaces lies **Kooralbyn Valley,** set in a cleft in the foothills of the MacPherson Ranges.

Kooralbyn offers country villa and motel lodge accommodation — and a 4,000-hectare backyard. It has its own tennis village, with ten all-weather day-and-night courts.

The Kooralbyn Championship golf course is rated number one among Australian resort courses, and coaching clinics are available with resident professionals.

Horse riding excursions take visitors up into the surrounding hills, and a network of bushwalks fan out from Kooralbyn for guests who prefer to do their exploring on two legs.

But relaxation is the name of the most popular game at Kooralbyn Valley. There are four swimming pools, three bars, and restaurants with dancing into the night.

43 A mountain hideaway set deep in the rainforest beside a mountain stream is an idyllic place to pass some time. **The Mouse's House** is just 45 minutes' drive from the Gold Coast and 100 kilometres south of Brisbane. It offers chalet accommodation at an altitude of 840 metres, in the seclusion of the mountainous rainforests of the Warrie National Park.

Eight Swiss-style chalets sleep up to six people each. The chalets have large double bedrooms and lofts, as well as plenty of space for relaxing in front of the fire or reading a book on the balcony, while taking in the view across the rainforest.

All kitchen facilities are provided, though guests must supply their own food.

The lodge has a sauna and plunge rooms, a hot tub spa, a half-tennis court and pleasant bicycle rides. Horse riding is only 20 minutes away. The Mouse's House has been highly recommended in the National Small Business Awards.

Burnham Beeches is Australia's finest example of Art Deco

Executive & Country Retreats Contacts

Operators

Select Hotels and Resorts of Australia is an association that has recently been formed, as part of a worldwide organisation, to group together quality accommodation establishments, and to maintain standards of excellence in these hotels and resorts.

Fairmont Resort (NSW), Burnham Beeches (VIC), Mt Lofty House (SA), Burswood Island Resort (WA) and Orpheus Island Resort (QLD) are all detailed below, but for information on other members of the association contact:

Richard Rosebery
The Profit Motif
Top Floor
175 Sailors Bay Road
Northbridge
Sydney NSW 2063
Ph. (02) 958 5599

New South Wales

1 Attunga Park

Nobby's Creek
Tweed Valley NSW 2484
Ph. (066) 79 1455

2 Linley House

PO Box 1070
Taree NSW 2430
Ph. (065) 50 5118 or
(02) 774 2244 (Sydney office)

3 Peppers Guest House

Ekerts Road
Pokolbin NSW 2321
Ph. (049) 98 7596

4 Kim's Resort

PO Box 1
Toowoon Bay NSW 2261
Ph. (043) 32 1566

5 Glenella

56 Govetts Leap Road
Blackheath NSW 2785
Ph. (047) 87 8352

6 Pegum's

25 Honour Avenue
Lawson NSW 2783
Ph. (047) 59 1844

7 Fairmont Resort

1 Sublime Point Road
Leura NSW 2780
Ph. (02) 327 6677 (Sales office)

8 Jenolan Caves House

Jenolan Caves NSW 2790
Ph. (063) 59 3304/3305/3306/3307

9 Macarthur Lodge Country Resort

Horderns Road
Wilton NSW 2571
Ph. (046) 30 9269

10 Milton Park Country House Hotel

Horderns Road
Bowral NSW 2576
Ph. (048) 61 1826 or 61 1522

11 Mount Broughton Country Resort

Kater Road
Sutton Forest NSW 2577
Ph. (048) 68 2355

Victoria

12 Lake Dartmouth Resort

PO Box 1
Dartmouth VIC 3701
Ph. (060) 72 4511
Or contact any Victour office

13 Mt Buffalo Chalet

PO Box 76
Porepunkah VIC 3740
Ph. (057) 55 1500

14 Akoonah

RMB 1585
Bengwarden Road
Stratford VIC 3862
Ph. (051) 49 8214

15 Howqua Dale Gourmet Retreat

PO Box 114
Mansfield VIC 3722
Ph. (057) 77 3503

16 Warburton Health Care Centre

Donna Buang Road
Warburton VIC 3799
Ph. (059) 66 2404

17 Burnham Beeches Country House

Sherbrooke Road
Sherbrooke VIC 3789
Ph. (03) 755 1903

18 The Tilba

Cnr Toorak Road West & Domain Street
South Yarra
Melbourne VIC 3141
Ph. (03) 267 8844

19 Narrabeen Cottage

16 Steele Street
Cowes
Phillip Island VIC 3922
Ph. (059) 52 2062

20 Boomerang Holiday Ranch

Tipperary Springs Road
Daylesford VIC 3460
Ph. (053) 48 2525

21 Bellinzona Country House

77 Main Road
Hepburn Springs VIC 3461
Ph. (053) 48 2271

Tasmania

22 Cradle Mountain Lodge

PO Box 153
Sheffield TAS 7306
Ph. (003) 63 5164

23 The Pines Resort

Surf Road
Seven Mile Beach TAS 7170
Ph. (002) 48 6222

24 London Lakes Resort

C/- Post Office
Bronte Park TAS 7140
Ph. (002) 89 1159

South Australia

25 The Hermitage of Marananga

PO Box 330
Tanunda SA 5352
Ph. (085) 62 2722

26 Lawley Farm

PO Box 103
Tanunda SA 5352
Ph. (085) 63 2141

DENNIS SCHULZ

Herding cattle, above, or rounding up sheep, it's all in a day's work for the active visitor on a farm holiday

on the style of accommodation provided. Bunkhouse accommodation, often in old shearers' quarters, is best suited to family or other groups since privacy is limited. Host farms generally provide accommodation within the family homestead, on a guesthouse basis, and meals are usually eaten with the family. The third category usually offers accommodation in separate cottages or other buildings on the property, on a self-catering basis.

The activities available also vary, depending on the farm and its location. For those who don't want to stay on a farm but would like to see how it operates, a few farms offer day tours in addition to overnight accommodation. The most common pastimes include assisting with the seasonal work, horse riding, bushwalking, swimming and fishing or yabbying in dams and creeks. Most country folk are only too delighted to 'show you the ropes' and provide assistance to visitors who are new to such things as four-legged animals and the hazards of swimming in real rivers rather than swimming pools.

For those city slickers who wish to dive head first into the country life — perhaps even with a future job on a farm in mind — one of the NSW properties offers a jackaroo/jillaroo training school which is open to holiday-makers and serious country aspirants alike. The same property offers a five-day cattle drive along old stock routes for those interested in sitting in a saddle and camping under the stars.

Families and children are well provided for, with a wide selection of properties to choose from. The most suitable are probably the larger ones and those offering self-contained accommodation. Children have the opportunity to meet other kids — often from overseas — and to have some quiet family life at night.

One NSW farm accepts children with or without

PHILLIP QUIRK

their parents, but there is a lower age limit. So, if families really want to get away — from each other — the kids can be sent there, while mum and dad take off for a cosy retreat elsewhere!

Some farms, on the other hand, do not encourage children, and they may not offer everything that city-folk think a farm should have, such as horse riding. It is a good idea to itemise what you require and to make a short list of the most likely farms. Some hosts prefer direct bookings; others prefer to use agencies. Whichever is the case, specify your requirements when booking so that there is no disappointment on arrival.

All of the farms listed are accessible either by car or public transport. If travelling by the latter, the farm's hosts usually provide transport from the nearest rail or bus destination.

Visitors who are unsure of what they want, or who have only a vague itinerary in mind and aren't sure of what to do in between, may like to contact one of the groups listed under Contacts who advise and arrange farm holidays.

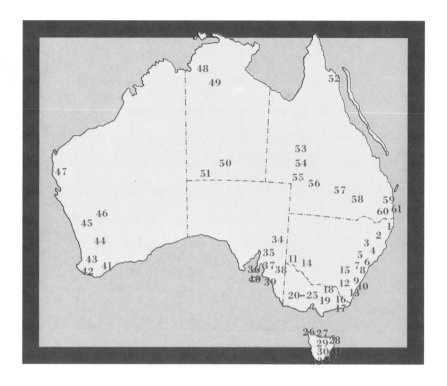

Locations

New South Wales

1 **Barula Park,** outside Alstonville near Lismore on NSW's northern coastal plateau, is a 22.5-hectare professional horse spelling property, caring for up to 22 horses. And one of the delights of staying on the property is helping to feed and groom the horses. Cart-rides with the resident Clydesdale, cycling, badminton and archery are also available.

The hosts, the Campbell family, provide daily escorted picnics and tours to the region's main attractions which include national park rainforests, superb beaches, local avocado and tropical fruit farms, and weekend markets operating in the region. Other activities include sailing, scuba diving, deep-sea fishing, windsurfing, hang-gliding, river cruising, golf and bowls.

Barula Park is easily accessible by air, rail and road from Sydney to Lismore, and the Campbells will meet guests either there or at nearby Alstonville.

Guests stay with the family in their large, modern homestead, but in a private section of the house comprising one twin and three double bedrooms serviced by separate bath and shower rooms.

2 **Wattleridge** is an eight-hour drive north of Sydney or a short flight from Sydney to Armidale. A grazing property running Merino sheep and Angora goats, it was awarded the Most Successful Exhibitor prize at three New England shows in 1987.

The property offers bush holidays in an isolated environment and activities include guided hunting trips (by arrangement only), cross-country bushwalk-

ing and swimming. Special bushriding activities (again by arrangement only) are available through the property's 1,200 hectares, with access to a further 6,000 hectares. Abseilers can bring their own equipment and practise on the escarpment running through the middle of the property.

The proprietors of Wattleridge are a talented team. Dr Judy Harris has a PhD in Agricultural Science, while her partner, Brian Humphries, is a professional wool and mohair classer who has an extensive knowledge of the gemstones and minerals to be found in the five kilometres of river running through the property. Both are proficient in bushcraft, including the use of native flora, as well as skin tanning and leathercraft.

Visitors can take advantage of the full-board homestead accommodation, or stay in the self-contained cabins, supplying their own food and linen.

At night, the Log Cabin Club provides a get-together atmosphere with a wood fire and table tennis and pool tables.

3 The brainchild of Brian Skerrett, a farmer of 40 years, **Leconfield Jackaroo/Jillaroo School** is unique as far as farm holidays go. A 1,600-hectare sheep, cattle and horse property on the Mulla Creek in rich isolated country 50 kilometres north-east of Tamworth and 450 kilometres north of Sydney, Leconfield offers both a training course for prospective jackaroos as well as a cattle drive in the great Australian tradition. Both courses are tailored for people with little or no experience of country life.

The Jackaroo School offers a basic, practical trainee course of 12 days. Everyone works at the same tasks. This means getting up early — rain, hail or shine — and learning a variety of skills ranging from mustering and branding cattle to shoeing horses and fencing, as well as studying pasture improvement, bushcraft and native animals.

Most trainees attend Leconfield to increase their chances of obtaining jackaroo work and students often do well on other properties. Other trainees go for a brief respite from the city and for the challenge of country life. Some love it so much they never return to the city!

Separate male/female dormitory accommodation is provided, with all meals prepared by the homestead cook.

Cattle drives are arranged periodically and inquiries should be made well in advance. The drive involves five days on horseback, driving 150 head of young Hereford cattle along the old stock routes of the Dungowan-Wooloomin area near Tamworth. Visitors are taught, amongst other things, how to ride drover style, crack a whip, handle working dogs and drove stock. The camp cook provides genuine Aussie campfire tucker, and communal get-togethers around the campfire are a major attraction. Weather permitting, everyone sleeps under the stars.

At the end of the course, a Drover's Certificate is given to all participants.

The lowest age limit for both activities is 16, with certain exceptions. Families wishing to go droving can bring younger children.

Although it can be hard work, visitors have a great time. As one visitor commented, 'I'm leaving with a worn-out, bruised and battered body, but I loved it.'

4 Bob and Sue Moore, the proprietors of **Lalla Rookh,** 20 kilometres south of Tamworth — Australia's Country Music Capital — provide the care and friendliness of country hospitality while allowing visitors the privacy of a guest wing in their modern country home.

As the area has a wide range of excursions and activities, the Moores can make arrangements to cater for particular interests. Some of the activities available are the Tamworth Country Music Festival in January and the Armidale Wool Expo and Agricultural Show in March. In May, amateur horse racing fans can enjoy the unique experience of the Wean Picnic Races, while in August, one of Australia's premier primary industry field days, the Ag. Quip, takes place in Gunnedah.

Bob also arranges visits to specialist farms, and guests can visit Sue's pottery studio where she produces individual pieces and functional stoneware.

The guest wing has panoramic views of the surrounding countryside and up to six guests can share a double and two twin rooms with share guest bathroom. Children must be over 15 years.

The tariff includes all meals and transport to and from Tamworth, which visitors can reach by train, bus or plane.

5 **4D Host Farm** on almost 1,200 hectares of land near Quirindi, approximately 400 kilometres north-west of Sydney, has been held by the Willis family for five generations. It is a working grain and beef property, with a large old Australian-style homestead complete with verandahs and a shady garden.

The emphasis is on relaxation. Guests can observe a farm at close quarters, take leisurely walks through the garden and property looking for kangaroos and birdlife, and picnic at some of the best spots in the region with views for miles across the Liverpool Plains. Or they can take in a game of tennis or ping-pong, or try their hand at catching crayfish in the dams.

Visitors can stay with the family in the homestead with Australian home-cooking provided, or opt for privacy in the farm's nearby self-contained cottage. Both the homestead and the cottage accommodate four guests.

Day trips are made to Tamworth, the lovely Warrumbungle National Park and Siding Spring Observatory, or to Lake Keepit and Chaffey Dam.

6 **Karanilla** (Aboriginal for 'cool water in high places') has six kilometres of creek frontage and views across the countryside for up to 110 kilometres. Set on 1,800 hectares near Tamworth in north-east New South Wales, it is a cattle property and flora and fauna sanctuary.

Karanilla has been owned by the Crossing family for over 40 years. For the past 14 years, proprietors Bob and Di have been providing bush holidays for vacationers from all over the world. In fact, the whole concern has been such a success that some guests have returned up to eight times.

Karanilla is quite a large complex, offering accommodation for around 36 people. Visitors can be accommodated in the homestead or opt for the self-contained bush bungalows scattered around the property. Home-cooked meals are provided in conjunction with a central dining room and restaurant.

A range of activities are provided to keep visitors entertained — tennis, croquet, swimming and crayfishing in the local waterholes, bushwalking and horse riding. Bob also takes guests on picnicking safaris in his 11-seater four-wheel-drive.

7 Located three and a half hours' drive north-east of Sydney on the Turon River, a few kilometres from the historic goldmining town of Sofala, **Chesleigh Guest Ranch** makes a perfect leisurely weekend getaway.

Set in the foothills of the Great Dividing Range, the 1,200-hectare property provides old-fashioned Australian hospitality, with a touch of history. Hosts Jan and Mike Cody provide outdoor Aussie barbecues and fresh homestead meals.

A feature of the weekend is trail rides through the mountains and timberland to the goldrush town of

Sofala. Gold panning, fishing and swimming in the river are also popular.

Guests can stay in the old main homestead or in the property's self-contained cabins. Accommodation is from Friday night to Sunday afternoon, and the property attracts an adult clientele. Mike advises that the terrain may be a little too rugged for the elderly or disabled.

8 **Millamolong** station, on the Central Tablelands of New South Wales and four and a half hours' drive west of Sydney, specialises in farm holidays for children — with or without their parents.

Hosts John and Mary Newman run sheep and cattle on their 3,200-hectare property which provides a great opportunity for children from the city and from overseas to participate together in farm life while enjoying fresh air and country food. Many children return year after year.

Visitors can watch mustering and shearing, milk cows, crack a stock whip, and play tennis, cricket, table tennis or pool. Swimming and canoeing are available at the nearby Belabula River which runs through the property. Excursions can be arranged to nearby goldmines and to historic Carcoar and Cowra.

Horse riding is another occupation for all standards of rider, and instruction is given in horse and saddle care. Visitors are welcome to bring their own horses (as long as they are not stallions!).

Accommodation is available for 30 children and the minimum stay is two days, except over Easter (four days), public holiday weekends (three days) and school holidays (five days).

Transportation to and from the railway station at Blayney or the airport at Cowra can be arranged.

9 **Kyabra,** a two and a half hour drive south of Sydney, is surrounded by rich grazing land and river flats. This 1,214-hectare cattle and merino sheep property is also an Australian stockhorse stud.

As well as farming activities, guests may enjoy boating, bushwalking, cricket, tennis, horse riding, swimming, chuck wagon rides and barbecues. Touring nearby includes the historic towns of Bowral, Berrima, Moss Vale and Goulburn, the Wollondilly River and the Wombeyan Caves.

Four self-contained guest cottages are set in three hectares of natural parkland and offer accommodation for up to 28 guests. Guests provide their own linen and food.

Guests will be met at Wingello railway station.

10 A two-hour drive and 120 kilometres south-west of Sydney is **Rotherwood**, a stately 30-room early colonial homestead set on 66 hectares supporting cattle and sheep.

Part of the property is now classified by the National Trust and the gatehouse is on the National Heritage Register. The homestead is furnished with fine antiques.

Guests may watch farming activities, go swimming

or horse riding and play croquet. Bushwalking, golf and fishing are nearby, as are the historic towns of Berrima and Bowral, the beautiful Kangaroo Valley, and Fitzroy Falls Reservoir.

The main homestead has eight double rooms with shared facilities for guests who join the homestead family for meals.

The proprietors will meet guests at Moss Vale railway station.

11 The historic **Avoca Station** homestead built in 1868 is set amidst beautifully tailored English gardens looking through river red gums to the famous Darling River near the south-west New South Wales-Victorian border. A stone and pine building with many historic pine log outbuildings, it was featured as one of the bush houses in the Australian TV mini-series, *The Flying Doctor.*

The owners, Mary and Alan Dawes, run sheep and cattle on their 28,300-hectare property, which is also a wildlife reserve. It is located in the Murray Valley Basin near the famous Sunraysia district which produces wine and dried and citrus fruits. The Dawes also grow stone and citrus fruits and vegetables and provide their own eggs, meat and poultry in typically self-sufficient country style.

Visitors can watch stock and field work, fish for freshwater callop or Murray cod, catch yabbies and

Two riders gallop their horses along a tree-lined track

MICHAEL LANGFORD

rabbits, ride horses (by arrangement), swim, boat and play tennis and table tennis. (Bring your own racquets and balls.)

Young overseas guests often visit the property to work for a short time to gain farm experience.

Full in-house accommodation is provided for overseas guests in addition to two fully self-contained pine log cabins. Families are welcome.

There is an airstrip for light aircraft, but most visitors drive from Wentworth (24 kilometres) or Mildura (55 kilometres).

12 Located on the Numerala River on 480 hectares of Monaro grazing country one and a half hours' drive from Canberra is 'Yarrabin', a working sheep property and the location of **Litchfield Farm Holidays.**

A large 30-square farmhouse with separate bunkhouses to accommodate 16, its location near Mt Kosciusko National Park provides easy access to the ski fields in winter and to local trout fishing spots. There is also gold panning at Kiandra diggings, exploring at Yarrangobilly Caves, and swimming in the river or in Lakes Eucumbene and Jindabyne.

Hosts Chere and Max Litchfield offer supervised horse riding on 4,000 hectares, allowing both beginners and experienced riders to enjoy the spectacular Snowy Mountains scenery. Visitors can also play tennis and ping-pong or join in with mustering sheep and feeding the animals.

Log fires and home cooking are a country treat, especially in winter. Children are welcome.

13 **Crown Tree Farm,** 500 kilometres south of Sydney, is an eight-hour drive or a five-hour flight. The proprietors will meet guests at Merimbula bus depot or airport.

A river bank in a picturesque coastal valley is the setting of the original colonial homestead. Cattle and goats are the mainstay of this 300-hectare property, where guests may join in farm activities or go canoeing, swimming, fishing and horse riding.

Swimming and surfing are possible at Merimbula which is a 40-kilometre drive to the coast. A beach house is also available.

Accommodation is in a self-contained, fully restored colonial cottage for up to seven people. Guests may cater for themselves or join the homestead family for meals.

14 **Nindethana,** situated on 129 square kilometres of semi-arid and desert land and fronting on to 35 kilometres of the Anabranch River in NSW's far south-west, provides what has been described as 'the authentic Australian outback experience'.

A working property producing some of Australia's best merino sheep, its owners, Meredyth and Andrew

Wearing the Australian stockman's uniform raincoat, a Driazabone, a stockman heads off to the stable

MICHAEL LANGFORD

Cunningham, work hard to ensure that their many overseas and Australian guests experience at first hand what traditional Australian farm life is all about.

Guests can observe station activities, ride horses, canoe, swim and go on wildlife safaris through national park bush with their hosts preparing Australian damper and billy tea. Much talk about the latter prompted one recent Japanese visitor to quietly ask, 'And who is this Billy Tea?'

The property accommodates up to four guests in a pretty cottage in the garden with a view of the river.

Visitors are welcome year round, except during February.

A courtesy car is available for plane, bus and train travellers to and from nearby Mildura.

A stockman leads a herd across a river

Australian Capital Territory

15 **Country Life Tours** is ideal for overseas guests staying in Canberra who wish to sample a taste of the country. Operators David and Pennie Mitchell conduct tours of small groups to one of the region's most historic sheep stations. Overnight stays can be arranged for up to two couples.

Visitors are collected in the morning from their hotel, embassy, or the Tourist Bureau in Canberra and taken by four-wheel-drive vehicle to their destination where they are greeted with a traditional Australian 'smoko' — morning tea, bush style. There follows a demonstration of working dogs mustering sheep, a drive over the large property to spot kangaroos and other wildlife, a campfire-cooked lunch of Australian steak and lamb accompanied by salads and washed down with Australian wines and beer, followed by what the Mitchells call 'David's Delicious Damper'.

The day's proceedings conclude with a trip to a local winery or an Australian afternoon tea, before visitors are returned to Canberra around 5 pm.

For those who wish to stay a little longer, accommodation is provided in two large, comfortable double bedrooms overlooking the swimming pool and the large garden. These are complete with en suite bathrooms and kitchenette. A private sitting room with an open fire is also available.

Victoria

16 Some 380 kilometres east of Melbourne is **Gillingall Station**. A vast holding of over 20,000 hectares on the edge of the Snowy Mountains region, Gillingall is one of the last remaining substantial Australian mountains stations.

The countryside and wildlife are spectacular. Guests may join station activities and participate in swimming, fishing, four-wheel-drive bush touring and horse riding.

Accommodation in the gracious colonial homestead is one double and two twin bed/sitting rooms. Guests join the station family for meals.

Private charter flights may land on Gillingall's private airstrip. Guests arriving at Bairnsdale railway station will be met.

17 **Riverlea**, situated on the beautiful Snowy River in Victoria's East Gippsland area some 375 kilometres east of Melbourne, has been in the Lynn family for four generations. Today, Kaye and Margaret Lynn and their son Brett and his wife Denise continue the family's farming tradition, with both couples opening their homes for farm holidays.

The Snowy River flats on which Riverlea is situated have the second most fertile soil in the world after the Nile River delta. Guests can canoe and fish on the river, play golf, bowls and tennis and go horse riding. There are caves nearby and magnificent forests, with surfing and boating at the beach only one kilometre away. Guests can also join in farm activities, helping with lambing and calving in season.

Children under three are welcome free of charge.

Visitors can travel by rail and bus to Orbost from Melbourne and a pick-up service is provided by the family.

18 Six years ago, Arthur and Pat Shone 'retired' and bought historic **Brookfield** at Numurkah, 217 kilometres north of Melbourne, from the grandson of the original settler. A wonderful example of early Australian settlers' architecture, it is classified by the National Trust.

The Murray pine log settlers' hut on the property was built in 1876 and the timber homestead was built in 1900. The huge old shearing shed is a museum packed with early Australian furniture, farm machinery, tools, kitchen utensils and homewares dating from the 1870s to the 1950s.

Farmhouse holidays, with all facilities supplied, are offered in the original farmhouse with room for up to eight people. The farm also caters for weddings, parties and bus and school excursions. There are barbecue facilities and Brookfield has a BYO licence.

Children can join in with all activities, go on pony rides or just do their own thing.

Horsemen drive a large herd across a rain-swollen Northern Territory river

The Shones do all the cooking and find that guests love the camp-oven cooking done outside the settlers' hut. When it's wet, guests crowd into the new log cabin to enjoy Devonshire tea followed by a sing-along around the log fire and old pianola.

The farm is open from 10 am to 5 pm year round, except for Christmas Day and Tuesdays — save for private party bookings.

19 **Dorilla Park** is located 180 kilometres north of Melbourne between the Strathbogie Ranges and the rich fruit-producing region of the Goulburn Valley. Excursions to the surrounding orchards and canneries are easily organised, while the Chateau Tahbilk and Mitchellton wineries are just a couple of hours away. Visitors can get a more sobering view of the countryside by hiring a glider in nearby Benalla, taking in the patchwork landscape from above. Longer excursions can be taken through the wild mountain scenery of Mt Buller or to beautiful Lake Eildon.

Closer to home, guests can play golf or learn about the running of the farm.

The farm's four-bedroomed, self-contained cottage accommodates up to eight people.

Guests can drive (about two hours from Melbourne) or take a one and a half hour train trip to Euroa or Shepparton where they will be met by their hosts.

20 Doreen and Bruce Orchard have fully restored their turn-of-the-century homestead, **Dunbar,** tastefully refurbishing it with antique furniture. Here, a couple of hours' drive north-west of Melbourne, visitors can escape the bustle of city life and experience Australian farm life. The property runs 1,400 fine wool Merino sheep plus a Jersey cattle stud. It is great for bushwalking and gold prospecting, and there are several scenic drives to nearby Kyneton and Bendigo.

Available for holidays all year round, up to ten people can enjoy the Orchard's hospitality at one time. Families with children are welcome.

21 **Holcombe Homestead** is a wonderfully restored, solid brick homestead (circa 1891) filled with antiques, with commanding panoramic mountain views.

Annette and John Marshall have successfully retained the building's original features such as open fireplaces and mantlepieces and acid-etched glasswork, while providing modern conveniences for their guests. They pay a lot of attention to detail and John has stocked the farm dam with plenty of trout for the keen fisherman.

Daylesford and Hepburn Mineral Springs, wineries, country restaurants, tennis, golf and bowls are all nearby.

The house sleeps from six to eight guests in three spacious bedrooms, each with their own fireplace.

Guests can take the short drive from Melbourne or land their light plane on the property.

22 **Naringal,** in Victoria's famous Western District, is one of the oldest sheep and cattle properties in the state and only one of the five in Victoria still in the same family.

Established in 1841, the 1,400-hectare property

is 161 kilometres north-west of Melbourne, near Ballarat. Its hill-top homestead is set in undulating country, and its original owners, William and Mary Rowe and their family, led a challenging life, opening up the land in this then wild colonial country.

Mary Rowe became friends with the women of the local Aboriginal tribe, the Naringales, after whom the property was named. On one occasion, she arrived at the Aborigines' camp with some broth for a new mother just in time to see the newborn baby being flung into the creek. Horrified, she was about to leap in after it when it paddled to the surface. It was then taken from the water and dried. The baby had presumably passed its first survival test.

Elizabeth Rowe and her son Michael no longer need to provide broth for Aboriginal babies. But they do provide first-rate farm fare for their guests — Elizabeth is a cordon bleu chef.

There is an all-weather tennis court, a swimming pool, and activities include shearing, fishing in the creeks and lots of bush walks. There is also a replica of the original slab hut homestead, filled with family heirlooms, as well as a family cemetery classified by the National Trust.

The surrounding countryside offers tours along the wonderful coastline and across mountain country, and visits to fishing villages, vineyards, crater lakes, old mining villages and craft shops.

Naringal features a gracious colonial homestead set in one and a half hectares of garden. Six people can be accommodated in the homestead, plus six in one Victorian cottage and ten in another. Everything is supplied except food. Forty guests can be housed in the simple modern shearers' quarters.

School tours are catered for, and Naringal is open year-round.

23 Families with children are welcome at **Old Strathconon**, set in 800 hectares of hilly grazing land near Elmhurst in Victoria's Pyrenees Ranges. Owners Roma and Ian Macdonald invite guests to stay in their century-old timber and mudbrick homestead.

There are plenty of safe playing areas for the children to have fun and enjoy the country air, and the Macdonalds provide many toys for extra amusement. Older children can swim, take rides on the station's horses and play table tennis. There are also local goat and deer farms to visit.

Mum and Dad won't be idle either, with visits to local wineries, walks in the hills and the odd game of tennis and golf a few miles away.

For the historically minded, the station boasts a good collection of pioneer tools and kitchen utensils.

Capacity accommodation is five adults or four adults and two children.

24 Pat and Norman Reid, owners of **Bellellen Rise** near the beautiful Grampian mountains, take great pride and interest in the abundant flora and fauna of the region. There are over 1,000 species of

flora in the mountains, 18 of which are peculiar to the area. Over the past 150 years or so these have attracted great interest from botanists.

Today, nature lovers can see over 200 of these species at the Halls Gap Annual Garden and Wildflower Exhibition held in October. Here, there are flower displays arranged by locals whose families have been collecting flora for over 50 years, as well as displays of paintings and photographs.

The Reids belong to the local Naturalist Club — a society for the growing of native plants — as well as to the Bird Observers' Club and the Historical Society, so they have a wealth of information on what is to be found in the mountains.

They run Merino sheep on their farm which is ten kilometres west of Stawell and 233 kilometres northwest of Melbourne, and can accommodate up to six guests at one time, supplying country-cooked meals and picnic hampers if desired.

Bellellen's rates are all-inclusive, including tours for guests into the Grampians and to other sights and activities. Visitors can also catch yabbies in the dams, play tennis and visit local wineries and museums. Swimming and bicycling are also available, with plenty of opportunity for bushwalking and looking at the flora, wildlife and Aboriginal art in the mountains.

An Aboriginal stockman takes a break at the end of a long day

A comfortable three and a half hour drive along the Western Highway from Melbourne, Bellellen Rise is also accessible by rail and bus, and guests are met at Stawell.

25 **Glenisla Homestead** is a beautiful old mountain sheep station, four and a half hours' drive northwest of Melbourne. It is one of Victoria's oldest sheep properties, growing fine Merino wool since 1843. The large verandaed colonial homestead, which is made from local Grampian sandstone taken from the region, is classified by the National Trust.

Views of the nearby mountains are magnificent and the area, adjoining the Grampian Mountains National Park, abounds in wildlife and flowers, with lovely bush tracks, rock formations and waterfalls. Only 15 minutes' drive from the homestead, visitors can see

PHILLIP QUIRK

A farmer pens his sheep after their day's grazing on lush Tasmanian pastures

Aboriginal rock paintings that are hundreds of years old and believed to have been done by the Buandik tribe.

For the past 15 years, Eric and Evelyn Barber have been entertaining and cooking for guests in their large, spacious home. In an informal and relaxed atmosphere, up to ten visitors can be accommodated at one time. Nearly half of their guests — mainly from overseas — come back for more.

Glenisla is 322 kilometres from Melbourne, and there are regular coach, rail and air services to the district. The Barbers provide free mini-bus transportation to and from the nearest terminals.

Tasmania

26 The north-west coast of Tasmania is a rich farming area with lush forests, wild rivers and some stunning coastland and island scenery. The region is steeped in history, with its buildings originating from the time of the island's convict era. **Woolnorth**, a 22,100-hectare farm tucked away right on its north-west tip, was established in 1825 by direct charter from King George IV. It has been breeding Hereford cattle longer than any farm in the country and also runs sheep, horses and cashmere goats as well as raising crops.

Four-wheel-drive tours of the farm are conducted daily, setting out from hotel/motel accommodation in nearby Smithton. Guided by locals with an extensive knowledge of the area, visitors are taken across the farm to Cape Grim, the site of many shipwrecks, which boasts the 'cleanest air in the world' (according to the

Department of Science and Technology), and along the Doughboys Island Walk and Woolnorth Point Beach, stopping for a lunch of Tasmanian scallops and local steaks. The day finishes with a visit to the Lacrum Experimental Dairy Farm.

The operators, Farnor West Tours, also conduct tours through Tasmania's timber country and along the Arthur River and West Coast.

27 **Kentford Park**, in Tasmania's Cape Country, is a small family operation set in rich undulating farmland 171 kilometres west of Launceston. Situated near picturesque Table Cape, the farm offers guests a touch of the country life, with plenty of good sea and estuary fishing in the nearby Flowerdale and Inglis rivers.

The countryside around Kentford Park is a mixture of cliffs, beaches, green fields and volcanic soils. It is a beautiful spot for city folk to get away from it all in fresh, invigorating, country sea air.

There is a golf course close by in Wynyard, and horse riding not far away in the Oldina State Forest.

The tariff includes bed and breakfast, with other meals by arrangement. According to critics, their country breakfasts are marvellous. Up to four guests can be accommodated at one time. Open year round, non-smokers are especially welcomed.

28 **Seasons Host Farm** is a small 'organic' farm on the aptly named Retreat Road in Lebrina, a small farming community 30 kilometres from Launceston. Owners Juliet and David Kimber grow most of their own vegetables and raise wool sheep, as well as horses, goats, cows, chickens, ducks and geese.

There's also a lake stocked with trout — which is also home to the occasional platypus, which guests can glimpse at dusk.

The Kimbers live in an old verandaed farmhouse which is close to many scenic spots, including Lavender Farm, Lilydale Falls Park, the Walker Rhododendron Reserve, and the Tamar Valley, as well as beaches and several vineyards.

Accommodation is one twin and one double room, with an adjoining private lounge. Breakfast is included, but the evening meal is optional. The couple specialise in vegetarian meals.

29 **The Stonehouse** (so-called because it is made from local blue stone) is just the place for visitors to Launceston who would like to do a bit of trout fishing in a quiet hideaway not far from the city.

Set in half a hectare of gardens overlooking 100 hectares of cattle property, it is only 24 kilometres north-east of Launceston and close to great trout fishing and wonderful beaches.

Klaus and Eleonore Wulf, who own The Stonehouse, provide an intimate family atmosphere for those wanting to escape the city and enjoy country hospitality and home cooking. They also run a market garden which is well-known for its organically grown vegetables.

The property has many beautiful walks and some wonderful views. In warm weather, barbecues are held outside, taking in the fresh air and magnificent surrounding countryside.

Klaus and Eleonore will gladly pick guests up in Launceston.

30 Lynne Agnew is a bundle of innovation and energy, able to turn her hand to wood and brick work, repair jobs, antique hunting, decorating, making curtains and everything else that goes into the restoration and renovation of old buildings.

Proprietor and manager of **Waverley Cottage Colonial Accommodation**, 84 kilometres north of Hobart, Lynne began offering quality accommodation in the late 1970s after renovating the family home with her husband. There followed renovation of a nearby hay shed and other neighbouring buildings.

The buildings are quite special and have an intimate warmth and character. They have even been featured in the *House and Garden Year Book* and the *Australian Women's Weekly*.

Much attention is paid to detail and the rooms are filled with homely touches and marvellous bric-a-brac from antique shops and secondhand stalls. Lynne and her mother have even made the patchwork bedspreads and knitted the top blankets for the beds.

Her work has won her the Tasmanian nomination in the 'National Tourism Awards for Outstanding Achievement'.

Located in peaceful countryside, the cottages are a perfect escape for honeymooners as well as for families. One group of mahjong players has booked the long weekend in June until 1995!

There are four cottages in all — Waverley Cottage, Waverley Croft, Amelia Cottage and Forget-Me-Not-Cottage, accommodating a total of 26. They are all self-contained, with bed and breakfast included in the tariff.

Situated in the 'heart' of Tasmania, one hour from Hobart, Launceston and the east coast, Waverley is a good base from which visitors can view Tasmania.

31 Situated 70 kilometres north of Hobart in a natural bush setting, **Ellesmere** supports sheep and cattle on its 1,821 hectares. The homestead was built in the early 1800s from sandstone and bricks made by convicts.

Cowboys rope cattle for branding

Guests may play tennis, go bushwalking, fishing, swimming, horse riding, sailboarding and enjoy farm and historic tours. Nearby are golf, fishing and many tourist attractions including the 'Mudwalls of Jericho' and the historic towns of Oatlands and Richmond.

A self-contained log cabin accommodates six people. Guests provide their own meals, although there are home-grown breakfast provisions supplied in the cabin. Proprietors will meet guests at Jericho bus depot.

32 **Morville Farm** is only 30 kilometres from Hobart and is set in green rolling hills within view of Mt Wellington. Morville's hosts, Merle and Dona Kehn, migrated to Tasmania four years ago from Washington State, USA and have been hosting farm holidays ever since.

Morville is located a few kilometres north of the historic village of Richmond and is ideally located for a day trip to Port Arthur, famous for its convict origins.

It is a modern, two-storey colonial-style home set in 75 hectares of land which supports sheep and chickens along with some crops. Guests can go on long walks taking in the views, play golf on a nearby course, and generally have a quiet, relaxing time.

Dona loves to cook and serves vegetables and fruits freshly grown by her husband in the garden. She is happy to cater for any special dietary requirements.

Full bed and board is offered, with special rates for three-day stays.

33 **Holly Tree Farm**, 50 minutes' drive south of Hobart, is a delightfully restored 1920s timber and iron Federation-style country home. Sited above the D'Entrecasteaux Channel, it is surrounded by a garden of roses and fruit trees. It is one of the few buildings in the region to have survived the disastrous bushfires of 20 years ago.

The farm is owned by Dr Henry Brigden and his wife Wendy, and one of the delights of the farm is the couple's unusually friendly animals. The donkeys accompany guests on walks down to the Channel, while the sheep answer to their names.

Annual musters of near-wild cattle are a feature of the large outback stations

The farm's location provides easy access to nearby Talune Wildlife Park, with its wombats and Tasmanian devils. Caves, museums and many cottage and craft industries are also found in the area.

Holly Tree Farm is perfect for artists and for people wishing to escape city living for a while. Bed and breakfast are inclusive, and other meals are by arrangement. Vegetarians and picnickers are welcome. Wendy's rose-petal jam, made from roses grown in the garden, and the farm's free-range eggs, are quite special.

There is accommodation for four or five people and twin and double suites, each with private bathroom. Rooms have a private entrance and a TV/sitting room.

South Australia

34 **Maraby**, located 375 kilometres north of Adelaide, in South Australia's impressive Flinders Ranges, is very popular with professional people seeking a private, relaxed holiday with friends in delightful country surroundings. The Telfers have been offering guests a quiet, get-away-from-it-all stay in their holiday cottage — a four-bedroom self-contained old stone farmhouse — for the past eight years.

There are no worries about noise from nearby neighbours; only birds and kangaroos abound. The country is great for bushwalking and trips are arranged to nearby national parks.

The farm attracts a cross-section of ages and accommodates up to ten people. Up to 70% of their guests like it so much that they return for more.

Maraby is closed in summer.

35 **Bungaree**, one of Australia's largest Merino studs, is more like a small town than a family property. Indeed, at one time it was home to around 100 people. Established in 1841 by George C. Hawker, today the fourth generation of the Hawker family continues to run the property as a family operation.

The property, 12 kilometres north of the famous wine-growing area of Clare Valley, and 92 kilometres north of Adelaide, is classified by the National Trust. Its sandstone buildings, erected between 1841 and 1869, include a church, with beautiful Italian wrought-iron gates, a Council Chamber, where the District Council met last century, an office/store, stables and blacksmith's shop, the manager's house, a shearing shed and a Swaggies Hut which was kept open for swagmen until well after the Second World War.

Many of the buildings have their original contents still in place for visitors to see. But the beauty of the place, as Sally Hawker says, is that 'the complex is alive. It is a working property, not a museum.'

The ivy-covered homestead has more than 34 rooms, four of which are underground — a far cry from the original homestead, which was a slab hut.

When it's not shearing time, guests can be accommodated in the Shearers' Quarters. Sixteen adults in twin accommodation or 30 schoolchildren — sardine-style. Rates are very good, with breakfast an option. It's BYO linen and blankets, with cooking facilities available.

Access to some of the buildings is difficult for people in wheelchairs, but a ramp has been built to the Shearers' Quarters where eight children from a Spastic Centre recently spent a week quite comfortably.

The station is open by prior arrangement for conducted tours, but a minimum of six people is required. Sally takes visitors around and lunch can be provided.

36 **Get-Away Holidays — Farm Holidays** of South Australia has been offering hospitality to visitors for 15 years, and is current holder of Yorke Peninsula's Excellence in Tourism award.

Run by Veronica and Jim Finlayson of the Stansbury Holiday Motel, Get-Away Holidays provides holidays in self-contained stone farmhouses on working farms situated on the Yorke Peninsula, around 200 kilometres west of Adelaide.

Farm life begins in April-May, when the new calves and lambs are born, and shearing takes place in July-September. From then through to December, hay is cut and the crops are harvested.

Sandalwood Park, established in 1875, is set

amidst old stone buildings and 20 hectares of natural scrubland. Located between the peninsula's two major towns, Minalton and Yorketown, it accommodates eight and is only a short drive from swimming and fishing beaches.

An easy walk from the white shores of Hardwicke Bay is *Hardwicke House*. As it is the most protected bay on the western coast of the peninsula, there is safe swimming for children and easy boating, with boats also available for hire.

The Lodge lies between Sandalwood Park and Hardwicke House. Fallow deer graze just beyond the front lawn and guests can play tennis or hire ponies. The Lodge is just a short distance from local beaches.

Further south lies *Paling Hut*, a 2,000-hectare property with an eight-kilometre beach frontage within walking distance of the house. With rooms for seven, it encompasses a sanctuary with kangaroos, emus and birds living peacefully in their native surrounds. The farm carries Merino sheep and stud Poll Hereford cattle, and has produced state champion malting barley.

37 **Apple Tree Cottage** is a secluded haven in the Adelaide Hills. Steeped in farming history, the beautifully restored two-storey settler cottage, built in 1853, attracts a constant flow of honeymooners (who often return to celebrate anniversaries), couples getting away for the weekend, and families.

What brings them back is Gai and Brenton Adcock's attention to detail and the home-away-from-home touches such as fresh flowers and pot-pourris around the house.

The farm, 30 kilometres south-east of Adelaide, is near Oakbank, home of the Great Eastern Steeplechase, and near several historic German towns. For wine buffs, it's only a short drive to South Australia's famous wineries. A variety of festivals take place in the area throughout the year and to fill the gaps between, guests can amuse themselves horse riding, visiting the many local cottage industries, and playing golf.

There is also plenty to do on the farm itself: blackberrying and mushrooming in season, fishing on the dam for redfin and rainbow trout, feeding the goat-come-lawnmower, catching yabbies and tadpoles, and collecting watercress.

The cottage overlooks a large dam and an apple orchard. The orchard was one of the largest in the country in the 1880s and today has 4,000 trees. The property is also home to Australia's own beef breed stud, the Amorilla Murray Greys.

Accommodation in the cottage is self-contained, with room for up to four people. It has lots of character, with scrubbed furniture, patchwork quilts and log fires, and guests need only bring their own food and linen. Bed and breakfast can be supplied if so desired.

The cottage won the Adelaide 1987 Tourism Award for Family and Specialised Accommodation.

38 **Old Mallee** is a sheep and grain property situated north-east of Adelaide in the Riverland of the Murray River. Around one-eighth of the property is natural scrub and home to native wildlife, including mallee fowls, emus, kangaroos and parrots. Guests can bring their own horses or go bushwalking or trail-bike riding, or they can participate in the farm's daily tasks. Shearing demonstrations can be arranged. There is also what is known as the 'Cockshell's Country Challenger', which provides quite an interesting challenge to city-reared golfers.

Guests are accommodated in a self-contained stone house which sleep six. Camping facilities are also available on the property.

39 **Poltalloch** is an historic homestead situated on the southern shores of Lake Alexandrina, 138 kilometres south-east of Adelaide. Classified by the National Trust and included in the Register of the National Estate, Poltalloch was built in 1873. It boasts the only inland lighthouse in the southern hemisphere.

Guests can boat on the lake, take in some tennis, go birdwatching and bushwalking and are welcome to work with the station's cattle, sheep and angora goats. Calving and lambing occur in May, with shearing from August to September.

Open year round, seven days a week, the Poltalloch homestead accommodates guests in three limestone, pioneer self-contained cottages and one bed and breakfast cottage.

In 1986-7, the homestead won the Lower Murray Region Tourist Resort award. Owner/manager husband and wife team, the Cowans, encourage an 18-plus age group.

A one and three-quarter hour drive from Adelaide, guests travelling by public transport can be met at Meningie bus depot.

40 **Narnu Pioneer Holiday Farm** on Hindmarsh Island, only 80 kilometres south of Adelaide, is accessible by car and ferry. Guests will be met at Goolwa station or bus depot.

A typical mixed farm of a century ago, Narnu is 33 hectares in size. Guests are encouraged to join farming activities including animal feeding, making butter and flour by traditional methods, hand-ploughing and sheep-shearing. Fishing and horse riding are also available. The island has fine beaches, scenery and wildlife, and many historical buildings.

Four self-contained two-bedroom cottages each accommodate four people. One large two-bedroom and two three-bedroom self-contained cottages accommodate four to six people. Guests cater for their own meals and are asked to bring their own linen. Bunkhouse accommodation is available for groups (minimum number 30) with shared facilities. The farm specialises in facilities for handicapped visitors.

STEVE LOVEGROVE

The helicopter is playing an increasingly important role in outback cattle mustering

Western Australia

Maileup Downs, 380 kilometres south-east of
41 Perth, is the perfect farm holiday for amateur
botanists as it harbours one of the most comprehensive collections of native trees and shrubs in Western
Australia. And in September, the Ongerup Wildflower
Show is held nearby, displaying 300-400 species of
wildflowers collected from the immediate area.
Western Australia's premier shearing event is also held
during the show.

Maileup Downs is a 2,800-hectare property
running 4,000 Merino sheep and Angus Stud cattle
and producing wheat, barley, peas and lupins. Guests
can participate in all farm activities.

Hosts Keith and Dulcie Davis arrange scenic
flights for guests in their light plane, taking them over
the magnificent Stirling Ranges, the Fitzgerald National Park and along the beautiful Brimmer Bay
coastline.

A typical country house, Maileup accommodates
guests in two twin rooms with en suite bathroom.
Guests join the family for meals. A three-roomed on-site caravan is also available, with guests cooking for
themselves.

Leyburn is located at the 'Gateway to the South-
42 west' of Western Australia, close to many south-
west tourist areas, particularly the Pemberton karri
forest.

A 4,800-hectare property overlooking the Black-wood River Valley, some 234 kilometres south-west of
Perth, it is situated in terrain itself timbered with the
state's famous karri trees.

Host Caroline Creek likes to make guests feel at
home by preparing fabulous fare for her many
overseas visitors. She comments that Australian farm
life is very different from what many have experienced
before. Many of her guests see farm animals and the
fruit 'on the tree' for the first time.

Up to six people can be accommodated in the
house, with use of a private lounge. Bed comes with a
home-cooked breakfast. Caroline will also cook an
evening meal on request.

A three and a half hour drive from Perth, guests
can also catch a train or bus to nearby Bridgetown
where they will be picked up.

Oulnina Farm, two and a half hours' drive south-
43 east of Perth, is a 1,400-hectare property raising
sheep, barley and oats.

Guests become part of the family at Oulnina, staying in the homestead and participating in daily farm
activities. Up to five guests can be accommodated in
the homestead's two twin guestrooms.

Catering for a 35-plus age group, guests can go
birdwatching, walk through the bush, swim, or go
trout fishing on a nearby farm.

Accessible by car or bus, Oulnina's hosts, Mr and
Mrs Klug, will greet bus travellers at Williams bus
depot.

44 A stay at **Bimbijy Station** is a perfect bush holiday for city families wishing to experience a touch of old-fashioned station life.

A pastoral property located in flat, dry country dotted with salt lakes 400 kilometres north-east of Perth, its owner Norm Bates and his brother Ron are tried-and-true bushmen. Ron is particularly knowledgeable in all aspects of Western Australian bush lore and its early explorers.

City folk can observe the various station activities, go on guided tours looking out for wildlife, and visit caves and waterholes and learn about the region's unique vegetation. Particularly wonderful are the wildflowers in bloom.

Up to 40 people can be accommodated in the shearers' quarters, which have showers, a laundry and a kitchen. The accommodation is self-catering and guests should bring stores for their own requirements.

Special concessions are available for school groups, but the station is closed in summer.

45 The drive to **Thundelarra**, around six hours north of Perth, takes visitors past the vineyards of the Swan Valley, through rolling green hills and fields of wheat on to the red dust gravel tracks which cut across rocky outcrops and grey-green mulga scrub. In spring, the ground is covered in the yellow, pink, white and mauve blooms of Western Australia's famous wildflowers.

A 155,400-hectare sheep station running between 12,000 and 16,000 sheep, Thundelarra (an Aboriginal word meaning 'spring waters'), sits between two small historic goldmining settlements where modern-day prospectors with metal detectors are sometimes lucky enough to find the odd gem. The station has a good variety of wildlife: goannas, dingoes, wild turkeys, mallee fowl, possums, kangaroos, goats, parrots, emus and wedge-tail eagles. The emu is responsible for the widespread growth of sandalwood on the property. The nut of the sandalwood is eaten by the emu and then acts as a grinding stone in its stomach, passing out of the emu's system when it's of no further use.

The big old stone homestead is ringed by turn-of-the-century palm trees and its wide verandas are surrounded by green lawns with a swimming pool and tennis court behind. Guests are accommodated either in the homestead or in the self-contained shearers' cottage or quarters. Camp groups are also catered for.

An airstrip is situated adjacent to the homestead and arrangements can be made for guests to be met from the bus at Paynes Find or Yalgoo.

46 The oldest property in the Murchison River area is **Yuin Station,** a 580-kilometre drive north of Perth. Part of the road is unpaved and difficult when wet, but the long drive is well worthwhile. The surrounding desert country has fascinating geological formations.

Yuin station runs 16,000 sheep on 200,000 hectares. Guests may join in station activities.

The buildings are classified by the National Trust and there is an old goldmine and mining museum on the property.

Three self-contained one-bedroom cottages each accommodate four people. Guests may join the homestead family for meals. The proprietors will meet guests at Mullewa bus depot.

47 **Nyang Station Homestead,** 20 minutes drive off the North-west Coastal Highway, was established as a sheep station in 1891. Today, it runs 10,000 Merino sheep.

Nyang is an Aboriginal word meaning 'junction of the two waters' and the property is watered by the Yannarie River and Emu Creek, along with 18 sub-artesian bores.

Because of its easy access to the highway, the homestead is an ideal one or two nights' stopover for those heading further north or returning south. Proprietors David and Mary Weir are able to meet guests at Barradale bus depot on the highway. There are also two airstrips on the property for light and twin-engine aircraft.

Nyang station accommodates up to 12 people, with guests residing in a wing of the house. Each room opens onto a veranda looking on to the lawns and surrounding trees. Part of the homestead has been constructed from an old hotel.

A typical outback station seen from the air

The nearest property is 70 kilometres away and David warns guests that teenagers might find it a little too peaceful as the homestead has neither TV nor newspapers. However, everyone is encouraged to become involved with the shearing, mustering, lamb marking and other activities.

Tours around the station and to nearby gold diggings are offered. Meals are served with the family. The homestead is closed for summer.

Northern Territory

48 **Springvale Homestead** is situated on the magnificent Katherine River, around four hours' drive from Darwin. Built in 1879, in the late 1800s it was the destination of Australia's longest cattle droving epic. The river is home to a lot of native wildlife, including the Johnstone River crocodile which, despite its teeth, is quite harmless, as well as several colonies of fruit bats.

Guests can swim and fish, take boat cruises and go horse riding. The best time to visit is from April to October, when the weather is not so hot.

Accommodation is in air-conditioned motel units or on the caravan and camping grounds. Tents are available.

49 **Mataranka Homestead,** five hours' drive south-east of Darwin, was established in 1916 as an experimental cattle station. It is now a major tourist attraction, largely due to the unique thermal pool nearby which is set in lush tropical rainforest.

The homestead has modern motel facilities — 29 airconditioned motel units with private facilities and pub-style homestead rooms with shared facilities — a youth hostel, and a caravan/camping ground.

Guests may go fishing, swimming, bushwalking and boating.

A number of package coach tours are available from Darwin.

50 Some 80 kilometres south-east of Alice Springs lies **Ross River Homestead.** This 15,000-square-kilometre cattle station is in the heart of the Red Centre. Colourful and spectacular scenery surrounds the homestead, with fossils and interesting geological formations nearby. The rugged Eastern MacDonnell Ranges, rocky gorges with beautiful ghost gums and Aboriginal rock carvings dating back more than 30,000 years are a short distance away.

Activities guests may participate in are boomerang throwing, bushwalking, damper making, supervised horse riding (for an extra fee) and swimming. Of interest nearby are rock carvings at N'Dhala Gorge, goldfields, and the Ross River dry river bed which runs through the station.

Guests are accommodated in 22 units, with four people to a unit. Self-sufficient campers are welcome. Although the units are self-contained, catered meals are available in the dining room.

51 **Curtin Springs Roadside Inn** and cattle station is only one hour's drive from Ayers Rock. The stone homestead is set amongst rolling hills, gum trees and spacious lawns. There is a general store for all guests' supply needs, a full takeaway liquor licence and accommodation for 35, with country-cooked meals provided.

Owner/manager Peter Severin can arrange tours to Mt Conner, which is on the station, as well as to Ayers Rock and King's Canyon which is accessible via the station's direct road.

The station is open to visitors year round, and office hours are from early morning to late at night.

Queensland

52 **Butchers Hill Homestead,** 322 kilometres north of Cairns, is over 120 years old. Cattle, corn and peanuts are produced on this 243-hectare property.

Activities guests may enjoy include bushwalking, fishing, gold panning and horse riding; experienced riders may join in cattle mustering. Interesting places to visit are Laura with its Aboriginal cave paintings, the city of Cooktown and Lakefield National Park.

Accommodation is in ten single cabins and seven double cabins with shared facilities. Meals are served in the communal dining room.

53 A 400-kilometre drive west of Townsville is **Silver Hills Outback Station,** set in a remote area of Queensland. The area has changed little since it was first explored by Europeans less than 100 years ago. This 14,175-hectare property is a cattle and sheep station.

Guests may join in with the station activities if experienced, otherwise spectating is encouraged. The station has a hot mineral spa. Native wildlife such as kangaroos and emus abound, and country race meetings and rodeos are held nearby.

Meals are served in a communal dining room. Guests are accommodated in either one of the nine units which accommodate two people or in one of the eight units which accommodate three people. All units have private facilities. Self-sufficient campers are welcome on powered or unpowered sites.

Proprietors will meet guests at Richmond bus depot or airport.

54 **Lorraine Station** lies in outback Queensland, 126 kilometres north of Longreach, in the rolling Mitchell grass downs.

Carrying 31,000 hectares of sheep, it is situated in true Waltzing Matilda country near Combo Waterhole, the site that inspired 'Banjo' Paterson to write Australia's unofficial national anthem in 1895.

The station organises day tours to Combo and to the ghost town of early Opalton (one of Queensland's oldest opal fields), as well as to the world's most extensive fossilised dinosaur trackway — site of a dinosaur stampede 100 million years ago. Other nearby attractions include Aboriginal paintings and bora ring sites, and Longreach and its Stockman's Hall of Fame and Heritage Centre.

Tennis, windsurfing on the dam and swimming are available for sports lovers. And sheep-shearing demonstrations can be arranged on request.

Sixty-two people can be housed in the outback shearers' quarters, which have shared facilities. Camping and caravan sites are available. So, too, is a licensed bar, canteen and barbecue areas.

The station is open from April to November.

55 A cattle property of 400,000 hectares, **Vergemont Station** is situated 145 kilometres west of Longreach. It was established over 100 years ago and

is sited on what were once the shores of an ancient inland sea where dinosaurs roamed, leaving behind their fossilised remains.

Vergemont runs cattle and sheep, and one of the highlights of a stay on the property is helping with the mustering which is done not only by horse and bike, but also by plane and helicopter. Guests can camp with the musterers in true outback style.

Back at the ranch, there's plenty of interest to see and do. There is the old station homestead, the blacksmith's shop filled with hand-made tools from a bygone era and lots of other interesting farm buildings to explore.

Guided tours with full and detailed explanations of the ins and outs of Queensland farm life are conducted for interested guests. Opal fossickers can try their luck, while guests handy with a line and hook can dangle for yellow bellies in the property's billabongs. There's even pig hunting for those so inclined.

Four-wheel-drive vehicles and trail-bikes are available for hire. Guests can feed the animals and participate in seasonal farm activities. Or they can simply take it easy, soaking up the expansive vista, or play tennis on the night and day court, followed by a swim and a barbecue. There are also plenty of indoor games for quiet, relaxing evenings.

Approximately 20 visitors can be accommodated and there are camping and caravan sites. The station is closed during the very hot summer season.

56 **Dalkeith Station** has been in the McClymont family since the 1920s. The property, 128 kilometres west of Longreach, carries 8,000 Merino sheep and 200 cattle.

As the property offers accommodation for only two people, with a recommended minimum of four days' stay, it is ideal for overseas tourists to experience fully Australian outback life in a true country family atmosphere. Guests stay with the family in their 'cottage' farmhouse in a timber-floored twin room with private bathroom.

When not helping out, guests can visit an old Aboriginal corroboree ground situated on the station and fossick for semi-precious stones.

The property is closed during summer.

Air and bus services are regularly available to Longreach from Brisbane and the McClymonts greet guests on arrival in either their car or light plane. During wet weather, the roads can sometimes be impassable and air transport is dependent on the state of the landing strip.

57 **Planet Downs** is 750 kilometres north-west of Brisbane and set amongst the rolling hills, scrub and forests of the Dividing Range. The owners, the Bloxsom family, have capitalised on the natural beauty of their 100,000-hectare working cattle station to create a luxurious resort for city-weary guests where activity or the lack of it are both acceptable pursuits.

For the active, early-morning cattle mustering on horseback or by four-wheel-drive vehicle is a highlight of a visit to the property. Planet Downs has over 200 horses available for horse riding, either for short rides or overnight campouts with the property staff. Swimming in rock pools beneath cascading waterfalls, walking, lounging around the pool or playing tennis are other options.

Planet Downs has its own wildlife sanctuary and Aboriginal bush art gallery. The latter was discovered only recently and the cave paintings are estimated to be around 3,000 years old — the largest collection yet discovered on a private property.

The Gunyah (the main resort building), which has been crafted from Tasmanian cedar, has its own licensed restaurant and bar and also offers bush barbecues as an alternative at meal times. The accommodation has been tastefully designed and rooms feature king-sized beds, air conditioning and pot-belly stoves. Traditional Australian bush dances are held regularly for evening entertainment.

Guests can be transferred to Planet Downs from Gladstone, Rockhampton, Emerald or Biloela, which is on the Burnett Highway from Brisbane to Rockhampton. Transportation and transfer details are available from the resort's Brisbane booking office.

58 **Reedy Creek Homestead**, a 40,000-hectare cattle station, is a bush-lover's paradise. Located at the junction of the Reedy and Ruined Cattle Creeks, seven hours north of Brisbane, in a valley surrounded by rugged hills in Queensland's Dividing Range, it boasts wind-eroded gorges, waterfalls, springs, Aboriginal rock paintings, native orchids and rare ferns and staghorns amidst a landscape of eucalypts and craggy sandstone ridges. Bush enthusiasts can either walk or be taken by four-wheel-drive vehicle to experience the scenery.

Guests can stay with the family in their Queensland colonial homestead, enjoying country food and a family atmosphere.

Special-interest groups, safari tours, trail riders and school groups are catered for. A bus pick-up service is provided to and from nearby Taroom-Reedy Creek. There is also a 1,220-metre airstrip.

59 **Susan River Homestead** is a holiday health and recreation ranch set on 670 hectares of pasture, bush and lazy river just minutes from the sea.

Only three and a half hours' drive north of Brisbane, the homestead was built by Norman and Faye McLean in 1976 and offers everything that holiday-makers could desire in a country farm holiday complex. It also caters for the disabled, offering wheelchair access.

Faye, a qualified naturopath, treats visitors' health problems with natural therapies and remedies, and nutritional advice. Swedish and therapeutic massage is available along with yoga, exercise classes, deep relaxation classes, saunas and spas.

Cattle mustering is always hot and dusty work in the arid interior

Some of the other activities are paragliding, volleyball, trampolining, waterskiing, billiards, bushwalking and table tennis. Golf and lawn bowling are minutes away. Tame kangaroos, wallabies and farm animals keep children amused.

The McLeans encourage guests to visit lovely Hervey Bay, only 15 minutes away, and to take a day tour of beautiful Fraser Island, the world's largest sand island boasting bush, beaches and rainforest.

With the help of five of their six children, the couple take great care in catering to individual needs. After breakfast, two-hour horse rides leave the ranch and make their way to the Susan River. Mounts are carefully selected depending on riders' capabilities, but Faye says they had to draw the line when one frequent guest, a young lady of 88 years, insisted that she could still handle a horse.

Guests not inclined to horse riding can go on a four-wheel-drive trip to the river, or simply laze about in the bush, the garden or around the open fire.

Up to 45 guests are accommodated in the verandaed twin and triple-share rooms. Faye's hearty, healthy meals, morning and afternoon teas and most of the activities are included in the tariff.

60 Peter and Janet Stephens have been accommodating guests at **Cedar Glen** in their 1901 colonial family home for the past six years. They are the third generation to work the farm.

The property sits peacefully at the head of the Albert River Valley, bordering on Lamington National Park, 100 kilometres from Brisbane and the Gold Coast.

The Stephens' raise Arabian horses as a hobby, using them for cattle mustering and other farm activities. They produce all their own beef, vegetables and milk, and rear peacocks and fancy poultry.

Six people can stay with the family in their home as house guests, waking to the call of cockerels and en-

joying Janet's wonderful home-made bread baked in the wood stove. Later, guests can join in the farm activities, go bushwalking, rockclimbing and riding, or just relax with their feet up, soaking in the wonderful colours of the surrounding hills.

To get there, visitors can drive to Cedar Glen or catch a bus from Brisbane or the Gold Coast to Beaudesert, where Peter and Janet will meet them.

61 Only 68 kilometres south of Brisbane, **Nindooinbah** is well located for holiday-makers who wish to experience a bit of gracious country living but don't have time to travel great distances.

A 1,200-hectare farming and grazing property, Nindooinbah features an old homestead furnished in its original 1840s style and surrounded by gardens.

High ceilings, decorative floral wallpapers, open fireplaces, rich timber fittings in mahogany and cedar and expansive gardens adorned with roses exude a warmth and style that move visitors back in time.

Illustrated in both American and British *House and Garden* magazines, and featured in virtually every book on Australian historic homesteads, Nindooinbah can offer much to keep visitors occupied and entertained.

Patrick and Margaret Hockey, owners of the homestead, show the same hospitality to their guests as they would to close friends and family, planning activities according to guests' needs. Farm inspections, visits to nearby Lamington National Park, watching polo at Kooralbyn, or spending time on the shady veranda admiring the hills reflected in the lake at the bottom of the garden are some of the possibilities. Dinner in the evenings is always a special highlight.

Accommodation and all meals are included, as well as excursions on the property and chauffeur transport between the homestead and Brisbane Airport.

Farms & Station Holiday Contacts

Operators

Bookings are required for all the farms and stations listed below, and these can be made direct with the properties concerned. Reservations for many of the farms can also be made with state tourist bureaus.

Several organisations throughout Australia specialise in farm holidays; we have listed some of these below:

The Australian Farm & Country Holiday Association, run by Tony and Rosemary Rich, offers holidays to farm seekers. They are currently in the process of forming a national association of farms with a long-term view of producing a brochure listing every host farm in the country.

PO Box 384
Woollahra
Sydney NSW 2025
Ph. (02) 387 6681

Hazelton Airlines operates 'Meet a Cocky' day tours to working properties in the central west of New South Wales. Trips operate from both Canberra and Sydney.

PO Box 12
Cudal NSW 2864
Ph. (063) 64 2104

The Host Farms Association, run by Cheryl Inglis, provides bookings for farms in Victoria, and a smaller number in New South Wales and South Australia.

'Fairview'
RMD Pollocksford Road
Gnarwarre VIC 3221
Ph. (052) 65 6159

In Western Australia, tourists can contact Jean Smiley of *Homestay of WA* who include farm holidays in their programme.

40 Union Road
Carmel
Perth WA 6076
Ph. (09) 293 5347

Australis Tours of Brisbane operates trips to a variety of Queensland stations, in both the outback and closer to Brisbane. Guests are flown from Cairns, Brisbane or the Gold Coast to properties for stays ranging from two to seven nights.

GPO Box 389
Brisbane QLD 4001
Ph. (07) 221 6404

New South Wales

1 Barula Park

PO Box 64
Alstonville NSW 2477
Ph. (066) 28 0914

2 Wattleridge

Guyra NSW 2365
Ph. (067) 79 7593

3 Leconfield

Kootingal NSW 2352
Ph. (067) 69 4230

4 Lalla Rookh

Duri NSW 2344
Ph. (067) 68 0216

5 4D Host Farm

Quirindi NSW 2343
Ph. (067) 47 4712

6 Karanilla

Quirindi NSW 2343
Ph. (067) 46 5660 or 46 1140

7 Chesleigh Guest Ranch

Hill End Road
Sofala NSW 2795
Ph. (063) 37 7077

8 Millamolong

Mandurama NSW 2792
Ph. (063) 67 5247

9 Kyabra

Paddy's River
via Moss Vale NSW 2577
Ph. (048) 84 1522

10 Rotherwood

Illawarra Highway
Sutton Forest NSW 2577
Ph. (048) 78 9146

11 Avoca Station

Wentworth NSW 2648
Ph. (050) 27 3020

12 Litchfield Farm Holidays

PO Box 48
Cooma NSW 2630
Ph. (064) 53 3231

13 Crown Tree Farm

Rocky Hall
via Wyndham NSW 2550
Ph. (0649) 4 1233

14 Nindethana Station

via Wentworth NSW 2648
Ph. (050) 27 0210

Australian Capital Territory

15 Country Life Tours

GPO Box 1275
Canberra ACT 2601
Ph. (062) 36 8182

Victoria

16 Gillingall Station

Buchan VIC 3885
Ph. (051) 55 9380

17 Riverlea

PO Box 133
Orbost VIC 3888
Ph. (051) 54 2031 or 54 1442

18 Brookfield

RMB 4478
Numurkah VIC 3636
Ph. (058) 62 2353

19 Dorilla Park

Arcadia VIC 3613
Ph. (058) 27 1383

20 Dunbar

C/- Metcalfe PO
Metcalfe VIC 3448
Ph. (054) 23 2388

21 Holcombe Homestead

Holcombe Road
RMB 3683
Glenlyon VIC 3461
Ph. (053) 48 7514

22 Naringal

Private Bag
Wallinduc VIC 3351
Ph. (055) 96 5122

23 Old Strathconon

Elmhurst PO
Elmhurst VIC 3469
Ph. (053) 53 7273

24 Bellellen Rise

RMB 2032
Stawell VIC 3380
Ph. (053) 58 2750

25 Glenisla Homestead

via Cavendish VIC 3408
Ph. (053) 80 1532

Tasmania

26 Farnor' West Tours

Woolnorth
Bridge Hotel/Motel
PO Box 327
Smithton TAS 7330
Ph. (004) 52 1083

27 Kentford Park

RSD 263 Smarts Road
Wynyard TAS 7325
Ph. (004) 38 1154

28 Seasons Host Farm

Retreat Road
Lebrina TAS 7254
Ph. (003) 95 6148

29 The Stonehouse

Brown Mountain Road
Karoola TAS 7254
Ph. (003) 95 4240

30 Waverley Cottage

Oatlands TAS 7120
Ph. (002) 54 1264

31 Ellesmere

Jericho TAS 7030
Ph. (002) 54 4140

32 Morville

PO Box 52
Richmond TAS 7025
Ph. (002) 62 4299

33 Holly Tree Farm

Channel Highway
Middleton TAS 7163
Ph. (002) 92 1680

South Australia

34 Maraby

PO Box 93
Hawker SA 5434
Ph. (086) 4891 (ask for 22W)

35 Bungaree Station

Bungaree Box 231
Clare SA 5453
Ph. (088) 42 2677

36 Get-Away Holidays

Brentwood
via Minlaton SA 5575
Ph. (088) 53 4201

37 Apple Tree Cottage

PO Box 100
Oakbank SA 5243
Ph. (08) 388 4193

38 Old Mallee

Box 1757
Meribah
via Loxton SA 5333
Ph. (085) 87 2263

39 Poltalloch

Tailem Bend SA 5260
Ph. (085) 74 0043

40 Narnu Pioneer Holiday Farm

Hindmarsh Island
via Goolwa SA 5214
Ph. (085) 55 2002

Western Australia

41 Maileup Downs

Borden WA 6338
Ph. (098) 27 6017 or 27 6060

42 Leyburn

RMB 138
Boyup Brook WA 6244
Ph. (097) 61 7506

43 Oulnina

RMB 508
Williams WA 6391
Ph. (098) 85 7026

44 Bimbijy Station

PO Box 73
Bencubbin WA 6477
Ph. (096) 85 1242

45 Thundelarra Station

via Wubin WA 6612
Ph. (096) 64 5056

46 Yuin Station

Yalgoo WA 6635
Ph. Radio Telephone — Yuin 1
(Ph. 011 Trunk calls)

47 Nyang Station

Carnarvon WA 6701
Ph. (099) 43 0534

Northern Territory

48 Springvale Homestead

Katherine NT 5780
Ph. (089) 72 1044

49 Mataranka Homestead

Mataranka NT 5780
Ph. (089) 75 4544

50 Ross River Homestead

GPO Box 84
Alice Springs NT 5750
Ph. Radio Telephone — Alice
Springs 135
(Ph. 011 Trunk calls)

51 Curtin Springs Station

C/- Alice Springs PO
Alice Springs NT 5751
Ph. (089) 56 2906

Queensland

52 Butcher Hill Homestead

PMB Lakeland
via Cairns QLD 4870
Ph. (070) 60 2155

53 Silver Hills Outback Station

Richmond QLD 4822
Ph. (077) 41 3289

54 Lorraine Station

Winton QLD 4735
Ph. (074) 57 1693

55 Vergemont Station

Longreach QLD 4730
Ph. (074) 58 2913

56 Dalkeith

via Longreach QLD 4730
Ph. (074) 58 2912

57 Planet Downs Tourist Resort

PO Box 420
Zillmere QLD 4034
Ph. (07) 265 5022

58 Reedy Creek Homestead

via Taroom QLD 4420
Ph. (071) 77 7315

59 Susan River Homestead

Hervey Bay Road
Hervey Bay QLD
Ph. (071) 21 6846

60 Cedar Glen

Darlington
Beaudesert QLD 4285
Ph. (075) 44 8170

61 Nindooinbah

Beaudesert QLD 4285
Ph. (075) 41 1070

Historic Houses & Inns

Australia's history has been short, colourful and tough. It is no land of sleepy villages and stately homes, evolving through the centuries. There has simply not been the time, and Australians have not had the leisure.

Many of Australia's historic dwellings were built as the lonely and often spartan outposts of farming folk, struggling to consolidate their grip on a hostile land and yet retain some link with civilisation. Others have even harsher stories etched in their stones, hewn with convict labour under the lash of red-coated guards.

The other side of the picture is gentler. In Australian cities, the inns and hotels strove to retain the style and even elegance of the European establishments which most of their patrons remembered. They strove all the harder because of their immense distance in space and time from a civilised world which sometimes seemed to have forgotten them.

Australians nowadays are, of course, cosmopolitan members of a more fluid world community. But they have not forgotten: there has hardly been time to forget.

They value with a special devotion dwellings that would barely be considered old at all in other countries, and they are the richer for it. Victorian and Edwardian hotels are lovingly restored and preserved, especially in the longer-established eastern states, with an attention that would be rare elsewhere in the world.

Modest stone cottages in the country and outback homesteads have been saved and renovated by people whose fathers and grandfathers would remember how once they were the only outposts of comfort and friendliness in a vast and alien landscape.

Today, the outback has been conquered, the bush tamed, and the cities have grown to take their place among the world's most sophisticated. But Australia's old buildings carry their stories and their histories with dignity.

A great many of the old city hotels which remain are still plying the trade for which they were built. Homesteads, while still homes, have often been converted to accommodate guests. Though they now provide modern facilities that would astonish the original inhabitants, they retain their pioneer atmosphere or their Victorian elegance — often under the protection of the National Trust.

This trend is fortunate for the international and inter-state visitor, whether on business or on vacation. A little effort will usually uncover one of these historic gems within range of any major town — often in the town centre itself. Ritzy hotels and motels are fine, but the imaginative traveller usually does have a quieter alternative if he wants it.

Holiday-makers and those who can stretch their business trips for just a few days can venture into another, older Australia, only hours from the major cities. It is an Australia that remembers its colonial past, its fierce independence of spirit, and the rugged values on which it was built.

It seems a pity to miss this other Australia — often so close to the 20th-century surface of the modern nation, and at the same time so much a part of the Australia of today. The locations detailed below should make it easier to uncover at least some elements of that other Australia.

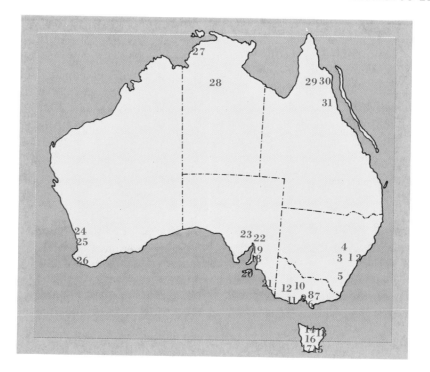

Locations

New South Wales

1 Tucked between the span of the Harbour Bridge and the high-rise buildings of Sydney's downtown district is the old commercial heart of the city — The Rocks area. Once a jumble of grog shops, warehouses and winding streets, The Rocks is now the centre of a multi-million dollar restoration project designed to give the district new life as a tourist town. The **Russell Hotel**, built in 1887, is a jewel of period architecture and still retains all of its Victorian style and grace.

Four-poster beds and open fireplaces give the visitor the opportunity to travel back in time from the centre of one of the southern hemisphere's most progressive cities. Surrounded by colonial pubs, stores and buildings not much changed since the district's heyday 100 years ago, the Russell is a small hotel with only 18 rooms, catering both to residents and to the passing trade.

Proud of its Victorian past, the Russell nevertheless offers 20th-century views of Circular Quay and Sydney Harbour from its penthouse suites high above George Street. The staff, too, play their part, dressing in period costume.

2 The **Jackson Hotel**, located in Victoria Street, Potts Point, a short distance from Sydney's lively and somewhat notorious nightlife centre of Kings Cross, is reminiscent of the appealing and romantic small hotels of Europe.

Now classified by the National Trust, the Jackson is two beautifully restored terraces dating back to 1880. The rooms have high ornate ceilings and decorative plaster work, original marble fireplaces, and French doors opening out on to iron lace work verandas.

There is a delightful courtyard in which to enjoy a continental-style breakfast. The service is friendly and the atmosphere homely.

3 Once a quiet retreat where nuns engaged in prayer and meditation, the **Little Company Guest House** in the Blue Mountains west of Sydney still retains an atmosphere of other-worldliness for visiting city-dwellers.

Set in fine grounds just a kilometre past Leura on the Great Western Highway, it is within two hours of Sydney. Guests travelling from Sydney by rail will be collected from the station.

The guesthouse has a tennis court, swimming pool, croquet lawn and a lawn bowling green. Beautifully restored, it dates back to the early 1900s, when it was originally built as a private home. Its ten rooms with leadlight windows are large and airy and guests eat in a magnificent panelled dining room.

4 In the heart of NSW's famous wine-growing district, the Hunter Valley, the **Neath Hotel** on Cessnock Road is slightly more than two hours from Sydney by road and can also be reached by rail from Sydney to Cessnock.

Built just after the turn of the century, the hotel has been classified by the National Trust, and is fully restored and renovated. It has a fine restaurant, and two bars in which guests can taste some of the best wines produced in Australia, many of them from vineyards just minutes away. The hotel contains many fine antiques which add to its old-world charm.

Australian Capital Territory

5 Only a 30-minute drive from Canberra is the small town of Bungendore whose most notable building is the **Carrington Motel** and restaurant. Built in 1885, the Carrington has been fully restored and modernised, but it still retains its old Victorian atmosphere. Its rooms are furnished with antiques, and probably the hotel's *pièce de résistance* is the 120-year-old mahogany bar.

The Carrington can cater for the casual overnight visitor seeking a break from the pressures of Canberra, but it is also large enough to handle wedding receptions and small conferences.

New additions, including ten luxury suites with undercover parking, a spa and a sauna, have all been completed in keeping with the style of the original restaurant building.

Victoria

6 **Gordon Place** in Melbourne was built in 1884 as 'Coppin's improved dwellings'. It was designed for George Coppin, philanthropist, one-time Member of Parliament, and the father of Australian theatre, by the notable colonial architect, William Pitt. Renamed Gordon House in 1887, it flourished as first-class apartment-style accommodation. It was purchased and completely restored in 1981.

The building is built around two courtyards linked by covered walkways, so each apartment overlooks either the trellis-covered eating area and the 100-year-old palm tree that has grown and flourished with the building, or the second courtyard, which has a tempting pool and garden area laid out beneath the walkway. Glass lifts take guests to the upper levels and a huge glass atrium is opened on hot summer evenings to the stars.

Now a hotel, Gordon Place provides some of the best apartment accommodation in Melbourne, with elegant buildings and garden courtyards sensitively restored. Situated at the end of Little Bourke Street, Gordon Place is at the entertainment hub of the city. The Princess Theatre is just across the street and Her Majesty's and the Comedy Theatre are nearby. Cinemas, restaurants and Melbourne's Chinatown are also a mere stone's throw away, as is Parliament House and its beautiful Treasury Gardens.

In spite of its highly professional smoothness, there is a casual informality about Gordon Place thanks to its open areas and walkways, and to the constant flow of activity in and around the hotel.

7 A two-hour drive north of Melbourne and just 11 kilometres north-east of Warburton is the **O'Shannassy Guesthouse**, near the O'Shannassy Reservoir and its catchment area. The guesthouse captures the spirit of the traditional Australian homestead, with long sweeping verandas over gracious lawns and gardens — a short stroll from woodland.

8 In similar style and rather closer to Melbourne is the **Wallaby Creek Guesthouse**, some 15 kilometres north-east of Whittlesea and only an hour by road from the state capital. The guesthouse has been lovingly restored and it provides warm and comfortable accommodation.

9 At Queenscliff, on the eastern tip of Victoria's Bellarine Peninsula, is the elegant **Queenscliff Hotel**. Built in 1888, the Queenscliff has been restored to its former glory and a long winding staircase and stained-glass doors are features of the hotel's classic Victorian interior. Its 32 luxuriously appointed bedrooms are furnished with large brass beds and imported antiques.

The hotel is famous for its French cuisine, and is close to a number of sites of local historical interest. Among them is the lighthouse on the peninsula, and an after-dinner stroll to this landmark has become something of a tradition with guests. The Maritime Centre and Reserve are also nearby, as well as the historical museum which presents a picture of Victorian colonial life in the region. The Queenscliff is set in a charming district known for its old cottages and churches.

10 Right in the heart of Victoria's historic goldrush region is **Ravenswood Homestead**. Centrally positioned near the towns of Bendigo, Castlemaine and Maldon — in the north of the state — the homestead is set in 160 hectares of pastoral country-side.

A typical room at Sydney's Jackson Hotel

More than a century has elapsed since Ravenswood was constructed in 1857, but amazingly the passage of time has seen very few changes to alter the home's original structure. The addition of a kitchen wing and servants' quarters in the late 1890s are the only major renovations to have occurred. Now a comfortable guesthouse, Ravenswood offers fine dining, open log fires and views over a patchwork of paddocks and statuesque eucalypt groves.

11 About 32 kilometres from historic Warrnambool, in Victoria's western region, is the stylish **Quamby Homestead** set in 1.6 hectares of English gardens in the township of Woolsthorpe. Built in 1886, this colonial weatherboard cottage can today cater for up to 14 guests in well-appointed rooms. Golf, tennis and cycling are all available to guests and there are some fine ocean walks to be enjoyed along the nearby headlands.

12 Midway between the towns of Hamilton and Horsham on the Henry Highway in the mid-west of Victoria is **Glenisla Homestead**. Built with rock quarried from the Grampians' sandstone ridges, this colonial homestead was constructed by pioneers as a mountain station in 1842.

It offers dramatic views of the Grampian mountains and every modern comfort — a necessity in this district, which is one of Victoria's coldest. Guests can take tours into the nearby Grampians National Park, and have the chance to explore the surrounding bushland and even to participate in the daily activities of a working sheep station.

Tasmania

13 Overlooking the city of Launceston and the Tamar estuary is the Georgian-style **Hillview House.** Built in 1840, it has undergone full restoration in keeping with the architectural style of its period, while bringing its facilities up to the most modern standards. Hillview House is just five minutes' stroll from the centre of Launceston and offers a restful alternative to the city's larger and more cosmopolitan hotels.

14 **Kilmarnock House,** in Launceston, was built in 1905 as a townhouse for a well-known Launceston merchant. This grand old home has recently been fully restored and renovated in keeping with its original Edwardian style. Now classified by the National Trust, the double-storey terrace has eight main rooms for visitors.

15 Port Arthur is one of Tasmania's most prized historic areas, rich in architectural achievement and representing a blend of colonial design and European craftsmanship. One of the best examples of this is **Cascades.** Established in 1841, Cascades operated initially as an outstation of the convict settlement about 15 kilometres from Port Arthur. At one point in its history, the home housed almost 400 prisoners who were banished to the station to work as timber cutters and crop and livestock farmers.

Situated on Norfolk Bay, at Koonya, Cascades stands among other farm buildings and convict cottages against a backdrop of orchards and fields. It is now on the register of the National Estate and has

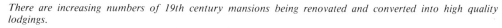

There are increasing numbers of 19th century mansions being renovated and converted into high quality lodgings.

received National Trust classification.

Self-contained accommodation for visitors is available in buildings which were originally erected by the convicts themselves. Faithfully restored, they remain true to the integrity of the original workmanship, executed in inhospitable conditions under the vigilant eyes of prison guards. Two particularly fine buildings in the complex are the old hospital and the officers' quarters, which won an Australian Heritage Award in 1986.

Horse riding is available nearby, and Cascades is also an ideal base for picturesque beach walks along the peninsula. The property has been privately owned since 1880, and the family that currently owns it took possession as long ago as 1915.

16 Perhaps the prettiest and certainly the most historic suburb of Hobart is Battery Point, with its narrow streets and charming cottages. **Cromwell Cottage,** right in the centre of Battery Point and over 100 years old, offers traditional hospitality and splendid harbour views.

With just four rooms of great character, Cromwell Cottage is within easy reach of the many Battery Point restaurants, antique shops and historic landmarks.

17 Richmond is a small township set in a fine rural environment just 20 minutes' drive from Hobart. One of the many notable historic buildings is **Laurel Cottage,** a convict-built home now listed by the National Trust.

Completed in 1830, and named in honour of the laurel tree which stood by its door, Laurel Cottage has been lovingly restored to accommodate its 20th-century guests in style. The cottage has just two guest bedrooms and visitors are wise to check availability well in advance.

South Australia

18 In 1912, **The Mansions** were Australia's first 'high-rise apartments'. Today, fully modernised, they are still a symbol of gracious living in Adelaide, itself the most gracious of Australia's cities.

The Mansions are conveniently located at the hub of Adelaide, with many attractions just a short stroll away — the Festival Centre, the casino, art gallery and museum. Theatres, department stores, airline offices and the central business district are also nearby. Some of Adelaide's finest restaurants are also in very close proximity, making dining out easy and exciting.

In modernising The Mansions, the most elegant of the old has been perfectly blended with the best of the new. Each apartment is bright and spacious and the most modern fittings assure guests of every comfort. A fully equipped kitchen is a feature of all rooms.

19 South Australia's most famous wine-growing district is the Barossa Valley, not far from Adelaide. In the heart of the valley is the township of Tanunda, with the fine old **Tanunda Hotel** in the centre of town.

The Tanunda Hotel was built from local stone in 1846 and though part of the building was destroyed in 1895, it was later rebuilt. Further additions were completed in 1945. A particularly attractive feature is the long veranda supported by wrought iron columns and iron and lacework. The hotel was renovated to fully modern standards in the 1970s.

20 Visitors travelling to or from Kangaroo Island off South Australia's coast should take the time to visit **Leonard's Mill** and the mill cottages in the pretty township of Second Valley not far from the Cape Jervis ferry wharf.

The mill was built in 1849 as a three-storey bluestone flour mill and has now been restored as a restaurant and function centre. The mill cottages can accommodate up to 23 guests in 20th-century luxury. Fine beaches are within easy reach, as are the nearby wineries of the Southern Vale and Hills districts.

21 One of the principal attractions of the small port of Robe in South Australia, on the easternmost cape of Guichen Bay, is the **Caledonian Inn.** In the late 1800s, the Caledonian gained a considerable reputation for providing the best in formal entertainment in the region. Among its clientele were travellers whose ships called in to the port of Robe, and men from the fishing fleets which worked the crayfish waters just offshore.

Now a pretty cottage swathed in ivy, it offers a number of fully self-contained units for its visitors.

22 **Martindale Hall,** a grand old mansion which combines old-world elegance with modern comfort, is situated in the tiny settlement of Mintaro in South Australia's mid-north.

The township, with a population of just 75, grew out of trade to and from the copper town of Burra. Martindale Hall was built in 1842. Much more recently, it achieved fame when it was used in the highly successful feature film, *Picnic at Hanging Rock.* It is now open for general viewing by the public between 1 pm and 4 pm daily, and overnight stays can be arranged by booking in advance.

A highlight of the building is the splendid master bedroom, decorated in wallpaper commissioned especially for Martindale Hall and designed and printed in England. The room and its adjoining bathrooms are beautifully maintained and furnished in period style. Martindale Hall is available for sophisticated dinner parties of between eight and 12 people, served by a maid and butlers in traditional style before an open log fire.

23 Just a stone's throw away from the Clare Valley wineries is the old **Stanley Grammar School,** now a fine guesthouse. Voted one of the three best guesthouses in South Australia by a gourmets' magazine, it was originally built as a school in 1860 and is now a registered State Heritage building.

Only four rooms are available to guests, a policy

which preserves the intimate atmosphere of the building.

The dining room, known as the Three Roses, is a former school classroom. Children's graffiti, which does not seem to have changed much over three or four generations, adorns the walls, and it is still possible to see pen nibs embedded in the Baltic pine ceiling.

Western Australia

24 The **Esplanade Plaza Hotel,** located opposite Fisherman's Harbour and the Fremantle Sailing Club, is a 140-room hotel faithfully restored to the grandeur of its architectural period.

The building was originally constructed in the 1860s for Simon Hubble, a shipping merchant and commission agent. In 1897 and 1903, extensions were added to turn the building into a hotel. Then, in 1984, the Esplanade Plaza saw major renovations take place which brought it to the standard of the luxurious hotel it is today.

There are two restaurants, three bars, a swimming pool and spa, health equipment, and function and conference facilities.

Colonial accommodation at its restored best is found at Cascades, a National Estate property overlooking Tasmania's Norfolk Bay

25 Built in 1887, Fremantle's **Norfolk Hotel** has been completely refurbished to accommodate 13 guests in its nine rooms. The hotel is ideally located — about 100 metres from both the yachting harbour and the city centre — with picturesque views. The building is made of limestone and a quaint terrace facade faces the main street.

Three of the rooms have en suite facilities, while the remainder share a communal bathroom. A separate television room and library are provided. There is a licensed basement restaurant open to the public, a cocktail bar and open fireplaces. The hotel is just a short drive from Perth.

26 **Darradup House** is a small beef cattle farm approximately 300 kilometres south-west of Perth on the Brockman Highway towards Augusta. Situated on the Blackwood River, the farm is ideal for those wishing to canoe, fish, swim, bushwalk or visit other towns in the south-west.

The 51-hectare farm is surrounded by heavily timbered undulating country where wildflowers are spectacular in spring and native birds proliferate year round.

Pioneer Cottage on the farm is a 19th-century colonial building with early 20th-century furnishings. It is self-contained, accommodating eight people, and guests need only provide their own meals and linen. The home is accessible by car, bus or rail (about three hours from Perth) and the proprietors are happy to meet guests at Busselton bus depot.

Northern Territory

27 The **Hotel Darwin** has 71 well-appointed rooms in a pleasant location bordering the esplanade of Darwin Harbour. There are excellent views of the water and surrounds.

The hotel boasts an outside eating area set in a lovely tropical garden with palm trees and fragrant frangipani flowers. There is also an à la carte dining room open to the public, a Green room, cocktail bar and the Kakadu Bar.

28 Larrimah was once the southern rail head of the North Australia Railway Line until it closed in 1976. Today, the town has a population of about 18, and is a stopover point for travellers along the Stuart Highway from Darwin to Alice Springs. The town is 179 kilometres south of Katherine.

The original Larrimah pub was built at Birdum, about two kilometres away, in 1924. In 1942, the Australian Army took over the premises and decided a year later to relocate the hotel in Larrimah. It then became the headquarters for the Army in the north. At the end of the war, concrete verandas were added and guest units were built to accommodate visitors. Over the years, **Larrimah Wayside Inn** has operated as a hospital and an army depot in an area characterised by subtropical terrain and numerous species of eucalypt trees.

Today, the inn provides modest yet comfortable accommodation in an environment which is very far indeed from the madding crowd.

Queensland

29 **Butchers Hill Homestead** is located 320 kilometres north of Cairns. Over 120 years old, it is surrounded by flat cleared countryside. Cattle, corn and peanuts are produced on the 243-hectare property.

The homestead itself was built by James Earl in 1874 of bush timber and it incorporates wide, open verandas characteristic of the period's colonial architecture.

Guests can go bushwalking, fishing, gold panning and horse riding. Experienced riders may also join in cattle mustering if they desire. At nearby Laura, Cooktown and Lakefield National Park, Aboriginal cave paintings date back tens of thousands of years.

Accommodation is in ten single cabins and seven double cabins, with shared facilities. Breakfast is served in a communal dining room.

30 The **Sovereign Hotel** in Cooktown, about three hours' drive from Cairns in north-eastern Queensland, is not strictly an historic building at all. The existing structure is in fact only a year or two old. Nevertheless, it is historically significant as a reproduction of a grand homestead built here in 1874. Its architecture was colonial in style, with the characteristic wide open verandas, open decking, and hardwood interiors.

Fire and cyclones damaged the original building so substantially that by the middle of this century, local residents dubbed the deteriorating home the 'Half Sovereign'. In 1986, however, the building was faithfully replicated and completely remodelled to incorporate a swimming pool, four separate bars, dining rooms, a mezzanine conference floor, a shopping complex, and a visitors' information centre.

It now provides accommodation of international standard and is a favoured destination in the Cooktown region.

31 The **Gunnawarra Homestead** is very much a monument to the tenacity and free spirit of Australia's early pioneers. Situated on the banks of the wild Hobart River, some 250 kilometres south-west of Cairns, the homestead stands alone in this remote region of Queensland. Built in 1878 of local cypress pine and ironbark shingles, the building blends perfectly with its surroundings. It remains modest in character and unadorned, but is as much an historic jewel of architecture as its more opulent contemporaries.

The homestead was one of the first to be classified by the National Trust in Queensland. It has a swimming pool and tennis court, and accommodates only six guests at a time in simple and comfortable bedrooms.

Evening meals at Gunnawarra are special affairs, upholding an old tradition of formal dining and home-style cooking, accompanied by fine wines. Day safaris from the homestead through some of the region's magnificent scenery are accompanied by picnic lunches.

Gunnawarra is accessible after a scenic drive across the Atherton Tablelands, or it is possible for the owners to pick up visitors by prior arrangement.

An interior setting at Glenisla Homestead, situated west of Victoria's Grampian Mountains

Historic Houses & Inns Contacts

Operators

New South Wales

1 The Russell Hotel

143A George Street
The Rocks
Sydney NSW 2000
Ph. (02) 241 2543

2 The Jackson Hotel

94 Victoria Street
Potts Point
Sydney NSW 2011
Ph. (02) 358 5144

3 The Little Company Guest House

2 Eastview Avenue
Leura NSW 2781
Ph. (047) 82 4023

4 Neath Hotel Guest House

Cessnock Road
Neath
Cessnock NSW 2321
Ph. (049) 30 4270

5 Carrington Restaurant and Motel

7 Malbon Street
Bungendore NSW 2621
Ph. (008) 04 6079 or 38 1044

Victoria

6 Gordon Place

24 Little Bourke Street
Melbourne VIC 3000
Ph. (03) 663 5355

7 O'Shannassy Guesthouse

Telephone Victour Properties for
bookings
Ph. (03) 619 9514

8 Wallaby Creek Guesthouse

Telephone Victour Properties for
bookings
Ph. (03) 619 9514

9 Queenscliff Hotel

16 Gellibrand Street
Queenscliff VIC 3225
Ph. (052) 52 1982

10 Ravenswood Homestead

Ravenswood
via Harcourt VIC 3453
Ph. (054) 35 3284

11 Quamby Homestead

Woolsthorpe VIC 3279
Ph. (055) 69 2395

12 Glenisla Homestead

via Cavendish VIC 3408
Ph. (053) 80 1532

Tasmania

13 Hillview House

193 George Street
Launceston TAS 7250
Ph. (003) 31 7388

14 Kilmarnock House

66 Elphin Road
Launceston TAS 7250
Ph. (003) 34 1514 or 44 2175

15 'Cascades'

RMB 1355 Koonya
Tasman Peninsula TAS 7187
Ph. (002) 50 3121

16 Cromwell Cottage

6 Cromwell Street
Battery Point
Hobart TAS 7000
Ph. (002) 23 6734

17 Laurel Cottage

9 Wellington Street
Richmond TAS 7025
Ph. (002) 62 2357

South Australia

18 The Mansions

21 Pulteney Street
Adelaide SA 5000
Ph. (08) 232 0033

19 Tanunda Hotel

51 Murray Street
Tanunda SA 5352
Ph. (085) 63 2030

20 Leonard's Mill

Cape Jervis Road
Second Valley SA 5204
Ph. (085) 98 4184

21 Caledonian Inn

Victoria Street
Robe SA 5276
Ph. (087) 68 2029

22 Martindale Hall

Manoora Road
Mintaro SA 5414
Ph. (088) 4 3901

23 Old Stanley Grammar School

Commercial Road
Watervale SA 5452
Ph. (088) 43 0013

Western Australia

24 The Esplanade Plaza Hotel

Marine Terrace
Fremantle WA 6160
Ph. (09) 430 4000

25 Norfolk Hotel

47 South Terrace
Fremantle WA 6160
Ph. (09) 335 5405

26 Darradup House

PO Box 80
Nannup WA 6275
Ph. (097) 56 1186

Northern Territory

27 Hotel Darwin

Herbert Street
Darwin NT 5700
Ph. (089) 81 9211

28 Larrimah Wayside Inn

Larrimah NT 5780
Ph. (089) 75 9931

Queensland

29 Butchers Hill Homestead

PMB Lakeland Downs
via Cairns QLD 4870
Ph. (070) 60 2155

30 Sovereign Hotel

Charlotte Street
PO Box 100
Cooktown QLD 4871
Ph. (070) 69 5400

31 Gunnawarra Homestead

PO Box 7
Mount Garnet QLD 4872
Ph. (070) 97 9005

Islands

The visitor to Australia's islands will discover that the picture-postcards don't in fact exaggerate. The seas *are* turquoise and the sands *are* as white as they appear to be. In fact, spectacular colour images are just the beginning. Australia's island havens are destinations where adventure, beauty, excitement and solitude can be found in surroundings that come close to paradise.

Australia has the longest coastline of any nation on earth, and it is ringed by islands of coral, volcanic rock and sand. One of them is even a state. Not all of these islands are palm-fringed and tropical, of course. Many to the south are barren, windswept and bleak, the haunt of seabirds, seals, and not much else. Though these have their attractions, too.

Other islands, now quaint and rural backwaters, hide violent and brutal histories. Norfolk Island, for example, was settled by the descendants of the *Bounty* mutineers. Norfolk was also a final desolate outpost for the more unmanageable convicts from Botany Bay.

Norfolk Island has today transmuted this sense of exile into a healthy independence, and holds semi-autonomous status granted by Queen Victoria. The most tangible sign of this is that it is the only Australian island to demand a passport of visitors from the mainland — not even New Zealand requires Australians to have a passport on entering.

Both Norfolk and Lord Howe Island, 700 kilometres northeast of Sydney, are havens for seabirds and vacationers alike, and both have taken steps to protect the former from the latter.

Birdlife of a different kind is also the attraction on tiny Phillip Island, just 50 kilometres south of Melbourne and sandwiched between Port Phillip Bay and Waratah Bay. Famous for its fairy penguin colony, it attracts many visitors keen to watch the remarkable parade of adult birds making their evening pilgrimage to feed their young, safely hidden on shore.

The very fact that islands are islands has enabled the unique wildlife on many on them to be preserved. Separated from their kin — and sometimes from later-introduced predators — by the action of continental drift and the rise and fall of oceans, species are left to adapt in isolation.

A good example is the Rottnest Island quokka, a wallaby so tiny that when early explorers saw it they mistook it for a large rat (hence the name of the island). Rottnest, which lies just 40 kilometres west of Perth, also has other weird and wonderful creatures, some of them human. People have rediscovered the warmer Australian islands, such as Rottnest. The combination of sun, sand and sea which most of them

The old convict settlement of Kingston Town, Norfolk Island

offer is proving irresistible. And nowhere is this more so than on the islands off the north-east coast of Australia's sunshine state of Queensland.

This is the true mecca for seekers of island paradise holidays. Each year, hundreds of thousands of tourists make their pilgrimage to island destinations such as Hamilton, Dunk, Brampton, Lizard, Heron, Fraser, Lindeman and Hayman's Island and the Whitsunday group.

And they are the real thing. Tropical. Beautiful. Palm-fringed. And with the finest and largest coral reef anywhere in the world on their very doorstep: in fact, the Great Barrier Reef *is* their doorstep.

Recent years have seen many of these islands developed into luxury resorts — pleasure palaces offering every conceivable form of activity for every budget, temperament, age and level of fitness.

and valleys — scenery that seems suited to a larger area. Norfolk Island is indeed tiny. It measures only eight by five kilometres, with a high point of just over 305 metres. The island's many beaches are reef-sheltered and the clear waters here are teeming with fish. Many varieties of seabird nest on the island and Norfolk is home to some 50 unique plant species. Forests abound, including stands of the famous Norfolk Island pine. The island has dedicated one-fifth of its area to public reserves and parkland.

Norfolk offers many other attractions to the visitor: horse riding, bushwalking, golf and tennis, coral reef diving, surfing and sailboarding are all popular activities. There is also a good selection of restaurants. The 160 kilometres of road and a good hire car service make exploring easy. Bicycles are also available for hire. The Norfolk government has made a

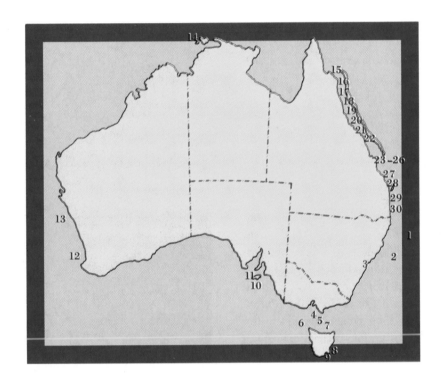

Locations

Norfolk Island

1 Despite its harsh and brutal beginnings, **Norfolk Island** is today a popular holiday destination. The island was discovered by Captain Cook in 1774 and established as Australia's first penal settlement in 1788. Convicts were sent here sporadically until 1855 when the jail was closed and the last of the prisoners were transported to Tasmania.

Norfolk Island is 1,600 kilometres north-east of Sydney and is reached after a two and a half hour flight. But it is a world away. Its volcanic origins have given it an undulating landscape of rolling green hills

wise decision to limit tourist numbers in order to preserve the natural and peaceful environment.

Accommodation ranges from a maximum three and a half 'pine trees' grading in hotels and apart-ments, to more simple guesthouse accommodation.

New South Wales

2 **Lord Howe Island** rises out of the Pacific Ocean 700 kilometres off the New South Wales coast. Ancient forest-clad volcanic peaks and a startlingly turquoise-blue lagoon provide a stunning finale to the one and a quarter hour flight from Sydney.

Lord Howe boasts the southernmost coral reef in the world and a subtropical climate. It would be easy to imagine crowded beaches and noisy resorts. However, while tourism is the major industry for the islanders, they have been spared this level of commercialisation. Lord Howe is protected, unspoilt and undeveloped, and it has deliberately restricted its tourist intake to preserve the delicate balance of its natural beauty.

Discovered in 1788 and first settled around 1834, the island's population still numbers only 300, many of whom are descendants of the original settlers. Life here is very different — there is no television, few street lights, the bicycle is the main form of transport, and the atmosphere is peaceful.

Lord Howe offers superb opportunities for water sports along its fine beaches surrounding the lagoon. Diving, fishing, sailboarding and boating are popular pastimes for the visitor. Landlubbers are also well catered for: there are numerous walking tracks for bushwalking, and nature lovers will find almost 120 species of birds and a unique vegetation, including the indigenous kentia palm. The island's small size (one by 11 kilometres) makes getting around very easy — on foot or by bicycle.

Island accommodation varies from the long-established Pinetrees Lodge and others like it, to self-catering apartments. All buildings on the island are designed to blend in with the environment and are generally of single-storey construction. Camping is not permitted on the island.

3 The NSW National Parks and Wildlife Service can provide three unusual venues for group outings within the Sydney Harbour National Park. **Clark, Shark and Rodd Islands** are available for hire to people interested in a secluded outing. Clark Island accommodates a maximum of 15 people, while Shark and Rodd Islands are suitable for up to 100 people.

Visitors must provide their own transport to the island and agree to abide by certain restrictions which prohibit dogs and other pets.

Victoria

4 In the centre of Westernport Bay, south-east of Melbourne, lies unspoiled **French Island**, a rugged bushland haven. Lagoons, swamps and sea cliffs are more in evidence than shops, facilities and roads, and the tiny population of 60 who have made this state park their home are more than content to live away from Melbourne's bustling metropolis.

This former prison settlement, which was mistaken for a promontory by George Bass in 1798, was finally discovered to be an island in 1802, and was first settled in 1854.

There is no shortage of recreational opportunities on the island for the visitor with a love for the outdoors who enjoys a simple lifestyle. Walking, horse riding, fishing, swimming and just relaxing are the most popular pastimes.

Guests wishing to visit the island and to use the camping facilities should consult with the Park Ranger for bookings.

5 **Phillip Island** is the better-known neighbour of French Island and is located at the southern edge of Westernport Bay. Its island status is sometimes contested because it is linked with the mainland at San Remo by a modern bridge, which forms one of the main access routes. Light aircraft from Melbourne or ferries from Stony Point are the only other means of transport to the island.

Phillip Island's strongest attraction is its plethora of diverse wildlife and vegetation. The landscape in some parts is totally untouched, and rugged bush and heathland and stands of eucalypt dominate. This accounts for the presence of a large koala population.

Surf beats against the rocky coast of Lord Howe Island

A large colony of seals occupies the rocky outcrops during the breeding season. Perhaps the most famous attraction is the nightly fairy penguin parade. These small penguins are the only species to breed on Australia's shores, and Phillip Island provides a large sanctuary for them.

Other activities such as surfing, fishing, walking, cycling, boating, golf and tennis are all popular. Motels and caravan parks are also available.

Tasmania

Treacherous and gale-swept Bass Strait lies in the notorious 'Roaring Forties' region between Tasmania and mainland Australia. This stretch of sea and its islands have a turbulent and adventurous past: shipwrecks, lawless sealers and the terrible fate of Tasmania's Aborigines. King and Flinders Islands are both located here.

6 **King Island**, slightly smaller than Flinders Island, is at the western end of Bass Strait, south of Melbourne. Less developed than Flinders, it offers 145 kilometres of unspoiled beaches, sand dunes and rocky cliff scenery. The diving here is excellent, and has the added attraction of more than 50 shipwrecks for experienced divers to explore. Fishermen can choose between casting for trout, or beach and rock fishing, and shooting is popular in the duck (March/April) and pheasant (June) seasons. Bushwalking, horse riding and beachcombing are added attractions.

King Island's European origins are rooted in the

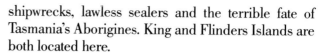

Dunk Island is one of many tropical resort islands off the Queensland coast

HEIDI ECKER

sealing trade of the early 1800s, and the population was later boosted when the post-war soldier resettlement scheme rapidly increased the numbers of people coming to settle on the island. Today, the island supports 2,500 people, who earn their livelihood from agriculture, fishing, mining of scheelite, and kelp harvesting.

Currie, the main town, has a modern hotel and several self-catering units. Similar units are also available on other parts of the island. Car rental can be arranged for visitors who wish to explore the island in comfort.

7 **Flinders Island** and the rest of the Furneaux Group lie at the eastern end of Bass Strait, beyond the north-eastern tip of Tasmania. Some 65 by 28 kilometres in size, Flinders and the nearby islands were discovered in 1773 by Captain Tobias Furneaux, a member of Captain Cook's party. In the early 1800s, the first settlement was made by sealers. From 1833 to 1847, a settlement at Wybalenna was created to house the already dwindling Aboriginal population who had been rounded up throughout Tasmania and trans-

ALLAN MOULT

ported here. Most eventually died on Flinders Island of sickness and despair.

Today, the 1,000 or so inhabitants are engaged mainly in farming, fishing, tourism and mutton-birding. The muttonbird, known also as the short-tailed shearwater, migrates to this region every September, and is hunted for its oil and food value. The island scenery is rugged and dramatic, and contains Mt Strzelecki National Park. Its slopes, fern gullies and granite peaks offer excellent bushwalking terrain and superb views of the Strait and islands. Some fine fishing can be found here, and boating, horse riding, diving, tennis, golf and birdwatching are all popular with visitors. The museums and the restored Wybalenna site are also of interest.

Camping is popular among visitors to the island, but establishments such as the Furneaux Tavern, Bluff House and several holiday cottages and host farms provide a range of alternatives.

Maria and Bruny Islands jut from the waters off the east coast of Tasmania. Both were first sighted by Abel Tasman in 1642.

8   **Maria Island**, 88 kilometres north-east of Hobart and some 12 kilometres off the coast, is presently uninhabited and was proclaimed a national park in 1972. It was set aside mainly for the breeding of wildlife and abounds with kangaroos, emus and Cape Barren geese which were introduced in the late 1960s and early 1970s. It was a penal colony from 1825 to 1852, and several original buildings still stand, adding historical interest to the island. Within its 260 square kilometres, this tranquil island presents a variety of vegetation and animal life.

For the visitor, this is very much a 'no frills' island. There are no shops or motor transport, and only a choice of camping or dormitory-style accommodation in the old Penitentiary at Darlington, built in 1830. However, the rewards for the more adventurous traveller make a stay here worthwhile — excellent fishing, walking, swimming, diving and rockclimbing are all possible on Maria, and a special bonus is the sense of peace and isolation that only an uninhabited island can provide.

9   **Bruny Island** is 35 kilometres south of Hobart and similar to Maria in that its two halves are joined by a narrow isthmus. Bruny, however, is in-habited by approximately 300 residents whose main occupation is mixed farming. Bruny has much evidence of a long period of Aboriginal settlement, which was rudely disturbed by European whalers and sealers in the early 1800s. Queen Truganinni, the last full-blooded Tasmanian Aborigine, who died in 1876, was born here.

Bruny contains several reserves under the auspices of the National Parks and Wildlife Service. Muttonbirds and penguins are common here, and vegetation varies from eucalypt forests and woodland to rainforest and heath with a variety of wildflowers.

Popular activities on Bruny are walking, surfing, fishing and diving, or just lazing around on the beaches.

Unlike Maria, Bruny offers a slightly more sophisticated holiday. The Whalers Inn Holiday Village and the House Sofia guesthouse provide an alternative to camping, as does the Alonnah Hotel, the most southerly in Australia.

Access to Bruny is by ferry from Kettering, 35 kilometres south of Hobart. Visitors to Maria Island have a choice of charter flights from Hobart or a ferry from Louisville, one and a half hours' drive from Hobart.

South Australia

10   Australia's third largest island — **Kangaroo Island** — lies 80 kilometres from Adelaide and guards the entrance to Gulf St Vincent. It is indeed large: 145 kilometres in length and 50 kilometres wide, with 450 kilometres of beautiful coastline that varies from rugged cliffs with pounding surf to sandy beaches and dunes.

Captain Matthew Flinders made the fortunate discovery of Kangaroo Island in 1802 during his voyage around Australia, and named it after the large number of kangaroos found there. The French explorer Nicholas Baudin visited the island in the same year and left a lasting reminder of his visit in the many French place names. D'Estrees Bay and Cape Gantheaume are two such examples. Early visitors included sealers and whalers and escaped convicts from South Australia. Official settlement did not commence until 1836 and was South Australia's first attempt at establishing a colony.

The major attraction of Kangaroo Island is the Flinders Chase National Park at its western end. Spectacular coastal scenery, a wide variety of flora and fauna (443 species of native plants, many birds, kangaroos, echidnas, brush-tailed possums and sea lions), and its isolated and undisturbed ecology make this one of South Australia's most important parks.

Visitors to the island find much to occupy their time. Bushwalking, fishing and boating opportunities abound, while diving, natural history study, horse or camel riding and four-wheel driving can all be arranged.

The choice of accommodation on Kangaroo Island is extensive. Camping, farm-stays, self-contained flats and cabins, and hotels such as the Sorrento Resort, Ellsons Motel, and the Ozone are available.

11   How often do dreamers contemplate what it would be like to own their own island, or at least to have sole access to one? This romantic fantasy can become a reality on **Boston Island**, just off the coast of South Australia, where it is possible to gain exclusive access by hiring the entire island.

Boston is tiny — just seven by two kilometres in size — and lies five kilometres off Port Lincoln, at the entrance to Spencer Gulf, west of Adelaide. The island has been declared a wildlife sanctuary and possesses extensive bird and animal life, including fairy penguins and wallabies; merino sheep also graze here.

Secluded sandy beaches and clear waters offer excellent swimming and snorkelling opportunities and a dinghy is available for fishing or just pottering around on the water. Perhaps the best that Boston offers, however, is total peace and relaxation.

Accommodation for up to 12 people is provided in a comfortable five-bedroom home. Guests bring their own food (this can also be pre-arranged with the owners) and linen, and create their own daily routine. There are no timetables on Boston Island.

Western Australia

12 Just 19 kilometres offshore from Perth is one of Western Australia's most popular holiday destinations, **Rottnest Island**. In the last century, however, the island had a much less savoury reputation. It was a penal settlement, which did little to make it popular either with those who lived there or with would-be travellers. These days the image of Rottnest Island is a far cry from prison, pestilence and rats. The island is a mecca for water sports, including swimming, diving, fishing and sailboarding.

Private vehicles are not permitted on the island, but bicycling offers an alternative which also gives the visitor the best views of Rottnest. The Rottnest Wreck trail has been set up especially for cyclists, and it traverses the whole island.

Other sporting facilities, including golf and tennis, are popular. For the historian, Rottnest has an interesting museum and some of the state's oldest buildings are to be found on the island. Educational tours of Rottnest Island, which is classified as a public reserve and wildlife sanctuary, are conducted by the Environmental Education Office.

In addition to the Rottnest Lodge Resort and the Rottnest Hotel, accommodation is plentiful in the form of flats, cottages and camping grounds.

13 The **Houtman Abrolhos Group** stretches in an 80-kilometre chain of reefs and low-lying islands

Cape de Couedic lighthouse, Kangaroo Island, South Australia

TREVERN DAWES

some 60 kilometres off the Western Australian coast beyond Geraldton. Discovered in 1619 by a Dutch sea captain, Frederik Houtman, these islands became the graveyard for many ships which sailed these uncharted seas. The most famous wreck is the *Batavia*, which fell foul of the reefs in 1629.

Today, the islands are a reserve administered by the Ministry for Fisheries and Fauna, and an important breeding ground for seabirds. The clear waters and colourful coral reefs provide an excellent environment for such recreational pursuits as fishing, diving and swimming. Camping is not currently permitted and the only access is by boat from Geraldton.

Tour operators in the district offer a range of holiday excursions, most of which have three or five-day itineraries planned. The luxurious cruiser MV *Western Success* gives passengers the chance to relax during pleasurable expeditions in and around the coastal fringes of the island chain.

Northern Territory

14 **Bathurst and Melville Islands** lie off the far northern coast of Australia, approximately 80 kilometres from Darwin.

The Aboriginal Tiwi people have lived here relatively undisturbed for thousands of years, having little contact with the mainland Australian tribes. The name 'Tiwi' means 'We, the people', suggesting that until the arrival of Europeans in the 18th century, this isolated group perceived themselves to be the only inhabitants of the world. Wood carvings, pottery and silk-screen printed fabrics reflect the Tiwi culture and the talents of the tribe's craftspeople.

Nguiu, on Bathurst Island, began life as a Catholic church mission in 1911 and is now the largest settlement, home to around 1,200 people.

The Tiwi are a friendly and outgoing people who welcome visitors into their isolated community, but individual travellers are not permitted to visit the islands unless accompanied by guides. This privilege has only been possible since 1980 when Tiwi Tours were successful in gaining permission from the Tiwi elders to bring visitors onto the islands and give them the opportunity to observe this remarkable community.

Anyone taking one of these tours must agree to abide by certain regulations to preserve the privacy of the Tiwi people, and this includes being presentably attired and refraining from taking any photographs of unwilling subjects. Tiwi Tours employ two Aboriginal women as guides, and they provide a wealth of information about the islands. Other tours include excursions to an Aboriginal burial site, and itineraries can be arranged for anthropologists and other special-interest groups.

Queensland

15 An island renowned for its game fishing is **Lizard Island**, located 27 kilometres from the mainland and 241 kilometres north of Cairns. It is an unspoiled national park covering 1,000 hectares, with 24 beaches and encircling reefs that are close to both the inner and outer Barrier Reef.

From August to December each year, game fishermen arrive at Lizard Island to seek out the biggest prize in big-game fishing — the black marlin. Fully equipped gamefishing boats are available for charter, and for those fishing from the shore there are light rods and reels for hire. With its giant clam gardens, Lizard is also a scuba diver's paradise, and diving packages are available for certified divers, plus introductory lessons for beginners.

The best way to discover Australia's islands is from the deck of a yacht

Snorkelling only requires the bare minimum

The resort, which recently took out the 'Best Resort' award at the National Tourism Awards, is nestled between coconut palms at Anchor Bay. It offers 30 private suites and two deluxe suites, and the Lizard Island Lodge contains a shop, lounge and bar, plus a dining room overlooking Prince Charles Island.

16 **Green Island** is a coral cay on the Great Barrier Reef, just 27 kilometres north-east of Cairns, covering an area of 13 hectares. It is reserved as a marine national park.

The Green Island Reef Resort has 27 units, in twin, double and family size. All have private facilities and a private patio. These can accommodate up to 90 guests. The resort also has a restaurant, bar and shop in the main building.

Attractions on the island include the Marineland Melanesia, with its display of colourful marinelife, and the Green Island Underwater Observatory. This is the first observatory of its kind in the world and is the only one on the Great Barrier Reef. From its 22 observation windows, visitors can see coral polyps, giant clams (the largest shellfish in the world) and giant sea anemones.

Snorkelling and scuba diving are popular pastimes on the island, as are fishing and walking.

17 **Fitzroy Island**, situated about 45 minutes off Cairns in far north Queensland, offers coral and sand beaches, clear waters, palm trees and lush rainforest vegetation. Access is by a large high-speed catamaran — the *Fitzroy Flyer* — which leaves from the Marlin Wharf at Cairns.

Accommodation on the island is reasonably modest, tending to entice the adventurous backpacker rather than those looking for luxurious modern conveniences. It has recently undergone a $5-million development, aimed at the budget-priced holiday-maker.

More luxurious accommodation facilities are available at the Villa units at Welcome Bay. These are two-bedroom units which offer shaded patios and private amenities. The long sweep of beach here has good views of the mainland and is made up of configurations of coral. There is also a well-maintained camping ground on the island.

Covering almost 324 hectares, the island features dense rainforest, tall eucalyptus stands, streams and waterfalls, and is almost surrounded by coral reefs. There are several bush trails to the island's lighthouse and beaches, and it is an ideal location for snorkelling, diving, fishing and swimming.

Lady Musgrave Island at the southern end of the reef is a true coral cay

RAY PEEK

18 The writer E.J. Banfield believed that **Dunk Island** was a true tropical paradise. He lived here for 28 years and the island inspired his classic account of island life, *Confessions of a Beachcomber*, published in 1908.

Dunk lies close to the mainland, 160 kilometres north of Townsville and 130 kilometres south of Cairns. A launch ride from Clump Point, near Tully, takes 45 minutes, and flights from Townsville and Cairns take 45 and 30 minutes respectively. Dunk was named by Captain Cook in 1770, and apart from the presence of a modern resort, the island has not changed much since those days.

A national park takes up much of the six by two-kilometre island, and within this wilderness area many sea and land birds and brilliantly coloured butterflies may be seen. Torres Strait pigeons, frigate birds and terns are regular visitors. Graded walking tracks provide excellent trails for bushwalkers, and for those who prefer to avoid resorts, camping is permitted on Dunk — with permission from the National Parks Service, and only in designated areas.

Dunk Island's resort has been tastefully created. Fifty units and cabanas have been designed to blend in with the tropical scene beneath beachfront palm trees. A maximum of 320 guests can stay at the resort at any one time.

19 Set in the tropical waters of north Queensland is a tiny island, 1.5 kilometres long and less than a kilometre wide. **Bedarra Island** is covered by rainforests and surrounded by white sandy beaches.

Bedarra Bay Resort accommodates just 32 people in 16 villas, all isolated from one another and all with sea views. The villas are a combination of two-level and split-level buildings and blend in with the natural surroundings. Bedarra Bay employs a gourmet chef to supervise the preparation of food which is served in the restaurant in the island's central complex. Other facilities include a spa, pool and tennis courts. Catamaran sailing, snorkelling and fishing are also popular activities.

20 **Hinchinbrook** is the world's largest island national park, located off the coast from Cardwell, 165 kilometres north of Townsville. Covering almost 37,500 hectares, it features thick vegetation, waterfalls, mountain country and long stretches of beach.

Wildlife is plentiful and includes wallabies, echidnas, goannas and 250 species of birds.

The owners of the resort at Hinchinbrook have gone to great pains to avoid commercialisation of the island, preferring to entice visitors with its seclusion and beauty. There are no discos, no organised entertainment, no impressive golf courses, but there is a wide variety of outdoor activities to be enjoyed. Fishing, snorkelling, scuba diving, sailing, windsurfing and bushwalking are all popular.

21 **Orpheus Island** has a limit of just 50 guests at any one time, making it one of the most exclusive Queensland resorts. It is a long, narrow island off the Queensland coast east of Ingham. The resort, on the south-western side of the island, is highly acclaimed for the natural beauty of its tropical landscape. Fully appointed guest units are available, as well as a restaurant, bar, reception area, boutique, swimming pool and spa.

The island itself is fringed with coral reefs, and has more than 1,360 hectares of national park, with a rainforest area on the western side of Iris Point.

Bush camping is allowed, though a permit must be obtained in advance at the Ingham Office of the Queensland National Parks and Wildlife Service.

Access is by Air Whitsunday's seaplane from Townsville, or via chartered helicopter or launch.

22 Just eight kilometres across Cleveland Bay from Townsville is Australia's largest tropical island, **Magnetic Island**. This granite-based island has a coastline of 40 kilometres. Served by a regular ferry service from Townsville, it is a popular spot with tourists. Two-thirds of the island is national park, while the remaining third includes a bustling township with a permanent population of around 2,300.

Holiday accommodation is provided at Picnic Bay, Nelly Bay, Arcadia, Alma Bay, Radical Bay and Horseshoe Bay, in the form of hotels, motels, guesthouses, self-catering units and a camping reserve.

Latitude 19 Resort lies below the spectacular forests of the national park, and nearby is a nine-hole golf course and a bowling club, as well as basketball, netball and horse riding facilities. Other activities available at the resort include tennis, yachting, fishing, snorkelling, coral viewing, paraflying and skiing.

23 **Hayman Island** covers 400 hectares of tropical palm-fringed beaches, headlands and luxuriant vegetation, surrounded by coral reefs.

Closed for 18 months to undergo redevelopment, Hayman re-opened in April 1986. The old resort has been demolished, and replaced by a spectacular new $200-million international hotel complex.

Hayman is 33 kilometres off the Queensland coast and their $2-million launch, the *Sun Goddess*, ferries guests to the island from Shute Harbour.

The deluxe hotel is contained within 13 hectares of grounds, fronting two white sand beaches on the southern side. The beaches are cleaned by hand every morning for the convenience of hotel guests. Accommodation is in the form of suites, rooms and 11 penthouses, all with private balconies and patios, and most with views of the beach or the landscaped gardens. There are four international restaurants, and a wide variety of bars. The Entertainment Centre features live dance music, weekend caberet performances, regular pool and dining entertainment, and special guest appearances by leading Australian and international artists.

The resort is set around a giant saltwater swimming lagoon with walkways, island bar and inner freshwater pool. For divers, there is a fully equipped dive shop, dive boat and training pool.

It also offers sailing, water-skiing, parasailing, big-game and sportfishing facilities, coral viewing, Great Barrier Reef cruises with snorkelling and diving, helicopter sightseeing and other cruises. There are assorted shops at the resort. It is generally regarded as being the best resort in Australia.

24 **Hamilton Island** is the only island in the Whitsunday group that can be reached by non-stop commercial jet — about two hours from Sydney and about one and a half hours from both Cairns and Brisbane. It is just 12 kilometres from the coast, and more than 500 hectares in area, representing one of the most highly developed resort islands in Queensland. Hamilton Island has also received a National Tourism award as Australia's foremost island resort.

The island is divided into two distinct areas, the resort and the harbour. The Hamilton Island Resort, fronted by Catseye Beach, houses the accommodation facilities. The main resort complex contains reception, activities, and travel desks, and a 200-seat dining room, a bar and a coffee shop. Accommodation ranges from individual Polynesian-style huts to hotel accommodation at Allamanda Lodge and Bougainvillea Lodge. There are self-contained suites at the Whitsunday Towers and luxury two and three-bedroom apartments available. The resort also has two excellent beachfront restaurants, a sports complex, convention rooms and a shopping terrace. At Catseye Beach, guests can hire catamarans, sailboards, surf skis, canoes, or go water-skiing, parasailing, or snorkelling along the reef.

On the island is Mountain Top Fauna Park, with kangaroos, emus, wallabies and deer, and bush-walkers can climb Passage Peak on the eastern side.

Diving courses can be undertaken at Hamilton, through H2O Sportz, the island's own dive centre. Sea access to Hamilton is by launch from Shute Harbour.

25 **Lindeman Island** is the largest of the resort islands in the Whitsunday Passage, with 800 hectares of national park and seven secluded beaches. It is located 70 kilometres north of Mackay.

Lindeman Island Resort is on the southern tip of the island, overlooking Royal Seaforth Island. Accommodation units are located near the pool, the beach or in elevated blocks. At Adventure Valley, there is a holiday camp for children.

The resort has a golf course, and activities include day or night tennis, fishing, sailboarding, catamaran sailing, cricket, snorkelling, scuba diving and a variety of night-time entertainment. There are two restaurants, an outdoor coffee shop and three bars at the resort, and a disco on a private beach.

On the coast, there are beautiful sights wherever you look

MICHAEL LEGGE

Access to Lindeman is via boat from Shute Harbour or light plane from Proserpine Airport.

26 **Brampton Island**, another island national park, lies in the Cumberland Group at the southern end of the Whitsunday Passage. This group was named by Captain Cook after the Cumberland Lake District of northern England. Some 380 kilometres south of Townsville, and 32 kilometres north of Mackay, this unspoiled island of volcanic origin supports forests of pine and eucalypt on its granite hills.

White sandy beaches are a particular feature of Brampton and many secluded coves can be discovered on a walk around the island's 12 square kilometres. The reef is a 45-minute boat ride away, but the waters around the island itself are full of tropical fish and brilliant coral. Walking trails through the unspoilt bush lead to hilltops and lookouts that provide views of the Whitsunday Islands and Passage.

Camping is not permitted on Brampton Island. Major upgrading has taken place since 1985 and the improvements have included the construction of 32 new units that are designed for tropical conditions. Brampton caters for a maximum of 300 guests at any one time. Activities provided by the resort include all watersports, plus fishing trips and cruises to the Barrier Reef. Archery, golf and tennis are other options for the visitor.

27 One of the lesser-known privately owned islands in Queensland is **Pumpkin Island** in the Keppel group. It is just 20 minutes by boat from Yeppoon. Its owners have long experience as island hosts, having owned nearby Orpheus Island for over 20 years.

Pumpkin Island has four self-contained cabins, each housing five people, and no phones, TV or shops. The owners drop in from Yeppoon on the weekend to make sure that guests are enjoying themselves, but leave them to their own devices in peace and solitude during the week.

Popular activities include snorkelling, fishing, swimming, coral viewing and sailing. The less energetic will enjoy strolling along its fine beaches.

28 **Heron Island** is a coral cay pushed up by the Great Barrier Reef. It can be reached by either boat or helicopter from Gladstone. It is relatively small, covering 17 hectares, and is surrounded by 24 square kilometres of coral reef, making it one of the world's best diving locations. The island is renowned for its green turtle nesting sites (October to February is the breeding season).

Visitors have a choice between self-contained units, called the Reef Suites, the more upmarket Heron Suites, or lodge accommodation. There is also VIP accommodation in the Beach House, popular with honeymooners. Packages include accommodation, all meals and optional transport.

Resort facilities include a swimming pool, restaurant, shop, bank and tennis court.

29 **Lady Elliot Island** is the most southerly coral cay on the Great Barrier Reef, approximately 320 kilometres north of Brisbane. It is a popular spot for divers, and there are professional diving instructors on the island who offer tuition through to certificate level.

Accommodation is available either in beach-side cabins or in safari tents. There is a dining room and bar for visitors. Line fishing trips are available for anglers, using the resort's motor craft with lines and baits supplied. Within reach of the island are some of the most magnificent reefs in the region, and an excursion in the island's glass-bottomed boat is a highlight of any visitor's stay. The island is also famous for its turtles, nesting sea birds and plentiful marine life.

Hamilton Island is one of the most highly developed island resorts in Australia

30 All visitors to **Fraser Island**, the largest sand island in the world, are required to have permits, obtainable from the National Parks and Wildlife Service. The island comprises 163,000 hectares of beaches, freshwater lakes and streams, sand dunes, open forests, mangroves and rainforests. It has virtually no roads usable by conventional cars, so access is best obtained by four-wheel-drive vehicles.

Camping is popular on Fraser Island, or accommodation is available at various beach houses, units and flats, or at one of the resorts.

Orchid Beach Resort is on the north-eastern tip of the island and consists of individual cabin-style accommodation, complete with swimming pool, netball court and licensed restaurant. It also offers tours of the island's main attractions.

The Great Sandy National Park covers the northern tip of the island and has two developed campsites.

Wildlife on Fraser Island includes dingoes, possums, squirrel gliders, echidnas, bandicoot, wild horses and an amazing range of birdlife.

Islands Contacts

Locations

1 Norfolk Island

Accommodation and Travel

East West Airlines
54 Carrington Street
Sydney NSW 2000
Ph. (02) 29 6676

230 Collins Streets
Melbourne VIC 3000
Ph. (03) 653 3911

PETER CAINE

Offices also in Brisbane, Canberra, Perth and other cities.

Norfolk Island Airlines
National Australia Building
Cnr Adelaide & Creek Streets
Brisbane QLD 4000
Ph. (008) 77 7011

Norfolk Island Government Tourist
  Bureau
64 Castlereagh Street
Sydney NSW 2000
Ph. (02) 235 3937

247 Collins Street
Melbourne VIC 3000
Ph. (03) 654 1393

Pacific Island Travel Centre
20 Loftus Street
Sydney NSW 2000
Ph. (02) 27 2867

Pacific Unlimited Holidays
50 York Street
Sydney NSW 2000
Ph. (02) 290 2266

New South Wales

2 Lord Howe Island

Accommodation and Travel

Norfolk Island Airlines
See (1) above for details

Pacific Island Travel Centre
See (1) above for details

Pacific Unlimited Holidays
See (1) above for details

Pinetrees Lodge
Lord Howe Island NSW 2898
Ph. (065) 63 2177

Travel Centre of New South Wales
16 Spring Street
Sydney NSW 2000
Ph. (02) 231 4444

3 Clark, Shark & Rodd Islands

General Information

National Parks and Wildlife Service
ADC Building
189-193 Kent Street
Sydney NSW 2000
Ph. (02) 237 6500

Victoria

4 French Island

Accommodation and Travel

French Island Discovery Tours
Avalon, Tankerton
French Island VIC 3921
Ph. (059) 80 1210

French Island Tourist Services
6 Governors Road
Crib Point VIC 3919
Ph. (059) 83 9633

5 Phillip Island

Accommodation and Travel

Phillip Island Information Centre
RMB 1305
Newhaven VIC 3925
Ph. (059) 56 7447

Victour
230 Collins Street
Melbourne VIC 3000
Ph. (03) 619 9444

Tasmania

6 King Island

Accommodation and Travel

Airlines of Tasmania
22 Edward Street
Currie
King Island TAS 7256
Ph. (004) 62 1365

Kendell Airlines
431 Little Collins Street
Melbourne VIC 3000
Ph. (03) 67 2677

Any Tasbureau office can also provide
information.

7 Flinders Island

Accommodation and Travel

Airlines of Tasmania

See (6) above for details

Flinders Island Travel Centre
Lagoon Road
Whitemark
Flinders Island TAS 7255
Ph. (003) 59 2004

8 Maria Island

General Information

The Ranger
Maria Island
C/- PO Triabunna TAS 7190
Ph. (002) 57 1420

9 Bruny Island

General Information

National Parks and Wildlife Service
16A Magnet Court
Sandy Bay TAS 7005
Ph. (002) 30 8011

South Australia

10 Kangaroo Island

Accommodation and Travel

Kangaroo Island Booking Centre
29 King William Street
Adelaide SA 5000
Ph. (08) 231 0133

Kangaroo Island Complete Travel
 Service
28 Hindley Street
Adelaide SA 5000
Ph. (08) 212 4550

General Information

National Parks and Wildlife Service
55 Grenfell Street
Adelaide SA 5000
Ph. (08) 216 7777

South Australia Government Travel
 Centre
18 King William Street
Adelaide SA 5000
Ph. (08) 212 1644

11 Boston Island

Rent the island from:

Peter Davis
Boston Island
Box 213
Port Lincoln SA 5606
Ph. (086) 82 1741 or 82 1708

He also arranges cruises to and around
the island via Investigator Cruises.

Western Australia

12 Rottnest Island

Accommodation and Travel

Holiday WA Centre
772 Hay Street
Perth WA 6000
Ph. (09) 322 2999

Rottnest Island Board
Rottnest Island WA 6161
Ph. (09) 292 5044

13 Houtman Abrolhos Islands
(non-residential)

Activities

Batavia Coast Charters
C/- Geraldton Tourist Bureau
PO Box 187
Geraldton WA 6530
Ph. (099) 27 1236

General Information

WA Department of Conservation and
 Land Management
50 Hayman Road
Como
Perth WA 6152
Ph. (09) 367 0333

Northern Territory

14 Bathurst & Melville Islands

Accommodation and Travel

Australian Kakadu Tours
GPO Box 1397
Darwin NT 5001
Ph. (089) 81 5144

Twin-share tents as part of two and
three-day tours to Melville Island.

Tiwi Tours
27 Temira Crescent
Darwin NT 5790
Ph. (089) 81 5115 or 81 5118
Non-residential day tours

Queensland

15 Lizard Island

C/- Australian Airlines
70 Hunter Street
Sydney NSW 2000
Ph. (02) 693 4444

Or call in at your nearest Australian
Airlines office.

16 Green Island

Green Island Resort
Green Island QLD 4871
Ph. (070) 51 4644

17 Fitzroy Island

Fitzroy Island Resort
PO Box 2120
Cairns QLD 4870
Ph. (070) 51 9588

18 Dunk Island

C/- Australian Airlines

See (15) above for details

19 Bedarra Island

C/- Australian Airlines

See (15) above for details

20 Hinchinbrook Island

Hinchinbrook Island Resort
Hinchinbrook Island
PO Box 3
Cardwell QLD 4816
Ph. (070) 66 8585

21 Orpheus Island

Orpheus Island Resort
PMB Ingham QLD 4850
Ph. (077) 77 7377
    (02) 32 3911 (Sydney)
    (008) 22 1837 (Toll free)

22 Magnetic Island

C/- Queensland Travel Centre
75 Castlereagh Street
Sydney NSW 2000
Ph. (02) 232 1788

Or contact any Queensland Travel
Centre.

23 Hayman Island

Ansett International Hotel
Hayman Island QLD 4801
Ph. (079) 46 9100 or
    (008) 07 5025 (Toll free)

Ansett Travel
Oxford Square
Oxford Street
Sydney NSW 2000
Ph. (02) 268 1555

Or contact your nearest Ansett Travel
office.

24 Hamilton Island

Hamilton Island Resort
Post Office
Hamilton Island NTH QLD 4803
Ph. (079) 46 9144
    (02) 327 1899 (Sydney)
    (03) 661 3805 (Melbourne)
    (075) 32 8422 (Gold Coast)

Ansett Travel

See (23) above for details

25 Lindeman Island

(Re-opening January 1988)

Lindeman Island Resort
Lindeman Island QLD 4741
Ph. (079)   46-9333 or
    (008) 777 3222 (Toll free)

26 Brampton Island

C/- Australian Airlines

See (15) above for details

27 Pumpkin Island

Pumpkin Island Cabins
12 Little Park Street
Yeppoon QLD 4703
Ph. (079) 39 2431

28 Heron Island

C/- P & O Resorts
482 Kingsford Smith Drive
Brisbane QLD 4007
Ph. (07) 268 8224

Ansett Travel

See (23) above for details

29 Lady Elliot Island

Lady Elliot Island Resort
LMB 6
Post Office
Bundaberg QLD 4670
Ph. (071) 71 5876

30 Fraser Island

Orchid Beach Resort
C/- Ansett Travel

See (23) above for details

The number of operators conducting
adventure and activity tours around the
Queensland islands is endless. We have
listed a few of the recommended
operators and the areas they cover.

Air Tours

Air Whitsunday
PO Box 166
Airlie Beach QLD 4802
Ph. (079) 46 9133

Operates around the Great Barrier Reef,
departing from several destinations
along the coast.

Boat Cruises and Charter

Australian Bareboat Charters
PO Box 357
Airlie Beach QLD 4802
Ph. (079) 46 9381

Offers a range of high-performance
sailing yachts or bareboat charter vessels
around the Whitsundays and Great
Barrier Reef islands.

Hayles Cairns Cruises
Wharf Street
Cairns QLD 4870
Ph. (070) 51 0455

Operate around Green Island, Fitzroy
Island and the outer Barrier Reef.

Diving

There are excellent diving facilities on
Hamilton, Hayman, Heron, Lady Elliot
and Lizard Islands. Other diving
operators are:

Barrier Reef Diving Services
The Esplanade
Airlie Beach QLD 4802
Ph. (079) 46 6204

Offer diving courses and diving
packages around the Whitsundays and
Great Barrier Reef.

Fishing

Calvin Tilley
Australian Pacific Charters
61 Livingstone Street
West End QLD 4870
Ph. (077) 72 4205

A fishing charter operation based in
Townsville.

JEAN-PAUL FERRERO

National Parks

Australia's national parks are vast in number and diverse in character. The country was still relatively undeveloped at the awakening of world interest in conservation and had the advantage of having massive areas of wilderness that were still in near-untouched condition. Australia's first national park, the Royal National Park, established just south of Sydney in 1879, was the second in the world after Yellowstone in the United States. Today, national parks spread right across Australia, representing almost a full range of life communities from rainforest to desert, alpine peaks and ocean reefs.

The primary function of these parks is to preserve a wide variety of natural habitats for intricate plant communities and native populations of mammals, birds, reptiles, insects and marine and freshwater life. It is only by maintaining a diversity of parks with varied soils, climates and vegetation that as many indigenous species as possible can be preserved. National parks also provide access for visitors to experience these fast-receding wonders, while causing as little intrusion as possible. They offer many recreational resources. Visitors can walk unbeaten tracks to secluded environments, climb mountains, explore rivers, gorges and reefs, or simply take the time to leisurely study the wide diversity of flora and fauna.

The parks are managed by National Parks and Wildlife Services in each state. Rangers direct visitors and advise on the weather and terrain. Camping facilities are provided inside or just outside most parks, while virtually all have conducted tours operating regularly within their bounds. At the same time, most parks have wild, rugged areas where visitors can enjoy complete isolation.

Walking is the key to enjoying national parks and all have some system of walking tracks fanning out from the central accommodation areas. These tracks are carefully maintained and generally well-signposted, being designed not only to make exploring easier but also to protect the parks themselves. Maps of the most popular tracks with leaflets describing the sights are generally available from the Ranger's Office.

Queensland's Lamington National Park has a 'Senses Nature Trail' designed for blind people who are able to obtain a better understanding of the sounds and textures of the bush by Braille signs and recorded descriptions along the way. It is also proving enormously popular with sighted people, who follow the trail blind-folded to rediscover and heighten their senses.

A major point to be considered in visiting the parks is Australia's seasonal weather patterns. These have a great effect not only on personal comfort, but also on the plant and animal life. The best times to visit parks in the southern states are summer and autumn; the northern parks are best visited in winter and spring.

New South Wales, Australia's oldest and most populous state, is as diverse as the country itself. In the north-east, a coastline of lakes, heathlands and sandy beaches is backed by high mountain ranges and rainforests. Inland lie jagged clusters of ancient volcanoes. The heavily forested eastern slopes of the Great Dividing Range, as in the New England National Park, have subtropical rainforests on the lower slopes and cool temperate rainforests of Antarctic beech on their heights. Much further west, where the Great Divide slopes gently out to the drier plains, are the volcanic Warrumbungle and Nandevar Ranges.

Further south is Myall Lakes National Park. Here,

Kosciusko National Park in southern New South Wales glows with its spring covering

swamp oaks and paperbarks line the margins of lakes and rivers, where visitors canoe on waterways among flowering waterlilies. Surrounding Mt Victoria, Blackheath and Katoomba in the Blue Mountains is some of the most spectacular mountain scenery in Australia. Although a misty blue from a distance, blue is only one of the moods of the mountains. At dawn, grey mists fill the valleys; at midday, the sandstone ridges reveal a warm hue, while the setting sun intensifies the bold red and golds of its facing cliffs.

On the border of New South Wales and Victoria is the Kosciusko National Park. This magnificent mountain region of snowbound granite outcrops, alpine plateaux and forested ridges is best known as a winter playground, having some of the finest and most extensive snowfields in Australia. The region is just as exciting in the summer months, when visitors fish for trout in cold, clear streams and horse ride along alpine roads and across the high plains ablaze with wildflowers.

Victoria also has great diversity in its terrain. The east-west spine of the Central Highlands, which forms the tail of the Great Dividing Range, is the main physical feature of the state. The uplands are densely forested and 30% of this area is still state forest. On the drier south-western slopes of the Dividing Range, Fraser National Park covers the hills partly surrounding Lake Eildon. Just over the border from New South Wales is Croajingolong National Park, with its wonderful river-mouth estuaries. And further south-west in the Gippsland district is Bulga National Park, where mountain ash soar to heights of more than 60 metres.

Across Bass Strait, Tasmania has more of its total area set aside as national parks than any other state. Because it is quite small, all the major parks are easily

accessible, most being around a half-day drive from either Launceston or Hobart. In the north, they offer everything from beaches to trout fishing. Swathes of wildflowers decorate the island's higher slopes and everywhere there are flowering trees and shrubs. In contrast, the south-west is a wilderness of wild rivers, jagged peaks and quiet lakes.

Tasmania is best seen in the summer months, though the 'Roaring Forties' can make any season cold, wet and windy. Visitors can fly to Hobart or Launceston and hire a car or take their own vehicle from Melbourne to Devonport on the overnight car ferry.

The north of South Australia is a vast wilderness of sparsely populated outback country with rugged mountains and deserts. Further south, to the north-east of Adelaide, are the spectacular red peaks of the Flinders Ranges with the rolling Mount Lofty Ranges further south. The coastline varies from the rugged Eyre Peninsula to the quiet beaches of St Vincent and Spencer Gulfs. Offshore, Kangaroo Island, with its abundant wildlife, is just a 30-minute flight from Adelaide.

Because South Australia has a range of climatic zones from the coastline to the desert, it is wise to select a particular area according to the season. In summer and autumn, the coastal parks are cooled by sea breezes, but they are cold and wet in winter. The parks in the Flinders Ranges are perfect in winter and spring, but can be unpleasant in summer.

Western Australia is Australia's largest state. Nearly four times the size of Texas, its 12,000-kilometre coastline is washed by the Southern and Indian Oceans and the Timor Sea.

In the spring months from September to November, the wildflower displays throughout the state, right up to the Pilbara region in the north, are truly magnificent. Some 250 kilometres north of Perth in the Nambung National Park are grey, weathered limestone columns known as The Pinnacles. One of Australia's more extraordinary geological formations, these rise from the red sandy-desert floor as high as six metres. They have no apparent base or foundation, but somehow never topple over. Geologists believe they were formed while still covered with sand, by a process similar to the growth of stalactites and stalagmites. It is an eerie experience walking amongst them, with the silence broken only by the sighing of the wind.

The Northern Territory is a primeval seasonally arid vastness, crowned by a fringe of tropical oases. The Top End includes the deeply eroded escarpments around Arnhem Land, the coastal plains of Darwin, and the rugged terrain of the Katherine region. The Red Centre has the world's most spectacular monolith, Ayers Rock (or Uluru, as it is also called), and the nearby Olgas. Further north are the Devil's Marbles, huge red granite boulders piled one upon the other as if scattered by a giant hand.

As it is largely a tropical state, Queensland's national parks are best visited in the winter and spring months. In summer, the northern part of the state is hot and sticky, with regular, heavy rainfall. Visits to the island parks are best made around the September equinox when the sea conditions are calm. Underwater sightseeing is quite spectacular from August to November when the water is at its clearest and least disturbed.

Locations
New South Wales

1 The **Border Ranges National Park** straddles the New South Wales and Queensland border some 900 kilometres north of Sydney and not far south of Brisbane. For those driving between the two cities, the park can make an interesting and worthwhile diversion at the cost of only a few extra kilometres.

It is a misty, high-rainfall area and the numerous rivers and streams have carved steep cliffs out of the volcanic landscape, over which magnificent waterfalls plunge into rainforested valleys below.

The 583-hectare park can be divided into three areas: the Tweed Range, Lion's Road and Mt Lindesay-Levers. The scenic drive passing through Tweed Range follows the rim of a gigantic crater which forms part of the Mt Warning volcano. Along the way, it leads to a number of spectacular geological formations, including Pinnacle Lookout. Here, a narrow finger of volcanic rock juts out of the range, dropping sheer on both sides to the valley floor far below.

The rainforest route along Lion's Road is not quite so daunting. This runs through the central part of the Border Ranges and provides a refreshing change of route for travellers heading to or from Brisbane.

Bushwalkers who want to trek in peace and quiet away from cars and roads will find Mt Lindesay-Levers plateau a rewarding challenge. The terrain is extremely rugged and there is no road access, but it is worth the trek. Walkers can follow several routes through the park and along the state border.

Rest areas throughout the park provide facilities for picnics and short-term camping. A particularly attractive area is at Forest Top, where an all-weather cooking area has been constructed in a grassy forest clearing.

2 **Myall Lakes National Park** is situated 236 kilometres north of Sydney on the NSW Central Coast. Road access is best made by driving from Sydney up the Pacific Highway to the Tea Gardens turn-off, some three and a half hours north. It is a comparatively easy drive except on holiday weekends.

The park has sweeping beaches, spectacular headlands, and three major freshwater lakes separated from the sea by dunes and swampy heathlands. Perhaps the best way to discover it is to hire a boat from Tea Gardens and cruise up the Myall River. This broad, deep river is bordered by mangroves which are alive with a striking variety of waders and water birds. It is flanked by rainforest and there are a number of wetland areas covered in melaleucas. Around the shores of the lake and along the length of this 25-kilometre stretch of the Myall River are many attractive spots for swimming, canoeing, boating and fishing. Water-skiing is also permitted.

Camping facilities are available at nearby Legges Camp, Mungo Brush and Seal Rocks. These sites are equipped with toilets, fireplaces, showers and laundries. Special permission is needed to camp outside the designated areas. Hotel and motel accommodation is available at Bulahdelah and at Forster and Tuncurry, both only a short drive away. Bush camping is permitted and houseboats can be hired from Bulahdelah. Canoe tours are also available.

3 The maps say that it is 30 kilometres north of Sydney on the Pacific Highway, but the **Ku-ring-gai Chase National Park** is more realistically described as a bush haven in Sydney's northern suburbs.

The park covers rough sandstone country and is dissected by deep, sheltered waterways that cut into the landscape. It is well known for its Aboriginal rock carvings and for the abundance of wildflowers that line its roads and walking tracks. Spectacular views of Pittwater, Broken Bay and the Hawkesbury River open out before the walker who takes the tracks to picnic spots such as The Basin and America Bay.

An ideal way for visitors to see the best features of

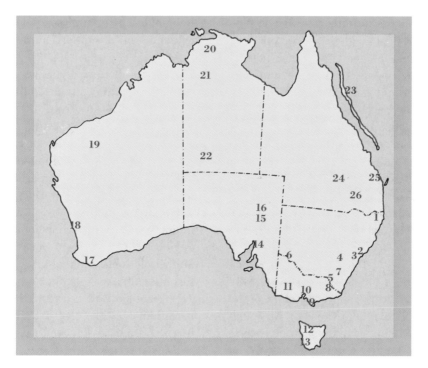

JEAN-PAUL FERRERO

Tasmania's rugged Wild Rivers National Park is home to the turbulent Franklin River

the park is to take a guided walk of the kind provided by Libby Buhring of Bush Picnics. These walks are designed for small groups, and include a gourmet picnic lunch served en route at one of the park's many scenic spots.

Although it is close to the centre of Sydney, it would be a mistake to think of Ku-ring-gai Chase as a suburban park. It covers many hundreds of hectares and is quite large and rugged enough for the inexperienced walker to become hopelessly lost. It has other dangers, too. Some of its tranquil waterways are inhabited by extremely untranquil sharks, but those wishing to cool off in the summer months can take advantage of safe swimming behind the shark nets at Appletree Bay and The Basin.

Camping facilities are available at The Basin, while there is plenty of motel and hotel accommodation along the Pacific Highway.

4   An easy drive 100 kilometres west of Sydney is the **Blue Mountains National Park.** Made up of sandstone canyons and hills, and clad in tall forests of bluegum, the Blue Mountains are the elevated remains of what was once a vast plateau. Over the centuries, it has been weathered by rivers and waterfalls, leaving flat-topped ridges on which the white man has built his towns. The Blue Mountains certainly look pretty enough, but in reality this is hard country that took the early settlers a generation to cross.

The heart of the park is the Grose and Jamison Valleys, carpeted with ferns and choked with gums. These lie north and south of the high narrow plateau on which the mountain towns of Blackheath, Katoomba and Wentworth Falls are perched. There

are a number of lookouts offering spectacular views.

The park offers several good walks of varying length and demanding different levels of endurance. The track system on the floor of the Grose Valley, for example, can be reached from Govett's Leap near Blackheath. Most of these tracks are clearly sign-posted, and though they follow the steep cliff-face down, there are plenty of lookouts where tired walkers can rest their legs. People who want to experience their thrills in comfort can take a cable car or an only slightly terrifying funicular railway from near Blackheath. Joy flights from Katoomba airfield are another alternative.

Canyoning is a popular sport in the area, with thrill-seekers descending between cliff walls that may be only a metre of so apart, but which are so high that the sky is hidden. The most popular location is the Grand Canyon, accessible by a track from Evans'

Lookout Road. Camping is permitted at Acacia Flat, Fortress Flat and Perry's Lookdown. However, both campers and rockclimbers need to obtain permits from the National Park Visitors' Centre at Blackheath. A wide range of hotel and motel accommodation is available throughout the region, most abundantly at Blackheath, Medlow Bath, Mt Victoria and Katoomba, which also has rapid rail access from Sydney.

5 **Kosciusko National Park**, situated 487 kilometres south-west of Sydney, and 60 kilometres west of Cooma, covers the highest mountains and the most extensive alpine snowfields in Australia. Ten peaks are above 2,100 metres, the highest being Kosciusko at 2,228 metres.

With alpine herb fields and bogs above the tree line and mountain forests below, the park has some wonderful alpine lakes and is a source of many of the state's rivers. It also includes all the major NSW ski-fields, the Snowy Mountains Hydroelectric System, the thermal pools and limestone caves of Yarrangobilly, the historic gold town of Kiandra, and the breathtaking wilderness area of Mt Jagungal.

Major ski facilities are provided at Thredbo, Perisher, Guthega and Mt Selwyn, and most of the snowfields are suitable for cross-country skiing. Between the beginning of June and 10 October, cars must be fitted with snow chains along the Kosciusko Road.

When the snows have melted, wildflowers make a beautifully colourful display with alpine bluebells, snow daisies and buttercups bursting into bloom.

Hotel and motel accommodation is available all year round at Thredbo Village, Perisher Valley, Charlotte's Pass and Cooma. Camping facilities are located at Sawpit Creek, just inside the park entrance on the road from Jindabyne to Perisher Valley. Bush camping is allowed in the park but permits must be obtained.

A variety of tours are also available in the region, including a five-day horse riding safari.

6 In the far west of New South Wales lies the extraordinary Willandra Lakes region, part of which is now included in the **Mungo National Park**. Willandra Lakes' unrivalled archaeological value led to its listing as one of Australia's five World Heritage properties by the World Heritage Committee in 1981, where it joined a prestigious list that includes Chartres Cathedral in France and the Serengeti of Tanzania.

This inaccessible and arid region is composed of saltbush plain and colourful sandscapes that illustrate the powers of wind erosion. The lakes here have been dry since the end of the last ice age, some 15,000 years ago, and the present landscape is a result of the wind, and (to a lesser degree in this dry plain) rain, creating gullies in the former lake beds, and piling up clay and sand into strange formations such as the 'Walls of China'.

Archaeological excavations since the 1960s have

been aided by natural erosion processes, and in 1969 evidence of a human burial was discovered and estimated to date back 25,500 years. Other discoveries of stone tools, ancient hearths and other skeletal remains indicate that human settlement extends back as far as 40,000 years. These finds have provided outstanding evidence of the antiquity of modern man and a fascinating insight into the life and culture of early Aboriginal societies. The Willandra Lakes region is one of the earliest known sites for man found anywhere in the world.

Within this 6,000-square-kilometre site it is believed that more archaeological treasures lie waiting to be discovered — a process aided by the constant and ruthless erosion that has created the landscape of this ancient lake system.

Access to Willandra and the Mungo National Park is difficult, but the easiest approach is from Mildura, on the border of New South Wales and Victoria. From Sydney, it is possible to drive via Bathurst and Griffith — a journey of eight or nine hours. A Visitors' Centre offers information on the area, as well as camping facilities. High temperatures in summer make this area best visited between March and November.

Australian Capital Territory

7 **Namadgi National Park** is only a short drive from Canberra, in the south-west of the Australian Capital Territory. Its fairly high altitude and sub-alpine climate ensure plenty of winter snow, but in summer it is a bushwalker's delight, covering 94,000 hectares of forested hills and ridges, softwood plantations, grasslands and mountain creeks.

Horse riding is permitted in certain areas of the park, but camping is limited to the Mt Clear camping ground at the southern end. A Visitors' Information Centre is located at Glendale, 24 kilometres south of Tharwa on the Boy Boyan Road.

Victoria

8 The **Snowy River National Park**, a 390-kilometre drive east of Melbourne, features magnificent unspoilt river country with cliffs, gorges and rapids. The Snowy River, one of the few wild rivers remaining in eastern Australia, is a paradise for white-water canoeists. Huge cliffs rise straight from its turbulent waters. Tulloch Ard Gorge is passable only by swimming or adventurous canoeing. For those willing to take the plunge, a couple of six-day rafting tours operate along the river.

However, not all of the park is wild and rough. There are some fine sandy beaches along the river, and comfortable campsites which lie 700 metres below the top of the surrounding ridges. The Snowy Valley's smaller creeks and tributaries are flanked by dense, luxuriant lowland forest.

Around McKillop Beach, located off the Buchan-

JIRI LOCHMAN

The Twelve Apostles is typical of the coastal scenery in the Port Campbell National Park, Victoria

Jindabyne Road, there are many sandy beaches ideal for swimming. A graded walking track from the McKillop Bridge camping site provides a scenic two-day walk south to an old mining area. And for those who aren't so energetic, the Buchan-Jindabyne Road, which goes through the park, provides panoramic views of the mountainous terrain.

The park is best visited from December to May, since water levels in the river are too high at other times.

Hotel and motel accommodation, and caravan facilities are available at nearby Buchan and Orbost.

Bush camping is also permitted in the park, and there is a picnic area at Raymond Falls.

9 **Wilson's Promontory National Park**, which includes mountainous country and stretches of beach, is on Victoria's southernmost tip, a 230-kilometre drive south-east of Melbourne via the South Gippsland Highway. Public transport is not available to the park. The promontory itself is a mass of granite which in places rises dramatically to nearly 800 metres.

More than 30 kilometres long and 20 kilometres at its widest, the park has tall forests on its mountain slopes, fern-filled gullies, and a coastline fringed by salt marshes. Norman Bay, lying in front of the park's accommodation area, is one of the promontory's finest and safest beaches. Excellent walking tracks beginning at Tidal River fan out across the promontory and take the bushwalker over steep mountain trails, across moorlands and through forested gullies to quiet beaches and picturesque coves. Day walks can be made to Sealers' Cove and there is also an overnight trek to Five Mile Beach. Organised weekend bushwalking through the park is also available. Permits are required for overnight camping. During the holiday season, ranger-naturalists lead daytime nature walks, as well as spotlight tours at night. Slide talks are given each evening at the Visitors' Centre. There are camping facilities at Tidal River, and hotel and motel accommodation is available in the neighbouring towns of Fish Creek and Foster.

10 **Fern Tree Gully National Park** is an ideal day excursion from Melbourne. Lying only 35 kilometres east of the city, it is a region noted for its thriving native population of lyrebirds and whipbirds, whose distinctive calls ring and echo across the bush valleys.

A track takes visitors to the top of the gully via a path lined and shaded by magnificent tree-ferns. At the top of the climb, trekkers reach fine open forests of red stringybark, box and peppermint trees.

Further east along the crest of the Dandenong Ranges is Sherbrooke Forest, a striking woodland of towering mountain ash, with streams cascading through ferns and green mossy banks. Here, the native lyrebirds have adapted so well to the park's many visitors that they now perform their bizarre mating rituals, displaying their enormous torquoise, blue and green-feathered tails, not only for their potential mates but for tourists as well. This display is best seen in the winter months.

Both Sherbrooke Forest and Fern Tree Gully are day parks, and camping is not permitted, though there are plenty of picnicking facilities.

11 The **Grampians National Park,** 260 kilometres west of Melbourne, is the largest of Victoria's national parks. Covering an area of sandstone ridges and peaks, it is noted for its abundant native wildlife, Aboriginal rock paintings, clear waters, and splendid displays of spring wildflowers.

With over 100 kilometres of walking tracks, there is plenty of space to get away from it all. During holiday periods, the park's rangers provide guided nature walks. Perhaps the best time to take advantage of these is when the wildflowers are at their most brilliant from August to November. But there is a feast of activities in which to take part year round.

Motel accommodation is available at Hall's Gap, which though not part of the park, is surrounded by it, and at neighbouring towns. Camping facilities are provided at Stawell, Horsham, Hamilton, Ararat and Cooper's Creek. Bush camping is also permitted.

Tasmania

12 The **Cradle Mountain-Lake St Clair National Park,** 155 kilometres south-west of Launceston, stretches across nearly 100 kilometres of Australia's finest mountain country. Only 95 kilometres south of Devonport on the island state's north coast, the park covers open moorland, deep gorges and forested valleys, and is noted for its lakes and tarns. Wildlife abounds and even day-trekkers can spot Bennett's kangaroos roaming the bush. In the evening, the cry of the native Tasmanian devil can sometimes be heard, and brushtail possums come to the lighted doorways of tourist cabins begging for scraps of food.

The Overland Track is probably the most famous walking trail in Australia. Leading for 85 kilometres past 22 mountain peaks from Cradle Valley to Lake St Clair, it crosses open heathland and dense forests of beech and snowgum, and skirts peaceful lakes and deep gorges.

From the Waldheim area in the north of the park, tracks lead across Cradle Valley towards Cradle Mountain and take the bushwalker through Weindorfers Forest under a canopy of beech pines with ferns and moss underfoot. Lake St Clair is an excellent trout-fishing spot, and is also suitable for swimming and sailing. Cross-country skiing in winter is possible at Mt Rufus in the south.

Storm-proof huts in the park are available for visitors, and bush camping is permitted. Self-catering cabins are situated in the northern and southern sections of the park, with hotel and motel accommo- dation available at the Bronte Park chalets near Lake St Clair, and at Pencil Pine Lodge, just outside the northern edge of the park. Organised walking tours and trail rides through the park and fishing trips on Lake St Clair can be arranged.

13 **South West National Park,** some 130 kilometres west of Hobart and covering nearly half a million hectares, is a vast tract of remote temperate wilderness. It features dolerite and quartzite-capped mountains, with magnificent glacial landforms and alpine vegetation. In the east, there are deep valleys with tall, dense forests of eucalypts. Particularly prominent is the leatherwood, a eucalyptus found only in Tasmania. Colonies of beehives are moved into the park when these trees are in blossom, resulting in a particularly aromatic honey that is in great demand worldwide. Vast areas of buttongrass plain and scrub cover the deeper valleys.

Adventurous bushwalkers can follow the park's two main walking tracks — the Port Davey and South Coast tracks — into the heart of the wilderness through virgin rainforest and across ocean beaches and mountain country.

The Pinnacles at Nambung National Park, Western Australia, com rock forms. They were first sighted by early Dutch navigators who

Bush camping is permitted inside the park, and there are camping facilities at Edgar Dam, Scott's Peak and Huon River. Hotel and motel accommodation is available at Strathgordon.

The best time to visit the park is from September to November and from January to May. Cruises and fishing tours can be organised on Lake Pedder and two-week walking tours are conducted along the South Coast Track.

South Australia

14 **Mt Remarkable National Park** is three to four hours' drive north of Adelaide. The slopes of the park are densely covered by a wide variety of eucalypts, including blue, red, sugar, grey and peppermint gums. Native pines and red river gums forest the valleys, while over 40 species of native orchid have been found throughout the park.

The deep valleys and gorges of the Flinders Ranges with their red-brown sandstone outcrops are quite spectacular — the most breathtaking being probably the narrow, steep, red-walled canyon of Alligator Gorge. The gorge has a couple of swimming

landscape of extraordinary
were ruins of an ancient city

JEAN-PAUL FERRERO

spots, but despite its name, neither alligators nor crocodiles are to be found in its waters.

Mambray Creek, which emerges from the park, is actually a river and its banks are home to emus and red kangaroos, while flocks of Adelaide rosellas sweep through its river red gums.

The best time to visit the park is during the cooler months from May to September. Bush camping is not permitted during the fire season from November to April, but is allowed at other times in designated areas. Facilities are available during the camping season at Mambray Creek and Alligator Gorge. Hotel and motel accommodation can be found at Wilmington, Melrose, Port Augusta and Port Pirie.

Four-wheel-drive tours through the park are another alternative.

15 **Flinders Ranges National Park,** which covers the central Flinders Ranges, is 330 kilometres north of Adelaide, and the journey by car takes five to six hours.

Standing at the entrance of the park is Wilpena Pound, one of the most extraordinary geological formations in Australia. It is a mighty rock wall, ringing a vast natural amphitheatre 17 kilometres long and seven kilometres wide, and flanked by quartzite ranges and peaks. It has a jagged summit, but its floor is flat and covered with trees and grass. The only entrance is via a narrow gorge that cuts through the rim of a creek.

There are five marked bush tracks in the Wilpena area and horse riding is permitted in the Oraparinna region of the park. Local operators offer horse-riding tours, four-wheel-drive safaris and hiking tours. Small planes can be chartered for a bird's eye view of Wilpena Pound.

The best time to see the park is between April and October. Hotel and motel accommodation and camping facilities are available at Hawker, and there is a tourist lodge at Arkaroola.

16 The **Gammon Ranges National Park** is a nine-hour drive 750 kilometres north of Adelaide and 250 kilometres from Port Augusta. It covers wild country of ranges and gorges, with very few tracks suitable for conventional vehicles.

The park encompasses many sites of sacred significance to the local Aboriginal people, the Adnjamathanha tribe. The rock carvings of these people testify to their deep relationship with the area and nowadays they work with the local ranger to manage and preserve the park in its original form. According to one of their legends, Arkaroo — a giant serpent — carved the gorge along the Arkaroola Creek as he slithered through the ranges, creating springs and waterholes where he rested his giant body.

The area is rich in wildlife, particularly red kangaroos, yellow-footed rock wallabies and Port Lincoln parrots.

There are very few walking tracks in the park, and

bushwalkers must contact the ranger before setting out.

The park is a gem-hunter's paradise, and its earth is rich in minerals. Permission is required, however, for visitors to collect specimens. Bolla Bollana Smelters, and the Bolla Bollana Brick Kiln, erected in 1873 to service the needs of what were then the Stanley and Daly copper mines, are still standing and can be viewed from the ridge-top walk.

Swimming and boating are options for the visitor, and boats can be hired from Port Lincoln. Seven-day hiking tours can also be organised. Camping facilities are provided at Surfleet Point and at Taylor's Landing. Bush camping is also permitted, but a permit is required by all campers. Hotel and motel accommodation is available at Port Lincoln.

Western Australia

17 **Walpole-Nornalup National Park** is 425 kilometres south of Perth and 112 kilometres west of Albany. It is famous particularly for its magnificent karri trees. Along with mountain ash, these massive eucalypts are the world's tallest hardwood trees and they live for several hundred years. In the park's rich, well-watered soil, they grow to heights of more than 100 metres. The park also embraces extensive coastal areas of dunes blanketed in heath, as well as 40 kilometres of superb ocean beach, and tranquil inlets and bays ideal for fishing, boating and water-skiing.

Perhaps the best way to see the park's dense forests is to take a boat up the Frankland and Deep Rivers. A trek especially popular with tourists is from the campsite at Coalmine Beach along a small, thickly forested promontory extending into Nornalup Inlet. The inlet is home to large populations of waders, pelicans and Western Australia's native black swans. The path is overshadowed by magnificent karri, and in spring and summer it is carpeted with a wonderful variety of wildflowers. Another walking track follows the forested Frankland River, while yet another leads through the wilderness area to the south coast.

Coalmine Beach in the centre of the park has a camping and caravan park and there are hotels and motels a little to the north at Walpole. At Nornalup in the east there is a guesthouse and holiday cottages.

18 **Yanchep National Park** is only a one-hour, 50-kilometre drive north of Perth. It straddles a belt of coastal limestone and its sandy soils are covered by low scrub with wildflowers in blossom in the spring and early summer.

An extensive and colourful cave system set in limestone hills rises 83 metres above Loch McNess, a large lake dotted with small islands in the centre of the park. A highlight of the cave system is the Crystal Cave, harbouring a superb collection of active stalactites and stalagmites. Visitors can view them on cave tours which are conducted daily. Other less accessible caves can be explored only with permission.

Another feature of the park is the large koala colony. It is one of the few places where visitors can see Australia's favourite marsupial in the wild. Rowing boats are available from the Loch McNess Information Centre and daily cruise trips take visitors around the lake. Fishing and swimming are possible at beaches only a few kilometres west of the park. Bush camping is permitted and hotel and motel accommodation is available in the town of Yanchep, five kilometres west of the park.

19 **Hamersley Range National Park,** 1,700 kilometres north-west of Perth, consists of a massive block of weathered iron-ore rock stretching for 320 kilometres. The range looms above the horizon in an undulating, horizontally striped band. It contains some of the largest known deposits of iron ore in the world. This is being mined from nearby Mt Newman and Mt Tom Price.

The park features many beautiful gorges, all within easy walking distance of the camping areas. Dales Gorge is a cool green oasis far below the park's stony, spinifex-dotted plateau. A track leads down from the hot slopes above the freshwater pools fringed with tall rushes and palms, forming a perfect environment in which to have a dip and relax after a hot walk. Another walking track leads through Knox Gorge, along the top of cliffs to spectacular lookout points with views down into forested chasms. The white trunks of the ghost gums make a surreal contrast to the gorge's vividly coloured layers of rock.

Camping facilities are available in the park at Yampire Gorge, Circular Pools, Joffe Campsite and Wearo Gorge. Hotels and motels are just two kilometres away in the town of Wittenoom.

Four-wheel-drive safari tours operate through the range and one-day coach tours of the park operate out of Wittenoom. Planes fly from Perth to Port Hedland where car hire is available.

Northern Territory

20 **Kakadu National Park** is a three or four-hour drive, 250 kilometres east of Darwin. Considered by many to be the jewel of Australia's national parks, it recently found international fame through Paul Hogan's successful film, *Crocodile Dundee.*

The park covers 13,000 square kilometres of varied terrain from coastal plains, tidal mangrove flats and flood plains to eucalypt forests, gorges and plateaux. It is also home to one-third of Australia's total bird species.

Water birds in their thousands gather on the park's billabongs and lagoons, the most noted of which is the Yellow Waters Lagoon which is home to ducks, ibises, black and white magpie geese, swans and pelicans. Boating tours along its waterways are operated from Cooinda Motel within the park. A quarter of Australia's freshwater fish species are also to be found in the park's waters, and it is particularly

Kakadu National Park, Northern Territory, features vast pools of exotic waterlilies

Rivers of salt are found in the Fitzgerald River National Park, Western Australia

renowned for its excellent barramundi. As viewers of *Crocodile Dundee* will know, swimming is not advisable since bathers can find themselves sharing the water with ferocious, gigantic saltwater crocodiles.

About 1,000 Aboriginal art sites have been recorded in Kakadu. Some of these rock paintings are 20,000 years old, with Obiri and Nourlangie Rocks being the two principal galleries.

Undoubtedly the best way to discover Kakadu is to head into the bush and camp for a few days. Beyond the plains, the red walls of the escarpment rise abruptly to form a backdrop for the rest of the park. Most of the cliffs and gorges are only accessible on foot, with the two main attractions being Twin Falls and Jim Jim Falls. The latter forms a spectacular sight, its water plunging several hundred metres into a deep pool in the centre of a massive natural amphitheatre.

The dry season from May to July is the best time to visit Kakadu and visitors will find camping facilities at Jim Jim Falls, Twin Falls, Nourlangie and Murella Park. Bush camping is only permitted with the ranger's approval. Motels are to be found at South Alligator, Cooinda and Jabiru as well as in Darwin. Camping safaris and air tours of the region can be arranged.

21 **Katherine Gorge National Park** is 370 kilometres south-east of Darwin and 32 kilometres north-east of Katherine. Katherine Gorge is a mighty waterway cut through a rock plateau by the Katherine River. Its waterfalls are spectacular during the wet season, and for most of the dry season (from May to August) tourists can see crocodiles happily sunning themselves on the gorge's rocks and sandy banks.

The dry season is ideal for camping, walking and boating, and fishing for barramundi and perch. Over 180 kilometres of marked walking tracks, varying in length from two and half to eight kilometres, begin at the park's camping area and end at various points along the gorge. There are plenty of pools and lagoons for swimming and boat cruises run twice-daily through the gorges. For separate trips, boats and canoes can be hired in Katherine.

The park is home to some spectacularly colourful wildlife, including the beautifully coloured rainbow bird, the red-winged parrot, the great bowerbird and the northern rosella.

There are camping facilities at the Gorge Caravan Park, and bush camping is permitted, though walkers should be warned that it's an eight-kilometre trek to the designated campsite. Both hotel and motel accommodation are available at Katherine.

Safaris, coach tours and scenic flights also operate throughout the region.

22 **Uluru National Park**, 450 kilometres south-west of Alice Springs, encompasses just a small portion of the vastness of central Australia. The spectacular Ayers Rock (Uluru) and the Olgas dominate the open barren landscape of sand plains and mulga woodland, rising up out of what is now a buried mountain range. These magnificent peaks are of great significance to the region's tribal Aborigines, and visitors to the park are able to see the many sights and cave paintings that form so important a part of central Australian Aboriginal mythology.

Ayers Rock — 353 metres high — is a gigantic monolith made up of a conglomerate of small pebbles. Its colours change constantly throughout the day with the course of the sun in a way that has fascinated painters and photographers for generations. Not far away, the Olgas are a cluster of bizarre soaring rock domes, separated by deep chasms, nestling into the terrain like a clutch of gigantic eggs. The main summit, Mt Olga, rises to 546 metres and the total circumference of the group is 25 kilometres.

Various forms of accommodation are available for visitors to Uluru. An international-class hotel, the Sheraton Ayers Rock, is the most luxurious, followed by the Four Seasons Ayers Rock Motel and the Ayers Rock Lodge. The Yulara Tourist Resort has a camping ground with laundries, washing facilities and a kiosk. On-site caravans are also available. Camping is possible around the Olgas, with prior permission from the park ranger.

Namadgi National Park, Australian Capital Territory

Queensland

23 In addition to a large number of mainland national parks, Queensland is fortunate in having the **Great Barrier Reef** on its doorstep. Island national parks include uninhabited islands, as well as resort islands such as Lizard, Hinchinbrook and Lindeman.

On a grander scale, the entire reef was included in 1981 as a listing in the UNESCO World Heritage List — an honour that only four other Australian locations have received. This incredible maze of islands and reefs stretches 2,000 kilometres along the Queensland coast and is the largest coral reef system in the world. Described as the most magnificent marine scenery on earth, this unique ecosystem attracts visitors of all types — scientists, divers, sight-seers and more than 1,500 species of fish. Underwater life also includes turtles, 400 species of coral, molluscs and a wide variety of sponges, marine worms, crustaceans and anemones. This marine wonder simply has to be seen to be believed.

Cairns, Townsville, Rockhampton and all major centres on the Queensland coast are ideal starting-off points for air or boat trips to the reef. Island resort holidays bring visitors a little closer, and most resorts offer day trips to the reef. Islands such as Lady Elliot and Heron are true coral cays on the reef itself and offer resort-type accommodation. The opportunities here for diving, snorkelling and coral viewing are superb, and literally a step away from your front door.

24 **Carnarvon National Park** is 718 kilometres north-west of Brisbane. It covers an uplifted sandstone plateau which is deeply dissected by the Carnarvon Creek. Some 32 kilometres in length, the walls of the gorge rise in places to 200 metres. Tributary gorges radiate out from the gorge, harbouring lush, sheltered gullies of cool green moss and ferns.

The surrounding sandstone terrain serves as a filter, forming part of the intake beds of the Great Artesian Basin. These beds are ideal swimming spots. There are many walking tracks in the gorge area, ranging from three to ten kilometres. However, there is no walking access from the gorge to the plateau country, which remains an undisturbed wilderness.

The most popular walk is the 16-kilometre trip to Cathedral Cave and back. The cave is adorned with Aboriginal paintings that are thousands of years old.

Bush camping is permitted, and the best time to visit is during the dry season, between June and August. Safari tents and cabin accommodation are available at Carnarvon Gorge Oasis Lodge, just outside the park.

Coach and camping tours as well as four-wheel-drive and walking safaris ranging from four days to over two weeks are regularly conducted through the park.

25 **Cooloola National Park** is located 248 kilometres north of Brisbane. With its sand dunes and sweeping beaches, it has a subtle beauty that is best appreciated on foot. The park includes rainforests growing on sand, lakes, desert-like sand blows, the striking Noosa River and the Noosa Plains with its carpet of wildflowers.

A number of walking tracks have been developed and a new 46-kilometre Wilderness Trail has recently been opened. There are a number of good beaches for swimming, and at Lake Freshwater, fresh water flows out from the dunes. The park has regular boat cruises with boats also available for private hire for those wishing to fish offshore.

There are camping facilities at Freshwater, Harry Springs Hut and Double Island Point, but visitors must bring their own drinking water and book in advance to ensure they obtain a site. Hotel and motel accommodation can be found at Rainbow Beach, Tewantin and Boreen Point.

The park is accessible all year-round. Camping and four-wheel-drive safaris are also offered.

26 **Bunya Mountains National Park** covers a ridge of low mountains rising from the flat plains of the Darling Downs. Some 250 kilometres north-west of Brisbane, the park is well known for its giant bunya pines. It also features waterfalls and streams, surrounded by native orchids and magnificent tree-ferns. Many Aboriginal rock paintings have been found within its boundaries.

The park's most colourful spectacle, however, is the morning and afternoon feeding of the brilliant green and scarlet king parrots and the crimson and blue rosellas. This ritual takes place at the Dandabah camping ground. Another sight for wildlife enthusiasts is the small red-shouldered wallaby and its cousin, the larger black wallaby.

There are several camping grounds in the park and permits are available from the ranger at Dandabah on the park's south-east border. Campers need to book well in advance, particularly for long weekends. Dandabah has well-appointed cabins and motel units, and there is a guesthouse at Mt Mowbullan, a further two kilometres to the south.

National Parks Contacts

Information Sources

Further information on all national parks listed can be obtained from the relevant state's headquarters as indicated below.

New South Wales and Australian Capital Territory

National Parks 1 to 7

NSW National Parks & Wildlife Service
ADC Building
189 Kent Street
Sydney NSW 2000
Ph. (02) 237 6500

Victoria

National Parks 8 to 11

Victorian National Parks Service
240 Victoria Parade
East Melbourne VIC 3002
Ph. (03) 651 4011

Tasmania

National Parks 12 and 13

National Parks & Wildlife Service of
  Tasmania
16 Magnet Court
Sandy Bay
Hobart TAS 7005
Ph. (002) 30 8011

South Australia

National Parks 14 to 16

National Parks and Wildlife Service of
  SA
55 Grenfell Street
Adelaide SA 5000
Ph. (08) 216 7777

Western Australia

National Parks 17 to 19

WA Department of Conservation & Land
  Management
Operations Headquarters
50 Hayman Road
Como
Perth WA 6152
Ph. (09) 367 0333

Northern Territory

National Parks 20 to 22

Conservation Commission of the
  Northern Territory
Alice Springs NT 5750
Ph. (089) 50 8211

Queensland

National Parks 23 to 26

Queensland National Parks & Wildlife
  Service
MLC Centre
239 George Street
Brisbane QLD 4001
Ph. (07) 227 4111

Fitzgerald River National Park, Western Australia

ALLAN MOULT

National Trust

The National Trust of Australia protects and preserves the integrity of historic buildings. It has autonomous state branches throughout Australia and is a private citizens' organisation which encourages membership from both individuals and companies.

Most of the places listed in the following section are classified by the National Trust. In most cases, it is the dedication and work of the National Trust that has ensured the buildings' survival. Very often when these historic buildings pass into the hands of the National Trust their state of disrepair is incredible, and it is only through time-consuming and costly renovation that a successful transformation has been brought about.

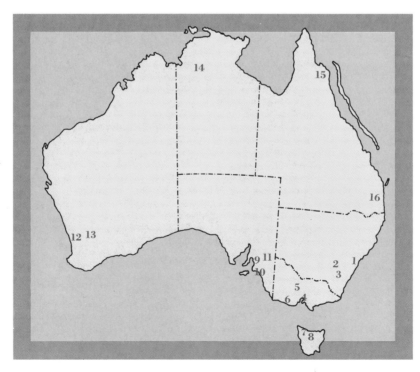

Locations

New South Wales

1 Close to Sydney's historic Rocks and Sydney Cove areas is NSW's National Trust Headquarters, **Observatory Hill.** The site of an old military hospital, Observatory Hill later became a school. It now houses the S. H. Erwin gallery, a specialist book and gift shop, a cafe and a real estate service.

The military hospital was constructed in 1815, and the new Georgian-style building had wide verandas on all four sides at the ground and first-floor levels. In the 1840s, the soldiers moved to Victoria Barracks in Paddington, which already had a hospital, thus rendering the Observatory Hill hospital redundant. In 1848, the building was handed over to the Department of Education for use as a school. It was extended to its present state, and became the Fort Street School, in its various forms, between 1850 and 1974. It was then bequeathed to the National Trust of New South Wales for use as its headquarters.

The site of the gallery was built in 1856 as classrooms for the expanding Fort Street School. It is named after Samuel Henry Erwin, a benefactor who financed the conversion of the school building into a gallery. The gallery contains important examples of paintings, graphics and sculptures that he collected. The Trust also mounts exhibitions of Australian art that relates to Australia's heritage.

2 The **Norman Lindsay Gallery and Museum,** near Springwood in the Blue Mountains, was the home of Australian artist and writer Norman Lindsay for 57 years. Lindsay and his wife Rose bought the humble stone cottage for 500 pounds in 1911, having been attracted by the beauty of its setting.

Rooms were demolished and replaced, existing ones were renovated, and an etching studio was added. This studio, with its enclosed veranda, later became the home of Lindsay's daughter, who in turn added two rooms, giving it the shape it has today. It was sold in 1968.

When Lindsay died in 1969, at the age of 90, he left to the National Trust a valuable collection of his work. However, it was a condition of his will that the Trust buy his house in order to display his work there. A public appeal was opened, sufficient funds were raised for the purchase, and the Gallery was officially opened in 1973.

Lindsay's range of watercolours, oil paintings, novels, ship models, sculptures and statuary are all on display at the Gallery.

Australian Capital Territory

3 Just a short drive from Canberra off the Monaro Highway is the historic **Lanyon Homestead,** built in 1859 and once the centre of a bustling pastoral community. Its extensive outbuildings and gardens blend in with the surrounding rural landscape.

The homestead's outbuildings include a barn, dairy, old kitchen, stables, stores and barracks. The homestead was named after John Lanyon, who moved to the area in 1834 and purchased the large tract of land upon which 'Lanyon' was eventually built.

When Lanyon died, a friend, James Wright, was left in control of the 1,690 hectares. With the use of convict labour, Wright managed the property. By 1841, 59 people lived there, all in temporary dwellings, and over one-third of them were convicts.

Severe financial troubles forced Wright to surrender 'Lanyon' to businessman Andrew Cunningham in 1849, and a decade later, Lanyon Homestead was constructed. Its original buildings were V-shaped, with stuccoed stone rubble walls and a shingled roof. Additional buildings were gradually added to the original structure.

In 1971, 'Lanyon' passed into the hands of the Australian government, which restored and finished it as an historic house museum. It now contains an art gallery in which some of the famous Sir Sidney

Nearly all Australian cities and towns contain a rich mixture of Victorian architecture, such as this Fremantle building

PHILLIMORE CHAMBERS

SIMON COWLING

Nolan's 'Ned Kelly' series of paintings reside.

Victoria

4 Arguably Melbourne's most beautiful Victorian mansion, **Como** was built in the 1840s and 50s by Edward Eyre Williams, a barrister. The land and later the house were named after Lake Como in northern Italy. In 1854, the house was sold to John Brown, an architect from Scotland, who enlarged and altered the existing building and improved the surrounding gardens.

The 1870s saw further enlargements and the addition of a ballroom, billiard room and sitting room under the care of the Armytage family, who eventually handed the house over to the National Trust in 1959.

Como sits in a gracious setting above the river in the Melbourne suburb of South Yarra. The original grounds of 21.5 hectares of gardens and orchards have been reduced to two hectares, which the National Trust has turned into lawns, a bluebell wood, and displays of azaleas, rhododendrons, irises and daffodils. The house itself consists of a central block surrounded by gracious verandas at both ground and first-floor levels and is built of brick faced with stucco. Its white facade provides a striking contrast to the lawn and driveway in front of the house.

The interior has retained its period feel, largely due to the fact that the National Trust has been fortunate enough to keep most of the original Armytage family furniture. Mostly of the Victorian era, this furniture includes pieces of walnut, oak, cedar and blackwood. The ballroom features a century-old Lipp grand piano, and was once the scene of balls for as many as 400 guests. The drawing room has some fine ornamentation and chandeliers, many of which originated from the Paris Exposition of 1879, and several French and Venetian items. Upstairs, the bedrooms feature some handsome furniture and ornaments and a display room contains some of the china, silver and glass originally used at Como.

This beautiful dwelling is a few minutes away from the city centre and is open daily for inspection.

5 The establishment of a special heritage Advisory Service in 1984 for residents of **Bendigo,** an old goldmining town 150 kilometres north-west of Melbourne, demonstrated its historical importance to Victoria.

The service offers Bendigo locals advice on materials, colours, design and architectural style when restoring the city's buildings. A flourishing place during the goldrush of 1851, mining continued in Bendigo until 1954.

The various ethnic groups who have settled in Bendigo over the years are reflected in the blend of building styles found there today, including early Irish, Cornish, Chinese and German.

About 30 buildings in the city have National Trust classification. The Sacred Heart Cathedral is one of the last built in Australia. It was begun in 1816 and completed only in 1977.

Visitors are particularly impressed by the Bendigo talking trams, which take passengers on an eight-kilometre trip through the city, detouring to the Tramway Museum and the Tass House at Emu Plains, built over a century ago.

Other historical focal points are Fortuna Village, the home of quartz king George Lansell; the last Bendigo mine, Central Deborah; the Bendigo Pottery; and the home of Fair Dinkum Eucalyptus, the Jim Eucalyptus Distillery at Sandhurst Town. Sandhurst Town lies 12 kilometres west of Bendigo, and provides examples of unusual buildings and paraphernalia from the goldrush days.

Bendigo is one of several old mining towns found in central Victoria. Other major ones are Ballarat and Castlemaine, and there are smaller mining settlements at Maldon, Clunes and Tarnagulla.

6 **Proudfoot's Boathouse** on the Hopkins River at Warrnambool, south-west of Melbourne on the coast, was opened in 1885, and is today regarded as the most notable of its type in the state. Together with its associated residence and jetties, it is included in both the Historic Buildings Register and the National Trust Register.

The boathouse began as a single-storey timber boatshed and jetty in 1885 and was used by the Hopkins Rowing Club. In 1888, a second single-storey timber shed was added, and a loading dock was constructed between the two. It was further extended in 1893, with the addition of a two-storey timber residence.

Boathouses played an important role in the social life of the Victorian era, which included family picnics, romantic boating excursions and fishing trips.

The boathouse was named after Thomas Proudfoot (1856–1900), its designer and builder.

Tasmania

7 Just 28 kilometres from Launceston, in the midlands of Tasmania, is one of Australia's finest Georgian homes, **Clarendon**. Completed in 1838 for a wealthy wool-grower and merchant, James Cox, 'Clarendon' was handed over to the National Trust in 1962, and was painstakingly restored over the following years. This was no easy task. Only 30 years after Clarendon's construction, builders discovered that the foundations were inadequate and the house was sinking. This problem had only been partly rectified, so the first major work of preservation facing the Trust was to underpin the entire foundations and rebuild the house's terrace, which had collapsed.

Today, the exterior of 'Clarendon' has been restored to its original appearance. It is set in 3.6 hectares of beautiful parkland.

Townsville church

ROB WALLS

The interior of the house is finished in Tasmanian Huon pine, blackwood and marble. There are two storeys, complete with library, nursery, drawing room, dining room, an 'oak' room, a costume room and the servants' wing to the east of the house.

8 Just outside Launceston, in Tasmania's midland region, the gleaming white mansion of **Franklin House** stands resplendent against the backdrop of an English countryside setting. The National Trust of Tasmania was founded in 1960 specifically to purchase and preserve the house.

Built by convict labour in 1838, it was sold shortly afterwards and became W. K. Hawkes School for Boys. The school was one of the leading educational centres in the colony during that era. The mansion was again sold in 1888 to a Greek family who renamed it 'The Hollies'. The house saw two more changes of ownership before the Trust acquired it and named it 'Franklin House'.

Described as late Georgian in style, it houses excellent pieces of colonial furniture in keeping with its era, much of it donated by locals. The house is also noted for its classic cedar interiors, most of which came from the forests of New South Wales.

South Australia

9 **Ayers House**, the National Trust headquarters of South Australia, was the home of one of the state's early and highly influential political figures. During a political career that spanned 36 years, Sir Henry Ayers held the office of Premier seven times in the late 1800s. Built in stages from a small cottage started in 1845, Ayers House took 20 years to complete. After Sir Henry leased the cottage from a young chemist, William Paxton, in 1855, several extensions were added including the family dining room and sitting rooms, a drawing room and the library and east-west hallway. The western wing was added later to accommodate a formal dining room.

When Sir Henry finally bought the house in 1874, the upstairs area, not visible from the front of the house, was built. The house looks today almost exactly as it did then.

Known in Sir Henry's days simply by its street number, 288 North Terrace, it was the venue for many parliamentary dinners and state functions. During the First World War, it became part of an entertainment centre known as Austral Gardens, and later was taken over by the Returned Soldiers' and Sailors' League.

Early in the 1970s, the SA government began to restore Ayers House, leasing the central western parts of the building to the National Trust for public inspection. The ground floor is used for National Trust offices, and there is a warder's flat upstairs.

The old coach house and harness rooms have been converted into Paxton's Restaurant, while the downstairs bedroom wing on the eastern side is now the more formal Henry Ayers Restaurant.

10 Nestled in the Adelaide foothills suburb of Springfield, **Carrick Hill** exhibits an architectural style reminiscent of the late Elizabethan period, though the house was built as recently as 1939.

Its original and only owners, Sir Edward and Lady Hayward, brought back from England several furnishings they purchased at a demolition sale of the historic Tudor mansion, 'Beaudesert', in Staffordshire. The Haywards instructed architects to design the building to house their collection of early 17th-century furnishings in fitting style.

Set in 39 hectares of Australian bush land and currently being developed as a sculpture park, the house has wonderful views of Adelaide. It contains one of the finest private art collections in Australia, with priceless works of art, silver, pewter and old English oak furniture. The building was bequeathed to the National Trust in 1983.

11 Close to Berri, north-east of Adelaide in the Murray Riverland area, the flora and fauna reserve of **Wilabalangaloo** (Aboriginal for 'the place of red, yellow and brown stones') features spectacular coloured sandstone cliffs, red gums and views of the Murray River.

Sydney's recently restored Queen Victoria Building

The reserve has walking trails, aviaries and native animals including emus, wallabies, wombats, peacocks, kangaroos and pheasants. Its indigenous plant collection is enormous and varied.

Its modern facilities include wood and electric barbecues, facilities for the handicapped, a snack shop and indoor and outdoor displays.

Wilabalangaloo was handed over to the Berri branch of the National Trust by the Department of Lands in 1972.

Western Australia

12 Over 150 buildings in the port of **Fremantle,** not far from Perth, are classified by the National Trust. The streets in this bustling city remain largely unchanged since the mid-19th century.

Named after Sir Charles Howe Fremantle, who took possession of the western coast of Australia for Britain in 1829, Fremantle owes its beginnings to the labour of convicts transported from Britain in the 1850s and 60s. The old stone terraces in Henderson Street were built to house warders at Fremantle Prison, and the jail itself was constructed by its convict prisoners. These buildings are still in use today for the same purpose. Other notable attractions are Fremantle Railway Station, opened in 1907, the international Motor Museum displaying over 34 restored vehicles, and the roundhouse at Austin Head, a civil jail which is the state's oldest surviving building, having been built in 1831.

The Fremantle Market building, opened in 1907, operates today as a lively marketplace at weekends.

With a population of over 23,000 people, 19 schools, over 200 manufacturing establishments and almost 700 retail and service outlets, Fremantle has grown from a tiny seaport in the last century to the popular tourist spot it is now.

13 The historic town of **York,** situated 97 kilometres east of Perth in the fertile Avon Valley, provides a welcome contrast to the hectic pace of the modern state capital. First settled in 1981, just two years after the establishment of the Swan River colony, its blend of historic churches, hotels and homesteads has made it one of Western Australia's most historic towns.

The list of historic buildings in York is almost endless. The magnificent ochre pillars and facade of the Town Hall, the architectural excellence of the Court House, Post Office and Police Station (built in the 1890s), and the gothic beauty of the town's three churches attest to the fine workmanship of Australia's early masons who have left such resilient legacies in stone and brick.

Of particular interest is York's Settler House, built in 1858 as a staging post and guesthouse. Standing as a monument to the 19th-century bourgeoisie, its paved courtyards, luxurious suites and impressive surrounds reflect the opulence the period.

Another noteworthy attraction in York township is Balladong Farm Living Museum, the only working farm museum in Australia. The staff, dressed in period costume, take visitors through the rigours of clip shearing, crutching, drenching, milking and blacksmithing.

York Motor Museum proudly displays one of the finest collections of racing cars in Australia.

Northern Territory

14 The old **Northern Australia Railway,** which was originally intended to link Darwin with Port Augusta but was never completed, is today one of the few National Trust classifications in the Northern Territory. Of particular interest is Katherine Railway Station, which was closed in 1976 when operations on the great railway ground to a halt. Work on the line commenced in the 1880s, reaching Pine Creek in 1889 and Katherine, south-east of Darwin (en route to Tennant Creek and Alice), in 1926. It was further extended to Birdum by 1929, at which point work on the railway was discontinued.

The railway station at Katherine, built in 1926, is the only concrete station in northern Australia. It was re-opened as the Headquarters of the National Trust

KATE WIMBLE

in Katherine on 29 June 1986, the 10th anniversary of the running of the last train. On view at the station are railway workshops which were once in constant use restoring locomotives. The railway bridge at Katherine was built between 1924 and 1926, and was the line's longest bridge.

An NBF Class Steam Locomotive, one of only two in the Northern Territory, resides at Rundle Park, on the Victoria Highway. Two other National Trust classifications along the North Australia Railway are Adelaide River Railway Station and Pine Creek Railway Precinct.

Queensland

About 160 kilometres north of Cairns in far north Queensland is the site where Captain James Cook beached his ship, the *Endeavour*, in 1770, marking Australia's formal discovery by Europeans.

15 **Cooktown** was named after Captain Cook, and his landing is celebrated every year with a re-enactment of the historic event.

At the Cooktown Sea Museum, Ossie Walker, himself an old seafarer, gives tourists a history of the town. The museum contains a reconstruction of a Chinese Joss House, the original anchor from the *Endeavour*, and a cannon given to the city fathers in the 1880s by the Queensland government to protect the town from possible invasion.

In the 1870s, Cooktown was established as the post of the Palmer River goldfields. It was at the time Queensland's second largest town, with 65 hotels.

Grassy Hill, the lookout used by Captain Cook to chart his passage further north, offers panoramic views across the reef township and hinterland. The Cooktown Historic Botanic Gardens, established in 1880, are one of Queensland's oldest.

16 The oldest section of the **Bellevue Homestead** at Coominya, just outside Brisbane, dates back to 1867, when it belonged to the North family. It was originally of timber construction and cedar-lined with a shingle roof, but it has been altered over the years. A western wing containing a dining room and guest suite was added in 1904.

In 1975, the property passed to the Co-ordinator General as part of the Wivenhoe Dam Project. With the construction of the dam, the Bellevue Homestead and its surrounding buildings were to have been flooded. Local feeling was so strong, however, that the National Trust and residents of Coominya decided on the mammoth task of moving the homestead and its outbuildings seven kilometres across the country.

The house was cut into pieces, the chimneys were dismantled, and the bathrooms, stables, aviary, garden shed and trellises were moved. The entire homestead was re-assembled beside a lagoon at Coominya. The homestead is still being restored and the garden is being replanted in its original pattern.

Historic Entally House at Hadspen in Tasmania

Clarendon House, a superior example of fine Georgian architecture to be found in Tasmania, complete with superb English-style gardens.

National Trust Contacts

Operators

For details of opening times, please contact the individual properties direct.

New South Wales

1 **Observatory Hill**

Watsons Road Observatory Hill
Sydney NSW 2000
Ph. (02) 27 5374

2 **Norman Lindsay Gallery and Museum**

128 Chapman Parade
Faulconbridge
via Springwood NSW 2777
Ph. (047) 51 1067

Australian Capital Territory

3 **Lanyon Homestead**

Tharwa Drive off Monaro Highway
Tharwa ACT 2620
Ph. (062) 37 5136

Victoria

4 **Como**

Como Avenue
South Yarra
Melbourne VIC 3141
Ph. (03) 24 2500

5 **Bendigo**

National Trust of Victoria
Tasma Terrace, Parliament House
Melbourne, VIC 3000
Ph. (03) 654 4711

6 **Proudfoot's Boathouse**

Hopkins River
2 Simpson Street
Warrnambool VIC 3280
Ph. (055) 62 2131

Tasmania

7 **Clarendon House**

Nile
via Evandale TAS 7212
Ph. (003) 98 6220

8 **Franklin House**

Young Town
Launceston TAS 7249
Ph. (003) 44 7824

South Australia

9 **Ayers House**

288 North Terrace
Adelaide SA 5000
Ph. (08) 223 1655

10 **Carrick Hill**

590 Fullarton Road
Springfield
Adelaide SA 5062
Ph. (08) 79 3886

11 **Wilabalangaloo Reserve**

Sturt Highway
Berri SA 5343
Ph. (085) 82 1804

Western Australia

12 **Fremantle**

National Trust of WA
The Old Observatory
4 Havelock Street
West Perth WA 6005
Ph. (09) 321 6088

13 **York**

National Trust of WA

See (12) above for details

KATE WIMBLE

Northern Territory

14 **Katherine Railway**

Railway Terrace
Katherine NT 5780
Ph. (089) 72 3956

Queensland

15 **Cooktown**

The National Trust of Queensland
Old Government House
1 George Street
Brisbane QLD 4000
Ph. (07) 229 1788

16 **Bellevue Homestead**

Coominya QLD 4311
Ph. (075) 86 4209

Information Sources

The Australian Heritage Commission
GPO Box 1567
Canberra ACT 2601
Ph. (062) 72 3966

New South Wales

The National Trust of Australia/NSW
Observatory Hill
Sydney NSW 2000
Ph. (02) 27 5374

Australian Capital Territory

The National Trust of Australia/ACT
6 Giels Court
Deakin
Canberra ACT 2600
Ph. (062) 81 0711

Victoria

National Trust of Australia/Victoria
Tasma Terrace, Parliament House
Melbourne VIC 3002
Ph. (03) 654 4711

Tasmania

National Trust of Australia/Tasmania
39 Paterson Street
Launceston TAS 7250
Ph. (003) 31 9077

South Australia

The National Trust of South Australia
Ayers House
288 North Terrace
Adelaide SA 5000
Ph. (08) 223 1196

Western Australia

The National Trust of Australia/WA
The Old Observatory
4 Havelock Street
West Perth WA 6005
Ph. (09) 321 6088

Northern Territory

National Trust of Australia/NT
Shop 1, 14 Knuckey Street
Darwin NT 5794
Ph. (089) 81 2848

Queensland

The National Trust of Queensland
Old Government House
George Street
Brisbane QLD 4000
Ph. (07) 229 1788

LEE PEARCE

Railway Journeys

To travel hopefully is better than to arrive. These sentiments of Robert Louis Stevenson are echoed by seasoned rail travellers in Australia. At least those for whom the rail journey is sufficient in itself, the destination being an added reward.

There is still something romantic about rail travel. In Australia the age of steam lives on in some places, while the intercapital expresses continue to offer an experience unparalleled by other forms of transport.

With plans for even greater comfort, speed and service, Railways of Australia are co-ordinating and improving the many long-distance trains which connect the capital cities and major centres in Australia. These trains are among the best in the world, and their unique journeys make rail the ideal way to explore the continent.

Australia's interstate express trains are all fully airconditioned, and offer a range of accommodation to suit all tastes. Economy or first-class sitting cars are provided on most services, while all overnight trains have sleeping carriages. The roomette sleeping compartment has a private washbasin and toilet facilities, with showers located at the end of each carriage. Designed for two people, the 'twinette' compartment has upper and lower berths, with an en-suite shower and toilet compartment. Most trains have a dining car, while some also have lounge and club cars serving light refreshments and drinks.

The *Indian-Pacific* leaves Sydney three days a week for its journey across Australia, arriving in Perth on the morning of the third day. As the train heads westward over the Great Dividing Range, the setting sun reflects on the exposed sandstone cliffs of the Megalong and Kanimbla Valleys. Passengers gather in the bar for an evening drink, and after dinner, the

piano and video in the lounge car are popular sources of entertainment. Next morning, the *Indian-Pacific* arrives at the mining town of Broken Hill, where there is time for a stroll down the main street. After an hour in the South Australian capital of Adelaide, the train heads north to Port Augusta, a town characterised by its old stone buildings and pepper trees.

The following day brings the train to the longest stretch of straight track in the world — 478 kilometres west to the horizon. The train stops at the small settlement of Cook on the Nullarbor Plain, where the traveller can purchase local artefacts and souvenirs, or visit the only significant building, a hospital with the slogan, 'If you're crook [ill], come to Cook'. Arriving in Kalgoorlie in the evening, there is time for a walk along the famous 'golden mile' of this city that continues to thrive on gold mining. The last night of the journey is spent travelling through Western Australia and along the Avon Valley before arriving in Perth in the morning — a 65-hour journey through three states and across mountains, deserts and dry lakes.

The *Trans Australian* is identical to the *Indian-Pacific*. It travels between Adelaide and Perth on the two days when the *Indian-Pacific* does not operate. It is particularly popular with young people, who choose the economy sitting carriages for an inexpensive, yet comfortable, trip to Perth.

Sydney and Adelaide share another set of twin trains — *The Alice* and *The Ghan* — which travel to Alice Springs in the centre of Australia. Departing from Sydney on Mondays, *The Alice* travels west to Broken Hill, where there is time for a short tour of the town. *The Alice* then continues on through Crystal Brook to Port Augusta before leaving the transcontinental line at Tarcoola. It then heads north, crossing the Finke River and the Northern Territory border before arriving in Alice Springs on the Wednesday morning.

The Ghan departs from Adelaide weekly (though in winter, a second service is provided) and follows the same route to the centre as *The Alice. The Ghan* was named after the Afghan camel drivers who provided the only transport in Central Australia before the arrival of the railway.

The standard-gauge track linking Alice Springs with the south is relatively new, having replaced an archaic and dilapidated narrow-gauge line. In the past, the train was often stranded for weeks because of flooding on the old line. A story goes that a woman protesting about the constant stopping of the train was assured by the guard that they would arrive eventually. She indicated some urgency, as she was about to give birth to a child. The guard exclaimed that she ought not to have boarded the train in such a condition, to which she replied, 'I wasn't *in* this condition when I boarded the train!' *The Ghan* now completes the journey in just 24 hours, a significant improvement on the tabled schedule of 48 hours for its narrow-gauge predecessor.

An interesting feature of *The Ghan* is its Conference Car facility — a unique venue for a convention or conference, and one that ensures a captive audience! The car joins the remainder of the train on its Adelaide to Alice Springs journey, and special packages can be arranged for delegates to remain in Alice Springs for a few days. The Conference Car offers three sections: a boardroom for 12 persons, a lecture room for 18, and a lounge area for discussions. All necessary electronic equipment is provided, and delegates are assured of *The Ghan's* normal high standard of service.

Adelaide, Melbourne, Sydney and Brisbane are linked by nightly expresses which provide a relaxed and civilised alternative to the domestic airlines. *The Overland*, which links Adelaide and Melbourne, is one of the oldest express trains in Australia. In its 100-year history, it has never required its passengers to change trains at state borders due to incompatible gauges. With a lounge car and refreshment facilities, the red and silver cars are often considered among the most comfortable in Australia. As the train winds its way through the Mount Lofty Ranges or Ballarat in the morning, sleeping-car passengers enjoy their breakfast in bed.

The *Sydney Express* and the *Melbourne Express* link the two great cities on the east coast. Passengers can entertain friends in the lounge car prior to departure, and enjoy one of life's great pleasures, an à la carte meal in the dining car, with cutlery and crockery jingling as the train speeds into the night. After a shower and hot breakfast, the 13-hour journey ends in the heart of the city before 9 am.

The *Brisbane Limited Express* links Sydney with the northern capital, and provides a scenic and relaxed overnight journey. Just north of Sydney, the train travels along the spectacular Hawkesbury River, which in the early morning and at dusk is an impressive sight. Near Queensland, the train climbs the Border Ranges through lush rainforest before traversing the flat plain and crossing the Brisbane River to arrive at the new Brisbane Transit Centre.

From Brisbane, rail lines head west to Cunnamulla and north to the tropical towns of Cairns and Townsville. *The Queenslander*, a weekly first-class train, is the newest of Australia's mainline expresses. With new lounge and dining cars, the train carries first-class passengers through the tropics of Queensland. Rainforests, sugarcane plantations, rivers and mountain ranges are viewed from the comfort of the lounge car. Meals which reflect the exotic foods of the state are a particular delight on this train.

Whilst these trains are the best known, Australia offers much more for the rail traveller who seeks adventure. The twice-weekly mixed goods train between Cairns and Forsayth takes 24 hours to travel 400 kilometres. With hours spent at Almaden, Mount Surprise and Einasleigh, there is plenty of time to visit the local pub, or explore the three buildings in the main street.

The sleek lines of a modern train contrast with the surrounding desert

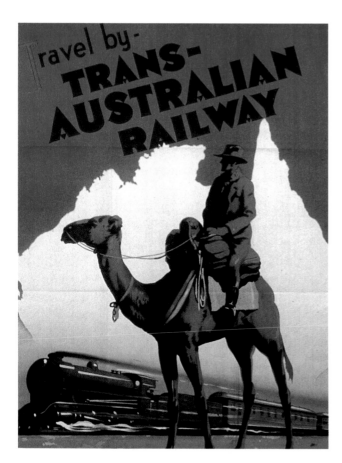

Or join the fast goods train from Mt Isa to Townsville — 39 hours in a combined guard/passenger van, with many hours to explore Cloncurry, Hughenden and Charters Towers.

The interstate express trains offer luxury and service across the continent, while each state offers an extensive rail and road coach network that will take you almost anywhere you want to go. In Western Australia, *The Prospector* and *The Australind* link Perth with Kalgoorlie and Bunbury respectively; the *XPTs* of New South Wales link Sydney with Albury, Canberra, Dubbo, Armidale and Grafton; in South Australia, *The Blue Lake*, *The Iron Triangle Limited* and *The Silver City Limited* link Adelaide with Mount Gambier, Whyalla and Broken Hill respectively; Victoria's *Vinelander* and *Sunraysia* provide services to Mildura; while in Queensland, *The Westlander*, *The Midlander*, *The Inlander*, *The Sunlander* and *The Capricornian* link Brisbane with Cunnamulla/Quilpie, Winton, Mt Isa, Cairns and Rockhampton.

To travel hopefully, to explore the country and to have time to savour the experience are desires we all share. With rail travel in Australia, these can become a reality.

Locations

New South Wales

1 The undoubted pride of the NSW State Rail Authority is the fast and luxurious **XPT Inter-City Express**, which now connects with most major centres in the state, and with the nation's capital, Canberra.

The *XPT* and Australia were made for each other. Certainly the train itself was quite literally made for Australia, even though its design is based on that of the successful *Intercity 125* of British Rail. The sleek express has been extensively modified for Australian conditions. It is lighter and quieter than its British parent, and its gearing has been adjusted to cope with steeper grades.

Powered by Paxman Valenta 12-cylinder, turbocharged diesel-electric engines rated at 2,000 hp, the *XPT* cruises at a top speed of 160 kilometres per hour, and it holds the Australian rail speed record of 183 kilometres per hour. Soon after its introduction, it won the Australian Transport Industry Award for Technical Excellence.

The *XPT* is not only Australia's fastest train, it is also the first to use the push-pull concept, having a power-car at each end. This reduces turnaround time at destinations. It also helps maximise the train's high-speed capabilities, as does the extreme lightness of the locomotives which, at 71 tonnes, weigh some 40% less than conventional mainline diesel-electrics. This has enabled the *XPT* to cut travel times dramatically, particularly from Sydney to Canberra, to the Central West (Orange and Dubbo) and to the New England

This old Railways poster recalls the days of steam and camel power

LEIGH HEMMINGS

region north of Sydney.

The train rides swiftly and smoothly over tracks originally designed for less advanced trains, and the stainless steel carriages are soundproofed, fully carpeted, and fitted with deep-cushioned seating and double-glazed anti-glare panoramic windows. There is a modern bar and buffet service, automatic doors (to allow hands-free passage along the train) and, of course, full airconditioning throughout.

While the *XPT* may be a world-beater, even the regular State Rail Authority (SRA) services in New South Wales have a great deal to offer. And while rail travel is important simply as an inexpensive means of transport in a state 75% the size of Western Europe, there is much more to it than that.

2. Increasingly, people are using the rail network as a base for a wide range of other activities — sports, sightseeing and entire holiday programmes among them. The SRA has catered for this with great success in recent years, and has taken out a number of major Australian tourism awards in the process.

It offers a bewildering variety of packages lasting up to a week or so and usually linking with coach services to take passengers to picturesque and sometimes remote areas of the state. There are 'adventures' to the Murray-Riverina region over the border in Victoria, to the Snowy Mountains and Canberra, to various parts of the coast, to the pretty New England and Hunter Valley areas north of Sydney, and to the Snowy Mountains and Canberra. Many of these involve travel on the *XPT*, and others use conventional trains — but all are well-planned and very economical.

One of the most interesting options is the **SRA's programme of farm holidays**. One of the most attractive holidays is to Mount Seaview Lodge on the state's mid-north coast, not far from the old logging and gold town of Wauchope. Visitors can spend from two to eight days on the 1,400-hectare property, taking safaris in four-wheel drives, gold-panning, canoeing, horse riding and walking in the rainforests or along deserted beaches. The less energetic will find that the property has its own bar and lounge with an open fire and a range of more sedate activities, such as tennis and mini-golf.

Yarrabin, near Bathurst in the central west of the state, claims to be Australia's first guest property. It can be reached by *XPT* from Sydney for holidays of between two and eight days. It specialises in horse riding, and offers instruction to beginners. It is set amid spectacular scenery and is surrounded by 800 hectares of gum forest.

At Karanilla, in the New England region, and reached by the Northern Tablelands *XPT*, guests are encouraged to become involved in the life of the farm. Karanilla is set in a wildlife sanctuary, and birds and other native Australian creatures — particularly kangaroos — abound. Karanilla offers self-contained bungalows for six-day family stays, and there is a range of activities including horse riding, bushwalking and freshwater crayfishing.

3. It wasn't always this easy to get around New South Wales by train. The Blue Mountains west of Sydney posed a particular problem for engineers — as they had for the early explorers, who only broke through to the rich western plains after a 30-year effort. The difficulty for rail pioneers in the mid-19th century was not so much getting up into the Blue Mountains, as getting down the other side. This became a more pressing problem when the rich gold finds of the central west added an extra incentive for crossing the mountains by rail.

Engineers overcame this obstacle by a feat of engineering which is still staggering to see. They built two 'zig-zags' down the western scarp, dropping down to the plains near Lithgow. It took just three years in the 1860s to build the Great Zig-Zag, though it involved construction of three one-in-42 grades, three stone viaducts and two tunnels.

The line led from the top of the mountains through deep-cut gorges, then switched direction and went back across the sandstone viaducts, through the tunnels, and reversed twice as it worked its way down the scarp to Lithgow Valley 150 metres below.

The Great Zig-Zag served its purpose well, and rail travellers were shunted along its gradients by labouring steam engines for half a century before the modern line all but bypassed it some 70 years ago. Thereafter, it lay neglected and overgrown until quite recently, when a band of enthusiastic volunteers came together to restore it.

The **Zig-Zag Railway Society** now has a number of restored steam engines and carriages running along sections of the Zig-Zag, taking passengers on a round trip of about an hour down and back up the scarp. Visitors have the odd experience of reliving the age of steam (and smoke) while watching the modern diesel-electrics whisper past on the main line below, along what was the bottom stretch of the Zig-Zag.

The views are magnificent, especially from the viaducts, which are as solid as when they were built a century and more ago. Local points of interest are indicated along the way, and the Society is currently restoring more engines and rolling stock. They are also restoring more of the original Zig-Zag and are aiming towards opening a new station at Clarence on the Bells Line of Road to mark Australia's Bicentenary. The journey from Clarence to Bottom Points will be about 7.5 kilometres each way.

The Zig-Zag Railway is open for visitors on weekends and public holidays (Wednesdays for some school trips), and can be reached by road from Blue Mountain resorts such as Katoomba after a drive of about 20 kilometres along the Bells Line of Road. The State Rail Authority (SRA) also organises a one-day rail excursion from Sydney which connects by coach to the Zig-Zag.

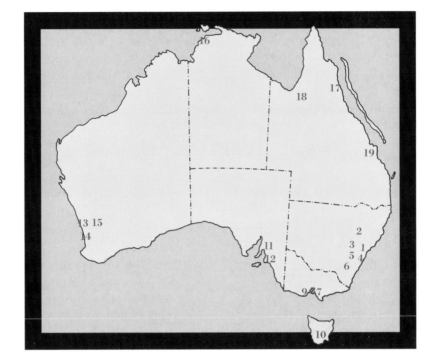

4 The SRA itself runs steam train excursions for enthusiasts, and one of the most popular is the four-hour run from **Sydney to Kiama** on the south coast. Both locomotive and restored carriages date from the early part of the century, and the ride is a leisurely one with a maximum speed of just 70 kilometres per hour. The locomotive has to make several stops to replenish its 24,000 litres of water.

All this is much as it used to be when the rail line was opened all the way to Kiama in 1888 with the construction of the final tunnel. Prior to this, rail passengers were ferried by horse-drawn carriage between North Kiama and the Kiama Inn.

It is ironic that the coming of the railway sounded the death-knell for Kiama as an important port serving the cedar-cutting industry and, before that, the quarries of the region. Now, the town of Kiama is best-known as a picturesque resort with its principal feature the famous blow-hole, through which the Pacific swells force great spouts of water high into the sky.

The day-trip allows time for passengers to disembark for a picnic or a stroll around Kiama before setting out on the return trip to Sydney after lunch.

5 No steam buff will want to miss the biggest collection of restored locomotives and rolling stock in New South Wales, on show at the **Thirlmere Railway Museum**, south-west of Sydney. Around 50 refurbished steam locomotives are on show, along with all sorts of historical railway paraphernalia.

The museum is on the almost-disused Picton-Mittagong line, part of the original single-track Great Southern Railway built in 1867. This section was bypassed in 1919 by a route via Bargo, but continued in use as a branch into the 1970s. Since 1976, some of the museum's exhibits have been able to run on this line, unaffected by regular trains.

The museum is open every Saturday, Sunday and public holiday (except Good Friday and Christmas). Its exhibits range from 'No. 18', built in 1864, to a giant 260-tonne Garratt locomotive built in 1956.

On the first and third Sunday of each month from March to November, passengers can take a steam train ride from Thirlmere to Picton and Buxton. The museum is the ideal place to gather information about other steam train excursions throughout the state.

Thirlmere is within easy reach of Sydney's western suburbs, and is 90 kilometres south-west of the city centre. It can be reached by road along the Hume Highway, turning off at Picton, and makes an interesting diversion on a sightseeing trip to Mittagong, just 34 kilometres further south. By choosing the right days, true enthusiasts can get there by train from Sydney, with the last leg behind a steam locomotive.

Australian Capital Territory

6 The **Australian Railway Historical Society** has a particularly active division in Canberra, based at the Canberra Railway Museum, not far from Canberra Railway Station. On certain days, they run nostalgic entertaining rail trips, using restored locomotives and carriages from the museum.

A regular programme of such events seeks to recreate a vanished era of elegance on the railways — which, if it didn't exist quite like this, certainly should have. Several of the tours are evening functions, leaving Canberra at 6 pm and returning around midnight, making them an original and amusing night out.

One particularly popular trip is to the colonial-style Carrington restaurant at Bungendore, just 45 minutes from Canberra and renowned as one of the best eating places in the state. A feature of the trip is that trains are usually hauled by 1920s 'rail motors', known to enthusiasts as 'tin hares'. They take the passengers on a champagne journey through the Molonglo Gorge and Pine Range tunnels to Bungendore's century-old railway station. Variations on the theme include bushdancing at Bungendore and Queanbeyan stations on the way back.

Another alternative is the Goulburn Gourmet Rail Motor tour, which follows a similar pattern, and the Jazz Train and Bush Dance Train, which features live music and meals served on board, as well as dancing at Queanbeyan and Michelago.

Other tours include day-long picnic outings with bushdancing which are ideal for social and family groups, and steam train trips up the Molonglo Gorge. With the aid of a Bicentennial grant, the Society is currently working to restore locomotive 1210 to haul these trains — at 120 years old, she will be the oldest operating steam engine in Australia.

Some trips go much further afield. The Hunter Valley Wineries Weekender, for example, features cedar-panelled Edwardian sleeping cars and vintage coach connections.

One special feature of the Society's activities is that it caters specifically for conventions or special-interest groups wishing to charter an entire train for an evening or day function. Special train tours can be customised to suit the client, and groups as large as 300-400 can be accommodated on board.

Victoria

The Dandenong Ranges have much the same relationship with Melbourne as the Blue Mountains have with Sydney — though at just 34 kilometres from Melbourne's city centre, they are much closer. The Ranges form a picturesque region of hills and valleys, known for its pretty resort towns with their antique shops and art galleries.

In 1900, an experimental narrow-gauge railway line was built from the town of Belgrave to open up communication and transport to the woodcutters and small farmers of the mountain interior of the Dandenongs. And it's been going ever since — with some hiccups, to be sure, but still running at least one of the same engines on the same line. The Fern Tree Gully line, as it is called, was commerically viable until 1953, when after faltering for some years a major landslide blocked it and it was finally deemed uneconomic to repair.

Two Melbourne journalists arranged a sentimental farewell for the line, whose small steam narrow-gauge Class A locomotives had become known to two

The Pichi Richi Railway in the Flinders Ranges region of South Australia

ALLAN MOULT

generations of Dandenong residents as 'Coffee-Potts', 'Hissing Jennies' and 'Pollys'.

As an experience, it was a wild success, but as a farewell, it was a wash-out. The line refused to die, and several more sentimental farewells were organised before a call for volunteers was launched in an effort to keep the line and its trains going. The volunteers poured in from all over the state and from every walk of life, and formed themselves into the now-famous **Puffing Billy Preservation Society.**

The volunteers, helped by the army, cleared the weeds, relaid the tracks, built a new platform at Belgrave, and bypassed the near-fatal landslide, carrying the line back to Menzies Creek Station and finally, in 1975, to Lakeside — reopening a 13-kilometre stretch of narrow-gauge to steam buffs of all ages. *The Puffing Billy* now runs every day of the year except Christmas Day, often making up to five trips daily on a set timetable. Only days of total fire ban stop the running of the train, and even then limited services continue with a diesel locomotive.

The trip takes in some excellent views over the Dandenongs to the flatlands below, as the old steam engine crosses wooden trestles and passes such railway landmarks as Nobelius Siding. The siding is named after an English settler who imported trees from his home country to plant in the area — many of them are still to be seen — and then shipped specimens all over Australia, starting their journey on the Fern Tree Gully Line.

The train stops at Emerald and terminates at Lakeside in the Emerald Lake Reserve, and many passengers use the train to reach the delightful picnic spots that dot the area.

The Society has restored a good deal of original rolling stock and is collecting more. Among its prized specimens are the magnificent VIP carriages, equipped with brass lamps and etched windows. The timber for some of the original carriages was pre-cut in Tasmania and shipped back to England for assembly. The VIP carriages are available for hire, and make a novel setting for a party.

The Puffing Billy Preservation Society also offers one of Melbourne's most imaginative nights out — The Night Train. This carries passengers to a choice of restaurants in Clematis or Emerald, providing drinks and entrees on the way and coffee and port on the return trip. Since *The Puffing Billy* can be reached direct by normal suburban train from Melbourne to Belgrave, this makes for an evening of old-world elegance. Coach connections can also be arranged, or guests can simply drive to Belgrave along the Burwood Highway, about an hour from Melbourne.

8 Although it is not strictly a railway, one other Melbourne attraction certainly runs on tracks. This is the now-famous **Colonial Tramcar Restaurant**, one of the most innovative dinner venues in Melbourne and winner of a coveted tourism award.

The moving restaurant started life as a 1927 tram, and is the only tramcar restaurant in the world. Gourmet food is served on board, with all the trimmings of silver service, and the tram has its own bar — and stabilisers to ensure that not a drop is lost.

Screened behind one-way windows, diners cruise past Melbourne's sights on the tram network for which the city is famous. The *Colonial Tramcar* can also be hired for social functions, weddings, promotions, afternoon teas and lunch.

9 Another steam train extravaganza in Victoria is organised by the Geelong Steam Preservation Society. The Society, with some government funding, has laid 16 kilometres of new narrow-gauge track to the town of Drysdale from Queenscliff, about 90 minutes south of Melbourne on the Bellarine Highway via Geelong, and also reached by ferry. Known as the **Bellarine Peninsula Railway**, the line skirts the shores of Swan Bay to Laker's Siding, and continues over rolling hills to Drysdale.

Many services are hauled by restored steam trains, and there are specials such as *The Queenscliff Carvery Express* and *The Pancake Express*. The original line had a much less peaceful purpose, and was largely inspired by military considerations (particularly the deployment of men to Queenscliff in the event of a feared Russian attack in the 1870s). The old fort at Queenscliff is one of the attractions of the area.

Steam trains now operate Sundays and public holidays, and on some midweek days during school holidays. Tours can be arranged from Melbourne. The Society has a collection of locomotives and rolling stock from the 1870s through to the 1950s, and a steam museum is being developed at Drysdale.

Tasmania

10 The **Tasmanian Locomotive Company** is an example of what volunteers can achieve with lots of labour, limitless love and little money. In 1979, Tony Coen and David Flecker bought a 1961 H-Class British-built steam locomotive from Australian National Railways for its scrap value of $2,500. After eight years of restoration, H2 made its inaugural run in its resurrected state from a northern suburb of Hobart, Derwent Park Junction, to the midlands town of Parattah, 86 kilometres away, on 4 April 1987. Now it runs regularly on the first Sunday of every month from Derwent Park Junction to the Mount Field National Park.

Leaving mid-morning, the steam train crosses some of the state's (and the country's) most picturesque countryside, following the Derwent River and crossing it four times, on a trip of two and a half hours. Passengers can stop over for two hours at the park, or go on to the Hydro-electric Commission village of Maydena, 16 kilometres further on. It returns to Derwent Park Junction in the late afternoon.

South Australia

11 The historic town of Quorn in South Australia is noted for its contribution to the reborn Steam Age — the **Pichi Richi Railway**. Originally built in 1879 (its stone embankments were constructed by British masons and Chinese labour), the line closed in 1957 for economic reasons. It was restored in 1974 and steam trains and steam motor coaches now carry scheduled passenger and freight services over 43 kilometres of track, departing from Quorn.

The Pichi Richi Railway Preservation Society now has steam locomotives from Britain, the United States and Australia, spanning 90 years of design, as well as some notable diesels. The two and three-quarter hour return trip takes visitors through the picturesque Pichi Richi Pass along parts of the routes of the original *East-West Trans* and *The Ghan*.

It is possible for visiting groups to hire their own observation car for a special celebration or business function. The carriage is the luxurious 16-passenger SA Railways Commissioner's Car, 'Flinders'. Another option for private hire is the 80-year-old steam motor coach known as the 'Coffee Pot'

12 A much longer steam adventure is that offered by **Steam Ranger Tours** from Keswick, an Adelaide suburb, to Victor Harbor on the Southern Ocean — a distance of 260 kilometres. Magnificently restored vintage engines and carriages take passengers through the splendour of the Mount Lofty Ranges, through six long tunnels, and finally along the scenic coastline between Port Elliot and the tourist venue of Victor Harbor.

The trip leaves Keswick at 9 am and returns by 7.45 pm, giving passengers four full hours in Victor Harbor. There is a buffet car, with souvenirs for sale, and an evening meal can be orderd.

Steam Ranger tours operate every Sunday, most public holidays, and the Wednesdays and Saturdays of school holidays. Conventions and social clubs can also arrange special packages.

Western Australia

In the 1870s, Governor Weld of Western Australia said of his colony, 'At last she moves'. He must have been referring to the opening up of some of the state's more remote regions by the miracle of steam travel. The steady development of the Western Australian wheat belt and the discovery of gold had made it imperative for rapid heavy transport to climb the Darling Range; logging of the region's magnificent hardwood forests was another incentive.

13 A line aimed at fulfilling this need was built in 1890 from East Perth to Pinjarra on the Murray River south of Perth as part of a rail connection to the south-west port of Bunbury. By 1910, the timber industry had drawn the line up to the logging centre of Dwellingup on its way to Narrogin.

During the 1970s, local people with vision began to realise that the old line still had a good deal to offer the people of Western Australia, and they formed a preservation society which established what is now known as the **Hotham Valley Tourist Railway.**

With help from local industry, the volunteers bought four W-Class mountain-type locomotives — the type used to work the Dwellingup line during the fading days of steam in the 1950s. They have since purchased, leased and been given a wide range of other engines and carriages, many of which have been faithfully restored and repainted in the line's original livery of traffic green and red.

A train with two steam locomotives, known as the *Dwellingup Forest Ranger,* now operates on most Sundays during the Western Australian steam season between May and October. The train leaves from Perth, and is hauled by a diesel through lush coastal dairy country. Steam locomotion takes over at Pinjarra, crossing the sandy river plain clothed in native wildflowers. On reaching the escarpment, the steam train assaults the 212-metre climb through the Darling Range and into the region's magnificent jarrah forest.

The railway now organises a whole range of other steam adventures. One of these is the *School Holiday Explorer* to the historic town of Toodyay through the picturesque Avon Valley. The Avon itself is a splendid sight, as it carries the winter rains to the coast in a torrent of foam. *The Explorer* connects with regular surburban trains.

The newest tour is a trip on the Etmilyn Forest Tramway to the very heart of the jarrah forests from Dwellingup on a one and a quarter hour round journey. Passengers ride in special refurbished open timber wagons in the tradition of the old logging trains. Regular services leave on Wednesday, Thursday and Sunday at 2 pm. The Tramway service can be chartered for groups of 20 or more. A variation on the theme is the Etmilyn Forest Diner Tour, which takes a twilight trip through the forests with a five-course country-style dinner served in a 1916 dining car. The tour leaves from Perth in the early evening and returns by about 11 pm, giving a new meaning to dining out.

14 The modern trains of Western Australia's state rail authority, Westrail, also have plenty to recommend them. Westrail has a wide variety of packages to offer the visitor, proving that rail is still the best way to see Australia's largest state.

Among them is the **Australind**, which completes the 185 kilometres south to Bunbury in just over three hours on a one-day excursion (every day except Sunday). It also picks up at Armadale on the way. A panorama of coastal plains unfolds as the train skirts the Darling Range and travels through the dairying and mixed farming lands around Pinjarra, Wagerup, Harvey, Brunswick and Picton.

Bunbury, now the capital of the state's south-west,

HENNA

Australia offers many opportunities for those who yearn for the days of steam

was founded in 1841 and became the region's principal seaport. With a population of 20,000 it is now a popular holiday resort, and *The Australind* connects with coach tours of Bunbury on three days a week. The train has a licensed buffet car and bar, and returns to Perth by early evening.

15 The fastest train in the west is **The Prospector.** Those with a touch of goldfever waste no time in getting from Perth to the gold town of Kalgoorlie to try their luck or to enjoy a weekender or explorer package with a choice of accommodation and local tours. Packages include visits to goldmines and the Flying Doctor Base.

In addition to its regular services, Westrail offers an interesting range of rail tours to destinations such as Esperance and the south coast, or north to Geraldton and areas such as the Kalbarri National Park or the Murchison River Gorges. Springtime wildflower tours to the south-west region are also available.

Northern Territory

In the 1880s, there were ambitious plans to build the Transcontinental Railway across the entire width of Australia from Darwin (then Palmerston) on the Gulf of Carpentaria to Port Augusta on the Southern Ocean. It never quite materialised, being overtaken by newer technologies and hampered by the incredible harshness of the central Australian terrain.

16 The southern half of the venture reached Alice Springs, but the northern stretch — though it reached as far south as Pine Creek in 1889 — took until 1926 to reach Katherine, 310 kilometres south of Darwin. After another three years, it limped as far as

Birdum, eight kilometres south of Larrimah, and there it stopped.

For many years, it provided a vital communications link and led to the founding of several settlements, but it was closed altogether in 1976. Many relics of it still survive, however, proving that the enthusiasm to keep it alive was still strong. Indeed, the **North Australian Railway** (NAR) enjoyed something of an Indian summer during the Second World War, when it achieved strategic importance, and from 1942 to 1946 Katherine was the headquarters of the NAR.

The old station at Katherine is especially interesting. A unique building, it was the only concrete station in north Australia, and its importance was recognised when it became the local headquarters of the National Trust in 1986 — on the tenth anniversary of the running of the last train.

Nearby is the line's longest bridge. Over 120 metres in length, it is 22.9 metres above the riverbed. Wooden planking, laid over the bridge deck, provided a secure wet season river crossing for road traffic. Built between 1924 and 1926, it led to the establishment of the modern town of Katherine.

Relics of the Transcontinental Railway survive at Pine Creek, reached by the Stuart Highway and about 100 kilometres north of Katherine. The Pine Creek Railway Precinct is of great architectural and historical significance.

Further north still is the Adelaide River Railway Station, also off the Stuart Highway and just 100 kilometres south of Darwin. Built in 1888, it was the only station on the North Australian Line to provide a refreshment room for passengers.

Queensland

17 The recent battle of the states to win Australia's massive submarine contract might look like big business, but it was nothing compared with the fight that took place between three tiny Queensland ports during the 1880s. The settlements were Port Douglas, Geraldton (now Innisfail) and Cairns — at that time townships barely clinging to the edge of the continent. And the prize? To become the coastal terminus for the first railway to climb the Atherton Tablelands, a railway that would supply the region's miners and open up the rich but unknown land of the hill country.

The three ports were in no doubt as to what was at stake. And no cigars will be handed out for guessing which one triumphed. Cairns is now a thriving centre of tourism, trade and industry, with an international airport — and it's still growing. It owes much of that prosperity to the **Cairns-Kuranda** rail line.

The 34-kilometre line was not built without cost. The contract for the arduous ascent section alone, which involved a climb of more than 300 metres over 24 kilometres, was worth nearly 300,000 pounds to engineer John Robb and his men — an enormous sum in those days. They earned every penny. The line employed nearly 1,500 Irish and Italian navvies, who built 15 tunnels, rounded 98 curves, and erected dozens of difficult bridges mounted hundreds of metres above ravines and waterfalls.

They braved landslides, sickness and hostile natives in shifting more than two million cubic metres of soil with buckets, picks and dynamite. They all suffered and some of them died. But in four years, by 1891, they had taken the line to the top of the scarp and launched the modern history of north Queensland.

Makeshift settlements sprang up along the way even while the line was building. The navvies played as hard as they worked and one camp at Kamerunga, at the foot of the range, boasted no fewer than five hotels. When the dizzying Stoney Creek Bridge was nearing completion, Robb hosted the Governor of Queensland to a banquet on top of the bridge, with tables, food and wine all balanced over the gorge.

Modern-day Queensland Railways have not forgotten all this. Today, they run a special tourist train up the awesome line from Cairns to Kuranda. There are spectacular views from the mountain line of the vivid canefields below and, far beyond, the jewel of Green Island set in the Coral Sea.

Passengers take a break at Barron Falls Station, where they see the spectacular Barron Falls. Though largely tamed by the local hydro-electric scheme, water is released daily to give visitors a glimpse of what nature had in mind. The final section of the journey to Kuranda with its 1915 station (thought to be the first precast concrete structure in Australia) is taken in restored carriages, some of which are older than the line itself.

18 **The Gulflander** sounds as if it should be a sleek high-flyer among Queensland trains. When it was first conceived a century ago (though it did not bear the name then) it certainly was a technological breakthrough.

A line was planned in the 1880s to run from Normanton in the gulf savannah country of north Queensland to Cloncurry. It was the brainchild of pioneer engineer George Phillips, then Inspecting Surveyor of the Southern Division of the Queensland Railways and a co-founder of the port of Normanton on the Norman River. Using his own patented steel sleepers, designed to withstand the region's frequent floods, Phillips hoped to open up the copperfields of Cloncurry, some 430 kilometres south.

In 1885, the discovery of gold 144 kilometres east of Normanton changed all that. The new field, named Croydon, rapidly boomed into a settlement of 6,000 tough, quarrelsome and near-starving miners — starving because the carriages and bullock teams could not get from Normanton in the wet season. It was probably Phillips who was behind the change in direction of 'his' railway. It was rerouted to the boom town of Croydon instead. Rail finally reach Croydon in July 1891, connecting it to Normanton after a journey of just five hours and having survived floods (which submerged it to two metres).

The Gulflander has been running ever since, still largely on Phillips' steel sleepers. It has declined a good deal, it is true. In its heyday in the 1890s, the service consisted of five carriages and 68 wagons. Now, leaving on Wednesday evenings from Normanton and returning the next day, it is drawn by a single 1922 rail-motor and consists of just two cars. But it remains one of the great railway journeys of Australia, taking passengers into the depths of the goldfield country and back a century in time.

19 The luxurious **Queenslander**, which travels from Brisbane to Cairns and return, has been described as 'Queensland's answer to the Orient Express'. This limited express service follows the scenic coastal route between the two cities, taking in some wonderful scenery on the way, while providing standards of comfort and luxury that are unsurpassed.

First-class passengers are treated to private, air-conditioned compartments, with the added touch of colour co-ordinated linen and towels. Some compartments include their own toilet and wardrobe. The dining car provides well-prepared food and a choice of Queensland wines. Other features of the train include a well-stocked bar, lush tropical plants and videos.

The Queenslander runs from Brisbane to Cairns on Sundays, and the reverse journey is made on Tuesdays. The trip takes 32 hours.

Railway Journeys Contacts

Operators

All of the major railway journeys described above can be booked with State Tourism Information Centres or with Railways of Australia. This is an association of the five government-owned railway systems: Australian National, the State Rail Authority of New South Wales, State Transport Authority — Victoria (V/Line), Western Australian Government Railways (Westrail) and Queensland Railways.

Head Office
85 Queen Street
Melbourne VIC 3000
Ph. (03) 608 0811

Booking centres are located as follows:

New South Wales

The Rail Travel Centre
State Rail Authority of NSW
Transport House
11-31 York Street
Sydney NSW 2000
Ph. (02) 290 4743 (Inquiries)
    (02) 217 8812 (Bookings)

Victoria

V/Line Travel
Transport House
589 Collins Street
Melbourne VIC 3000
Ph. (03) 619 1500
    (03) 62 3115 (After hours)

Tasmania

Tasmanian Tourist Bureau
80 Elizabeth Street
Hobart TAS 7000
Ph. (002) 30 0211

South Australia

Australian National Interstate Booking
 Office
108 King William Street
Adelaide SA 5000
Ph. (08) 217 4455

Western Australia

Interstate Booking Office
Westrail Centre
GPO Box S1422
Perth WA 6000
Ph. (09) 326 2222

Westrail Travel Centre
City Rail Station
Perth WA 6000
Ph. (09) 326 2690

Queensland

City Booking Office
Queensland Railways
208 Adelaide Street
Brisbane QLD 4000
Ph. (07) 225 0211

Information on the Forsayth Mixed Goods Train may be obtained from:

Queensland Railways
McLeod Street
Cairns QLD 4870
Ph. (070) 51 1111
Or from Queensland Government Travel Centres.

New South Wales

1   **XPT Inter-City Express**

The State Rail Authority of New South
 Wales
Rail and Travel Centre
11-31 York Street
Sydney NSW 2000
Ph. (02) 290 4743 or 217 8812

2   **State Rail Authority Farm Holidays**

See (1) above for details

3   **Zig-Zag Railway Society**

PO Box 187
Lithgow NSW 2790
Ph. (063) 51 4826 or (047) 57 3061

4   **Sydney/Kiama Steam Trains**

See (1) above for details

5   **Thirlmere Railway Museum**

NSW Rail Transport Museum
PO Box 31
Burwood
Sydney NSW 2134
Ph. (02) 744 9999

Australian Capital Territory

6   **Australian Railway Historical Society**

ACT Division Incorporated
PO Box 112
Civic Square ACT 2608
Ph (062) 51 5831

Victoria

7   **Puffing Billy Preservation Society**

PO Box 156
Belgrave VIC 3160
Ph. (03) 754 6800 or 754 6876

8   **The Colonial Tramcar Restaurant**

254 Bay Street
Brighton
Melbourne VIC 3186
Ph. (03) 596 6500

9   **Bellarine Peninsula Railway**

68 Heysen Drive
Sunbury VIC 3429
Ph. (03) 744 2276 or (052) 52 2069

Tasmania

10 **Tasmanian Locomotive Company**

123 Main Road
Austin Ferry
Hobart TAS 7011
Ph. (002) 28 7024 or 49 2591

South Australia

11 **Pichi Richi Railway**

South Australian Government Travel
 Centre
18 King William Street
Adelaide SA 5000
Ph. (08) 276 6232

12 **Streamranger Tours**

Shop 1
Woodsons Lane
Adelaide SA 5000
Ph. (08) 231 1707

Western Australia

13 **Hotham Valley Tourist Railway**

Hotham Valley Tourist Railway WA Inc.
PO Box 197
Pinjarra WA 6208
Ph. (09) 421 1908

14 **The Australind**

Westrail Travel Centre
City Rail Station
Wellington Street
Perth WA 6000
Ph. (09) 326 2159/2195/2690

JON GOLDEN

15 The Prospector

See (14) above for details

Northern Territory

16 North Australian Railway

National Trust of Australia (NT)
Shop 2
14 Knuckey Street
Darwin NT 5790
Ph. (089) 81 2848

Queensland

17 Cairns-Kuranda Railway

Queensland Railways
McLeod Street
Cairns QLD 4870
Ph. (070) 51 1111

Queensland Railways
305 Edward Street
Brisbane QLD 4000
Ph. (07) 225 0211

18 The Gulflander

See (17) above for details or contact any
Queensland Tourism office

19 The Queenslander

See (17) above for details

Museums

Various museums throughout Australia
contain displays of steam engines and
other railways memorabilia. Examples
are the Canberra Railway Museum, the
Melbourne Railway Museum, Adelaide's
Mile End Rail Museum and Casey's
Steam Museum in Tasmania.

Information on these can be
obtained from State Tourism Office. For
a directory of Australian Tourist Railways
and Museums, write to:

The Light Railway Research Society of
  Australia
PO Box 21
Surrey Hills
Melbourne VIC 3127

Or write to the Australian Railway
Historical Society (see addresses below).

Information Sources

Australian Railway Historical Society (ARHS)

The ARHS is a society committed to the
preservation of Australia's railway
heritage. The Canberra and Melbourne
branches, for example, run rail
museums, and the Brisbane and
Canberra offices operate steam rail trips.
For more information, contact the
Society direct.

New South Wales

New South Wales Division
PO Box E129
St James NSW 2000
Ph. (02) 212 1201

Australian Capital Territory

Australian Capital Territory Division
PO Box 112
Civic Square
Canberra ACT 2608
Ph. (062) 51 5831

Victoria

GPO Box 5177AA
Melbourne VIC 3001
Ph. (03) 596 3249

Tasmania

PO Box 162
Sandy Bay
Hobart TAS 7005

South Australia

GPO Box 507
Adelaide SA 5001
Ph. (08) 43 8462

Western Australia

GPO Box 51319
Perth WA 6001
Ph. (09) 279 7189

Queensland

Queensland Division
GPO Box 682
Brisbane QLD 4001
Ph. (07) 359 5132

To Forsayth by Mixed Goods Train

As the *Queenslander* crept into Cairns Railway Station on a humid Monday afternoon, we checked out the trains sitting in the adjacent yard. We were looking for the mixed goods train that would take us the 840 kilometres to Forsayth and back, and we knew that the airconditioned elegance of the *Queenslander* was going to be left far behind. For the next three nights, we would be back to basics.

The 40-minute wait between trains was spent stocking up our esky. Wine, fresh bread, quiche and fruit, some cheese and olives would be our staple diet until Thursday.

We headed off to the railway yard with our luggage and the overflowing esky. 'Forsayth?' said the station master. 'Why on earth do you want to go there? Nothing out that way, mate, and it's a slow old trip.' He was right about the speed, or lack of it, but during these three days aboard the mixed goods train we would be travelling through the Atherton Tablelands and the lower part of the Gulf country.

We climbed into one of the two passenger cars on the back of the train which seemed to go on forever. Although it was designated 'first-class', there seemed to be no difference between our compartment and the economy one. Or perhaps the difference was the adjoining washroom where the overhead water tank leaked, so that using the room was like having a shower.

We left Cairns at 6.30 and climbed the escarpment, crossing along the way the spectacular bridge over Stony Creek Falls. Constructed in the 1880s by John Robb, the track passes through 15 tunnels and around 98 curves on its climb to the quaint hilltop town of Kuranda.

We spent an hour exploring the township while more wagons were added to the train. Home to many small farm-holders and artisans, Kuranda has a 'back-to-nature' feel about it.

An hour and a half after leaving Kuranda, we arrived at Mareeba, a prosperous town serving the lower part of the Gulf country. Here the train was shunted and remarshalled in complicated manoeuvres while we walked the length of the town and chatted with some of the locals in the milk bar.

Back on board, we headed west and woke in the morning at the Almaden junction. Off to the north, a short branch line links Chillagoe and Mungana. Chillagoe was a prosperous goldmining town at the turn of the century, but today its fame lies in its immense caves.

We spent the next few hours in the company of the travellers in the adjoining car, all of whom worked on the railway. They were travelling to Wirra Wirra, just east of Forsayth, where they were to build a camp and work on the line. It occurred to us that this just might be a perfect Catch 22 situation: the only people who use the train are those who work on the tracks in order to keep the train running!

The train slowed to climb the hills and then raced down the other side. The last few hours into Forsayth were the most dramatically scenic, passing through gorges and around sharp curves.

We arrived at Forsayth at 7.30 pm, though we had been due in at 5.15. We booked into the new hotel — the old one burnt down a few years ago — and went into the bar for a drink and a meal. No one was surprised that we had come all the way from Sydney just for the ride. 'The train was late,' I said. 'No, mate. On time,' said the publican. 'It was due just after 5, and we arrived at 7.30,' I said. 'Listen,' he said. 'As long as the train is in before midnight, it's on time.'

We left at 6.30 the next morning on the return trip to Cairns and I rode with the guard for some time. 'It's a good job,' he told me. 'I'm my own boss. I work four days a week, and never on a weekend. It's good money.' It had been months since he had been to Cairns, and he couldn't remember the last time he'd been to Brisbane.

We decided to leave the train at Almaden, and stayed in the hotel next to the station while waiting for the weekly mixed goods train from Chillagoe which was due in the next morning. When it arrived, its one passenger van was crowded with a group of Aborigines on their way to a funeral at Mareeba.

I rode with the driver from Lappa to Dimbulah, and we boiled a billy of tea in the cabin and talked about everything from the weather to politics as the train rumbled towards Cairns, 150 kilometres and seven hours to the east.

After stops in Mareeba and Kuranda, where the markets were bustling with activity, we descended the range at dusk, the lights of Cairns becoming clear below us. Three days before, we had climbed this line to explore the tablelands and beyond, and during that time we had discovered a new part of Australia and the people who call it home.

The Ghan to Alice Springs

MILTON WORDLEY

Of all the long-distance passenger trains I have travelled on, *The Ghan* holds the greatest memories. As a small child, I rode *The Ghan* between Port Augusta and Alice Springs, with its late evening change at Maree from standard to narrow gauge, and as a teenager I travelled on one of the legendary old *Ghan's* last trips.

The old *Ghan* was the epitome of true travel. It arrived when it arrived, and timetable delays were measured in days or weeks rather than hours. The train lurched and creaked its way to Alice at a speed little faster than walking pace, and though definitely not built for speed, many passengers would also question its capacity for comfort.

The tracks of the old *Ghan* now lie abandoned. The route of the new *Ghan* has swung west, tracking the transcontinental line to Tarcoola and heading north over land that, unlike the old route, is flood-free. Floods were one of the major reasons for the old train's unreliable schedules.

Departing from Adelaide on a recent trip on the new *Ghan*, I ventured to the lounge car to meet fellow passengers. An academic from Nebraska University was on sabbatical and travelling around Australia by rail; an Alice Springs lawyer was returning home after visiting his parents in Adelaide; and a retired railway worker and his wife had decided to see the Red Centre, and to climb Ayers Rock.

Passengers always have different expectations of the journey. Many expect to see large numbers of kangaroos or emus and real outback scenery, but much of the journey takes place at night and it is not until morning that the country towns of South Australia are replaced by the expanse of central Australia.

The new *Ghan* bypasses Port Pirie and calls at the small settlement of Coonamia, a few miles to the east. Further on, at Port Augusta, I left the train and strolled the main streets of this historic rail junction. Travelling on the *Ghan* is an excellent way to visit country towns — with your accommodation at the station, it is easy to wander the streets before returning to the train for drinks in the lounge before dinner. If you are fortunate enough to claim a place at the last dinner sitting, it is often possible to linger over port and coffee before retiring to your compartment.

Lying in bed and looking out at the night sky was a very soothing experience, especially when combined with the sleep-inducing rhythmic sounds and movements of the train. In the morning I awoke to sun streaming through the window and a view of vast red plains.

At breakfast, my travelling companions and I discussed the strange juxtaposition of this barren land and our airconditioned dining car. Over fresh fruit, bacon and eggs, toast and coffee, we recalled the hardships of the Afghan labourers who built the original line to Alice.

Late in the morning we passed through Heavitree Gap, which heralded our arrival in Alice Springs. In just under 24 hours, we had travelled 1,500 kilometres. We had eaten, slept, showered, and travelled in comfort while the *Ghan* had effortlessly linked Adelaide and Alice Springs. What a contrast to the Forsayth journey!

Owen Johnstone-Donnet

PER ERICSON

Wine Country

In many ways, learning about Australian wines is much easier than learning about the wines of the old wine world of Europe. Australian and American wines are far more closely linked with the grape varieties from which they come than are the wines of the traditional wine-producing countries of Europe. The Europeans are far more parochial in their wine-drinking habits, with the generalised exception of the British who, growing little or no wine grapes of their own, have had to look to France, Germany, Spain and Portugal, to a certain extent Italy, and more recently to Cyprus, South Africa and Eastern Europe. The United Kingdom is in many ways, therefore, the wine centre of the world. Although English wine consumption is much lower than Australia's (the UK per capita consumption at present is only about nine litres a year, around the same as that of the US), there is a sophisticated international wine trade centred in London and a small but highly aware population of wine drinkers.

The British have understood the intricacies of European wine-making — the reds of Bordeaux, the dry whites and reds of Burgundy, the sparkling wines of Champagne, the fruitier wines of the Loire, the deliciously sweet white wines of Sauternes, the flinty whites of Chablis and the magnificent whites of Germany — the Mosel rieslings, the Hocks (from Hochheim) and so on. They gave the English names to some of the classic wine styles of the world, for example the Bordeaux reds ('claret', from clairette, or light red) and the fortified sweet red wines of Oporto ('port').

It is scarcely surprising, then, to find that when the English settled Australia, they retained the nomenclatures with which they felt at home. A lighter style of Australian red wine thus became 'claret', still a common name for red wine in this country, though its apparent connection with the reds of Bordeaux is harder to find today. A rounder, more generous red became Australian 'burgundy'. Whites became 'riesling', 'hock' or even 'riesling/hock', and drier whites became 'white burgundy', after the great wines made from the chardonnay grape in Burgundy itself. When drier styles became popular among the white wines, they were branded 'chablis' and this broad description of a wine style — today as broad as an Australian valley — remains in use and is understood by wine buyers looking for this type of wine. A sparkling wine became, of course, a 'champagne', despite legal action by the French Champagne makers to stop the use of the name.

As the Australian wine industry developed new customers in the 1950s, 60s and 70s, it therefore labelled much of its wine under these 'generic' labels. They had to do with a taste expectation rather than with any guarantee of the area of origin of a wine (which is their purpose in Europe) or of grape varieties. Use of these generic wine descriptions developed innocently, despite charges by some Europeans of plagiarism and labelling dishonesty, and the words certainly conveyed the required meaning to potential customers.

It went even further. Since the 1950s, some generic names have really had little to do with taste. The word 'riesling', for example, came to mean a more-or-less dry white wine, and this wine could be blended from just about any grape variety, not just the riesling grape. In the Hunter Valley, a widely grown white grape variety was for many years incorrectly called 'Hunter River Riesling', though it was in fact the semillon grape. In Australia, a wine labelled 'riesling' indicates a medium-to-dry white wine, just as 'chablis' means the same thing in the United States.

When it became apparent that the German clone of riesling was going to be immensely popular with Australian drinkers, wine-makers started calling it 'Rhine riesling' to differentiate it from a blended 'riesling' wine. The practice persists, though the use of the generic 'riesling' is slowly fading.

Many of the other generic labels are also slowly disappearing, though some (claret, white burgundy, chablis and champagne) will probably be around forever. In their stead come the 'varietal' wines, and it is the awareness of these few grape varieties that provides the best clue to appreciating and finding enjoyment in Australian wines today.

Barossa Valley landscape

The Wine Areas of Australia

There are over 550 wineries in the country today, including the multiple cellar doors or wineries of some of the major makers. The state-by-state breakdown is as follows:

New South Wales: 155, with the largest number (40) in the Hunter Valley, and 12 in the greater Canberra area.

Victoria: 125, and growing fast, with more than a dozen separate areas throughout the state and 23 in the central/southern areas.

Tasmania: 13.

South Australia: 155, with 41 in the Barossa Valley, 39 in the Southern Vales, 21 in Clare and 20 in Coonawarra.

Western Australia: 90, with 34 in the Swan Valley, close to Perth, and 22 in the Margaret River region.

Northern Territory: 1, near Alice Springs.

Queensland: 14, with 12 in the Granite Belt area south-west of Brisbane.

New South Wales

1 Sydney

The wineries in the greater Sydney metropolitan area are gone, though the signs remain in a suburb called Vineyard and the old Minchinbury Cellars of Penfolds. There are a few wineries on the outskirts of the city (in Richmond and Camden), but they are small. However, there are still a few places worth visiting, particularly the Australian Wine Centre (in Circular Quay West in Sydney's Rocks area, under the southern approach to the Harbour Bridge) and some excellent wine stores such as Camperdown Cellars, the Oak Barrel and Jarmans.

A number of wineries have their head offices in Sydney and at least one, McWilliams, can arrange tastings by appointment.

Sydney's position in the Australian wine industry, other than being the nation's largest wine market, is dominated by an outside presence. The Hunter Valley lies 160 kilometres, or just over two hours' drive, directly north of the city.

2 The Hunter Valley

Royal Navy Captain John Hunter was master of one of the ships in Captain Arthur Phillip's First Fleet which landed on the coast of eastern Australia on 26 January 1788. Adventurous colonists did not take long to explore north, and they found a river valley which they named after Hunter.

The early European settlers in the valley were quick to realise that its high levels of sunshine were suitable for growing ripe grapes. By the second half of

Grape Vine ready for picking

DAVID SIMMONDS

the 19th century, quite large volumes of table wine were being made in and around the valley, and some surprising grape varieties, including chardonnay and cabernet sauvignon, were widely grown. The Hunter was not — is not — an ideal place to grow grapes or make wine, but the vines seem to flourish against the many adversities, and some excellent wines were — still are — produced despite the area's droughts, hail, heat and floods. The flourishing wine industry in the valley was nearly wiped out not by such natural disasters but by the advent of Federation at the turn of the century. With the breakdown of trade barriers between the states, cheap and subsidised South Australian wine started flooding onto the Sydney market and the Hunter industry was very nearly decimated.

It was not until the 1960s, with the advent of the red wine boom, that progressive thinkers turned once again to the Hunter Valley to grow wine grapes. There was another boom and grapes were planted where they should not have been, on soil which would not generate crops good enough to support a viable wine production business. The quality makers, sited on the good volcanic soils sloping off the Brokenback Range, kept going during the hard years — the Tyrrells, Tullochs, Draytons and the legendary Maurice O'Shea, whose company was later taken over by the McWilliam family.

A number of makers learned these lessons the hard way. The Rothbury Estate, established under the imaginative chairmanship of Australian wine entrepreneur and judge Len Evans, nearly went broke a few times; and companies such as Tulloch, Hungerford Hill, Saxonvale and, further up the valley, Arrowfield struggled from crisis to crisis. The problem was that yields were often too small to produce wine economically and several makers soon learned that to compete in the market-place they would have to look elsewhere to supplement their grape intake.

But the Hunter and its wine-makers are survivors, and tourism has been their saviour. Over the past 15 years, a number of imaginative tourist-related enterprises have grown up. **The Rothbury Estate** helped lead the way, with its grand dinners, banquets, sophisticated tastings, wine auctions, operas, concerts and other events throughout the year. The Estate has also concentrated on wine quality, producing some admirable dry white wines, mainly from semillon but later from chardonnay. Rothbury seems to have surmounted its problems and, like many of the remaining Hunter wineries, come to terms with the realities of commercial life and people's wine needs. Visit Rothbury if you go to the Hunter, taste the wines and, if possible, attend one or more of the events organised during the year.

A dog-leg away from Rothbury is an older Hunter Valley winery operated by the Tyrrell Family since 1858. The family is still very much in control, with Murray Tyrrell, the head of the clan, and son Bruce running the show from their picturesque old wooden winery.

Tyrrell's produce a very wide range of wines, which are available in two tasting rooms. If you indicate a genuine interest in their better wines, they'll whisk you into the inner sanctum and show the best. As with the better Hunter wineries, the wines are made from semillon, shiraz and cabernet sauvignon. However, for all their traditionalism, the Tyrrells have been among the most pioneering of the vignerons of the valley. Murray Tyrrell quickly realised the potential of chardonnay, possibly before anyone else in modern Australian winemaking, and the company's Vat 47 Chardonnay is worth seeking out, though it is produced only in limited quantity each year. He also spotted the potential of cabernet sauvignon and in particular the pinot noir red grape for the Hunter. The Tyrrells astounded the wine world in the late 1970s when, at the Gault Millau 'Wine Olympics' in Paris, their pinot noir beat the great burgundies and other outstanding European reds by coming first in its class.

The Tyrrells have a bewildering range of vat numbers for many of their wines, but their wines are generally top class and full of flavour. Even the 'commercial' wines, such as their big-selling Long Flat Red (named after a vineyard), are excellent drinking. They make many wines which require cellaring.

McWilliam's are another family company with a strong presence here, though their head office is in Sydney and their largest winery interests are to the south in the Murrumbidgee Irrigation Area. They offer a very wide range of local and other products, being notable for value for money across the board with all their wine products.

'The Homestead', at McWilliam's Mount Pleasant winery, is typical of early Australian colonial architecture, though it has only recently been built. It has a homely feel, with an open fire and wood panelling. 'The Homestead' range of wines is sold exclusively at the winery.

Tulloch's was a family company, and still has family members working there, but several years ago it sold out to the Gilbey's group, and then went to the giant Penfold's/Kaiser Stuhl wine consortium. The company also makes, like Tyrrell's, some fine semillon

Grape vines in South Australia

and shiraz-based white and red wines in the distinctive Hunter styles. The chardonnay and champagnes are also good.

Among the smaller makers of the Hunter, one stands out for sheer individuality and commitment. Murray Robson, a Sydney businessman, founded his tiny and picturesque **Robson Vineyard** near the southernmost end of the valley in 1972 and has concentrated on parcels of wine almost small enough to be described as 'hand-made'. Although his boutique winery is crammed with the best equipment available, he signs each wine bottle label by hand, having perfected the art of signing two simultaneously while sitting in front of television at night. He has concentrated on the premium varieties including cabernet, pinot noir, shiraz and chardonnay, plus the Hunter staples of semillon and shiraz. His Squire Cottage, several hundred metres from the winery, is

Wine testing at the Leo Buring cellars of the Barossa Valley

available for hire and is thoroughly recommended for a stay of a few days.

Further north, towards the winding Hunter River itself, is one of the most significant wineries in the valley — **The Wyndham Estate.** The Wyndham Estate produces some of the biggest selling wines on the east coast and has been active in the past few years buying other, less successful, wineries, including Hermitage Estate and Saxonvale. Wyndham was established as Dalwood over 150 years ago, but when an active entrepreneur named Brian McGuigan took over in the early 1970s, the real action began. McGuigan made wines people *liked* drinking, not wines that wine-makers thought people *should* like drinking, and then promoted them aggressively. The winery is right alongside the river. It has a restaurant and other recreation areas plus a large cellar door. Bus tours are a speciality and while it is to be said that the complex is unashamedly aimed at mass tourism, there is no doubt that the better wines produced here are good. The Wyndham Estate is 20 minutes' drive from the central Hunter district of Pokolbin, but is well signposted.

One of the largest wine-making concerns in Australia, and one of the best in quality terms, is **Lindeman's,** named after an Australian wine pioneer, Dr Henry John Lindeman (one of many doctors who helped establish the industry, just as many continue to make wine today). Lindeman's is now owned by tobacco giant Philip Morris, and poor returns in the Australian wine industry over the past decade have caused Lindeman's Hunter River Winery some considerable heartache, contraction, retrenchments and property sales.

In the Hunter Valley, one finds the company's most visible presence where traditional valley wines are made. The semillons (labelled as 'riesling', 'white burgundy' and 'chablis') are outstanding; so, too, are many of the reds, usually labelled as 'hermitage' (shiraz). Other wines include chardonnay, verdelho (which at their best are exceptional) and some great sweet white wines. The wider range of Lindeman's other products is also available at this winery, which features a great picnic area and winery museum.

Hunter Estate is part of the Wyndham Estate empire, but is closer to the heart of the wine area of the valley. It is interesting as a tourist destination because it has a very good motel, Brokenback Motor Lodge, amid the vineyards alongside the winery and a good restaurant attached to the distinctive winery building. The large 'H' structure at the winery's front, on top of a rise, originally stood for 'Hermitage' winery. Now, under Wyndham parentage, the wine-making is overseen by Brian McGuigan's younger brother, Neil McGuigan. A wide range of traditional Hunter whites and reds, plus champagnes, fortifieds and other products are available.

Among the smaller Hunter producers, **Brokenwood** also stands out for the unremitting efforts made by the constantly changing band of owners who run it with spare time effort plus a full-time wine-maker, Iain Riggs. The winery, just a few hundred metres from the giant Hungerford Hill complex, specialises in premium dry reds and whites, including semillon, shiraz, chardonnay and cabernet.

One of the centrepieces of a visit or stay in the valley is the winery complex at the geographical centre of the area — the **Hungerford Hill** village. Sited at the intersection of two of the main roads at Pokolbin, the village includes a high-quality winery, a good motel, a very good restaurant run by an imaginative French chef, Robert Molines, tasting centres, a farmer's market, a curio shop, a horse-riding centre and extensive picnic and play areas. There's something for just about everyone here. Hungerford Hill also makes some very good wines at the winery itself, buried immediately behind the well-designed visitors' areas.

The Cellar restaurant is a delightful fern-filled semi-underground area with a very good local wine list and excellent meals. There are also convention and meeting areas, plus provision for small and large groups for tastings.

The valley is replete with restaurants, some great, some good and some not so good. Several of the better ones include Peter Meier's Casuarina, near the Hunter Estate winery, which is exceptional in most ways. So too, though less grand in ambience, is Frank Margan's Cottage Restaurant at Cessnock. Pepper's Restaurant and Motel is particularly good. It is *the* place for a weekend, or a few days, in the area. They also offer tennis, horse riding, tours and helicopter flights. You can even fly in from Sydney or Newcastle. There is a good airfield just north of the township of Cessnock for both light aircraft and commuter

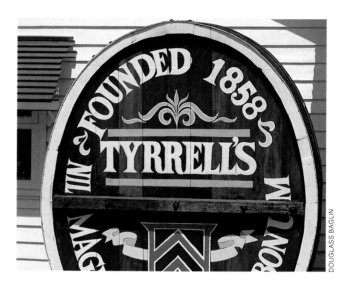

Tyrrell's winery in the Hunter Valley

services from Sydney and elsewhere, and there are also good connections to Maitland airfield, a little further away. Cars can be rented from both airfields.

Another restaurant, popular for lunch and very central to the area's major wineries, is Blaxland Barn, opposite the entrance to the Rothbury Estate. It can also help with area maps and information.

There are many other attractions in the Hunter Valley in addition to those already mentioned. There are walks, balloon flights, cart and hay rides, not to mention some good pub crawls. Two local hotels that stand out are the Wollombi Tavern and the Bellbird Hotel, which is a classic example of a restored Australian country pub. Drop in for a cool ale on a warm day. It also has some very pleasant accommodation and reasonably priced meals.

A leisurely wander around the valley, the best-known wine area in New South Wales and possibly in Australia, takes the best part of two days.

3 The Upper Hunter Valley

West of the Lower Hunter area, the Hunter Valley starts winding and curving through hills and rugged horse and cattle country. This Upper Hunter area is a new and quite different wine-growing district. The countryside is delightful and there are some lovely places to stop for lunch or a picnic, or to camp or caravan near the river with its sandy and gravelly curves, often shaded by gums or weeping willows. There is seldom much traffic and the townships and farm communities have a tranquil and rested feeling.

Three hours or so from Sydney (an hour and a half from the Lower Hunter), it's not a place you'd drive to in order to find great restaurants, though there are several reasonable ones in Muswellbrook. If there are no problems with fire bans, a better idea is to have an outdoor barbecue along the way. This is a very pleasant way of sampling a bottle of Upper Hunter wine on a sunny day.

The Barossa Valley's Wolf Blass winery

There are few widely known wineries here. **Arrowfield,** one of the largest, is a huge winery sprawling on the side of a hill at Jerry's Plains. Some good whites have been made here, at the eastern end of the Upper Hunter from Pokolbin.

Without a doubt, the best-known Upper Hunter winery, both within Australia and in several overseas countries including the United States, is **Rosemount Estate.** Rosemount has pursued an aggressive policy of making some exceptional chardonnays which have received great international acclaim. The Show Chardonnay, a lovely dry white wine of great fruit and wood flavours, is the best known. Other Rosemount whites are also good, ranging from commercial chardonnay to chablis and rieslings, and there are some very enjoyable reds, especially those (such as cabernet sauvignon) from the company's vineyards in Coonawarra in South Australia. The winery site is splendid, with its adjacent horse pastures and the narrow reaches of the Upper Hunter River just below. Picnics, tours and tastings are possible here, the most important port of call in this little-understood wine area of Australia.

4 Mudgee

Mudgee is another wine area of great scenic beauty — at certain times of year the 'nest in the hills' is quite breathtaking. The wineries are almost all small ones making very individualistic products, including mead (honey wine). Again, it's hardly worth driving to Mudgee to taste the wines alone, but a very scenic weekend drive might also include the Hunter areas.

Small wineries worth a visit include Huntington Estate (especially for reds), Botobolar, Miramar and Platt's (near the town of Gulgong). Winery maps and details are readily available in and around the local towns and at the wineries, and signposting is quite good.

The largest, and best, winery in the Mudgee area

is **Montrose.** The company is owned by an Italian group, Transfield, and the wine-maker/manager is Italian-trained wine-maker Carlo Corino. Some excellent, and some unusual, white and red wines are made here in a modern location. Tastings are encouraged, and are worthwhile. Close by is **Craigmoor,** a winery recently taken over by Montrose. This very old cellar had its first vintage in 1858, and now has a stylish Italian-type restaurant, tours, and barbecue and children's playground areas.

The upland and grazing country around Mudgee is typically Australian, and the town is representative of settlements of this type, with wide streets and country shops (such as Loneragans). The old Mudgee burial ground is a testament to the hardships of the early settlers, particularly the children, in this part of Australia.

5 The Murrumbidgee Irrigation Area (Griffith)

The waters of the Murrumbidgee River and its big brother, the Murray, have long provided a large proportion of Australian wines, and a very large proportion of the best value-for-money wines. Many of the vineyards in this area were established as 'soldier settler' blocks after the First and Second World Wars and plenty of sweat and water diverted from the rivers created emerald green oases out of the parched earth.

Areas such as Griffith and parts of the Victorian and South Australian Riverlands can never expect hordes of tourists. They are too far from the major population centres, they are very hot in summer, and with the exception of a few towns and the wineries there isn't much to see or do (except perhaps some river fishing or duck shooting).

If you draw a line between Sydney and Adelaide, it won't miss the town of Griffith by much. Situated in one of the drier parts of the country, the water from the river, out of sight to the south, nevertheless produces very large crops of grapes. The largest wine presence is that of **McWilliam's,** based in Sydney but with their largest winery here and at three other locations in the Riverina. Hanwood, some ten minutes' drive south of Griffith, is well worth a visit.

The large range of sparkling, table and fortified wines can be tasted at a most unusual tasting room, a huge 'barrel' along the lines of giant pineapples, oranges and lobsters in other tourist areas of Australia. The rieslings, chardonnays, semillons, blended whites, cabernets and shiraz dry wines are outstanding value for quality, and a superb range of ports and other fortified wines is also made. A giant green riesling bottle nearby is actually a wine museum.

Another winery in the area worthy of a visit is **San Bernadino,** which offers a huge range of well-made wines for sale. Perhaps some of the area's best wines come from another family maker, **de Bortoli.** The de Bortoli family, of Italian lineage, are excellent wine-makers and some excellent wines are to be tasted in their large, cool tasting room. Best known among them are some world-class sweet white (sauterne-style) wines.

Victoria

Victoria was once the wine state of Australia. Its climate emulates that of certain parts of Europe, and vines were widely planted around Melbourne and other areas in the colonial days. Apparently the wines made from these grapes were impressive until the vine louse *phylloxera* arrived from Europe, where it had wreaked havoc on the French and German industries. It did the same to Victoria, and wine production in South Australia and New South Wales soon exceeded that of Victoria.

Today, almost 100 years later, Victoria is experiencing a strong comeback, both in the quality and quantity of its wines. There are now some 125 wineries throughout the state and it appears that by the 1990s Victorian wineries will have outnumbered those in the other states though the quantity of wine produced will still be less.

6 **Melbourne** has always been a city interested in wine and food. It has some of the best wine outlets (Dan Murphy's, Crittendens and Nicks amongst others) and many excellent restaurants and wine bars (such as Jimmy Watson's and McCoppin's Wine Pub).

A good place to start a wine trek is the state-sponsored wine promotional body, Wine Victoria. Their office and tasting/function room is sited in Banana Alley, beneath the railway lines running into Flinders Street Station in the centre of the city. The area is beside an old banana market where bananas were unloaded from the nearby Yarra River. Wine Victoria can point you toward wines and wine activities that interest you around the state.

There are more than a dozen Victorian wine areas, but the key ones are the Yarra Valley, just east of Melbourne in the outer suburbs and near the town of Yarra Glen; the north-east region, around Rutherglen and Milawa; the long Murray Valley which stretches along the NSW/Victorian border to South Australia; the Goulburn Valley immediately north of Melbourne; Geelong around the north-western shore of Port Phillip Bay; and the central and southern areas of the state with some 23 wineries, plus a few wineries in the area of the town of Great Western.

The Yarra Valley wineries are generally small, though they produce some very good wines indeed. Among those with cellar door operations, the attractive **Fergussons** winery sells some good wines and has an entertaining restaurant/function area; **St Hubert's** turns out some most attractive wines, especially reds; and **Chateau Yarrinya** produces some excellent reds.

There are other activities in this appealing valley, which is upstream along Melbourne's River Yarra and about an hour and a half out of town. Golfing, tennis, walking and riding are among the semi-rural pursuits to be found in the area, together with a wide range of wildlife and birdlife.

The Goulburn Valley, also within easy striking distance of Melborne, is just north of Melbourne's Tullamarine Airport. There are only a few wineries, including two significant operations. **Chateau Tahbilk** dates back to 1860 and is among the best-known wineries in the state. Still owned by the Purbrick family, it makes some powerful cabernet sauvignon and shiraz whites, plus some interesting full-bodied whites, including some from the unusual grape variety, marsanne. Other activities include water-skiing and fishing on the nearby lakes and streams.

Mitchelton is one of the more modern showpieces of the Australian wine business, with its towering spire, excellent red and white wines, restaurants, picnic areas and children's playgrounds.

7 Around the bay from Melbourne is the **Geelong area,** put on the wine map by two main wine enterprises, **Idyll Vineyard** and **Hickinbotham Wines,** which has now moved closer to Melbourne.

8 The **central and southern areas** of the state, just east of the Pyrenees mountains, are the source of some very striking table wines, particularly reds. They are often said to have a 'mintiness' about them, especially the cabernet sauvignons. Several wineries that stand out are **Balgownie Estate,** which is owned by Mildara wines in the far north-west of the state, **Passing Clouds, Chateau Le Amon** and, for sparkling wines, **Yellowglen,** also now owned by Mildara Wines.

9 The area around the town of **Great Western,** some two hours north-west of Melbourne on good roads, is worthy of mention because of the endeavours of one company: **Seppelt's.** Their sparkling wines

*The Yalumba Winery in the Barossa Valley South Australia
is one of the many historically diverse constructions to be
found in and around the Barossa Valley.*

have put this isolated area on the wine map, and their large winery is certainly worth seeing if you are in the area.

The name Great Western is synonymous with 'champagne' in Australia, and the company makes a number of different styles, from very well-priced, well-known national brands to some special cuvees, sparkling burgundies and indeed some very attractive table wines with local fruit. They are not the only local vignerons, however; other notable locals include **Best's Great Western, Mount Langi Ghiran** and **McRae's Montara**, in the town of Ararat.

Some very distinctive and attractive wines are made in this area, and to the east in the Macedon district.

10 Leaving the best — and certainly the most varied — to last, the broad area of **north-east Victoria** may be the most appealing for travellers wishing to try some very different wines. The area around Rutherglen, stretching south to Milawa, is popular with travellers for a number of reasons. Horse riding, canoeing (on the Murray, King, Ovens or the many other rivers that flow from the nearby Great Dividing Range), water-skiing and fishing in the nearby lakes and streams, and snow-skiing in the Victorian Alps (very near Brown Brothers at Milawa) are some of the area's many other attractions.

Brown Brothers must be one of Australia's most interesting and appealing wineries in terms of what they make and sell, as well as the rustic, rural ambience of their winery and tasting areas. You can picnic, barbecue or just relax and enjoy one of the amazingly wide range of wines they produce. The quality is generally excellent across the board, and the Brown Family, who run the thriving business, are charming people.

The Rutherglen area, three-quarters of an hour further north, produces some of the most distinctive wines of Australia — the famous fortifieds of Victoria's north-east. These muscats, tokays, ports and sherries are stunning at their best. There are very few wines quite like them anywhere in the world. They are wines of incredibly intense flavour and often of great age — 50 years and more for the base materials. The wineries are friendly and a 'Winery Walkabout' (the name of the annual wine festival held in the area over the Queen's Birthday long weekend in June) is a great experience at any time of the year. There are plenty of hotels and motels in nearby Albury-Wodonga, Wangaratta, Rutherglen and in the historic town of Beechworth.

Most of the wineries are scattered close to Rutherglen itself, an old gold town, and some of those worth visiting include **Morris Mia Mia** which produces some excellent muscats and tokays, as well as good table wines, **Pfeiffer, Chambers' Rosewood** and **Buller's Calliope**. Closer to the Ned Kelly bushranger country of Glenrowan, just to the south,

Bailey's Glenrowan and **HJT Vineyards** also make some excellent wines.

Tasmania

Some fascinating and often very good table wines have emerged from Tasmania over the past few years. Climatically, the area has much in common with parts of Europe, being far to the south and quite cold, so vintage is often prolonged into May. But there are problems with frosts and winds as well as birds.

11 **Heemskerk** (at Piper's Brook, north of **Launceston**) and the nearby **Piper's Brook** wineries stand out. Operated respectively by Graham Wiltshire and Dr Andrew Pirie, both produce comparatively small amounts of table wine and some sparkling wine (Heemskerk is involved with the French Champagne house, Roederer). The chardonnays, rieslings, cabernets and increasingly the pinot noirs are, at their best, stunning, but they are also fairly expensive.

12 To the south, near **Hobart,** is a smaller almost 'hobby' winery operated by Claudio Alcorso and his son Julian. **Moorilla Estate** is right on the western banks of the Derwent River and the wines, again in miniscule quantities, are excellent.

If in Hobart, Graeme Lynch's admirable Aberfeldy Cellars — one of the better wine shops in Australia — stocks some Tasmanian wines. There is also a very good wine club and restaurant in the hotel section of the outlet.

The fruit of the vine

South Australia

Some 57% of Australia's wine comes from South Australia — the Wine State — including many of Australia's best wines. Many of the largest wineries in the country are either based here or have their principal production areas in the state. The SA Tourism Department has established that, apart from business, wine is the main motivation for visits to South Australia.

13 Adelaide and the Adelaide Hills

A truly delightful city of a million people, Adelaide is large enough to be reasonably cosmopolitan, yet small enough to be relaxed and comfortable for both visitors and locals alike. In the past few years, and especially since the first Formula One Grand Prix was held in the streets of Adelaide in 1985, some large hotels have been established and a very fine casino has opened. Some of Australia's best restaurants are also to be found in this city of churches.

The main geographical feature of the area, other than the Gulf of St Vincent to the west of the city (St Vincent was the patron saint of wine-makers), is the spine of hills — the Mount Lofty Ranges — running from the south-west to the north-east behind Adelaide. Scattered amongst these hills are many new vineyards and some new wineries, as well as some very good restaurants. There are also plenty of opportunities to go horse riding, trail walking and off-track driving and to visit craft and pottery shops.

A recommended way to see the spectacular Adelaide Hills, and to taste some of its wines, is by taking a trip on a 200-tonne steam engine, the Steamranger.

The best-known winery in the Adelaide Hills is **Petaluma,** which produces exceptional dry white and dry red wines, plus a sweet white. These can be tasted at the **Bridgewater Mill,** a lovely old mill with a giant working waterwheel and one of the best restaurants near Adelaide.

Grape picking in South Australia

14 The Barossa Valley

The Barossa Valley is Australia's best-known wine-growing district. It stretches as a shallow depression just west of the Mount Lofty/Barossa Ranges and is about one and a half hours' drive from Adelaide. A large wine area, it extends into the hills around the charming town of Angaston. An overnight stay is recommended if possible, and 36 hours is a fair estimate of the time required to see a reasonable slice of the Barossa.

The German influence is still very strong in many areas of the Barossa, dating to the mid-1800s, when many refugees from Europe fled religious persecution and came to South Australia. Their cultural heritage is evident in shop-front names, German wursts and sausages, lovely fresh breads and in the German-influenced food in several restaurants and wineries.

The wineries range from among the biggest in Australia (Penfolds/Kaiser Stuhl) to the very tiny (Gnadenfrei), and the wines cover the whole range but are generally of high quality.

The Barossa revolves around a trilogy of towns: Nuriootpa-Tanunda-Angaston, with a few smaller towns scattered around and in the hills. The most exciting time to be in the Barossa is during the biennial Barossa Vintage Festival. (Information is available through the SA Tourism offices or through the Barossa Winemakers' Association.) The Barossa Valley Highway (or Sturt Highway) can be used as a main road between Adelaide, the Riverland and Sydney. Some of the large wineries are located close to this road which goes through Tanunda and Nuriootpa if you avoid the high-speed by-pass.

Penfolds/Kaiser Stuhl, now the largest winery in Australia, is based in Sydney but has a huge winery complex just outside Nuriootpa. The vast range of wines from this group, which includes Wynn's, spans the entire range of Australian wines. Penfolds are noted for their red wines, headed by classics such as Grange Hermitage (Australia's most famous red), St Henri and the outstanding Bin 707 cabernet sauvignon. Kaiser Stuhl makes some excellent Barossa rieslings.

Entering the valley from the south, another large national wine-maker, **Orlando,** can be seen on the right. This company, now owned by Reckitt and Colman, ranks very high among large producers and exporters in Australia, with consistently good and often great table and sparkling Carrington wines. The tasting room welcomes visitors, including tour buses, and there is a restaurant for simple meals. Their rieslings and chardonnays are exemplary commercial wines, with an equally good series of Coonawarra reds. Orlando is also noted for its well-promoted Coolabah cask range of wines.

On the western side of the valley, off the Barossa Valley Highway and down a driveway lined with hundreds of palm trees, is **Seppeltsfield,** the largest production centre of B. Seppelt and Sons. The Seppelt family have sold out and the SA Brewing Company now owns this very large maker.

This huge winery is the site of regular hot-air ballooning championships, and the sight of 20 or 30 brightly coloured balloons rising from the open spaces between the Seppeltsfield vineyards is certainly memorable. The complex has tours and tastings and other regular entertainment events throughout the year; inquiries can be made at the winery or at the company's Adelaide headquarters. Their wines are of a very high quality, from a wide variety of vineyards. Where else in the world could you obtain, on an ongoing basis, a 100-year-old tawny port, though you'll pay $1,500 or so a bottle for it!

Nowhere in the Barossa is the Germanic influence more obvious than at **Wolf Blass** wines. The centre of this rapidly expanding empire is on the Sturt Highway a few kilometres from Nuriootpa, though the administration centre is in Adelaide. Trained in Germany, Blass came to Australia and worked for several large concerns, including Kaiser Stuhl, before launching his own small winery, Bilyara, in 1973. He buys grapes and wines from wherever he needs in order to get the full and intense flavours he and his wine-making team seek. The best results — which are undoubtedly his red wines — are superb. His Yellow Label riesling is among the most popular in Australia and his Classic Dry White is also gaining enormous popularity — a tribute to the enterprise and skill needed to pick just what people want to drink and to then find ways to make it better than most others. The winery is an amazing place, with a stunning tasting room.

Among the major makers of Australian wine, only a few are still family controlled. In descending order of production, they are McWilliams, Hardys and Yalumba. It would be difficult to find three more different families. The gregarious and omnipresent McWilliams from New South Wales date their huge company to the 1920s. Their most successful product is a cream sherry. The Hardys, with sailing in their blood, are deeply established in the Southern Vales of Adelaide. And the Hill Smiths of Angaston are gentlemen wine-makers as well as horse breeders and racers.

The image of the Hill Smiths belies an imaginative approach to their business, all the way through the grape-growing to wine-making and marketing. Behind the lovely old facade of the Yalumba winery, just outside Angaston on the side of the Barossa Range, is a heap of technology and a ready willingness to make innovative changes. Wines such as Pewsey Vale (from a vineyard they re-established) and other extraordinarily attractive rieslings, some very fine blended reds, and top-quality ports and champagnes are among their product range. Functions and tastings

are encouraged, with meals by arrangement. A look at their wine museum, containing wines dating well back into the 19th century, is a highlight of any visit.

A number of smaller wineries are scattered around the valley and back into the Barossa Ranges/Adelaide Hills. These include **Holmes' Springton** (which has a simple but very pleasant restaurant), **Krondorf** and **Mountadam.** Larger wineries making very good products but with less obvious cellar door operations include **Tollana** and **Peter Lehmann.** Peter produces some superior and well-priced wines and ports and offers, with his wife Margaret, family-style hospitality for those lucky enough to catch them at their lovely antique weigh station next to the winery.

Saltram, owned by the huge Seagram international liquor group, with a splendid winery and cellar door operation is just on the downhill side of Angaston (on the northern side of the road). Their wines are generally very good.

Wine bottles ready for labelling

The restaurant scene around the Barossa Valley is very diverse. Perhaps the most spectacular is the Pheasant Farm, west of Nuriootpa, which specialises in game. The restaurant sits out over a lake filled with trout and yabbies. It is wonderfully relaxing, with great food. Die Gallerie and Die Wienstube in Tanunda and between Tanunda and Nuriootpa respectively offer German food, both in most appealing surroundings. An al fresco meal, perhaps with some local sausage, bread and pickles and one of the rieslings or fine reds that have made the Barossa Valley famous among Australian wine drinkers is also highly recommended on a warm day.

15 The Clare Valley

A little way off the beaten track and producing some really good wines is the Clare Valley, located two hours or so north of Adelaide off the road that leads to Broken Hill. The valley itself is a delight, wending upwards (if you are heading north on Route 83) to the towns of Watervale, Sevenhill and then Clare. The drive is easy and pleasant unless the temperature is very high — and it can be! There are some good motels, and a homely hotel/motel in Clare. In the town of Mintaro is a superb set of restored stables and buildings, the Mintaro Mews, complete with a top-rate restaurant. It's very highly recommended for a few days' respite.

Clare prides itself on both fine wines and fine food. A wine and food festival is held each year, and top restaurateurs from Adelaide take their pots and pans north to the wineries of the district to join in with the local restaurants in the festival.

Stanley Leasingham, owned by the H. J. Heinz Company, is the largest wine-maker in the area, producing some excellent rieslings and red wines. The winery is close to town and this is a good place to start tasting. It provides a useful benchmark by which to judge other wineries in the area — and their prices!

On the way into Clare from the south are two other sizeable wine-makers. **Quelltaler** has historic and attractive cellars set amid rolling vineyards. The quality of their white wines, especially, has risen sharply in recent years since the French giant Remy bought them. Not far away, **Taylor's** are well known for their white burgundy and for their distinctive red wines, particularly cabernet.

Further up the main road to Clare, it's worth taking a small diversion into a piece of the past. The **Sevenhill Cellars** is a winery run by a Jesuit order. A beautiful chapel and crypt are located nearby. If this sort of thing interests you, this place — which makes quite a lot of wine, including export wine, for the

A view of the Heemskerk vineyard in Tasmania

Catholic Church — is certainly worth a visit. Brother John May's carefully made wines are distinctive, and some are very good indeed, and he's a delight to meet.

Tim Knappstein, a skilled and enthusiastic winemaker, is one of the valley's best-known. He still makes wine here, though he sold the business to Wolf Blass a year or two ago. His whites (chardonnay, fumé blanc and rieslings) are really good, and the reds are arguably as good. The winery is in an old brewery called Enterprise, the original name of Tim's business.

Families still make some fine wines in this area, among them **Jim Barry** and his sons. His wines are among the very best to come out of the district, and among the best in the state. **Mitchell Cellars** is run by Andrew and Jane Mitchell and their dedication to both wine-making — their rieslings and reds are terrific — and to the area itself makes a visit to the winery worthwhile. It is off the main road, but is sign-posted.

There are many other appealing and diverse wineries in the area, which includes the Polish Hill River sub-district just to the east, and such unremittingly traditional wineries as **Wendouree**. But go and see and taste; the Clare Valley wines are very good and getting better.

16 The McLaren Vale District

If the Barossa is the home of big wineries, the McLaren Vale District (also known as the Southern Vales) is the heartland of Australia's small wine-makers, with the exception of Hardy's, Chateau Reynella, Pirramimma and Seaview. And charmingly so, spreading along the bottom end of the Adelaide Hills down a shallow vale, through the growing town of McLaren Vale, to the Gulf of St Vincent.

The area is within easy striking distance of Adelaide — just 40 or so kilometres. It has some very good restaurants, some lovely (and well sign-posted) tourist drives, a smattering of stylish pottery and craft shops, plus the horticultural attractions of being the southern hemisphere's largest almond-growing region and one of the most successful rose nursery districts.

For the visitor, the beaches along the Gulf of St Vincent, stretching south from Hallett Cove to Sellick's Beach, where the Adelaide Hills meet the gulf waters, are a pure and simple summer delight. You can drive onto many of them for a token payment, park on the hard white sands, bathe, picnic and walk. Hang-gliders soar along the cliff faces through much of the year. There is seldom much surf because of the sheltering influence of Kangaroo Island across the gulf's mouth, but the Marine Park near Port Noarlunga welcomes skin divers, and the fishing in the gulf waters can be an angler's dream when the whiting are running.

Sailing in these brilliant blue waters, whether on simple surf skis or in 12-metre yachts, has nurtured world-class yachtsmen including Sir James Hardy, who grew up at nearby Seacliff, and a great South Australian wine-maker, the late Colin Haselgrove, who won the Sydney-Hobart ocean race in 1950.

For visitors, the great appeal of the Southern Vales is its closeness to Adelaide. You can get there by car, bus, train, taxi, or even by helicopter from the large Lloyd Aviation company based at Adelaide Airport, and spend an easy and rewarding day in this southern wine-growing area, and still be back in Adelaide in time for dinner or the theatre.

The restaurants in the area that are worth visiting include The Barn, a relaxed and leafy eatery fronted by a small art gallery in McLaren Vale. The food here is generous and the atmosphere relaxed, and the wine selection concentrates on local wines; it is one of the best-known and most consistent eateries around Adelaide. Other worthwhile spots to dine are Pipkins in McLaren Vale (take your own wine, which is simple as Hardy's winery is opposite, and so is the local hotel); Prewett's in Kangarilla, some 15 kilometres distant; the Hotel McLaren for simpler food; The Vines; and during weekends the Red Oven for oriental food.

A number of the smaller wineries in this area really do repay a visit if you are looking for high-quality wines. Among them are **Wirra Wirra**, whose dry whites and reds are very hard to fault; **Woodstock**, which is very small though with a range of very fine reds and superlative chardonnays; and **Pirramimma**, with its distinctive reds and fortifieds. The wines of **d'Arenberg** have distinction and character, most obviously in the reds and ports. Not far away, **Middlebrook** has a restaurant well worth seeking out for the quality of its food. The winery's chardonnays have been good, but the rest of its wines are more variable.

Old Clarendon Winery, in the hills south-east of Adelaide, includes two fine restaurants — the casual Wintergarden, and the refined Gillard's restaurant, housed in the original maturation room of this historic winery. Horse riding, golf, tennis and other activities can be organised in the immediate area.

Though some wine is produced here, this 'winery' is more an historic and well-situated resort, with shops, lovely rustic motel rooms with fine views, an art gallery and other attractions. An ideal location for a weekend away where one may taste a large variety of locally produced vintages, there is also a conference centre useful for business gatherings of up to 50 people.

One of the more unusual activities and certainly the adventure highlight of this area is a camel trek through the rugged and spectacular Onkaparinga Gorge. The Onkaparinga River runs from the Adelaide Hills down through Clarendon, entering into the Gulf of St Vincent near Port Noarlunga. The gorge is a largely unspoilt reserve snaking along the sea, providing unparalleled views including some of the McLaren Vale vineyards; all this from atop a camel.

McLaren on the Lake is a very large motel just outside the township of McLaren Vale, complete with an atrium-style restaurant, a huge lake with ducks, plus a winery operation run by the enterprising and talented Andrew Garrett. A superb location with tennis courts, pools, bars, walks and good wines, it is within easy walking distance of McLaren Vale and Adelaide is 45 minutes by road and a lot less by helicopter.

The wineries are scattered all over the area, amid almond trees, vineyards, and sheep and cattle. Others that would repay a call are Wynn's Seaview, Kay's, Maglieri and Norman's Chais Clarendon.

The largest wine enterprise in the Southern Vales is **Hardy's** at McLaren Vale and further north in the outer suburbs of Reynella. This family company, founded in 1853, now also controls **Chateau Reynella**. The Reynella property, particularly, is virtually a compulsory visit for anyone in the district. It is just off the Main South Road in Old Reynella, 23 kilometres south of Adelaide, and about 20 kilometres north of McLaren Vale township. Stunningly restored at enormous cost by the Hardy's, it is unquestionably the showplace of the Australian wine industry, with its rolling vineyards, botanic gardens, National Trust buildings dating to the early 1840s, and the

opportunity to taste, buy and drink on the premises a range of wines made by the Hardy's group from one side of the continent to the other. The Hardy's white wines and the Chateau Reynella reds (plus ports from both companies) are the jewels in a very lovingly constructed crown. Business and social functions and group visits are all possible by booking. There's a helipad, too.

17 Coonawarra

Here's a paradox. An area which many people think belongs to Victoria, and one which produces what many consider to be the best red wines of Australia, is one of the least interesting wine areas in the country, from the point of view of the tourist. Coonawarra (Aboriginal for 'place of the wild honeysuckle') is 380 kilometres south-east of Adelaide, on flat terrain overlying some rich terra rose soil. Many of the wineries are sited along or near the road that runs through on the way from Mount Gambier to Adelaide. It's pretty warm in summer and very cold in winter, with an icy wind coming off the Southern Ocean.

The coolness of the area is the clue to wine quality, since most years the grapes take a long while to become fully ripe. There's not much to see in the area and most of the companies that grow grapes and turn them into wine here either have head offices elsewhere or have others distributing their wines. The Chardonnay Lodge is the main and best

Visitors enjoy a wine tasting in the Clare Valley

motel/restaurant in the narrow belt of vineyard land that constitutes Coonawarra. A stop for lunch on the way between Melbourne and Adelaide or points between would probably suffice for most, though the smaller vineyard area of Padthaway some 70 kilometres to the north might entice you to stay the night at a splendidly restored colonial stone mansion called Padthaway Estate. The rooms are a trip back to bygone days of 'real' service, the food is superlative and the building is very attractive. It is a trip into the past amid vineyards and country walks. It is fairly expensive, but very worthwhile for a special occasion.

The major wineries have cellar doors in the Coonawarra region. Among them and worth a tasting are Wynn's, Rouge Homme (a division of Lindeman's), Redman, Hungerford Hill, Leconfield, Mildara, Hollick and Katnook. They are so close together that individual cellar door listings are unnecessary because they are generally open during normal working hours on most days. Cabernet sauvignon is king in Coonawarra, and some very good chardonnays and shiraz wines are being produced.

If you're driving toward the coast, arm yourself with a bottle or two and find a few Safcol crayfish at Beachport, Robe, Kingston or Millicent. The coasts are generally unspoilt, the fishing is terrific and the scenery is awesome and beautiful.

18 The Riverland

An enormous amount of Australia's wine comes from the Riverland area, stretching from the north-western Victorian reaches of the Murray and the areas near Waikerie, not far from where the 2,500-kilometre long river turns south for its run to the Southern Ocean. But the wineries are generally so far apart there is little to recommend them to wine visitors.

The large wineries of the South Australian and north-west Victorian areas produce some exceptionally good wines, and wines of superb value for price. At the top of this list has to be **Mildara Wines.** A large and aggressive public company, Mildara has acquired other wineries in the past few years (such as Yellowglen, Krondorf and Balgownie) and continues to produce some very high-quality wines from its base near the large river capital of Mildura. It makes some really excellent fortified wines, some fine Coonawarra and other reds, plus some well-styled whites and a good up-market champagne.

The winery is worth a visit for the wine quality, the very good cellar door operation and a great view of the River Murray. Further inland is Lindeman's giant **Karadoc** winery, with a large range of their very good wines.

There are many other river-based wineries, but few would claim to be a welcome haven for visitors. Nevertheless, the river from one end (Rutherglen in

A vineyard, above and a winery, right in Western Australia's Cape Leeuwin region

north-east Victoria) to the other (near Langhorne Creek in Victoria) has fathered some of Australia's best wine styles, from sherries to light table wines, and many of its most economical cask wines in four-litre packs.

The Riverland is also the centre of a tremendous amount of holiday activity, from sailboarding and fishing to hunting, bird watching, hiking and camping, and canoeing. The paddlesteamers once rivalled the great paddlewheelers of the southern United States in their derring-do and romance — and they live on in places such as Echuca, home of Tisdall's excellent wines. The Murray and Murrumbidgee valleys are home to a very large proportion of Australia's wild waterfowl.

Wineries exist along much of the civilised shore of the rivers, together with vineyards. Two activities that are particularly enjoyable on these great rivers are houseboating and gliding. Live-on houseboats are rapidly becoming popular in cities such as Renmark. The towns of Waikerie (centre of very large vineyards) and Tocumwal and Benalla in Victoria are all centres of gliding, having hosted world gliding championships.

DAVID SIMMONDS

Western Australia

Australia's largest state produces a very small proportion of its wine, yet some of the wines are very exciting. They are certainly very different, reflecting different climatic conditions, grape varieties and a unique approach to wine-making.

Houghton's White Burgundy is the best-known Western Australian white, a very large-selling dry and full-flavoured white wine with wood treatment. Its popularity obviously reflects consumer pleasure at the taste, and few outside Western Australia have come near emulating the complex, slightly nutmeg, taste of the wine. The next runner in the wine stakes is city blocks behind. Yet some fine reds have been coming from the Margaret River area for years, and Houghton themselves make very good cabernet rosé, a Frankland River Rhine Riesling and several chardonnays. Next in size to Houghton is Sandalford, with some enjoyable verdelhos, a few very good cabernets from the Margaret River area, and a superb fortified verdelho.

19 The rest of the field is very varied, though it's not hard to pick the worthwhile places to visit. In the **Swan Valley, Houghton** is a great starting place, with its old homestead and modern technology. They produce some varied white, red and fortified wines, and a few sparkling wines. It is a great spot for a picnic, as the Swan Valley vineyards are just 25 minutes out of Perth, and even closer to the international airport.

Sandalford is not far away, and it offers a luncheon area for those who book or who travel up the nearby Swan River by boat. Of the many other smaller wineries in the valley, **Evans and Tate** stands out, notably for reds and a few excellent dry white wines produced from several different grape-growing areas in the state.

There is a very strong Yugoslav influence in the Swan Valley, reminiscent in its origins of the German influence in the Barossa Valley of South Australia. There are literally dozens of family-owned wineries in this area, making very individualistic wines. They are not hard to find if you take a drive beyond the towns of Guildford or Midland.

South-west Western Australia

While the traditional Western Australian wine business grew up within a short cart ride of the capital of Perth, in the past ten years some very exciting things have been happening with wine in the region 200-400 kilometres south of Perth.

The trip to the south-west region is not a short one, whether by car, bus or plane. However, the scenery is often breathtaking — indeed unforgettable — whether during the wildlife season, when driving through the huge forests of karri, along the shores of the Indian

DAVID SIMMONDS

Ocean with its splendid beaches and labyrinthine caves, or looking over the old whaling station at Albany.

Much of this wonderfully rich, forested and densely green corner at the far south-west of the continent offers all sorts of adventures, from isolated walks or surfing on waves that may have travelled from East Africa to seeing a brace of emus or kangaroos on the road to Margaret River.

The wineries and vineyards are newcomers to the region, numbering around 40 — almost half the state's total. The region comprises a very large corner of the biggest state, embracing regions as far apart as Mount Barker, the Frankland River and the Margaret River.

20 The **Margaret River region** steals the limelight. There are good restaurants; the Captain Freycinet is a very good motel; and there are some of the best wineries of the south. This is the area in which American wine-maker Robert Mondavi became involved, originally with Leeuwin Estate. It has challenges: voracious grape-eating birds, salt spray from the Indian Ocean, and such menaces as kangaroos who like pinot noir grapes! However, the much sought-after Jimmy Watson Trophy from the Melbourne Wine Show has ended up here twice in recent years, and some of the biggest eastern states' wineries are now buying grapes from the region.

For all that, the wine production of the region is miniscule. It can be purchased only with difficulty through a handful of specialist distributors. There are limited supplies and it's expensive.

Nevertheless, try to see a few of the better wineries in these areas. **Leeuwin Estate** is a stunning winery set amid trees and glades. Their cabernets, chardonnays, rieslings and sauvignon blancs, among others, are good, though expensive. If you see the winery, you'll understand why! Most of **Cape Mentelle's** table wines are simply outstanding, particularly the cabernet sauvignons and semillons. **Cullen's Willyabrup**, a pioneer of the southern areas, has very good dry white and dry red wines. The wines of **Moss Wood** and **Vasse Felix** are also worth pursuing.

21 Western Australia is now making some outstandingly good table wines. It is a pity that the quantities are so small, but the wineries certainly merit a trip if you find yourself in the area. From Perth, allow at least two days to do the triangular trip between Perth, the Margaret River and **Mount Barker**, where a visit to **Plantagenet Wines** will complete a visit to an entirely new wine world.

Northern Territory

22 One of the most unusual wineries in Australia is **Chateau Hornsby**, a desert winery outside **Alice Springs** in the outback of the Northern Territory. Here, local pharmacist Denis Hornsby has the first

Brown Brothers Milawa Cellars in North - east Victoria

LEIGH HEMMINGS

vintage in Australia and once or twice he has started picking the grapes before the New Year arrives.

Queensland

23 Queensland has a dozen or so wineries, the most unusual being the **Romavilla Vineyards** at outback **Roma**. It has excellent fortified muscats.

24 The main thrust of the state's wineries is in the cooler **Granite Belt,** up in the Great Dividing Range some two hours south-west of Brisbane. **Robinson's Family Vineyards** is a good place to start tasting here, and the family has a tasting outlet closer to Brisbane in Toowoomba. There are another dozen or so wineries around the Ballandean general area, including Rumbalara, Sundown Valley Vineyards, Old Caves and Mount Magnus in apple country. It even snows in the vineyards occasionally!

Robert Mayne

Robert Mayne is one of the best-known figures in the Australian wine business. He spent five years as National Promotions Manager of The Australian Wine and Brandy Corporation, the Australian government's statutory wine authority, promoting Australian wines throughout Australia and overseas. He is the author of a number of books on wine.

Wine Country Contacts

Locations

New South Wales

1 **Sydney**

Australian Wine Centre
17-21 Circular Quay West
The Rocks
Sydney NSW 2000
Ph. (02) 27 2755

McWilliams
100 Bulwara Road
Pyrmont
Sydney NSW 2009
Ph. (02) 660 2066

2 **The Hunter Valley**

Winery Addresses

The Rothbury Estate
Broke Road
Pokolbin NSW 2321
Ph. (049) 98 7555

Tyrrell's Vineyards
Broke Road
Pokolbin NSW 2321
Ph. (049) 98 7509

McWilliams Mount Pleasant Winery
Marrowbone Road
Pokolbin NSW 2321
Ph. (049) 98 7505

J.Y. Tulloch
Glen Elgin
de Beyer's Road
Pokolbin NSW 2321
Ph. (049) 98 7503

Robson Vineyard
Mount View Road
Mount View NSW 2325
Ph. (049) 90 3670

The Wyndham Estate
Government Road
Dalwood
via Branxton NSW 2335
Ph. (049) 38 1311

Lindeman's Hunter River Winery
McDonalds Road
Pokolbin NSW 2321
Ph. (049) 98 7501

Hunter Estate
Hermitage Road
Pokolbin NSW 2321
Ph. (049) 98 7577

Brokenwood
McDonalds Road
Pokolbin NSW 2321
Ph. (049) 98 7559

Hungerford Hill
Broke Road
Pokolbin NSW 2321
Ph. (049) 98 7519

Accommodation

Accommodation

Neath Hotel
Cessnock Road
Neath NSW 2321
Ph. (049) 30 4270
Classified by the National Trust, a lovely
historic guesthouse, with renovated
bedrooms, restaurant, two bars, a
beergarden and convention facilities.
Five minutes from Cessnock.

Peppers Guest House
Ekerts Road
Pokolbin NSW 2321
Ph. (049) 98 7596
Luxury guesthouse, regarded as one of
the finest in the region, with five-star
accommodation and excellent food. It
has a swimming pool, spa, sauna,
gymnasium, horse riding and a tennis
court.

Brokenback Motor Lodge
Hermitage Road
Pokolbin NSW 2321
Ph. (049) 98 7777
Upmarket accommodation with licensed
restaurant, cocktail bar, swimming pool
and spa.

Bellbird Hotel
Wollombi Road
Cessnock NSW 2325
Ph. (049) 90 1094
Lovely old hotel with licensed restaurant.

Monte Pio Court
Dwyer Street
Campbells Hill
Maitland NSW 2320
Ph. (049) 32 5288
Newly opened hotel with a convention
and function centre, licensed restaurant
and stylish accommodation.

Recommended Restaurants

Casuarina
Hermitage Road
Pokolbin NSW 2321
Ph. (049) 98 7562

Blaxlands Restaurant
Broke Road
Pokolbin NSW 2321
Ph. (049) 98 7550

The Old George and Dragon Restaurant
Melbourne Street
East Maitland NSW 2333
Ph. (049) 33 7272

Hunter Valley Wine Society
Wollombi Road
Cessnock NSW 2325
Ph. (049) 90 6699

Cottage Restaurant
109 Wollombi Road
Cessnock NSW 2325
Ph. (049) 90 3062

The Pokolbin Cellar Restaurant
Hungerford Hill Wine Village
Pokolbin NSW 2321
Ph. (049) 98 7584

Clos de Corne
Hermitage Road
Pokolbin NSW 2321
Ph. (049) 98 7635

Wollombi Tavern
Main Road
Wollombi NSW 2325
Ph. (049) 98 3261

3 **The Upper Hunter Valley**

Winery Addresses

Arrowfield
Jerry's Plains NSW 2330
Ph. (065) 76 4041

Rosemount Estate
Rosemount Road
Denman NSW 2328
Ph. (065) 47 2467

Accommodation

John Hunter Motel
New England Highway
Muswellbrook NSW 2333
Ph. (065) 43 4477
Contains the Governor's Retreat
Restaurant, a swimming pool and spa
and a range of rooms.

Charbonnier of the Hunter
44 Maitland Road
Singleton NSW 2330
Ph. (065) 72 2333
Has an international restaurant, spa,
swimming pool, 70 luxury units, cocktail
bar and conference facilities.

Denman Motor Inn
8 Crinoline Street
Denman NSW 2328
Ph. (065) 47 2462
Middle-range accommodation in
pleasant surroundings with a swimming
pool.

Recommended Restaurants

Charades Restaurant
Charbonnier of the Hunter
44 Maitland Road
Singleton NSW 2330
Ph. (065) 72 2333

Black Hill Restaurant
New England Highway
Muswellbrook NSW 2333
Ph. (065) 43 2945

Loxton House Cellar
142 Bridge Street
Muswellbrook NSW 2333
Ph. (065) 43 3468

4 Mudgee

Montrose Winery
Henry Lawson Drive
Mudgee NSW 2850
Ph. (063) 73 3853

Craigmoor Winery
Craigmoor Road
Mudgee NSW 2850
Ph. (063) 72 2208

Huntington Estate
Cassalis Road
Mudgee NSW 2850
Ph. (063) 73 3825

Botobolar Winery
Botobolar Lane
Mudgee NSW 2850
Ph. (063) 73 3840

Miramar
Henry Lawson Drive
Mudgee NSW 2850
Ph. (063) 73 3874

Platts
Gulgong Road
Gulgong NSW 2852
Ph. (063) 74 1700

5 The Murrumbidgee Irrigation Area (Griffith)

McWilliams
McWilliams Road
Hanwood
via Griffith NSW 2680
Ph. (069) 62 1333

San Bernadino
Leeton Road
Griffith NSW 2680
Ph. (069) 62 1391

de Bortoli
de Bortoli Road
Bilbul
via Griffith NSW 2680
Ph. (069) 63 5344

Victoria

6 Melbourne

Wine Victoria
36 Banana Alley
Melbourne VIC 3000
Ph. (03) 614 5589

Fergusson's
Wills Road
Yarra Glen VIC 3775
Ph. (059) 65 2237

St Hubert's
St Hubert's Road
Coldstream VIC 3770
Ph. (03) 739 1421

Chateau Yarrinya
Pinnacle Lane
Dixon's Creek VIC 3775
Ph. (059) 65 2271

Chateau Tahbilk
Tabilk
via Nagambie VIC 3607
Ph. (057) 94 2555

Mitchelton
Mitchellstown
off Goulburn Valley Highway VIC 3608
Ph. (057) 94 2388

7 Geelong Area

Idyll Vineyard
Ballan Road
Moorabool VIC 3221
Ph. (052) 76 1280

Hickinbotham Wines
2 Ferguson Street
Williamstown
Melbourne VIC 3016
Ph. (03) 397 2949

8 Central & Southern Areas

Balgownie Estate
Hermitage Road
Maiden Gully VIC 3551
Ph. (054) 49 6222

Passing Clouds
Kurting Road
Kingower VIC 3517
Ph. (054) 38 8257

Chateau Le Amon
Calder Highway
Bendigo VIC 3550
Ph. (054) 47 7995

Yellowglen
White's Road
Smythesdale VIC 3551
Ph. (053) 42 8617

9 Great Western District

Seppelts
Western Highway
Great Western VIC 3377
Ph. (053) 56 2202

Bests Great Western
Mount Langi Ghiran
Warrack-Buangar VIC 3375
Ph. (053) 54 3207

McRae's Montara
Chalambar Road
Ararat VIC 3377
Ph. (053) 52 3868

10 North-east Victoria

Winery Addresses

Brown Brothers
Milawa Vineyard
The Mill Road
Milawa VIC 3678
Ph. (057) 27 3400

Morris Mia Mia
Mia Mia Road
Rutherglen VIC 3685
Ph. (060) 26 7303

Pfeiffer
Distillery Road
Rutherglen VIC 3685
Ph. (060) 33 2805

Rosewood Winery
Corowa Road
Rutherglen VIC 3685
Ph. (060) 32 9641

Bullers Winery
Three Chain Road
Rutherglen VIC 3685
Ph. (060) 32 9660

Baileys of Glenrowan
RMB 4160
Glenrowan VIC 3675
Ph. (057) 66 2392

H.J.T. Vineyards
Keenan Road
Glenrowan VIC 3675
Ph. (057) 66 2252

Accommodation

Red Carpet Motor Inn
10 Moodemere Street
Rutherglen VIC 3685
Ph. (060) 32 9776
There are 16 units, a pool, playground
and barbecue area.

The Victoria Hotel
90 Main Street
Rutherglen VIC 3685
Ph. (060) 32 9610
Classified by the National Trust, this has
15 rooms and a licensed restaurant.

The Heritage Motor Inn
25 Edward Street
Corowa NSW 2646
Ph. (060) 33 1800
The motor inn has 18 units for
accommodation.

Wingrobe Motel
Federation Avenue
Corowa NSW 2646
Ph. (060) 33 2055
The motel has ten units and a swimming
pool.

The Rose Cottage
42 Camp Street
Beechworth VIC 3747
Ph. (057) 28 1069
There are four rooms and bed and
breakfast accommodation in this lovely
renovated cottage.

Recommended Restaurants

The Shamrock
Main Street
Rutherglen VIC 3685
Ph. (060) 32 9439

Tuileries
Drummond Street
Rutherglen VIC 3685
Ph. (060) 32 9922

Old Emu Gallery
Milawa VIC 3678
Ph. (057) 27 3410

Peter's Cellar 47
54 Ryley Street
Wangaratta VIC 3677
Ph. (057) 21 6309

Chatlers Restaurant
Murray Valley Highway
Rutherglen VIC 3685
Ph. (060) 32 9773

Tasmania

11 **Launceston**

Heemskerk Vineyards & Pipers Brook
  Vineyard
PO Box 1408
Launceston TAS 7250
Ph. (003) 82 7197

12 **Hobart**

Moorilla Estate
655 Main Road
Berriedale
Hobart TAS 7011
Ph. (002) 49 2949

South Australia

13 **Adelaide & the Adelaide Hills**

Petaluma
Bridgewater Mill
Mount Barker Road
Bridgewater
Adelaide SA 5155
Ph. (08) 339 3422

14 **The Barossa Valley**

Winery Addresses

Penfolds/Kaiser Stuhl
Sturt Highway
Nuriootpa SA 5355
Ph. (085) 62 1633

Orlando
Barossa Valley Highway
Rowland Flat SA 5352
Ph. (085) 24 4500

Seppeltsfield
Seppeltsfield
via Tanunda SA 5352
Ph. (085) 62 8028

Wolf Blass International
Sturt Highway
Nuriootpa SA 5355
Ph. (085) 62 1955

Yalumba
Angaston SA 5353
Ph. (085) 64 2423

Krondorf
Krondorf Road
Tanunda SA 5352
Ph. (085) 63 2145

Mountadam
High Eden Ridge
Eden Valley SA 5235
Ph. (085) 64 1101

Tollana/Penfolds
PO Box 21
Nuriootpa SA 5355
Ph. (085) 62 1433

Peter Lehmann Wines
Tanunda SA 5352
Ph. (085) 63 2500

Saltram
Stockwell Road
Angaston SA 5353
Ph. (085) 64 2200

Accommodation

Lawley Farm
Krondorf Road
Tanunda SA 5352
Ph. (085) 63 2141
Accommodation in The Cottage and The
Barn situated behind the central
farmhouse of Lawley Farm. These are
self-contained suites with breakfast-
making facilities.

DAVID SIMMONDS

The Landhaus
Bethany Road
Bethany
via Tanunda SA 5352
Ph. (085) 63 2191
A cosy cottage with accommodation for
just two, log fires and a vine-covered
courtyard. A master chef and baker
combine to produce hearty meals in
their restaurant.

The Hermitage
Cnr Seppeltsfield & Stonewell Roads
Marananga
Barossa Valley SA
Ph. (085) 62 2722
Large, homely suites offer comfortable
accommodation and their Barossa
Dining Room serves delicious food.

Blickinstal
Rifle Range Road
Tanunda SA 5352
Ph. (085) 63 2716
There are six fully self-contained units,
and country fresh breakfast food is
provided each day. The farm is set in
lovely bushland overlooking the valley.

Vineyards Motel
Stockwell Road
Angaston SA 5353
Ph. (085) 64 2404
Single and double rooms are available,
and there is a swimming pool and spa
for guests.

Barossa Motor Lodge
Murray Street
Tanunda SA 5352
Ph. (085) 63 2988
This motor lodge is centrally located in
Tanunda, with a view of the vineyards to
one side. It has single and double
rooms, a licensed restaurant, cocktail
bar and swimming pool.

Buckbury End Farm
Rosedale SA 5350
Ph. (085) 24 9035
This farm is located on the North Para
River in the lower valley, and there is a
lovely stone cottage, fully self-contained,
available for rental.

Lyndoch Motel
Barossa Valley Highway
Lindoch SA
Ph. (085) 24 4268
This motel has a selection of single and double rooms, together with a restaurant, cocktail bar and pool.

The Lodge
via Greenock
Seppeltsfield SA 5360
Ph. (085) 62 8277
A gracious and quiet country residence with four private en-suite rooms, a lawn tennis court, swimming pool and lovely gardens. Dinner, bed and breakfast available.

Recommended Restaurants

Pheasant Farm Restaurant
Box 301
Nuriootpa SA 5355
Ph. (085) 62 1286

The Vintners Restaurant
Nuriootpa Road
Angaston SA 5353
Ph. (085) 64 2488

The Hermitage of Marananga
Cnr Seppeltsfield & Stonewell Roads
Marananga
Barossa Valley SA
Ph. (085) 62 2722

The Landhaus
Bethany Road
Bethany
via Tanunda SA 5352
Ph. (085) 63 2191

Barossa Junction
Barossa Valley Way
Dorrien SA
Ph. (085) 63 3400

Die Gallerie
66 Murray Street
Tanunda SA 5352
Ph. (085) 63 2788

Postkutsche Cellar Restaurant
Barossa Valley Highway
Lindoch SA
Ph. (085) 24 4015

15 The Clare Valley

Winery Addresses

Stanley Leasingham
7 Dominic Street
Clare SA 5453
Ph. (088) 42 2555

Quelltaler Estate
via Watervale SA 5452
Ph. (088) 43 0003

Taylors Wines
Mintara Road
Auburn SA 5451
Ph. (088) 49 2008

Sevenhill Cellars
Collage Road
Sevenhill
via Clare SA 5453
Ph. (088) 43 4222

Tim Knappstein's Enterprise Wines
2 Pioneer Avenue
Clare SA 5453
Ph. (088) 42 2096

Jim Barry Wines
Main North Road
Clare SA 5453
Ph. (088) 42 2261

Mitchell Cellars
Hughes Park Road
Skillogalee Valley
via Sevenhill SA 5453
Ph. (088) 43 4258

Wendouree Cellars
Wendouree
Clare SA 5453
Ph. (088) 42 2896

Accommodation

Old Stanley Grammar School
Watervale SA 5453
Ph. (088) 43 0013
A fine two-storey stone building, once a school, offering accommodation and restaurant facilities.

Martindale Hall
Mintaro SA 5415
Ph. (088) 43 9011
Built in 1842, Martindale Hall has been beautifully maintained and furnished in period style. It offers lovely, old-world accommodation.

Mintaro Mews
Burra Street
Mintaro SA 5415
Ph. (088) 43 9001
This historic building contains 11 rooms, six with en-suites. It has a spa and swimming pool, restaurant and bar.

Tatehams
Auburn SA 5461
Ph. (088) 49 2030
Tatehams has five bedrooms and bed and breakfast-style accommodation.

Clare Valley Motel
74a Main North Road
Clare SA 5453
Ph. (088) 42 2799
This has a restaurant, conference facilities and motel-style rooms.

Clare Hotel-Motel
Main North Road
Clare SA 5453
Ph. (088) 42 2816
This has a restaurant and motel accommodation.

Bentley's Hotel-Motel
191 Main North Road
Clare SA 5453
Ph. (088) 42 2815
Hotel-motel with 15 self-contained units and a restaurant.

Recommended Restaurants

Brice Hill Vineyard Restaurant
Wendouree Road
Clare SA 5453
Ph. (088) 42 2786

Crawleys Old Shop Restaurant
Watervale SA 5453
Ph. (088) 43 0136

Three Roses Restaurant
Old Stanley Grammar School
Watervale SA 5453
Ph. (088) 43 0013

Kilkanoon Restaurant
Penwortham SA 5453
Ph. (088) 43 4277

Clare Valley Motel
Licensed Restaurant
74a Main North Road
Clare SA 5453
Ph. (088) 42 2799

16 The McLaren Vale District

Winery Addresses

Hardy's Tintard
Main Road
McLaren Vale SA 5171
Ph. (08) 323 8676

Chateau Reynella
Reynell Road
Reynella SA 5161
Ph. (08) 381 2266

Pirramimma
Johnstone Road
McLaren Vale SA 5171
Ph. (08) 323 8205

Seaview
Chaffey Road
McLaren Vale SA 5171
Ph. (08) 323 8250

Wirra Wirra
McMurtie Road
McLaren Vale SA 5171
Ph. (08) 323 8414

Woodstock Wine Cellars
Douglas Gully Road
McLaren Flat SA 5171
Ph. (08) 383 0156

d'Arenberg
Osborn Road
McLaren Vale SA 5171
Ph. (08) 323 8206

Middlebrook
Sand Road
McLaren Vale SA 5171
Ph. (08) 383 0004

Old Clarendon
Main Road
Clarendon SA 5171
Ph. (08) 383 6056

Accommodation

McLaren on the Lake
Kangarilla Road
McLaren Vale SA 5171
Ph. (08) 323 8911
A large motel with restaurant, pool and
bars.

McLaren Vale Motel
Cnr Main Road & Caffrey Street
McLaren Vale SA 5171
Ph. (08) 323 8265
This motel has a choice of standard
doubles and executive suites with two-
person spas.

Port Noarlunga Motel
39 Salt Fleet Street
Port Noarlunga SA 5167
Ph. (08) 382 1267
This motel is right near the beach and
offers modern motel suites.

Recommended Restaurants

The Barn
Main Road
McLaren Vale SA 5171
Ph. (08) 323 8618

Pipkins
Main Road
McLaren Vale SA 5171
Ph. (08) 323 8707

Prewetts
Main Street
Kangarilla SA 5157
Ph. (08) 383 7274

Hotel McLaren
Main Street
McLaren Vale SA 5171
Ph. (08) 323 8208

The Vines
Cnr Kangarilla & Foggo Roads
McLaren Vale SA 5171
Ph. (08) 323 8958

Red Oven
4 Martins Road
McLaren Vale SA 5171
Ph. (08) 323 8849

Carters
218 Old South Road
Old Reynella SA 5161
Ph. (08) 381 6963

17 Coonawarra

Wynns Coonawarra Estate
Memorial Drive
Coonawarra SA 5263
Ph. (087) 36 3266

Rouge Homme
Naracoorte Penola Road
Coonawarra SA 5263
Ph. (087) 36 3205

Redman Wines
Coonawarra SA 5263
Ph. (087) 36 3331

Hungerford Hill Wines
Coonawarra Road
Penola SA 5277
Ph. (087) 37 2613

Leconfield
Naracoorte Penola Road
Coonawarra SA 5263
Ph. (087) 37 2326

Mildara Wines Limited
Naracoorte Penola Road
Coonawarra SA 5263
Ph. (087) 36 3380

Hollick Wines
Naracoorte Penola Road
Coonawarra SA 5263
Ph. (087) 37 2318

Katnook Estate
Naracoorte Penola Road
Coonawarra SA 5263
Ph. (087) 37 2394

18 The Riverland

Mildara Wines
Wentworth Road
Merbein VIC 3505
Ph. (050) 25 2303

Karadoc Winery
Karadoc VIC 3496
Ph. (050) 24 0303

Western Australia

19 The Swan Valley

Houghton
Dale Road
Middle Swan WA 6056
Ph. (09) 274 5100

Sandalford
West Swan Road
Caversham WA 6055
Ph. (09) 274 5922

Evans & Tate
Swan Street
Henley Brook WA 6055
Ph. (09) 296 4329

20 The Margaret River Region

Leeuwin Estate
Gnarawary Road
Margaret River WA 6285
Ph. (097) 57 6253

Cape Mentelle
Wallcliff Road
Margaret River WA 6285
Ph. (097) 57 2070

Cullens Willyabrup
Caves Road
Cowramup WA 6284
Ph. (097) 55 5277

Moss Wood
Metricup Road
Willyabrup WA 6284
Ph. (097) 55 6266 or 52 1526

Vasse Felix
Harman's South Road
Cowramup WA 6284
Ph. (097) 55 5242

21 The Mount Barker Region

Plantagenet Wines
46 Albany Highway
Mount Barker WA 6324
Ph. (098) 51 1150

Northern Territory

22 Alice Springs

Chateau Hornsby
Petrick Road
Alice Springs NT 5750
Ph. (089) 52 5771

Queensland

23 Roma

Romavilla Vineyards
Northern Road
Roma QLD 4455
Ph. (074) 22 1822

24 The Granite Belt Region

Robinson's Family Vineyards
Lyra
via Ballandean QLD 4382
Ph. (076) 84 1216

Sundown Valley Vineyards
Sundown Road
Ballandean QLD 4380
Ph. (076) 84 1226

Old Caves Winery
Warwick Road
Stanthorpe QLD 4380
Ph. (076) 81 1494

Mt Magnus
Donnelly's Castle Road
Pozieres QLD 4352
Ph. (076) 85 3213

Rumbalara
Fletcher Road
via Glen Aplin NSW 2381

Kay Brothers Winery seen from the air in McLaren Vale, south of the Barossa Valley.

Seven Hill Winery in the Clare region near the Barossa Valley, South Australia.

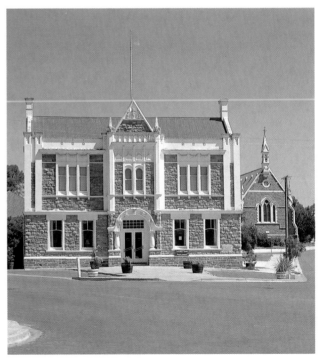

Historic Angaston Town Hall in Barossa Valley.

ACTIVITIES

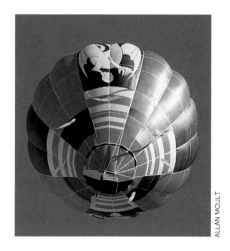

ALLAN MOULT

Ballooning

Few sports are both gentle and exhilarating at the same time. And if the list of activities which qualify is a short and exclusive one, ballooning has to come at the very top of it. No one is ever quite the same again after experiencing the sensation of space, freedom and peace to be found in a wicker basket swinging high above the mountains in the calm morning air, or drifting into a fairytale sunset over the sea. And perhaps no country on earth can offer the variety of terrain and wilderness that Australia unfolds below the balloon traveller.

Generally regarded as both a romantic and an aristocratic pastime, the sport of hot-air ballooning originated in France in 1783 — not long before Australia was settled — when the Montgolfier Brothers flew their primitive balloon across the roof-tops of Paris. They descended into the vineyards of the French aristocracy and their flight was toasted with the finest French champagne. While 20th-century technology has made its mark on ballooning, some traditions die hard and balloon flights are, to this day, associated with the good life, champagne and caviar.

Today's hot-air balloons have moved a long way from the paper construction adopted by the intrepid Montgolfier Brothers. Nowadays, the fabric is manufactured of rip-stop nylon, while propane burners heat the air which fills the balloon and gives it lift. One tradition which has survived, however, is the use of the wicker basket or gondola. Wicker is still preferred by balloonists because of its light weight and classic style.

Although relatively new to Australia, ballooning has become remarkably popular in a very short time, and now some 90 balloons fly regularly from different locations throughout the country.

Its popularity is not surprising. Suspended in space and time, passengers and their qualified licensed pilots can drift across some of the world's most picturesque rural scenery, spectacular rock formations and dramatic beaches.

Sunrise and sunset offer the best conditions for a balloon adventure because they are the least windy times of the day and allow passengers to experience the peculiar Mediterranean-like intensity of the Australian light. Most flights vary between 30 minutes and two hours and carry their passengers into a new dimension guided only by the prevailing winds.

Each Australian state has something unique to offer the balloonist. Tasmanian flights take in the Tamar Valley near Launceston and run out to sea along 45 kilometres of estuary. Early morning flights in Victoria view the rock formations of the majestic Grampians in the state's largest national park — only hours from the centre of Melbourne. In both South Australia's Barossa Valley and the Hunter Valley of New South Wales, balloon passengers fly over a patchwork of vineyards which are even more captivating from the air than from the ground.

In Queensland, flights provide spectacular views of the booming city of Brisbane and of the fast-growing sun-lovers' paradise of the Gold Coast. From Alice Springs, in the very heart of Australia's Red Centre, balloon passengers gain a unique perspective on the empty red, brown and ochre wastes which took early explorers so many decades to conquer.

The Western Australian capital of Perth will feature as the starting point of an event which will mark the coming of age of ballooning as a sport in Australia. Early in 1988, a Bicentennial Trans-Australia Ballooning Challenge will be held in which

50 of the best international ballooning teams will cross the entire width of the island continent. The 600-kilometre fly/drive event, organised by the Australian Ballooning Federation and supported by the Bicentennial Authority, will start in Perth on 30 March 1988 and will be conducted in 12 stages over 16 days. Balloonists, followed by their back-up crews, will fly over selected locations in Western Australia, South Australia, Victoria and New South Wales.

The magnitude of the event, the huge distance involved and the leap-frogging style in which it crosses Australia will set it apart from ballooning contests anywhere else in the world. The contestants will move over a land of stark contrasts, across the arid outback, through rich rural belts, and finally on to Sydney. It will be Grand Prix ballooning, unlike anything attempted before in the world.

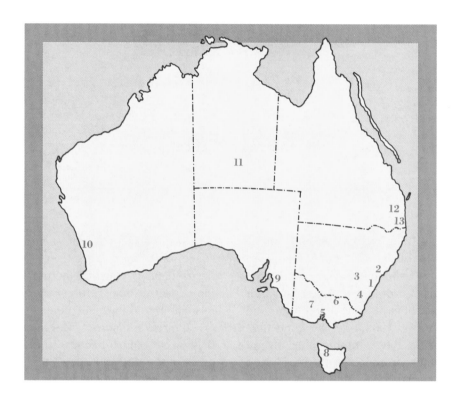

Locations

New South Wales

1 The **Camden Valley,** just an hour or two from the centre of Sydney, is a prime ballooning location. Set between the skyscrapers of Sydney and the Blue Mountains of the Great Dividing Range, Camden Valley sits between two of New South Wales' richest pockets of natural flora and fauna, the Royal National Park and the Blue Mountains National Park. The valley is a picturesque rural environment with widely diverse agriculture, ranging from horse breeding for thoroughbred racing to intensive vegetable and grape cropping.

Dawn ballooning takes place daily, and one-hour flights catch the calm morning conditions and spectacular light. Balloon passengers drift over the valley itself and view the patchwork of fields below and the Nepean River that waters them. A champagne breakfast is served after the flight and passengers can take several hours to enjoy the beauty of the valley before returning to Sydney by midday.

2 A few hours' drive north-west of Sydney lies the **Hunter Valley,** one of Australia's most famous wine-producing regions. Its red wines in particular are gaining a world-wide reputation.

The landscape which produces these wines is both striking and diverse and has been the centre of the Australian wine industry for 150 years. It is rich country, with deep red and black soils covering the region's huge coal deposits. Coal and wine may seem unusual bedfellows, but between them they offer some of the most interesting landscapes for the air traveller to observe. Ballooning takes place over wineries such as Arrowfield, Penfolds, Rosemount Estate and Lindemans scattered among lush grazing country. The Hunter River meanders through this scene, its valley dotted with small villages and settlements so characteristic of the area.

As flights move over the Lower Hunter and its rural hinterland, historic colonial homesteads give the balloon passenger a peaceful glimpse into the early years of the colony of New South Wales.

Balloon flights last about an hour and begin at dawn. A traditional champagne breakfast normally follows the journey.

3 Situated on the banks of the Belubula River, **Canowindra** is a delightful township just over

four hours' drive west from Sydney, two hours from Australia's federal capital, Canberra.

Set among gently undulating hills and wide open tracts of pasture land, the town is the centre of a prosperous horse-breeding region which has won acclaim for the many fine animals bred at studs throughout the district.

The fact that Canowindra is so far inland is one of its most important assets as far as the sport of hot-air ballooning is concerned. The warm thermal currents that rise from the land's surface provide some of the best uplift to be found at any ballooning location in the country, and the town is recognised by many as the 'ballooning capital' of Australia.

Accommodation and all facilities are included in a weekend package at either the Blue Jacket Motel or the Canowindra Hotel, both in Canowindra town.

Lift-off is usually at sunrise, and afternoon flights can be scheduled on Saturdays if weather conditions are suitable.

Australian Capital Territory

4 Australia's capital, Canberra, is a young city. Designed by Walter Burley Griffin in the 1920s, it provided a neutral site for the federal Parliament between the rival cities of Melbourne and Sydney.

A balloon flight over Canberra is a remarkable experience and offers the rare opportunity to view a city planned specifically for the 20th century. The central focus is Parliament House, from which tree-lined avenues radiate around Lake Burley Griffin. Beyond the lake, majestic Black Mountain stands as a backdrop to the city and is the doorway to Australia's snow country.

Balloon flights are early morning or afternoon affairs conducted by a pilot-guide. The traditional champagne celebration caps off each flight.

Victoria

5 Travelling by balloon over **Melbourne,** Australia's second largest city, provides an interesting and unusual sight-seeing perspective. From the air, the city centre's grid of wide tree-lined streets, the Yarra River winding its way through the urban sprawl, and the many parks and gardens seem quite different from a ground-level view. Further afield, Port Phillip Bay to the south and the hills that surround Melbourne are a pleasant contrast to the flatness of the plain on which the city has spread.

The past decade has seen hot-air ballooning become an accepted feature of Australian skies in winter

ALLAN MOULT

6 About 270 kilometres north-east of Melbourne, and very close to the border town of Albury-Wodonga, lies **Rutherglen**, a popular Victorian ballooning venue. Early morning and sunset flights depart every weekend from the second week in March to the first week in November. Weekend packages can be arranged which include the balloon flight itself, bunk-house accommodation, champagne, and all meals from late supper on Friday night to brunch on Sunday — and a support vehicle with driver.

7 Another Victorian champagne ballooning district is **Stawell**, a four-hour scenic drive west from Melbourne. The temperature and winds in this region, among the Grampian hills, are settled and predictable, particularly in the cold winter months, which makes for excellent flying.

The sandstone rock formations of the Grampians rise from the tableau below like the raised letters on a page of braille. Waterfalls, lakes, forests and national park scenery afford some of the best views to be had in Victoria, and are a spectacular backdrop for early-morning flights above the region's wineries. Balloons fly over farms and villages and land in sheltered clearings in forests or in small secluded valleys. Gourmet cooking is available at the Walmsley Guesthouse, which is located in the hills around the Stawell base camp.

Tasmania

Tasmania — known to Australians as the Apple Isle — is a popular haven for travellers and tourists in its own right. The scenery in the north of the island is reminiscent of England, with orchards, gentle hills, and a colonial backdrop of old sandstone cottages.

8 The centre of this district is **Launceston,** a couple of hours' drive north of the state capital Hobart. Daily balloon flights operate throughout the summer months from the Launceston Federal Country Club Hotel-Casino, departing at 6 am and 6 pm. Each flight, which lasts about an hour, carries five passengers, together with a fully qualified pilot. Journeys of between 10 and 30 kilometres provide spectacular views of the rolling meadows and forests of northern Tasmania.

South Australia

9 South Australia's **Barossa Valley** has played as important a part in the development of Australian wines as has the Hunter Valley in New South Wales. It also gives balloonists similar glimpses of Australia's heritage and of the unusual pattern of agriculture that is characteristic of wine-growing districts.

The Barossa is just 65 kilometres north-east of the South Australian capital of Adelaide. It has a rich German heritage and the descendants of the original settlers are proud of their culture and tradition and of the part they have played in the development of fine Australian wines.

Farming architecture still bears the stamp of German styles introduced more than a century ago and it is an extraordinary experience to observe them from the air. Balloon flights in the region are scheduled several days every week and flight time is usually about an hour.

Western Australia

10 Western Australia's favourite ballooning spot is situated one hour east of Perth in the **Avon Valley.** Flights operate out of Northam and York airfields, depending on weather conditions.

One of Western Australia's best-known balloonists, Sally Smith, has been awarded the Winston Churchill Fellowship for outstanding achievements in air sports and her invaluable contribution to hot-air ballooning. She has also made frequent appearances in international aviation shows and has authored several books on the subject.

Northern Territory

11 Balloon flights from **Alice Springs** take place every day of the week. Early balloon safaris leave an hour before dawn, while evening flights take travellers around the famous township during the luminescent orange glow of a spectacular Red Centre sunset. Touring packages of four, seven and nine days are also available.

Flights cruise over the Simpson Gap National Park, Emily and Jessie Gaps Nature Park, and other wildlife sanctuaries within a 20-kilometre radius of the township. The balloons are followed by four-wheel-drive vehicles carrying chase crews who can be commissioned to make a video recording of the flight.

Queensland

Queensland, Australia's sunshine state, is a land of wild contrasts. Brisbane itself is a booming state capital and the nearby Gold Coast is a glittering metropolis of high-rises and tourist centres dedicated almost entirely to pleasure. Yet not far away are unspoiled tracts of rainforest and wilderness.

12 Even short balloon flights from the **Brisbane** region take in some of this colourful variety. Queensland's magnificent weather means that flights are normally available year-round. Weekend excursions are also offered, leaving from close to the city of Brisbane itself.

13 Passengers on flights from the **Gold Coast,** 65 kilometres south of Brisbane, are likely to get one of the most experienced pilots in the country. Michael Conran has been Queensland's champion pilot three times, and was selected as Australia's representative in the 1987 World Championships held in Austria.

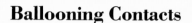

Ballooning Contacts

Operators

For information on the Bicentennial Trans-Australia Ballooning Challenge contact:

Flag Inns Limited
132 Bank Street
South Melbourne VIC 3205
Ph. (03) 698 7700

New South Wales

1 Camden Valley

Balloon Aloft
Judy Lynne and Peter Vizzard are the owners of this company which, from its base in Sydney, organises balloon flights in Camden, the Hunter Valley, Canberra, Benalla in Victoria, and the Sunshine Coast. Peter, the 1983/84 World Hot-Air Balloon Champion and twice Australian Champion, is one of the six professionally trained pilots. Judy was also a national champion in 1984. They love their work and want to share their experience with you. Book direct or through your hotel (they have a hotel pick-up service), the NSW Travel Bureau or Victour. Flights are available all year round from 5 am to 11 am.

RMB 56
Hume Highway
Cross Roads
Sydney NSW 2170
Ph. (02) 607 2255

Balloon Flights Australia
Balloon Flights Australia offer ballooning weekends at Canowindra as well as one-day flights at Camden and in the Hunter Valley. It's a friendly operation. Their Hunter Valley trips include private wine-tasting at selected vineyards. Bookings through the NSW Tourist Board, Trading Post at Pokolbin, or direct to their Sydney and Canberra offices.

PO Box 460
Rozelle
Sydney NSW 2039
Ph. (02) 818 4599

Balloon Sunrise
Most travel agents will book your dawn-to-midday ballooning adventure with Balloon Sunrise who are part of Peregrine Adventures in Sydney. Their chosen destinations are in the Camden and Hunter Valleys, Melbourne, Launceston and Cowra. They are the oldest balloon operators in Australia and offer hotel pick-up services in Sydney and Melbourne.

1st Floor 117 York Street
Sydney NSW 2000 Ph. (02) 264 6033

World Expeditions
Balloon weekends, balloon charter, destinations in the Camden Valley, Hunter Valley, Devonport in Tasmania, the Red Centre at Alice Springs, Canowindra and Springhurst — you'll not find it difficult to catch one of these flights wherever you're staying. They offer a complete service and you can book direct.

3rd Floor 377 Sussex Street
Sydney NSW 2000 Ph. (02) 264 3366

2 Hunter Valley

Balloon Aloft
See (1) above for details

Balloon Flights Australia
See (1) above for details

Balloon Sunrise
See (1) above for details

World Expeditions
See (1) above for details

3 Canowindra

Balloon Flights Australia Pty Ltd
PO Box 39
Canowindra NSW 2804
Ph. (063) 44 1840

World Expeditions
See (1) above for details

Australian Capital Territory

4 Canberra

Balloon Aloft
See (1) above for details

Balloon Flights Australia
See (1) above for details

Victoria

5 Melbourne

Balloon Sunrise
See (1) above for details

Suite 9A, 9th Floor
343 Little Collins Street
Melbourne VIC 3000 Ph. (03) 602 3066

6 Rutherglen

Balloon Aloft
See (1) above for details

World Expeditions
See (1) above for details

Suite 602 Wellesley House
126 Wellington Parade
East Melbourne VIC 3002
Ph. (03) 419 2333 or 419 2920

7 Stawell

Balloon Rise
They offer several ballooning trips to the champagne districts of Victoria, centred around Stawell. Their ten-day Outback Camping Safari includes camping and ballooning over the Barossa Valley and Flinders Ranges. Morning flights are also available.

19 Seaby Street
Stawell VIC 3380
Ph. (053) 58 3086

Tasmania

8 Launceston

Balloon Sunrise
See (1) above for details

C/- Launceston Country Club
Prospect Vale
Launceston TAS 7250
Ph. (003) 44 8855

ROBBI NEWMAN

South Australia

9   Barossa Valley

Balloon Academy
The Murray River Champagne Safari is their special feature. They operate all year round and are planning trips over Adelaide, too. If you don't make the sunrise trip, they also have late afternoon flights.

Bagshaw Road
Kersbrook
Adelaide SA 5231
Ph. (08) 389 3195

Balloon Adventures
Their three-to-four-hour champagne balloon flights take you over the picturesque vineyards and rolling farmland of the Barossa Valley. They operate all year round. Late afternoon flights are available, too. Proprietor Simon Fisher founded Balloon Safaris in Kenya, the world's first balloon passenger operation. Book via the SA Government Travel Centre offices or through your travel agent.

PO Box 382
Tanunda SA 5352
Ph. (085) 24 4383 or 24 4568

Western Australia

10   Avon Valley

Perth Hot Air Ballooning Centre
The Centre specialises in flights over the beautiful Avon Valley, one and a half hours from Perth. They operate from York airfield or Northam, seven days a week from March to December. Sally Smith, who runs the operation, received a Winston Churchill Fellowship for her services to air sports.

Duck End Farm
Wilura Road
Mundaring
Perth WA 6073
Ph. (09) 295 1168

Windward Adventures
Apart from the summer months, they offer champagne day flights in the Avon Valley from Northam. They say that one of their pilots likes to land in nudist camps! Book through Holiday WA and Golden West Travel.

PO Box 1
Northam WA 6401
Ph. (096) 22 0242

Northern Territory

11   Alice Springs

Aussie Balloons
Ken Watts has been flying here for over 20 years. They pick you up one hour before dawn and you're off on your ballooning adventure over the Red Centre. At the end of your flight, tuck into a champagne brunch and savour the flavour of your wonderful journey. April through October, seven days a week.

PO Box 2055
Alice Springs NT 5750
Ph. (089) 52 4369

Toddy's Balloon Safaris
With over 1,000 hours of ballooning under his belt, Michael Sanby offers you flights over the national parks and wildlife areas near Alice Springs. They fly morning and evening and also run travel packages of four to nine days. Adventure day tours, mainly walking, are complemented by longer 4WD and camping excursions. Your hotel will book for you.

41 Gap Road
Alice Springs NT 5750
Ph. (089) 52 1322

Queensland

12   Brisbane

Lovely! Champagne Balloon Flights
These flights operate from a variety of launching pads around Brisbane and the Gold Coast. The traditional champagne breakfast is executed with great flair. The Meadmores who run the operation have some accommodation and also run the Annonay Balloon School from their home location. It's a year-round operation.

21 Avebury Street
Hill End
Brisbane QLD 4101
Ph. (07) 844 6671

Sunshine Balloons
Three times Queensland Ballooning Champion, Michael Conran is their chief pilot and flew for his country at the World Championships in 1987. They arrange pick-ups for you to their locations in Brisbane, Gatton, Beenleigh and the Gold Coast. Your travel agent will fix a booking for you on one of their early morning flights which are followed by a champagne breakfast.

PO Box 463
Springwood
Brisbane QLD 4127
Ph. (07) 208 6527

13   Gold Coast

Lovely! Champagne Balloon Flights
See (12) above for details

Sunshine Balloons
See (12) above for details

Information Sources

The Australian Ballooning Federation
The Federation can supply further information on the sport of hot-air ballooning in Australia.

Ms Gaye Murray
Secretary
8/78 Wolseley Road
Point Piper
Sydney NSW 2017

Mr Adrian Clements
President
PO Box 100
Northam WA 6401

ALLAN MOULT

Bicycling

Bicycling is a sport more usually associated with Europe than with Australia. Yet some of the world's best cyclists have been born and bred in Australia, and a closer look at what the country has to offer makes it easy to see why.

Bicycling holidays are an ideal blend of fresh air, exercise and escape. There are terrains to suit all ages and levels of fitness, taking the enthusiast along high mountain tracks, through tropical rainforests, or along country lanes that could be in rural England.

For off-the-beaten-track cycling, mountain bikes are the answer. This type of bicycle, which is becoming increasingly popular with cyclists all over the world, allows the rider to venture into rough or mountainous terrain. Cyclists using these machines have reached such inaccessible areas as the Nepal Himalaya and the summit of Mount Kilimanjaro in Tanzania. Mountain bikes are generally smaller than touring cycles; wide tyres, an upright seating position and straight handlebars are other common features. This type of bicycle is perfect for many rugged areas of Australia that would defeat the normal two-wheeler.

There are many organised cycling tours available, catering for both the novice and the more experienced cyclist. Many tours include the hire of bicycles and the cost of accommodation and, in some cases, even a guide and a support vehicle for the weary. Some cycle tours embrace other activities as well, such as bushwalking and canoeing.

In addition to these packaged tours, there are a number of independent cycling associations which can be contacted for advice. Such groups occasionally conduct their own tours.

Australia's national touring organisation, Bicycle Australia, is a good place to start researching bicycle tours and holidays. It provides a number of bicycling programmes as well as insurance and mail-order bicycle touring information for the whole country. The organisation is planning a special programme of rides for the Bicentenary year. The event, 'Bicycle Australia in '88', will commence in June of 1988 from Cape York in far north Queensland, travel the length of the east coast, including part of Tasmania, and across the southern coast, finishing in Perth in December. Cyclists will have the option of forming their own small groups, or joining a supported group organised by Bicycle Australia. One or more stages can be tackled, or the really keen cyclist can undertake the entire journey of approximately 8,200 kilometres. Further details are available from Bicycle Australia.

Locations

New South Wales

New South Wales offers enormous variety for the cycling enthusiast. The countryside varies from flat farmland to mountainous slopes, and while most roads are sealed there are many rougher tracks, particularly in the Snowy Mountains.

From Sydney, a good place to begin is the **Hunter Valley**, one of Australia's prime wine-growing areas and only a couple of hours from the state capital. The Hunter Valley is a popular tourist destination in its own right, and can be reached easily from Sydney by train or road.

Cycling through the vineyards is ideal for those who prefer sedate pedalling along sealed and relatively flat roads. Most vineyards encourage passersby to sample their wares and the level of temptation is so great that the cyclist is unlikely to break any speed records.

There are many fine old colonial homes and other places of historical interest to visit in addition to the vineyards. And for weary bones after a hard day's cycling, some of the country's best local pubs provide comfortable beds and good breakfasts.

2 The **Snowy Mountains** straddle the border of New South Wales and Victoria. The region is relatively easy to reach from Sydney and easier still from the national capital, Canberra. The terrain is ideal for cyclists seeking a more alpine environment and the additional effort it demands is well worthwhile. Sealed roads climb through forests of mountain ash and snow gum and wind along high alpine valleys that could be in Switzerland. The air is wonderfully clear and the views are magnificent, with snow visible most of the year.

Experience is not as important as general fitness in this region. Those who take their rough country cycling seriously can leave the tarmac and explore the mountains on tracks of graded gravel or on four-wheel-drive fire trails. One of the tours operating in the area provides support vehicles to carry gear when the going gets too tough. And tough it certainly can be, particularly when attempting the steep grade up the flank of Australia's highest mountain peak, Mt Kosciusko.

For those with the time, there are a number of excellent camping spots in the Snowy Mountains, and there is plenty of lodge accommodation for cyclists who want a base camp for day outings. In the high peaks, weather is a limiting factor and it is wise to check conditions well before setting out.

Australian Capital Territory

3 **Canberra** is the perfect place for cyclists. Its generally flat terrain and extensive network of cycle tracks provide the ideal means of seeing the sights or just dawdling around the shores of Lake Burley Griffin. A little further afield, the historic houses of Lanyon and Cuppacumbalong, or spectacular Ginninderra Falls with its picnic area and scenic nature trails, are all possible day trips. From Canberra, short trips can be made to the southern highlands area of New South Wales, visiting historic towns such as Braidwood, which was founded during the gold boom in the 1830s.

Victoria

4 Victoria is probably the most popular state in Australia with cyclists. The area around **Glenrowan,** in the north of the state, is particularly beautiful when clothed in autumn or spring colours. Despite its peaceful aspect, the area is alive with history — some of it violent.

This was the stamping ground of Australia's most notorious bushranging family — the Kelly Gang. Glenrowan itself was the settlement where the most famous of them all, Ned Kelly, was finally captured. Among the attractions of the region are old goldrush towns and historic pubs that were serving beer even before Kelly was born.

As in New South Wales, the wineries of the area are a big attraction. Rutherglen produces some of Australia's best muscat and port, perfect for warming up chilly cyclists in the colder months of the year. The area is well catered for in terms of cycle tour operators, with half a dozen different types of tours available year round.

5 In **Melbourne,** the visitor can hire a bike for a quick trip along the banks of the Yarra River. While this hardly qualifies as the great outdoors, it is a delightful way to spend an afternoon and gives an unusual perspective on one of Australia's great cities.

Tasmania

For travellers with enough time — it takes about two weeks — it is possible to cycle all the way around the island state of Tasmania. A number of operators offer such tours, as well as shorter tours and excursions.

6 The countryside around **Launceston** is reminiscent of rural England, with rolling green farmland

A group of cyclists enjoy the Tasmanian scenery

and lanes winding along the coast through quiet fishing settlements where fresh seafood is plentiful and the beaches are deserted. Magnificent forests and natural woodland pools are to be found not too far away in Douglas Apsley Gorge.

A popular cycle tour is from Launceston to Hobart. The picturesque route takes in Coles Bay, a well-known scallop fishing town, and the entrance of Freycinet National Park.

7 Closer to **Hobart**, cyclists can travel through history in the old convict settlement of Port Arthur or visit rainforest areas and enjoy some of Tasmania's finest mountain landscapes in the Mt Field National Park. The adventurous (and those with any energy left) can cycle down to the Upper Derwent Valley and take in some exhilarating river rafting.

Accommodation for cyclists in Tasmania varies from place to place. While camping is probably the most common option, it is also possible to stay in shearers' quarters and in many of the island state's pretty fishing villages. For the less avid explorer, day trips based at for example the Launceston Youth Hostel are also available.

Tasmania, like the more northern countries it resembles, has weather which is temperamental in the extreme. It is a good idea to come prepared for wind and rain before setting out on two wheels.

South Australia

8 South Australia will become something of a cycling mecca in 1988. In late April, the South Australia Touring Cyclists Association is holding a festival of cycling at **Oakbank** in the Adelaide Hills. This promises to be quite an occasion, bringing together cyclists from all over the world. The event will include displays and exhibitions of vintage bicycles and other cycling memorabilia, as well as races and competitions.

9 If the Oakbank Festival doesn't fit into your calendar, there are many other cycling adventures to experience in what is known as Australia's Festival State. Only an hour's drive from the state capital of Adelaide is South Australia's answer to the Hunter, the **Barossa Valley.** A broad, shallow valley filled with wineries and orchards, the Barossa was settled in 1842 by Prussian immigrants who brought with them their wine-making skills as well as their German language, architecture and culture, and perhaps the best way to discover these is on two wheels. It's easy cycling, with plenty of opportunities to sample the Barossa's famous wines. Country pubs are probably the best places to stay, although during the tourist season they are frequently fully booked and it's a good idea to check in advance.

ALLAN MOULT

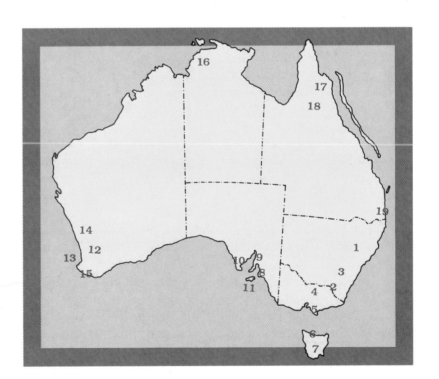

10 For those interested in history, the **Yorke Peninsula** is only a few hours' drive from Adelaide. While it is possible to cycle all the way, you may prefer to put the bike on the car or hire bicycles in the region.

Settlements in the area were founded on the copper-mining industry and there are many historic towns, museums and old mines to visit. The Yorke Peninsula is also a major grain-producing region and its farmland is an added attraction to the cyclist. The coastline is rugged, with high cliffs dominating empty beaches, and there is abundant wildlife. Kangaroos are common and the birdlife is varied and colourful.

11 **Kangaroo Island,** the third largest island off the Australian coast and 113 kilometres as the crow flies from the centre of Adelaide, can be reached after a 30-minute flight from Adelaide Airport. Bicycles can be hired on the island, or taken on board the ferry from Port Adelaide or Cape Jervis.

Flinders Chase National Park on the island is a wild heathland environment with very few trees, ringed by cliffs and white sandy beaches. It is home to thousands of kangaroos, as the name of the island implies, as well as other native animals, and it has a thriving seal colony.

Western Australia

12 Probably because of its remoteness from the more populated eastern areas of Australia, Western Australia is the state least well covered by organised cycle touring groups. But it is worth looking out for the bi-monthly newsletter of the Cycle Touring Association of Western Australia in the better bicycle shops in the state capital, **Perth.** The Association organises occasional jaunts — visitors are welcome — and fairly regular weekend tours to destinations in and around Perth.

13 Easy and picturesque cycling is to be experienced on **Rottnest Island,** 19 kilometres west of Perth and reached by ferry. Once a penal colony for Aborigines, the island boasts some of the state's oldest buildings. The countryside consists mostly of heathland, with plenty of fine sandy beaches for cooling off after a hot, dusty ride.

14 Some 135 kilometres north-east of Perth on the Great Northern Highway is the historic town of **New Norcia.** Situated in easy cycling country in the heart of Western Australia's rolling wheat belt, the town is the site of a fine Benedictine Monastery. Built in the old Spanish style, many of its buildings are classified by the National Trust.

15 The **south-west region** of Western Australia is a cyclist's paradise. About 200 kilometres from Perth, the area features unique karri and jarrah hardwood forests. The karri can grow up to 90 metres in height, rising from an undergrowth of lush ferns. The region is most spectacular in spring, when Western Australia's famous wildflowers burst into bloom. There are also many good surfing beaches for those who can manage to carry their surfboards on their bikes.

Western Australia's better vineyards are to be found in the region, too, with plenty of interesting historic houses to look at between the obligatory stops to taste the local produce.

Northern Territory

16 Although the Northern Territory's rugged reputation might deter cyclists, there are, in fact, some interesting cycling possibilities here for the adventurous. Hire cycles are available in **Darwin** for exploring the town and surrounding area, or for an exciting trip into Kakadu National Park. Using the Cooinda Motel or the caravan and camping park as a base, tours can be made to the Aboriginal art site at Nourlangie Rock, or to the East Alligator River, which borders on Arnhem Land. Cooinda is on the western edge of the park, and a three or four-hour drive from Darwin.

Queensland

Cycling through rainforest along roads overhung with vines and creepers is an experience hard to come by anywhere but in Australia. And Queensland is the best state for it. Cairns, in the north of the state, is close to one of the world's largest remaining tropical rainforests, the Daintree.

17 The **Daintree** contains an incredibly complex and diverse range of vegetation which stretches right down to the sea with its spectacular reefs. Rainforests worldwide are dwindling at an alarming rate, but the Daintree — largely because of the unstinting efforts of Australia's growing band of conservationists — is still largely untouched. It is the perfect venue for the cyclist who is serious about getting back to nature.

18 Closer to Cairns is the village of Kuranda on the **Atherton Tableland.** The tableland rises from the coastal plateau, and features fringed volcanic crater lakes and deep cool mountain pools, giant fig trees, and the ubiquitous Queensland sunshine.

A brief train ride from Cairns, Kuranda has fine markets and forms the centre of a web of tracks leading to pools, waterfalls and quiet tropical glades.

19 The hinterland of the **Gold Coast,** one and a half hours' south of Brisbane, is one of Australia's more picturesque highland regions. Cycling here is relatively sedate, taking the traveller through lush agricultural land and peaceful country valleys. The air is crisp and clean, and the district could be a thousand miles from the bustling Brisbane and Gold Coast conurbations.

Bicycling Contacts

Operators

For those people wishing to organise their own bicycle tours, the *Yellow Pages* telephone directory should be consulted for a list of the bicycle hire sources in each capital city. Further information on bicycle routes and recommended destinations can be obtained from the local tourist associations and information contacts listed at the back of this section.

New South Wales

1 **Hunter Valley**

World Expeditions
Their weekend tour includes visits to historic sites, as well as wine tasting at Pokolbin and Rothbury Wine Estates. You start from Cessnock and are provided with a 10-speed touring bike. Your guide has a support vehicle to carry the baggage and the trip includes all meals and accommodation in country pubs. The tour departs on the first weekend of each month, all year round.

3rd Floor
377 Sussex Street
Sydney NSW 2000
Ph. (02) 264 3366

Bicycle Hire
Pokolbin Trading Post
Broke Road
Pokolbin NSW 2321
Ph. (049) 98 7675

2 **Snowy Mountains**

Kosciusko Expeditions
From December to March, weekend or five-day trips on mountain bikes are available from this operator, a franchise of the famous Paddy Pallin chain of equipment shops. You need to check on the weather conditions before confirming your trip. Then you're off on an exciting tour following the path of the Snowy River, staying in lodges or using the great camping spots of the region.

PO Box 72
Jindabyne NSW 2627
Ph. (064) 56 2458

Wilderness Expeditions
Their seven-day tour offers excellent alpine bicycling. You circumnavigate Australia's highest peak, Mt Kosciusko, starting from Cooma and going through Adaminaby, Kiandra, along the Alpine Way to the peak. Here you celebrate your achievement with a champagne picnic while contemplating the ravishing mountain terrain and lush meadows below. Support vehicles guarantee that

you get the best from the tour whatever your level of experience. Road surfaces range from sealed to well-graded gravel. The mountains, forests, valleys and crystal streams are a wonderful tonic for all.

100 Clarence Street
Sydney NSW 2000
Ph. (02) 29 1581

26 Sharp Street
Cooma NSW 2630
Ph. (064) 52 1587

Australian Capital Territory

3 **Canberra**

Tailwinds Bicycle Touring
Tailwinds can take you on a day trip to explore the sights of Canberra, complete with a comprehensive map and a good quality 10-speed bicycle. Canberra's good selection of bicycle paths makes this an easy and enjoyable meander. The trip departs every day at 9 am, returning at 5 pm, and takes in some interesting spots just outside Canberra.

9 Sargood Street
O'Connor
Canberra ACT 2601
Ph. (062) 49 6634

Victoria

4 **Northern Victoria**

Bogong Jack Adventures
Bogong Jack Adventures offer a variety of cycling tour holidays through north-east Victoria. Tours vary from two days to a week, and prices include most meals, share accommodation, geared touring bikes, a local guide and a support vehicle. The famous vineyards of the Rutherglen region are included, as well as the lovely historic towns of Wangaratta, Beechworth and Yackandandah. Tours operate virtually all year round.

PO Box 209
Wangaratta VIC 3677
Ph. (057) 21 2564

World Expeditions
Staying in old country pubs, and exploring the vineyards, historic goldrush towns and some of the haunts of Ned Kelly's gang are the highlights of this circular weekend tour by World Expeditions. Included in the price are 10-speed touring bicycles, a guide, all meals, accommodation and a support vehicle to carry all loads. The tour departs the first weekend of each month for most of the year, except during the depths of winter.

Suite 602, Wellesley House
126 Wellington Parade
East Melbourne VIC 3002
Ph. (03) 419 2333

5 **Melbourne**

Bicycle International & Christies Cycles
Although this company does not hire out bicycles, it is an agent for organised bicycle tour operators throughout Australia, and a useful source of information.

85 Burwood Road
Hawthorn
Melbourne VIC 3122
Ph. (03) 818 4011

Bicycle Hire
A number of places around Melbourne hire out bicycles for cycling around the city. Two that are centrally located are:

Penny Farthing Cycle Shops
100 Canterbury Road
Middle Park
Melbourne VIC 3206
Ph. (03) 690 3469

Hire A Bicycle
95 Eley Road Box Hill
Melbourne VIC 3128
Ph. (03) 288 5177

Tasmania

6 **Launceston**

Rent-a-Cycle Tasmania
Douglas and Janice Snare are a husband-and-wife team based in Launceston who offer a variety of bicycle trips around Tasmania. Accommodation is organised at Launceston Youth Hostel, which has well-equipped kitchens and dormitory accommodation. Bicycles are available through Rent-a-Cycle Tasmania, and are equipped with rear panniers, puncture kits, tools and safety equipment. Camping equipment is also available.

36 Thistle Street
Launceston TAS 7250 Ph. (003) 44 9779

DAVID McGONIGAL

Tropical Bicycle Odysseys
Tropical Bicycle Odysseys operates two bicycle tours in Tasmania, one of six days' duration, and the other of two weeks. Both take place only during summer, from December to March. The six-day tour takes in mainly the northern and central regions of Tasmania, while the longer trip provides a more extensive look at Tasmania, from Launceston right down to the southern tip of Eaglehawk Neck. Maximum tour size is 15, and the price includes all meals, accommodation mainly in colonial inns, bicycles, experienced guides, maps and directions.

PO Box 5092
Cairns QLD 4870
Ph. (070) 56 2100

7   Launceston to Hobart

Peregrine Adventures
Peregrine operate a ten-day tour, starting in Launceston and finishing in Hobart. The tour takes in Ben Lomond National Park, the pretty east coast village of St Helens, and a stop-off at Maria Island. The tour operates from December through to March. Cost includes all camping equipment, sleeping bag, air mattress, support vehicle and guide. Bicycle hire and contribution to the food kitty are additional costs.

Suite 9A, 9th Floor
343 Little Collins Street
Melbourne VIC 3000
Ph. (03) 602 3066

Wilderness Expeditions
Wilderness Expeditions offer a 12-day cycle tour in Tasmania, staying at specially selected campsites, shearers' quarters and mountain huts. From Launceston, the group travels toward the east coast to Freycinet Peninsula, and then inland toward the rainforest regions of Mt Field National Park. Rafting in the southern Derwent Valley region is a special highlight of this tour. Cost includes bicycles, maps, group camping gear, supply vehicle, accommodation, food and guides.

See (2) above for details

World Expeditions
Travelling through the rolling green farming country from Launceston to Evandale, along the South Esk River, makes a welcoming start to this two-week tour of Tasmania. Travelling along this island's lovely east coast, the group visits Coles Bay, Freycinet National Park and Swansea en route. Places of historic interest and good eating spots are regular stop-off points. Along the way, you will camp in farmers' fields, shearing quarters, quiet fishing villages and a former flour mill. Included in the cost is a guide, all camping equipment and a support vehicle.

See (1) and (4) above for details

Bicycle Hire
Graham McVilly Cycles
65 King Street
Sandy Bay
Hobart TAS 7005
Ph. (002) 23 7284

Seven Mile Beach Hire & Rental
2 Winston Avenue
Seven Mile Beach
Hobart TAS 7170
Ph. (002) 48 7397

South Australia

The *South Australian Touring Cyclists Association* conducts tours to the following places at certain times of the year, providing they can obtain a minimum number of participants.

8   **Adelaide Hills**

9   **Barossa Valley**

10   **Yorke Peninsula**

11   **Kangaroo Island**

GPO Box 1508
Adelaide SA 5001
Ph. (08) 388 8331

Western Australia

The *Cycling Touring Association of Western Australia* organises a variety of cycle tours. The following locations are a sample of some of the destinations they include:

12   **Perth**

13   **Rottnest Island**

14   **New Norcia**

15   **South-west Region of Western Australia**

PO Box 174
Wembley
Perth WA 6014
Ph. (09) 330 3659 or 325 9366

Northern Territory

16   **Darwin**

Lamaroo Lodge
Phil Heenan at Lamaroo Lodge has a bicycle hire service and also provides maps, suggested itineraries and camping gear for those wishing to venture into Kakadu National Park. Bicycles can be taken on the bus from Darwin to Cooinda for a bicycle trip in the park. Otherwise, the bikes are suitable for day use to see the sites of Darwin.

69 Mitchell Street
Darwin NT 5790
Ph. (089) 81 9733

Bicycles are also available for hire in Alice Springs from:

Melanka Lodge
94 Todd Street
Alice Springs NT 5750
Ph. (089) 52 2233

Queensland

17 Daintree

Tropical Bicycle Odysseys
Tropical Bicycle Odysseys are based in Cairns, and operate tours in North Queensland from April to November. Their 'Daintree Odyssey' is a seven-day trip through this spectacular rainforest region. The itinerary takes in Barron Gorge National Park, the lovely coastal scenery around Port Douglas, and snorkelling on the Great Barrier Reef. Cost includes accommodation in country hotels and cabins, all meals, a support vehicle and a Great Barrier Reef cruise.

See (6) above for details.

Wilderness Expeditions
This company includes a cycle through the Daintree National Park as part of a multi-adventure holiday entitled 'North Queensland Tropical Adventure'. The seven-day tour cost includes hotel accommodation, all meals, snorkelling gear, bicycles, canoes, rafts, safety and first-aid equipment, support vehicles and a guide. The trip includes crocodile spotting on the Daintree River, canoeing on the Mulgrave River and white-water rafting on the Tully River.

See (2) above for details.

18 Atherton Tablelands

Tropical Bicycle Odysseys
This seven-day trip starts with a scenic train ride on the Kuranda Railway up the coastal range, through country markets and forest trails. It then diverts through lush rainforests, ending with a canoe trip down the Mulgrave River. Tour cost includes accommodation in country hotels and cabins, all meals, bicycle and helmet and canoe and safety equipment. It is a moderate-grade trip, suitable for first-timers. Tropical Bicycle Odysseys also has a two-week trip that takes in both Daintree and the Atherton Tablelands.

See (6) above for details.

World Expeditions
This seven-day trip departs quite regularly from April through to October. It follows a similar itinerary to the trip that Tropical Bicycle Odysseys offers, with a flexible schedule that allows for shorter or longer stays at a place, depending on the whims of the group.

See (1) and (4) above for details.

19 Gold Coast

Tropical Bicycle Odysseys
The 'Gold Coast Hinterland' tour conducted by Tropical Bicycle Odysseys starts at the golden surf beaches along the Gold Coast and then heads inland. The five-day tour gradually winds its way south, crossing the state border into New South Wales, through the Tweed Valley to Tyalgum. The trip concludes at Byron Bay, Australia's most easterly point, and a bus returns the group to Surfers Paradise. Cost includes cabin and hotel accommodation, bicycles, guide and all meals. Tours depart through December to the end of January.

See (6) above for details.

Bicycle Hire
ABC Bicycle Hire
3090 Gold Coast Highway
Surfers Paradise QLD 4217
Ph. (075) 38 8422

Silly Sycle Rentals
10 Beach Road
Surfers Paradise QLD 4217
Ph. (075) 38 6991 or 38 4011

Information Sources

Bicycle Australia
PO Box K499
Haymarket
Sydney NSW 2000
Ph. (046) 27 2186

Australia's national bicycle touring organisation.

New South Wales

Bicycle Institute of New South Wales
802 George Street
Sydney NSW 2000
Ph. (02) 212 5628

NSW Cycling Federation
157 Gloucester Street
Sydney NSW 2000
Ph. (02) 241 1870

Victoria

Bicycle Institute of Victoria/Victorian
  Pedal Club
Shop 15/16, City Square
Melbourne VIC 3000
Ph. (03) 650 2500

Victorian Cycling Federation
347 Victoria Street
North Melbourne VIC 3051
Ph. (03) 328 4391

Tasmania

Northern Districts Amateur Cycling Club
10 Frederick Street
Perth TAS 7300
Ph. (003) 98 2400

South Australia

Amateur Cyclists' Association
  of South Australia
14 Homington Road
Elizabeth North
Adelaide SA 5113
Ph. (08) 255 1639

Northern Territory

Darwin Amateur Cycling Club
30 Freshwater Road
Jingili
Darwin NT 5792
Ph. (089) 85 4572

Queensland

Queensland Amateur Cyclists'
  Association
C/- Sleeman Complex
Tilley Road
Chandler
Brisbane QLD 4155
Ph. (07) 390 1489

Boat Charter & Hire

Australia is an island. And, not surprisingly, for a people surrounded entirely by sea, Australians are noted for their love of sports involving being in, on, or under water. With some of the most spectacular coastal fringes in the world and a labyrinth of waterways meandering through the vast inland reaches of the continent, it is easy to understand why boating enjoys an enormous popularity.

There are many boat charter and hire facilities available to those who wish to experience the wonders of a water holiday in Australia, whether it be on a yacht, a sleek cabin cruiser, or a comfortable old houseboat.

A houseboat holiday can be great fun, especially for families looking to find an unconventional vacation alternative. A houseboat offers a relatively large amount of deck and interior room. It is more like a large caravan than a boat, allowing easy manoeuvrability for those with little sailing experience. The shallow draft of the pontoons means that even a large houseboat can be navigated in very little water.

If a yachting excursion is more to the vacationer's taste, there are numerous operators who can cater for these needs. According to the sailor's level of competence, they can make available a wide assortment of cruising craft, from small two-berth skiffs to large, luxuriously-appointed motor cruisers.

The charter or hire of yachts, motor cruisers or houseboats falls into three quite distinct categories. Bareboat charter does not, as the name implies, indicate an empty boat. The idea of this type of chartering is that an operator provides the boat and you do the skippering. Houseboat hire always falls into this category. This type of craft is relatively easy to operate, and hire companies should provide detailed instructions before sending you out onto the waterways. Linen is generally provided on houseboats, but you should check this when booking. Provisioning is almost always your responsibility, but some operators will assist with this if it is pre-arranged. The charm of a houseboat holiday is that you dictate the pace of travel. Some people choose to moor in one spot for days at a time, or there is the option of travelling longer distances and seeing more of an area.

Yacht and motor cruiser charter is also often on a bareboat basis. As with houseboats, the freedom of moving around at your own pace is the attraction of bareboating. Experience of sailing or cruising is usually not required, and it is not difficult to master the essentials of manoeuvring your craft.

Linen is usually supplied with bareboat charters, and provisioning can often be organised by pre-arrangement with the charter company.

The second category is crewed charter. This type of boating appeals more to those who prefer a relaxing holiday with first-class service. The crew is provided along with the boat, and they are at your disposal for the duration of the charter period. Crewed charters are rather more expensive than the bareboat variety, but the crew will generally know the area well and be able to make suggestions as to mooring locations. Some charter companies also provide crews with specialist knowledge of such topics as fishing, diving or marine biology who are able to cater for special-interest groups. Both motor and sailing craft can be chartered on a crewed basis, and everything is provided for guests in what might best be described as a floating hotel.

Shareboat holidays are a third charter option that will suit the individual or small group. These holidays have scheduled departures, and you can book one or more places. The advantage of this type of charter is the opportunity to meet other people and to sail on craft that would not otherwise be available for charter. The Whitsunday region of Queensland is the major centre for shareboating. It is even possible here to join a group on a square-rigged ship for a sailing safari.

Once the decision has been made to charter a cruiser or hire a houseboat, everything else is easy and relaxing. The opportunity to enjoy scenic views, to feel the caress of balmy breezes while sunbathing on spacious timber decks, to swim and snorkel in clear shallow inlets or to fish calm rivers or test your angling skills in the ocean, to dine at waterfront restaurants, or simply to observe the wildlife are some of the reasons why a boating holiday is so pleasurable. And every Australian state provides such opportunities.

New South Wales, for instance, has some fine coastal harbours, bays and rivers for cruising and boating. Sydney Harbour is one of the deepest and most visually captivating harbours in the world. From the beaches near the harbour entrance to the distant backwaters of the Parramatta River into which the harbour eventually tapers, there are many pleasant places to visit.

Perhaps the most beautiful waterway is the Broken Bay-Hawkesbury River area, 40 kilometres north of Sydney. Broken Bay leads into Pittwater, a boating playground.

The Hawkesbury River was for many years the chief route between Sydney and the rich farming land of the Hawkesbury Valley, with ships of up to 300 tonnes carrying goods and passengers between Sydney and historic Windsor. The temperate climate, sun-soaked days and soft, still nights of the region are ideally suited to a cruising sojourn.

Not to be outdone, Queensland's Whitsunday Passage provides another excellent location for a cruising holiday, offering turtles, dolphins, coral gardens, deserted beaches, a surfeit of island resorts and spectacular scenery. The legendary north Queensland hospitality is part of the hire package in this idyllic setting.

Though New South Wales and Queensland could claim to be the premier boating states of Australia, particularly along their coastal fringes, Victoria and South Australia offer some fine inland locations for leisurely river jaunts. The Murray River is the most popular of these watercourses, with numerous charter and hire operators along its length.

The Murray commences its chequered 2,500-kilometre journey to the sea as a clear, icy stream high in the Australian Alps in far eastern Victoria. It meanders westward to spill unceremoniously into South Australia's Lake Alexandrina. Echuca, Swan Hill, Mildura and other one-time river ports are reminders of the days when cumbersome paddlesteamers lugged cargo and passengers up and down the river's length.

Western Australia, too, offers pleasant boating localities close to Perth. One of these regions is Mandurah, a small town on the west coast, south of the

Queensland's Whitsundays offers spectacular views from the water or the air

city. Armed with full operating instructions and a map of the area, passengers can set out along the idyllic waterways of Peel Inlet, Harvey Estuary and the Serpentine River.

Surprisingly, the Northern Territory and Tasmania have something in common where boating is concerned. Although separated by enormous distance and great variations in climate, their unadulterated wilderness regions provide a wealth of flora and fauna for travellers to observe on unique boating expeditions.

With its superb waterways, it is little wonder that Australians and visitors alike are increasingly choosing boating charter and hire as a holiday option.

Locations

New South Wales

1 **Gold Coast Houseboats** was founded to provide an answer to the perennial holiday question: 'Where will we go and what will we do?' It offers the opportunity to do something totally different in a wonderfully relaxed environment.

Luxury is the order of the day as you cruise the Tweed River, about 200 kilometres south of Brisbane. The journey takes in lush pastures and vast expanses of sugarcane plantations in this rich, subtropical agricultural region. Along the way, some of the best fishing on the east coast of Australia can be enjoyed.

All modern conveniences are available on board and guests need only bring linen and towels.

2 The Myall Lakes consist of four interconnecting lakes exceeding 10,000 hectares in area. The largest natural freshwater system on the NSW coast, it is the breeding ground for many species of fish and prawns. The area abounds in natural beauty, with a wide variety of flora and fauna. Stands of angophora and paper barks fringe the lakes' edges, and kangaroos, wallabies and possums frequent the campsites.

Myall Lakes Water Safaris, situated at Bulahdelah on the Myall River, is the closest access point to the lakes system. Being non-tidal, there are no problems with anchorages or currents, and it is a pleasant two-hour trip downstream from Bulahdelah to the first of the four main lakes. Passengers can spend an enjoyable weekend fishing, sightseeing, cruising, or just sitting about in the sun doing nothing except feeding the pelicans and marvelling at the flight of the resident osprey eagles and black swans.

A lead boat will guide those who are a little unsure of their sailing capabilities around the lakes, showing passengers the better anchorages and assisting with any difficulties.

3 On a **Tea Gardens Cruiser**, passengers can explore the bluewater wonderland of nearby Port Stephens, famous for its brilliant white beaches. The boats are designed for easy handling and even the novice will feel confident and comfortable as a navigator. Two to eight-berth houseboats come fully equipped with a gas stove, pressurised hot and cold water, a refrigerator, cutlery and cooking utensils; hirers need only supply sheets and towels. Ship-to-shore radios are fitted to all cruisers, as well as first-aid kits and lifejackets.

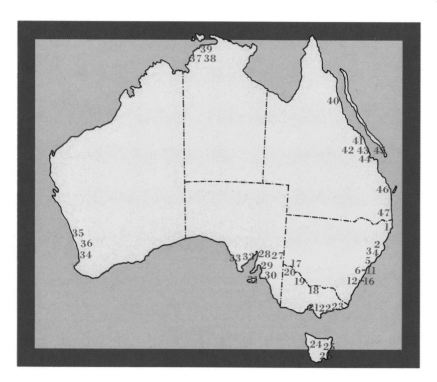

4 **Sail-Cruise Port Stephens** has fully equipped luxury six and eight-berth yachts and cruisers which enable visitors to experience one of the loveliest cruising regions in Australia. Soldiers Point and Nelson Bay are the better-known resort areas and waterways in the locality.

Sail-Cruise Port Stephens offers a well-fitted range of boating craft to accommodate the tastes and skills of sailing enthusiasts.

5 **Newcastle Holiday Houseboats** provides the relaxation of a roving holiday on beautiful Lake Macquarie. One of the largest seaboard lakes on Australia's east coast, it is only 100 kilometres north of Sydney.

Lake Macquarie has much to offer the houseboat enthusiast, including kilometres of deserted coastline, natural bushland seclusion on Pulbah Island, excellent fishing and exploring in the shallow waters around Dora Creek, which is inaccessible to other boats, and a fine selection of restaurants and clubs on the waterfront at overnight moorings.

Houseboats can be hired for two days up to a week, and costs include virtually everything: a dinghy with oars, a television, blankets and pillows, all cooking and eating utensils, secure car-parking facilities, a radio-cassette player, LP gas and up to 180 litres of fuel.

6 The fascination of the Hawkesbury River is as strong today as it was for Governor Phillip when he explored this 112-kilometre waterway in 1788. It is the longest navigable river on the east coast of Australia, with scenery that has a beauty all its own.

With many kilometres of the river unchanged since it was first discovered, it is easy to re-live the excitement of the pioneers who first navigated the Hawkesbury's mighty course. Passengers on an **Able Hawkesbury River Houseboat** have this opportunity, but they can explore in comfort aboard a floating home.

The houseboat is a spacious, eight-berth vessel that comes complete with all amenities. A licence or experience are not required to handle the craft.

7 In one of the most scenic areas of Australia, passengers can enjoy the company of fellow mariners as they explore the proven fishing grounds of the magnificent Hawkesbury River or take a meal at one of the riverside clubs, hotels or restaurants. There is the opportunity to discover ancient Aboriginal carvings and unspoiled waterways in a river system that has 320 kilometres of spectacular shoreline.

Situated 50 kilometres north of Sydney at Brooklyn on the Hawkesbury, **Fenwicks Hawkesbury River Houseboats** is one of the largest operators in the area, and its craft can readily accommodate up to six people. The houseboats are powered by reliable Evinrude outboard motors, which provide very comfortable cruising without the noise, vibration and fumes associated with diesel motors.

The boating haven of the Great Barrier Reef is best viewed from the air

8 **Halvorsen Boats** enables passengers to enjoy the landscape and superb climate of Sydney's northern beaches, Pittwater and the Hawkesbury River. Passengers can guide their pleasure craft on the meandering scenic waterways from Bobbin Head in the Ku-ring-gai Chase National Park, along the historic Hawkesbury River to Windsor. The McDonald and Colo Rivers also provide a marvellous retreat for a cruising expedition. The birdlife, unspoiled beaches, fishing, and out-of-the-way locations make for a memorable holiday.

Halvorsen Boats accommodates up to nine people on their well-fitted cruisers which are equipped with modern facilities, including a dinghy.

9 **Skipper a Clipper** offers comfortable self-drive cruisers out of Akuna Bay on the Hawkesbury River. The marina is in a sheltered cove on General San Martin Drive, and the staff provide helpful advice to the most inexperienced boating enthusiast.

All cruising craft are fully equipped with modern conveniences and can be hired for weekends or week-long sailing trips.

10 **Berowra Waters Boatshed** is a must for anyone wanting to take a small open boat and explore the beautiful waters of the Hawkesbury in the Berowra and Bear Island areas.

What's different about this boatshed is the way i is run by proprietors Ulrich and Anne Steiner. Ulrich came to Australia from Switzerland a number of years ago and has used his exceptional skills in boat building to turn Berowra Waters Boatshed into the sort of friendly, welcoming operation most people return to again and again.

11 Dominated by Lion Island, so-named because of its resemblance to a crouching lion, Pittwater offers countless inlets and bays to explore. It is actually the southern arm of Broken Bay, between Barrenjoey Headland and West Head. Known as the 'Yachtsman's Paradise', this idyllic cruising haven is 10 kilometres long and over one kilometre wide.

Passengers will find that even the water takes on different characteristics as they explore Pittwater. Near Scotland Island, it's the deep blue of the Pacific Ocean, while upstream it turns a dark green. In the backwaters, it's a haven for blackfish and bream.

The waters of Coal and Candle Creek are very deep, with the only shallows at the entrance to the creek itself. This nine-kilometre creek is within the confines of a national park and it offers a good anchorage as well as excellent fishing and swimming.

There are six different yacht types available from **Pittwater Yacht Charter**. All are fully equipped with safety gear, and come complete with bedding, linen and towels, a galley, and bathroom facilities. Most craft accommodate six passengers comfortably.

12 **Eastsail**, at the Rushcutters Bay marina, is right on the spot for people visiting Sydney. It is both a sailing school and yacht chartering organisation, with a variety of yachts on offer for sailing around Sydney Harbour. All are equipped with radio communication and high-standard facilities.

13 **Flagship Charters** arranges bookings and charters in Sydney Harbour and Pittwater. The range of vessels includes 7.3 and 10.9-metre yachts, with or without crews, a 17.3-metre sailing ketch, a 13-metre fast gaming cruiser, a 15-metre motor yacht, an 18-metre traditional motor vessel, a 22.8-metre sea-going motor vessel and a 21.3-metre catamaran hull cruiser.

14 **Magna Charter** is a yacht broking organisation based in Sydney which is able to provide both bareboat charters and crewed yachts throughout Australia. Of particular interest are the two yachts that sail out of the Northern Territory on a cruising basis. The two yachts are *Zachariah* and *Alegrias*, the first being a 12-metre steel ketch and the second a 22.8-metre schooner.

Magna Charter also offers bareboat charters of Cavalier 26's in Tasmania for challenging sailing and extensive cruising in the D'Entrecasteaux Channel and the Derwent River. In addition to these venues, an extensive range of boats is available in Cairns, Sydney,

Melbourne, Adelaide and Perth.

15 **Racing Yacht Charters** in Sydney has, as the star of its fleet, the classic 12-metre yacht *Vim*. *Vim* was designed by Olin Stephens and built in New York for H.S. Vanderbilt. Up until the late 1950s, she was a champion 12-metre. She was brought to Australia by Sir Frank Packer as a trial horse for *Gretel I*, Australia's first challenger for the America's Cup. *Vim* is now available for charters, along with a first-class crew.

Racing Yacht Charters also offers speedboats and private charters as part of their boat hire facilities.

16 The headquarters of **Sail Australia** at Lavender Bay, North Sydney, look out under the Harbour Bridge to the Opera House and the bustling life of the city. Sail Australia enables passengers to see Sydney Harbour at its best aboard their own charter yacht. Hire periods can be as short as an afternoon, or as long as a week or two.

Boats are also available for charter in the waters of Pittwater, the Hawkesbury River and Cowan Creek, all of which offer tranquil waters. There are no reefs or large tides to worry about.

Sail Australia's fleet includes the comfortable *Marauder 27* (up to six passengers), the *Cavalier 32* (up to eight passengers) and the spacious *Mottle 33* (up to ten passengers). In its power fleet, it has the *Persuader 21* (half-cabin for six), the *Clipper 34* (up to 12) and one large luxury motor cruiser, the *Janthe* (up to 70 passengers).

Sail Australia also provides instruction in yacht and dinghy sailing, catering for everyone from beginners to those wishing to gain radio operator, navigation or skipper's certificates.

17 At the turn of the century, the Murray and Darling Rivers were alive with steam paddleboats carrying cargo and passengers into the pioneering settlements of inland Australia. Today, these great waterways provide an impressive setting for holidays aboard a well-equipped **Adventure Houseboat.**

Passengers captaining their own craft have the choice of cruising through bushland to Nangiloc, about 60 kilometres upstream from Mildura (850 kilometres west of Sydney) or downstream through Lock II to the old river trading port of Wentworth, where the Murray and Darling Rivers meet.

Adventure Houseboats are smartly decorated with spacious kitchens, bathrooms and sleeping accommodation. They do not require passengers to possess a boating licence to operate the vessel.

Victoria

18 Echuca, just two hours' drive from Melbourne, is the base for **Rich River Holiday Houseboats.** This riverboat port still retains its 100-year-old wharf and some well-preserved historic buildings, some of which date back to the founding of the city in 1850.

The Echuca to Swan Hill stretch of the Murray

River, once the heart of a thriving riverboat industry, is now yours to explore by houseboat. The boats are easy to operate and skilled instruction is given before you leave Echuca. Rich River Houseboats operates a fleet of eight craft, including an eight-berth boat with a full-sized double bed. Kitchens are well-equipped and supplies can be purchased from Echuca and from Barmah — upstream and past the junction of the Goulburn and Murray Rivers. A cruise downstream will take you past orange groves and impressive river red gumtree forests.

19 Located at Mildura, **Serenity Houseboats** runs a fleet of boats ranging in size from four to eight berths, with a minimum hire period of three nights.

Mildura is further downstream from Echuca and closer to the point where the Murray River winds its way into South Australia. Irrigation has transformed this dry area of river flats into Australia's major dried fruits producing region. It is also famous for its citrus fruits and wineries. Mildura itself was founded in the 1880s when the irrigation scheme brought settlers to what had previously been a struggling sheep station.

Cruising the Murray is a relaxing pastime. Shore excursions can be made to historic towns such as Wentworth, on the northern bank of the Murray, in New South Wales.

Serenity's boats are easy to operate, well appointed and comfortable.

20 **Riverqueen Houseboat Holidays**, also based in Mildura, offers houseboats of the 'apartment afloat' variety on the Murray River. They have a houseboat fleet at Bruce's Bend Marina in Mildura and provide a range of boats and facilities to enable passengers to enjoy the delights of the Murray River.

21 **Le Yacht** provides yachts for chartering on the Gippsland Lakes. The yachts are safe, comfortable, well-equipped cruisers, with accommodation for up to six adults. They are simple to sail.

The Gippsland Lakes cover over 400 square kilometres of navigable water, with access to the famous Ninety Mile Beach. The beach is separated from the lakes by a narrow strip of coastal dunes and native scrub. From the lakes there is access to national parks and picturesque rivers such as the Tambo, Nicholson and Mitchell Rivers and their nearby townships, as well as lakeside hotels. Fishing is popular on the lakes.

22 In this delightfully unspoiled Gippsland Lakes area, about three and a half hours' drive from Melbourne, **Riviera Nautic** provides an opportunity for a different holiday in one of the prettiest waterways in Australia. Their small marina in Metung offers 20 boats for hire: ten motor cruisers and ten yachts.

Operating the motor cruisers requires no previous boating experience, while the yachts can be managed with only a little sailing knowledge. Accommodation is available for up to six people, and all craft are comfortably appointed with the best facilities.

23 **Webster Marine** is based at Paynesville, the boating centre of the Gippsland Lakes. Charts of

Holidaymakers on a Gold Coast houseboat

the lakes are provided to show passengers the location of spots like Sperm Whale Head, Box's Creek and Bunga Arm.

Some of the favourite destinations for overnight moorings include Ocean Grange, Newlands Arm, Bunga Arm and Barrier Landing. All are set in quiet, undisturbed bays and inlets, affording passengers privacy and peace to explore this bushland haven.

Webster Marine yachts sleep six adults in comfort and come with a fully-equipped galley.

Tasmania

24 The latest cruise vessel to ply Hobart's Derwent Estuary and surrounding waters is the 12-metre wooden craft **Carmel D,** which has been upgraded to provide safe, comfortable accommodation. *Carmel D* offers all-inclusive daily charters for up to 15 passengers in an area extending from New Norfolk, north of Hobart, to Southport, at the southern extremity of the D'Entrecasteaux Channel, and to the narrows at the entrance to Blackman Bay — some of Australia's most varied and interesting waterways.

The vessel is manned by professionals and is powered by twin-diesel motors. It carries two-way radios, a stereo radio-cassette player, and safety and navigational equipment.

25 **Channel Charters** of Hobart provides a bareboat charter service for sailing on the waters of the D'Entrecasteaux Channel and the Huon and Derwent Rivers — all close to Hobart. Sailors must have some prior experience to sail these eight-metre Cavalier yachts, which are fully equipped for chartering. Charter periods can vary from one to two weeks, and shorter charters can be made by arrangement. The boats sleep a maximum of four, but can be handled by two people with sailing experience.

The waters around Hobart provide some excellent sailing, with opportunities to visit locations such as Bruny Island, and the pretty bays and headlands of the Channel.

26 Houseboating is not a well-known Tasmanian holiday activity, but the opportunity exists both in the Hobart area and on Bathurst Harbour in the south-west of the state. The calm water of Bathurst Harbour is the venue for a houseboat holiday with **King Neptune Adventure Cruises.** The area is remote and unspoiled, and is contained within the South-West National Park. Since access is difficult, guests are flown into the region to commence their houseboat charter.

The houseboats are totally self-contained and comfortably appointed. A test drive must be taken before setting out, and instruction and advice are provided on handling the boat.

Boats are also available in Hobart for use on the D'Entrecasteaux Channel and the Derwent River.

South Australia

27 **Swan Houseboats** at Berri, about 160 kilometres north-east of Adelaide and close to the Victoria/South Australia border, offers ideal holiday packages all year round. Their well-equipped houseboats accommodate up to ten people and include all kitchen facilities as well as linen and blankets; customers need only supply their food and drinks.

A spectacular highlight of these houseboat journeys is the scenery. The wilderness of the magnificent Katarapko Reserve, the forests of Rilli Island, long white beaches and tall towering cliffs predominate as travellers negotiate downstream through willowy backwaters before reaching the long creek that stretches to the Gurra Gurra Lakes.

Swan Houseboats has the distinction of receiving the Riverland Tourism Award for their excellent tour services and tourist transportation.

On board the NT's Zachariah

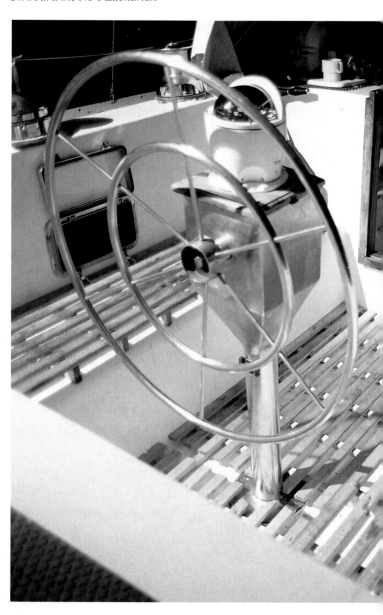

28 Passengers who charter a craft from **Koala House-boats** can experience the beauty and tranquillity of the Murray River. The journey begins at Morgan, 167 kilometres north-east of Adelaide, and travels the scenic riverland region where tall river gums and weeping willows dominate the vegetation on the banks which, in some parts, drop away to large cliffs and escarpments. The winding journey passes the townships of Waikerie and Barmera on the way to the river town of Loxton, close to the border of New South Wales.

The houseboats have been designed to ensure simple handling and no experience is necessary to hire any of their fleet of six to ten-berth luxury diesel-powered craft.

29 Operating along the picturesque Goolwa, Coorong and Great Lakes waterways of South Australia, **Afarr Yacht Charter** provides the largest range of power and sailboats in the area.

The different environments of the lakes offer an excellent variety of holidays. Downstream from Afarr's marina base at the heritage town of Goolwa, passengers pass the famous Murray Mouth and enter the Coorong — a 140-kilometre time capsule of golden beaches, undisturbed birdlife, and waters teeming with fish. Beyond a row of sandhills is the pounding Southern Ocean, a stark contrast to the tranquil anchorage enjoyed by travellers on their chartered craft.

Designed specifically for Afarr, the *Traditional Tug* is a pocket cruiser. At around 8.5 metres, she is easily managed by two people but has accommodation for up to six.

30 **Yacht Charter SA** invites passengers to be part of a relaxing lifestyle as they board a luxury yacht and cruise in sheltered waters amongst 42 uninhabited, unspoiled islands and anchor at night in tranquil bays and inlets.

Yacht Charter SA ensures that guests have a memorable journey. Not only can passengers enjoy lazy days on deck, marvelling at the spectacular sights of the coastline of South Australia, but they can also participate in a range of recreational activities during the cruise. There's the chance to fish for King George Sound whiting or snapper, both abundant in these waters, or to dive for scallops, lobsters or razor fish.

Qualified skippers lead the expedition, and the highest safety standards are maintained. An on-board cook is available if desired, enabling passengers to get away from daily routines.

31 **American River Yacht Charter** provides chartering facilities in the sheltered waters in and around American River on Kangaroo Island, some 140 kilometres due south of Adelaide.

The company charters a ten-metre sloop and a Farr design eight-metre shoal draft yacht. The Duncanson sloop has accommodation for six and is equipped with all regulation safety equipment.

Passengers can be taken as far west as Emu Bay on the north coast in the Duncanson, while the Farr yacht is available in Eastern Cove and Pelican Lagoon. In addition to excellent fishing and sailing, this area boasts magnificent beaches and bays.

American River Yacht Charter also offers sailing instruction, and they are happy to arrange a one-day course for anyone wishing to learn the basics of boat-handling whilst enjoying a holiday on Kangaroo Island.

32 **Lincoln Cove Yacht Charter** offers passengers the chance to indulge in cruising luxury aboard a Beneteau 305. This light and airy craft accommodates up to six people and has spacious cabin room, ample lockers, and a fully equipped galley.

This chartered sailing holiday takes place in the Port Lincoln region of South Australia. The islands in the area proliferate with native wildlife, including seal colonies, sea eagles, Cape Barren geese and reptiles. The waters teem with fish.

DAVID MCGONIGAL

33 Freedom, excitement, adventure, solitude and relaxation are offered by **Yacht Away Cruising Holidays** to travellers interested in a sailing holiday or sail training in the Adelaide and Port Lincoln areas or nearby Kangaroo Island.

Yacht Away was established in 1975, and it was the first cruising charter service in Adelaide. The yacht, skipper and all provisions are supplied so that passengers need only bring clothing, sleeping bags and any recreational gear such as snorkels, fishing rods or diving equipment.

Port Lincoln, on the eastern tip of Eyre Peninsula, nestles in a harbour three times the size of Sydney Harbour. The cruising area includes Boston Bay and over 30 islands within a 40-kilometre radius.

While on board, passengers have the opportunity to learn to sail if they so desire. Skippers will provide instruction in general seamanship, compass and chart work, and sail setting.

Western Australia

34 **Mandurah Holiday Cruisers** provides the perfect opportunity to get away from the hectic schedules of a working week and to relax while cruising through Peel Inlet, Harvey Estuary, and up and down the picturesque Murray and Serpentine Rivers. Explore the islands of the Murray River delta or rendezvous with friends at a land destination such as the historic Ravenswood Hotel.

Comfortable accommodation in four or six-berth cruisers includes all amenities: deep foam mattresses, a galley equipped with gas stove and all cooking utensils, and toilet and shower. Passengers need only bring linen and blankets.

35 Only five hours' drive from Perth, Walpole is situated on the southern coast west of Albany. It has inlets, coves, lazy rivers and islands to explore and is the ideal departure point for a leisurely holiday on the water. **Houseboat Holidays** operates from Walpole and offers two houseboats for self-drive for as little as a day.

The *Laze-Away* is a four to six-berth ten-metre boat supplied with blankets, cutlery and crockery for six, outdoor furniture for the sundeck, plus a small stove and griller, caravan fridge, radio-cassette player, UHF radio, first-aid kit, a full fuel tank and water.

36 **Phil Curran Charters** are brokers who have a range of vessels available for charter. They are based in Fremantle and Jandakot in Western Australia and will provide boats ranging from small yachts and motor vessels to large luxurious sea-going vessels. They are well-equipped with two marinas. The first is situated at Jervois Bay. Here they offer excellent facilities for guests, including transport, hire cars, parking, security, and even secretarial services.

A hospitality tent serves as a general meeting area at the marina. The marina at Nedlands offers similar facilities as well as fuelling.

They have an extensive range of craft for all manner of clients, whether they are professional sailors or simply keen boating novices. Weekends and holiday trips to remote areas can be organised using charter aircraft as well as vessels.

Northern Territory

37 Victoria Settlement, founded in 1838 and the first major European township in northern Australia, is deep inside Port Essington on the Cobourg Peninsula, 150 nautical miles from Darwin. It is in this remote tropical wilderness region that **Cobourg Marine** has established regular one and three-day tours between March and November, as well as providing a full boat charter service on their yacht, *Zachariah*, which takes passengers along the north coast.

Zachariah comes equipped with everything except sleeping bags. This 13-metre, ketch-rigged Van Der Stadt offers the ultimate in luxury for six passengers.

38 **Mary River Houseboats,** based in Darwin, operates a fleet of houseboats on the Mary River, just 60 or so kilometres from the city. Houseboating in this tropical region is delightful; the vegetation is lush and includes rainforest, palm trees and colourful flowers. Wildlife is prolific, too, with a vast variety of birds, crocodiles and buffalo. The presence of crocodiles is the only drawback to boating on the river, as they make swimming a hazardous pursuit!

Houseboats are available for hire for a minimum period of two days. The boats are fully carpeted and sleep from four to six people. All cutlery and linen are supplied, and facilities include a shower and hot and cold water supplies. Fishing tackle may also be hired. The dry winter season is the best time for houseboating in the Northern Territory.

39 **V & J Charters** operates out of Darwin and offers their 12.8-metre cruiser for charter. The boat is fully equipped for both diving and fishing trips, with facilities for offshore, onshore and game fishing. The boat can also be hired for less energetic pursuits as pleasure boaters are also catered for.

V & J takes charters into the coastal waters of the Northern Territory, and into the waters off the north coast of Western Australia. Fish such as trevally, bream and snapper are abundant in these waters and provide the perfect big-catch opportunity for the keen fisherman. The diving is also excellent in this region.

Queensland

40 **Tinaroo Tropical Houseboats** is a family business run by Margaret and Peter Dollman. Their boats cruise Lake Tinaroo on the Atherton Tablelands just inland from Cairns in tropical north

Queensland. Lake Tinaroo is perfect for family holidays, with safe year-round swimming, fishing, water-skiing, sailing, canoeing and sailboarding.

The houseboats, which resemble floating apartments, are split-level in design, affording passengers spacious, well-appointed living quarters.

41 **Australian Bareboat Charters** of Shute Harbour offers a good range of high-performance sailing yachts or bareboat charter vessels for sailing around the Whitsunday Group and the Great Barrier Reef islands. The company will teach basic sailing if required.

The yachts, designed by the international yacht designer Bruce Farr, have such names as *Farr Dinkum*, *Farr More* and *Farr Lap*.

42 The yacht **Pegasus** is a luxury charter yacht which sails the Whitsunday Islands region. Two facilities are offered. One is charters for seven days or longer for 12 passengers. The second is regular scheduled departures, which they call luxury laid-back holidays, and these depart regularly throughout the year.

43 **Queensland Yacht Charters** provides bareboat yachts and flybridge cruisers around the Whitsunday Islands. Home base is Airlie Beach. The company has a large fleet of good quality boats with a staff of well-trained and knowledgeable enthusiasts.

Their mini cruise ship, *Pacific Challenge*, which operates around the Great Barrier Reef, is of particular interest as it was launched in late 1986 as the mother ship for the challenge by New Zealand for the America's Cup. It is 27.4 metres long, with luxuriously appointed living quarters.

Pacific Challenge has three decks, all airconditioned, with accommodation for 20 guests in private cabins.

44 **Whitsunday Rent-a-Yacht** of Shute Harbour has a wide variety of yachts and motor cruisers for hire, providing access to the uncrowded waters of the Whitsunday Islands. There are over 74 islands in the Whitsunday group, making up a vast subtropical haven for those who want pleasant cruising in quiet idyllic surroundings.

45 **Hamilton Island Charters** has yachts and power boats available for charter, as well as game-fishing and speed boats. Home base is Hamilton Island, in the Whitsunday Islands.

They offer a very high standard of service. Their boats come equipped with stereo systems, a large area of refrigeration space, and push-button sail furling and anchor winch gear. All boats have two-way radios and excellent facilities. The company also provides crews. They are regarded by many as the best charter operator in the Whitsunday region.

46 **Fraser Island Rent-a-Yacht** in Tin Can Bay in southern Queensland offers bareboat charter yachts and motor cruisers. Passengers can visit the smooth waters of the Great Sandy Straits and nearby Fraser Island, a huge sand island off the Queensland

Relaxing on deck in the Whitsundays

CRAIG LAMOTTE

coast. Fraser Island Rent-a-Yacht offers a unique opportunity for visitors to skipper their own boat in a wilderness area that is only three hours by car from Brisbane.

Fraser Island is a wildlife haven, especially for marine creatures such as turtles and the rare and strange dugong. Opportunities for leisurely bushwalks, swimming, snorkelling, or angling in the island's shallow waters make for a memorable holiday.

47 **Sail-a-Holiday,** based at Runaway Bay on the Gold Coast, offers yachts for bareboat charter to explore this area. Their RL 28s accommodate up to six adults in comfort and are fully equipped for extended cruising. Comprehensive charts and books are provided to guide you around the waterways of the region, and sailing experience is not necessary. Sail-a-Holiday also charters its yachts in the Broadwater and Nerang River, close to the Gold Coast.

The secluded waterways of the Gold Coast are a perfect sheltered location for boating. The Broadwater, just north of Southport, is protected by South Stradbroke Island and The Spit and it contains many beautiful and unspoilt islands.

ALLAN MOULT

Boating Charter & Hire Contacts

Operators

New South Wales

1   Gold Coast Houseboat Hire

161 Pacific Highway
Murwillumbah NSW 2484
Ph. (066) 72 3525

2   Myall Lakes Water Safaris

Myall Lakes Marina
Crawford Street
Bulahdelah NSW 2423
Ph. (049) 97 4664

3   Tea Gardens Houseboats and Cruisers

Marine Drive
Tea Gardens NSW 2324
Ph. (049) 97 0555

4   Sail-Cruise Port Stephens

14 Warruga Street
Corlett NSW 2301
Ph. (049) 81 2405

5   Newcastle Holiday Houseboats

PO Box 50
Boolaroo NSW 2284
Ph. (049) 63 5700

6   Able Hawkesbury River Houseboats

River Road
Wiseman's Ferry NSW 2255
Ph. (045) 66 4299

7   Fenwicks Hawkesbury River Houseboats

31 Brooklyn Road
Brooklyn
Sydney NSW 2253
Ph. (02) 455 1333

8   Halvorsen Boats

PO Box 21
Turramurra
Sydney NSW 2074
Ph. (02) 457 9011

9   Skipper a Clipper

PO Box 63
Terrey Hills
Sydney NSW 2084
Ph. (02) 450 1888

10   Berowra Waters Boatshed

Berowra Waters
Sydney NSW 2082
Ph. (02) 456 1025

11   Pittwater Yacht Charter

Lovett Bay
via Church Point
Sydney NSW 2105
Ph. (02) 99 3047

12   Eastsail

d'Albora Marine
New Beach Road
Rushcutters Bay
Sydney NSW 2011
Ph. (02) 328 1118

13   Flagship Charters

d'Albora Marine
New Beach Road
Rushcutters Bay
Sydney NSW 2011
Ph. (02) 327 4999

14   Magna Charter

3rd Floor
377 Sussex Street
Sydney NSW 2000
Ph. (02) 264 1747

15   Racing Yacht Charters

16 Shadforth Street
Paddington
Sydney NSW 2021
Ph. (02) 357 6202

16   Sail Australia

23a King George Street
Lavender Bay
Sydney NSW 2060
Ph. (02) 957 2368

17   Adventure Houseboats

PO Box 213
Buronga NSW 2648
Ph. (050) 23 4787

Victoria

18   Rich River Holiday Houseboats

PO Box 375
Echuca VIC 3564
Ph. (054) 82 2994 or 82 3485

19 Serenity Houseboats

PO Box 255
Merbein
via Mildura VIC 3505
Ph. (050) 25 2534

20 Riverqueen Houseboat Holidays

PO Box 924
Mildura VIC 3500
Ph. (050) 23 2955

21 Le Yacht

Jetty Road
Nurgurner VIC 3909
Ph. (051) 56 3344

22 Riviera Nautic

185-187 Metung Road
Metung VIC 3904
Ph. (051) 56 2243

23 Webster Marine

39 Slip Road
Paynesville VIC 3880
Ph. (051) 56 6700

Tasmania

24 Leisure Cruises

1 Nutgrove Avenue
Sandy Bay
Hobart TAS 7005
Ph. (002) 34 7981

25 Channel Charters

GPO Box 977K
Hobart TAS 7001
Ph. (002) 25 1558

26 King Neptune Adventure Cruises

Prince of Wales Marine Park
49-55 Jepp Parade
Moonah
Hobart TAS 7009
Ph. (002) 72 6699

South Australia

27 Swan Houseboats

PO Box 345
Berri SA 5343
Ph. (085) 82 1622

28 Koala Houseboats

PO Box 106
Morgan SA 5320
Ph. (085) 40 2257

29 Afarr Yacht Charter

PO Box 390
Goolwa SA 5214
Ph. (085) 55 3777

30 Yacht Charter SA

PO Box 14
Kingswood
Adelaide SA 5062
Ph. (08) 277 4642

31 American River Yacht Charter

PO Box 39
American River
Kangaroo Island SA 5221
Ph. (0848) 3 3101

32 Lincoln Cove Yacht Charter

PO Box 929
70 Lincoln Highway
Port Lincoln SA 5606
Ph. (086) 82 1124

33 Yacht-Away

'Glengoulda' Koppio Road Mail
via Port Lincoln SA 5607
Ph. (086) 84 4240

Western Australia

34 Mandurah Holiday Cruisers

PO Box 137
Mandurah WA 6210
Ph. (095) 35 1149

35 Houseboat Holidays

2a Creekview Close
Rossmoyne
Perth WA 6155
Ph. (09) 457 9935

36 Phil Curran Charters

6 Parry Street
Fremantle
WA 6160
Ph. (09) 335 9966

Northern Territory

37 Cobourg Marine

GPO Box 1529
Darwin NT 6923
Ph. (089) 85 6923

38 Mary River Houseboats

Territorian Tourist Services
14 Knuckey Street
Darwin NT 5790
Ph. (089) 81 1244

39 V & J Charters

Box 3942
Winnellie
Darwin NT 5789
Ph. (089) 83 1213

Queensland

40 Tinaroó Tropical Houseboats

PO Box 44
Kairi QLD 4872
Ph. (070) 95 8322

41 Australian Bareboat Charters

PO Box 357
Airlie Beach QLD 4802
Ph. (079) 46 9381

42 Pegasus Cruises

PO Box 84
Airlie Beach QLD 4802
Ph. (079) 46 9381

43 Queensland Yacht Charters

16 McLachlan Avenue
Rushcutters Bay
Sydney NSW 2011
Ph. (02) 331 1211

44 Whitsunday Rent-a-Yacht

Bay Terrace
Shute Harbour QLD 4741
Ph. (079) 46 9232

45 Hamilton Island Charters

The Charter Base
Hamilton Island QLD 4802
Ph. (079) 46 9144

46 Fraser Island Rent-a-Yacht

Pacific Marina
Tin Can Bay QLD 4570
Ph. (071) 86 4507

47 Sail-a-Holiday Yacht Charters

20/249 Bayview Street
Runaway Bay QLD 4216
Ph. (075) 57 2533

DAVID MCGONIGAL

Boating Cruises

Australia is the biggest island in the world, with a coastline longer than that of any other country. Consequently, the variety of cruising adventures it offers the seafarer is vast. And the freshwater adventures on Australia's inland waterways and lakes are equally diverse.

From square-rigged brigantines in the idyllic tropical waters of Queensland to paddlesteamers on the Murray River and catamarans exploring the rugged coastline of north-west Western Australia, there is a water holiday/adventure to suit all tastes.

Queensland offers the greatest number of water-based options. The Great Barrier Reef, with its magnificent coral and deserted islands, and the long stretches of white sand flanked by lush rainforest and mangroves, provides exciting options for those wishing to brush up on their sailing skills, or to cruise in pampered luxury while soaking up the sun.

In New South Wales, not far north of Sydney, the Hawkesbury River and Lake Macquarie offer relaxed cruising on inland waters bordered by some of Australia's richest farmland. Sydney Harbour itself is one of the most magnificent harbours in the world. Several tours operate around its waters, providing a unique view of this beautiful city.

The Murray River, which forms the border between Victoria and New South Wales and finally reaches the sea in South Australia, has in recent years revived the old colonial days. In the early years of settlement, the river was the main transport and trading route between the inland farming country and the southern coastal ports. Today, several magnificent paddlesteamers, based in ports in both Victoria and South Australia and equipped with all modern facilities, ply its waters.

Western Australia, host of the recent America's Cup Defence, boasts some magnificent coastline in the remote north-west of the state. Travellers can sail these seas in total luxury, or experience thrills and adventure while sailing in a restored pearling lugger along the Kimberley coastline.

Visitors to the Northern Territory's Top End need not step ashore to see this region's exotic wildlife at close range. Several cruises venture into its national parks, through mangroves and along gorges, allowing visitors to see the magnificent abundance of birdlife as well as man-eating crocodiles from the safety and comfort of a boat.

One operation that deserves a special mention is Adventure Under Sail, which owns and operates the *Eye of the Wind*, a square-rigged sailing vessel which cruises Australia and the south-west Pacific islands. One of the pleasures of travelling on this boat is working as part of the crew, enabling passengers to participate in the fun and adventure of sailing the high seas. With a permanent crew of eight, *Eye of the Wind* provides for 16-18 share-expenses crew. It visits the South East Cape, the South West Cape of Tasmania, and the beautiful Pacific islands.

Many cruises available in Australia combine activities such as diving, snorkelling, sailboarding, fishing and inland trekking. There is an option to suit all pockets, schedules and tastes in adventure.

Locations

New South Wales

Lake Macquarie, four times the size of Sydney Harbour, is one of the largest lakes in Australia. Located between Newcastle and Sydney, the lake is a popular destination for water-lovers. It borders the

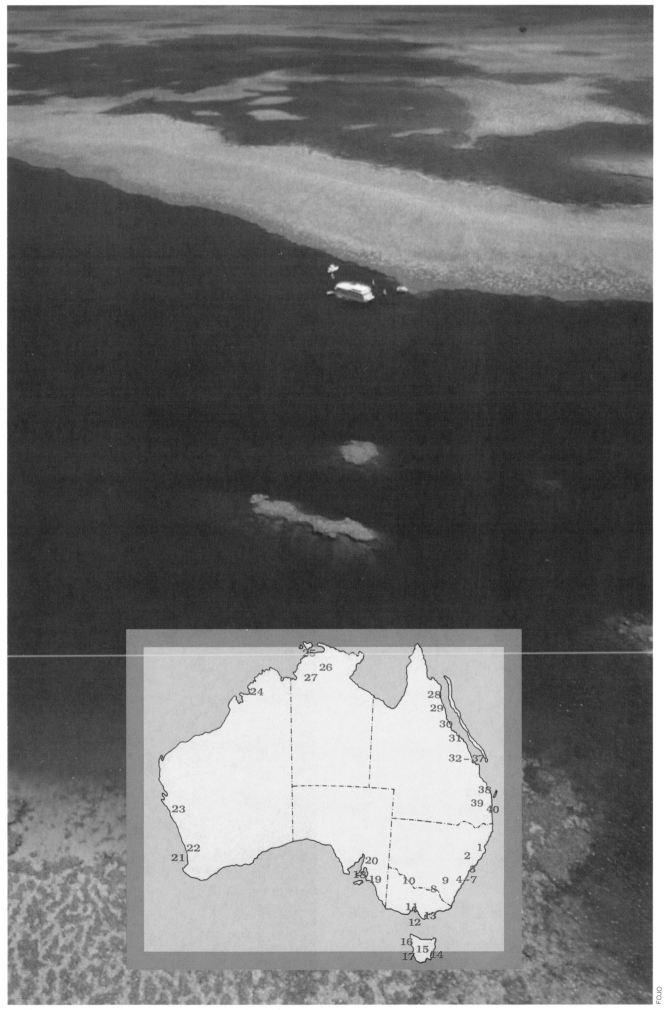

Hunter Valley, and is a central point for day tours to the surrounding areas.

1 The **Wangi Queen Showboat,** operated by Lake Macquarie Cruises, offers three short cruises around the bays and islands of this extensive waterway. The *Wangi Queen* is a carefully restored and maintained 1922 cruise ferry which provides numerous services, including facilities for the handicapped.

2 The **Lady Hawkesbury,** the newest addition to New South Wales' luxury boating fleet, is in fact the only large luxury cruising boat plying the state's inland waters. With 60 luxurious cabins, a swimming pool, bars, staterooms, airconditioning, sauna, sundeck, dance floor and conference centre, she emulates the old-world elegance of Germany's Rhine cruises.

Her flat-bottomed design allows access to many of the Hawkesbury River's shallow waterways. A 250-kilometre Heritage Cruise takes passengers as far as Windsor, on the upper reaches of the river, taking in sights of historical interest along the way. There are also two-night weekend 'escape' cruises from Kangaroo Point.

3 Just north of Sydney, **Boatshed Cruises'** *Stockton* carries up to 176 passengers along the waterways and around the shores of scenic Pittwater and Broken Bay in the Hawkesbury River region.

The *Stockton* also operates Sydney day tours. For two hours, it mingles with the many craft on the harbour, while gliding past sandy beaches, inlets with sheltered blue waters, small bays and the many other sights of this busy harbour.

The *Stockton* may also be privately chartered in the summer, being fully fitted out for elaborate entertaining.

4 **Captain Cook Cruises** provides the greatest number of sightseeing cruises around Sydney Harbour. These include a four-hour Coffee Cruise, a Luncheon River Cruise (which takes in the sights of Sydney Harbour and the Parramatta and Lane Cove Rivers), and the Sydney Harbour Budget Cruise. In the evening, candelight cruises include dinner, music and dancing.

One of the many vessels operated by Captain Cook Cruises is the *Sydney Harbour Explorer,* which visits five famous harbourside attractions — the Sydney Opera House, The Rocks, Taronga Park Zoo, Watsons Bay (a seafood village) and Pier One. The advantage of this type of cruise is that it is possible to disembark at any one point and rejoin the next *Explorer,* which calls at each stop at 90-minute intervals.

5 **Matilda Cruises** operates a large, comfortable, catamaran cruiser on Sydney Harbour. It is especially fitted out for wining and dining in the most romantic surroundings. Designed to operate in comfort in all weather conditions, the MV *Matilda* can be completely closed in if there is unfavourable weather. In summer, the wide outside upper and lower decks offer outstanding views.

One of the main features of the *Matilda* is that guests are welcome on the bridge. Passengers can also embark or disembark at pre-arranged vantage points on the harbour.

The *Matilda* is available for charter for conferences, seminars, weddings and parties.

6 The **PS Sydney Showboat,** in operation since late 1987, is the largest sightseeing cruising restaurant on Sydney Harbour. Offering both day and evening cruises, this 42-metre vessel, reminiscent of the early paddlewheelers, is berthed at No. 2 Jetty, Circular Quay. The *Sydney Showboat* is the first stern-driven paddlewheeler ever to cruise Sydney's waters.

The 33 metres of luxury which is the Elizabeth E II explores the Outer Reef

There is a wide variety of cruises available and one of the many attractions is the nightly cabaret. The *Sydney Showboat* provides set menus for some cruises, and an à la carte menu when required. All food is prepared on board by master chefs.

7 The **Solway Lass,** a topsail schooner, was built in Holland in 1902. Totally and lovingly restored, she is Sydney's official entrant in the 1988 Bicentennial Tall Ships race. Boasting a magnificent set of sails, she is considered to be the belle of Sydney Harbour. In addition, she has a six-cylinder diesel engine (for difficult manoeuvring) and is fully fitted out with the most up-to-date regulation safety equipment.

The *Solway Lass* operates daily tours, dinner cruises, and shorter 'Lunch Under Sail' tours every weekend. The below-deck dining saloon, panelled with cedar and upholstered in leather, provides first-class food and service for up to 60 guests. As a special treat, keen sailors are welcome to sail as hands on this topsail schooner just for the fun of learning the ropes.

8 The **Upper Murray Steamship Company,** with sponsorship and assistance from the federal government as part of a Bicentennial project, has built an exact replica of a 19th-century steam-powered paddlewheeler. It is an authentic working exhibit of an historic mode of travel. The three-decked PS *Cumberoona,* powered by two elderly steam engines, operates daily cruises from Albury on the New South Wales/Victorian border. It is also available for group

A gracious paddlewheeler plies the waters of the Murray River at Echuca

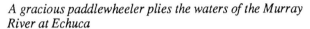

bookings during the day and evenings.

Australian Capital Territory

Lake Burley Griffin is the heart of the city of Canberra. Named after the architect of the city, the lake has 36 kilometres of foreshore and is one of the most popular recreation areas for both visitors and residents. Many of Canberra's famous buildings overlook the lake, adding to the interest of a lake cruise.

9 **Murrays Australia** is one of Canberra's largest tour operators, and included in its programme of tours are several lake cruises. A Lake Burley Griffin cruise can be combined with a trip into the Molonglo River and Jerrabomberra wetlands. Luncheon cruises are also available.

An unusual way to view the night skyline of Canberra is on board a dinner cruise. Four hours of fine food, music and pleasant surroundings make this a great night out.

Victoria

The Murray River system, which includes the Murrumbidgee and Darling Rivers, is one of the longest in the world. The Murray itself flows for a distance of 2,300 kilometres and forms the border between New South Wales and Victoria.

Despite the building of several weirs along its system, the Murray still boasts 1,800 or so kilometres of navigable water. And paddlesteamers, relics from the past, have come to life again, this time bringing tourists to visit one of Australia's most historic waterways.

10 The **PS Emmylou** is powered by a restored 1906 steam engine and is the only wood-fired, steam-driven, overnight paddlesteamer in the world. She runs on timber found along the banks of the river, a legacy of 80 years of railway sleeper cutting in the area.

The PS *Emmylou* carries 20 passengers and offers weekend and midweek cruises. With sundecks, dining and bar areas, a sound system, videos and an on-board chef, she has all the conveniences expected by the modern traveller while reliving the past.

The *Emmylou* is based in Echuca on the Murray River, two and a half hours' drive north of Melbourne. She is available for private charter, except in winter.

11 The Yarra River valley was selected in 1835 by John Batman as the site for the new settlement of Melbourne. In 1851, with the discovery of gold in central Victoria, it entered into a boom period and by 1861, Melbourne was the biggest city and port in Australia.

Melbourne Cruises offers sightseeing trips along the Yarra in three luxurious cruisers. Tourists glide past the Royal Botanic Gardens and the magnificent National Gallery of Victoria complex, and pass under the river's historic bluestone bridges. A commentary

The 27.5 metre James Kelly II on a cruise to Limekiln Reach on the Gordon River

is provided on the passing sights. The *Yarra Empress, Queen* and *Princess* each hold up to 128 passengers and are available for private functions. They operate year-round, seven days a week.

12 The **Spirit of Victoria** is the world's first wave piercer catamaran. She is designed to pierce the waves instead of riding over the top of them, ensuring a smoother ride for her passengers. This 27 by 13-metre, three-storey catamaran operates cruises around Melbourne's Port Phillip Bay. Passengers visit resort towns and beaches, and Fort Island with its 19th-century underground fort and 'disappearing' guns. They can also see the bay's delightful seals, and stop at one of its seafront restaurants for lunch.

13 The steam tug **Wattle,** built in 1933 at Cockatoo Island in Sydney, spent her working life based with the navy at the Garden Island Dockyard. She was kept busy berthing ships and manoeuvring barges in the harbour. Upon retirement, she was restored and refitted by the Victorian Steamship Association. The *Wattle* is now one of the few surviving steamers in Australian waters, and today she conducts day excursions around Port Phillip Bay, as well as Sunday and public holiday cruises in the Port of Melbourne.

Portarlington, a picturesque country town on the Bellarine Peninsula, is the destination for excursions around Port Phillip Bay.

Tasmania

14 The **Carmel D** is a recently refurbished and modified 12-metre wooden vessel which takes guests along the lovely Derwent River and

DAVID McGONIGAL

D'Entrecasteaux Channel. Although it is licensed to carry 15 people, its owners place priority on safety and comfort and prefer that it carries only eight to ten passengers.

The vessel is available for short sightseeing cruises and day-long cruises, as well as for longer overnight cruising and private charter. It operates year-round.

The *Carmel D* has all modern amenities including hot and cold water, a sound system, gas stove, refrigerator, deep freezer and microwave oven. Powered by twin diesel motors, she carries the latest in safety and navigation equipment.

15 **Devil Jet**, in New Norfolk, on the beautiful upper reaches of the Derwent River close to Hobart, provides the only white-water jet boating in Australia. Their boat, the *Hamilton Jet 52*, was designed and developed in New Zealand and has won many national and international jet-boat marathons.

Although it is not suitable for babies and mums-to-be, potential thrill-seekers with any doubts can take courage from the oldest passenger to partake of this 30-minute ride along the wild Derwent River rapids. He was 92, and he brought along his 86-year-old wife for company! Trips are available year-round.

16 The Gordon River is one of the longest and most remote of Tasmania's rivers. It was the focus of worldwide attention a few years ago when the Tasmanian government proposed to dam its waters as part of a hydro-electric scheme.

For 44 years, the Morrisons, one of the pioneering families of the river port town of Strahan, have been providing cruises along this magnificent river. Their luxurious cruiser, the **Gordon Explorer**, takes visitors into the second largest harbour in Australia — the landlocked Macquarie Harbour — to the notorious Hell's Gates (the harbour entrance), and up the Gordon River. Operating year-round, seven days a week, the cruise operates from Strahan.

17 **Scenic Gordon and Hells Gate Charters** also operates cruises around the 285 square kilometres of Macquarie Harbour and past Hell's Gates. One of its boats, the *Wilderness Seeker*, is the only vessel in Tasmania's south-west World Heritage area to venture as far upstream as the Franklin River. This shallow water jet boat travels past Sarah Island (once Tasmania's most brutal penal settlement) before leaving the harbour and cruising along the Gordon with its gorges and rapids to its junction with the Franklin.

South Australia

18 **Murray River Cruises** offers the choice of three riverboats, allowing tourists to relive the days of yore along the historic Murray River.

The PS *Murray Princess* is the largest vessel of its kind in the southern hemisphere. She is styled after the magnificent old riverboats of the Mississippi River in the United States, but her interior reflects the days of colonial Australia. She also caters for modern times, with a lift for handicapped passengers, as well as a spa and sauna. The *Murray Princess* departs from Renmark, in the heart of South Australia's citrus-growing area, for six nights of idyllic cruising along 300 kilometres of the Murray's inland waters.

The PS *Murray River Queen* departs from the historic town of Goolwa, which was the first major shipping port in South Australia. The *Queen* takes passengers upstream, crossing Australia's largest freshwater lake, Lake Alexandrina, and stops at places of historic interest so that passengers can learn more of this important colonial trading route.

The MV *Murray Explorer* is styled after the German cruise boats of the Rhine River, and it treats passengers to a standard of accommodation normally found only in a first-class hotel. Departing from the historic Old Mildura Homestead (settled in 1846), she takes passengers to the junction of the Murray and Darling Rivers.

19 The **Proud Mary**, a Murray River passenger vessel, is moored at Murray Bridge, only 45 minutes' drive from Adelaide. Conducting five-day midweek and weekend tours up the beautiful Murray River, the *Proud Mary* operates year-round. She sweeps past historic towns set amidst willow and gumtree-lined river banks, allowing passengers to retrace the early pioneering routes and to learn about the colourful history and ecology of this famous river system.

Passengers are accommodated in 18 well-appointed cabins, each with private facilities. The

Proud Mary also has a large saloon dining room, bar, sundeck, souvenir shop and dance floor. Experienced chefs prepare meals, often including the delicious local Murray River fish in their extensive menus.

20 With their new riverboat, the *Ginny Christmas,* the **Cruising Matilda Company** emulates the luxurious style of the hotel-barges which ply the waterways of Europe. With emphasis on personalised service, *haute cuisine* and excellent wines, the *Ginny Christmas* offers a variety of cruises year-round. Passengers enjoy the luxury of sailing through beautiful countryside and can also take part in onshore adventures, including hot-air ballooning, gliding and bushwalking. They can also visit a conservation park, the vineyards of the Barossa Valley, historic settlements and a pioneering property.

Western Australia

21 **Oceans International Adventure Tours** operates out of Cottesloe, near Perth. Their boat, *That's Life!,* is a 19-metre luxurious modern sailing craft capable of carrying 11 passengers.

That's Life! sails to Rottnest Island from October to March for one-day adventures which include snorkelling around shipwrecks, sailboarding, shore tours, and lunch on board.

The ultimate get-away-from-it-all trip is their one or two-week land, sea and air Kimberley Adventure Tour (April to October). The Kimberleys are world renowned and the region is considered by many to be the last frontier, most of it being total wilderness.

22 **Swan River Cruises** operates cruises along the Swan River to and from Fremantle and across to Rottnest Island. They also offer a 'champagne cruise' 15 kilometres north to the historic town of Guildford. Transferring to a coach, guests tour Guildford's many historic sights before driving on to Midland and the Swan Valley for wine-tasting at one of the area's vineyards. Dancing is held on board on the return journey at the end of the day. Private charter is available.

23 **Wave Spirit Charters** runs the *Wave Spirit* from Geraldton and Broome on the north-west coast of Western Australia. The *Wave Spirit* visits two of the most extraordinary locations in Australia, the Rowley Shoals and the Kimberleys, both in north-western Australia. The Rowley Shoals are one of the finest diving sites in the world.

An 18-metre aluminium-hulled vessel working between May and October, she accommodates up to eight people for diving and fishing expeditions. On diving expeditions, a fully qualified divemaster is on board in addition to the crew.

The boat has a range of 1,000 nautical miles and a cruising speed of 15 knots, and is fully equipped with the most modern facilities, including a radio-telephone.

Explore Queensland's Whitsunday Passage in a luxury cruiser and discover paradise

24 The **Kimberley Explorer** is a 34-metre catamaran which recently saw service as the Royal Perth Yacht Club's viewing vessel for the America's Cup Defence. Refitted for extended cruising, she now offers scenic cruises from Broome to Wyndham in the remote Kimberley region of Western Australia.

Travellers fly from Perth to Broome, at the southernmost tip of the Kimberleys, where they join their luxurious cruising home.

With 16 well-appointed cabins, a restaurant, bars, video facilities, telephone and telex, the *Explorer* also has four landing craft which enable exploration of normally inaccessible areas. She takes passengers past some of the most rugged and remote territory in the world, cruising through tropical seas and meeting the Bardi Aborigines. Travellers also view magnificent bird and wildlife and spectacular waterfalls and gorges.

Northern Territory

25 The **Alegrias** is a 22.8-metre, three-masted sailing ship based in Darwin Harbour. It has recently circumnavigated Australia. For those with a few days to spare, the schooner is probably the most exciting way to see the Top End coastline.

The *Alegrias* offers three and five-day cruises of the islands, as well as day and sunset cruises of Darwin Harbour. The three-day cruise links up with an optional four-day four-wheel-drive adventure through Kakadu National Park. After visiting remote waterfalls, seeing wildlife and Aboriginal rock art, and cruising in a swamp boat on Yellow Waters Lagoon, visitors can join the *Alegrias* on a three-day Island and Coastal Fishing Adventure Cruise to Perron Island.

The five-day cruise — the Cobourg Adventure Cruise — is perfect for total relaxation. Passengers can enjoy great fishing, bushwalking, visit historic ruins, spot giant saltwater crocodiles, go oystering off island rocks and view some of the Top End's wonderful birdlife. There is also a tour of the Bathurst Island Aboriginal settlement with its various arts and crafts.

Sailing year-round, except during the summer's wet season, the schooner can accommodate eight people. It is also available for private charter.

26 The **Adelaide River Queen** allows visitors to see some of the best of the Northern Territory's wildlife from the safety of its decks. Passengers cruise along the beautiful Adelaide River, looking out for crocodiles, birdlife (including magpies, brolgas, jabirus, kites and dollar birds) wild buffalo and pigs.

Two cruises are available: a two and a half hour 'Croc Spotter' Cruise, and a half-day tour which also includes crocodile spotting and a visit to Gow's Reptile World and the scenic Fogg Dam. It is a 50-minute drive from Darwin to the river, and cruises operate year-round except during February.

27 The Victoria River Gorge, 400 kilometres upstream from the mouth of the 800-kilometre long Victoria River, boasts fantastic red sandstone cliffs and a wide diversity of fauna and flora.

The river flows through the new Gregory National Park, one of the biggest parks in the Northern Territory. Its 200-metre-high sandstone cliffs change from rich red to brown in colour as the sun moves through the course of the day.

Max Sharam, with his wife Edna, has run **Red Valley Boat Tours** for the past five years and is on close terms with the river's crocodiles. Crocs come from the water at his call to be fed meaty tid-bits and to be given the odd scratch behind the ear.

Tours depart from the Victoria Wayside Inn, which has motel and camping accommodation and is located 195 kilometres west of Katherine and 315 kilometres east of Kununurra in Western Australia. Tours operate during the dry season from April to the end of October.

Queensland

28 **Quicksilver-Low Isle Cruises**, based in Port Douglas, a scenic 60-kilometre coastal drive north of Cairns, offers two daily cruises for visitors to the Great Barrier Reef. Visitors have a choice of travelling on the 30-metre catamaran, *Quicksilver*, to Agincourt Reef, 63 kilometres from Port Douglas, or catching the 20-metre *Low Isles Reef Express* to Low Isles, a coral cay surrounded by 22 hectares of reef.

Both tours provide visitors with the opportunity to snorkel and swim, enabling close viewing of the spectacular coral formations and tropical fish through the glass walls of their underwater viewer.

29 The **Hayles** family were pioneers in the Queensland tourist industry, opening up one of the seven great wonders of the world, the Great Barrier Reef, to sightseers more than 60 years ago. Today they offer visitors to Cairns an extensive variety of cruises through the beautiful waterways of this magnificent coral reef.

Cruises depart twice daily from Cairns for the coral cay of Green Island, 40 minutes offshore. Passengers can view the coral through a glass-bottomed boat, or they can don scuba or snorkelling gear.

Passengers can choose to travel to the Outer Barrier Reef, 40 minutes further on from Green Island, to view the coral from the unique semi-submersible vessel, *Reef Pioneer*.

30 Just 45 minutes south of Cairns, beside the Mt Bellenden Ker, passengers can board the historic **Jungle Queen** and embark on a cruise along the tranquil Mulgrave River. Here they will see rain-forest-clad mountains rising from the river's edge, as well as a wealth of birdlife and mangrove swamplands.

A stopover at Russell Heads allows time for a relaxing tropical beach barbecue and the chance to have a quick swim or to drop a fishing line or two. The *Jungle Queen* then cruises on into the Russell River to give passengers a breathtaking view of the Graham Range National Park before afternoon tea is served and the boat returns to the jetty.

31 Townsville is home port for the luxurious **Coral Princess**. Every Monday, the *Coral Princess* departs for a reef and island cruise through the most picturesque islands and coastline in Australia. Carrying up to five crew and a maximum of 24 passengers, the *Princess* offers informal holidays in a relaxed, friendly atmosphere.

The itinerary encompasses the world's largest marine park, the Great Barrier Reef. The *Coral Princess* cruises for three or four hours each day, making its way from one beautiful island to the next.

A *Coral Princess* five-day cruise includes all meals, hotel transfers and all snorkelling equipment and fishing tackle.

32 **Club Whitsunday** provides two luxury holidays on the waters of the beautiful Whitsundays. With deserted islands, magnificent coral, fishing and oystering and white sandy beaches, the Whitsundays are a water-lover's paradise.

Holiday-makers can choose from a seven-day cruise in one of Australia's largest and most luxurious yachts, the *Pegasus*, or opt for the comfort of a 21-metre motor cruiser, the MV *Nocturn*.

33 Built at a cost of almost $4 million, the **Coral Cat** has three spacious deck levels and 21 cabins and suites, all with private bathrooms, to accommodate passengers in luxury as they sail the Whitsundays.

Onboard entertainment varies from day to day depending upon the interests and requirements of passengers. The extensive range of activities to choose from includes sailboarding and other water sports, clay pigeon shooting, board games and videos.

34 **Coral Sea Line** offers two unique sailing holidays through the magnificent Whitsundays. Passengers sail through seas filled with coral reefs and tropical fish, laze on long white stretches of beach, camp on uninhabited islands, snorkel, dive, swim and sailboard.

Passengers have a choice of two vessels: the *Golden Plover*, a 30-metre square-rigged brigantine built in Melbourne in 1910, or the *Cygnus*, a nimble 16.7-metre ketch that sometimes flies along in the breeze. Both sail a similar route, with camping, sailboarding and snorkelling gear provided. The *Plover* also provides diving gear.

35 The sight of a full spinnaker swelling resplendently on an ocean-racing yacht as it moves gracefully across the water is one worth savouring. The opportunity is now available to be a part of the action and excitement on a cruise aboard Australia's first America's Cup Challenger, **Gretel.**

This grand old racing yacht sails daily to Langford Reef from Shute Harbour Jetty near the Whitsunday Islands. It affords passengers not only the chance to sailboard, snorkel and observe the intricate coral formations around the reef, but also to take part in a sailing experience on a world-famous vessel that has won acclaim for its sporting endeavours.

36 The most advanced cruising passenger ship in the Great Barrier Reef waters is the luxurious **Elizabeth EII**, based at Mackay. This 33-metre vessel takes passengers to some of the most glorious regions of Queensland's north, including the Whitsundays, and Brampton, Lindeman, Dent, South Molle, Daydream and Hamilton Islands, as well as the beautiful stretches of the Outer Barrier Reef.

The *Elizabeth EII* accommodates 28 people in modern airconditioned cabins with en-suite facilities.

Four days are spent travelling through the Whitsunday Islands and out to the Great Barrier Reef, where passengers can explore the reef on foot, in the water, or through a glass-bottomed boat. They may also disembark at any of the resort islands for a longer holiday if they wish, and connect with the *Elizabeth EII's* return journey a week later.

37 The **Spirit of Roylen** is a modern, high-speed, 250-passenger catamaran that cruises from Mackay through the fabulous waterways of the Whitsunday Passage to the beautiful Brampton and Hamilton Island resorts.

Passengers enjoy a day of activity, excellent food and spectacular sights around the coral reefs. The *Spirit* moors at Credlin Reef beside a spacious, shaded pontoon platform complete with underwater observatory. This is also a perfect place for swimming, snorkelling, scuba diving and relaxing.

38 Noosa's **Cooloola Cruises** has been working the Noosa River and Everglades area for 60 years and offers a complete range of day and half-day tours around this scenic wonderland.

The slow, comfortable cruisers are designed for the ultimate in passenger relaxation. Space to move freely about the boat, morning and afternoon tea, and an open top deck for sunbathing and photography are some of the features guests can enjoy when they embark on a Cooloola cruise.

39 The **Kookaburra Queen**, a 30-metre, 19th-century-style paddlewheeler, gracefully plies the Brisbane River, conducting cruises and providing special facilities for social and trade functions. The paddlewheeler has three enclosed decks, two of which provide restaurant and function facilities.

The *Kookaburra Queen* offers a wide range of cruises, from a 90-minute Devonshire Tea cruise to a three and a half hour dinner cruise on the Brisbane River. The *Queen* also sails on regular morning and lunchtime cruises, as well as offering a very popular once-a-month excursion to Bishop Island at the mouth of the river.

40 The **MV Brisbane Explorer** is a 52-metre ship, based in Brisbane, offering two and four-day tours of the waterways and sights south of Brisbane to the Gold coast. She accommodates up to 130 people in comfortable private rooms, each with airconditioning and en-suite facilities. The *Explorer* boasts a spa, sauna and sun-deck and two well-stocked bars. Meals are complemented by a wide range of Australian wines, and on-board entertainment is provided by musicians and singers.

The *Explorer* cruises through beautiful Moreton Bay with its huge sand islands, through Canaipa Passage and Broadwater, past long white beaches and marinas and along secluded channels and waterways.

Boating Cruises Contacts

Operators

The Eye of the Wind
Adventure Under Sail
90 Ferris Street
Annandale
Sydney NSW 2038
Ph. (02) 560 4035 or 27 8877

New South Wales

1   Wangi Queen Showboat

6 Morse Street
Speers Point NSW 2284
Ph. (049) 59 5072

2   The Lady Hawkesbury

Captain Cook Cruises
No. 6 Jetty
Circular Quay
Sydney NSW 2000
Ph. (02) 27 4548

3   Boatshed Cruises

PO Box 304
Newport Beach
Sydney NSW 2106
Ph. (02) 997 4010 or 949 1977

4   Captain Cook Cruises

See (2) above for details

5   Matilda Cruises

PO Box 420
Willoughby
Sydney NSW 2068
Ph. (02) 552 1677

6   PS Sydney Showboat

Blue Line Cruises
Suite 7, 'The Vintage'
281 Sussex Street
Sydney NSW 2000
Ph. (02) 264 3510 or 264 3432

7   The Solway Lass

See (6) above for details

8   Upper Murray Steamship Company

PO Box 923
Albury NSW 2640
Ph. (060) 41 1355

Australian Capital Territory

9   Murrays Australia

PO Box 60
Red Hill
Canberra ACT 2603
Ph. (062) 95 3677

Victoria

10   PS Emmylou

PO Box 123
Moama NSW 2739
Ph. (054) 82 3801

11   Melbourne Cruises

Vault No. 3 Princes Walk
Yarra River
Melbourne VIC 3004
Ph. (03) 63 2054

12   The Spirit of Victoria

10th Floor
3 Bowen Crescent
South Melbourne VIC 3205
Ph. (03) 820 1533

13   Steam Tug Wattle

GPO Box 5316BB
Melbourne VIC 3001
Ph. (03) 328 2739

Tasmania

14   Carmel D

Leisure Cruises
1 Nutgrove Avenue
Sandy Bay
Hobart TAS 7005
Ph. (002) 34 7981

15   Devil Jet

PO Box 125
New Norfolk TAS 7140
Ph. (002) 61 3460

16   Gordon Explorer

Morrison's Tourist Services
Esplanade
Strahan TAS 7468
Ph. (004) 71 7179

17   Scenic Gordon and Hell's Gate Charters

PO Box 38
Strahan TAS 7468
Ph. (004) 71 7187

South Australia

18   Murray River Cruises

151 Franklin Street
Adelaide SA 5000
Ph. (08) 211 8333

19   Proud Mary Cruises

33 Pirie Street
Adelaide SA 5000
Ph. (08) 51 9472

20   Cruising Matilda

Far Horizons
2 River Lane
Mannum SA 5238
Ph. (008) 08 3141 (Toll free) or
(085) 69 1895

Western Australia

21   Oceans International Adventure Tours

PO Box 79
Melville
Perth WA 6156
Ph. (09) 384 3756

22   Swan River Scenic Cruises

No. 3 Jetty
Barrack Street
Perth WA 6000
Ph. (09) 325 3793

23   Wave Spirit Charters

10 Broadhead Avenue
Tarcoola Geraldton WA 6530
Ph. (099) 21 3796 or
(091) 92 1127

24   Kimberley Explorer Cruises

Suite 25
Merlin Centre
3 Plain Street
Perth WA 6000
Ph. (09) 323 6200

Northern Territory

25   Schooner Alegrias

C/- Australian Kakadu Tours
GPO Box 1397
Darwin NT 5794
Ph. (089) 81 9899 or 81 5144

26   Adelaide River Queen

PO Box 37913
Winnellie NT 5789
Ph. (089) 32 2892 or 81 1186

27   Red Valley Boat Tours

PO Box 306
Katherine NT 5780
Ph. (Radiophone) 1389 or
(089) 81 6611 (NT Tourist Bureau,
Darwin)

Queensland

28   Quicksilver — Low Isles Cruises

PO Box 171 Port Douglas
QLD 4871 Ph. (070) 98 5373

29   Hayles Cairns Cruises

PO Box 898
Cairns QLD 4870
Ph. (070) 51 5644

30   Jungle Queen

Rainforest River Cruises
Ross Road
Deeral QLD 4871
Ph. (070) 67 5286

31   Coral Princess Cruises

78 Primrose Street
Townsville QLD 4810
Ph. (077) 72 4675

32   Club Whitsunday

Shute Harbour Jetty
Shute Harbour QLD 4802
Ph. (079) 46 9381

33   Coral Cat Cruises

Hamilton Island
PMB Mackay QLD 4740
Ph. (079) 46 9144

34   Coral Sea Line

PO Box 497
Airlie Beach QLD 4802
Ph. (079) 46 6049

35   Gretel Cruises

PO Box 109
Airlie Beach QLD 4602
Ph. (079) 46 6184 or 46 6224

36   Elizabeth EII

102 Goldsmith Street
Mackay QLD 4740
Ph. (079) 57 4281

37   Roylen Cruises

Harbour Road
Mackay QLD 4740
Ph. (079) 55 3066

38   Noosa's Cooloola Cruises

PO Box 283
Tewantin QLD 4565
Ph. (071) 49 9177 or 49 7884

39   Kookaburra Queen

247 St Paul's Terrace
Fortitude Valley
Brisbane QLD 4006
Ph. (07) 52 3797

40   MV Brisbane Explorer

GPO Box 2796
Brisbane QLD 4001
Ph. (008) 88 8524

ALLAN MOULT

Bushwalking

In this age of motors and mechanisation, many people choose not to walk to the nearest shop, let alone get out into the bush. But escaping from city pressures — be it for a day or a week — while experiencing the joys of the bush is a relaxing and stimulating pastime that is gaining in popularity.

Bushwalking as a sport or pastime is easily organised and relatively inexpensive. Day walks require only appropriate clothing, a sturdy pair of boots or shoes, a good rucksack and such equipment as a water bottle. Extended walks need a dependable tent, a sleeping bag and mattress, a stove and other cooking equipment.

All the states are served by bushwalking clubs for those who know little about the bush and who prefer to join in with others on organised walks. This is an ideal means of learning more about bushcraft, equipment and safety in the wilderness, and walkers often progress from the club system to arranging their own excursions with friends or family.

Several outdoor travel operators offer courses in bushcraft, navigation and wilderness medicine. Many of Australia's bushwalking trails are in true wilderness areas that deal ruthlessly with the unprepared or inexperienced walker.

Even in accessible areas, however, safety is of prime importance and it is possible to get lost quite close to relatively well-populated areas. It is vital to be well prepared with the correct clothing and equipment, maps, a compass perhaps, and sufficient food and water.

Travel companies serve a valuable role in arranging guided walks for small groups, removing the difficulties of organising transport, equipment and food and ensuring a sense of security in unfamiliar areas. Most of the guides also possess a good knowledge of local history, wildlife and vegetation.

Why walk in Australia? Much of this vast continent is untouched by human settlement and offers some unique wilderness experiences. There is a tremendous variety of bird and wildlife, terrain and vegetation waiting to be discovered by anyone with a sense of curiosity and adventure.

Apart from the more remote walking areas such as the fabulous Bungle Bungles of northern Western Australia and the historic Simpson Desert in the heart of the continent, most Australian cities have excellent walking trails virtually on their doorsteps. Sydney's Blue Mountains, Melbourne's Dandenong Ranges, and Lamington National Park in the Gold Coast hinterland are all classic examples of inspiring and accessible walking locations for city-dwellers.

Many of the walking regions are under the auspices of the National Parks and Wildlife Service or the Forestry Commission. These bodies can be of assistance in providing maps and detailed information on walking trails, and should be consulted especially if it is intended to walk in an unfamiliar area.

Bushwalking is simple, rewarding and, most importantly, fun. Kids can do it, people in their 70s can do it, families can have some of their most memorable holidays doing it. There is no better way of seeing Australia close up.

Locations

New South Wales

Fortunately for Sydney and its visitors, some of the state's best bushwalking areas are to be found within easy reach of the city. But if walkers have the time to spend, the whole state offers a great diversity of land to

DAVID McGONIGAL

explore and experience on foot.

1 To the west of Coffs Harbour on the north coast on the edge of the escarpment that forms the steep eastern side of the Great Dividing Range, lie the **New England and Dorrigo National Parks.** Stretching as far as the eye can see is an untouched landscape of volcanic ridges and rich forested valleys.

The New England park is the second highest region in New South Wales and only experienced walkers should attempt to explore its steep valleys. For the novice, the Lyrebird Trail is one of the best walking tracks in this part of the bush.

Closer to Coffs Harbour, surrounded by land that has been cleared for dairy farming, Dorrigo National Park also provides some wonderful rainforest walks. The vegetation here is truly luxuriant, with huge trees, native orchids, palms, waterfalls and streams cutting through the undergrowth.

2 Some 70 kilometres south are the **Warrumbungle Ranges** which were created by massive volcanic activity millions of years ago. The Ranges have some magnificent views and rock formations.

The bushland in the Warrumbungles is virtually untouched and is a haven for native wild animals and birdlife. The wildflowers are prolific, including 25 species of wattle.

The best time to walk through the Ranges is during autumn and spring. Walks can vary from very short nature scouts to day-long treks.

3 The **Blue Mountains,** with some of the best bushwalking country in the state, are only 100 kilometres west of Sydney. The region has over 40 walking trails suitable for day and longer walks, appealing to both the novice and experienced hiker. There are plenty of organised bushwalks through the region, including walking excursions from the spectacular Jenolan Caves — limestone grottoes that are millions of years old.

The region boasts wonderful clifftop walks and deep forested gorges. Around two-thirds of the original ancient sandstone plateau has been washed away onto the plains by the rivers that course through its valleys. One of the best walks in the park is down into the Blue Gum Forest of the Grose Valley. The walk takes a day.

Visitors can camp on nearby Acacia Flat, with permission from the Ranger, or find accommodation in Blackheath, a short drive from the ridge top. Trains run regularly into the mountains from Sydney.

4 **Kosciusko National Park,** a seven-hour drive south-west of Sydney, offers some very exhilarating walks through its alpine forested mountains and valleys. Covering 629,708 hectares, the park encompasses the highest mountains in the country as well as the most extensive alpine snowfields. Life begins anew in the late spring when the snows have melted and the streams have filled. This is followed by a short summer, which is the best time for walkers to take advantage of this spectacular and varied country.

Several tours operate through the region, varying in length from a weekend to a week.

Australian Capital Territory

5 **Namadgi National Park,** which takes up a large part of the Australian Capital Territory, is a recent addition to Australia's park system, providing some challenging bushwalking within a short distance of Canberra. The area includes some of Australia's

Previous page: The Blue Gum Forest in the Blue Mountains near Sydney

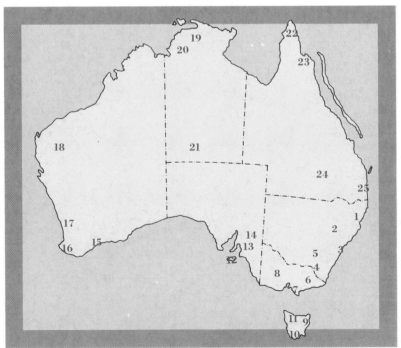

highest peaks after Mt Kosciusko and adjoins the Kosciusko National Park. This is a significant wilderness area which contains large tracts of forested hills and a wide variety of plant and animal life. As there is often snowcover in winter, the park is best visited between October and May.

Easier walking trails are to be found in the Tidbinbilla Nature Reserve and around Ginninderra Falls, both within a few minutes of Canberra.

Victoria

Victoria's walking regions vary from outstanding coastal areas to the high country of the north and east and the semi-arid areas in the west. The Victorian high country, north-east of Melbourne, includes the national parks of the Snowy River, Bogong and Mt Buffalo, which have many walking trails suitable for both the novice and the more experienced walker.

6 The ten highest mountain peaks in the state lie just to the west of the Snowy River region in **Bogong National Park.** The park, once the stamping ground of Bogong Jack, a horse thief who roamed the area in the 1850s, is an important region for bushwalkers. One of the many good walking tracks goes from Mt Hotham to Mt Wills via the Bogong High Plains. Mt Bogong is part of an extended walking route connecting the Baw Baws and New South Wales. Organised walks are conducted to the Falls Creek and Mt Hotham areas, with hardier trekkers climbing 1,986 metres to the top of Mt Bogong, the highest point in Victoria.

Bush camping is allowed and accommodation can be found at the various nearby ski resorts. The best time for walking in Bogong and the high country generally is during the warmer months from November to April.

7 Victoria's coastal bushwalking areas are quite outstanding. Some 230 kilometres south-east of Melbourne lies **Wilson's Promontory,** the most southerly part of mainland Australia. The promontory itself is a huge mass of granite, with over 700 species of native plants ranging from gum and eucalypts to ferns. There are also open heaths and salt marshes. It provides good hill and coastal walking country and a variety of campsites. There are 80 kilometres of walking tracks in the park, with easy self-guided nature trails making excellent short walks. Permits are required for overnight hikes.

8 The **Grampians National Park,** just under 500 kilometres north-west of Melbourne, has some good walking opportunities, including a traverse from north to south for the experienced hiker. The region is well known for its magnificent rugged scenery and excellent displays of wildflowers. It is also believed to have once been home to 80% of Victoria's Aboriginal population and today has the greatest concentration of Aboriginal rock paintings in the state.

The park boasts more than 800 plant species and more than 200 bird species. Echidnas, platypus, koalas and kangaroos comprise just some of the wildlife.

Tasmania

Tasmania's relatively small size means that many superb bushwalking areas are quite accessible from the major centres of Hobart and Launceston.

9 Situated virtually halfway between the two cities, the **Freycinet Peninsula** on the east coast

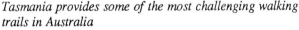

Tasmania provides some of the most challenging walking trails in Australia

ALLAN MOULT

Activities

provides some easy scenic walking. Its picturesque bays and beaches contrast with its rugged red granite peaks, making it a popular area for day walks and longer hikes.

There are several good coastal and bushwalking tracks, as well as organised walking tours. Camping facilities are available, and nearby Coles Bay and Swansea offer hotel and motel accommodation.

10 For the more experienced and well-equipped walker only, the **South West National Park,** which includes the well-known South Coast Track, provides some truly amazing wilderness and terrain. Some 130 kilometres south-west of Hobart, and covering 442,240 hectares, the park includes Federation Peak.

There are several walking tracks traversing virgin rainforest, eucalyptus forests, ocean beaches and mountain scenery. The Port Davey Track takes walkers 60 kilometres through the depths of the wilderness. The waterways of Port Davey and the Bathurst Harbour are unique, containing Australia's only fjord, its mountains rising 1,000 metres from the shore. The South Coast Track passes through a variety of spectacular and contrasting scenery, with views across mountains and coastline to islands just offshore.

Full camping equipment must be carried by all walkers and registration of itineraries must be lodged with the Rangers or the police. Sections of the tracks are subject to high rainfall, so it's advisable for walkers to have suitable boots and wet-weather gear.

11 **Cradle Mountain-Lake St Clair National Park** is also part of the South West World Heritage Area and contains Australia's most famous walking track — the Overland Track. Starting just over 170 kilometres north-west of Hobart, the track's 85 kilometres of moorland and peaks — including Tasmania's highest, Mt Ossa — should not be attempted by the inexperienced.

Its muddy conditions are notorious, even in summer, and the Overland Track takes walkers of average fitness up to six days to complete. Huts are provided along the way, but walkers are advised also to carry tents as the area experiences sudden weather changes. It is also advisable to register departure and arrival. Organised walking expeditions are also conducted throughout the park.

South Australia

South Australia has more than 1,000 kilometres of marked walking trails through some wonderfully contrasting environments. Its parks offer a profusion of wildlife which can be seen at close quarters.

12 Some 200 kilometres south of Adelaide on the western end of Kangaroo Island, **Flinders Chase National Park** has several short marked walks. The coastal walks feature sheer cliffs and sea-carved arches, woodlands of stringybark to the north and heath and mallee scrub to the south. There are 12 species of Australian mammal native to the island, including the famous Kangaroo Island kangaroo.

13 To the north, on the mainland, more than 600 kilometres of South Australia's first long-distance trail — the **Heysen Trail** — have been established. Named after world-renowned local artist, Sir Hans Heysen, it has the potential to be one of the world's greatest long-distance walking trails, stretching eventually from Flinders Chase to the Northern Flinders Ranges, more than 300 kilometres north of Adelaide — a total of more than 1,800 kilometres.

Although it is a long-distance trail, it is divided into various sections and walkers can join and leave it at various points. The trail passes through the Mt Lofty Ranges which bound Adelaide. These contain a cluster of nature reserves comprising bushland and parks which are home to many birds including lorikeets and honeyeaters.

14 Further north, about 330 kilometres from Adelaide, the **Flinders Ranges National Park** has five marked walking trails. One section of the Heysen Trail finishes at Wilpena Pound, the main feature of the park. A huge natural amphitheatre, 17 by 7 kilometres, the Pound is circled by quartzite ranges with Aboriginal paintings visible in the gorge.

Organised bushwalks operate in the region. Bush camping is permitted and camping facilities are provided. Motel accommodation is available at Wilpena. The trip by road from Adelaide to Wilpena takes around seven hours.

A footbridge across Tasmania's upper Derwent River leads into great walking country

Western Australia

Western Australia's vastness means that bushwalking areas are widely scattered throughout the state — from rugged gorges in the north to coastal headlands and beaches in the south.

15 The **Stirling Ranges**, 322 kilometres south-east of Perth, are considered to be one of Australia's most outstanding botanical reserves. The isolation of the flora of Western Australia from the rest of the country has allowed the evolution of 100 species that are endemic to the region. The area is spectacular in spring when the flowers come into bloom.

The Ranges reach to 1,073 metres, with stark cliff faces, flats and some salt lakes. There are several walking tracks ranging from two to eight hours return. The best time to visit is during September and October.

The region from Albany to Augusta, along the western section of the **southern coast region,** has some great areas of karri forests. The karri tower over surrounding trees, reaching to more than 100 metres. Today, only a few areas of mature tree survive and one of these is in Walpole-Nornalup National Park. Their canopies and the cool, shaded bases of their huge trunks provide a unique home for many birds and local wildlife, including western rosellas, the red-capped parrot and purple-crowned lorikeets.

16 **Walpole-Nornalup National Park,** south-west of the Stirling Ranges, has some 40 kilometres of coastline, dotted with beaches, inlets and quiet bays.

One walk which should not be missed in spring and summer is from the park's campsite at Coalmine Beach around the Knoll, which is a thickly forested promontory jutting into Nornalup Inlet.

Many organised walks are conducted throughout the south-west. Guides well-versed in the terrain, vegetation and animal life of the area provide excellent tours for curious walkers.

17 Only 50 kilometres north-east of Perth is the **Darling Range** which runs through the Avon Valley National Park. The park follows the course of the Avon River and is a transitional region from the jarrah forests to the state's wheatbelt area.

The Range comprises steep forested hills, with rocky gullies, waterfalls and crystal clear water. There are some short easy walks along guided nature tails which point out the geology and plantlife of the region. One of Australia's longest marked tracks, the Bibbulmun Track, also traverses the Range.

18 **Hamersley Range National Park** is about two days' drive north-east of Perth. A massive block of weathered rock around 320 kilometres in length, it boasts a number of easy walking tracks leading from the park's camping areas to the deep gorges that cut through its flat arid plains. Walkers pass through mulga and brightly flowering shrubs in the valleys and along lush green gorges covered in mosses and ferns.

The other tracks traversing the region are suitable only for the very experienced. All intending walkers must notify the Park Rangers before setting out.

Northern Territory

Isolated and rugged walking areas are a feature of the Northern Territory, and most visitors prefer to join organised tours, especially for longer walks.

19 **Kakadu National Park,** 250 kilometres east of Darwin, presents some superb walking. The region has a rich abundance of birds and other wildlife as well as ancient Aboriginal cave paintings.

Intending walkers and campers must first obtain permits from the Ranger. Motel accommodation can be found at South Alligator, Cooinda and Jabiru within the park.

Several trails have been established throughout Kakadu, ranging from short walks to bushwalks of several days' duration. Some enable access to the galleries of Aboriginal rock art for which western Arnhem Land is perhaps most famed.

20 Just south of Kakadu, in **Katherine Gorge,** more than 180 kilometres of trails have been marked for walkers, passing through a terrain of sandstone plateau, waterfalls, rock pools and gorges. The Katherine River zigzags through deep, canyon-like ochre and red sandstone cliffs, its path marked by waterfalls and bounded by wonderful river scenery including tropical rainforest.

Most people choose to see the gorge from the

DAVID MCGONIGAL

comfort of a boat. However, if walkers have the endurance and are equipped for rough backpacking, it is well worth the effort. All walkers require permits.

21 Ormiston Gorge and Pound in the **MacDonnell Ranges,** 32 kilometres west of Alice Springs, is one of Australia's most spectacular canyons. The Ormiston Creek cuts through the MacDonnell Ranges and flows into a waterhole in the Ormiston Pound. This is a basin-like enclosure that is ten kilometres across and completely surrounded by high ridges and peaks. More than 400 species of hardy plants are to be found here.

To see the full magnificence of the gorge it is necessary to walk through at least a part of it. There is a marked trail which guides walkers along the creek to where it enters the Pound — a total of eight kilometres return.

Queensland

Bushwalking in Queensland encompasses the tropical rainforests of the north and the sandstone gorges of the south. Most of its major cities are close to good walking areas.

22 In Queensland's far north, the **Cape York Peninsula** remains one of Australia's least disturbed and last remaining large wilderness areas. A region of high rainfall, it contains rich tropical rainforests, mangroves, swamps, gorges and mudflats. It is an area that should only be tackled by the very experienced walker.

23 The **Quinkan Reserve,** around the Laura River, was established in 1977 to protect the Aboriginal rock art of the region. This art was first discovered in 1959 by artist and anthropologist Percy Trezise.

Quinkan takes its name from the large human spirit figures depicted in almost every gallery. The paintings are probably around 5,000 years old, while the rock engravings are at least 13,000 years old.

A four-day tour operates in the Quinkan region — a combination of four-wheel driving and trekking. It explores the art galleries, details the local flora and fauna, and visits nearby Lakefield National Park.

24 About ten hours' drive north-west of Brisbane, **Carnarvon Gorge National Park** offers around 200,000 hectares of palms, gums, eucalypts and mahogany trees. Side gorges run off from the main one and there are many caves, some featuring Aboriginal art. The park offers panoramic views and the only way to see the gorges properly is by taking to the walking tracks which range in length from three to ten kilometres.

There are camping facilities within the park, but advance bookings are required. Bush camping is permitted. The access road into the park is impassable during wet weather.

25 **Lamington National Park** is handy to both Brisbane and the Gold Coast. Situated on the ranges overlooking Surfers Paradise, it has many graded walking tracks ranging from one hour to half-day and longer excursions. These tracks pass through rainforests filled with orchids, ferns, mosses and lianas and take walkers to caves and some magnificent waterfalls — there are more than 500 in all.

Operators

New South Wales

1   New England and Dorrigo National Parks

Bushwhacker Expeditions & Tours
An ideal way to explore the Dorrigo National Park is to take the Rainforest

ALLAN MOULT

Bushwalking Contacts

Discovery Tour operated by this company. You will spend six days with a small group of companions (maximum 16), visiting and exploring some of the best rainforest areas of northern New South Wales.

Darkwood Road
Thora NSW 2454
Ph. (066) 55 8607

2   Warrumbungle Ranges

Balmain Hiking and Bushwalking Expeditions
This company offers you a weekend hike in the Warrumbungles. Accommodation is provided in a hotel or motel in Coonabarabran and light day packs are provided.

PO Box 133
Balmain
Sydney NSW 2041
Ph. (02) 810 8187

3   Blue Mountains

Balmain Hiking and Bushwalking Expeditions
With this group you can spend a day exploring the Blue Mountains. A light day pack and lunch are provided. Also offered is a walk from the Jenolan Caves to Katoomba, travelling the Six Foot Track'.

See (2) above for details

4   Kosciusko National Park

Wilderness Expeditions
A programme of walks in the Snowy Mountains is offered by Wilderness Expeditions. An easy lodge-accommodated walk will appeal to those who prefer their walking to be spectacular yet comfortable, and special wildflower walks are available in December and January.

100 Clarence Street
Sydney NSW 2000
Ph. (02) 29 1581

World Expeditions
The Snowy Mountains are the setting for a six-day backpacking walk run by World Expeditions. The trip traverses the valleys and peaks of the high country.

3rd Floor
377 Sussex Street
Sydney NSW 2000
Ph. (02) 264 3366

Australian Capital Territory

5   Namadgi National Park

Bush Quest
Based in Canberra, Bush Quest specialises in naturalist-accompanied walks to the bushland and lakes of the ACT. Short walks or day outings are available.

29 Millen Street
Hughes
Canberra ACT 2605
Ph. (062) 81 2879 or 51 1549

Victoria

6 Bogong National Park

Bogong Jack Adventures
Bogong Jack Adventures specialises in tours of north-east Victoria. Bushwalking tours vary from easy day walks that return to a lodge each night, to extended camping trips.

PO Box 209
Wangaratta VIC 3677
Ph. (057) 21 2564

7 Wilson's Promontory

Walkabout Adventure Tours
One of the many areas covered by Walkabout Adventure Tours is Wilson's Promontory. You can either take a three-day walkabout adventure, on which you camp, or spend three days walking returning to a well-appointed lodge each evening.

105 Brown Street
Heidelberg
Melbourne VIC 3084
Ph. (03) 439 2501

8 Grampians National Park

Base Camp and Beyond
This specialist Grampians operator provides both bushwalking and rockclimbing/abseiling itineraries. Bushwalking trips can be made by arrangement with proprietor David Witham, who can cater for individuals or groups.

PO Box 37
Hall's Gap VIC 3381
Ph. (053) 56 4300

Tasmania

9 Freycinet Peninsula

Paddy Pallin Adventure Equipment
Bushwalking trips on the Freycinet Peninsula lasting one or two days are available through Paddy Pallin, an outdoor equipment store in Launceston.

124 St John Street
Launceston TAS 7250
Ph. (003) 31 4240

10 South-west National Park

Wilderness Tours
Wilderness Tours specialises in lightweight hiking and base camp walking tours mainly of eight days' duration throughout the south-west. Access to many of these walks is via light aircraft. There are no walks in winter.

Geeveston TAS 7116
Ph. (002) 97 1384

11 Cradle Mountain-Lake St Clair National Park

Craclair Tours
This well-established operation specialises in walks in the Cradle Mountain-Lake St Clair National Park.

PO Box 516
Devonport TAS 7310
Ph. (004) 24 3971

Open Spaces
A six-day guided walk through the park is offered by Open Spaces. Each of the five nights is spent in comfortable private huts along the route. The final night of each trip is spent at the Cradle Mountain Lodge. Walks take place from December to April.

28 Criterion Street
Hobart TAS 7000
Ph. (002) 31 0983

South Australia

12 Flinders Chase National Park

Australian Odysseys
Tim Williams of Australian Odysseys has long been exploring the wild, rugged country of Kangaroo Island and now offers a variety of tours for visitors. He caters for bushwalkers and birdwatchers and provides accommodation in farmhouses and beach cottages.

PO Box 144
Kensington Park
Adelaide SA 5068
Ph. (08) 31 5321

13 Heysen Trail

Ecotrek
Ecotrek runs an exciting range of bushwalks through some of the most impressive national park and wilderness regions of South Australia. Walks range from two to six days. Of particular note is their six-day gently graded trip along the rugged Flinders Ranges section of the Heysen Trail.

24 Gibbon Lane
North Adelaide SA 5006
Ph. (08) 267 1442

14 Flinders Ranges National Park

Thor Adventure Travel
Thor operates a small programme of trips into South Australia's most beautiful environments. One of these is the Wilpena Walk in the Flinders Ranges. This five-day hike is for those who are prepared to carry a ten-kilogram pack.

40 Waymouth Street
Adelaide SA 5000
Ph. (08) 212 7857

Western Australia

15 Stirling Range

WA Adventure Treks
This bushwalking operation covers a variety of areas in Western Australia. They run tours of five, seven and ten days' duration, as well as weekend treks, and will take you into the Stirling Range National Park.

PO Box 1013
Booraggon
Perth WA 6154
Ph. (09) 330 4948

16 Walpole-Nornalup National Park

Adventure West
Vern Delgade and Peter Adamson of Adventure West both have military and outdoor education backgrounds. One of the areas in which they take trips and offer instruction is Walpole-Nornalup National Park. They run their tours from September to June.

15 Hepburn Way
Balga
Perth WA 6061
Ph. (09) 342 8678

17 Darling Range

Action Tours
Action Tours offers guided bushwalking with the emphasis on education and relaxation in the Darling Ranges and Kalamunda region. Tours operate on Wednesdays and Sundays.

PO Box 279
Kalamunda
Perth WA 6076
Ph. (09) 480 9301

18 Hamersley Range National Park

Nangar Wilderness Expeditions
This operation is run by Arthur Weston, a professional botanist with ten years' experience in leading bushwalking expeditions. He will guide you backpacking in the Hamersley Range National Park, taking you to remote areas and teaching you about the natural history of the region.

PO Box 1209
East Victoria Park
Perth WA 6101
Ph. (09) 458 9738

Northern Territory

19 Kakadu National Park

International Parktours
International Parktours offers an impressive number of well-organised

walking tours of varying lengths around Australia. They will take you to the national parks of the Top End, including magnificent Kakadu National Park.

Binna-Burra Lodge
Beechmont
via Nerang QLD 4211
Ph. (075) 33 3583

20 Katherine Gorge

Willis's Walkabouts
Walks from two days to three weeks in the Top End are offered by Willis's Walkabouts. Among the many areas you might wish to explore with them is Katherine Gorge National Park.

12 Carrington Street
Millner
Darwin NT 5792
Ph. (089) 85 2134

21 MacDonnell Ranges

Toddy's Tours & Safaris
Toddy's runs tours in the western MacDonnell Ranges twice a week. You will have the opportunity to walk about five kilometres in Serpentine Gorge, Glen Helen and Ormiston Gorge.

41 Gap Road
Alice Springs NT 5750
Ph. (089) 52 1322 or 52 5999

Queensland

22 Cape York Peninsula

Cape York Wilderness Lodge
The Lodge at the tip of Cape York, was established as a fishing and wildlife lodge to allow visitors to experience the wilderness in comfort and safety. A new bush camp has been built for overnight camping trips and to accommodate bushwalkers.

C/- 62 Abbott Street
Cairns QLD 4870
Ph. (070) 50 4305

23 Quinkan Reserver

Trezise Bush Guide Service
The Quinkan Reserve was established in 1977 to protect the Aboriginal rock art in the hundreds of galleries in the region. On their four-day trip, commencing with a flight from Cairns, Trezise Bush Guide Service will guide you on inspections of the few sites that may be visited. You will spend your nights in the comfort of Jowalbinna Bush Camp.

Jowalbinna Station
Laura QLD 4781
Ph. (070) 60 3236

HANS & JUDY BESTE

24 Carnarvon Gorge National Park

International Parktours
The 18-day Reef, Rock and Rainforest tour takes you through the islands of the Whitsunday Group to the rugged ranges and gorges of Carnarvon National Park, before travelling on to Lamington National Park. Tours operate ex-Brisbane.

See (23) above for details

25 Lamington National Park

Binna Burra Mountain Resort
Binna Burra Lodge is perched on top of Mt Roberts amidst the magnificent scenery of Lamington National Park. The daily programme includes guided walks and adventure hikes through rugged terrain.

Beechmont
via Nerang QLD 4211 Ph. (075) 33 3622

Information Sources

Bushwalking Clubs

The following organisations can provide information on bushwalking clubs:

New South Wales

NSW Federation of Bushwalking Clubs
GPO Box 2090
Sydney NSW 2001

Australian Capital Territory

Canberra Bushwalking Club
PO Box 160
Canberra ACT 2601
Ph. (062) 47 3064

Victoria

Federation of Victorian Walking Clubs
GPO Box 815F
Melbourne VIC 3001
Ph. (03) 428 7211

Tasmania

The Hobart Walking Club
28 Criterion Street
Hobart TAS 7000
Ph. (002) 31 1753

South Australia

Adelaide Bushwalkers
PO Box 178
Unley SA 5061
Ph. (08) 31 5339

Western Australia

Perth Bushwalkers Club
PO Box 8321
Stirling Street
Perth SA 6000
Ph. (09) 362 1614

Northern Territory

Darwin Bushwalking Club
PO Box 41568
Casuarina
Darwin NT 5792
Ph. (089) 85 1484 (After hours)

Central Australian Bushwalkers Club
PO Box 1818
Alice Springs NT 5750
Ph. (089) 52 7120

Queensland

Queensland Federation of Bushwalking
  Clubs
GPO Box 1573
Brisbane QLD 4001

Outdoor Equipment Shops

The following outdoor equipment shops are all recommended. In addition to selling clothing and equipment, these shops are valuable sources of books, guides and maps. Some shops also hire out equipment and are agents for adventure travel companies.

New South Wales

Mountain Designs
494 Kent Street
Sydney NSW 2000
Ph. (02) 267 8238

Mountain Equipment
291 Sussex Street
Sydney NSW 2000
Ph. (02) 264 3146

Paddy Pallin
507 Kent Street
Sydney NSW 2000
Ph. (02) 264 2685

Australian Capital Territory

Paddy Pallin
11 Lonsdale Street
Braddon
Canberra ACT 2600
Ph. (062) 57 3883

Victoria

Mountain Designs
377 Little Bourke Street
Melbourne VIC 3000
Ph. (03) 67 3354

Paddy Pallin
55 Hardware Street
Melbourne VIC 3000
Ph. (03) 670 4845

Tasmania

Paddy Pallin
32 Criterion Street
Hobart TAS 7000
Ph. (002) 31 0777

South Australia

Paddy Pallin/Thor Adventure Travel
40 Waymouth Street
Adelaide SA 5000
Ph. (08) 212 7857

Western Australia

Mountain Designs
862 Hay Street
Perth WA 6000
Ph. (09) 322 4774

Paddy Pallin
Shop 11, 105 Lord Street
Perth WA 6000
Ph. (09) 325 5984

Northern Territory

Refer to the *Yellow Pages* telephone directory.

Queensland

Jim the Backpacker
76 Wickham Street
Fortitude Valley
Brisbane QLD 4006
Ph. (07) 839 6609

Mountain Designs
95 Albert Street
Brisbane QLD 4000
Ph. (07) 221 6756

MILTON WORDLEY

Camel Trekking

The first camels were introduced into Australia in 1840, when the early explorers and pioneers recognised the invaluable role these ships of the desert could play in opening up and supplying the continent's vast, dry regions. In 1860, the Victorian government imported 24 camels from India for the ill-fated Burke and Wills expedition. Five years later, Sir Thomas Elder imported 120 camels. His breed was built up to be the country's healthiest and best, fetching 50 pounds more than any other on the market. In 1886, two Afghans imported 259 camels to carry supplies to the Western Australian goldfields. From this herd they also built up an enterprising camel farm. Such camels were used in many expeditions, traversing the territory between Adelaide and Darwin, and delivering produce, mail and missionaries to the outback. In 1912, they worked on the Trans-Australian Railway, carrying water for the workers between camps as far as 480 kilometres apart. By 1922, there were an estimated 20,000 camels serving as outback railroads and automobiles, often carrying enormous burdens. Today, their life is somewhat easier as they provide an unorthodox mode of transport for tourists wishing to see Australia's more remote regions, if at a somewhat slow and swaying pace.

There are only a few camel trek operators in Australia. New South Wales, Western Australia and South Australia are represented, but the majority operate out of the Alice Springs area in the Northern Territory. The operators are usually well-versed in local knowledge and their tours provide an interesting insight into the outback as well as into the animals themselves. They are quite remarkable creatures and are capable of great endurance. A female camel galloping flat out can travel at over 20 kilometres per hour; a speed she can maintain, if pushed, for several hours. There are stories from the Middle East of camels travelling 150 to 200 kilometres a day for several days on end (and dropping dead on their arrival).

Interest in camels has grown over the past few years. The spontaneous camel races conducted in Central Australia late last century, with the camels being urged on by their 'Ghan' masters, have now grown into quite a significant sport and tourist attraction, and Australia now offers four major camel races annually. The Alice Springs Camel Cup, held in May, is the premier event.

Not all of the so-called 'Ghans' were actually from Afghanistan. Many simply pretended they were, because of the true Afghan's tough reputation, in order to protect themselves from any problems with the white pioneers. Following the completion in 1929 of the last leg of the Ghan railway from Adelaide to Alice Springs (which followed the camel route known as the Ghan Track), many of these now-redundant camels were set free.

In 1988, a Great Australian Camel Race across the outback, covering a distance of 3,260 kilometres, has been planned to help celebrate the country's Bicentenary. It will set out from Australia's most westerly tip, Steep Point, at the beginning of March and the contestants will travel across the mainland to Byron Bay on the NSW coast. The journey will be done in ten stages, ranging from 16 to 22 days each.

Australia's camel trek operators usually offer one-day treks for first-timers to test their endurance, as well

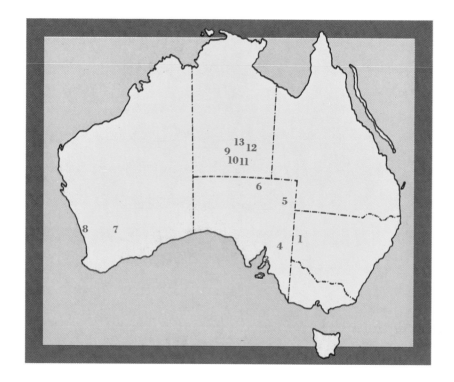

as treks lasting several days with overnight camps. Groups generally travel in a camel train linked by nose lines and halter ropes. Riders alternate between riding and walking in order to stretch their legs.

Camel trekking is an interesting jaunt for those seeking an unusual experience. Or, for the more adventurous, it is a novel and relaxed way of seeing the country's more remote regions.

Locations

New South Wales

1 The flat outback country around **Broken Hill** in the west of the state — with its wide open plains of red semi-desert, grey saltbush, scrub and gum trees, and what are supposedly the best sunsets in Australia — is the ideal setting to capture the romance of a bygone era when this country was a vast mystery to the white man.

The region around Broken Hill has some great, typically outback, terrain. Silverton, an old ghost town only 25 kilometres north-west of Broken Hill, has been the location of many films, including *Mad Max II*, *A Town Like Alice* and *Razorback*. The Menindee Lakes, huge natural lakes seven and a half times the size of Sydney Harbour, are a few hours away in Kinchega National Park.

Broken Hill, 508 kilometres from Adelaide and 1,165 kilometres from Sydney, is the site of massive deposits of zinc, silver and lead and was opened up to mining around 1855. The town has many historic buildings, mining, rail and train museums, and an Afghan Mosque, as well as some excellent art galleries featuring such esteemed Australian artists as Pro Hart and Jack Absalom.

According to local man Billy Cannard, who has

been riding camels since he was six, the best time to take a long camel trek around Broken Hill is in the cooler months from March to September. He runs Silverton Camel Treks, which offers a variety of rides ranging from 15 minutes to two days. For the longer jaunts, visitors need to bring their own camping gear. Billy supplies the food and cooks it over the campfire under the stars.

Visitors travelling by air to Broken Hill can fly with either Air NSW or Kendell Airlines.

South Australia

2 South Australia offers a variety of terrain for those wishing to experience it at a slow pace and at close quarters. A bit over 100 kilometres off the south-west coast as the crow flies is **Kangaroo Island.** Covered in scrub and bush and surrounded by rugged coastline, it abounds with native wildlife, particularly kangaroos. It is also home of one of South Australia's two camel farms.

3 Only 40 kilometres from Adelaide is **McLaren Vale,** with some of the country's best vineyards set amidst rolling hills and valleys. Camel tours operating in the region are made even more interesting, and perhaps a trifle more unsteady, with riders stopping to sample the region's produce as they pass through. In stark contrast, just outside the vale, is Onkaparinga Gorge, where riders can experience some rugged bushland.

4 Further north in the **Flinders Ranges,** 440 kilometres from Adelaide, the terrain gets rougher still at the site of Wilpena Pound, a huge oval rock bowl measuring 20 by eight kilometres with gorges and creeks bounded by river red gums. The region is home to kangaroos, emus and eagles. Just west of the park, out in the red sand dune desert country, is the

Veteran camel train leader, Noel Fullerton

saltwater Lake Torrens.

5   There are several camel treks operating through this eastern part of the state. One-day rides are offered on both Kangaroo Island and through the wineries of the McLaren Vale. For the hardier, there are 16-day treks retracing the ill-fated steps of explorers Burke and Wills. These treks leave Adelaide for Innamincka where Burke and Wills died in 1861, continuing on to the **Strzelecki Track,** which was pioneered as a stock route over 100 years ago, and then to Cooper's Creek and into the Coongie Lakes region.

6   For the hardier still, there are 24-day expeditions through the **Simpson Desert.**

Operators are well-versed in the South Australian bush. The ancestors of Dick Lang (Desert-Trek Australia) were among the first white settlers in the state, while Rex Ellis of the Outback Camel Company has written books on the subject and offers probably the widest range of camel expeditions in the country.

Western Australia

7   **Coolgardie,** once a thriving goldrush town of 20,000 people, is renowned today as Australia's most famous ghost town. It is situated on the dry red plains of southern central Western Australia, nearly 600 kilometres east of Perth on the Great Eastern Highway, just west of Kalgoorlie. Today, Kalgoorlie is still dependent on its goldmines for its prosperity. Back in 1893, when gold was first discovered here, it took less than a week for 1,400 prospectors to arrive to try their luck on the fields. In 1902, with a population of 30,000, the town boasted 93 hotels and eight breweries!

Despite its ghost town label, Coolgardie is far from dead. The town features a goldfields exhibition where visitors can see the history of the region's colourful boom-to-bust past. There is also a wildlife park and still the odd bit of gold to be dug up by lucky prospectors. Four kilometres west of the town is the Coolgardie Camel Farm. In addition to the riding facilities and treks it offers, there is a museum which provides educational displays as well as talks given by owner Noel McKay, who has a wealth of knowledge on the history and characteristics of this remarkable and often maligned creature.

8   Western Australia's other camel farm, the Blue Gum Camel Farm, lies closer to Perth in the **Avon Valley** near the town of Northam. Visitors to the farm can look at the animals or take day trips through the surrounding rich sheep and wheat-farming country.

Northern Territory

The Northern Territory is the heart of Australia's camel trekking industry. The vast open deserts of the area are still home to wild camels, and several camel farms are in operation, particularly in the Alice Springs region.

Several operators run treks of varying length through the Central Australian deserts, valleys and gorges. All of these operators are based in and around Alice Springs, and treks can range from an hour to two weeks.

The Northern Territory, and the camel business, are full of characters, and one of the most well-known must be Noel Fullerton of Alice Springs Camel Outback Safaris. Noel is a true outback identity who has spent many years as a camel train leader and camel farmer. His long white flowing beard and enormous knowledge of camels have made him the subject of countless articles and television programmes.

Camel farms in the area export their animals to

several parts of the world — Japan, the United States and even to Arab countries — and supplement their industry by offering camel treks to tourists and visitors.

Much of the outback may be near-desert now, but it contains a multitude of ancient watercourses with a distinct flora and fauna.

9 The **Finke River** is regarded as the oldest watercourse in the world. The first European exploration of its route was conducted in 1872 by Ernest Giles. Camel trekkers are able to follow this exploration, heading along the Finke River into the valleys branching off from its sides.

10 Home base for another of the treks is the **Rainbow Valley**, 100 kilometres south-west of Alice Springs. From here, exploratory journeys are taken into the fascinating valleys and oases of the Hugh River system. The region is rich in Aboriginal sites and there are fossil remains of what was once a huge inland sea.

11 Very rugged tours are available for the real camel enthusiast. These take about two weeks and travel through unexplored terrain in the **Krischauf and James Ranges**.

12 Other treks are taken to a working cattle station and to historic **Arltunga Goldfields,** north-east of Alice Springs.

13 For those who would like the experience of just a little jaunt, one-hour treks can be taken down **Alice Springs'** Todd River to the Chateau Hornsby winery for a cellar tour and wine tasting before dinner.

Camel Trekking Contacts

Operators

Information on the Great Australian Camel Race is available from:

Ausventure Holidays
PO Box 54
Mosman
Sydney NSW 2088
Ph. (02) 960 1677

New South Wales

1   Broken Hill

Silverton Camel Treks
Silverton Camel Treks is run by Billy Cannard. Billy has been riding camels since he was a boy and he offers a variety of camel rides, ranging from a 15-minute tour of Silverton to two-day treks. A two-hour sunset trek is also available. The best time of year for long treks is during the winter months. For the two-day treks you will need to bring your own camping gear, but Billy will provide the food and cook it for you. He maintains that his camels are all extremely well behaved.

PO Box 121
Broken Hill NSW 2880
Ph. (080) 88 5327 or 88 5306

South Australia

2   Kangaroo Island

Outback Camel Co.
Author Rex Ellis' Outback Camel Co. has been in operation since 1976 and presents the widest variety of camel treks and expeditions in Australia. He offers half-hour rides plus one, three and five-day treks on Kangaroo Island, enabling you to enjoy the many aspects of this unspoilt island and become acquainted with its varied wildlife.

PMB 251
Kingscote
Kangaroo Island SA 5223
Ph. (0848) 93 256

3   McLaren Vale

Outback Camel Co.
If you are interested in camel trekking in the McLaren Vale area, they will take you on a one-day Southern Vales winery trek on which you will visit up to six wineries and be given lunch. They also offer a one-day Onkaparinga Gorge trek which takes you through vineyards and bush country to the rugged gorge where you have lunch by a large permanent waterhole, and where you can fish and swim.

See (2) above for details

4   Flinders Ranges

Outback Camel Co.
A variety of treks ranging from one to 15 days are offered in the Flinders Ranges. The shorter treks are based at Merna Mora station, a few kilometres west of Wilpena Pound, where there are self-contained flats and on-site vans available. Both the longer treks are ex-Adelaide, the 15-day Heart of the Flinders trek providing the most comprehensive coverage available of the northern Flinders.

See (2) above for details

5   The Strzelecki Track

Ausventure Holidays
Starting out from Adelaide, Ausventure Holidays will arrange for you to take a 26-day Strzelecki camel expedition, which will take you to some of the remotest desert country anywhere: Cooper's Creek, the Strzelecki Desert and Sturt's Stony Desert. You will spend 21 days travelling with the camels, walking up to 16 kilometres a day and helping with loading, wood-gathering and camel herding. A high level of physical fitness is therefore necessary.

PO Box 54
Mosman
Sydney NSW 2088
Ph. (02) 960 1677

Desert-Trek Australia
In addition to their four-wheel-drive safaris, Desert-Trek Australia offers a 16-day 'Burke and Wills' camel trek which follows much of the route taken by these famous explorers. Departing from Adelaide, the trek takes you from Innamincka on to the Strzelecki Track, Cooper's Creek and into the red sand dune desert of the Coongie Lakes area. A radio-equipped four-wheel-drive vehicle accompanies the trek, carrying water and all camping equipment. Treks run from May to October.

Box 80
Highbury
Adelaide SA 5089
Ph. (08) 264 7200

Outback Camel Co.
They run a 21-day Strzelecki Desert camel expedition, which takes you to Cooper's Creek, the Strzelecki Desert

and the north Flinders Ranges. This trek allows the adventurous tourist to venture far from the beaten track, into regions that are closed even to four-wheel-drive vehicles. You will be required to walk a good deal and to help with the camels, so you must be fit.

See (2) above for details

6 Simpson Desert

Outback Camel Co.
A number of camel treks and expeditions to the Simpson Desert are offered, one operating from Alice Springs and three from Adelaide. The longest expedition, which lasts 23 days, takes you across the Northern Simpson Desert via Lake Caroline to Lake Phillips, east of the Mulligan River on Kamaran Downs station. This is one of the great adventures available in Australia today.

See (2) above for details

Western Australia

7 Coolgardie

Coolgardie Camel Farm
The farm is located four kilometres west of Coolgardie, Australia's most famous ghost town. Camel rides and treks are available for any length of time from one hour to one week, depending on the requirements of particular groups. In addition to the riding facilities, the farm boasts a museum where there are displays on the history and characteristics of camels, and educational talks are given. Owner Noel McKay is a fan of these much-maligned animals and will explain their behaviour, personalities and idiosyncracies.

Great Eastern Highway
Coolgardie WA 6429
Ph. (090) 26 6234

8 Avon Valley

Blue Gum Camel Farm
Located near Northam, close to Perth, the Blue Gum Camel Farm is open to the public and runs day-long camel rides which include lunch at the nearby Spencer Brook Tavern. Extended trail rides can be arranged for those who would like a longer 'camel experience' and camels are also available for hire.

Spencer Brook Road
Clackline
via Northam WA 6401
Ph. (09) 574 1480

Northern Territory

9 Finke River

Alice Springs Camel Outback Safaris
A seven-day camel safari along the Finke River is provided and your guide will be veteran camel train leader, Noel Fullerton. You will ride through the Glen of Palms and explore the valleys that lead from the gorge. The safari is a package which includes camels, guide, a cook, camping equipment, meals and accommodation.

PO Box 3244
Alice Springs NT 5750
Ph. (089) 56 0925

10 Rainbow Valley

Alice Springs Camel Outback Safaris
On their seven-day Rainbow Valley safari, base camps are established in Rainbow Valley and exploratory journeys are taken into the fascinating valleys of the Hugh River system. The area is rich in Aboriginal sites and fossil remains of what was once a huge inland sea. The safari is an all-inclusive package.

See (9) above for details

11 Krischauf and James Ranges

Alice Springs Camel Outback Safaris
The Across the Ranges Safari takes 14 days and is limited to six people. This safari, which is pretty rugged and for enthusiasts only, explores the Krischauf and James Ranges. The safari is an all-inclusive package.

See (9) above for details

12 Arltunga Goldfields

Central Australian Camel Treks
This group offers half-hour rides, day rides, overnight safaris and extended treks of from three to 14 days in the Arltunga area of central Australia. The treks operate with the assistance of a four-wheel-drive vehicle and the longer safaris include tours of national parks, the Arltunga goldfields and a working cattle station. Camels, camping gear, the vehicle and meals are included in the package.

PO Box 84
Alice Springs NT 5750
Ph. (089) 52 7611

Ross River Homestead Tours
Based 80 kilometres east of Alice Springs, they offer a variety of camel safaris, from half-hour rides to treks of up to 14 days. You might like to go on their camel sunset dinner tour, riding to Old Loves Creek Homestead which was once used as a depot for the camel trains bringing supplies for the goldfields at

Arltunga.

PO Box 84
Alice Springs NT 5751
Ph. (089) 52 7611

13 Alice Springs

Camel Expeditions Australia
A seven-day camel expedition from King's Creek to Curtin Springs is operated by Camel Expeditions Australia. They pick you up from your accommodation in Alice Springs, and at the end of the expedition you tour Ayers Rock before being taken back to your hotel. The guides and handlers are experienced and you will ride through a variety of fascinating country. Expeditions are not run during the summer.

Box 3594
Alice Springs NT 5750
Radio Ph. 536 (Ph. 011 for Trunk call)

Camel-Time Walking
Bushwalks with pack camels, lasting a minimum of one week, are on offer at Todd River station near Alice Springs. Owner-operator H. Duell will take you exploring in the country east and south of Alice Springs, walking in mountain ranges and over sandhills. You will need to be physically fit as the walking is strenuous.

PO Box 2764
Alice Springs NT 5751
Ph. (089) 52 8466

Frontier Tours
Several camel treks are run by Nick and Michelle Smail, who also operate a camel farm and reptile sanctuary. Their hour-long trek takes you down the Todd River at sunset to visit the Chateau Hornsby winery for a wine tasting before dinner. On their two-day camel safari you ride along the Todd River, camp at Emily Creek and head back to the camel farm after a hearty breakfast the following day.

PO Box 2836
Alice Springs NT 5750
Ph. (089) 53 0444

ALLAN MOULT

Canoeing, Kayaking & Rafting

The pioneers found that Australia's waterways were crucial in the exploration and settlement of this huge and unknown land. All their early settlements were founded on rivers or river mouths where there was a ready supply of water, and from where they could ship out their farm produce.

The first tentative probing into the interior was along the veins of Australia's rivers — the Parramatta River, the Hawkesbury, the Yarra and the Swan. These waterways have now declined in economic importance. But the Australian love affair with running water continues, as expressed by a new breed of explorers. Canoeing, kayaking and white-water rafting enthusiasts in growing numbers are rediscovering Australia's wilderness areas from the water. Theirs is a sport of contrasts, offering everything from a wild slalom down rocky rapids to lazy paddling in sheltered lagoons.

The sport attracts all kinds of participants, from the competitive to the contemplative. While white-water pursuits can be exhilarating, demanding nerve and muscle and even a love of danger, canoeing and kayaking can be peaceful, safe family sports.

New South Wales and Victoria offer some splendid white-water experiences in the high country of the Snowy Mountains and the Victorian Alps, within reach of Sydney, Canberra and Melbourne. Both states also have more leisurely options for the less experienced on their lowland waterways and lakes.

Tasmania boasts some of the wildest and coldest canoeing and rafting water in the country, as well as sea-kayaking around the jagged coasts of one of the world's last great temperate wilderness areas.

South Australia, in addition to conventional canoeing and kayaking, offers the bizarre option of 'desert canoeing'. It is possible to get very wet indeed

following the trail of explorers who dragged their way, parched almost to death, across the Red Centre.

Western Australia's empty and remote regions are probably best explored by canoe, and in some cases they can be reached in no other way. The state also hosts one of the world's premier white-water canoe races, the Avon Descent, staged each year near Perth.

In the Northern Territory, canoeists can take part in adventurous options such as a 'canoe and Kakadu' trek to Australia's most famous national park.

Queensland has some of the world's fastest and most exhilarating white-water torrents, spilling from the catchment of the Atherton Tablelands down through the rainforests to the sea, and constantly replenished by seasonal monsoons. It also offers the gentler attraction of sea kayaking around the coral islets of the Great Barrier Reef.

For the beginner in the world of kayaking or canoeing, many clubs and associations throughout Australia have courses teaching the basic skills. Many adventure travel operators also have excellent trips for those wanting to learn.

White-water rafting has gained in popularity in Australia in recent years. Most rafting is organised through adventure travel companies, mainly because of the logistics of organising people and equipment, and the expense of a raft. Made of inflatable rubber, rafts can accommodate anything from two to nine people, with additional space to carry food and equipment for extended trips.

Rafting trips generally provide a boat captain, and participants paddle while the captain steers the craft through the rapids. The only exception to this is where single-person inflatables are used.

Rafting tours have become very popular because they allow even inexperienced paddlers to visit wild-water areas that would otherwise be beyond their capabilities.

There is a large range and style of equipment available for this sport. The most obvious choice is between canoes and kayaks. The main difference between the two is the type of paddle used. Kayaking uses a double-bladed paddle, while canoeing uses a single-bladed paddle. Kayaks are usually single-seated and the paddler sits fully enclosed in the boat. Canoes can be double or single-seated, open or enclosed, and the paddler frequently kneels.

Courses are offered throughout the year, so finding a suitable time is never a problem. The summer tends to be the most popular time, with its warmer and longer days. It is best to start on a flat section of the river or lake to get a feel of the boat before taking on moving water.

Enthusiasts who are keen to pursue the sport further may well consider buying their own canoe or kayak, and the necessary clothing and equipment. Australia has many specialist canoeing suppliers and shops that can be approached for advice. These can be located through the state Canoe Associations. (See the Contacts section.)

It is also possible to hire canoes, kayaks and paddles in most of the areas discussed below. Local canoeing shops are listed in the *Yellow Pages* telephone directories.

River trips can range from several hours to a week or more. Many rivers, because of their remote and infrequent access points, demand several days on the water well away from civilisation. On such trips, full camping gear, first-aid and repair kits and spare paddles are essential. This level of commitment is fully rewarded by the wild, undisturbed country that is encountered.

Afternoon or day trips are a good way to start. Weekend or extended tours are for the more experienced paddler. Some states have a canoeing guide to their rivers (available from canoe shops) and these are a mine of information, including descriptions of the river, the degree of difficulty, access points and so on.

Rivers are graded on an international scale of 1-6 for difficulty. These gradings vary with water levels, and usually the higher the water level, the higher the grading.

White-water canoeing or rafting is a potentially hazardous activity, but like any sport involving risk, the element of danger can be reduced when sensible safety precautions are observed. Canoeists should always canoe with a partner, be able to swim well, leave a plan of their trip and expected arrival time, take all essential safety gear and ensure that it is waterproof, and above all, they should be honest with themselves about their abilities.

Without doubt, Australian rivers have all the ingredients for great rafting. Undisturbed natural beauty, abundant bird and wildlife, the tranquillity of broad waterways and the heart-stopping action of big white waters. Whether they are after furious action or gentle paddling, canoeists at all levels of experience agree on two things — it's always challenging and it's always fun.

Rafters enjoy a quiet reach on the Franklin River, Tasmania

DAVID McGONIGAL

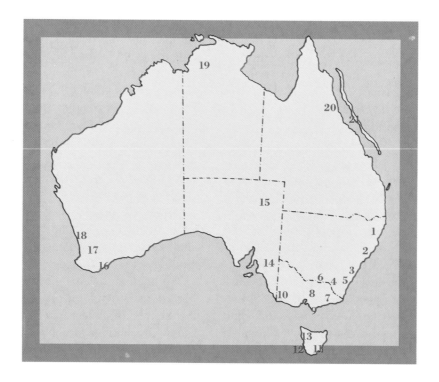

Locations

New South Wales

New South Wales has much to offer the paddler — an enormous range of rivers, estuaries and lakes, a generally attractive climate, and no 'dry' season to speak of over most of the state.

The wide range of waterways and climate means that there is something for everyone, from the hardy all-season canoeist to the warm-weather enthusiast. An equally broad span of topography ensures also that every conceivable kind of waterway is within reach — dramatic white-water mountain torrents and placid reaches of lowland river. Some of the calmer stretches are within easy reach of suburban Sydney, while other waterways are close to regional centres such as Coffs Harbour and Gloucester, in the north, and Nowra and Canberra in the south.

1 The adventurous rafting enthusiast, or the experienced canoeist, will find excitement and challenge on the rivers of **Northern New South Wales** — between the centres of Byron Bay and Coffs Harbour, and inland around Armidale, atop the slopes of the Great Dividing Range.

The magnificent Nymboida and Gwydir Rivers have some of the most heart-stopping white water to be found anywhere in Australia. Stretches of these rivers are definitely for the experienced paddler only, but even novices can share the thrill of rocks and rapids on rafting trips lasting one day or more. They can even be trained in the skills of skippering a raft if they are really committed to excitement.

The nearby Manning and Clarence Rivers are generally of a more moderate grading, though various stretches of these rivers contain different grades of water. Paddling is possible all year. There are plenty of rapids on both, mostly of an easy Grade 2 standard, and the wildlife to be seen on the banks makes the effort well worthwhile.

2 Further south, between **Kempsey and Gloucester,** lie the hills of the Dividing Range and the beautiful Barrington Tops area, a region of wild natural beauty cut by the Barrington, Barnard, Macleay and Manning Rivers. A number of small canoeing tour operators serve this area, arranging waterborne camping tours lasting typically from one to three days, and including lodge accommodation, canoeing and kayaking instruction, and canoe hire. Several dovetail river expeditions with bushwalking or four-wheel-drive trips and at least one company picks up participants from the Sydney area.

3 Less spectacular, but just as peaceful, is the **Shoalhaven River** to the south of Sydney. It is placid enough for family canoeing holidays, but extensive enough for trips lasting several days. Some tour operators offer loosely structured packages for families on the Shoalhaven, and include instruction in basic canoeing skills.

4 The **Kosciusko National Park,** in the south-west of the state and within a few hours' drive of Sydney and Canberra, is one of Australia's prime high country wilderness areas, surrounding the country's highest peak. To see it by water is a rare and memorable (if sometimes chilly) experience, though usually one best enjoyed by the competent paddler.

There are a number of rivers to choose from. The Goobarragandra River is a fast-flowing alpine stream, providing excellent white water which can challenge even the expert. It rises on the north-west side of the park and joins the Tumut River just upstream from the township of Tumut itself. The higher reaches are the most turbulent, while the rapids on the lower part of the river are less demanding and are suitable for paddlers at an intermediate level. By contrast, the Tumut River into which it flows has some placid stretches suitable for leisurely family holidays of three or four days' duration.

Just about any level of rafting or canoeing is to be had on the great Murrumbidgee, which also rises in the north of the park and travels fully 1,500 kilometres before joining the Murray south-west of Balranald in the far south-west of the state. There is exciting white water on the upper reaches and lazy placid stretches further downstream.

Australian Capital Territory

5 Although **Canberra** and its rivers hardly conjure up pictures of wild white water, there are some excellent canoeing and kayaking locations around the city. The Cotter River, located within the Cotter Reserve, and Lake Burley Griffin — the heart of Canberra — both provide some good flat water for paddlers. Canoes can be hired around the shores of the lake. Canberra is also close to some great canoeing and rafting possibilities on the Tumut and Murrumbidgee Rivers, for those who prefer more adventurous paddling.

Victoria

6 The **Murray River,** Australia's mightiest river, runs from the mountains of New South Wales and forms the border of New South Wales and Victoria before finally entering the sea in South Australia. From the raging white water of the Murray Gates in the Snowy Mountains to the gently flowing lower reaches, rafting and canoeing possibilities abound. While the flatter water is easily tackled by the independent canoeist, the higher reaches and all the excitement they present attract only the experienced paddler. Several companies offer adventurous white-water rafting trips in this area.

7 The **Snowy River** also rises in the Snowy Mountains, but probably the best canoeing and rafting on the Snowy are to be had as it flows through Victoria's far eastern region — where another national park bears its name. Rafting trips of 70 kilometres or more take the adventurous through some of the most exciting river wilderness country in Australia.

The course of the Snowy features steep canyons and white beaches, between rapids with whimsical names like 'Gentle Annie' and the more sinister 'George's Mistake'. Wedge-tailed eagles ride the thermals overhead, and waterdragons, goannas, herons, ducks, cockatoos and kangaroos are all likely to put in an appearance during the trip. Canoe tour operators can organise camping expeditions from one to six days or more, including instruction.

8 More restful canoeing and rafting is to be enjoyed on the **Goulburn River,** closer to the state capital, Melbourne. It provides ideal conditions for the learner. It is also near enough to the city to attract Melburnians seeking a weekend away from it all on the water.

This alpine area contains beautiful foothills and quiet valleys, as well as Lake Eildon, a large man-made body of water that is suitable for canoeing and other water sports, such as fishing and boating.

9 Exciting sea kayaking is a feature of the **Wilson's Promontory** region, 230 kilometres south-east of Melbourne. The nearby Gippsland Lakes offer calmer waters for beginners and learners. Packages available for the Wilson's Promontory area can include instruction weeks (which are offered all year round).

10 The **Glenelg River,** near the Victorian-South Australian border, has cut a spectacular gorge, 50 metres deep in some places, through the Miocene limestone deposits for a distance of some 35 kilometres. Canoeists travelling these waters find themselves in the centre of a thriving river-country habitat teeming with wildlife.

Tasmania

11 Close to Hobart, in the settled but still picturesque countryside of the island state's east coast, some restful canoeing trips can be taken on the **Huon River.** As an alternative to camping or driving out for the day from Hobart, visitors can use one of the local guesthouses as a retreat and a base for bushwalking and other activities in the pretty Huon Valley. A good example is Balfe's Hill Farm, which offers hotel/motel-style accommodation and arranges rafting and canoeing trips on the nearby Huon and Picton Rivers.

12 **Bathurst Harbour** is the jewel of Tasmania's wild and magical south-west region. From here, two-person touring sea-kayaks thread their way down the intricate channels of Melaleuca Inlet to a first camping site, then move on the following day past the Celery Top Islands and down the Bathurst Narrows. Paddling to the edge of the Southern Ocean brings the kayaker to the calm waters of Port Davey, where the cold ocean swells from Antarctica converge.

The history, flora and fauna of this remote region are quite unique, and the local penguins are a particular attraction. Short bushwalks from the campsite are well worth the effort, and for those who take the trip as part of an organised expedition, the local knowledge of guides and instructors is a big bonus.

13 Another and even more exhilarating Tasmanian adventure is to be had in the dramatic surrounds of the **Franklin River** valley, now classified as part of a World Heritage area. This is one of the world's last

temperate riverine wilderness regions, fiercely fought over by conservationists and politicians alike some years ago — with the conservationists winning out in the end.

The Franklin River is considered by many paddling afficionados to be the hardest river run in Australia, and it demands dedication and fitness from those who attempt it. But the rewards are worth the effort. Canoeists will remember not only the breathtaking rapids, but also the water-worn gorges of quartzite and limestone, and the ancient stands of now-rare Huon pine and Antarctic beech which flank the torrent.

Rafting expeditions are an option, using single or multi-person rafts and led by experienced guides trained not only in the ways of the river, but also in first aid. Some of these adventures last as long as 16 days.

South Australia

14 The fertile **Murray-Darling Basin**, between Wentworth in New South Wales and Morgan in South Australia, affords some fine canoeing and kayaking on these broad rivers. The splendid wetland areas are indeed best explored in this way, and paddlers can venture to riverside environments inaccessible to vehicles and larger boats.

The region is ideal for long-distance canoe touring, either on guided expeditions or on self-guided trips.

15 South Australia has another adventure up its sleeve for the canoeist who thinks he or she has seen everything. Known as 'desert canoeing', it means just that. **Cooper's Creek** is near the Red Centre of Australia, yet despite its remoteness it is one of the country's most historically renowned waterways — if it can properly be described as a waterway.

It was near Innamincka and this desert oasis that the explorers Burke and Wills met their deaths in 1861 after missing their support party by a matter of hours. Their fatal steps can be followed now by water, taking in such landmarks as the 'Dig Tree', which still bears the marks of the explorers' knives, and Wills' grave.

Western Australia

16 The **Southern Region** of Australia's largest state is still largely untouched by humans, and much of it is protected by its inclusion in the Walpole-Nornalup and other national parks. Kayak and canoe trips are available on the Deep River and on the wild and remote Broke Inlet. The region features luxuriant karri and jarrah forests, and it has only recently begun to attract tourists.

This remote area is probably best explored with an organised group in order to get the benefit of the knowledge and experience of local guides. Some tour operators offer other adventure options such as rockclimbing and four-wheel driving.

17 More accessible and much closer to Perth is the **South-west Region**, centred around Margaret River and Bunbury, one of Western Australia's most popular holiday regions. This beautiful area of farmland, forest and streams contains the Collie and Blackwood Rivers, the waters of which are well-suited to the needs of the canoeist, and offer some good, generally easy-grade paddling. Canoeing trips are arranged on the Blackwood and Collie by one or two local operators, who also provide instruction.

18 Much closer to Perth is the **Avon River**, which features one of the most famous white-water rafting events in the world — the Avon Descent. More

Wild and wet adventure on the Franklin River

than 700 determined and intrepid enthusiasts descend the turbulent Avon during August each year, battling the foaming waters in a race that can last as long as 20 hours for some contestants.

The competitors paddle through picturesque locations like Northam, Toodyay, Emu Falls and Syd's Rapids and then on through the rough country of the Walyunga National Park, some 80 kilometres east of Perth. Meanwhile, less energetic spectators line the banks and create their own entertainment with rock bands, country singers, spit-roasted sheep and campfires, making it a memorable weekend.

It's not necessary to be a masochist to enjoy the waters of the Avon by canoe or raft, however. Easy-grade one-day raft runs are organised on the Avon, with rather harder and longer expeditions on the nearby Murray, including white-water sections.

Northern Territory

20 Canoeists on the Northern Territory's **Daly and Katherine Rivers**, located between Darwin and Katherine, in the north, can often glimpse some of the creatures that share the waters with them, particularly crocodiles. Other wildlife is also abundant, especially buffaloes and wild pigs. Some organised groups roast pigs over the campfire for the evening meal.

No-one travelling these northern rivers should miss tasting the excellent barramundi and bream which thrive in these waters. Bushwalking and photography are other very popular options in the region, and it is possible to link canoe trips with four-wheel-drive expeditions into Kakadu National Park to the south.

Queensland

20 In far north Queensland, the **Cairns area** provides some of the world's best white-water rafting and canoeing. The region's torrential seasonal rainfall turns its high mountain ranges into a catchment area from which rivers spill down to the coast and the plains. On the way, rivers like the Mulgrave, the North Johnstone, the Herbert, the Tully and the Barron carve their way through deep gorge country which can only be reached by water. Canoeists and rafting enthusiasts can battle through fast-flowing water and across treacherous rapids in a landscape of creeks, waterfalls and rainforest.

It's not all danger and excitement, though. The North Johnstone River, for example, has placid stretches suitable for beginners before the rapids — in several grades of difficulty — start making life really interesting. One other advantage of these tropical rivers is that the water is unusually warm, which is a rare and welcome luxury for devotees of the sport.

It is possible for visitors to make short trips of just a day or two, but some of the grandest stretches of the north Queensland rivers are very remote indeed and access to these is usually only by helicopter.

21 Offshore, the clear warm waters of Queensland's **Great Barrier Reef** are generally considered the preserve of tourists on leisurely island holidays who like to swim, snorkel and surf. But these same waters also afford an unforgettable experience for kayaking enthusiasts.

It is a rare thrill to glide smoothly and silently through the world's largest island national park, almost at one with the fish below. The sheltered shores of the mainland offer sweeping beaches and secluded bays, against a backdrop of rainforested mountains. Organised packages can be arranged for a week's paddling around the coral islands of the reef.

JIM SCHWALBACH

Canoeing, Kayaking & Rafting Contacts

Operators

New South Wales

1 Northern New South Wales

Canoe Tours Australia
This group, based in Melbourne, offers canoe tours in Victoria and New South Wales. They have a nine-day trip in northern New South Wales on the Bellingen and Nymboida Rivers.

PO Box 26
South Oakleigh
Melbourne VIC 3167
Ph. (03) 548 1838

Nymboida Whitewater Rafting Expeditions
This group, based near Coffs Harbour, offers white-water rafting on the wild Nymboida River. Trips run from Saturday to Thursday.

PO Box 224
Woolgoolga NSW 2456
Ph. (066) 54 1788

Wilderness Expeditions
One of the many rafting trips that this organisation offers is a five-day 'Nymboida Whitewater' run. The trip is graded easy to moderate, but there is some exciting whitewater.

100 Clarence Street
Sydney NSW 2000
Ph. (02) 29 1581

26 Sharp Street
Cooma NSW 2630
Ph. (064) 52 1587

World Expeditions
Their range of activities includes a canoeing and rafting programme.
They offer a five-day white-water camp on the Nymboida River.

3rd Floor
337 Sussex Street
Sydney NSW 2000
Ph. (02) 264 3366

2 Kempsey/Gloucester Area

Adventure Outdoors
This group specialises in canoeing and camping trips in the Barrington area. They offer one to three-day trips in two-person Canadian canoes on the Barrington, Barnard, Manning and Gloucester Rivers.

PO Box 21
Tuncurry NSW 2428
Ph. (065) 54 6167

Trekabout Bushtours
Based at Gloucester, just four hours north of Sydney, their programme of activities includes canoeing for both the uninitiated and the converted.
They have one to three-day guided tours of the Barrington and Barnard Rivers.

Barrington Road
Gloucester NSW 2422
Ph. (065) 58 2093

3 Shoalhaven River

Shoalhaven Adventure Camps
They offer canoe treks on the Shoalhaven and Kangaroo Rivers over three or more days. Their camps cater for up to 40 participants in tented accommodation.

PO Box 3063
North Nowra NSW 2541
Ph. (044) 46 0130

Sportrek Australia
This group offers a comprehensive range of outdoor activities. Among their white-water rafting destinations is a two-day trip on the Shoalhaven River. This is graded moderate, requiring an average level of fitness. Each raft is captained by an experienced instructor.

10 Elouera Road
Cronulla
Sydney NSW 2230
Ph. (02) 523 2132

4 Kosciusko National Park

Canoe Tours Australia
They offer tours on the Murrumbidgee and Tumut Rivers, in addition to several other destinations in Victoria and New South Wales.

See (1) above for details

Wilderness Expeditions
Based in both Sydney and Cooma, Wilderness Expeditions offers a four-day canoeing trip on the Tumut River. This trip operates from October to April.

See (1) above for details

Australian Capital Territory

5 Canberra Rivers and Lakes

Gone Camping
Based in Canberra, this company arranges canoeing trips as part of their multi-adventure programme. Special camps are operated for children.

PO Box 37
Scullin
Canberra ACT 2614
Ph. (062) 54 8693

Victoria

6 Murray River

Wilderness Expeditions
Wilderness Expeditions offers a moderately graded canoeing trip on the Upper Murray River.

See (1) above for details

World Expeditions
They offer a three-day rafting trip on the Murray River. The cost includes all rafting equipment, guide, meals, camping equipment and return transport to Khancoban.

See (1) above for details

7 Snowy River

Peregrine Adventures
Peregrine offers a wide curriculum of rafting holidays at a variety of locations. Their five-day Snowy River trip is graded moderate. Rafts, camping gear, meals and experienced guides are all included in the package.

Suite 9A, 9th Floor
343 Little Collins Street
Melbourne VIC 3000
Ph. (03) 602 3066

Snowy River Expeditions
This group runs spectacular rafting and canoeing trips through the massive gorges and rapids of Victoria's Snowy River. Trips range from one to six days and include paddling instruction, experienced guides and equipment.

PO Buchan VIC 3885
Ph. (051) 55 9373 or (03) 55 9353

8 Goulburn River

Canoe Tours Australia
They have a five-day Eildon Safari, including two days on the Upper Goulburn River, using a motel at Jamieson as a base. They also have a Goulburn weekender, offering two days of canoeing on the Upper Goulburn River.

See (1) above for details

Peregrine Adventures
Peregrine offers a two-day rafting tour on the Goulburn River. The package includes rafts, camping and safety

equipment, experienced guides and vehicle transfers.

See (7) above for details

9 Wilson's Promontory

Spindrift International Guiding
This specialist guiding organisation offers weekend sea-kayaking trips around Wilson's Promontory National Park.

PO Box 455
Maffra VIC 3860
Ph. (059) 67 1659

10 Glenelg River

Ecotrek
Ecotrek offers a five-day canoeing trip along the Glenelg River, and there are opportunities to hike along sections of the Great South West Walking Trail. You camp by the river, enjoying wine and good food.

24 Gibbon Lane
North Adelaide SA 5006
Ph. (08) 267 1442

Tasmania

11 Huon River

Tasmanian River Rafters
This group offers canoeing day trips and weekends on the Huon River, close to Hobart. They operate from the comfortable Balfes Hill Farm, which offers hostel-type accommodation.

PO Box 89
Huonville TAS 7109
Ph. (002) 95 1573

12 Bathurst Harbour

Open Spaces
This group operates an eight-day sea-kayaking trip around Bathurst Harbour. The introduction and finale to this trip is a spectacular 40-minute flight over the Hartz Mountains National Park and past majestic Federation Peak.

Travelling in two-person sea-touring kayaks, you will explore the inlets of Bathurst Harbour.

28 Criterion Street
Hobart TAS 7000
Ph. (002) 31 0983

13 Franklin River

Tasmanian River Rafters
This group offers a 16-day rafting trip down the Franklin River, taking a maximum of eight people. Each person paddles his own raft in the company of two experienced guides.

See (11) above for details

Wilderness Expeditions
Wilderness Expeditions includes in its rafting programme a ten-day trip down the Franklin River.

See (1) above for details

World Expeditions
Their 11-day rafting trip on the Franklin is graded as extremely difficult and is suitable for experienced outdoors people only. Five-person rafts are used and wetsuits can be hired from the company.

See (1) above for details

South Australia

14 Murray River

Riverland Canoeing Adventures
This group provides guided four and six-day canoeing tours, and self-guided tours of up to 14 days along the Murray River.

Alamein Avenue
Loxton North SA 5333
Ph. (085) 84 1494

15 Cooper's Creek

Canoe Tours Australia
They offer a 14-day desert canoeing trip which paddles Cooper's Creek and follows the trail of the famous explorers, Burke and Wills.

See (1) above for details

Ecotrek
One of the popular destinations of this group is the Cooper's Creek area, where they offer various canoe tours.

See (10) above for details

Western Australia

16 Southern Region

Great Southern Wilderness Expeditions
This organisation specialises in short raft and canoe trips through karri and jarrah forests on the Deep River and Broke Inlet.

'Bonnie View'
Little River Road
Denmark WA 6333
Ph. (098) 48 1341

Wildside Adventure Excursions
They have a five-day Deep River rafting trip, labelled a 'laid-back' wilderness experience. This trip departs from Perth and uses one-man rafts.

PO Box 96
Bassendean
Perth WA 6054
Ph. (09) 279 1750

17 South-west Region

Blackwood Expeditions
These canoe trips, catering for beginners and the more experienced, range from half-day to five-day tours on the Blackwood River.

Canoes and equipment are available for hire to experienced canoeists, and flexible arrangements can be made for private groups.

PO Box 64
Nannup WA 6275
Ph. (097) 56 1081 or 56 1209

Wildside Adventure Excursions
Two-day rafting trips take place on the Collie River during the summer months (November to March). Two-person inflatable rafts are used and trips include all transport and equipment, plus an experienced guide.

See (16) above for details

18 Avon and Murray Rivers

Adventure Out
Based in Fremantle, Adventure Out caters for all groups including the physically and mentally handicapped.

Two-day instructional canoe courses take place on the Avon River and other rivers close to Perth. Both basic canoe techniques and flat-water and challenging white-water canoeing are taught.

33A Adelaide Street
Fremantle WA 6160
Ph. (09) 335 9299

Northern Territory

19 Daly and Katherine Rivers

Breakwater Canoe Tours
Four and seven-day canoeing safaris are offered on the Daly and Katherine Rivers. No canoeing experience is required.

Canoe trips can be linked with walking and four-wheel-drive trips to Kakadu National Park and the Finnis River region.

PO Box 641
Darwin NT 5794
Ph. (089) 27 2532 or 81 1244

Pandanus Canoe Safaris
Pandanus offers four and six-day canoeing trips on the Daly River. Swimming, bushwalking, fishing and photography may also be enjoyed on the trip. They only operate during summer.

GPO Box 1486
Darwin NT 5794
Ph. (089) 85 3475

ALLAN MOULT

Information Sources

Canoeing Associations

Australian Canoe Federation Inc.
Sports House
157 Gloucester Street
Sydney NSW 2000
Ph. (02) 27 2933

General information on rivers and
waterways, canoe safety, and a source of
educational and training services for
canoeists.

New South Wales

New South Wales Canoe Association
Sports House
157 Gloucester Street
Sydney NSW 2000
Ph. (02) 241 3866

Australian Capital Territory

ACT Canoe Association Inc.
34 Angophora Street
Rivett
Canberra ACT 2611
Ph. (062) 88 6799

Victoria

Victorian Amateur Canoe Association
1 Byrne Court
Cheltenham
Melbourne VIC 3192
Ph. (03) 583 4260

Victorian Board of Canoe Education
140 Cotham Road
Kew
Melbourne VIC 3101
Ph. (03) 817 6130

Tasmania

Tasmanian Canoe Association
PO Box 230
Scottsdale TAS 7254
Ph. (003) 56 1612

South Australia

South Australian Canoeing Association
1 Garden Road
Westbourne Park SA 5041
Ph. (08) 272 2372

Western Australia

Western Australia Amateur Canoe
  Association
7 Cygnet Place
Lynwood WA 6155

Queensland

Queensland Amateur Canoe Federation
PO Box 590
Woodridge QLD 4114
Ph. (07) 207 3415

Queensland

20 Far North Queensland Rivers

Butlers Canoes Tours
This group specialises in one or two-day
paddling trips on north Queensland's
Mulgrave River. The tours involve an
overnight camp-out and it is preferred
that participants have some canoeing
experience.

C/- Going Places Travel
26 Abbott Street
Cairns QLD 4870
Ph. (070) 51 4055

In the Wild Canoe Tours
This organisation takes small groups
(maximum 12 people) on canoeing trips
on the North Johnstone River. Two-
person canoes are used, and prior to
commencing the one-day tour, they give
paddling instruction. Each trip offers
nine rapids of varying grades.

19 Terka Street
Innisfail QLD 4860
Ph. (070) 61 3961

The Raft 'n Rainforest Company
Their tours include the Tully, North
Johnstone and Barwon Rivers. They
operate all year round.

PO Box 1938
Cairns QLD 4870
Ph. (070) 51 7777

Raging Thunder
They offer rafting trips down the Tully,
Barron and North Johnstone Rivers.
Their North Johnstone River trip is of
two or five days' duration, the Barron
River trip is of three hours' duration,
and the Tully River trip lasts one day.
They operate out of Cairns and
Townsville.

PO Box 2172
Cairns QLD 4870
Ph. (070) 51 4911

21 Coral Sea

Raging Thunder
Raging Thunder offers a relaxing seven-
day sea-kayaking trip around the Coral
Sea Islands of the Great Barrier Reef.
The trip requires a total of eight hours'
paddling, with single and double-seat
kayaks.

See (20) above for details

MICK TURNER

Diving & Snorkelling

Australia is no doubt unique. With over 20,000 kilometres of magnificent coastline, we have superb diving in the tropical waters of the Great Barrier Reef and northern Western Australia, as well as brilliant temperate-water diving in the southern states and Tasmania. Indeed Lord Howe Island in the Pacific, a part of New South Wales, has both tropical and temperate marine life. Australia offers excellent shipwreck diving on vessels sunk in the 17th century through to early this century. We have the finest freshwater cave diving in the world, and huge ocean kelp forests. Underwater photography is popular due to the prolific marine life. And there is excellent snorkelling at most dive sites and offshore islands.

One of the main problems that we face in Australia is the remoteness of many excellent diving sites. Although over 95% of our population lives within easy reach of the sea, we tend to congregate in the state capital cities and the moderate-sized coastal towns, many of which are hundreds of kilometres apart, particularly in the northern half of the continent. This limits diving facilities, such as dive shops with air compressors and charter boats, to a few select locations.

Each Australian state has something different to offer. Western Australia, with the longest coastline, provides the most varied conditions from the temperate waters off Esperance and Albany to the isolated coral reefs of Rowley Shoals, 14 hours by boat off Broome in the Indian Ocean. The most popular area is Rottnest Island, only 18 kilometres out of Fremantle, site of the 1987 America's Cup Defence.

South Australian divers venerate the freshwater cave system at Mt Gambier, where the crystal clarity of the waters attracts specialist cave divers from all over the world. (A permit to dive is required.) The best

ocean diving is south of Adelaide on the St Vincent Gulf, at nearby Kangaroo Island, and around the more remote Flinders and Pearson Islands to the west. Some divers may be reluctant to dive these waters, however, for it is here that the Great White Shark is to be found.

Bicheno on the eastern coast of Tasmania has some of the finest temperate water marine life in Australia, and it is readily accessible. Of greater historical significance are the numerous 19th-century shipwrecks scattered throughout the island waters of Bass Strait which separates Tasmania from mainland Victoria.

Melbourne divers often travel several hours to reach a good dive site, though the most popular area is at the entrance to Port Phillip Bay, only 90 minutes by car from the city. The coastline west of Melbourne is arguably the most beautiful in Australia, but it is somewhat too treacherous to dive regularly despite the attraction of several excellent shipwrecks. To the east, Wilson's Promontory National Park and the offshore islands are very popular despite restricted access.

New South Wales has the largest number of divers in the country. Its relatively mild climate and highly populated coastline with dive facilities in most coastal towns ensures easy access to excellent offshore diving. The most popular areas are within easy driving distance of Sydney, but there is also excellent diving in the south and north of the state. Green Cape, near the Victorian border, is superb; and Byron Bay near the Queensland border has become a holiday resort for divers. Jervis Bay has brilliant marine life and is only two hours by car from Sydney.

Of all the states, however, Queensland rates as the mecca for Australian divers and overseas visitors. The Great Barrier Reef is one of the natural wonders of the world and the diving here is excellent, with professional dive charter boat facilities and exotic island resorts. From Lady Elliot and Heron Islands in the south to the remote Ashmore Reefs way up north near Papua New Guinea, each section of the reef is sheer delight.

Although there is no law in Australia specifically requiring a licence to dive in ocean waters, dive shops and dive charter operators require the diver to be certified to a recognised standard. Australian divers are trained to one of three major scuba diving standards — the Federation of Australian Underwater Instructors (FAUI), the Professional Association of Diving Instructors (PADI), and the National Association of Underwater Instructors (NAUI). Overseas visitors may well be qualified to other standards; most will be recognised.

Dive courses are available in all capital cities and in many coastal and inland towns and resort islands. Courses may be taken over evenings and weekends spanning several weeks, or over an intensive five days. The training is thorough, yet at a pace that suits the student. Australia has arguably the highest standard of diving instruction, and hence divers, in the world.

An experience of scuba diving, without going to the expense of a full course, is possible through 'resort' courses at most island resorts. These provide a half-day of theory and pool instruction, followed by a 'hand-hold' dive with an instructor. Invariably, the non-diver becomes hooked on diving and continues with a full course of instruction at some later time.

Divers visiting new destinations like to feel that they are in professional hands and that they are offered the best in equipment and charter boats. Most overseas visitors make the Great Barrier Reef their objective. All charter boats provide scuba tanks and weights — you need to bring the rest of your equipment or hire it from a dive shop in town or through the charter boat or booking agent. There is usually only limited spare equipment on board.

There are only two resort islands actually on the Great Barrier Reef — Heron Island and Lady Elliot Island. Lizard Island, north of Cairns, has fast boat access to the reef, as do Hamilton and Hayman Islands in the Whitsundays. All resorts have ample equipment — you don't even need to bring a mask.

When booking a dive holiday, charter boat or island resort, consult a recognised travel agency specialising in scuba diving holidays who can make all the arrangements, including transport and accommodation. The weather plays a large part in what you can expect from each dive site, so get expert advice before travelling.

The diving areas we have detailed are generally the more accessible areas within each state and they are well served by instructional and charter operators. There are, of course, many other excellent diving regions around Australia.

Locations

New South Wales

New South Wales has the largest number of resident divers and tends to have the most facilities for offshore diving. The warm climate adds to its attraction as a great diving location.

1 Most locations are easily accessible from Sydney, and both the north and south coast of New South Wales offer excellent diving. One of the most spectacular spots is **Lord Howe Island**, 700 kilometres north-east of Sydney. The island has the southernmost coral reef in the world. Areas such as the Admiralty Islets are a marine photographer's dream.

2 **Byron Bay,** on the New South Wales north coast, is the most easterly point along the coast, and is close to the edge of the continental shelf. It is an important cattle-producing area, with fine grazing and dairying land.

Apart from its rural heritage, Byron Bay also boasts some of the best diving sites in Australia. Diving within the bay offers very good reefs. One section, known as Little Reef, is a series of bomboras which break during big seas and low tides. Within the bay there are also two kelp reefs — Wilsons Reef and Bait Reef — inhabited by thousands of yellowtail, whiting and herring.

3 **Coffs Harbour,** located in the heart of banana plantations south of Byron Bay, is another great spot for keen divers. The best local diving feature is the Solitary Islands, located off the coast and accessible only by boat. Schools of kingfish, mackerel and Queensland groper are common, and extensive coral formations and diverse tropical and subtropical marine life are spectacular sights for divers in and around the islands. Visibility is excellent, between 13 and 18 metres. Several dive shops service the Solitary Islands with regular charter trips and escorted dives.

4 Around the **Sydney** metropolitan area there are three major dive locations — Port Hacking, Sydney Harbour and Broken Bay. Port Hacking offers many good spots, including the Baron's Hut, Marley Reef and Hanging Rock. These usually offer good visibility inshore and offshore.

Sydney Harbour has several good dive locations, especially North Head, Clovelly and Shelley Beach. Long Reef on Sydney's northern beaches has great offshore diving at Ship Reef. There are also wrecks off Avalon and South Head. Broken Bay has good diving at Maitland Bay and Barrenjoey Head. Most areas are accessible from headlands so charters are not usually required, thus minimising costs.

Diving courses are available throughout Sydney, with many dive shops offering equipment hire and maintenance, especially in the coastal suburbs from the east through to the northern beaches.

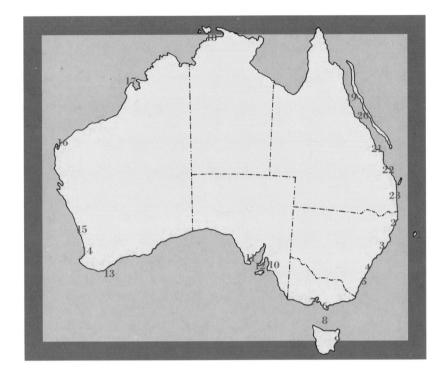

5 The **Jervis Bay area** in southern New South Wales deservedly has the reputation of being one of the best diving locations in the state. The physical beauty of the region is outstanding, with sheltered bays and white sandy beaches, and almost impossibly turquoise-coloured water.

The underwater scene is just as interesting. An abundance of marine life inhabits the waters of the bay — sponges, sea ferns and fish — all in waters that generally give visibility of around 20 metres. The underwater terrain contains huge boulders, caves and tunnels from the surface down to around 50 metres, and many of the most interesting sites are close to the cliffs that surround the bay.

Jervis Bay's protected waters provide good diving all year round, and several operators in the area can offer diving courses, boat charters and dive-holiday packages with accommodation included. Jervis Bay is 190 kilometres south of Sydney, and also within easy reach of Canberra, 230 kilometres to the west.

Victoria

Climatic conditions inhibit diving in many areas of Victoria, but there are several locations that provide excellent diving. Port Phillip Bay and Heads, and the Bellarine Peninsula are two of the most popular diving locations.

6 **Wilson's Promontory** is classified as a national park, and for divers wanting to camp there are sites available. Wilson's Promontory is one of the most picturesque spots divers can visit in Australia, with large mountains of thick granite jutting out from the waters below.

Divers without a boat and powerful outboard will need to base themselves at Tidal River, as the distance from Port Welshpool, Sandy Point and Walkerville South is too great for small boats. Tidal River has good amenities for campers, with showers, laundries and a general store.

The best diving is approximately nine kilometres from Tidal River at Shellback Island, or there is Norman Island at five kilometres, and the Glennies, six kilometres from Tidal River. The most effective way to dive the promontory is by charter boat, and several are available from eastern Victoria.

7 The entrance to **Port Phillip Bay** is the most popular area for Victorian and visiting divers. The bay's appeal lies in the fact that it provides varied diving to enthusiasts of all standards and interests. There are vast areas of largely unexplored reefs, a number of shipwrecks and a large range of marine life.

Most diving in Port Phillip Bay is done at the southern end, but visitors to Melbourne may find some spots closer to the city and to the north. One problem with diving at the northern end of Port Phillip Bay is the poor visibility, but on a good day the reefs can be clearly seen.

Access to all dive sites is good, especially from the coastal resorts of Queenscliff and Portsea. The area is also well serviced by a number of professional dive charter operators. Good shore diving is available on the reefs from Point Gellibrand to Point Cook, with varying depths to choose from.

The best time to dive is after a long period of dry, calm weather, usually during April and May, though most areas are protected from bad weather. Visibility varies depending on the weather conditions, but on

One of the many vast coral gardens available to divers, where underwater life abounds, even at depths of only two–three metres

most days it is at least ten metres.

A short power boat ride out the entrance of the Barwon River at Geelong, south-west of Melbourne, puts scuba divers within range of kelp forests, reef formations and shipwrecks.

Following its recent discovery by a group of Geelong divers, 'Chimney Rock' has become a very popular dive location. This underwater feature, approximately one kilometre south of Barwon Heads Bluff, rises ten metres from the seabed in a reef formation supporting a wide variety of fish. If planning a dive on Chimney Rock, it is advisable to seek information and advice from local clubs and associations, as markers are not very precise.

Victoria has hundreds of other diving locations, most of which have good services with charter boat operators, dive courses and equipment hire.

One of the Reef's thousands of unique species

8 At the western entrance of **Bass Strait,** King Island is a world-renowned 'ship's graveyard', with over 100 wrecks. The island is only accessible by air and does not offer the best conditions for diving in the southern waters.

In contrast to King Island, Flinders Island, in the Furneaux Group of Islands at the eastern end of Bass Strait, offers superb diving. The western shores and the north-east of the island have excellent beaches. The eastern shores, however, are largely inaccessible.

Flinders Island offers great wreck dives and marine life studies. The area is largely unexplored, with only a few divers visiting the island each year. However, improved accommodation facilities and organised group dive tours from Melbourne have increased diving opportunities.

There are scheduled flights to Flinders Island from Essendon in Melbourne, Hobart and Launceston, and light aircraft charters can be taken from Welshpool and Moorabbin in Victoria and Launceston.

Tasmania

The cold Tasmanian waters may deter many visitors from diving, but there are several locations well worth attempting.

The most accessible areas are along the east and north coasts of Tasmania, though land access is restricted. Hobart divers tend to favour Maria Island, the Tasman Peninsula, or the D'Entrecasteaux Channel to the south where visibility is often up to 30 metres and extensive marine life can be seen.

9 On the **east coast of Tasmania**, about 160 kilometres by road from Launceston, Bicheno offers great diving for the enthusiast.

Bicheno is an appealing little town, based predominantly on fishing and tourism. The Gulch is famous throughout Australia for its all-weather safe anchorage for boats. About two years ago, Bicheno had no facilities for divers, but one operator now has superb professional facilities.

Bicheno offers some of the finest temperate water diving in the world, with water cooler than Victoria or New South Wales. From March through to July, visibility often exceeds 45 metres, and offshore winds create calm conditions and clear skies.

South Australia

10 Close to **Adelaide,** and offering excellent diving, is Port Noarlunga Reef. Access to the reef is precarious in some places, and the area has claimed the lives of at least eight divers since 1951.

The reef — a recently declared marine reserve — is possibly the most dived spot in Australia, excluding Heron Island on the Barrier Reef.

Aldinga Beach, with easy boat launching which enables divers to go to the Aldinga 'drop-off', is another great location. It affords spectacular sights for the avid marine photographer. Another nearby attraction is the wreck of the *Star of Greece.*

11 **Port Lincoln** is a 700-kilometre drive west of Adelaide on the Eyre Peninsula. Diving offshore is limited due to the shortage of good roads. However, Wanna Beach and Memory Cove can be reached by road. Whaler's Way, south-west of the township of Port Lincoln, is a popular tourist attraction. The cliff at Cape Wiles puts many people off diving there, and divers must obtain permission before entering the water. At the base of Cape Wiles, a large lagoon provides an excellent sheltered dive site.

The lagoon is surrounded by huge cliffs, and entrance is obtained through a narrow channel at its eastern end. A boat is needed to reach Cape Wiles, with Fishery Bay providing a good launching site if a four-wheel-drive vehicle is used.

12 The **islands off the South Australian coast** provide some excellent diving. Apart from Kangaroo Island, which has its own dive operators,

This blue angel fish has a luminous quality

charters are available to other islands such as the Sir Joseph Banks Group.

Several charter boat operators run trips to a variety of South Australian islands. Some provide accommodation on board, or tented accommodation on certain islands, while Wedge Island has a comfortable homestead available to divers.

Diving is possible all year round, but September is best avoided due to high winds. Visibility is best in the early winter and in summer.

Western Australia

Western Australia has many excellent diving locations all along its extensive coastline. Some of the most popular areas are the south coast, Rottnest Island, the Abrolhos Islands, and Rowley Shoals off Broome, in the far north of the state.

13 The **south coast** of Western Australia, particularly between Augusta and Esperance, and including the Recherche Archipelago, has some exciting diving conditions, though it is not as accessible as the west coast.

The Denmark/Albany region offers some excellent diving, with good facilities available at Albany. Further east, the thriving port of Esperance is the gateway to the Recherche Archipelago Nature Reserve. This chain of islands stretches for around 200 kilometres south-east of Esperance and the Cape Le Grand National Park.

The close proximity of the continental shelf to the south coast makes the water here generally very deep, making for interesting diving.

14 **Rottnest Island** offers various attractions for divers of all standards — wrecks, reefs and pelagic schools are just a few of the drawcards. Rottnest Island is the major attraction for divers visiting Western Australia because of its spectacular marine life and wreck sites, and also because of its proximity to Perth and its excellent facilities. Private boats can travel the 18 kilometres to the island's

One of the delights of the underwater world

eastern tip if the weather is suitable, and ferries operate from Perth daily.

The wrecks around Rottnest Island can only be visited by boat, and the diver is usually taken to the ocean side of the island where visibility ranges between nine and 18 metres, considerably less than on the harbour side.

Perth has several excellent dive shops providing instructional courses, charters and equipment services. Many of these offer trips to Rottnest and to the waters surrounding Perth and Fremantle.

15 Another favourite location is the **Abrolhos Islands**, situated 60 kilometres off Geraldton, north of Perth. These islands have been the resting place of the famous *Batavia* since 1629, and also have some of the finest coral gardens in Australia — fine enough, some say, to rival the Great Barrier Reef.

The Abrolhos offer some of the best diving in Australia, and are served by several dive charter operators from Geraldton and Dongara, and by diving holiday operators based in Perth. The islands, properly named the Houtman Abrolhos group, are uninhabited and are protected as a nature reserve. Consequently, camping is not permitted, and dive trips need to be boat-based.

16 North of the Abrolhos Islands on one of the most western extremities of the coast is **Exmouth,** another great location for keen divers. The only restriction on diving is the weather. During summer

months it is often too hot, and the waters are inhabited by sharks and sea snakes, making diving extremely dangerous. However, there are plenty of fish and shells in the area, and the coastline is accessible as far as Coral Bay if visitors are without a boat.

17 Broome, on Western Australia's northern coastline, has a fascinating history as an early pearling port. The pearling industry was established here in the late 1800s.

Northern Territory

Tropical temperatures mean that diving in the Northern Territory is great all year round. However, there are various hazards to be avoided. During October and May, sea wasps infest the waters off the coast, and sharks and crocodiles make swimming dangerous. High tides near Darwin also restrict the diving season. There is little offshore diving and boats with expert guides are a necessity. Boat charters are available in Darwin.

18 **Darwin Harbour** has several wrecks, some — such as *Megis*, a 15,000-tonne freighter and the *Peary*, an old destroyer — dating back to the Second World War. There are also many coral reefs, some with outstanding soft coral gardens. All these sites are easily accessible by boat.

Water temperatures are warm all year round, reaching around 32°C during November and April when wetsuits should be worn to avoid box-jellyfish stings. For the rest of the year, water temperatures average 24°C.

Queensland

The Great Barrier Reef commences near the mouth of the Fly River in New Guinea and extends down the Queensland coast as far as Lady Elliot Island, southeast of Gladstone. It is not a single reef, but rather a system of coral reefs and islands on the edge of the continental shelf, varying in distance from 20 to 250 kilometres offshore.

It is the largest and most beautiful coral reef system in the world. Little wonder that it attracts people from all over the world — especially divers and snorkellers. The Reef is the most popular visitors' dive spot in the world. It is accessible only by boat from over 100 charter operators based in centres such as Bundaberg, Gladstone, Yeppoon, Rockhampton, Cairns, Port Douglas and Townsville. Most of the coastline is accessible throughout the year, yet access to offshore reefs can cause problems. Small reliable outboard-powered boats provide the easiest transport to these areas.

Charter boats usually operate on a total charter basis, where 8-12 passengers book the whole boat out for 6-15 days. Individuals can join these groups or regular scheduled departures. Everything is included — meals, diving equipment and unlimited airfills.

Day sightseeing cruises to the reef operate from Gladstone, Shute Harbour, Townsville, Cairns and Port Douglas, offering snorkelling only if pre-arranged with the operators. Divers may take day trips providing they bring their own gear.

19 **Cairns** is well known as the gateway to the northern Great Barrier Reef and all the incomparable diving it contains. A wonderful way to explore the 20 or more reefs that lie off Cairns is on the MV *Esperance Star.* Scheduled charters throughout the year visit the Ribbon Reefs, Cod Hole and Lizard Island. MV *Esperance Star* is a 19-metre luxury steel-hulled cruiser with four triple cabins. The cruiser is fully equipped for diving, with ten 63 psi and two 80 psi tanks as well as weights and belts.

The Coral Sea lies some 150 kilometres from the Great Barrier Reef and approximately 300 kilometres east of Cairns. It is a distinctly different area to the Great Barrier Reef, with its own coral reefs.

Diving in the Coral Sea is superb, with generally excellent visibility and schools of pelagic species. The corals are excellent, but not so diversified as on the Great Barrier Reef due to the extreme vulnerability of the exposed ocean reefs.

Some 95 kilometres east of Cooktown lies beautiful Lizard Island (a national park). The waters around the island and along the reef are renowned for big-game fishing. Keen divers use Lizard Island as a base for diving trips to the Great Barrier Reef. Snorkelling

is also popular over the lagoon coral.

20 The Great Barrier Reef off **Townsville** comprises a large number of individual reef areas ranging in size from 400 metres across to 15 kilometres long. These reefs are separated by channels, and anchorage is available in sheltered waters inside the lagoons or on the lee side of the reefs. Underwater visibility is generally in the range of 15-25 metres. Diving is possible in all tides and in all weather.

One of the most popular dive spots out of Townsville is the wreck of the *Yongala.* Lying ten kilometres off Cape Bowling Green, it is a superb dive with plenty of marine life and several good and safe areas to penetrate. Although the wreck is difficult to find without radar, the MV *Watersport* has no difficulty in tethering to the wreck.

21 Diving the **Whitsunday Group** can be as interesting as the Great Barrier Reef, though visibility tends to decrease further out. There is a profusion of soft corals, hard corals and sponges, as well as tropical reef species. Pelagics are not as common as on the reef, but there are some schools, as well as the occasional manta ray and shark. The north side of Hook Island offers some of the best diving in the group.

The Whitsunday region is one of Australia's main holiday centres. There are 74 islands, six of which have holiday resorts — South Molle, Lindeman, Royal Hayman, Hamilton, Whitsunday 100 and Palm Bay on Long Island, and Daydream Island. Most Whitsunday Island resorts have their own dive operation, or arrange diving from one of the several cruise boats that operate in the area. Full dive services are available on Hamilton and Hayman Islands.

Airlie Beach, on the mainland, is an accommodation and holiday centre for the Whitsunday region, with good hotels, flats and camping grounds in the vicinity. Barrier Reef Diving Services at Airlie Beach will help plan a diving trip to the reef.

22 Divers keen to stay closer to the reef can visit any of the resorts surrounding the Great Barrier Reef. Heron Island, situated on the southern end of the reef, off **Gladstone,** is excellent. Visitors to Heron Island should see the reefs of Wistari, Mast, Wreck and Wilson Island, and the famous 'Bommie'.

Heron Island has permanent dive facilities, including escorted dives and charter boats, which are fully supervised. Divers must show a certificate of their diving standard, and some scuba instruction is available.

Lady Elliot Island, 85 kilometres north of Bundaberg, is the southernmost island on the Great Barrier Reef. Access is by air: 90 minutes from Brisbane or 20 minutes from Bundaberg. The island offers excellent unlimited diving at basic rates. Diving is mainly off the reef edge, though there is a boat dive to the Blowhole. Report in at the dive shop near the airstrip, log in, obtain the necessary gear, and the divemasters will take all equipment to the beach edge.

The 16-metre steel motor sailer, *Tropic Rover*, can be chartered from Gladstone for tours of the Capricorn and Bunker Groups. Accommodation is provided in five two-berth private cabins. The charter includes full catering and all diving equipment.

23 **Brisbane and southern Queensland** divers are fortunate in having Moreton Island and the Stradbroke Islands at their doorstep. The 'Rufus King' (off Moreton Island) is a reasonably shallow dive on a good day. As an artificial reef, the wreck is excellent for fish and macro photography, but it can be a treacherous dive because of the strong current.

Cape Moreton and the nearby reefs can only be reached by a long boat trip when conditions are calm. The best area to dive is in the area north of Cape Moreton — Roberts and Brennan bommies, Smith Rock, Flinders Reef and Hutchison's Shoal.

The main reefs east of the Gold Coast can be reached by launching a boat in the Tweed River or across the beach at Rainbow Bay. Close to the mainland, Cook Island is a popular diving spot and whenever the water is clear the northern side offers pleasant diving.

Diving & Snorkelling Contacts

Operators

The following three companies are recommended as travel agents specialising in dive travel. They operate diving tours to various destinations around Australia.

Aquarius Dive Travel
38 Taylor Street
Ashburton VIC 3147
Ph. (008) 33 8409

Dive Magic Tours
100 Clarence Street
Sydney NSW 2000
Ph. (02) 805 0088

Sea Life International
27 Alfreda Street
Coogee
Sydney NSW 2034
Ph. (02) 665 6335

In addition to the instructional diving and dive charter companies detailed below, over 200 dive shops around Australia provide a variety of services to the local or visiting diver. Many of these shops also provide gear and equipment hire services.

New South Wales

1   Lord Howe Island

Sea Life International
In addition to diving instruction courses along the Queensland and New South Wales coast, they offer specialist diving holiday packages to Lord Howe Island.

27 Alfreda Street
Coogee
Sydney NSW 2034
Ph. (02) 665 6335

2   Byron Bay

Byron Bay Dive Centre
This dive centre offers the newcomer a comprehensive programme, with groups limited to eight persons. At the end of each five-day course, an international diving certificate is obtainable. For the experienced diver, they offer package adventure tours to various locations around Byron Bay.

9 Lawson Street
Byron Bay NSW 2481
Ph. (066) 85 6587 or 85 7149

3   Coffs Harbour & The Solitary Islands

Dive Quest
This group owns a fully equipped dive charter vessel, *Divequest II*, operated by fully qualified coxswains and instructors. They operate daily dive charters, dive holiday packages, holiday dive courses, and sell dive, surf and beach gear.

53 Beach Street
Woolgoolga NSW 2456
Ph. (066) 54 2771

4   Sydney Area

Dive 2000
Dive 2000 has over ten fully certified instructors, and offer a variety of courses. They have various specialty courses such as Underwater Photography or Wreck Diving. All local dives operate from their 7.2-metre Shark Cat diving vessel, *Dive 2000-Tasman Encounter*. They operate special charters, take group bookings, and have scuba equipment sales and service, secondhand scuba sales and scuba hire.

2 Military Road
Neutral Bay
Sydney NSW 2089
Ph. (02) 953 7783

Sea Life International
Based in Sydney, this specialised diving travel agency also offers instructional diving courses and charters in the Sydney area.

See (1) above for details

5   Jervis Bay

Jervis Bay Sea Sports
This dive centre, with its charter boat *Sea Life III* and team of instructors, runs both full-time and part-time dive courses. Their own lodge provides comfortable accommodation, and they have a complete range of rentals, sales and services. They also offer holiday packages for the experienced diver, and their boat is available for charter.

47 Owen Street
Huskisson NSW 2540
Ph. (044) 41 5012 or 41 5598

Victoria

6   Wilson's Promontory

Polperro Charters
This outfit offers group charter upon the *Polperro II*, a 14-metre, nine-berth boat with an in-built compressor. It is an excellent dive charter boat, with full facilities.

Port Franklin VIC 3964
Ph. (059) 88 8437

7   Port Phillip Bay

Diver Instruction Services
This company offers instruction from basic to advanced levels. They have air fills and gear hire at their outlets in Beaumaris and Portsea. They operate dive charters to southern Port Phillip Bay, Phillip Island, Flinders Island and Wilson's Promontory from their boat, *Osprey*. Their Divers' Lodge at Blairgowrie offers excellent accommodation and facilities.

34 East Concourse
Beaumaris
Melbourne VIC 3193
Ph. (03) 589 2084 (Sales, Air, Hire)
     (03) 589 5474 (FAUI Certification)

Melbourne Diving Services
This is a full dive shop, with compressor
sales and service. It has a PADI Five
Star Training Facility and Instructor
Development Centre, with boat charter.

144 Bell Street
Heidelberg
Melbourne VIC 3081
Ph. (03) 459 4432 or 459 4111

8   Bass Strait

Polperro Charters
Boat charter to the islands of Bass Strait
aboard *Polperro II*. Weekend, weekly
and fortnightly charters are available, as
well as limited day charters.

See (6) above for details

Tasmania

9   East Coast

Bicheno Dive Centre
This company has boat charter, diving
courses up to instructor level, and a full
diving hire service. They provide lodge-
style accommodation at the centre, and
have a range of diving holidays.

4 Tasman Highway
Bicheno TAS 7215
Ph. (003) 75 1138

South Australia

10   Adelaide Area

Adelaide Skindiving Centre
This full dive shop with sales, service
and hire is regarded as one of the best-
stocked dive shops in Australia. They
have a charter boat operation, and offer
scuba diving training.

7 Compton Street
Adelaide SA 5000
Ph. (08) 51 6144 or 51 6140

11   Port Lincoln Area

*Port Lincoln Skindiving and Surfing
Centre*
This centre has a complete range of dive
gear for hire and offers fast and clean air
fills. They have a range of dive tours and
diving courses.

73 Mortlock Terrace
Port Lincoln SA 5606
Ph. (086) 82 4428

12   South Australian Islands

Falie Project
This ketch is available for charter
around the islands off South Australia's
coastline. Accommodation aboard the
Falie is in four two-berth cabins and
three four-berth cabins with shower and
toilet facilities, laundry and dining room.

No. 1 Berth
Port Adelaide SA 5015
Ph. (08) 47 3658

Western Australia

13   South Coast

Australasian Diving Centre
This centre offers its services throughout
Western Australia. It provides
professional instruction courses from
basic scuba diving to instructor level,
and also operates various diving tours.

259 Stirling Highway
Claremont
Perth WA 6010
Ph. (09) 384 3552 or 384 3966

Perth Diving Academy
This is a full dive shop, offering
instruction at all levels. They operate a
boat charter service, and serve as a
sales, service and hire outlet for diving
gear. They have escorted diving holidays
for the experienced diver.

281 Wanneroo Road
Nollamara
Perth WA 6061
Ph. (09) 344 1562 or 334 7844

14   Rottnest Island & Perth Area

Both the *Perth Diving Academy* and
Australasian Diving Centre listed above
service the Rottnest Island and Perth
area for all diving needs.

See (13) above for details

15   Dongara & The Abrolhos Islands

The *Australasian Diving Centre* listed
above also extends its operations to this
area.

See (13) above for details

Batavia Coast Charters
Batavia Coast Charters operates from
Geraldton, Kalbarri and Dongara to the
Abrolhos Islands. Its 16.5-metre luxury
cruiser is fully fitted, including
accommodation, for all diving needs.

Lot 14
Port Leander Drive
Dongara WA 6525
Ph. (099) 48 1222

16   Exmouth Area

'The Gun' Fishing Charters
Although primarily geared for fishing
charters, *The Gun* is a 14-metre charter
vessel and can be hired for skin diving
off the coast. They also provide
extended island tours, and cater for
limited diving tours.

Murat Road
Exmouth WA 6707
Ph. (099) 49 1094

17   Broome & the Rowley Shoals

The *Perth Diving Academy* offers live-
aboard trips on its charter vessel to the
Rowley Shoals during August and
September. The *Australasian Diving
Centre* also operates here. Its vessel, the
Jodi Anne, conducts diving tours in the
area.

See (13) above for details

Northern Territory

18   Darwin Area

Territory Diving Services
This is a professional dive store which
operates a reliable charter service to the
local and distant dive sites around
Darwin. They conduct diving courses of
various levels, and have the widest range
of diving equipment for sale and hire in
the territory.

Shop 9
Fannie Bay Place
Darwin NT 5790
Ph. (089) 81 7665

Queensland

19   Cairns & Far North Queensland

Coral Sea Diving Services
This group offers a comprehensive range
of diving packages to some of the best
dive sites around the Great Barrier Reef.
They run scuba diving instruction
courses, and are an outlet for diving and
scuba gear.

Box 122
Port Douglas QLD 4871
Ph. (070) 98 5254 or 98 5710

Lizard Island
This island has some excellent diving
opportunities, and Air Queensland
packages several diving tours to the
island. It has full scuba diving facilities
and all dive sites are accessible by the
resort's dive boat.

C/- Air Queensland
62 Abbott Street
Cairns QLD 4870
Ph. (070) 50 4305

MV Esperance Star

The *Esperance Star* is for certified divers wishing to explore the marine life of the Great Barrier Reef. They operate a seven-day 'Lizard Island and Northern Great Barrier Reef Dive Cruise', anchoring at night in the quiet protection of the reef lagoons.

Seaboard Charters
14 Yorkeys Knob
Cairns QLD 4870
Ph. (070) 55 7235 or 51 9436

Reef Explorer Cruises

Reef Explorer Cruises operates four vessels, all fully equipped for diving around the Great Barrier Reef. These offer a variety of diving excursions from Cairns and Lizard Island to the dive sites of the Ribbon Reefs. They have both scheduled cruises and private charters.

49 Abbott Street
Cairns QLD 4870
Ph. (070) 51 6566

20 Townsville Area

Mike Ball Watersports

Mike Ball Watersports own and operate two large live-in dive boats, *Watersport* and *Supersport*. Their training facility and retail shop are combined in the one complex, especially designed for scuba training. They have a variety of dive packages for the certified diver around the reefs.

252-256 Walker Street
Townsville QLD 4810
Ph. (077) 72 3022

TSMV Coralita

The *Coralita* is a luxury dive vessel fitted out with a licensed bar, chef-prepared meals, a hostess, and room for just 12 divers. Both the Northern and Southern Coral Seas, and the Ribbon Reefs are regular destinations for their diving tours. Individual charters are available.

Barrier Reef Cruises
PO Box 6605
Cairns Mail Centre
Cairns QLD 4870
Ph. (070) 53 7477

21 Whitsunday Area

Barrier Reef Diving Services

This is the longest established dive training facility in the Whitsundays. They have introductory dive courses, open-water scuba certificate courses, and advanced and specialty courses. They also operate a variety of fully accommodated dive courses. Their diving tours for the certified diver visit a number of sites around the Whitsundays and Great Barrier Reef. They are a retail outlet for all diving needs and equipment hire.

The Esplanade
Airlie Beach QLD 4802
Ph. (079) 46 6204

H2O Sportz Dive Centre

This dive centre at the Hamilton Island Resort offers a variety of dive courses, and specialty courses. They have a retail section and equipment hire. For the certified diver there are day trips aboard one of Hamilton Island's luxury vessels to dive sites around the Whitsundays or helicopter trips out to their fixed pontoon on the outer reef.

Hamilton Island Resort
Post Office
Hamilton Island NTH QLD 4803
Ph. (079) 46 9144

Hayman Island Resort

Hayman Island has a complete dive shop, full service, a photographic laboratory, a purpose-built high-speed dive boat and a training pool. The island boasts a number of spectacular dive sites around its reefs.

Hayman Island QLD 4741
Ph. (079) 46 9100 or
    (008) 07 5025 (Toll free)

22 Gladstone Area

Heron Island

The dive shop on Heron Island has a complete range of diving and snorkelling gear, available for either hire or purchase. There are full resort facilities on the island, and dive courses are conducted every week commencing on Sundays and lasting seven days. There are also qualified divers' packages. Heron Island is internationally recognised as *the place* to dive on Australia's Great Barrier Reef.

C/- P & O Resorts
482 Kingsford Smith Drive
Brisbane QLD 4007
Ph. (07) 268 8224

Lady Elliot Island

Specialised scuba diving courses to certificate level are available on Lady Elliot Island. The island's dive shop supplies all equipment. A special attraction for divers is the underwater trail which is clearly marked by nylon rope for easy guidance while diving. There are also dive packages for the certified diver.

C/- Aquarius Travel Service
38 Taylor Street
Ashburton VIC 3147
Ph. (03) 25 8863

Tropic Rover

Ron Isbel has over 25 years of diving experience along the Great Barrier Reef. His vessel, the *Tropic Rover*, is a 16-metre, fully equipped vessel, with accommodation in five two-berth private cabins.

13 Auckland Street
Gladstone QLD 4680
Ph. (079) 72 1680

23 Southern Queensland

Sunreef Diving Services

This group offers basic and advanced diving courses, and full-day dive trips aboard their vessel, *The Sundiver*, to Moreton Island and reefs off the Sunshine Coast. They provide dive gear hire, sales and service at their dive shop.

40 River Esplanade
Mooloolaba QLD 4557

Ph. (071) 44 5656 or 44 5545

Information Sources

Diving Associations

Federation of Australian Underwater
    Instructors (FAUI)
PO Box 246
Tuart Hill
Perth WA 6060
Ph. (09) 344 7844

This federation can recommend diving instructors throughout Australia.

Professional Association of Diving
  ˙Instructors (PADI)
181 Elizabeth Street
Sydney NSW 2000
Ph. (02) 267 8020

This association can recommend diving training facilities throughout Australia.

National Association of Underwater
    Instructors (NAUI)
PO Box 183
Capalaba
Brisbane QLD 4157
Ph. (07) 390 3113

This association can recommend good dive shops and scuba diving instructors throughout Australia. They run courses for certified divers to become instructors.

Australian Underwater Federation
PO Box 1006
Civic Square
Canberra ACT 2608
Ph. (062) 88 5374

General information source for most underwater sports, including diving.

Fishing

There are more anglers in Australia than devotees of any other sport. Almost everyone picks up a rod and reel at some time in their life and every Australian state can boast recognised fishing havens, from the world-famous reefs off the Queensland coast — home of big-game marlin — to the fast-flowing, shallow streams of inland Tasmania where rainbow trout proliferate.

The travelling fisherman has in Australia some of the most exciting angling opportunities in the world. The contrasts in fishing styles and geography are matched by the range of species and the great distances which the angler might travel in pursuit of his sport.

There are some remarkable indigenous fish, more than a fair share of global-wandering species, and even a few successful imports like brown and rainbow trout.

There are many opportunities for both light and heavy tackle fishing. You can fish for wild trout in alpine eucalyptus forests or rolling grasslands, chase barramundi and other exciting sport fish in the tropical estuaries and floodplains of the north, or hunt the cobalt currents for massive gamefish like giant black marlin, shark and tuna. If a fishing enthusiast were to design a country as an ideal fishing destination, he'd have a hard time creating anything better than Australia.

Wilderness and remote areas both on and off-shore are reached by fast transportation operated by people who know their country. The world-class fishing experience in Australia is a heady mixture of comfort and challenge.

Nevertheless, the best can elude you if you don't have the right information and guidance. Australian anglers are used to the unstructured nature of our fishing. They are accustomed to finding their own fish and think nothing of taking half a lifetime to become proficient at it. Visiting anglers don't have that luxury. And, until recently, very little had been done to help them surmount the twin hurdles of locating good local guidance and suitable gear.

Today, things are changing. Fishing package holidays to many destinations are being developed and local services are also improving.

The main kinds of fishing in Australia are trout fishing, blue-water gamefishing, tropical sportfishing, and fishing from the beaches and rocks. General freshwater fishing is also important. The highlands of New South Wales, Victoria and Tasmania are the prize areas for trout fishing.

In Tasmania, the lakes of the Central Highlands provide the best trout fishing in the state. In the south-west wilderness area, the trout from Lake Pedder and the Gordon River are fabled for their size. Indeed, Tasmanian brown trout are among the largest in the world.

The New South Wales township of Adaminaby in Snowy Mountains country — an area famous for its lakes, rivers and streams — is surrounded by some of the best trout waters in the state. Brown and rainbow trout are caught in Lake Eucumbene and its tributaries.

Rainbow trout predominate upstate in the New England region, though brown trout are also found.

When it comes to gamefishing, far north Queensland, around Cairns and the Great Barrier Reef, has won world acclaim for its record-breaking giant black marlin.

A fleet of modern charter launches operates from Cairns to the big gamefishing grounds which also provide mackerel, turrum, tuna, barracuda, sailfish and other tropical fighting fish. The light tackle scene also offers good sport. Nearby Townsville and the waters of Cape Bowling Green provide exciting gamefishing for the mercurial sailfish.

Barramundi is the big drawcard for game fishermen in the Northern Territory. The reasons for its popularity include its fighting ability, handsome appearance and good eating qualities. Some of Australia's best light tackle sportfishing is found in the coastal waters of the Northern Territory. Queenfish, Spanish mackerel, longtail tuna, giant trevally, threadfin salmon and barracuda are common.

In South Australia, Tumby Bay provides a gateway to the Sir Joseph Banks Group of Islands. This is a popular spot with game fishermen. The Coffin Bay area is a mecca for fishermen looking for whiting, trevally, salmon, garfish, Tommy Ruffs, flathead and snapper.

Exmouth, in Western Australia, is another big gamefishing area, particularly known for its black marlin, sailfish and sharks.

In New South Wales, the southern coastal towns of Eden, Merimbula and Bermagui are major gamefishing areas. In Bermagui, particularly around Montague Island, the reefs and submarine canyons attract marlin, tuna and sharks.

In Victoria, East Gippsland, Mallacoota Inlet and Gypsy Point are among the state's finest gamefishing areas. Tuna and marlin are varieties you can expect to find here, and there are southern bluefin tuna off Portland in the west of the state.

Tasmania's main gamefishing area is off the Tasman Peninsula around Eaglehawk Neck.

Australia also offers much in the way of surf fishing. The east coast of New South Wales has many long sandy beaches and imposing sandstone cliffs which are popular places to fish. The best surf and rock fishing areas are north of Port Stephens where beaches predominate, with only short rocky outcrops in between.

Fraser Island, off the coast of Queensland, is a paradise for the amateur fisherman. Its 126-kilometre length makes it the largest sand island in the world.

Running almost parallel with the mainland between Gympie and Bundaberg, it offers surf beach and rock fishing on the Pacific Ocean side and sheltered water fishing and crabbing along its Sandy Strait shores, with almost untouched shallow water gamefishing between Wathamba Creek and the mainland.

Not far from the New South Wales/Queensland border, the twin towns of Forster/Tuncurry, on

Seasonal Fishing Guide

Type of Fishing	Summer (Dec-Feb)	Autumn (March-May)	Winter (June-August)	Spring (Sept-Nov)
Trout Fishing	Highlands of NSW, Victoria and Tasmania	As for summer	NSW: Season closed June-Sept inclusive VIC: Season closed June-Sept inclusive TAS: Season closed June-July inclusive	NSW VIC TAS Some good early stream fishing
General Freshwater Fishing	South-eastern states for cod, bass, perch	As for summer	NSW: cod in northern areas & perch in lakes VIC: perch in lakes	NSW: cod and some bass in northern districts VIC: cod QLD: bass
Bluewater Gamefishing	East coast: marlin, kingfish, shark, tuna West coast: kingfish, marlin, shark, tuna NT: sailfish, shark, tuna SA: Great white shark	As for summer NSW: yellowfin, tuna QLD: sailfish S.A. Great white shark	NSW: big kingfish & very long yellowfin tuna until early July QLD: mackerel and kingfish VIC: bluefin tuna on the west coast WA: mackerel and tuna	Small tuna species prolific in NSW and QLD Mako sharks follow tuna schools Early kingfish in NSW & QLD
Tropical Sportfishing	QLD: barramundi, jacks, queenfish, trevally NT: jacks, threadfin, salmon, queenfish, tarpon WA: queenfish, trevally, estuary cod, jacks	QLD: As for summer, except barramundi slow NT: As for summer WA: As for summer. Good barramundi	QLD: mackerel, tarpon, barramundi, saratoga, jacks NT: saratoga, jacks, barramundi, tarpon WA: barramundi, queenfish, trevally, jacks	QLD: jacks, queenfish, trevally, cod NT: barramundi, jacks, trevally, mackerel WA: barramundi, trevally, queenfish, jacks.

opposite sides of the entrance to Wallis Lake, provide great fishing opportunities for both the amateur and professional fisherman. Deep-sea, beach, rock and lake fishing are all possible here.

No matter where the angler travels around the great Australian land mass, from the Gulf region of the Northern Territory to the waters of the Great Australian Bight, chasing fish for sport will always provide the ultimate in enjoyment and satisfaction.

Locations

New South Wales

Trout fishing in the lakes and rivers of the Snowy Mountains and New England rates as some of the best fishing available. Elsewhere in the state, other lakes also carry good stocks of fish. The Murray cod, for example, is the recognised 'king' of the river. Other species are catfish, yellow belly, redfin, eel, silver perch, bass and European carp. On the coast, shark, mackerel, jewfish, blackfish, bream, drummer, snapper and kingfish are found. At dawn and dusk especially, the New South Wales coastal waters have the drawing power of a magnet. This is when most fish species are frenetically active, biting often and in large numbers.

1 In the highland areas of the **Snowy Mountains**, a favourite haunt is the township of Adaminaby. Here, rainbow and brown trout species thrive in the waters of Lake Eucumbene. The lake is 14 kilometres from the town.

Trout tours are available using trolling and harling bait methods, or evening fly sessions. You can venture further afield on the Eucumbene and Murrumbidgee Rivers or visit the reservoir at Tantangara. On the western side of the Great Dividing Range, at Khancoban, the popular Fly Fisherman's Clinic takes students to the upper Murray River and other fishing locations in the area.

2 **Lord Howe Island**, located 720 kilometres north-east of Sydney, is a remote fishing paradise with an abundance of marine life. The predominant species in the clear blue waters are yellowtail, king-fish, yellowfin tuna, dolphin fish, whaco, blue and black marlin. The best way to enjoy fishing here is by taking up one of the package tours on offer.

Victoria

Most offshore fishing in Victoria is confined to the bigger bays and inlets. In Port Phillip and Western-port, most fishing is done between September and late March, largely because the waters here are too cold in winter. Flathead can be caught in Port Phillip through-out the year, while Corio Bay is outstanding for snapper, usually caught in great numbers along the coast to Queenscliff. The reefs of Mornington, Frankston and Rickett's Point are also excellent locations for this very popular fish.

Mallacoota Inlet and Gypsy Point in East Gipps-

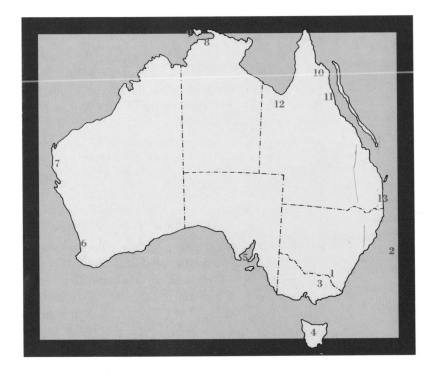

Rock fishing is one of Australia's most popular forms of angling - and also the most dangerous!

LEIGH HEMMINGS

land are the state's finest gamefishing territories, with regular catches of tuna, marlin and barramundi. The best inland places are found on the Murray River and in the lakes and streams of the Snowy Mountains.

3   The **Snowy Mountains** feature in Victoria's fishing scene, too, as the border between Victoria and New South Wales follows the left bank of the **Murray River.** Your fishing pursuit will, of course, take you across the border at times in search of trout, Murray cod and redfin. The rain-fed streams and rivers offer excellent sport. Victoria has a year-round season. The region is also an excellent location for combining fishing with horse riding, kayaking, bicycling and walking.

Tasmania

The cool moist climate and mountainous terrain of Australia's island state, Tasmania, make it a marvellous freshwater fishing venue. Since it is endowed with many lakes and streams, anglers can pursue their sport with the knowledge that a good catch is almost always guaranteed.

4   The **Central Highlands,** with its large cluster of lakes, is the main trout fishing area in Tasmania. The south-west wilderness areas, Lake Pedder and the Gordon River boast some of the largest brown trout in the world. In addition, the English redfin, perch, eel and the native blackfish can be found in the network of lakes and streams.

South Australia

5   Fine trout fishing can also be enjoyed in South Australia, almost on **Adelaide's** back doorstep. Only 15 kilometres from the heart of the city, the Onkaparinga River, a tributary of the River Torrens, yields brown and rainbow trout of impressive size. It meanders from the sea at Port Noarlunga through the Adelaide Hills, and down through a spectacular valley, known as the Gorge.

South Australia is also fortunate in having some excellent shore-based fishing. Outer Harbour and the Port River are close to Adelaide, and it is in these waters that the big mulloway can be found. Bream are also prolific, and small salmon, silver whiting and mullet are frequently present in large numbers. From Cape Jervis to Victor Harbor, an exciting and beautiful stretch of coastline unfolds — from the rolling hills of Fisheries Beach to the breathtaking terrain of Aaron and Deep Creeks. The Coffin Bay area is also a favoured location for fishermen looking for whiting, trevally, salmon, garfish, Tommy Ruffs, flathead and snapper.

Western Australia

Although Western Australia possesses few freshwater systems of any real significance, it does boast numerous gamefishing grounds of enormous potential, and many anglers are attracted by the challenge.

6   Just south of Perth, **Mandurah** is a very popular fishing location. Inland you can fish the Murray River, and offshore there are excellent catches of jewfish, pink snapper, sand whiting and herring. Mandurah's famous crabs and prawns are also fished here. Perth also boasts a prolific marlin ground just offshore.

7   **Exmouth,** near the continental shelf, is renowned for its marlin, sailfish and most other light gamefish varieties. The Dampier Archipelago and Port Hedland attract many enthusiastic anglers who recognise the gamefishing potential of the region. Fishing mainly from launches, the most regular catches include species such as mackerel, yellowfin tuna, wahoo, yellowtail kingfish, hammerhead and bronze whaler sharks, and the occasional mako west of Rottnest.

LEIGH HEMMINGS

Northern Territory

Barramundi is the big drawcard for game fishermen in the Northern Territory. The barramundi inhabits both salt and fresh waters along Australia's tropical north coast and it is exploited commercially for its superb flesh. One of the reasons for its popularity is the incredible size it can attain — up to 50 kilograms in some cases.

The abundance of barramundi in the Northern Territory is due largely to the area's high rainfall. Some 177 centimetres of rain falls annually, and most of this occurs between November and March. Since the amount of rainfall is directly proportional to the availability of fish, most anglers hope for a good wet season and an even distribution of rain.

8   Trips may be organised from **Darwin** to explore these wonderful fishing grounds.

9   An exciting alternative is to visit **Bathurst Island** and to stay at the Fishing Lodge at Barra Base. From this wilderness lodge, anglers can explore some of the best game and estuary fishing in Australia. Only 40 minutes from Darwin by air, Bathurst Island is the home of the Tiwi, an Aboriginal tribe which has lived on the island for thousands of years. They have granted rights to the people who run the lodge to take visitors on fishing tours throughout the island.

Apart from barramundi, the other prized fish are threadfin salmon, mangrove jacks, bream, queenfish, tuna, trevally (jacks), shark, mackerel and many others.

MARK HANLON

Queensland

10 When it comes to game fishing in Australia, the far north of Queensland around **Cairns** and the spectacular coral formations that make up the Great Barrier Reef form the most coveted location, winning world acclaim for its record-breaking catches of black marlin. From September to December, blue water, big boats, big fish, and a blazing sun are the order of the day. Millions of dollars change hands when luxury gamefishing cruisers chase the world's greatest fish, the black marlin, which will leap for the sky and plunge to incredible depths in its fight for freedom.

Hundreds of wealthy international anglers, and some not so wealthy, make an annual pilgrimage to Cairns in quest of this majestic fish. It is not uncommon for big game boats to be booked years in advance just for the opportunity to conquer the marlin in its most important spawning ground in the world.

11 The waters around **Townsville and Mackay** are renowned for their reef fish. Mackerel are plentiful between August and October, while sweetlip and emperor are available all year round.

Whiting, flathead and bream are found along rivers, creeks and beaches, and salmon can be caught during the winter months. Barramundi are found in estuaries and inshore waters extending upstream to the freshwater reaches.

Townsville has become the central attraction for anglers wanting to tangle with sailfish and marlin. The waters off Cape Bowling Green, some 50 kilometres east of the harbour, contain the densest population of these fish yet discovered in Australia.

12 The waters of the remote **Gulf of Carpentaria** offer excellent fishing. The large numbers of fish can be attributed to the fact that the area is protected from commercial fishing, other than prawning, and both reef and sport fishing are practised here.

The Gulf boats a great variety of fish — red emperor, coral trout, cod, reef sharks and sweetlip for reef fishing, and mackerel, tuna, salmon, barracuda and trevally for sport fishing.

For visitors to the region, one operator runs a resort on Mornington Island out in the Gulf itself.

Back on the mainland, Dorunda Station also offers fishing holidays. This working cattle station has a 25-kilometre private lake that is well stocked with barramundi and saratoga, in addition to the waterways of the nearby Staaten and Wyaaba Rivers. An added attraction for visitors is the opportunity to observe the running of the cattle station. Dorunda is near Normanton, the isolated main town of this rugged region.

13 In **south Queensland,** Brisbane and Moreton Bay provide excellent fishing all year round, with good catches of cod, snapper, sweetlip, drummer, parrot and crabs. Outside Moreton Bay is some of the finest deep-sea and gamefishing to be found off the Australian coast. It is well catered for with charter vessels operating out of Brisbane.

Along the Sunshine Coast, stretching from Bribie Island to Noosa, the beaches, bays, rivers and lakes provide great catches all year round.

Large flathead and top-quality whiting are a feature of summer fishing in the Noosa River, with bream and tailor in the winter. On deep-sea reefs off Noosa, Mooloolaba and Caloundra, there are good catches of snapper, pearl pearch, parrot, mackerel, sweetlip, emperor and cod.

Fishing Contacts

Operators

The Finz Fishing Tours' Barra Base Lodge on Bathurst Island and their Townsville tour are mentioned below. Finz is the largest package tour operator in Australia and they also cover destinations in Cape York and at London Lakes in Tasmania. Tours are operated in conjunction with Australian Airlines. Contact Finz at the address under (9) below or inquire at any Australian Airlines office.

New South Wales

1 **Snowy Mountains**

Anglers Reach Lakeside Village
The Village offers both fishing and ski holidays in a beautiful mountain and lake setting on Lake Eucumbene.

John and Ada West offer trout tours on their specially equipped vessel *Relaxation 1,* which can take seven people out on the lake in search of rainbow and brown trout. They organise four-wheel-drive tours for those wishing to fish the local rivers and Tantangara reservoir.

Accommodation is provided in fully self-contained lodges and units. Fish caught by clients are kept in the freezer, or smoked overnight, if they cannot be eaten fresh. A full tackle hire service is also available.

For those wishing to relax after a day's fishing, a private spa and sauna is also available.

PO Box 30
Adaminaby NSW 2630
Ph. (064) 54 2276

Mike Spry's Fly Fisherman's Clinic
Mike Spry runs a live-in school for fly-fishermen in the alps of the Kosciusko National Park at Khancoban. Mike has been operating as a trout-fishing guide and fly-fishing instructor for over 12 years. Students attending the school stay at the nearby Alpine Inn Hotel-Motel at Khancoban.

Instruction throughout the five-day course includes lessons on the basics of fly-fishing: flies, insects, learning to cast, and general information about fishing rods and lines. These lessons take place both in the classroom and out in the field. A 15-seat bus transports students to selected fishing locations throughout the region, and an inflatable raft is used to navigate the upper Murray River, where students are also taken for tuition.

Each student is supplied with a complete range of fishing equipment, and picnics, barbecue lunches and

relaxed evenings lend an informal, friendly feel to the course.

Some previous experience in fly-fishing is recommended, though it is not compulsory.

Courses start on a Sunday and finish on Friday.

PO Box 7
Khancoban NSW 2642
Ph. (060) 76 9496

Motel Nimmitabel
John Killip offers excellent guided fly-fishing for trout from his motel at Nimmitabel, a small town 1,100 metres above sea level. He works on a one-to-one basis with beginners, people who want to brush up on technique, and experienced fly-fishermen who simply want to be guided to the best spots.

John knows the streams of the region well, and takes you to selected spots where the fertile waters support plump trout averaging three pounds in weight.

He supplies all your tackle needs and, with Margaret, provides pleasant motel accommodation and food.

Snowy Mountains Highway
Nimmitabel NSW 2631
Ph. (064) 54 6387

2 **Lord Howe Island**

Sportfishing Tours Pty Limited
This company operates trips to Lord Howe Island, on a 12-metre yacht which takes a maximum of six anglers. These expeditions are usually of four days' duration and eight hours is spent at sea each day.

Some tackle is available on board, and the amateur game fisherman is welcome to make use of this equipment. The serious angler, however, may wish to purchase additional line and tackle.

The package includes return airfare to Lord Howe Island ex-Sydney flying Norfolk Island Airways. Twin accommodation is provided at the Sea Breeze Lodge.

C/- Green Travel Service
2/114 Hampden Road
Artarmon
Sydney NSW 2064
Ph. (02) 411 4944

Victoria

3 **Snowy Mountains and Murray River**

Snowy Mountain Fishing Holidays
River and stream fishing is available at this resort, nine kilometres east of

Corryong. Fully self-contained accommodation houses up to six guests at a time.

Ron and Sarah Vise specialise in fly-fishing, and fly-tying facilities are available. Guests also have the opportunity to enjoy guided canoe trips on the nearby river.

Five evening meals are supplied on weekly holidays, and two evening meals on a three-day holiday. On the remaining nights, patrons are encouraged to dine out in one of the neighbouring towns.

Guests should provide their own general tackle, chest waders and rod and reel, although some limited rental is available.

PO Box 122
Corryong VIC 3707
Ph. (060) 76 8252

Tasmania

4 **Central Highlands and South West**

Jet-Fly Trout Guiding Services
Noel and Lois Jetson's colonial accommodation at Cressy is just 20 minutes from Launceston Airport in the north of the state. Guests can either stay caravan-style or in stone cabins.

Informal fishing tours operate from spring to autumn. Guests are taken in a four-wheel-drive vehicle to various fishing locations around Tasmania. The majority of these rivers and lakes lie in Tasmania's wilderness areas.

78 Main Street
Cressy TAS 7302
Ph. (003) 97 6272

London Lakes Fishing Resort
Guests staying at this resort in central Tasmania can fish in the private waters of Lake Samuel and Lake Big Jim. These waters offer excellent nymph and dry-fly fishing from the shores. London Lakes also operates tours of public waters within five to 30 minutes of the lodge, where brown, rainbow or brook trout can be found. Fishing guides are available on a one to three, or two to four basis.

The lodge itself was completed in 1984, and accommodates ten guests in five twin rooms. It was handcrafted from logs and stone, is panelled with rich Tasmanian timbers, and has in-floor control heating and open log fires. Food at the lodge is of a very high standard.

Rates include all meals and accommodation, an angling guide, waterproof clothing, angling licence, transport to angling waters and all equipment including waders and flies.

C/- Post Office
Bronte Park TAS 7140
Ph. (002) 89 1159

South Australia

5 **Adelaide and the South Australian Coast**

Recommended saltwater, deep sea and bay charters:

West Coast Charters
PO Box 9
Ceduna SA 5690
Ph. (086) 25 2654

Top of the Gulf Charters
8 Kleeman Street
Whyalla SA 5600
Ph. (086) 45 2817

Cape Jervis Charter Services
89 Darkana Way
Cape Jervis SA 5204
Ph. (085) 98 0222

Western Australia

6 **Mandurah**

Toucan Charters
Operating out of Mandurah, this charter company is run by Roger Curnow and has a fully surveyed 8.5-metre Sharkcat vessel. It is licensed to carry up to six passengers offshore or eight on the Murray River.

The Toucan is available for full or half-day charters, and a qualified master is included in the service. All fishing equipment is supplied.

20 Riverside Drive
Furnissdale WA 6210
Ph. (095) 35 3525

7 **Exmouth**

Capricorn Travel
Shane King is the angling expert here. He specialises in fishing holidays to Exmouth in Western Australia's north-west. Exmouth has three species of marlin, plenty of reef fish and offers a range of beach fishing and light tackle game fishing. The King family has been involved in Exmouth's commercial fishing industry for over 20 years.

A 15-metre charter boat, *The Bun*, is used to explore the Ningaloo reef system around Exmouth.

Capricorn Travel can arrange fully inclusive package holidays to Exmouth, a mecca for game fishermen, from almost anywhere in Australia.

Capricorn Travel
11 Church Street Northbridge
Perth WA 6000 Ph. (09) 227 8506

Northern Territory

8 **Darwin and the Top End Coast**

Top End Angling
This operator takes fishermen on trips through Arnhem Land in the east and along the north coast to the Western Australian border. Some of the fishing areas are located on Aboriginal land and private property with entry fees payable.

All tackle, boats, camping equipment and meals are included in the package. Four-wheel-drive vehicles provide transport from fishing locations. Barramundi is the main fish in this area.

Fly-fishermen are required to provide their own gear as none is available on the trips.

Maximum group size is six, and all tours leave from Darwin.

PO Box 37129
Winnellie
Darwin NT 5789
Ph. (089) 88 1260

9 **Bathurst Island**

Finz Barra Base Lodge
This has ten twin-share airconditioned rooms and excellent facilities including fish-freezing.

Their boats include the 7.9-metre *Sportfisher,* two centre console boats, and dinghies for estuary fishing. Professional guides help you make the best of your stay backed by full gear for purchase and hire. It is one of Australia's premier sportfishing operations.

Tours start on Saturdays and run for nine days, all year round.

GPO Box 2189
Canberra ACT 2601
Ph. (062) 47 6117

Queensland

10 **Cairns and Far North Queensland**

John & Barry Cross Specialized Sport Fishing Safaris
This offers a comprehensive range of fishing in far north Queensland. Tours are conducted to tropical freshwater streams, saltwater estuaries and headlands, and along inshore coral reefs around the Great Barrier Reef.

Their services cover light and heavy tackle game fishing for marlin and sailfish, and every aspect of line and fly fishing, as well as bait fishing.

Their estuary and freshwater fishing trips range from one day trips in the Cairns area to extended safaris throughout Cape York Peninsula.

Between them, John and Barry Cross have over 30 years of sportfishing knowledge to draw on.

PO Box 84
Earlville
Cairns QLD 4870
Ph. (070) 55 1641

Tropical sportfishing charters:

Gary Wright
C/- Cape York Wilderness Lodge
via Bamaga QLD 4876
Ph. (070) 50 4222

Going Places Travel, based in Cairns, also offer barramundi fishing holidays at Punsand Bay Private Reserve, located near the tip of Cape York. Five or eight-day trips are available and include a return flight from Cairns to Bamaga.

26 Abbott Street
Cairns QLD 4870
Ph. (070) 51 4055

11 **Townsville and Mackay**

Finz Fishing Tours
They offer an excellent weeklong tour to Townsville which provides accommodation at the Sheraton Breakwater Casino Hotel, your skipper and crew on a fast fully rigged gamefish craft, tackle, and refreshments at sea.

See (9) above for details

ALLAN MOULT

Hamilton Island Charters
This charter operation has game boats fully rigged for light and heavy tackle game fishing, as well as reef and bottom fishing. Their locally experienced game crews will take you fishing around the Whitsundays' 74 islands.

Cruising time from Hamilton Island to good fishing grounds varies from 45 to 90 minutes.

Hamilton Island
PMB Post Office
Mackay QLD 4740
Ph. (079) 46 9144

Other charters in the Townsville area are:
Calvin Tilley
Australian Pacific Charters
61 Livingstone Street
West End
Townsville QLD 4870
Ph. (077) 72 4205

Jim Dalling
4 Dahl Crescent
Wulguru
Townsville QLD 4811
Ph. (077) 78 1950

12 Gulf of Carpentaria

Birri Fishing Resort
This resort is located on Mornington
Island, 50 kilometres out in the gulf.
Guests are flown in from Mt Isa and
generally book by the week. This
isolated resort provides comfortable
accommodation for a maximum of 15
people and excellent reef and sport
fishing. All fishing is carried out within
sight of the resort, which means little
time is wasted on travel, and a fleet of
boats is provided for the use of guests. A
large variety of fish inhabit these waters
— coral trout, red emperor, cod, reef
sharks, mackerel, tuna and barracuda
may all be caught.

The Queensland Experience
152 Jubilee Terrace
Bardon
Brisbane QLD 4065
Ph. (07) 38 1611 or 38 3416

Dorunda Station
This huge property of 1,200 square
kilometres has its own airstrip and is
reached by air from Cairns; a journey of
one and a half hours. The station is also
a fishing resort and its many waterways
are under strict surveillance to prevent
poachers from fishing the rivers illegally.
The property incorporates the Staaten
National Park.
    Guests are flown to Dorunda, and
meals, accommodation and fishing
safaris are all included in the holiday.

PMB 16
via Normanton QLD 4890
Ph. (070) 53 4500

13 South Queensland

The following are fishing charter
operators:

Noosa Blue Water Charters
Noosa's Game Fishing Wharf
Gympie Terrace
Noosaville QLD 4566
Ph. (071) 46 1614 or 47 4909

Bob Jones
35-37 Thompson Crescent
Clontarf
Brisbane QLD 4019
Ph. (07) 283 3568

Klahlua Charters
126 Picton Parade
Wynnum
Brisbane QLD 4178
Ph. (07) 396 2149

Sunreef Diving Service
44 River Esplanade
Mooloolaba QLD 4557
Ph. (071) 44 5656

Information Sources

Fisheries Information Offices and Angling Clubs

New South Wales

Division of Fisheries
C/- Department of Agriculture
Ph. (02) 217 6110

Fisheries Information Officer
PO Box K220
Haymarket
Sydney NSW 2000
Ph. (02) 217 5093

Sydney Game Fishing Club
The Wharf
Watsons Bay
Sydney NSW 2030
Ph. (02) 337 5687

The Fishing Connection
68 Mulgoa Road
Mulgoa NSW 2750
Ph. (047) 73 8824

Detailed independent information on all
Australian fishing services. Tackle,
fishing holidays, charters, books, videos
and magazines are available.

Victoria

Victorian Fisheries and Wildlife Division
250 Victoria Parade
East Melbourne VIC 3002
Ph. (03) 450 8600

Victorian Game Fishing Club
186 Station Street
Aspendale
Melbourne VIC 3195
Ph. (03) 580 8846

Tasmania

Department of Sea Fisheries
23 Old Wharf
Hobart TAS 7000
Ph. (002) 30 8011

Inland Fisheries Commission
127 Davey Street
Hobart TAS 7000
Ph. (002) 23 6622

Tuna Club of Tasmania
103 Leslie Road
Kingston TAS 7150
Ph. (002) 39 6446

South Australia

South Australian Department of
  Fisheries
GPO Box 1625
Adelaide SA 5000
Ph. (08) 227 2788 or 227 2790

Western Australia

Department of Fisheries and Wildlife
108 Adelaide Terrace
Perth WA 6000
Ph. (09) 325 5988

Australian Anglers' Association
WA Division
12 Galahad Way
Carine
Perth WA 6020
Ph. (09) 448 5169

Australian National Sport
  Fishing Association
WA Branch
39 Groyder Way
Padbury
Perth WA 6025
Ph. (09) 401 3131

West Australian Trout & Freshwater
  Angling Association
95 Dean Road
Bateman
Perth WA 6155
Ph. (09) 332 7779

Northern Territory

Senior Licensing Officer
Department of Port and Fisheries
Cnr Harry Chan Avenue
  & Cavenagh Street
Darwin NT 5794
Ph. (089) 89 7514

Queensland

Department of Primary Industries
Division of Dairying and Fisheries
Mineral House
41 George Street
Brisbane QLD 4000
Ph. (07) 227 4111

Blue Fin Fishing and Social Club
Lilac Street
Inala
Brisbane QLD 4077
Ph. (07) 372 4334

Manly Game Fishing Club
114 Mountjoy Terrace
Manly QLD 4179
Ph. (07) 396 0114

MALCOLM HOLMES

Golf

To golfing enthusiasts, Australia is indeed 'the lucky country'. No long winter hiatus waiting for the snow to melt: our temperate climate enables golfers to play year round. Golf can be enjoyed at the end of a long, hot summer's day or savoured on a crisp, brisk winter's afternoon.

Australia has a high standard of private, semi-private and public courses with several championship courses. Most of the 18-hole golf courses in Australia have a professional instructor. As well as giving lessons, the 'pro' can answer any queries on the course layout and advise on dress regulations and equipment hire.

Nationwide, there are 320,000 affiliated male amateur golfers, and 1,000 professional golfers, as well as hundreds of thousands of social golfers. Australia is rated amongst the top five in the golfing world and can be proud of such golfing luminaries as Greg Norman ('The Great White Shark'), David Graham and Rodger Davis. The highlight of the Australian golf year is the Australian Open, held in November at different venues around Australia. In 1988, it will be held at Royal Sydney Golf Club.

In each state, the Golfing Association administers all events held within that state, services all the needs of the clubs under its jurisdiction and represents those clubs in union matters. Members pay annual fees to the Association.

In the capital cities, most of the private clubs will not accept visitors who do not have reciprocal membership unless, of course, they have been invited by a club member. Reciprocal membership varies from club to club: some accept reciprocal membership with only a few clubs in Australia and overseas, while others have quite a wide selection. A quick check can be made with the relevant golf club's office.

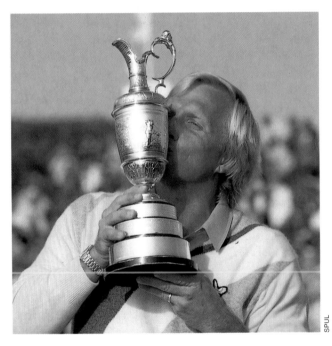

SPUL

While Greg Norman kisses yet another victor's cup, fellow champion Graham Marsh concentrates on his putt

In country areas, private clubs tend to welcome visitors.

City and country golf courses play host to golf clinics, 'get-away-from-it-all' golf weekends, week-long competitions, and tours. All of these provide ideal opportunities to sample one or more courses, meet a variety of people, and have instruction from the resident professional on a new and different course. Golf tours are sometimes the only way to play at private clubs unless the player is invited by a member. Sportsbiz is one operator which arranges golf tours; they even offer to pair golfers up with partners. Golf tours usually include pick-up and delivery, green fees,

18 holes of golf, booked starting times, course layout and hole-by-hole information, and sometimes an electric golf cart. Available for rental are matching sets of clubs and a wide range of golf shoes. Brochures on golfing packages are available from travel agents, and from organisations such as the NRMA, the Department of Sport and Recreation, the State Tourism Commissions, and airlines.

Golfing is growing in popularity amongst Australian youngsters. The Junior Pennants are fought as keenly as any adult competition. A lot of public golf courses hold school holiday golf clinics and welcome high school students who play golf as part of their physical education programme. The Jack Newton Junior Golf Foundation is an organisation responsible for the introduction, promotion and development of golf for kids in New South Wales. The Foundation holds coaching camps and runs clinics.

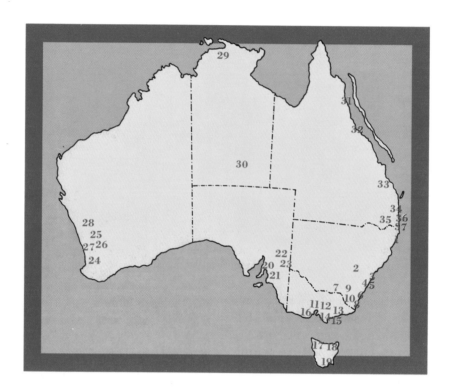

Locations

New South Wales

In the Sydney metropolitan area there are 69 affiliated golf courses and in country areas there are about 296. Couch is the most common grass, with kikuya found on a lot of country courses.

The main professional golf tournament, which attracts wide overseas interest, is the NSW Open, held in October at a host Sydney course. The venue changes each year. For the first time, Enterprise Sports Promotions is holding an Enterprise Sports Promotions Open at the Royal Canberra during 1988 with $500,000 in prize money.

The general consensus of opinion seems to be that the cream of Sydney's metropolitan golf courses are Royal Sydney at Rose Bay, the Australian at Rosebery (established in 1882, it is the oldest in the state), and Elanora Golf Club at Elanora Heights. Not surprisingly, the only way to get a game at any of the above courses is as a guest of a member on an invitation day or as part of an inter-club team.

1 **Terranora Lakes Country Club** is one of the most complete sporting complexes in Australia. As well as an 18-hole, 5,400-metre, par 70 golf course with magnificent views, they offer bowls, tennis, touch football, cricket, hockey, softball, clay target shooting and squash. Terranora is only a short drive from Coolangatta Airport, an hour or so from Brisbane, and a full day's drive from Sydney. If arranging a golfing tour, it is wise to check whether any competitions or special events conflict with your preferred time of visit to the course. Time-share accommodation is being built.

2 **Duntry League Country Club** at Orange, 265 kilometres north-west of Sydney, is a must for the golfer who enjoys a challenging course and the opportunity to stay in a magnificent 19th-century mansion.

The course is a 6,061-metre, par 70 course. Features like the 17th hole, which is a 170-metre par three with water-carry to an elevated green, and the almost impossible 386-metre par four 15th hole, make this a memorable course on which to play.

When the visitor wants to relax away from the

greens, there are tennis courts, full-size billiard tables, and interesting tourist attractions nearby.

3 Half an hour's drive from Sydney on the northern beaches is **Long Reef Golf Course**. Situated on a prominent headland, the course is a true links layout with the Pacific Ocean on three sides. This 5,963-metre par 72 championship course has been the location for many major amateur championships. Long Reef is known for its lack of trees, exposed fairways, uphill and downhill lies and great greens. Visitors are welcome and arrangements for a game can be made through the club's office or professional. Open day is Wednesday. There is no accommodation at the course, but there are excellent motels in Collaroy.

4 In close proximity to the city, **Eastlake** at Kingsford was built on a government stipulation that a public course be built alongside The Lakes Golf Course on Crown land. This 5,420-metre, par 70 course is known for its friendly atmosphere and visitors can play by making arrangements through the club. It has an interesting layout with an outward nine leading directly away from the clubhouse and the homebound nine wending its way side by side with the front nine. No accommodation is provided in the golf club, but with the variety of city accommodation only a ten-minute drive away there is really no need.

5 Only a few minutes away from Eastlake, **Bonnie Doon** in Pagewood has a long tradition dating back to 1907. The 5,910-metre, par 72 course has a championship layout — eight holes out, ten holes in. Visitors are welcome on open day (Monday). The club still claims the world record mark for a woman golfer. June Howe shot a 65 in 1956. No accommodation is provided on the course, but there is ample available nearby.

6 **Dormie House** in Moss Vale, a two-hour drive south of Sydney, is one of the most popular golf links in the state. The 5,770-metre, par 71 course is mainly flat and is set in beautiful countryside with an abundance of trees. A creek meanders through the golf course. The traditional 1930s-style clubhouse has 33 bedrooms, all with ensuites. The feel of the place is English and, in keeping with tradition, jackets and ties are required for dinner.

7 The **Wagga Wagga Country Club** is situated on the foreshores of Lake Albert in the heart of the Riverina, midway between Melbourne and Sydney. A 6,084-metre, par 72 championship course, Wagga Wagga Country Club hosts the pennant match between Sydney and Melbourne golfers each year. The course has excellent grass greens and fairways, with a multitude of trees and bunkers to make it interesting and challenging. Visiting golfers are most welcome, either in competitions or socially. The city of Wagga Wagga itself has good accommodation, licensed clubs, restaurants and nightlife.

8 On the far south coast of New South Wales, 460 kilometres south of Sydney, is the **Pambula-Merimbula Golf Club**. The 5,513-metre, par 72 course has large greens set in natural bushland. Wildlife is a feature of the course — grazing kangaroos, kookaburras and magpies are plentiful. The most popular tournament in the area is the Sapphire Coast Week of Golf which starts on the first Saturday in October.

Australian Capital Territory

9 Befitting Australia's capital, **Royal Canberra Golf Club** is maintained in top condition, being ranked among the best five courses in Australia. Located on the shores of Lake Burley Griffin, midway between Sydney and Melbourne, Royal Canberra was the scene of the Dunlop Open won by Gary Player in 1970. Visitors have the chance of playing this superb 6,138-metre, par 72 course on Mondays, Thursdays and Fridays, provided they have a letter of introduction from their home club. The club's restaurant and bar may be used by visiting golfers.

10 The **Yowani Country Club**, in Canberra, also offers golfers a beautiful tree-lined course. This 6,334-metre, par 72 course has well-bunkered greens on most holes, with water posing an additional hazard on four holes — the 17th is virtually a double water carry. Yowani welcomes visitors seven days a week. The club boasts one of Canberra's finest restaurants, Oodles, which is open from Tuesday to Saturday.

Victoria

Victoria's capital city, Melbourne, claims to be 'the golf capital of Australia'. In fact, there are few cities in the world that have more world-class golf courses than Melbourne. There are approximately 60 clubs in the metropolitan area and 270 plus in the country areas. There are about 87,000 male affiliated members in Victoria, in addition to thousands of social players.

The main event on the Victorian golfing calendar is the Victorian Open, held in Melbourne in February.

The main concentration of golf courses lies 77 kilometres south of Melbourne in an area known as the Sand Belt. This undulating land, covered with fine grasses and indigenous trees, contains many championship courses, some of which were designed in consultation with the famous Scottish golf course architect, Dr Alistair Mackenzie. The three top clubs in the area are the Royal Melbourne Golf Club, the Commonwealth Golf Club and Kingston Heath Golf Club. Most of the private clubs along the Sand Belt won't accept visitors without reciprocal membership. But there are many beautifully designed country courses outside the metropolitan area which do.

11 Some 25 kilometres north-east of Melbourne is the **Yarrambat Golf Club**. This is one of Melbourne's newest and longest courses (6,215 metres)

Seaside golf course near Sydney

with a par 72 and a course record of 70. The hilly, wide-open course has impressive views of the nearby Whittlesea Ranges and the South Morang Gorge. Visitors are welcome.

12 **Ringwood Golf Course** (23 kilometres east of Melbourne) is a hilly course with lots of trees. This 5,263-metre, par 69 public course has an unusual 8th hole at a 90⁰ angle — imagine teeing-off! The abundance of trees and the dam on the 16th and 17th holes makes for challenging golf for regulars and newcomers alike.

13 Built on part of the old Royal Melbourne course is **Sandringham Golf Course**, a 14-kilometre drive south of Melbourne. It's a 5,559-metre, par 69, tree-lined public course and visitors may play on any day of the week. The back nine holes feature a few well-bunkered difficult holes.

14 The **National Golf Club** at Cape Schanck opened in November 1986. It features a public course (5,615-metres, par 70), and a private members-only course is being constructed. The public course offers rolling valleys and steep, tree-covered dunes, with spectacular views from many of the tees and greens.

15 The **Peninsula Country Golf Club** is 45 minutes south of Melbourne on the lovely Mornington Peninsula. There are two courses: the North Course (5,900 metres, par 71) and the championship South Course (6,148 metres, par 72). Both are open to guests with reciprocal membership of the main clubs in each state or overseas, or as guests of a member. A true country club, the facilities offered include accommodation, three tennis courts, a bowling green and swimming pool, and conference facilities. The Peninsula runs clinics and is host to many interstate golf weeks.

16 **Anglesea Golf Club** is situated 109 kilometres south-west of Melbourne. This 5,965-metre course boasts 70 bunkers, undulating watered fairways and many kangaroos — which often form a gallery for players. Par for the course is 73 and the course record is 68.

Tasmania

Tasmania, Australia's most southern state, has 9,106 male affiliated members in 61 clubs. Although most of the courses are private, visitors are welcome. Three of the top courses are Woodrising Golf Club on the north-west coast, the Royal Hobart Golf Club and the Tasmania Golf Club in Hobart. The Tasmanian Open is held in the early part of the year in Hobart.

17 Situated ten kilometres from Devonport Airport in northern Tasmania is **Shearwater Country Club.** It offers the complete holiday: golf, tennis, swimming,

a games room and a playground for children. Guests literally step out of their suites onto the first tee. A 5,335-metre, par 68, nine-hole course, it appeals to long shot players.

18 At **Launceston Federal Country Club** there are so many diversions it's possible to stay here and not hit the golf course at all for the first few days. This country club boasts a casino, disco, cabaret shows, tennis courts, swimming pool and horse riding. The 18-hole, 4,807-metre, par 68 course is set around a lake with views of the Derwent River.

19 **Rosny Park Public Golf Course,** in the Hobart suburb of Rosny Park, will appeal to the 'short hitter'. This 18-hole, par 68 course is only 4,807 metres in length. Great views of the Derwent River, plus a quick round, make this a popular course for locals and visitors alike. Visitors are made to feel welcome.

South Australia

South Australia's dry climate is great for golf. There are 25,981 male affiliated members in South Australia, as well as plenty of social golfers. The metropolitan area has 12 private and eight public clubs. In the country area, there are about 150 clubs. Most of these are private courses, but they do welcome visitors with a letter of introduction from their home club. The climax of the South Australian golfing calendar is the South Australian Open held in Adelaide during October/November each year. The three best-known courses in Adelaide are the Kooyonga Golf Club, Royal Adelaide Golf Club and The Grange Golf Club, the all of which are members only.

20 The **City of Adelaide Golf Links** in North Adelaide has superb city views. The Links is comprised of two 18-hole public courses — the North and South Golf Links. The North Links is a par 70 5,030-metre course, and the South Links is a par 71, 6,075-metre course. All the usual facilities — cafeteria, golf tuition and buggies for hire — are available to the visitor.

21 Located in the Glenelg Beach area of Adelaide, just opposite Marineland and a couple of minutes from the beach, is **Patawalonga Golf Links**. There is a north and south 18-hole course — par 60, 3,210 metres and par 71, 5,810 metres respectively.

22 There is no shortage of accommodation for golfers who have a game at **Berri Country Club,** 238 kilometres north of Adelaide. As well as the Berri Golf Course Motel, the nearby Berri Hotel Motel offers golf packages to Berri Country Club. The 18-hole course is a par 71 and is 5,990 metres in length. Activities nearby include water-skiing, fishing, golf, bowls, wine tasting and tennis.

23 Ten minutes further north of Berri Country Club, and three hours' drive from Adelaide, is **Renmark Country Club.** This flat 18-hole, 6,152-metre,

par 72 course is maintained in good condition year round. The long par four, 17th hole will test any golfer. The 40 motel units have views of the golf course. Other facilities include tennis, a swimming pool and spa, and a barbecue.

Western Australia

There are 210 affiliated clubs in Western Australia, with 19 affiliated clubs and 15 public courses in the metropolitan area.

Most of the private clubs in Perth's metropolitan area have reciprocal membership requirements and exclude visitors. However, the majority of private courses in the country areas welcome visitors. Generally, the quality of courses in the country areas is good.

The highlight of the golfing year is the Western Australian Open, held in November at different Perth courses each year.

The top golf courses are the Royal Perth Golf Club, Lake Karrinyup Golf Club and Mount Lawley Golf Club, all in the Perth metropolitan area.

24 **Busselton Golf Course** is a two and a half hour drive south-west of Perth. Although it is a private course, it is open to the public with an honour system for green fees. The par 72, 6,170-metre, 18-hole course is very popular with tourists who flock to this picturesque area. The course has the services of a golf pro once every three weeks. There are plenty of activities in the area to enjoy such as fishing, windsurfing and swimming in Geographe Bay, and the nearby Margaret River is a well-known surfers' paradise.

25 The biggest golf complex in Perth is the **City of Perth Golf Club,** ten minutes from the GPO. The club has a driving range for practice and four golfing professionals who offer private and group tuition. This 36-hole, par 73, 6,500-metre course is open to the public. Motorised buggies can be hired.

26 **Collier Park Public Golf Course** is a ten-minute drive south of central Perth. This 18-hole, 6,123-metre, par 72 course is flat and open, and surrounded by pine trees.

27 Perth's massive Burswood Island Resort and Casino project, situated along the scenic Swan River foreshore, will boast an unusual 18-hole championship golf course by the end of 1987. Built on the site of a rubbish dump, the course will feature eight lakes. One lake 900 metres in length will double as a water driving range. Players will hire special floating balls that can be easily retrieved from the lake after practice. Robin Nelson designed the course to provide a challenging 6,040-metre layout for championship tournaments and a shorter 5,540-metre course for handicapped players. **Burswood Golf Course** will be open to the public.

28 Internationally renowned architect Robert Trent Jones Jr designed the 18-hole, 6,275-metre, par

The Dandenong Ranges near Melbourne boast several fine golf courses

72 championship golf course at **Joondalup Country Club.** The course, acclaimed by many experts as one of the best in Western Australia, is an easy 25-30 minutes' drive north-west of central Perth. All the estate's facilities, which include tennis courts and restaurants, are open to visitors, although they are encouraged to book ahead, especially for golf.

Northern Territory

Golf in the Northern Territory comes under the jurisdiction of the South Australian Golf Association. There are only nine clubs in the Northern Territory, with 1,533 affiliated male members. The two main championship courses are Alice Springs Golf Club and the Darwin Golf Club, both of which welcome visitors. The golfing event of the year is the Northern Territory Amateur Championship held in either Alice Springs or Darwin, usually on the Queen's Birthday weekend in June.

29 **Darwin Golf Club** is a 15-minute drive east of Darwin. Visitors are welcome to this private 18-hole, par 72, 6,047-metre championship course. The two most difficult holes are the 7th and the 14th. Both are long and narrow par fives, with out-of-bounds on both sides. This can be a tricky course to play because of extreme wind variation at times. Although

there is no accommodation at the clubhouse, excellent first-class hotels are to be found in Darwin.

30 Adjacent to the Sheraton Hotel in Alice Springs is the **Alice Springs Golf Club.** This is an 18-hole, 6,223-metre, par 72 course. The clubhouse bar and lounge are open to visitors. Golf tuition is available by booking a lesson with the pro shop. The Sheraton Hotel has all the amenities needed for a total holiday: a swimming pool, two tennis courts floodlit for night playing, sauna, spa and gym.

Queensland

Nearly all of the private golf clubs in the Brisbane metropolitan area accept visitors and do not require reciprocal membership like clubs in most other states.

There are approximately 44,000 male affiliated members in Queensland, and 18,000 female associate members in the 214 affiliated clubs. Six of the clubs are resort courses, such as Palm Meadows.

The standard of golf courses in Queensland is high, and the generally recognised top courses in Brisbane are the Royal Queensland Golf Club, Indooroopilly Golf Club, Brisbane Golf Club and Pacific Golf Club.

31 On the far north coast of Queensland, **Cairns Golf Club** is set amidst palm trees and surround-

ed by mountains. This beautiful, tropical, 5,812-metre, par 70 course is ten kilometres north of Cairns and is the only 18-hole golf course north of Townsville (400 kilometres to the south). Visitors will appreciate the recently reconstructed greens and renovated clubhouse with restaurant, bar and change rooms.

32 Just over 1,000 kilometres north of Brisbane is **Townsville Golf Club,** which will be a 27-hole course by the end of 1987. Visitors are welcome to this 6,213-metre, par 71 public course. A word of warning — watch out for the treacherous dam on the 14th hole.

33 Situated near the picturesque Rockhampton Botanic Gardens is **Rockhampton Golf Club,** an eight-hour drive north of Brisbane. This 18-hole grass green course is 6,157 metres, and a par 72. The course is open seven days a week, and competitions are held on Wednesday, Thursday, Saturday and Sunday. Rockhampton has a full range of clubs, buggies and other equipment for hire.

34 **Pacific Golf Club** in Mt Gravatt (a suburb of Brisbane) is a private course. However, it is open to the public at certain times during the week. Anyone with reciprocal membership with the main interstate clubs may play in the competition golf. There is a nine-hole course as well as the 18-hole course. The length of the nine-hole course is 4,344 metres (twice around), and that of the 18-hole course is 6,276 metres, with a par 72. The club house has two bars and a restaurant. Motorised buggies may be hired from the pro shop.

35 Professional golfer Graham Marsh designed **Palm Meadows** public golf course at Carrara, a five-minute drive from Surfers Paradise. This superb course is open seven days a week from 7 am and is very popular with guests staying at the nearby Jupiters Casino. This is a long 6,340-metre, par 72 course.

36 Situated on the border of Queensland and New South Wales is **Coolangatta Tweed Heads Golf Club,** comprising two 18-hole courses built on the Tweed River. The River Course is 5,947 metres long with a par 72, and the West Course is 6,120 metres with a par 72. The course is tree-lined and well-bunkered, with fantastic water views. There is a daily golf competition open to members, guests and visitors. The clubhouse caters to a continuous stream of tourists. It has four bars, a club bistro that is open day and night, and a superb international restaurant.

37 Just an hour's drive inland from both Brisbane and the Gold Coast, and near to Beaudesert, is the Kooralbyn Valley Resort. Set in the foothills of the MacPherson Ranges, the resort prides itself on civilised living in rural surroundings of rolling hills, creeks and the Australian bush.

The **Kooralbyn Championship Golf Course** is based on American design lines and offers the best resort golfing in Australia. World-class standards are maintained by daily grooming of the course, which offers a challenge to most golfers. This public golf cart

The challenges of golf - a long drive across a water hazard, top, and a bunker-lined green at the Kooralbyn course, above

course has 11 kilometres of sealed tar, and to play here it is compulsory to use one of the 80 motorised carts. The 6,338 metre, par 72 public course has three resident golf professionals who offer golf clinics and lessons for in-house guests. Kooralbyn also has both day and night-time driving range facilities.

The 182 metre, par three 17th hole has a tricky water shot over a lake to the green nestled on the other side. Packages of four, six or eight days are available, which include all accommodation, golf clinics and competitions, and use of the sauna, spa and swimming pool.

Kooralbyn also offers tennis, horse riding, bowls and bushwalking if you tire of the golf course. Three bars, restaurants and dancing into the night are also available for night-time relaxation.

Golf Contacts

Operators

Golf — The Victorian Way
The Department of Sport and Recreation and the Victorian Tourism Commission have combined to produce a series of golfing packages to a number of championship courses around Victoria. Each package includes limousine and/or helicopter transfer from your city accommodation to the selected course and return, plus green fees.

Victour
230 Collins Street
Melbourne VIC 3000
Ph. (03) 619 9444

Sapphire Coast Holidays
The 'Sapphire Coast' in southern New South Wales has some of the state's finest country golf courses. This golfing package takes in the Pambula-Merimbula, Bega, Narooma and Tura Beach golf courses.

The package price includes accommodation at the Black Dolphin Motel in Merimbula, all meals, golf fees and a barbecue cruise down the Pambula Lake and River.

PO Box 193
Merimbula NSW 2548
Ph. (0649) 5 2197

Sportsbiz Golf Tours
This group operates a tour package to some of the finest private golf courses around Sydney. The package includes round-trip mini-bus from your hotel, 18 holes of golf and electric golf cart. Some of the courses are Monash, The Lakes, Bonnie Doon and St Michaels.

17 Northcliff Street
Milsons Point
Sydney NSW 2061
Ph. (02) 957 2160

Tourist Sports Promotions
This company can organise golf on an individual or group basis on championship courses in New South Wales, Victoria and Queensland. Participants can choose to play at any one of their listed locations around Australia, or all of them. They have locations in Sydney, the Gold Coast, Cairns and Melbourne. The package includes transfers and all golfing arrangements.

18-21 Chalmers Crescent
Mascot
Sydney NSW 2020
Ph. (02) 669 5068

New South Wales

1 **Terranora Lakes Country Club**

Marana Street
Bilambil Heights NSW 2486
Ph. (075) 90 9223

2 **Duntry League Country Club**

PO Box 82
Orange NSW 2800
Ph. (063) 62 3602

3 **Long Reef Golf Club**

Anzac Avenue
Collaroy
Sydney NSW 2097
Ph. (02) 98 8188

4 **Eastlake Golf Club**

Gardeners Road
Kingsford
Sydney NSW 2032
Ph. (02) 663 1374

5 **Bonnie Doon Golf Club**

Banks Avenue
Pagewood
Sydney NSW 2035
Ph. (02) 349 2101

6 **Dormie House**

Arthur Street
Moss Vale NSW 2577
Ph. (048) 68 1014

7 **Wagga Wagga Country Club**

PO Box 77
Wagga Wagga NSW 2650
Ph. (069) 22 6444

8 **Pambula-Merimbula Golf Club**

Princes Highway
Pambula NSW 2549
Ph. (0649) 5 6154

Australian Capital Territory

9 **Royal Canberra Golf Club**

Westbourne Woods
Yarralumla
Canberra ACT 2600
Ph. (062) 81 2409

10 **Yowani Country Club**

Federal Highway
Lyneham
Canberra ACT 2602
Ph. (062) 41 2303

Victoria

11 **Yarrambat Golf Club**

Yanyean Road
Yarrambat
Melbourne VIC 3091
Ph. (03) 436 2201

12 **Ringwood Golf Club**

352 Canterbury Road
Ringwood
Melbourne VIC 3134
Ph. (03) 870 7496

13 **Sandringham Golf Club**

Cheltenham Road
Cheltenham
Melbourne VIC 3192
Ph. (03) 598 3590

14 **National Golf and Country Club**

Boneo Road
Cape Schanck VIC 3939
Ph. (059) 88 6257

15 **The Peninsula Country Golf Club**

Skye Road
Frankston VIC 3199
Ph. (03) 786 4133

16 **Anglesea Golf Club**

Noble Street
Anglesea VIC 3230
Ph. (052) 63 1582

Tasmania

17 **Shearwater Country Club**

C/- Post Office
Port Sorell TAS 7307
Ph. (004) 28 6205

18 **Launceston Federal Country Club**

Country Club Avenue
Prospect Vale
Launceston TAS 7250
Ph. (003) 44 8855

19 **Rosny Park Public Golf Course**

Rosny Hill Road
Rosny Park
Hobart TAS 7018
Ph. (002) 44 1297

South Australia

20 The City of Adelaide Golf Links

Cnr Hills Street & Strangeways Terrace
North Adelaide SA 5006
Ph. (08) 267 2171

21 Patawalonga Golf Links

Military Road
Glenelg
Adelaide SA 5045
Ph. (08) 356 4811

22 Berri Country Club

PO Box 399
Berri SA 5354
Ph. (085) 82 1974

23 Renmark Country Club

Renmark Avenue
Renmark SA 5341
Ph. (085) 85 1401

Western Australia

24 Busselton Golf Club

Strelley Street
Busselton WA 6280
Ph. (097) 53 1050

25 City of Perth Golf Club

The Boulevard
Floreat Park
Perth WA 6014
Ph. (09) 387 1496

26 Collier Park Public Golf Course

Hayman Road
Como WA 6152
Ph. (09) 450 6488

27 Burswood Island Resort

Great Eastern Highway
Victoria Park
Perth WA 6100
Ph. (09) 362 7777

28 Joondalup Country Club

Country Club Boulevard
Connolly
Perth WA 6027
Ph. (09) 306 1538

Northern Territory

29 Darwin Golf Club

Links Road
Marrara
Darwin NT 5973
Ph. (089) 27 1322

30 Alice Springs Golf Club

Cromwell Drive
Alice Springs NT 5750
Ph. (089) 52 1921

Queensland

31 Cairns Golf Club

Bruce Highway
Woree
Cairns QLD 4870
Ph. (070) 54 1208

32 Townsville Golf Club

Benson Street
Rosslea
Townsville QLD 4812
Ph. (077) 79 0133

33 Rockhampton Golf Club

PO Box 729
Rockhampton QLD 4700
Ph. (079) 27 3311

34 Pacific Golf Club

430 Pine Mountain Road
Mt Gravatt
Brisbane QLD 4122
Ph. (07) 349 4411

35 Palm Meadows Public Golf Course

Springbrook Road
Carrara QLD 4217
Ph. (075) 52 9450

36 Coolangatta-Tweed Heads Golf Club

Sooley Street
Tweed Heads South QLD 2486
Ph. (075) 54 4644

37 Kooralbyn Championship Golf Course

Kooralbyn Valley Resort
PO Box 216
Beaudesert QLD 4285
Ph. (075) 44 6222

Information Sources

State Golfing Associations

For further details on golf courses in each state contact:

New South Wales & Australian Capital Territory

17 Brisbane Street
Darlinghurst
Sydney NSW 2010
Ph. (02) 264 8433

Victoria

6 Riddell Parade
Elsternwick
Melbourne VIC 3185
Ph. (03) 528 1555

Tasmania

2 Queen Street
Hobart TAS 7000
Ph. (002) 44 3600

South Australia & Northern Territory

PO Box 256
Cowandilla
Adelaide SA 5033
Ph. (08) 352 6899

Western Australia

49 Melville Parade
South Perth WA 6151
Ph. (09) 367 2490

Queensland

Cnr Wren Street & Walden Lane
Bowen Hills
Brisbane QLD 4006
Ph. (07) 854 1105

ALLAN MOULT

Horse Riding

In the romantic traditions of early Australian poetry and prose, dominated by figures such as Henry Lawson and 'Banjo' Paterson, the image of a man and his horse stands for strength and unity — a bond of faith and friendship based on the importance of the horse to our pioneering forebears. And that feeling endures, despite the developments in science and technology which have all but replaced the horse as a mode of transport and a beast of burden.

Every state in Australia offers recreational facilities for people wishing to experience a horse-riding holiday. Riders can experience, from the comfort of a well-oiled saddle, a new perspective on Australia's diverse landforms and vegetation. It is also a great form of exercise for both the novice and those who are at home in the saddle.

Horse riding enables you to appreciate the sweet aroma of country air and to explore some of the most picturesque parts of the country. Riders can venture out on their own, with a few friends, or on an organised tour lasting for a few hours or a few weeks.

Organised tours provide the perfect opportunity for inexperienced riders to gain the maximum benefit from their adventure. Skilled guides accompany the group and provide information and assistance when necessary. On longer expeditions, overnight stays are usually arranged in comfortable lodges, or weather permitting, a night or two may be spent camping under a star-filled sky.

Australia has some of the best country in the world for exploring on horseback. The high country in the Snowy Mountains of New South Wales offers views of snow-clad peaks, carpets of wildflowers and stands of eucalypts. Further north, in the New England district, riders can retrace the paths of the pioneers along bullock wagon trails and old stock routes. A

horse, a sleeping bag, a sense of humour, and a spirit of adventure are all that are required.

Victoria is a horse-rider's heaven. There are numerous horse trails to explore around the Bogong and Otway National Parks, Falls Creek and the Gippsland region. Guides lead visitors on spectacular High Country rides around the Victorian Alps and through thousands of hectares of state forest and national park. The area is a naturalist's and photographer's paradise, with snowgums, sub-alpine peat bogs and grasslands. Riders can also enjoy excursions into the agricultural regions north of Melbourne where dairying, grazing and wheat farming activities form a neatly ordered grid pattern across the fertile landscape.

In Tasmania, riders can enjoy horse-riding tours into one of the world's last great temperate wilderness areas in the Franklin River region.

And a visit to Australia's more arid areas of South Australia, Western Australia and the Northern Territory would not be complete without an outback excursion on horseback. Riders can sample the stark grandeur of the desert or the gentler beauty of karri and jarrah forests. The vast expanses of inland desert plains are hot and unrelenting by day, but at night they are a camper's heaven where tents are pitched under a sea of flickering stars while the billy boils on the campfire.

Horse riding in Queensland is a different experience again. Here, thick rainforests hug the northern coastline which is rich in unique flora and fauna. Wildlife abounds, though species such as the pademelon, bandicoot and native marsupial mouse are very shy and rarely seen. Not so lyrebirds, parrots, bower birds and bellbirds, which serenade riders as they make their way through lianas and ferns hanging in the filtered sunlight. However, Queensland has more than rainforest to offer the horse rider. The glorious, sweeping beaches for which the state is renowned provide idyllic locations for a romantic horseback jaunt at sunset.

Australia's Bicentenary year, 1988, will see the opening of the Bicentennial National Horse Trail which has taken 16 years to develop with the financial assistance of the Australian Bicentennial Authority. Starting at Cooktown in Queensland, the trail uses historic stock routes, pack-horse tracks and coach roads as it heads south. Covering a breathtaking diversity of wilderness from the far north to New South Wales through 5,000 kilometres of bush to Melbourne in the south of the continent, the National Trail will be the longest horse trail in the world.

The trail has been designed so that campsites and water are no more than a day's walk or ride apart (15-25 kilometres) and it links with other recreation trails along the way. The facilities will be minimal to encourage users to develop bush skills and to minimise their impact on the environment.

Information and maps will be freely available to anyone wishing to take a horse-riding or walking trip along the trail. Solid granite marker posts will not only divide the trail into sections, but will also identify sites of historical significance.

Locations

New South Wales

1 Just south of **Coffs Harbour,** on the mid-north coast of New South Wales, lies the Pine Creek State Forest, an area of natural bushland that is ideal for leisurely trail rides. Riders can explore the magnificent scenery, flora and birdlife for which this region is renowned on escorted two-hour scenic rides or on weekend treks into the more isolated areas. Children are also catered for with weekend and five-day holiday camps designed to introduce them to the joys of riding in the Australian countryside.

A sleeping bag and a pillow are all that is needed to appreciate this forest wilderness, but for those who prefer to sleep indoors, bunkhouse-style accommodation with the use of a pool and a barbecue provides a base from which to explore the bush.

2 A journey through the townships of Singleton, Muswellbrook, Tamworth and Armidale brings travellers to the **New England district** of New South Wales, some 400-500 kilometres north-west of Sydney. In the remote ranges of this area, riders can experience the austere beauty of the Australian bush. Five-day treks across the Great Dividing Range enable riders to follow the original bullock wagon trails and old stock routes of the pioneers. Riders are taught

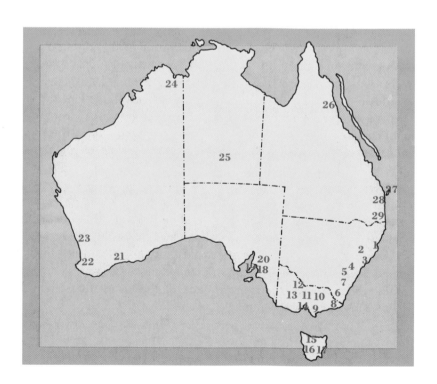

bushcraft skills and survival techniques by competent guides. They can also catch and prepare such local bush delicacies as yabbies, brown and rainbow trout, and even snake. No expedition would be complete without instruction in the fine arts of making damper and brewing a good cup of billy tea over the fire. Travellers can choose to combine a four-day bush trek with a three-day stay on an Australian property.

3 North of the Hunter Valley, about three hours' drive from Sydney, is the **Barrington Tops** area. Gateway to the Tops is Gloucester, a picturesque township on the Gloucester River. This mountainous location is ideal for horseback adventures.

Guided camping and horse treks of between five and 12 days' duration enable riders with some degree of experience and a love of the outdoors to explore alpine grasslands, forest trails, timbered ridges and cattle country during the temperate months from October to June.

4 South-west of Sydney in the Blue Mountains, and a short drive from the towns of Katoomba and Blackheath, lies the **Megalong Valley.** Horse-riding excursions through the valley are guided by versatile 'rough country' horsemen and women with wide experience of the bush.

5 The fertile **Southern Tablelands** — one of the earliest settled inland areas of Australia — is a region of plains, rivers and historic towns. Goulburn (approximately 150 kilometres south-west of Sydney), one of the oldest cities in inland New South Wales, is the centre of this prosperous agricultural region.

Bushrangers roamed this countryside in the 19th century, and horse riding is still a popular pastime.

One of the most pleasant ways to experience horse riding in this area is at one of the farms or historic homesteads dotted around the region. The Berrebangalo Country Resort is located just 20 minutes from the town of Yass, or 45 minutes from Canberra. In addition to horse riding, the area offers fishing, golf and limestone caves to explore.

6 In the Snowy Mountains region of New South Wales, near the town of Adaminaby, is the **Kosciusko National Park.** An area of mountain ranges with awesome alpine scenery, it was immortalised in the poems of 'Banjo' Patterson.

Visitors ride through carpets of wildflowers and stands of gnarled and hardy snowgums on four or five-day Landrover-supported rides, exploring the Yarrangobilly Caves, fishing for trout in mountain streams or relaxing in thermal pools. Or, in the spirit of 'The Man from Snowy River', they can ford rivers, climb steep mountain passes and cross the high plains on six-day wilderness pack rides designed for the more adventurous and experienced rider.

The area is one of the few remaining alpine wildernesses on the continent, and trek organisers can arrange camping at carefully selected sites within the park. Lodge accommodation is also available.

Australian Capital Territory

7 The growing popularity of horse riding in the **Canberra** area has prompted the development of the Equestrian Trail System, which is soon to be completed. The trail system will cover 57 kilometres, linking the city's northern and southern suburbs and providing safe routes for equestrian riding. The sprawling suburbs of Canberra, connected by wide areas of natural bushland and rural scenery, make it an ideal location for horse riding. Some of the local horse-riding schools are already using those sections of the Equestrian Trail that have been completed. These trails lie mainly within or on the periphery of the city area, and are connected to rural tracks.

The outlying areas of Canberra, with their dense pine forests, mountains and rivers, also provide a lovely setting for longer trail rides.

Victoria

8 The town of Buchan, nestled in the foothills of the Victorian Alps, boasts in its immediate vicinity two national parks, the biggest gorge in Victoria, extensive limestone cave systems and the **Snowy River.** All are within easy reach of the town.

Throughout the year, experienced guides lead visitors through this spectacular area on High Country horse rides, weekend and five-day camping trips, and on two-hour round trips which depart twice daily.

Country cooking and crisp mountain air add to the overall enjoyment of this Snowy River adventure.

9 The **Gippsland** area of Victoria, located 240 kilometres east of Melbourne, provides alpine trail rides through the **Great Dividing Range,** and the high alpine plains, rivers and creeks, cattle country, wilderness areas and national parks of the Victorian Alps.

During spring, summer and autumn, mountain-bred horses take riders to such delights as the legendary Lake Tarli Karng. Formed by a natural landslide and fed by the tumbling waters of the Nogothoruk Creek, it is sacred to the Wellwenduk tribe of Aborigines. Overnight accommodation is available, with riders enjoying the best in home-cooked meals and hospitality.

The hill country around Briagolong in this region provides riders with the opportunity to discover the Australian bush.

Down-to-earth holidays in the area provide participants with accommodation in self-contained rustic log cabins, complete with log fires and candle-lit bunkrooms and bathrooms. As well as instruction in the many aspects of horse care, riders can learn a little philosophy. At least one operator stresses this aspect of a horse-riding holiday, claiming that riding through the countryside enables one to 'look away from self', to gain inspiration and stimulation, and to develop a more positive and peaceful outlook on life.

The foothills and high plains of the Dividing Range of this area are also the setting for fully catered adventure horseback safaris. These expeditions can involve negotiating mountain slopes and mud slides. Organisers therefore require that riders be confident and at least be able to canter their animal.

At the end of each day's ride, a chuck wagon is waiting, with billies boiling, fires blazing and tents already pitched.

Riders climb through rainforests with snow crunching underfoot, fuelled with hot food and mulled wine. Both weekend camping rides and VIP rides operate in old-world comfort, and nights are spent indoors at an old gold town where riders are transported back in time and reminded of the excitement of the goldrush era.

10 Some 320 kilometres north-east of Melbourne is Mt Bogong and the surrounding hill country of the **Bogong High Plains.** Riders can take one to ten-day trips, meandering from one cattleman's hut to the next along the route. Meals are usually cooked for the riders, but it is normal for riders to look after their own horses and saddles, and to set up the tents and help break camp each morning.

Day rides from nearby Falls Creek, Victoria's snow-skiing capital, are possible during January. These include camp lunches out on the plains, and visits to cattlemen's huts and scenic lookouts.

11 The town of **Mansfield** in north-east Victoria lies in the high country region of state forest. From horseback, visitors can see sub-alpine wildflowers, native birds, kangaroos, wombats, dingoes, wallabies and echidna.

On excellent mountain-bred horses, riders of all ages and levels of experience explore the countryside on supervised trail rides and safaris. These range in duration from full-day to overnight rides. An indoor equestrian centre in the area also provides riders with expert tuition in the finer arts of horsemanship.

Visitors can enjoy luxurious accommodation and elegant dining in a timber, rock and slate homestead equipped with a pool and hot spa. Or they can experience the lifestyle of the early settlers in an original bush hut which offers pioneer-style living with campfires and bush tucker.

Riders can extend their holiday with a visit to the nearby slopes of Mt Buller, Mt Stirling or Mt Feathertop for skiing, or to Lakes Eildon or Nillacootie for fishing.

12 In the rich dairying, grazing and grain-growing country of the **Echuca area,** in the Murray Riverland region of Victoria, about 200 kilometres north of Melbourne, visitors who yearn for the open road and the gypsy life in a traditional horse-drawn caravan will find what they are looking for.

Expert tuition is given in harnessing and unharnessing the Clydesdale which pulls the caravan before the adventurer escapes along country roads for

Horseriders enjoying the northern New South Wales scenery above, and the companionship of a horse, right

four days or more of relaxed sightseeing.

13 The Bridgewater area in the fertile farming region of the **Loddon Valley,** north-west of Melbourne via Bendigo, is the ideal setting for a similar holiday in a colonial-style wagon drawn by powerful yet docile Clydesdale horses.

Once the techniques of caravanning with Clydesdales are explained, adventurers can travel at a leisurely pace across the countryside, fishing, fossicking and visiting historic landmarks.

LEE PEARCE

ALLAN MOULT

ANDY MORGAN

The Australian Adventure

470

Travellers can also savour the delights of camping on their journey. Well-protected bushland with numerous streams and rivers offers fresh water supplies and provides idyllic surroundings far removed from the pressures of modern life.

14 The town of **Winchelsea,** adjoining the Otway National Park about 150 kilometres south-west of Melbourne, provides an excellent venue for trail riding. Palamino and chestnut horses are available for novice or experienced riders to explore the surrounding countryside on two-hour, day rides or extended rides of two or more days with overnight stays at Lorne or Bambra. There is also the option of safari-style camping in the bush.

Accommodation is available in large log cabin bunkhouses and motel suites, and guests can extend their knowledge of the Australian bush during their stay through observing shearing demonstrations or the farming techniques practised at a nearby dairy.

Tasmania

15 **Launceston,** the second largest city in Tasmania, is located at the head of the Tamar River in the north of the state. The city lies in the wide valleys formed by the river system and is surrounded by rugged mountains. It is this lush rural setting which makes horse riding such a pleasurable activity in the area. The countryside is dotted with stately mansions and old cottages.

16 Tasmania's **Central Highlands,** with its rugged plains and lakes and vast tracts of wilderness is a perfect spot for horse riding. Rides range from two to ten days, or longer if required. Guides familiar with the area will take care of the horses, do the cooking and arrange hot showers. Some of the destinations are Quamby Bluff, the Western Tiers, Frenchman's Cap National Park and the lakes around the plateau.

17 An area rich in history, with its convict buildings and remnants of old colonies, is the **Tasman Peninsula.** This southern area is the home of the famous penal settlement of Port Arthur. The coastal scenery is quite stunning, taking in Eaglehawk Neck, a narrow sandy isthmus linking the Tasman and Forestier Peninsulas. Black dolerite cliffs jut from the Tasman Sea, and the coastal road weaves around the bays and inlets, offering unsurpassed sea views. Some lovely towns are scattered along the peninsula, providing old-fashioned accommodation and a relaxing drink at one of its pubs.

South Australia

18 About 100 kilometres south of Adelaide on the **Fleurieu Peninsula,** two, three and four-day pack-horse treks, as well as half-day beach and cliff-top rides, offer some pleasurable exploring in South Australia's southern regions.

Riding in tropical north Queensland, left, and trail riders in New South Wales, above

On some two-day excursions, groups can camp in comfort at a homestead. On the longer rides, however, campsites at picturesque locations are preferable. Riders can try a little fishing and rabbit trapping before night falls, after an exhausting but enjoyable day in the saddle.

19 Horse wagon holidays are available along the quiet country roads and scenic coastline of the state's **Yorke Peninsula.** Available in all seasons, wagons normally accommodate a maximum of five, with two double beds and one single. Pillows are provided and travellers need only bring their own linen, bedding or sleeping bags.

Before travellers embark on their wagon adventure, instruction is given in horse harnessing and handling. Other information will include how to make camp and where to find the best beach and bush locations. Feed and water for the horses are supplied and riding horses are also available for hire.

Each of the gipsy wagons travels a separate route unless a number of vans are booked among friends. To the steady clip clop of hooves and the chinking of the harness, the route takes visitors along the high-water mark of Hardwicke Bay or inland to Sandalwood Park.

20 The wild and jagged terrain of the **Flinders Ranges** covers around 78,500 hectares. Its high ridges and peaks contrast with wide valleys, creeks and a colourful expanse of wildflowers. Trail rides through this area are for the adventurous rider who can cope with rugged territory. However, it is not all rocky and difficult terrain. Parts of this national park consist of rolling hills, groves of red gums, and white cypress and peppermint box trees.

Western Australia

21 The Esperance region of Western Australia on the **South Coast** has more coastline protected by

national park than any other area of the state. Its stretches of white beaches and secluded bays contrast with the farming country inland. The Esperance Plains produce beef, wool, oats and other crops. This rich farmland changes colour with the seasons: the green rolling hills in winter alter to a sea of gold in summer. It is an area with few rivers and only a scattering of towns through its countryside. Trail riding through the Ravensthorpe Ranges, and down the Jerdacuttup and Phillips Rivers to the sea is popular.

22 A slow and relaxing way of exploring the picturesque **South-west Region** of Western Australia is by horse-drawn wagon. No previous experience with horses is required, and operators in the Margaret River area demonstrate, before departure, how to harness, groom, feed and handle the Clydesdale horses.

Each horse-drawn wagon sleeps up to five people and contains a gas fridge, a two-burner griller and gas stove, gas lanterns, sink, fresh rainwater, and all the other necessities for self-catering. Travellers must provide their own food.

Clydesdales are known for their docile and peaceful nature, so there is no problem with troublesome or temperamental horses.

Travellers have the opportunity to enjoy the beauty of the karri forest and jarrah bush, the riverland, dairy and cattle farms, and the Margaret River vineyards and wineries. The nearby area of Manjimup is a rugged landscape of giant, aged karri forests, sand dunes and towering cliffs.

Riders can sample the wonders of this area on hourly or daily tours, while longer holidays of one week or more enable the robust adventurer to camp overnight in real mustering huts or fishing shacks where close encounters with kangaroos, emus, black swans, and even dingoes as they roam in their natural habitat enhance the experience of this unspoilt bushland area.

23 Just seven kilometres from the small town of Midland Junction, 22 kilometres east of Perth, riders can explore the spectacular scenery of the **John Forrest National Park**. The park's wildflowers and kangaroos are certain to capture the interest and imagination of the city dweller.

Of special interest in this area are residential courses for school children. Children spend a week learning the rudiments of horse care and grooming, as well as show ring riding and jumping. Guests will be collected from the local station.

24 An area of nearly half a million square kilometres, **the Kimberleys** in far north Western Australia is twice as large as Victoria and three times the size of England.

It is rough country, containing some of Australia's best cattle country. Wyndham is the most northerly port in the state and the most consistently hot town in Australia, with temperatures rarely falling below 19°C. During the wet season, from November through to March, dry creek beds and yellow grassy plains quickly become roaring waterfalls amongst the lush vegetation. This area around the Cambridge Gulf contains five rivers, including the Ord River, which discharges more water into the sea than the River Nile. The surrounding district includes the rugged Cockburn Ranges. In this remote and beautiful country, trail riding is a rewarding pastime.

Northern Territory

25 The Northern Territory is a place of mysterious beauty, the site of Aboriginal mythology and tales of the 'Dreamtime', an ancient land where red desert is transformed in the wet season into a place of vivid colours. For riders wishing to discover the real outback, **Alice Springs** is the ideal departure point.

On trail rides of one hour to two days' duration, riders can follow the path of the ancient Todd River as it winds between gnarled river gums out into the eastern desert, or explore the rugged country of the western MacDonnell Ranges with its swamps, claypans and some of the finest desert waterbirds in the world.

Queensland

26 The **Atherton Tableland**, south-west of Cairns, is a rich agricultural area with an ideal climate for enjoying riding and farm activities.

On organised trail rides, riders follow old timber tracks while passing through rainforest and cypress woods into open forest country studded with ghost gums.

27 **Fraser Island**, the largest sand island in the world, is a paradise for the lover of the outdoors. Its fine fishing potential, long sandy beaches, four-wheel-drive tracks and inland trails makes it perfect for a wide variety of outdoor ventures.

Horse riding is popular here. The large network of trails around the island makes it possible to get away from the crowds and to enjoy some fine riding across sand dunes, wildflower-strewn heaths, and past streams and clear lakes.

Six or eight-day horse treks are available on Fraser Island, one of which commences from Noosa, on the Sunshine Coast. This trek starts off with a ride north along Forty Mile Beach to the ferry which crosses to the island.

Riding holidays from six to 14 days' duration are

28 available in south-east Queensland on the **Sunshine Coast** and its **hinterland**. Treks operate from Conondale to Nanango, about 180 kilometres north-west of Brisbane, through heavy tropical rainforest, open grazing lands, pine plantations, creeks and stands of eucalyptus.

Approximately five hours a day are spent in the saddle. Campsites are located near streams, where facilities and a temporary kitchen are installed by a support team before the riders arrive.

At nearby Noosa, treks cater for both the novice wishing to have just a few hours on horseback and the keen rider who wants to take a ride lasting a few days. Half-day rides are available, complete with gourmet lunch. These rides pass along pleasant bush tracks at an easy pace. The full-day rides for the more competent rider cover up to 40 kilometres of native bush, scenic ridges and beaches.

29 The Gold Coast region, just a short drive south of Brisbane, in **Southern Queensland**, is not just beaches, nightlife and high-rise hotels. The beautiful, often ignored, hinterland offers much for bushwalkers, nature lovers and horse-riding fans.

Kooralbyn Valley Resort, in the foothills of the MacPherson Ranges, is a great location for anything

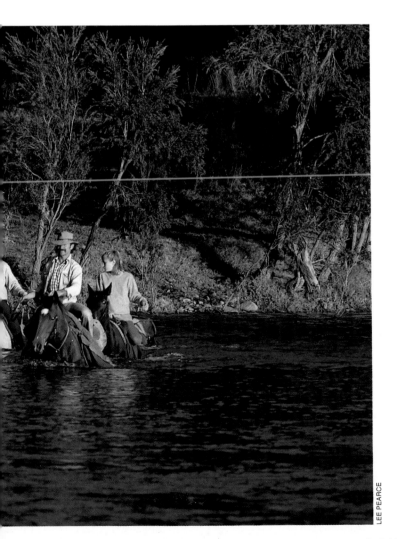

A group fording a river, left, and a team of Clydesdales pulling a laden cart

from golf and tennis to bushwalking and horse riding. Horse rides are conducted into the surrounding hills on a regular basis, and saddle-sore guests are offered swimming pools, bars and restaurants for a relaxing contrast to the great outdoors.

Further west, near Warwick in the Condamine River Valley, a mere two hours' drive south-west of Brisbane or 25 minutes by plane, horse riders can enjoy the charm of a genuine Aussie homestead which boasts the utmost in luxury in a natural bushland setting.

Regardless of the experience, trail rides are available into the surrounding countryside where native trees, plants, wild orchids and a great variety of birdlife enhance the rider's experience of the Australian bush.

Horse Riding Contacts

Operators

The Bicentennial National Trail
GPO Box 1
Brisbane QLD 4001
Ph. (076) 38 3501

New South Wales

1 Coffs Harbour Area

Valery Trails
This group, just south of Coffs Harbour, offers four types of trail rides for different interests and levels of experience. There is the escorted two-hour ride through Pine Creek State Forest, two-hour rides into more isolated areas, the off-season Ladies Day ride of two hours, offering free instruction and child-minding, and weekend treks for the more adventurous.

Valery & Repton Roads
Valery
via Bellingen NSW 2454
Ph. (066) 53 4301

2 New England District

Tim and Julie's Mountain Horseback Treks
These treks are available all year round in the New England Ranges. They have five-day treks in the Great Dividing Range, and camping accommodation on the property. Along with treks, they teach the art of bushcraft and bush survival techniques.

'Bimboola'
Kootingal NSW 2352
Ph. (067) 69 4328 or (02) 969 9515

3 Barrington Tops

Saddle Treks
These camping horse treks of either five, six or 12 days' duration start and finish at Base Camp, 11 kilometres from Dungog. Some riding experience is necessary for these treks through Barrington Tops country which operate from spring to autumn.

PO Box 114
Dungog NSW 2420
Ph. (049) 92 1713

4 Megalong Valley

The Packsaddlers
This group is located in the Megalong Valley, and has been operating for 24 years. No riding experience is necessary for hourly or one-day trips. A full day's mountain bush ride leaves from the homestead at 9 am, trekking all day through untouched wilderness.

Rides are available all year round and they offer overnight motel-style accommodation for up to 20 guests. There is a games room and swimming pool at the homestead.

'Green Gully'
Megalong Valley NSW 2785
Ph. (047) 87 9150

5 Southern Tablelands

Berrebangalo Country Resort
This resort is situated in a peaceful valley 260 kilometres south of Sydney, and just 45 minutes' drive from Canberra. More luxurious than the average horse stud, it has two floodlit tennis courts, a large swimming pool, a croquet lawn and a wildlife aviary.

Appaloosa horses, famous for their speed, stamina, intelligence and pleasant disposition, are bred on the property, and are available for guests to use for various day rides.

Accommodation is available in the 45-room homestead.

Lade Vale Road
Gunning NSW 2581
Ph. (048) 45 1135

6 Kosciusko National Park

Kosciusko Trails
Kosciusko Trails offers treks, predominantly of five days' duration, through the Kosciusko National Park. The areas they explore include the Happy Jacks Plain, Tantangara, Table Top and the Kiandra goldfields area.

They have vehicle support, and all treks are ex-Wagga Wagga. They also run 4WD adventure safaris ex-Wagga Wagga and Canberra.

PO Box 783
Wagga Wagga NSW 2650
Ph. (069) 22 5156

Reynella Rides
The property of Reynella at Adaminaby has become quite an institution with horse riders in New South Wales. All treks take place through the Kosciusko National Park, and are mostly of five days' duration. Half and full-day rides can be taken in the hills around Reynella, and they offer accommodation in alpine-style cabins.

Reynella
PO Box 57
Adaminaby NSW 2630
Ph. (0645) 42 386 or 42 469

Australian Capital Territory

7 Canberra Area

Marcel's School of Riding and Trekking
Located on the western side of Canberra, Marcel's offers one-day or several-day treks in the pine forests. They provide professional instruction in general riding and dressage, and follow some of the completed sections of the Equestrian Trail.

Lady Denman Drive
Curtin
Canberra ACT 2605
Ph. (062) 81 2212

Victoria

8 Snowy River Region

Snowy River Trail Rides
Snowy River Trail Rides are located near Buchan in the foothills of the Victorian Alps, at the heart of Snowy River country. They offer tailored rides of various days' duration to suit all guests.

Weekend and five-day camping trips are available, with secluded campsites set up along the Murrindal River.

'Hume Park'
Old Basin Road
Buchan VIC 3885
Ph. (051) 55 9290

9 Gippsland/Great Dividing Range

Alpine Trail Ride
This group, with 20 years' experience, conducts trail rides in Gippsland through high alpine plains, cattle country and wilderness areas.

Vehicle support is supplied for longer treks, while overnight accommodation for 25 is available at their base for one-day treks. They operate from spring through to autumn, seven days a week.

Valencia Creek
RMB 6865
Maffra VIC 3860
Ph. (051) 45 4293

Walhalla Mountain Saddle Safaris
They provide fully catered adventure horseback safaris from two to six days' duration in the foothills and high plains of the Great Divide. They also have one-day and weekend rides.

PO Box 26
Erica VIC 3825
Ph. (051) 65 3365

10 Bogong High Plains

Bogong Horseback Adventures
This group operates day trips, as well as three, four, five and ten-day treks in the high plains and surrounding country of Mt Bogong.

Supplies are carried by pack-horses. Day rides from nearby Falls Creek operate during January.

PO Box 230
Mt Beauty VIC 3699
Ph. (057) 57 2849

Bogong Jack Adventures
They specialise in outdoor holidays through north-east Victoria. Horse treks are only scheduled for summer, with groups of maximum 15, and pack-horse backup.

Treks are of two, three, four, five and ten days' duration, and take place around the Bogong High Plains.

PO Box 209
Wangaratta VIC 3677
Ph. (057) 21 2564

11 Mansfield/Mt Buller

Sawpit Gully Lodge
At Sawpit Gully Lodge, there is an indoor equestrian centre with expert tuition, and trail rides into the state forests around Mansfield. They offer accommodation in a luxury homestead. They have two-hour, half-day, full-day and overnight safaris. Mts Buller, Stirling and Feathertop are all within easy reach.

PO Box 421
Mansfield VIC 3722
Ph. (057) 76 9562

12 Echuca

Rich River Horsedrawn Caravans
Located in the Echuca-Rochester area, these horse-drawn caravans travel through dairying, grazing and grain-growing country. The caravans are fully equipped to accommodate five people, although guests must bring their own food and sleeping gear. The minimum booking is for four days.

RMS 422
Rochester VIC 3561
Ph. (054) 86 5274 or 86 5430

13 Loddon Valley

The Colonial Way
Their colonial-style wagons are available for hire in an area south and west of Bridgewater-on-Loddon. They can accommodate five people, with minimum bookings of four days.

Bridgewater-on-Loddon
VIC 3516
Ph. (054) 37 3054

14 Winchelsea Area

Seamist Palomino Stud
This stud lies on a 13-hectare property and adjoins a state forest. Facilities include a BYO restaurant, swimming pool, spa, and accommodation for 64. The horses are all palamino and chestnuts. There are regular two-hour and one-day rides to a number of locations around Winchelsea. Extended rides of two or more days are available, with overnight stays at Lorne or Bambra, or safari-style in the bush.

Wensleydale Station Road
Winchelsea South VIC 3241
Ph. (052) 88 7255 or 88 7365

Tasmania

15 Launceston

Launceston Federal Country Club
This club/casino in Launceston offers a variety of activities other than gambling. Horses are stabled nearby for guests to use around the Launceston countryside. Visitors are welcome.

Launceston Federal Country Club
 Hotel-Casino
Country Club Avenue
Launceston TAS 7250
Ph. (003) 44 8855

16 Central Highlands

Central Highlands Trail Rides
This property is situated in Golden Valley, 15 kilometres from Deloraine in northern central Tasmania.

Their rides range from two to ten days, or longer if required. Guides familiar with the area will take care of the horses, do the cooking and arrange hot showers. Some of the destinations include Quamby Bluff, Frenchman's Cap National Park and the lakes around the Central Plateau.

PO Box 60
Deloraine TAS 7304
Ph. (003) 69 5298

17 Tasman Peninsula

Seaview Riding Ranch
The Seaview Riding Ranch is located at Koonya on the Tasman Peninsula. Bunkhouse accommodation is available for up to 24 people, and they offer treks of varying length around the peninsula. They have been established for ten years, and operate all year round.

RMB 1371
Koonya TAS 7187
Ph. (002) 50 3110

South Australia

18 Fleurieu Peninsula

High Country Trails
They offer two, three and four-day pack-horse treks around the Fleurieu Peninsula. They also have half-day beach and cliff-top rides. Accommodation is available at their homestead for the short day rides.

Willis Drive
Normanville SA 5204
Ph. (085) 58 2507

Wirrina Holiday Resort
Located near Yankalilla, a small town on the Fleurieu Peninsula, Wirrina is a popular resort with holiday-makers from Adelaide. Amongst the many activities available, horses can be hired for rides around the area. For the novice rider, lessons can be arranged.

PO Box 63
Yankalilla SA 5203
Ph. (085) 59 4001

ALLAN MOULT

19 Yorke Peninsula

Get-Away Holidays
This company offers horse-drawn wagon holidays along the quiet country roads and scenic coastline of the southern Yorke Peninsula. Each wagon accommodates five people, and you must bring your own sleeping gear and food.

Get-Away Holidays Gipsy Wagons
PO Box 107
Stansbury SA 5582
Ph. (088) 52 4455 or 52 4147

20 Flinders Ranges

Flinders Rides
This popular company has a couple of base camps in the Flinders Ranges, from where it conducts trail rides in the northern and southern Ranges. Rides also operate in the Coorong area. Rides are of varying length. The base camps have comfortable quarters.

PO Box 273
Gawler SA 5118
Ph. (085) 28 2132

Western Australia

21 South Coast Area

Ravensthorpe Range Trail Rides
Just inland from the south coast, trail rides are available at Ravensthorpe. There are half-day and full-day rides around the local rivers, down the coast and through the Ravensthorpe Ranges. Longer treks of up to six days can be arranged.

PO Box 138
Ravensthorpe WA 6346
Ph. (098) 38 1163

22 South-west Region

Shannon Horseback Adventures
This group conducts trail rides through the karri forests of the south-west to the Shannon River Basin and the southern coast of Broke Inlet. They cater for hourly, daily, weekly or longer holidays, with no more than 12 to a party.

RMB 134
Manjimup WA 6258
Ph. (097) 73 1234 or 73 1296

Vardo Horse Drawn Holidays
In the picturesque Margaret River area, a horse-drawn holiday provides a slow and relaxing means of seeing the region. These wagons are equipped for five people, and only food and sleeping gear need be brought by guests. Toilets and hot showers are available at each overnight camp and some sites have electricity.

RMB 343
Bullant Drive
Forest Grove WA 6286
Ph. (097) 57 7510

23 John Forrest National Park

Swan View Equestrian Lodge
The Lodge takes parties of up to 20 through the John Forrest National Park. Lessons are given on the property, and rides operate all year round. Accommodation is bunk-style.

Lot 17
Pechey Road
Swan View
Perth WA 6056
Ph. (09) 294 1476

24 The Kimberleys

Kimberley Pursuits
This group is situated in Wyndham, at the southern end of Cambridge Gulf in the extreme north of the state. They conduct horse-back treks through the Cockburn Ranges, usually of two or three days' duration. They also have day treks through the outlying areas of Wyndham.

PO Box 5
Wyndham WA 6740
Ph. (091) 61 1014

Northern Territory

25 Alice Springs Region

Glenrowan Trail Rides
Located six kilometres from Alice Springs, this group takes riders into the outback and through the rugged country of the western MacDonnell Ranges. A maximum of five people is required for each trek, the duration of which depends on the group's wishes.

PO Box 2785
Alice Springs NT 5750
Ph. (089) 52 6447

Ross River Tours
Ross River Tours operates from their base, 80 kilometres east of Alice Springs. They conduct horse rides through the Ross River area, where they have a homestead for overnight groups.

PO Box 84
Alice Springs NT 5750
Ph. (089) 52 7611

Queensland

26 Atherton Tablelands

Double D Holiday Ranch
The Double D Holiday Ranch on the Queensland tablelands, just east of Malanda, operates all year round except during autumn, which is the wet season. They have motel-style units for guests and all the usual farm activities. They organise horse rides through the rainforest and open forest country along the tablelands.

PO Box 284
Malanda QLD 4885
Ph. (070) 96 5882

27 Fraser Island

Clip Clop Treks
Clip Clop Treks at Noosa, on Queensland's Sunshine Coast, have horse treks of varying length. On Fraser Island, they conduct six-day treks, camping on the island. To reach the island, groups trek north from Noosa along the beach and catch a ferry.

C/- Post Office
Noosaville QLD 4566
Ph. (071) 49 7408

28 Sunshine Coast & Hinterland

Clip Clop Treks
Clip Clop Treks also have half-day rides, complete with gourmet lunch. These treks amble along quiet bush tracks. Their full-day rides, for the more competent rider, cover up to 20 kilometres of native bush, lakes and beaches on the Sunshine Coast.

See (27) above for details

Horse Trek Australia
Horse Trek Australia conducts riding holidays of six and 14 days' duration in south-east Queensland. Their treks stretch from Conondale to Nanango, (about 180 kilometres north-west of Brisbane), through tropical rainforest, open grazing lands, pine plantations and creeks. Campsites are prepared in advance for groups.

MS 16
Aherns Road
Conondale
via Maleny QLD 4552
Ph. (071) 94 4580 or 94 4586

29 Southern Queensland

Cherrabah Homestead Resort
Located in the Condamine River Valley, two hours' drive from Brisbane, Cherrabah Homestead Resort has its own airstrip and luxury accommodation. Golf, tennis, sailing and trout fishing are just some of the activities that this homestead offers. Trail-riding with guides who know the area takes place in all the surrounding parts of the valley.

MS 162
Warwick QLD 4370
Ph. (076) 67 9177

Kooralbyn Valley Resort
This resort caters for most tastes, with its wide range of activities and luxurious accommodation.
    Horse-riding excursions take visitors up into the surrounding hills.

PO Box 216
Beaudesert QLD 4285
Ph. (075) 44 6100 or 44 6222

Information Sources, Clubs and Associations

National Organisations

Australian Trail Horse Riders' Association (ATHRA)
GPO Box 1
Brisbane QLD 4001

Equestrian Federation of Australia
Federal Secretariat
77 King William Road
North Adelaide SA 5006
Ph. (08) 267 2319

New South Wales

Equestrian Federation of NSW
GPO Box 4317
Sydney NSW 2001
Ph. (02) 332 2990

Australian Capital Territory

ACT Equestrian Association
PO Box 4
Curtin
Canberra ACT 2605

Victoria

Equestrian Federation of Victoria
Royal Showgrounds
Epsom Road
Ascotvale
Melbourne VIC 3032
Ph. (03) 376 3733

Tasmania

Equestrian Federation of Tasmania
PO Box 94
Glenorcy
Hobart TAS 7010
Ph. (002) 72 6812

South Australia

Equestrian Federation of South Australia
1 Sturt Street
Adelaide SA 5000
Ph. (08) 213 0627

Western Australia

Western Australia Equestrian Federation
PO Box 376
Midland
Perth WA 6056
Ph. (09) 296 1323

Northern Territory

Equestrian Federation of Northern Territory
PO Box 38314
Winnellie
Darwin NT 5789
Ph. (089) 88 1170

Queensland

Queensland Equestrian Federation
PO Box 385
Fortitude Valley
Brisbane QLD 4006
Ph. (07) 52 9796

The Australian Adventure

BARBARA HEMMINGS

Motoring — Campervans

Sleeping out under the Southern Cross is one of the world's great experiences, but not even Australia is warm and dry all the time.

Many people prefer to observe the southern skies through the perspex roof of a campervan. Though Australians have not yet raised this form of leisure activity to the status of a religion — as Americans have done — campervans are now widely available, and the whole of Australia can be regarded as the mobile camper's playground. In fact, the island continent's vast distances and relatively sparse settlements make campervanning one of the best ways to get around and see as much as possible.

Visitors to the United States will know that campervans (known appropriately as motor homes) in that country contain everything that opens and shuts, whirls and whistles. A few of these mobile palaces have found their way to Australia and it is possible to tour the country in a driver's seat which doubles as a full-size armchair. On the road, drivers of these vehicles tap into lusty V-8 motors with automatic gears and cruise controls. And at the campsite, all the comforts of home await the traveller: four-burner stoves with ovens, full-size fridges and freezers, hot showers, toilets and thermostatically controlled room-heating units. Such motor homes are the ultimate in on-the-road luxury, but the traveller pays for them in high rental and insurance premiums and often in weighty fuel bills. Even driven conservatively, some of these beasts devour a gallon of petrol every nine kilometres or so.

The more likely alternative for a campervanning holiday in Australia is the Kombi-type vehicle. For many years in Australia, the Volkswagen Kombi, converted by amateurs and professionals, was the only type of unit available. Today, Japanese makes predominate. Rental rates and fuel consumption, especially for diesels, are much lower than their big brothers.

On the road they may look like delivery vans, but with the semi-automatic roof raised they provide a surprising amount of room and a high level of comfort. 'Semi-automatic' is a suspiciously vague term. Raising the roof is simple in some campervans and a task bigger than Ben Hur in others.

Pulling the roof down again can be just as semi-automatic as pushing it up. Lightweight people have been known to haul themselves entirely off the floor without managing to close the lid. It's a good idea to practise roof raising and lowering before signing the rental form.

It may be tempting to leave the roof up (it's also very easy to forget that it *is* up), but beheading the campervan with shop awnings or overhanging trees can be very expensive, and most rental insurance policies exclude the roof.

Once these techniques have been mastered, driving a small campervan presents no particular problems and requires only a standard or international licence. It is worth remembering, however, that on the road the extra weight of camping fittings and increased wind resistance means that campervans accelerate and decelerate more slowly than ordinary cars. Allow extra time for safe overtaking and greater stopping distances.

In certain areas, road signs warn drivers towing caravans about severe side wind gusts, and these apply also to campervans. Australian roads, particularly in country areas, sport some fairly enormous trucks and road-trains, and the slip-streams of these monsters will also affect the handling of a small campervan.

If you are travelling through the outback or over rough terrain, it may be advisable to hire a four-wheel-drive campervan, though these are more cramped and more expensive. Some drivers prefer to opt for manual gears on their vehicles to allow for greater control, particularly for descending steep winding roads.

It is always a good idea for the driver unused to this type of vehicle to keep speed down as much as possible, particularly when roads are wet. If the road has not been graded for some months, the gravel builds up at corners and it is quite easy to skid or even roll a vehicle of this sort. Unseen dips and humps in the road taken at speed can quickly make the campervan airborne. When it comes back to earth, the crockery mixes with the cutlery, and then with the contents of the pantry and the frozen foods and milk from the fridge.

Although living space in a Kombi-type campervan is limited, it will usually accommodate two adults and two children. Four adults need to be extraordinarily compatible, or rent a larger unit. For an extended holiday, a roll-out annexe, a table and a few camp chairs will double the space of any campervan.

Campervan rental companies proliferate in every state in Australia, making it worthwhile to shop around for competitive rates and bonus extras. Some operators will deliver the campervan to the airport or collect it from your destination. Rates should include unlimited kilometres or at least a generous free allowance. Comprehensive insurance is essential, but renters should always check on the size of the excess payable in case of accident. They should also check both the roof and the underside of the vehicle for unnoticed damage caused by a previous client. Before setting off from the rental yard it's the hirer's responsibility to check that everything works and that he knows how to make it work. It is frustrating to find, some kilometres from the nearest shop, that an internal fluorescent light has blown, that the fridge does not work on gas, or that the 12-volt lead to the TV is missing.

In some parts of Australia, water is scarce or almost undrinkable. It is vital therefore to check that the drinking water supplied is clean and plentiful. In country areas, there may also be very long distances between petrol stops. Drivers should be quite sure that they are aware of the capacity of the tank and of the vehicle's estimated consumption. When planning their next fuel stop, they should also bear in mind that strong head winds can cause these vehicles to gulp down fuel.

The charm of a campervan is the freedom it gives the occupants to camp where and when they like, even on rough stony ground where it would be impossible to hammer in a tent peg. As with regular camping, it can pay dividends to be sure that a campsite is selected before dusk. A level site is better for fridge efficiency and for a good night's sleep, and attractive dry creek beds can quickly become rivers after heavy overnight rain.

The experienced traveller will take a torch, toilet paper, tissues, a couple of books, a small umbrella and at least one change of clothes. Soft bags are better than suitcases, and it may be a good idea to pack the camper at the rental yard and store empty suitcases there.

Cooking can either be fun and creative or a real hassle, but many modern campervans have microwave ovens, and it is possible to prepare meals quite quickly using oven bags. Another good tip is to stow picnic lunches for day walks.

Locations
New South Wales

1 In the winter skiing season, the **Snowy Mountains** can be life in the fast lane, but the warmer months bring a gentler, more relaxed pace. The mountain highways are excellent, with some of Australia's most spectacular scenery. From Canberra, head south to Cooma, then through the picturesque village of Berridale. Skirt around Lake Jindabyne and enter Kosciusko National Park. Beyond the cash register at the park entrance is Sawpit Creek. After setting up at Sawpit, exercise the leg muscles with an afternoon walk to a nearby waterfall. Next day, head off to Perisher Valley. From the end of the road there is a marvellous day walk to Blue Lake.

The following day, travel to Thredbo where the most popular walk in the region is to the roof of Australia, Mt Kosciusko. The main chairlift to Crackenback operates year round. This takes the traveller above the treeline into a special alpine environment where rocks, lichens, sphagnum moss and glacial lakes dominate. It's a rugged landscape of almost overpowering desolation.

Back in the campervan, head over Dead Horse Gap down a gravel road to Tom Groggin campsite, close by the Murray River. Beyond Tom Groggin there is a full circuit of alpine roads going back to Cooma. On the way are marvellous bush camps near rivers and lakes containing good numbers of trout. Experts favour fly fishing, but for the beginner a little spinning outfit and a few Celta lures should bring good results.

Victoria

2 Construction began on the **Great Ocean Road** in 1919 and it took 13 years to complete. Today, it stretches for more than 300 kilometres along a rugged section of the Victorian coastline — one of the most

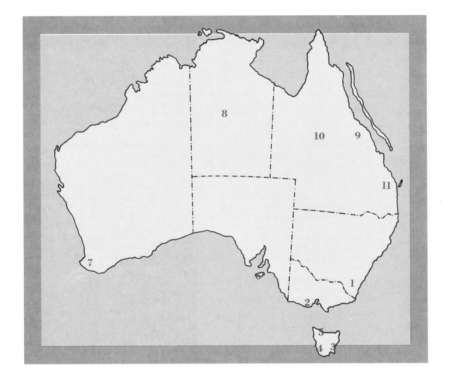

scenic drives in the world. The winding bitumen road begins just south of Geelong (75 kilometres from Melbourne) and ends at Warrnambool in the south-west corner of Victoria. From Melbourne, a pleasant hour of campervanning takes you down the Princes Highway to Geelong. Ideal for a luncheon stop, this city of grand old stone buildings has many fine restaurants.

From Geelong, travel south to Torquay and the beginning of the Great Ocean Road. Detour to the surfing mecca of Bells Beach and spend the night in Lorne. For many years, this has been a popular weekend playground for Melbourne folk, and it's a good location in which to spend a day or two. At the fishermen's co-operative, fresh fish and local delicacies such as crayfish are reasonably priced. Heavy rain in the hinterland can cause flash flooding around Lorne, so avoid riverside caravan parks during prolonged wet weather.

Lorne Forest Park is well worth a visit. The walking tracks pass beside and through creeks and rivers, amidst tree ferns, and past waterfalls. Some tracks with easy gradients follow old timber-hauling tramways; others zigzag down steep hillsides. On a clear morning, Teddy's Lookout gives sweeping views of a coastline washed by Bass Strait.

After clinging precariously to a toe-hold above the waves, the Great Ocean road temporarily departs from the coast and heads west behind Cape Otway. There are two spectacular alternative roads: Skenes and Wild Dog. After climbing steeply up the Otway Ranges you will find Turton's Track. This pretty road has a guard of honour beside the gravel: tall, straight mountain ash with tree ferns crowd in on the edges.

Between where the Great Ocean Road rejoins the ocean and Warrnambool, it skirts rugged coastline with many striking limestone formations. These are part of Port Campbell National Park which reaches from Peterborough to Princetown. At the information centre and camping area in Port Campbell an informative display explains how the stormy Southern Ocean has sculpted this coast.

Some 142 wrecks were recorded off the coastline beside the Great Ocean Road between 1836 and 1958. The Loch Ard, a three-masted clipper, is the most famous. She foundered, losing 52 lives, but amazingly two people and a huge porcelain peacock statue survived. The statue is on display at Flagstaff Hill in Warrnambool.

Beside the last section of the Great Ocean Road are vantage points from where you can see weather-worn cliffs, deep gorges, bridge-like arches, tiny islands and roaring blow-holes — beautiful photographs in the warm glow of late afternoon.

Tasmania

3 Situated on the **Tasman Peninsula,** Port Arthur is one of the most visible vestiges of our colonial past. For more than 40 years, Port Arthur served as a penal station for well over 12,000 convicts. Responses to the buildings, especially the cells, range from utter revulsion to complete fascination. The convicts stayed against their will, but the savage guard dogs which were once chained across the isthmus of Eaglehawk Neck have now gone. Even the surrounding waters don't seem as thick with sharks as in the past. Just before Eaglehawk Neck crossing on the left is the

Tessellated Pavement, a fascinating geological structure.

Instead of heading straight for Port Arthur, a five-kilometre detour takes the traveller along the precipices of rock that form a shoreline of outcrops offering unforgettable ocean views. Tasman's Arch, the Blow-hole and Devil's Kitchen are awesome to contemplate. This is one place where visitors hope for the roughest, wildest weather, for that's when the blow-hole really performs. The road to these attractions passes through the little village of Doo. Every house in this tiny village incorporates the word 'doo' in its name — 'Sheil-doo', 'Doo-little', 'Love-me-doo'.

For keen walkers, there is a wealth of coastal heath country to explore on the peninsula. Leave the camper, take a small day pack with map, lunch, waterproofs and a warm jumper and tramp the track out from Fortescue Bay which leads to some rugged outcrops named Candlestick and Matchstick. The path begins with a tough 200-metre uphill section, and after meandering through a wildflower-strewn landscape, the trek ends at cliffs that plunge straight down to the sea. Walkers can stand on the windswept edge and watch the breakers caress giant kelp.

4 On the way to **Lake Pedder,** the campervan will slip silkily along a ribbon of bitumen. Discounting landslides, erosion, washaways and ugly scars beside the tar, this road is the only means of access to the area. And it's a lonely road. Bustling little Hobart is but an hour and a half away, yet seeing another campervan mid-week is a rarity. Locals and visitors who do journey out here come to chase the trout that lurk beneath the cold waters of Lake Pedder.

The mythology in which trout are steeped is built on fact: they are as wily as foxes, fantastic fighters, beautiful to look at, and delicious when gently poached in white wine. It is little wonder that anglers come from all over the world to dabble in the waters of Lake Pedder.

In the days before the hydro-electric tide swallowed the pristine shores of the real Lake Pedder, these fish were caught only by dedicated anglers. Now, with a highway to their breeding ground, anyone with a licence can try their fishing prowess. The fish initially responded to the flooding of the lake by breeding up in numbers and size. Displayed over the bar at the Lake Pedder Motor Inn are pictures of anglers struggling to hold up gigantic trout, while taxidermic specimens adorn the walls.

5 **Devonport** is the Tasmanian terminus for *Abel Tasman,* the vehicular liner that plies between Melbourne and Tasmania. Campervans driven off the vessel turn either south or east. Few journey west. Yet this northern section of the coastline is a picturesque area of Tasmania. Venturing west from Devonport, there are two routes: the Bass Highway which sweeps along the coast, and the old highway which meanders through farms of poppies to Forth. The two routes

A comfortable campsite alongside a placid river makes for a delightful

merge near Ulverstone and a single scenic route continues on to Penguin.

Between Ulverstone and Penguin, coastal bird sanctuaries protect seagull and fairy penguin rookeries. At the village of Penguin, the locals don't let visitors forget this little bird's endearing qualities. Even the litter bins are penguins. From Penguin on to Burnie, the highway sweeps past the smoke-belching stacks of the Associated Pulp and Paper Mills. Burnie is one of the oldest cities on this stretch of coast, and much of its history is preserved in the Pioneer Village museum, where original shops, old wares, tools of trade and domestic appliances recreate the atmosphere of an early village street.

Further west from Burnie is Stanley, an excellent example of an historic seaside settlement. It snuggles under the cone of an extinct volcano called 'The Nut' — a great spot for an all-round view of the district. Between Stanley and the far west is rich grazing, dairy and timber country. The furthest point west is Marrawah. On wild days, the campervan will be buffeted by winds that have travelled over many thousands of kilometres of open ocean.

South Australia

6 **Kangaroo Island** is an ideal place in which to travel by campervan but the corrugations tend to

rs experience

Kangaroo Island wildlife has taken to the idea that it is their island and visitors are for their amusement. On the south coast, a special beach has been set aside for the use of fur seals and sea lions. These marvellous creatures are the island's top animal attraction. Swimming, sleeping, basking, playing, roaring and fighting, they will captivate the most jaded visitor. Photographs are no problem, but getting too close or in the way is out. It's worth remembering that the bull sea lion who owns the beach weighs a great deal.

Western Australia

7 The 225 kilometres from Perth to Western Australia's **south-west region** can be covered with ease before sundown. Spend the night in Busselton, a shire with 83 kilometres of coastline. From Busselton, there's a pleasant drive out to Cape Naturaliste lighthouse. Whales are often seen on both sides of Cape Naturaliste between early spring and late summer. Back in 1845, they were hunted, killed and boiled down. Today, anglers find this stretch of coastline worth a cast or two. A long beach rod is impractical to carry in a campervan, but there are some excellent multi-section rods.

Between Cape Naturaliste and Cape Leeuwin is cave country. There are as many as 380 known caves in this area, but only four are open for public access. The 'young' ones are about 35,000 years old and some are very active. The formations are still growing. Yallingup Caves, discovered in 1899, are probably the best known. Further south is Mammoth Cave (easily accessible and known for its fossil remains), Lake Cave (noted for its steep natural entrance and suspended table formations), and Jewel Cave (which has the longest straw stalactite).

Just off Caves Road, four kilometres south of Lake Cave, is a 14-kilometre alternative. Boranup Drive winds through some of the prettiest karri forest in the west. A spectacular tree stretching to 87 metres, karri is second in height only to the Californian sequoias. Sadly, the Australian karri lacks the protection offered the Californian giant and is under severe threat from overlogging and introduced diseases.

South of Augusta, the road heads out to Cape Leeuwin where the waters of the Indian Ocean mingle with the Southern Ocean. The old lighthouse is pebbled with stones disgorged as ballast from early freighters. Nearby is an old wooden water wheel slowly being turned to stone by the calcifying action of water.

Northern Territory

Although the Northern Territory's rugged terrain might not seem to be suitable for campervanning, the availability of four-wheel-drive campervans and the upgrading of many of the territory's roads makes this a feasible alternative to a four-wheel-drive/camping holiday.

give most vehicles a real hammering. At Adelaide Airport, it is simple to pick up a hire campervan and take the pleasant road south. Alternatively, just change aircraft and fly direct — there's a campervan firm based on the island. The landing point for the Philanderer vehicle ferry is the historic little village of Penneshaw. If you arrive on the night ferry, a nice caravan park is located a few hundred metres from the landing jetty.

Given a week's holiday, you can gently circumnavigate the island. Obtain provisions, fuel and a good map at Penneshaw and then head off. Kangaroo Island offers plenty to the adventurer — not much in the way of facilities, but many wild beaches and a lot of wilderness. At one location on the northern side of the island a tight passage wriggles through ancient rocks giving access from one beach to another.

A French influence decorates Kangaroo Island's maps, a tradition dating back to 1803–5 when Captain Baudin in *Le Geographie* accidently preserved the only complete specimens of Kangaroo Island emu. The others were all exterminated in the 1830s. Today the island is home to a range of animals and birds, introduced ostensibly to prevent their extinction on the mainland. Most of these have become so overfriendly that the national parks service has had to build enclosures — for the visitors.

8 In 1987, the upgrading of the **Stuart Highway** which stretches from Darwin to Port Augusta in South Australia was completed, providing a sealed and properly constructed road-link across the continent. The highway is named after John McDouall Stuart who led, in 1862, on his seventh attempt, the first successful crossing of the country from south to north. The removal of dusty and uneven sections of this highway has made the journey from Darwin to the southern border of the Northern Territory, and beyond, much more comfortable for campervanners.

Travelling south along the highway from Darwin, where campervans are readily available for hire, there are many interesting and scenic places: historic Pine Creek (220 kilometres), with its goldmining past; the spectacular rock formations of Katherine Gorge (310 kilometres); Mataranka's lush rainforest and thermal pools (415 kilometres); picturesque Lake Woods (730 kilometres); and the strange natural granite formations of the Devil's Marbles (970 kilometres), just before Tennant Creek. From here to Alice Springs (1,480 kilometres), small settlements such as Wauchope and ti-tree provide food and fuel for travellers en route to 'The Alice' and the outlying attractions of Ayers Rock, the Olgas and Finke Gorge National Park.

The journey on to South Australia passes through the MacDonnell Ranges, past the Henbury meteorite craters, formed several thousand years ago, and on into the flat grey gibber plains that herald the beginning of South Australian territory (1,780 kilometres).

Other trans-territory routes that provide the traveller with spectacular scenery and a real taste of outback Australia are the Barkly Highway from Tennant Creek to Mount Isa in Queensland, and the Victoria Highway from Katherine to Kununurra and the Kimberley region of Western Australia. Both of these roads are sealed and suitable for campervans, and open up great possibilities for interstate touring from the territory.

Queensland

9 North Queensland has some great holiday spots for campervanners, especially those keen on a little fishing. Any place described as 'the climate capital of Australia' and an 'untouched sportfishing paradise' has to be a worthwhile destination and **Bowen,** just north of Proserpine, has been given both titles. The northern suburbs of Bowen extend around Queens Bay, taking in a two-kilometre curve of golden sand, rocky headlands, sheltered coves and a sparkling expanse of ocean. There are numerous caravan parks in the area.

At the eastern end of Queens Beach is Horseshoe Bay, an ideal family holiday site and one of the few all-tide sandy beaches in northern Queensland. From here you can wander to the granite boulder-strewn headland of Cape Edgecumbe. Fishing is good from any of the rocky headlands, and within a short distance of Horseshoe Bay Caravan Park in Greys Bay is a boat launching ramp. On a suitable day, head out from the ramp in a small aluminium dinghy to Innamincka Rocks or Raywards Reef in search of coral trout, sweetlip and blue parrot. Trolling for mackerel is also excellent here.

Bowen is in the dry tropics, which tends to make for fine weather even when rain is deluging townships to the north and south. Occasionally the weather becomes a bit too rough for offshore fishing, but there are 17 good fishing creeks within easy driving distance. When the tides are wrong for fishing, take a drive to Mt Nutt Reservoir. From the top of the tank, a 360° view encompasses the mouth of the Don River, Queens Beach, Cape Edgecumbe, fields of mangoes and hectares of tomatoes. Bowen mangoes have a top reputation and tomatoes too ripe to send south are sold locally and sometimes given away. They are so delicious they are like a completely different fruit — prepared as a sauce, they make a perfect complement to fish.

10 **Carnarvon Gorge** in central western Queensland offers many things: green tranquillity in a dry brown country, superb Aboriginal paintings and carvings, soaring golden faces of sandstone, and groves of ancient ferns. The first sight of Carnarvon Gorge is spectacular, the only disadvantage being that it is a long way from anywhere. The township of Injune

Campervans make the outback experience a comfortable one

BARBARA HEMMINGS

is 710 kilometres north-west of Brisbane and Carnarvon is a further 150 kilometres.

Once at the gorge, there is a popular free national park camping area, but forward bookings are essential. Alternatively, accommodation is available at Carnarvon Oasis Lodge. The main walking track winds up the gorge, criss-crossing Carnarvon Creek. By the time Cathedral Cave is reached, the walker has covered ten kilometres and 18 river crossings. For keen walkers, there is a bush camping area just beyond the cave.

The side gorges hold great fascination. A steep little climb past Lower Aljan Falls leads to Angiopteris Ravine, the home of an ancient, rare king fern (*Angiopteris evecta*). Further into the ravine, you can step out on to a rock surrounded by water and peer into a little cave sheltering the softly lit Upper Aljon Falls. At the art gallery, a boardwalk helps protect fragile paintings and carvings. Don't rush the experience. Sit down and let your eyes wander over the wall art. Dating back more than 3,500 years, some of the shapes are faint. Like much of Carnarvon Gorge, a quiet, reflective time spent looking at paintings and drifting in the atmosphere of the place can have a deep and lasting effect.

11 If you are campervanning north of Brisbane, keep a look out for the turn off to Lake Cootharaba. The largest lake in the Noosa River system, on weekends it is a kaleidoscope of sails. Nestle the camper into one of the van parks at a sleepy little spot called Boreen Point, or try Elanda Point where sailboards, catamarans and canoes are available for hire. Few pleasures can compare with the delight of gliding a canoe along a tranquil river, especially the Noosa which flows through magnificent **Cooloola National Park.**

In a canoe, the first contact with Cooloola is at the information centre on Kinaba Island. Take time to stroll along the boardwalks and visit the bird hide. Beyond Kinaba is pretty Lake Figtree, and then 'The Narrows', where the combination of dark, tannin-stained water, vibrant banksias and a breathless hush is a delightful experience.

After returning the canoe, drive along a bush track grandly called the Cooloola Way which connects Tewantin with Rainbow Beach. It's rough in the dry, and slippery in the wet, but there are compensations. Christmas bells create a haze of yellow and red. Just past an ancient scribbly gum, the track passes over an old log bridge which spans a trickling stream. This is the upper reach of the Noosa River.

Rainbow Beach, at the northern end of the park, makes a good base, or drive into the national park camping area at Freshwater. A beautiful sandy beach leads to Double Island Point and an historic lighthouse. If time is no problem, instead of taking the Cooloola Way to Rainbow Beach, take the bush track to the national park camping area at Harry's Hut. This track can be found using 'Cooloola Coast', a very detailed local map. Harry's is a peaceful camping site where inquisitive goannas usually put in an appearance.

The roads of inland Australia are often long, hot and dusty, and carrying the comforts of home on board helps to ease the pain

BARBARA HEMMINGS

Motoring — Campervan Contacts

Operators

Campervan and motorhome rentals are easily arranged in all states, and some recommended companies are listed below.

The four companies listed below operate Australia-wide and have offices in most large cities. For details of their locations, contact the Head Offices as indicated.

Allaussie Campervans
20 Norwich Avenue
Thomastown
Melbourne VIC 3074
Ph. (03) 469 2186

Budget Rent-a-Car
21 Bedford Street
North Melbourne VIC 3051
Ph. (03) 320 6222

Holiday Motorhome Rentals
314 Princes Highway
Banksia
Sydney NSW 2216
Ph. (02) 597 2533

Newmans Campervans Australia
16-20 Parramatta Road
Summer Hill
Sydney NSW 2130
Ph. (02) 797 6133

New South Wales

1   Snowy Mountains

John Terry Motors
Cnr Hillcrest Street & Parramatta Road
Homebush
Sydney NSW 2140
Ph. (02) 764 3444

Victoria

2   Great Ocean Road

Brits-Rentals
13 Orion Street
Vermont
Melbourne VIC 3133
Ph. (03) 873 2395

Off Road Rentals
1370 North Road
Huntingdale
Melbourne VIC 3166
Ph. (03) 543 7111

Tasmania

3   Tasman Peninsula

Avis-Tasmanian Mobile Motels
39 Campbell Street
Hobart TAS 7000
Ph. (002) 34 4222

Thrifty Car Rentals
156 Harrington Street
Hobart TAS 7000
Ph. (002) 23 3577

4   Lake Pedder

Avis-Tasmanian Mobile Motels

See (3) above for details

5   Devonport

Avis-Tasmanian Mobile Motels
PO Box 147
East Devonport TAS 7310
Ph. (004) 27 9797

Southern Cross Campervans
  & Motorhomes
10 The Esplanade
East Devonport TAS 7310
Ph. (004) 27 9119

South Australia

6   Kangaroo Island

Go Touring
730 Port Road
Beverley
Adelaide SA 5009
Ph. (08) 243 2055

Touralong Travel Homes
344 North East Road
Klemzig
Adelaide SA 5087
Ph. (08) 261 8833

Unit 3/84 Todd Street
Alice Springs NT 5750
Ph. (089) 52 9633

Western Australia

7   South West Western Australia

Koala Campers
44 Great Eastern Highway
South Guildford
Perth WA 6055
Ph. (09) 478 3200

Westland Travel
708 Canning Highway
Applecross
Perth WA 6153
Ph. (09) 364 5529

Northern Territory

8   Stuart Highway

NT Territory Holidays
3rd Floor
418 St Kilda Road
Melbourne VIC 3004
Ph. (03) 820 0822

Thrifty Rent a Car
131 Stuart Highway
Darwin NT 5790
Ph. (089) 81 8555

48 Hartley Street
Alice Springs NT 5750
Ph. (089) 52 6555

Queensland

9   Bowen

Holiday Motorhome Rentals
289 Ingham Road
Garbutt QLD 4810
Ph. (077) 79 3338

Townsville Leisure Homes
31 Ralston Street
Townsville QLD 4810
Ph. (077) 71 2585

10   Carnarvon Gorge

Holiday Motorhome Rentals

See (9) above for details

Townsville Leisure Homes

See (9) above for details

Apollo Motorhome Holidays
698 Nudgee Road
Northgate
Brisbane QLD 4013
Ph. (07) 260 5064

Sunrover Rentals
11 South Pine Road
Alderley
Brisbane QLD 4051
Ph. (07) 352 5888

11   Cooloola National Park

Apollo Motorhome Holidays

See (10) above for details

Sunrover Rentals

See (10) above for details

NOEL LEVY

Motoring — Four-wheel-drive

The ultimate ticket-to-ride in Australia's outback is the four-wheel-drive (4WD) vehicle. The development over the past 20 years of relatively economical, safe and even comfortable 4WD vehicles has brought them a long way from the bone-shaking work-horses they used to be. In the process, 4WD vehicles have opened up areas of outstanding beauty not previously accessible even to adventurous travellers. They have put within reach of most normally experienced drivers the overwhelming vastness of the Nullarbor Plain and the claustrophic tangle of tropical rainforests. Outback tracks, thick with bulldust, creeks that flood past the wheel arches, and broad expanses of white sandy beach are no more than a rented 4WD away. All that is necessary to explore them is a vehicle in first-class order which is packed skilfully and driven with care.

In the past, a rip and tear, bush bash approach existed to four-wheel driving. This not only damaged fragile ecologies, but also lowered the image of 4WD travel. Today, such attitudes have been replaced by more responsible vehicle use on bush tracks and this, combined with walking, can bring anyone within reach of untouched wild country, some of it barely explored.

To cope with the roughest of Australian bush tracks, 4WD vehicles are structurally sound, with beefed-up suspensions and powerful motors. Most vehicles cope with hundreds of kilometres of bone-jarring corrugations probably better than the passengers' kidneys. Four-wheel drives need high ground clearance to negotiate sand tracks and to avoid underbody damage on jagged rocky ground.

On the highways, high-range gearing (often with overdrive) allows for comfortable cruising at top speed limits. Off sealed roads and into true 4WD country, the driver can walk a vehicle in low range over

LEIGH HEMMINGS

Outback creeks are no obstacle for today's 4WD vehicles

boulder-strewn ground or climb steep, loosely gravelled terrain.

Thanks to the advent of power-assisted steering and braking, it takes no great strength to handle a 4WD vehicle. However, coping with the wide variety of Australian terrain requires skill and experience. It is still possible in a 4WD to become hopelessly bogged in mud or defeated by a deep sand track. Knowing when to lower tyre pressure and select the right gear will keep most drivers out of trouble, but this takes experience. For this reason, at least two vehicles should travel together for mutual assistance when heading out into the bush.

For those travelling solo, there is another safety alternative. Many 4WD tour operators, and there are hundreds of them throughout the country, run convoys of privately owned or rented vehicles. These operators provide routes, planning expertise, on-track mechanical repairs, and will even supply provisions and cook all meals along the way.

In very remote, harsh locations — particularly the desert — a convoy is the only wise mode of travel. Where possible, solo drivers (any drivers for that matter) should develop the necessary skills by joining a 4WD club, and taking part in outings and driving courses. Special driving skills courses are available to take drivers through the theory and practice of four-wheel driving.

In planning any trip by 4WD to a remote location, it is essential to establish a checklist. Such a list should read something like this:

> Travel with other vehicles
> One member of the group to have mechanical experience
> Carry an extra spare tyre and tubes plus essential spares (fan belt, radiator hose, coil, condenser, fuse, light bulbs, etc.)
> Don't overload the vehicle
> Take a good jack, tyre pump, shovel, saw and tow rope
> Carry a first-aid kit and a fire extinguisher
> Reserve steel petrol drum plus oil and brake fluid
> Five litres of water per person per day
> Avoid travelling at night or in the late afternoon
> Gain permission for travelling over private roads
> Let others know your itinerary
> Leave gates as you find them

Locations

New South Wales

1   Some of the most dramatic 4WD country in the state lies just a couple of hours to the west of Sydney in the **Blue Mountains.** The Blue Mountains may appear to be little more than a range of picturesque hills when viewed from Sydney's western suburbs, but in reality they encompass rugged bush-choked country which barred explorers for more than three decades after the first settlement of the colony. Operators working from Katoomba, easily reached by train from Sydney, can explore less well-known areas of the Blue Mountains and the western slopes on eight-to-nine hour 4WD tours in air-conditioned vehicles.

Longer overnight trips take travellers to historic Hill End and Yerranderie. Gold fossicking is popular on both day and overnight trips.

2   In **northern New South Wales,** the eastern slopes of the Great Dividing Range and the unspoilt coastal region between Taree and Coffs Harbour provides some scenic driving country. Inland, the heavily forested hills contain stands of both subtropical and cool temperate rainforests, including Antarctic beech. Many state forests are located here, between the numerous rivers that wind their way to the coast. The coastline of lakes, heathland and long stretches of white beach is a striking contrast to the pastoral and woodland scenery of the hinterland with its thriving dairy and timber industries.

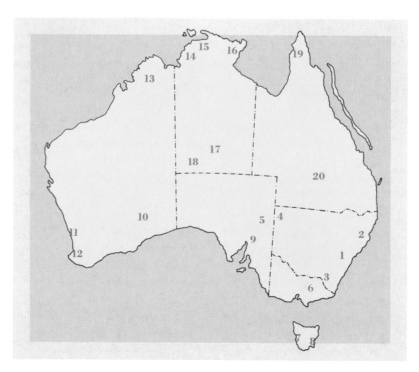

3   The alpine scenery and high plateau country of the **Snowy Mountains** in the south of the state make it another superb location for four-wheel driving. And the area is very accessible from both Canberra and Sydney. Both the winter and summer here have their own special characteristics. Wildflower-carpeted grasslands are transformed in winter by a covering of snow that makes this region one of Australia's most popular skiing venues. A trip to the Snowies can easily be extended into the alpine areas of Victoria, just across the border.

4   Accessible to 4WDs is the aptly named **Corner Country.** The region, at the meeting point of New South Wales, Queensland and South Australia, is an inhospitable land of gibber plains and rolling red sand hills, where shimmering heat plays tricks on the eyes. It is fascinating country for four-wheel driving. The area was first surveyed by John Cameron in 1881, and the dingo fence runs close by.

The region is accessible in autumn, winter and spring. The closest settlement, Tibooburra, was originally at the centre of a goldrush. It is now a drowsy settlement, but still retains its unique character with wide streets composed more of grit, sand and dust than of bitumen, and the paintings of bush artists displayed on the walls of the local pub.

Visitors should stock up on food and water and then visit the NSW National Parks and Wildlife Office. North of Tibooburra is the Sturt National Park, once Mt King and Mt Wood stations, encompassing a wide expanse of desert covering nearly 300,000 hectares. A feature of the park is the abundant glossy black and scarlet Sturt pea.

From here, travellers can head for Innamincka in one of two ways. One route continues along the Silver City Highway, entering Queensland through the dingo fence at Warri Gate. From here on, the track crosses gibbers, loose sand and bulldust and tackles numerous creek crossings.

The other route heads for Cameron's Corner and travels past Bollard's Lagoon to Murti Murti. Just short of the town, the route joins the famous Strzelecki Track to Innamincka. This involves some classic four-wheel driving beside spectacular red sandhills that are awesome in the warmth of a desert sunset.

5   Innamincka boasts the stark ruins of the Inland Mission hostel. Once an important base for the famous Flying Doctor Service, today the town caters mostly for 4WD and coach traffic. It is a simple matter to find a secluded campsite on the banks of **Cooper's Creek** among the coolabah trees. Those who like to read up on their history in advance should get hold of a copy of Alan Moorehead's *Cooper's Creek.*

Sleeping in the open under the stars in this region is an experience not to be missed. On this side of the Black Stump (that's Australian for 'back of beyond'), the Southern Cross and its neighbours take on unmatched brilliance. Sleeping late in the morning is

TREVERN DAWES

Australia's overland tracks are notorious for unpredictable terrain

much less pleasant. Screeching, wheeling flocks of white corellas make enough noise to wake the dead. Once awakened, the newcomer should take time to visit the Dig Tree, made famous during the tragic journey of Burke and Wills, and still standing. There are memorials to the two explorers nearby, and the Cullyamurra Lagoon where they rested is not far away. The country around here is rugged, particularly the route along the northern side of Cooper's Creek to the Dig Tree site.

From Cooper's Creek, head out to the oasis of Coongie Lakes, which have water in all but the driest years. As the dry season progresses, more and more animals and birds congregate near the water. Each morning while the dew is still on the ground, the evidence of their nocturnal wanderings is to be seen in intricate tracks etched on the fine red sand.

Victoria

6 The Snowy River country in the **Victorian Alps** in north-eastern Victoria was made famous by Australia's unofficial poet laureate, 'Banjo' Paterson, at the turn of the century. A major Australian film named after Paterson's famous poem 'The Man from Snowy River' has already made the region well known to cinema-goers world-wide, and a sequel now in the making will extend its reputation.

The area can be reached with comparative ease from Canberra and Melbourne. Travellers can make the 200-kilometre drive from Melbourne, or rent vehicles in the region. In addition, a number of tour operators run 4WD trips of varying duration through the high country.

The Snowy River country is studded with old cattlemen's settlements and former goldmining sites, and most tours include visits to both.

And it is memorable country. The mist rises through the tallest hardwood forest in the world and visitors camped in forest glades can listen to the rush of mountain streams that provide some of the best trout fishing in the country. The region is rich in history, and many tours take travellers along forest trails little used since early bushmen drove cattle along them a century ago.

Trips vary in length from one day to a week or more and are not confined to athletic adventurers. Several operators boast that their tours are suitable for people of any age who are in reasonable health and there are plenty of opportunities for bushwalking and for relaxing within sight of the best views in the state.

A feature of alpine 4WD trips is the nightly campfire and singalong. Some are so well catered for that all a visitor needs to bring is a good voice. In many cases, tour operators will organise an itinerary to fit individual needs. For those who like everything to be organised, tours that start and finish in both Canberra and Melbourne are available.

It's as well to be prepared, however. The weather in the high country is fickle even in summer and warm, waterproof clothes are advisable.

Tasmania

Tasmania, Australia's smallest state, is known for its orchards and gardens and for the comfortable, settled pattern of its agriculture. But this is only part of the story.

7 Conservationists and adventurers alike know Tasmania as one of the main areas of undiscovered Australia. Much of **central and southern Tasmania,** consisting of rugged mountain country clad in temperate rainforest, has been barely touched by man. Some of it, particularly the area around the Franklin River, is understandably restricted.

Nevertheless, 4WD operators do offer tours to the region. These normally set off from Hobart or Launceston in the more settled regions of the state.

Day trips are available, but those with the time should experience an extended tour of a week or so in a luxury 4WD vehicle to the south-west wilderness. Some trips involve cruises on the Gordon River — in country conservation groups fought over and won just a few years ago. Tours take in old mining settlements such as Zeehan, little-seen rainforests and abandoned railway tracks.

Despite the rugged terrain, operators cater for anyone of reasonable health and fitness as well as for the disabled.

8 There are 4WD tours, too, in the more populous areas of Tasmania, including half-day and one-day trips around the **Tasman Peninsula** starting from Port Arthur. These can pack 130 kilometres of travel into a day trip, visiting convict ruins, oyster and mussel farms and secluded ocean coastlines.

South Australia

Tours by 4WD are available through many areas of South Australia, and some of them link up with optional activities such as camel trekking and aircraft safaris. The many cattle roads in the state, notably the Gunbarrel Highway, attract four-wheel drivers in their own vehicles on trips of varying duration.

9 A popular area for explorers is the **Flinders Ranges.** The region encompasses Oodnadatta, at the start of the Birdsville Track, and the subterranean opal-mining centre of Coober Pedy. Four-wheel drive tours to the region normally end in a campfire singalong, and some feature real Australian-made damper prepared on the hot coals. Guests can even bed down in an Aussie swag. Visitors with limited time can still experience the outback, staying at bunk-houses in the Rawnsley Park camping centre, for example.

Some operators are well versed in Aboriginal dreamtime legends and in the history of the Flinders Ranges and surrounding districts. There is even the opportunity for the visitor to learn a little bush craft along the way. Most operators offer motel or camping options and use well-appointed 4WDs so that the visitor's outback experience need not be an uncomfortable one. Several boast that they have taken passengers 80 years old or more. In many cases, the drivers and guides are themselves well-known Australian outback personalities.

10 Spanning the borderlands of Western Australia and South Australia is the vast, flat **Nullarbor Plain.** The Nullarbor is well named: far from being an Aboriginal word, Nullarbor is Latin for 'without trees'.

Both rail and road links cross the plain from Port Augusta in South Australia, and although it is a hot and dusty haul through the barren scrub-covered

The Devils Marbles, over 30 disconcertingly round and perfectly balanced rock shapes to be found near Tennant Creek in the Northern Territory.

A four-wheel-drive is essential to discover the heart of Australia - a land of constant surprise where the sun can turn the sky blood-red at the end of a long day's drive

MARK HANLON

landscape it can be done in comparative comfort, given time. This was not always so. A 4WD alternative to mindlessly following the bitumen is to turn off the highway at Medura and follow the old telegraph line at the foot of the Hampton escarpment.

In this age of high-tech telecommunications, it is easy to forget how much struggle and sweat went into making the first tentative connections between Western Australia and the eastern states — a distance roughly equivalent to the entire span of Europe or the United States. Travelling down the old telegraph line gives the driver some appreciation of just how tough the conditions must have been. The area is protected within the Nuytsland Nature Reserve and the journey is enlivened by sightings of emus, buzzards, mallee fowl and kangaroos.

One magnificent campsite is set among the picturesque ruins of the old Bunabbie Telegraph Station. Shell kerosene tins were used as building materials and the faint classic imprint of their emblem can still be seen, though it is gradually crumbling to rust and dust. From here it is only a short drive along a soft sand track to the ocean with its rolling white dunes, and to the Eyre bird observatory, one of the most remote in the world.

Trekking out on the dunes is something like being on foot in a moonscape of sand. In the late afternoon, as white dunes turn gold in the reflected sunset, the traveller might catch a breathtaking glimpse of pink and red from a flock of Major Mitchell cockatoos.

The 4WD track to the head of the Great Australian Bight is a little obscure, but it is worthwhile persisting until you find it. From a camp among the dunes, it is possible to walk to the very edge of Australia and to watch the Southern Ocean pounding against rugged limestone cliffs — a scene once described by the explorer Edward John Eyre as 'a rich and gorgeous view for a painter'.

Another explorer, Giles, described the Nullarbor as 'a region utterly unknown to man, and as utterly forsaken by God'. Travelling in the comfort and security of a 4WD vehicle, it is possible to have a more charitable view of this awesome landscape.

The whole region was once the floor of the ocean, and fossilised shells are to be found well inland. The Nullarbor caves were formed when the sea retreated and fresh rainwater seeped down from the surface. These caves, while rugged, are cooler than the ground-level Nullarbor.

Observing the horizon from a camp in the centre of this endless plain is rather like standing on a cliff viewing a becalmed ocean. At night, the Nullarbor sky is one of the biggest and brightest in the world. A number of operators take visitors to the Nullarbor on tours lasting typically five or six days. At least one Perth-based group offers the option of flying back from the Nullarbor so as to maximise the time available.

Western Australia

11 Travellers based in **Perth** will find a number of trips of varying duration available to them. Western Australia, the country's largest state and one of the least populous, offers almost unlimited opportunity to the four-wheel driver. A driving skills course is also available in Perth for drivers who wish to improve their four-wheel driving techniques.

12 The **south-west region**, some 270 kilometres from Perth, is a largely unoccupied area. The Perth-based traveller can explore this region in his own vehicle or travel with an experienced local 4WD operator. A three-day tour includes fishing and swimming at deserted beaches, bushwalking in the karri forests, and freshwater lakes and waterfalls.

13 One area of Western Australia deserves special mention. This is the remote and rugged **Kimberley region**, which borders on the Northern Territory in the far north of the state. Ancient mountain ranges, a spectacular coastline and isolated settlements characterise the area. Mysterious rock formations such as the weathered sandstone of the Bungle Bungles, only recently added to the tourist itinerary and still a little-known wonder of Australia, provide a backdrop to the surrounding plains.

A variety of 4WD tours cover the Kimberley Ranges. Some trips touch the coast at settlements like the old pearling lugger town of Broome and then mount the Mitchell Plateau to traverse the cattle savannah plains of the West Kimberley region. These safaris sometimes dovetail with even more adventurous 4WD tours which explore in depth the north of Western Australia. Still others conduct Aboriginal heritage tours which offer visitors overnight accommodation in isolated communities while Aboriginal guides explain the traditions and culture of the Aborigines.

Northern Territory

The Northern Territory embraces within its boundaries some of the wildest and emptiest country in Australia — and also some of the most varied terrain. It is now possible for the four-wheel driver to travel with comparative ease halfway across the continent from Alice Springs in the south of the state to the port town of Darwin in the tropical north. But there's not much human settlement on either side of the road. The southern half of the territory in particular is a land of awesome red desert and scrub and of enormous cattle properties larger than some European principalities.

14 The **Darwin region** has plenty of history to attract the visitor with his own 4WD or a rented vehicle, and a number of tour operators work from the city. Darwin was bombed by the Japanese in the Second World War (the only major Australian town to be

Ever-changing scenery is a feature of Australia - a dusting of snow in the mountains, above, a river crossing or wide, empty beaches, opposite

accorded this privilege) and was flattened by the devastating Cyclone Tracy in the 1970s.

But the Darwin region was an exciting place to live long before that. Towns like Pine Creek, about two and a half hours' drive from Darwin, were the scene of goldrush activity in the 1870s which drew thousands of Europeans and Chinese to the diggings. The relics of this romantic past remain, with vestiges of the once-thriving Chinatown and abandoned diggings forming a focal point for a number of local tour operators.

Hunting is permitted in the area, subject to certain restrictions, and some tour operators organise buffalo hunting safaris.

15 South-east of Darwin lies **Kakadu National Park.** Kakadu is a microcosm of the Northern Territory, with its gorges, waterfalls, Aboriginal rock art, crocodiles and buffalo. Four-wheel driving in Kakadu takes on the character of an old-style safari, with plenty of face-to-face encounters with wild game including buffalo. The difference is that on this game chase, the only shooting allowed is with a camera.

Travellers to Yellow Waters can leave their vehicle and board a stable outboard-powered punt to explore lagoon waters that are home to huge saltwater crocodiles. These creatures can live to a venerable age and grow to a frightening size. Sightings of reptiles three metres in length and more are not unusual, and getting close enough to spot one of these creatures is about as close as anyone would want to get.

Aboriginal involvement with the Kakadu region goes back 20,000 years, so it is fitting that the Aboriginal presence is strong today. The park itself is owned by Aborigines and many of the traditional owners work there as rangers helping to administer the region.

Aboriginal rock art in the area depicts the Tasmanian devil, barramundi, catfish, magpie geese,

DAVID PRICE

LEIGH HEMMINGS

European man, and the so-called x-ray paintings show the internal organs and skeletons of animals.

The living creatures in the park, and particularly the birds, are at least as colourful as the Aboriginal paintings that recorded them tens of thousands of years ago.

Three hours of rough driving will take the devoted driver to Twin and Jim Jim Falls. Freshwater crocodiles have made their home in the green water beneath red ochre cliffs at Twin Falls.

Operators based in both Darwin and Alice Springs will take visitors on 4WD Kakadu safaris of varying length.

16 It is in the Northern Territory that Australia's Aborigines have been able to maintain their age-old culture with the least interference. Much of **Arnhem Land**, in the territory's far north-east, is a restricted area in order to help preserve the Aboriginal heritage, and many communities live there much as they have always done.

While it is understandably not permitted for four-wheel drivers or anyone to go barrelling through the Aboriginal homelands in this region, at least two licensed ground tour operators are allowed into Arnhem Land. One tour takes visitors through the Stone country with an Aboriginal guide to observe living areas and examples of dramatic Aboriginal rock art. Typical images include explicit paintings in a spirit gallery which dates back 23,000 years. The operator, based in Darwin, also takes tours to other parts of the Northern Territory.

17 **Alice Springs** was made famous by novelist Neville Shute in the 1950s. The town — surprisingly large and sophisticated these days — occupies a point at the very heart of Australia's Red Centre. Every second vehicle in this region is a 4WD, and there is no lack of places to use them.

18 A matter of hours from Alice is perhaps Australia's most famous — and now infamous — geological monument, **Ayers Rock**. This vast mound of red stone has fascinated painters and photographers for generations, and has held equally magical significance for the Aborigines in the area for many thousands of years before that. The Rock is now owned by the Aboriginal people, who lease it back to the white man so that all Australians and visitors from all over the world can enjoy it. Having arrived there, it is traditional to climb Ayers Rock, and though hardly an alpine ascent this undertaking has its dangers. In particular, there is only one quick way down.

Purists may find that the tourist activity around the Rock lessens its attraction somewhat. In that case, it is worth driving on a few miles to explore the nearby Olgas and King's Canyon. These sights are less well-frequented and retain rather more of their lonely majesty.

For people with limited time, operators in Alice Springs offer a variety of one- or two-day local tours in 4WD vehicles that include visits to local Aborigines and working cattle stations. Some of the spectacular gorge country is within easy reach of the town, as are the historic telegraph station and the Northern Territory's only winery, Chateau Hornsby, where visitors can have lunch and taste the local produce.

Queensland

19 The far northern tip of Australia is one of the top attractions for 4WD adventurers in the country. Queensland's **Cape York Peninsula** is a remote and still predominantly wild area, encompassing thousands of kilometres of dusty dry track, tropical rainforest, and swamps and rivers inhabited by huge saltwater crocodiles.

The Cape is no day trip. Even from Cairns on the north Queensland coast, where many tour operators are based, it can take five days or more of testing four-wheel driving to get within striking distance of the Cape. The route, crossed by dozens of creeks and rivers, is a wild and sparsely populated wilderness trafficable only from May to November, and then only by 4WD. To many, it is the last frontier. One regular driver has described the road to the Cape as 'designed to rearrange your kidneys and shake the fillings from your teeth'.

However, civilisation is not left behind entirely. Many operators use enormously expensive, relatively comfortable and highly sophisticated vehicles, equipped with powerful motors and winches. They also maintain radio contact with the Flying Doctor Service in case of an emergency.

Four-wheel-drive tours take up to 16 days, but an eight-day trip is possible if passengers opt to fly back from the Cape. Some trips include the nearby Torres Strait islands, which lie between Australia and Papua-New Guinea.

But there is really no limit to the time the four-wheel driver could spend in the Cape York area without seeing anything twice. The region is just slightly smaller than the state of Victoria and could easily absorb a six-month odyssey. For some, it does just that — but only if they can meet the high price of staple foods and fuel, and resist being carried off into the mangroves by the sandflies.

The most popular national park on the Cape is Lakefield, which can be entered with a permit obtainable from the Ranger Station. With an area of more than 500,000 hectares, Lakefield is the second largest national park in Queensland. It is home to more than 200 species of birds, mammals and reptiles and that great fighting fish, the barramundi. Pick up a set of locally made lures in Cairns on the way north and try slow-speed trolling from a boat or casting and retrieving from the bank. But landing a barramundi is no easy task. Like everything that survives up here, the fish is tough and smart.

20 The **Central Highlands** of Queensland are dotted with national parks and campsites which are almost always uncrowded. The Carnarvon Gorge National Park is well worth a visit by the four-wheel driver, and it is within striking distance of the gem fields of western Queensland. Fossicking for precious stones is almost a national sport up here, and while fortunes are rarely made, the industrious and the patient have a very real chance of making a find, if they chance upon the right places to look.

Old goldmining towns in the area, such as Mt Morgan and Clermont, are testimony that some prospectors did find their fortunes in the region.

Some of the Central Highlands' most interesting features are to be found on private properties. These include extraordinary rock formations and Aboriginal sites. Access to these properties is restricted, however, and the four-wheel driver in his own or a rented vehicle may benefit from joining one of the area's tour groups.

During the spring, autumn and summer seasons, a number of tour groups work the Central Highlands, and a crowded seven or eight-day 4WD safari is a good way to get to know the region quickly. Tours of this kind are within reach of people staying in the Rockhampton area, where some of the operators are based.

Ayers Rock forms a dramatic background to a Range Rover, above, while a vehicle tackles an outback track, right

21 **Fraser Island**, north of Brisbane and within easy reach of that city, is the largest sand island in the world. It encompasses vast freshwater lakes, clear streams and dense rainforest. Fraser Island is criss-crossed with sand tracks suitable only for 4WD vehicles — a legacy of its timber felling past. Its hard-packed beaches make for easier driving, but remember to keep an eye on the tide.

A fee must be paid on entering the island and camping permits are required. Access is gained by a vehicle barge from Hervey Bay or Rainbow Beach, and 4WDs may be hired from either location or in Brisbane.

The northern part of the island is a national park, and the southern part is state forest. Both have camping areas and there are a number of private camping grounds. Motel-style accommodation is also available for those visitors who are less committed to the outdoors.

The ultimate 4WD campsite on Fraser Island is at the back of the eastern beach, close to drinkable freshwater streams. Rising at dawn, the camper may catch sight of wild brumbies galloping along the empty beach.

Fishing is splendid almost all year round on both sides of the island and on the offshore reefs. The peak fishing time is August/September when the tailor run. Tailor — bluefish to Americans and shad to South Africans — draw hundreds of excited anglers in the season and make the island a mecca for 4WD vehicles. Fishermen have to compete with sharks for their catch and it's not unusual for them to have to cast their bait beyond the sharks to reach the tailor.

TREVERN DAWES

Motoring — 4WD Contacts

Operators

Many of the operators detailed below arrange 4WD expeditions that traverse large sections, or the whole, of Australia. Some examples are:

AAT King's
Their 23-day 'Western Frontier and Gunbarrel Highway Expedition' goes from Alice Springs to Western Australia's Kimberley area, returning via the Gunbarrel Highway and the Gibson Desert.

Australian Pacific Tours
A 29-day 'Great Frontier Expedition' goes from Alice Springs to the Gulf of Carpentaria, Kakadu National Park, Western Australia's Mitchell Plateau area and back to Alice Springs via the Tanami Desert.

Centralian
The 'Transcontinental Safari' is a 30-day 4WD convoy adventure that travels from Sydney or Melbourne to Birdsville, the Simpson Desert, Alice Springs, then through Western Australia and South Australia before returning to Sydney/Melbourne.

Desert-Trek Australia
A 26-day Cape York expedition travels from Adelaide through New South Wales and Queensland to Cape York, in Northern Queensland, and returns via the Gulf of Carpentaria and the outback to Adelaide.

Trekabout Expeditions
This 106-day 'Round Australia Expedition' is the most comprehensive itinerary offered. From Brisbane, the group proceeds north to Cape York, then into the Northern Territory, Western Australia and across the Gunbarrel Highway and the Simpson Desert before returning to Brisbane.

Contacts for all of the above operators are detailed below.

Four-wheel-drive vehicles are available for hire in most Australian cities — refer to *Yellow Pages* telephone directories. The following companies hire vehicles in all major cities:

Avis Rent-a-Car
PO Box 205
Alexandria
Sydney NSW 2015
Ph. Toll Free (008) 22 5533

Budget Rent-a-Car
21 Bedford Street
North Melbourne VIC 3051
Ph. Toll Free (008) 33 1331

New South Wales

1 Blue Mountains

Venture Out
Based in the Blue Mountains, about two hours to the west of Sydney, Venture Out runs 4WD tours that are both adventurous and educational. Full-day tours take in the more remote regions of this rugged country, and overnight trips provide the opportunity to see the old goldmining towns of Hill End and Sofala, as well as the Jenolan Caves. You are welcome to try your hand at gold fossicking on both day and overnight trips.

PO Box 82
Katoomba NSW 2780
Ph. (047) 82 5022

2 Northern New South Wales

Mount Seaview Safaris
Half-day and full-day safaris, plus two and three-day escorted camping safaris are offered at the Mount Seaview Resort, 80 kilometres from Port Macquarie, midway between Sydney and Brisbane. You can go gold panning, explore rugged mountainous country, visit bush pubs and discover out-of-the-way beaches. Various styles of accommodation are provided at the resort, and all meals are available. There are also guest kitchens. Mount Seaview Safaris also offer 24 and 26-day safaris, either camping or accommodated, all over Australia.

Oxley Highway
via Wauchope NSW 2446
Ph. (065) 87 7155

3 Snowy Mountains

Scobie's Walkabout
Naturalist and former ranger Paul Scobie provides 4WD treks complete with knowledgeable local guides to show you the alpine plants, animals and scenery away from the more predictable locations. Walking is combined with four-wheel driving in these holidays, but there is no backpacking. Walks, graded easy to medium, operate from a base camp. Accommodation is in walk-in, insect-proof tents, motels, hotels or lodges, as appropriate.

PO Box 43
Newcastle NSW 2300
Ph. (049) 2 3025

4 Corner Country

Sambell's Scenic Tours
In their luxury landcruisers, equipped with radio telephones and fridges, Sambell's Scenic Tours offer a five-day, three-state outback tour which takes in Broken Hill, Sturt National Park and Cameron's Corner, the spot where South Australia, New South Wales and Queensand meet. You will be picked up from and returned to Adelaide, staying at motels and hotels along the way. The Sambells bring to their business a wide knowledge of South Australia and the outback.

7 Melaleuca Drive
Gawler SA 5118
Ph. (085) 22 2871

5 Cooper's Creek

Desert-Trek Australia
Desert-Trek Australia is the oldest 4WD company in Australia and one of the smallest. Owner-operator Dick Lang's ancestors were among the first settlers in South Australia and he maintains a long tradition with the outback. Desert-Trek has been crossing the centre of the Simpson Desert and visiting the Cooper's Creek area regularly for the last 20 years. The company also offers camel and aircraft safaris.

PO Box 80
Highbury
Adelaide SA 5089
Ph. (08) 264 7200

Outback Expeditions
Outback Expeditions offer outback tours in the style to which the original Australian bushmen would have been accustomed. And that means visiting remote places such as Innamincka and Cooper's Creek, sleeping in a swag under the stars (or in a tent if you prefer) and enjoying bush cooking on an open fire. This is a chance to learn a little bush craft and at the same time have a great 4WD holiday.

PO Box 651
Blackwood
Adelaide SA 5051
Ph. (08) 270 2032

Transcontinental Safaris
Rex Ellis, owner of Transcontinental Safaris, has many years' experience as a tour operator and has an intimate knowledge of the outback. He runs his tours in the cooler winter months, and travellers sleep under the stars in cosy swags. The trips include fossicking for opals in Andamooka, a visit to the Coongie Lakes for fishing and boating, Aboriginal rock carvings and various locations associated with Burke and Wills' famous trip. Transcontinental also runs boat safaris and extensive outback camel safaris.

PMB 251
Kingscote
Kangaroo Island SA 5223
Ph. (0848) 9 3256

Victoria

6 Victorian Alps

Bogong Jack Adventures
Bogong Jack was a cattle duffer and
horse thief who roamed the high country
of the Victorian Alps in the 1850s, and it
is to this country that Bogong Jack
Adventures take their groups. Trips are
often combined with walking in the
Bogong and Dargo High Plains, and
visits to rustic cattlemen's huts and old
goldmining sites. Tours only operate in
the summer.

PO Box 209
Wangaratta VIC 3677
Ph. (057) 21 2564

Mansfield Mountain Safaris
This company operates out of Mansfield,
nestled at the foot of Mt Buller, gateway
to the Victorian Great Dividing Range.
This is real Australian horseman
country, remote, rugged and steep, made
famous in the film, *The Man from Snowy
River*. Tours operate in spring, summer
and autumn. Bring a warm, waterproof
coat as even in summer the weather can
be cold. 4WD vehicles are available for
hire.

137 High Street
Mansfield VIC 3722
Ph. (057) 75 2606

Snowy River Outriders
Snowy River Outriders take 4WD tours
through this magnificent country of
hardwood forests and wild mountain
streams. There are frequent stops, and
walks are a feature of all tours. Also
available are horse riding, rafting,
bushwalking, canoeing and rockclimbing.

PO Box 399
Orbost VIC 3888
Ph. (051) 54 1089

Upper Murray 4WD Tours
Greg Coysh, owner-operator of Upper
Murray 4WD Tours, maintains that the
view from the top of Mt Pinnabar, only
accessible by 4WD, is the best in
Victoria. Gold and tin-mining areas can
be visited, and for keen anglers there is
access to some of the best trout fishing
in the country. The company will supply
a vehicle and driver to lead a maximum
of six private 4WDs.

43-45 Hansen Street
Corryong VIC 3707
Ph. (060) 76 1664

Tasmania

7 Central and South Tasmania

Bushventures 4WD Tours
Bushventures 4WD Tours is the only
organisation permitted entry to the
restricted World Heritage area of south-
west Tasmania — a wilderness of
temperate rainforest and wild
mountains. Day and extended tours are
run, with the overnight trips fully catered
and accommodated. A six-day excursion
to the Franklin River is available, which
includes cruising the Arthur and
Gordon Rivers and walking on Cradle
Mountain.

4 Heath Court
Kingstone TAS 7150
Ph. (002) 29 4291

Centralian
Centralian offers nine-day wilderness
convoys all around Tasmania. You can
travel in a Centralian escort vehicle, hire
a 4WD, or join the group in your own
4WD. Accommodation is mainly in tents
(a couple of nights are spent in cabins),
and most meals are provided.

1 James Street
Clayton
Melbourne VIC 3168
Ph. (03) 544 8644

*Tas-Trek Four Wheel Drive Adventure
   Tours*
Tas-Trek are entirely at home in the
wildest, most spectacular parts of the
state. One of their five-day tours takes
you through the Central Plateau to Lake
St Clair, Mt McCutcheon, Mt McCall, the
Franklin River Gorge, Queenstown, the
Gordon River, Black Bluff and Cradle
Mountain National Park before returning
you to Devonport.

PO Box 100
Longford TAS 7301
Ph. (003) 97 6340

8 Tasman Peninsula

Tasman Peninsula Detours
Tasman Peninsula Detours is based at
Port Arthur, the most popular tourist
destination in Tasmania. Owner-operator
Andrew Simmons has eight years'
experience guiding tours of the Tasman
Peninsula and thus has an intimate
knowledge of the peninsula and its flora
and fauna. Half-day and full-day tours
take in rainforests, old convict ruins,
oyster and mussel farms, trout farms and
secluded ocean coastline, including
Roaring Beach. Special 4WD fishing
tours can be arranged.

Arthur Highway
C/- PO
Port Arthur TAS 7182
Ph. (002) 50 3355

South Australia

9 Flinders Ranges

G'Day South Australia Adventure Tours
Jim Larsen is a true bushie, with a great
love of the untouched country through
which he takes his clients. Regular 4WD
tours head out to the Flinders Ranges,
Oodnadatta, Coober Pedy and down the
Coorong, south of Adelaide. A
particularly appealing tour is the four-
day Flinders trip which takes in the
'Great Wall of China'. Small numbers
and a flexible mode of travel enable an
unhurried schedule: there is always time
for an extra photo or a spot of fishing.

Lot 10 Bassett Street
Nairne SA 5252
Ph. (08) 388 6000

Outback Expeditions
Bill Temby, the owner of Outback
Expeditions, is an enthusiastic Flinders
Ranges explorer, photographer and
mineral collector, who virtually
pioneered hang-gliding in the region. He
is currently researching the Aboriginal
dreamtime legends of the area. His
4WD tours enable travellers to sample
the style of life the bushmen once
enjoyed — cooking on an open fire, even
sleeping under the stars if you wish.

See (5) above for details.

Sambell's Scenic Tours
Operating out of Adelaide, Sambell's
provide a variety of tours in the region,
including three, four and five-day tours
to the Flinders Ranges, taking in
Arkaroola, Leigh Creek, Blinman,
Wilpena Pound and Hawker.
Accommodation is provided in hotels
and motels. A maximum of six people
are taken on any one tour. The
airconditioned 4WD vehicles are
equipped with a radio telephone and
fridge.

See (4) above for details

Treckabout Safaris
Treckabout Safaris aim to make outback
safaris comfortable for the less
adventurous, priding themselves on their
high standards of service, well-appointed
vehicles and a good range of
accommodation. A popular trip is the
Arkaroola-Top of the Range safari, which
is a tour through the Gammon Ranges
National Park, visiting many almost
inaccessible areas. Motel
accommodation or two camping options
are provided.

30 Berryman Drive
Modbury SA 5092
Ph. (08) 264 3770

10 Nullarbor Plain

Desert-Trek Australia
Dick Lang, who operates Desert-Trek Australia, has years of experience in taking small groups to some of the remotest parts of the country. Among the safaris he offers is a 15-day round trip from Adelaide taking in Coober Pedy, Curtin Springs, Ayers Rock, Docker River, the Gunbarrel Highway, the Great Victoria Desert and finally Rawlinna, where you board the *Indian Pacific* to cross the Nullarbor.

See (5) above for details

Off-Road Safari Tours & Aboriginal Heritage
Based in Perth, Off-Road Safari Tours operate day tours as well as extended outback expeditions. Their Nullarbor Plain five and six-day 4WD tours give you the chance to experience the superb wilderness of the Nullarbor. An option on these trips is to fly back to Perth. Aboriginal Heritage Tours take groups on overnight trips to isolated communities in the far north of Western Australia. Aboriginal guides give clients a privileged insight into their traditions and culture.

49 Pearson Street
Floreat
Perth WA 6014
Ph. (09) 387 5564

Transcontinental Safaris
Among the safaris on offer from Transcontinental is the 14-21-day Nullarbor Wilderness Safari, which operates out of Adelaide. This tour enables visitors to experience the vast empty distances of the northern Nullarbor and the Great Victorian Desert, a botanist's paradise. On the 21-day trip, visitors travel on to Rawlinna, visit a Nullarbor sheep station, and then travel south to the Great Australian Bight, the Nullarbor Cliffs and Lake Tallacootra. The last few days take in Lake Everard and the Gawler Ranges.

See (5) above for details

Western Australia

11 Perth

Venture Skills West
This company runs a number of adventure tours and instructional courses in outdoor recreational pursuits. The 4WD instructional courses comprise two evening sessions for two weeks, followed by one and a half days of practical experience. To conclude, Venture Skills West runs a three-day tour in a challenging area of the south-west of

Western Australia for you to try out your new skills. Instruction courses are also run on rockclimbing, canoeing and mountain biking.

34 Wellesley Way
Samson
Perth WA 6163
Ph. (09) 337 3856

12 South-west Region

Milesaway 4WD Tours
Located in popular tourist country some 270 kilometres from Perth, Milesaway 4WD Tours will take you far away from the better-known spots. Their three-day, 450-kilometre Black Point and Beyond tour, for example, takes visitors to deserted beaches, vast rolling sand dunes, karri forests and freshwater lakes and waterfalls. Day tours operate from Busselton to Cape Naturaliste and spectacular local caves.

'Marnup Park'
Cape Naturaliste Road
Dunsborough WA 6281
Ph. (097) 55 3574

13 Kimberleys and Bungle Bungles

Amesz Adventure Tours
The ten-day Amesz Mitchell Plateau Kimberley 4WD Adventure sets off from the old pearling town of Broome, and takes in the cattle plains of the west Kimberleys, bushcamping and trekking the gorges as you ascend the Mitchell Plateau. This trip dovetails with an eight-day Bungle Bungle 4WD Adventure. There is also an in-depth exploration of the north of Western Australia on a 22-day Grand Kimberley Adventure.

223 Collier Road
Bayswater
Perth WA 6053
Ph. (09) 271 2696

Centralian
Centralian, one of the country's principal tour operators, offers an eight-day Bungle Bungle air safari, operating out of all major cities, which gives visitors five days in this remote region. You join the 4WD vehicle at Kununurra, the nearest town of any consequence, which is several hundred kilometres distant. Bungle Bungle is a 'lost world' of beehive-shaped sandstone hills, sheer cliffs, valleys of palms and stony riverbeds which have been visited by a mere handful of white people.

See (7) above for details

Kimberley Pursuits
Wyndham is about as far north in Western Australia as you can go without getting wet, and it is on a working cattle station not far from Wyndham that you

will find Kimberley Pursuits. They operate three-night 4WD treks in the Saw Ranges where you can sleep in a swag under the stars, fish and swim in the billabongs and learn all you wish to know about the Kimberleys from your guides. Tours do not operate during the summer.

PO Box 5
Wyndham WA 6740
Ph. (091) 61 1014

Kimberley Safari
Kimberley Safari is run by Sam Lovell, known as 'Mr Kimberley'. Of Aboriginal descent, Sam has an extensive knowledge of the area and of its traditional inhabitants. About the only requirements to join one of his trips are the ability to walk and a fair level of fitness. Kimberley Safari runs two 14-day tours, one to the Mitchell Plateau and the other to the Bungle Bungles.

PO Box 63
Derby WA 6728
Ph. (091) 91 1084

Northern Territory

14 Darwin Region

Back o' Beyond Tours
Based in Pine Creek, two and a half hours from Darwin, Back o' Beyond Tours will show you the remains of this goldrush town which had its heyday in the 1870s, attracting thousands of Europeans and Chinese to the diggings. Owner-operators Earl and Elaine Gano have lived in the area for 14 years. Earl, once a park ranger, uses his extensive local knowledge in organising tailor-made sightseeing tours and buffalo hunting safaris.

159 Gunn Alley
Pine Creek NT 5782
Ph. (089) 76 1221

Terra Safari Tours
Terra Safari Tours operate a wide range of tours out of Darwin, from a one-day sampling of Kakadu to an 11-day Top End Explorer, which will take you to Kakadu, the Kimberleys and Broome. Owner-operator Tom Winter says all his staff are competent bushmen and women and experts in their field.

5 Moil Crescent
Darwin NT 5790
Ph. (089) 27 0881 or 45 0863

15 Kakadu National Park

Australian Pacific Tours
Australian Pacific, a sizeable tour operator, has a small, highly specialised division which runs 15-passenger 4WD tours out of Alice Springs. The 15-day

and 21-day tours take in Kakadu National Park as part of their itinerary. The patrol captain and the camp cook are chosen for their expert knowledge of the outback, and each vehicle has a lending library stocked with literature relating to the area being travelled. An aluminium dinghy travels on the roof, to be used for fishing expeditions and general exploring. Tours do not operate between November and February.

475 Hampton Street
Hampton
Melbourne VIC 3188
Ph. (03) 598 5355

Dial-a-Safari
A wide range of Kakadu tours is offered by Dial-a-Safari, from one-day trips for those whose time is limited, to a 16-day adventure special taking in Wangi, Katherine and Kakadu. Several seven-day tours are offered which combine canoeing with travelling by 4WD to reach some of the least accessible parts of the park. Some tours operate year round, while others are restricted to certain seasons.

14 Knuckey Street
Darwin NT 5790
Ph. (089) 81 1244

N.T. Territory Holidays
Many safaris in Kakadu National Park are provided by N.T. Territory Holidays, with tented or lodge accommodation, depending on how far afield you travel. The 11-day Port Essington and Kakadu tour is conducted by charter flight, boat and 4WD. The 13-day Arnhem Land Kakadu tour includes a visit to Wigram Island by helicopter. Visitors spend three days as guests of Terry Yumbulul, the traditional owner, before flying back to Darwin and then beginning the Kakadu visit. Or you can explore Kakadu by canoe and 4WD. Some of the tours do not operate during the summer.

3rd Floor
418 St Kilda Road
Melbourne VIC 3004
Ph. (03) 820 0822

Scobie's Walkabout
Scobie's Walkabout run a Kakadu National Park tour: a 12-day camping holiday exploring Aboriginal rock art at Obiri and Nourlangie Rocks, walking in the area surrounding the East Alligator River, Jim Jim and Twin Falls, and bird watching while cruising on the Yellow Waters lagoon. The company aims to provide the maximum level of comfort compatible with experience of the wilderness.

See (3) above for details

16 Arnhem Land

Arnhemland Adventure Safaris
Terry Yumbulul's Arnhemland Adventure Safaris include Aboriginal tour guides. One of the nine tours available is a three-day Cape Arnhem safari. Visitors fly to Gove, spend a day cruising to Melville Bay, and then spend the next day exploring Cape Arnhem by 4WD. Safaris are limited to four or six people and the emphasis is on a sense of freedom and total remoteness. Lodge accommodation is provided.

C/- Hideaway Safari Lodge
Gove
via Nhulunbuy NT 5797
Ph. (089) 87 1833

Terra Safari Tours
One of the two ground tour operators allowed into Arnhem Land is Terra Safari Tours. Their three-night Arnhemland Tour commences with a visit to Kakadu before crossing the East Alligator River and entering Arnhem Land. Here, an Aboriginal guide shows visitors the magnificent wetlands and stone country of the Gummulkbun Clan, explaining their way of life and the Dreamtime. Visitors will also see Aboriginal rock art.

See (14) above for details

17 Alice Springs

AAT King's
AAT King's Tours, one of Australia's largest and most diversified operators, runs a great variety of tours from Alice Springs. There is a nine-day Red Centre tour and a 23-day western frontier tour taking in Meekatharra, Hamersley country, Derby and Halls Creek before returning to Alice Springs. There are also one and two-day 4WD adventures around Alice Springs itself.

108 Ireland Street
West Melbourne VIC 3003
Ph. (03) 329 8022

Rod Steinert Tours
Rod Steinert Tours seeks to share the traditions of the central Australian Aborigines with visitors to Alice Springs. Rod operates a variety of 4WD day tours which include visits to local Aboriginal people, a working cattle station, the bush races and campdraft meetings.

PO Box 2058
Alice Springs NT 5750
Ph. (089) 52 4610

Rover 4WD Escorts
Rover 4WD Escorts leads convoys of privately owned 4WDs, often tracing the treks of early explorers and pioneers. Co-owners Irene and David Murtagh

have a mass of qualifications between them, plus 20 years of 4WD experience. David is a qualified mechanic — essential for peace of mind on an arduous 4WD trip. They provide the expertise necessary for novice 4WD owners to travel the outback in safety, and enjoy sharing their love of geology and natural history with their clients. Trips include three days fossicking in the Harts Range, 14 days exploring the Gulf country, and a six-day Simpson Desert crossing. Tours do not operate during the summer.

PO Box 8331
Alice Springs NT 5750
Ph. (089) 52 6111

18 Ayers Rock

N.T. Territory Holidays
N.T. Territory Holidays offers, among many trip options commencing in Alice Springs, 4WD self-drive safaris which give you the greatest possible flexibility in visiting Ayers Rock and the Red Centre. Vehicles fitted out with all the necessary gear are available for hire and the price includes camping equipment, unlimited kilometres, insurance and stamp duty. You can plan your own itinerary or they will plan it for you.

See (15) above for details

Spinifex Tours
Spinifex Tours, a small operation based in Alice Springs, has recently won two local tourism awards. A number of one-day tours are offered to familiarise the traveller with the style of central Australia, and there are two and three-day tours to Ayers Rock, the Olgas and King's Canyon. Phil Bourke recommends that you come equipped with a sense of adventure, and he keeps groups small to maintain a friendly atmosphere and to enable tours to run at a relaxed pace.

PO Box 2433
Alice Springs NT 5750
Ph. (089) 52 2203

Queensland

19 Cape York Peninsula

AAT King's
AAT King's offer a 16-day trip from Cairns to the tip of Cape York and across to Thursday Island. Travellers visit the Atherton Tablelands, see Aboriginal art, cross the Jardine River, see the bauxite mine at Weipa, visit Lakefield National Park, Cooktown and the Daintree rainforest. The peninsula is a remote region of tropical rainforest and savannah and the roads are the roughest of tracks. Unpredictable weather can

mean that from time to time itineraries have to be altered. Tours run from June to November.

See (17) above for details

Cape York Guides to Adventure
Cape York Guides to Adventure is a guiding service for people in their own or hired 4WDs. Scotty and Mary-Anne Wales provide a fully equipped guide and recovery vehicle and a complete catering service. The Wales take each 21-day Cape York trip out personally and while they have an agenda it is only a guideline and can be changed to suit the desires of participants. Vehicles should be in good condition and must be inspected within 48 hours of beginning the tour. All repairs must be carried out before leaving Cairns. Tours do not operate in the summer.

23 Sandwich Street
Kamerunga
Cairns QLD 4870
Ph. (070) 55 1406

New Look Adventures
New Look Adventures is a well-established operation based in Cairns, offering a variety of trips to the Cape York Peninsula. To cope with the rough road conditions they have specially designed vehicles and a Flying Doctor radio to maintain contact with the outside world. Trips run for either eight or 16 days, the shorter trip being achieved by four-wheel driving to the Cape and then flying back. Camping is in easily erected pyramid tents and you sleep on air mattresses. Meals are prepared by imaginative cooks.

PO Box 357
Smithfield
Cairns QLD 4870
Ph. (070) 51 7934

Oz Tours Safaris
Beginning in Cairns, Oz Tours Safaris run a number of trips to Cape York lasting from eight to 16 days. It takes five days of testing 4WD travelling before you are in striking distance of the Cape, and in that time you will have splashed, pushed and floated your way in the vehicle across more creeks and rivers than you can remember. The Oz Tours photographer will record highlights of the trip on video, including the boat trip through the Torres Strait islands, the Weipa bauxite mine and crocodiles at Lakefield. A copy of the video is yours, free. For 4WD owners, Oz Tours will act as tour leaders, providing all camping equipment, food and expertise.

142 Sheridan Street
Cairns QLD 4870
Ph. (070) 51 4869

20 Central Highlands

Bush Explorer Holidays
The home base of Bush Explorer Holidays is a property near Carnarvon National Park. This connection between properties and national parks reflects the style of trip run by the organisation, as both feature strongly in their eight-day tour. Bush Explorers is the only tour group permitted access to many of the private properties visited — properties steeped in history, with numerous rock formations and Aboriginal sites. Campsites are uncrowded and serene. Bush Explorers invite you to tag along in your own 4WD and take advantage of their experience. Tours do not operate during winter.

19 Stumm Street
Toowoomba QLD 4350
Ph. (076) 35 0530 or (074) 26 1271

Central Highlands Safaris
Their seven-day safaris begin in Rockhampton. From there, the tour travels through the historic goldmining town of Mt Morgan before arriving at Carnarvon Gorge National Park, a steep-sided natural oasis of lush vegetation and clear freshwater streams. Next day, the tour heads towards Springsure, Anakie and the gemfields, and from there to the goldmining town of Clermont, the coal-mine at Norwich Park and the bat caves at Mt Etna. Tours do not operate during summer.

PO Box 4021
Rockhampton Base QLD 4700
Ph. (079) 27 8168 or 58 1696

21 Fraser Island

Holiday Coast Adventure Safaris
Operating out of Coffs Harbour, Holiday Coast Adventure Safaris run seven-day accommodated safaris on Fraser Island. You have a 4WD vehicle and driver at your disposal to go where you like, when you like. There are any number of beaches to visit, 40 freshwater lakes and magnificent areas of rainforest.

8/42 Karuah Avenue
Coffs Harbour NSW 2450
Ph. (066) 52 7433

Sunrover Rentals
A wide range of 4WD holiday options on Fraser Island are offered by Sunrover Rentals, operating out of Brisbane. A number of different current model 4WD vehicles are available, including campervans. If you choose to camp, you can hire all the equipment you need from Sunrover, and if you want an alternative to a tent you can hire a camper trailer. Packages including self-catering units or resort-style accommodation are also offered.

11 South Pine Road
Alderley
Brisbane QLD 4051
Ph. (07) 352 5888

Trekabout Expeditions
Trekabout Expeditions run a wide variety of tours. On the 13-day Whitsunday and Fraser Island Explorer, you island-hop along the Queensland coast, cruising, snorkelling and swimming, lingering for four days on the largest sand island in the world, Fraser Island. It is here that you have the exhilaration of four-wheel driving on great stretches of deserted beach.

GPO Box 2637
Brisbane QLD 4001
Ph. (07) 357 5741

LEIGH HEMMINGS

JONATHAN CHESTER

Rockclimbing, Abseiling & Mountaineering

Many people are surprised to learn that the world's flattest continent offers some of the best rockclimbing imaginable. Yet Australia is dotted with ancient mountain ranges whose weathered bones of rock provide a playground for those who seek the thrills and challenges of a vertical environment.

Though exploratory climbs of many of Australia's more inaccessible rocky summits were made as early as the 1930s, serious rockclimbing did not begin until the 1960s. Most instrumental in this development was John Ewbank, a young member of the Sydney Rockclimbing Club, whose obsession with rockclimbing lasted until he turned 22. He left behind a list of over 300 first ascents in New South Wales, Victoria and Tasmania, many of which remain classic climbs today, and the most daring of which have rarely if ever been repeated.

Apart from these climbs, Ewbank's legacy to rockclimbing is his grading system. A simple walk was graded 1, and a scramble was 3 or 4, while climbing which definitely needed ropes began at 6 or 7. When Ewbank traded his EB climbing boots for a guitar and became a folksinger, the hardest climbs in the country were graded 21. At the time of writing, the hardest climb in Australia is graded 32.

The grading of climbs is, of course, a matter of argument for the afficionados and not something that need bother novices. Their concern is how to learn the safest techniques of climbing and descending rockfaces. Like playing a musical instrument or dancing Swan Lake, rockclimbing is an activity which cannot be learnt from books. Direct instruction is necessary from either a competent friend, a club or a commercial organisation. Unfortunately, competent friends usually wish to climb more challenging routes than those that appeal to a beginner. Climbing clubs and

commercial organisations bring together novices, who after learning the basics can continue to learn together at their own speed. Climbing with someone of equal ability has the advantage of making sure that decisions are shared, and that both climbers take turns at leading (finding the way and fixing the rope).

In recent years, the teaching of rockclimbing has become more the province of professionals than of clubs. This trend is due to an increase in the number of people who wish to make a living from the sport they love. Consequently, most of the popular cliffs have professional guides living nearby, or are serviced by the larger adventure travel operators.

Experienced climbers, both residents of Australia and visitors, will usually be aware, through the climbing grapevine, of the extensive climbing possibilities that Australia offers. Also, good information sources exist in the form of outdoor equipment shops in all major cities who stock detailed and localised guidebooks providing information on routes and gradings, and such outlets are often able to hire equipment to the visitor wishing to climb. Private guiding services are also available for the experienced climber in need of a partner with local knowledge, and these are detailed in the Contacts section.

Our main purpose is to illustrate to the beginner the ways and means of learning how to climb or abseil, and the best areas in which to do this. Aspiring climbers with some previous experience will also find this information useful, as several climbing schools cater for people of various levels of competence and provide an opportunity to gain greater confidence and degrees of skill while under expert instruction.

Anyone contemplating learning the ropes of rockclimbing should be in good health and have a reasonable standard of fitness. It is not a sport suitable for young children, although abseiling presents a lower degree of difficulty for the young. It is also not essential to be super-fit to enjoy a day or two out on the rock.

The mecca for Australian rockclimbing is undoubtedly Mt Arapiles in north-western Victoria. Good camping facilities, easy access and superb rock make these sandstone cliffs a destination for the world's top rockclimbers. There are quality climbs at all levels of difficulty from the easiest grade to the hardest.

Mt Buffalo National Park is the other famous climbing area in Victoria. Australia's best aid-climbs are found on the dramatic 250-metre northern wall of Buffalo Gorge. Free-climbs exist by the hundreds, not only in the gorge, but also on outcrops of granite across the Mt Buffalo plateau.

Tasmania has much to offer the rockclimber — both on accessible cliffs like the dolerite columns of Hobart's Mt Wellington and the granite slabs of Freycinet National Park on the east coast, as well as on the big and more remote quartzite cliffs such as Frenchman's Cap and Federation Peak. Other areas worth visiting are Geryon, the Acropolis and Ben Lomond.

South Australia also has good rockclimbing. Close to Adelaide are the small cliffs of Morialta Gorge. Several hundred kilometres to the north in the Flinders Ranges is Moonarie, a steep and awesome cliff often included on the itinerary of overseas climbers.

The Blue Mountains, near Sydney in New South Wales, is not so much a mountain range as a huge plateau surrounded by sandstone cliffs. Much of this rock is unsuitable for climbing because it is either crumbly or inaccessible. Only the solid cliff faces close to roads have been well developed, and there are many of these. Climbing is focused around Mt Victoria, where good climbs abound at Mt Pidding-ton, Mt Boyce and Mt York. Cosmic County, closer to Lithgow, is a cliff where the best routes are delicate face climbs, a genre for which the Blue Mountains have become famous. The cliffs around Katoomba are often well over 100 metres high, and though the rock is often bad, the setting is spectacular enough to entice climbers.

The sea cliffs of Sydney are climbed upon extensively, since they are handy for the many Sydney-dwelling climbers. The infamous 'Fear' at North Head is a moderately difficult climb which goes out underneath a huge roof while the waves crash on the rocks 100 metres below.

Several hundred kilometres to the north lie the volcanic plugs of the Mt Kaputar and Warrumbungle National Parks. The routes here, particularly on Bluff Mountain, are serious undertakings since the climbs are long and the route-finding is difficult. Many climbers have spent nights huddled on small ledges

PETA PRIMROSE

A lead climber edges up a sandstone cliff in the Blue Mountains

dressed only in shorts and T-shirts after losing their way.

Similar climbing exists on the volcanic Glass House Mountains in south-eastern Queensland. However, the focus of rockclimbing in this state is at Frog Buttress, west of Brisbane. This steep 40-metre-high cliff is the home of crack-climbing in Australia. Many full-time climbers head to Frog in the winter when cold and rain make the southern cliffs a less-pleasant prospect.

Booroomba Rocks, in the Gudgenby Nature Reserve close to Canberra in the Australian Capital Territory, is a cliff of weathered granite which provides balance climbing on steep and often poorly protected slabs.

In sparsely populated Western Australia, climbing is not well developed except for areas within a few hours' drive of Perth. Short climbs can be found at Willyabrup, and there are routes up to two pitches long at West Cape Howe, and longer routes, complete with longer approaches, in the Stirling Ranges.

Very little climbing has been done in the Northern Territory, though the potential is enormous. Chambers Pillar near Alice Springs has been climbed, but climbing is prohibited on Uluru, otherwise known as Ayers Rock. Visitors are allowed to ascend the famous monolith by the approved tourist route only.

Abseiling can be practised at most of these cliffs. Unlike rockclimbing, abseiling has the advantage of being possible at any sheer drop (provided one's ropes are long enough!), regardless of the quality of the rock. Abseiling is becoming a popular sport in its own right, and not merely as an accessory to rockclimbing. The difference is that abseiling is the *descent* of rockfaces using ropes and other equipment, and once the basics are learnt it is a sport that people of all ages can enjoy. An interesting development of abseiling is canyoning, which is the descent and exploration of

reach Tasmania's higher summits during winter, but the remoteness of these peaks makes them unsuitable for use as training grounds.

There is no permanent snow in Australia, and thus no glaciers or permanent ice-faces to test the really serious mountaineer. Only in the high regions of New South Wales, Victoria and Tasmania is snow cover such, during the winter months, that ice climbing is possible.

An indication of the growing popularity of both rockclimbing and mountaineering in Australia is the number of very competent climbers that the country has produced. Many Australian rockclimbers are of world class, and in the mountaineering field the name of Australia has, within the last few years, been firmly placed on the map. The 1984 Everest success was a world first — an oxygen-less lightweight alpine-style

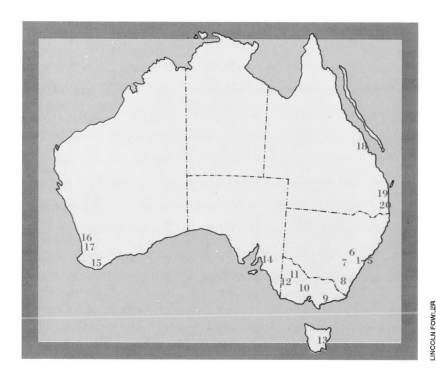

Belougery Spire forms a dramatic outline in the Warrumbungle National Park

narrow gorges by abseiling and swimming.

Rockclimbing and abseiling can be enjoyed for most of the year, though summer heat can be a problem in the more northerly regions. Equally, winter in the south could deter all but the most avid climbers and force them to seek their thrills elsewhere. However, in New South Wales, Victoria and Tasmania mountaineering techniques can be practised during winter. Blue Lake and Watson's crags in the Kosciusko National Park, and Mt Feathertop in Victoria, have steep slopes of snow and ice where basic techniques can be learnt. Mountaineering skill may be needed to

expedition that pioneered a new route on the north face of the mountain, using only five main climbers, and putting two of them on the summit. Several other Australian expeditions have had both success and failure on other Himalayan peaks, and 1988 will see a major Bicentennial attempt on Mount Everest.

Locations

New South Wales

The Blue Mountains, around 100 kilometres west of Sydney, is undoubtedly one of the most popular climbing areas in the state, both for beginners and experienced climbers. The proliferation of companies giving rockclimbing and abseiling instruction in this area is a good indication of the suitability of many rock faces for teaching beginners.

The surroundings are magnificent. The sandstone plateau of the range has been deeply cut and eroded by rivers, leaving valleys, gorges and cliffs that provide climbs of varied grades. Blue gums, ferns, streams and waterfalls all help to make this area a deservedly popular bushwalking and camping venue for Sydneysiders.

Further south (approximately 500 kilometres from Sydney, and close to Canberra), the Kosciusko National Park is the best location in Australia for mountaineering. Several companies offer instructional courses here, teaching all the basics of ropework, snowcraft and survival in snow and ice environments. Although not high by most overseas standards, this is Australia's highest region, with Mount Kosciusko standing at 2,228 metres.

1 **Vertical World,** based in Sydney, has been providing wilderness experiences in the Blue Mountains for over five years. Most of their trips utilise a base camp in the form of a lodge, which provides a comfortable and relaxing environment after a day of activity in the mountains.

One, two and five-day courses in abseiling, canyoning, river liloing, caving, bushwalking and rockclimbing are all available. A rockcraft certificated course and specialised rope technique instruction can be arranged, as can private guiding and teaching for those who prefer a more personalised service.

2 **Geoff Weigand,** one of Australia's leading rockclimbers, provides a private instruction and guiding service in the Blue Mountains and other areas of New South Wales. Arrangements are very flexible and should be discussed with Geoff.

3 Greg Mortimer's **Risky Business** offers a special opportunity to climb with an Everest summiteer. Greg reached the top of Mount Everest in 1984 as a member of the Australian North Face Expedition, and is now sharing his expert knowledge and experience with those who want to learn the sport.

Both rockclimbing and mountaineering are instructed and guided on a private basis, and Risky Business can cater for people of all levels of experience — from beginners to the more advanced.

Most instruction takes place in the Blue Mountains, but arrangements can be made for guiding and teaching in other areas of New South Wales.

4 **Wilderness Expeditions** is one of the few organisations to offer a winter snow mountaineering course. Understandably, this activity is not easy to pursue in a land of only seasonal snow and no high mountains, but the best conditions are to be found in the Mount Kosciusko area of southern New South Wales.

Although the five-day course is graded as strenuous, it caters for beginners and teaches the technical skills of climbing, the reading of mountain weather, and safety in mountain environments.

Abseiling and canyoning weekends in the Blue Mountains, close to Sydney, are also available. A day's instruction in abseiling is followed by a descent of the fabulous Claustral Canyon.

Instructors are very competent and include Tim Macartney-Snape, an Everest summiteer.

5 **World Expeditions'** large programme of activities and holidays includes rockclimbing, mountaineering, abseiling and canyoning trips.

Abseiling and canyoning are available in the Blue Mountains. Courses are graded as moderate, and are of two days' duration. The course is designed for beginners and will introduce you to the fun and excitement of this activity. Participants must be able to swim as there are some water sections between abseils.

The introduction to rockclimbing course is also a weekend trip, and is offered in the Blue Mountains.

World Expeditions also operates a six-day snow mountaineering course for those with cross-country skiing experience. This takes place in the Kosciusko National Park and covers the essential techniques of mountaineering, snow camping and snow survival. On completion of the course, participants will be qualified to extend their climbing experience on more challenging climbs overseas.

6 The **Blue Mountains Climbing School,** based at Katoomba, is a specialist climbing outfit that presents a wide range of services and activities for people of all abilities.

Two-day rockclimbing courses are available for both beginners and intermediates, and similarly graded one-day trips are offered for those with an interest in abseiling and canyoning. A five-day beginners' course covers both rockclimbing and abseiling, and a special climbing camp in the beautiful Wolgan Valley near Lithgow can be arranged at any time for private groups.

The company can also cater for those who prefer personal tuition, or provide private guiding on various climbs in the Blue Mountains area.

7 Another Katoomba-based operation is the **Rockcraft Climbing School.** With their reputation for quality instruction and eight years of operation, they have enjoyed seeing many hundreds of people discover the delights of rock sports and come back for more!

Rockclimbing courses are graded Rock I, Rock II and Rock III. They range from two to five days, and are intended to allow the beginner to progress by completing the full series.

A continuation of this process is the 'Blue Mountains Classic Climbs' weekend, where those with experience can visit four different climbing areas with well-qualified guides. Abseiling courses of one day's duration are available for young and old — as Rock-craft says, 'If you can walk, you can abseil!'

Australian Capital Territory

Booroomba Rocks and the Tidbinbilla and Brinda-bella Ranges are located within the Australian Capital Territory and are a short distance from Canberra. Summer and winter rockclimbing and abseiling are both possible here, and climbs of all difficulties can be found within the ranges. The bush and gumforest-covered hills of the area are composed of granite — an ideal surface for rockclimbing purposes.

8 The **Australian Outward Bound Federation** has existed for 31 years and is associated with 35 similar schools throughout the world. Courses in challenging outdoor experiences such as rockclimb-ing, abseiling, canoeing and expeditioning take place in various locations and are for people of all ages.

Three main programmes are in operation: Pack and Paddle camps for boys and girls of 12-16 years; the standard course for ages 17-29; and an adult course. The National Outward Bound School is based just south of Canberra and many of the courses give the basic training here. Abseiling and rockclimbing courses are carried out in the Brindabella and Tidbinbilla Ranges and in the Shoalhaven region of New South Wales. Instruction in these activities is part of a full programme of outdoor skills that range from nine to 26 days' duration.

Victoria

This state is fortunate in rockclimbing terms. Mount Arapiles is not just a mecca for Australian climbers, but is on the world rockclimbing circuit and is visited every year by many outstanding overseas climbers, including Britain's well-known Himalayan mountain-eer, Chris Bonington. The nearby Grampians also offer some excellent climbing, and should not be overlooked by those aiming for the Arapiles.

The Arapiles are located 25 kilometres from Horsham (325 kilometres from Melbourne), and the Grampians are close to Hall's Gap, some 250 kilo-metres from Melbourne. The rocks of both areas are composed of sandstone and offer climbs of all diffi-culties and a choice of over 2,000 routes.

Both areas are excellent for beginners as well as the most experienced of rock stars, and several schools and climbing companies offer courses.

9 **Spindrift International Guiding** is a small operation specialising in private guiding and instruction in several activities, including rockclimbing. Owner Malcolm Cowell offers instruction in both the Grampians and Arapiles areas, and is also prepared to accompany climbers to most parts of Australia. Mountaineering instruction and programmes for schools and teachers can also be arranged.

A climber on a sandstone rock face

10 **Base Camp and Beyond**, is located at Hall's Gap, and specialises in rockclimbing, abseiling and bushwalking trips in the Mount Arapiles and Gram-pians regions. Owner David Witham has 25 years' experience of instruction in outdoor activities, including a five-year period as Director of the Australian Outward Bound School.

Rockclimbing and abseiling courses are for both beginners and those who wish to extend their previous experience, and vary from two to five days. Emphasis is placed on practical and thorough instruction, with a safe and personal bias. The client/instructor ratio does not exceed four to one.

11 The **Arapiles Rockclimbing School** is based at Natimuk, close to the best-known climbing region of Australia — Mount Arapiles.

Basic and advanced rockclimbing instruction and guiding is provided for men and women of all ages by Eric Jones, who has 20 years' experience in this field.

This rockclimbing school emphasises that its priorities are safety, patience, skill and personalised service — an important factor in teaching and learning the art of coming face to face with rock.

12 Louise Shepherd's inspirationally named **Sheer Height** rockclimbing school is an all-female oasis in the male-dominated world of rock. Five years of operation, and Louise's reputation as one of Australia's leading rockclimbers, make this organisation a must for women who wish to learn this exciting and challenging sport.

Louise caters for both beginners and those of a more advanced standard, and trips are operated in the Mount Arapiles region. Courses range from two to five days, and all climbing equipment is provided.

Tasmania

The island state offers some great rockclimbing and mountaineering possibilities and some challenging stuff for the more experienced climber. Snow cover in the higher regions means that mountaineering skills can be practised in winter, but many of these rock faces are very inaccessible, and would appeal to the devotee only.

Rockclimbing venues include Mount Wellington — right on Hobart's doorstep and very accessible. This dolerite mountain is the backdrop to the city of Hobart and offers several hundred climbs of all grades.

Freycinet National Park is located within 190 kilometres of both Hobart and Launceston and it provides some good climbing in a magnificent coastal and bush setting. Climbing is possible all year on the granite slabs, and camping facilities are available at nearby Coles Bay.

The demand for climbing trips in Tasmania is not high enough to warrant regular and advertised commercial programmes. Most climbing here is organised through the club system, and residents of Tasmania who wish to pursue the sport should contact The Climbers Club of Tasmania. (See the Contacts section.)

13 An alternative for visitors to Tasmania would be to contact **Open Spaces** in Hobart who can arrange guided excursions on demand. Open Spaces is also the Paddy Pallin Outdoor Equipment outlet in Hobart and can provide equipment, advice and guidebooks to various regions of Tasmania.

South Australia

Morialta Gorge is only eight kilometres from the centre of Adelaide, yet it offers some excellent climbing — particularly for beginners. The hard sandstone here is a good surface on which to learn the basics of rockclimbing and abseiling, and one Adelaide company provides instructional courses for beginners.

Further afield in the Flinders Ranges, around 350 kilometres north of Adelaide, good climbing for all abilities is found at Moonarie — a sandstone cliff that offers several hundred climbs. Basic camping facilities are available here, and as no climbing schools provide instruction in the area, Moonarie would be best approached by the experienced climber.

14 **Thor Adventure Travel** in Adelaide is an offshoot of an outdoor equipment business. Their Morialta Gorge climbing course is designed to teach beginners the basic skills of both rockclimbing and

abseiling. The two-day course on this excellent instructional cliff will teach you to be at home with rock and rope, and hopefully inspire you to continue with this satisfying pastime. George Adams, who has been climbing since the late 1950s, and his son Luke are among the instructors for the courses.

Western Australia

Many of Western Australia's climbing possibilities have not been fully explored, but a few operators are now offering rockclimbing courses and instruction in several areas.

Close to Perth, the Darling Escarpment, set in rolling hills, forests and fertile farmland, provides

The famous Three Sisters rock formation in the Blue Mountains of New South Wales

LEO DUYCKERS

some good granite rock faces that may be climbed all year and which are suitable for beginners.

Coastal climbing is a popular activity on the south coast of Western Australia, particularly on the stretch of cliffs between Albany and Denmark, including West Cape Howe. Climbing on the granite cliffs of this beautiful coastline is superb and climbers of all grades will find routes suitable for their standard of climbing.

15 **Great Southern Wilderness Expeditions** arranges two-day introductory rockclimbing courses on the granite cliffs of Western Australia's south coast region, between Albany and Denmark. This is a truly different way to enjoy an unspoiled part of Australia.

16 In addition to **WA Adventure Treks'** bushwalking programme, basic rockclimbing, abseiling and canyoning are also available for private groups. Locations and times are flexible and should be discussed with the company.

17 **Adventure Out** offers two-day instructional courses in caving, abseiling and beginners' and more advanced rockclimbing. Locations include the Darling Escarpment, close to Perth; the Willyabrup sea cliffs near Margaret River; and the granite cliffs near Armadale.

GLENN ROBBINS

A 'second' climber removes a runner from Mt Piddington in the Blue Mountains

Northern Territory

Despite the Northern Territory's excellent climbing possibilities there are no tour operators or rockclimbing clubs to guide the interested visitor. The nearest thing to climbing here has to be the Ayers Rock ascent, which is strictly walking and is an option offered by many tour operators in the Alice Springs and Ayers Rock area.

Queensland

Rockclimbing in Queensland is very much a sport for the experienced, though a few organisations provide instruction for beginners.

Mount French National Park, south-west of Brisbane, contains Frog Buttress, a well-known crack-climbing venue. The rhyolite rock of the buttress offers several hundred climbs that are suitable for all grades of climber.

The Glasshouse Mountains, just 90 kilometres north of Brisbane, is another popular and accessible climbing area. The peaks here rise abruptly from the plain and are best climbed in periods other than summer when the heat and humidity make climbing unpleasant.

Lamington National Park, in the Gold Coast hinterland, offers some sheer rock walls of volcanic origin that are ideal for abseiling. The park contains rugged mountains, rainforest and a great variety of wildlife that can all be appreciated during a stay at one of the lodges based in the park itself.

Further north, the Cape Hillsborough region near Mackay is the venue for Queensland's most comprehensive programme of rockclimbing and abseiling courses — organised by a Mackay climbing school.

18 Bruce Parr's **Mackay Rocksports** is a surprising discovery in this central Queensland city. For three years, Bruce has been instructing in the fields of abseiling and rockclimbing to school groups, youth programme groups, adults of all ages and even for the mines rescue service.

Cape Hillsborough National Park is the location for most courses. Both abseiling and rockclimbing are offered for beginners and those with some experience in half-day modules, two-day certificate courses, and a seven-night adult expedition.

19 **Mountain Designs** is primarily a manufacturer and importer of high-quality outdoor clothing and equipment. They have won Australian design awards and supplied a considerable proportion of the gear used on the 1984 first Australian Mount Everest ascent. In addition to this, some of their retail outlets offer courses and trips in the bushwalking and rock-climbing fields.

The Brisbane shop, managed by Tony Young, is one such outlet. Located between the Glasshouse Mountains to the north, and Mount French to the south of Brisbane, they are ideally placed to run instructional rockclimbing trips or private guiding services to those who already have some experience but are lacking in local knowledge.

20 **Binna Burra Lodge**, in Lamington National Park, offers in addition to its other activities, a comprehensive abseiling programme.

Two-day trips for both beginners and those with abseiling experience are run in a variety of locations, and guides are used on all departures. Itineraries include a stay at the famous Lodge, which is featured in our Activity Lodges section.

Rockclimbing, Abseiling & Mountaineering Contacts

Operators

New South Wales

1 Vertical World

12 Terrigal Road
Terrey Hills
Sydney NSW 2084
Ph. (02) 450 2382

2 Geoff Weigand

Ph. (02) 80 2487

3 Risky Business

GPO Box 2601
Sydney NSW 2000
Ph. (02) 997 1302

4 Wilderness Expeditions

26 Sharp Street
Cooma NSW 2630
Ph. (064) 52 1587

100 Clarence Street
Sydney NSW 2000
Ph. (02) 29 1581

5 World Expeditions

3rd Floor
377 Sussex Street
Sydney NSW 2000
Ph. (02) 264 3366

6 Blue Mountains Climbing School

21 Wells Street
Katoomba NSW 2780
Ph. (047) 82 1271

7 Rockcraft Climbing School and Mountain Guides

166 Katoomba Street
Katoomba NSW 2780
Ph. (047) 82 2014

Australian Capital Territory

8 Australian Outward Bound Federation

GPO Box 4213
Sydney NSW 2000
Ph. (02) 29 7784

Victoria

9 Spindrift International Guiding

PO Box 455
Maffra VIC 3860
Ph. (051) 48 2499

10 Base Camp and Beyond

PO Box 37
Hall's Gap VIC 3381
Ph. (053) 56 4300

11 Arapiles Rockclimbing School

Main Street
Natimuk VIC 3409
Ph. (053) 87 1371

12 Sheer Height

PO Box 20
Natimuk VIC 3409
Ph. (053) 87 1329

Tasmania

13 Open Spaces

28 Criterion Street
Hobart TAS 7000
Ph. (002) 31 0983

South Australia

14 Thor Adventure Travel

40 Waymouth Street
Adelaide SA 5000
Ph. (08) 212 7857

Western Australia

15 Great Southern Wilderness Expeditions

Bonne View
Little River Road
Denmark WA 6333
Ph. (098) 48 1341

16 WA Adventure Treks

PO Box 1013
Booragoon
Perth WA 6154
Ph. (09) 330 4948

17 Adventure Out

33A Adelaide Street
Fremantle WA 6160
Ph. (09) 335 9299

Queensland

18 Mackay Rocksports

22 Lindeman Avenue
Lambert's Beach
Mackay QLD 4741
Ph. (079) 55 1278

19 Mountain Designs

95 Albert Street
Brisbane QLD 4000
Ph. (07) 221 6756

GLENN ROBBINS

20 Binna Burra Mountain Lodge

Beechmont
via Nerang QLD 4211
Ph. (075) 33 3622

Information Sources

New South Wales

The Sydney Rockclimbing Club
PO Box A592
Sydney South NSW 2000
Ph. (02) 232 4848

Australian Capital Territory

Australian National University
Mountaineering Club
ANU Sports Union
Australian National University
Canberra ACT 2600
Ph. (062) 46 5648

Victoria

The Victorian Climbing Club
GPO Box 1725P
Melbourne VIC 3001

Tasmania

The Climbers Club of Tasmania
C/- Tasmanian Environment Centre
102 Bathurst Street
Hobart TAS 7000

South Australia

The Climbing Club of South Australia
C/- Luke Adams
Thor Adventure Travel
40 Waymouth Street
Adelaide SA 5000
Ph. (08) 212 7857

MICHAEL LANGFORD

Skiing

Australia's premier skiing slopes are to be found on the east coast in the mountain ranges between Sydney and Melbourne. This is Australia's 'High Country', home of the Man from Snowy River, bushrangers and silver brumby horses.

The northern access to the Snowy Mountains is from the Cooma region of New South Wales, around six hours' drive south of Sydney and just one and a half hours from Canberra.

Eleven major alpine and nordic resorts and uncharted cross-country ski areas stretch south and west, through Victoria, to within two hours' drive of Melbourne.

The High Country is vast and wild, and to preserve its fragile ecosystem it is now almost entirely under the care of Australia's National Parks and Wildlife Service. Visitors marvel at how it has retained its delicate balance of ecologies, which is quite unique by world standards.

The Snowy region is especially remarkable considering that Australia is the world's flattest continent. Australia's location has created a unique geographical pattern, which survives here, offering remoteness and tranquillity (beloved of cross-country skiers), a temperate sunny climate, and the rich scenery and wildlife normally found only at lower altitudes. Deep gullies and winding creeks criss-cross the stands of beautiful Australian snowgums which border the downhill runs, creating challenging ski trails, and the dense bushland shelters skiers from the harsh wind.

The Australian Alps are ideal for the skiing family. All the New South Wales and Victorian resorts include well-groomed beginners' slopes and intermediate slopes with lift facilities. Children love the animals, ducks and wombat holes found in the low-altitude resorts such as Thredbo Village. Meanwhile, advanced skiers have found that Thredbo's moguls on the Merritt's Schuss and down the Funnelweb Run are comparable to Val d'Isere's La Plan or Squaw Valley's Black Mogul Piste.

Cross-country (or Nordic) skiing is one of Australia's best-kept secrets. Skiers can choose between marked ski trails adjacent to most resorts or take off on a back country ski adventure into the heart of the winter wilderness. The terrain of the Alps is perfect for ski-touring.

Although low in altitude, the Australian mountains require knowledge and expertise if skiers intend to venture beyond the resorts. What the mountains lack in height, they make up for in extreme weather conditions. High winds and heavy snowfalls are common during the winter season. Luckily, the avalanche danger is low, but skiers not familiar with the mountains are recommended to travel with an experienced tour guide.

Numerous tour companies offer instruction in cross-country skiing and arrange ski tours. Intending participants should check all details of these trips before booking and ensure that instructors have ASF (Australian Ski Federation) teacher/instructor qualifications.

Cross-country skiers should be well-equipped for any emergency that could present itself in remote situations. A skier's basic checklist should include a first-aid kit, water bottle, food, spare ski tip, compass, map, matches, torch and warm waterproof clothing.

Snowshoeing, a more leisurely pursuit, is also gaining popularity and is suitable for all age groups. Although this activity is not widely practised, a couple of operators in Victoria conduct one-day or weekend snowshoeing trips.

Visitors are often surprised to learn that Australia was probably the first place where skiing was practised as an organised sport. In 1859, when gold was discovered at Kiandra in New South Wales, people flocked to its remote snow-covered plains, and skiing became an amusing pastime for the prospectors. Early photos of the miners show them skiing in boots nailed or strapped to planks of wood with a pole between their legs to enable them to manouevre and stop. The Norwegian miners then introduced the long sharp-pointed ski in vogue in Scandinavia, and around 1863 skiing emerged and spread as an organised sport. The first ski club was formed in Kiandra in 1870, two years before the first clubs in the United States. Australia's first slopes and chalets were opened up at Kosciusko in New South Wales in 1909 and at Mount Buffalo in Victoria the following year.

Ski racing events are organised at national, state and regional levels, and date back to the old 'Flying Furlong' at Kiandra. The Thredbo Cup, held in New South Wales, is an official FIS Olympic event and attracts many competitors. Regular events are also held at Perisher-Smiggins and Charlotte Pass.

Although pre-dating Austria and Switzerland as the scene of organised skiing as a sport, Australia's snow country was too remote from the post-goldrush population centres to develop resorts and lift facilities that were comparable to European standards. And it was only after the establishment of the Snowy Mountains Authority in 1949 that major ski resorts developed.

Based at Cooma, the northern gateway to the Snowy Mountains, the Authority planned to provide New South Wales with electricity and irrigation water for the state's dry western plains. Now ranking as one of the largest undertakings of its kind in the world, the project introduced resources, new roads, housing and many enterprising European migrants. The resorts close to Cooma — Thredbo, Smiggin Holes, Charlotte Pass and Guthega — still retain the old ambience of the European resorts in their architecture, food and ski instructors' styles. This is a direct result of Australia's high post-Second World War immigration intake from Europe and the enormous impact these migrants made while working and living in the resorts.

All of Australia's major ski resorts provide varied standards of accommodation, with most lodges being only a short walk from the lifts or a short trip in a shuttle bus. The largest resorts are booked out months ahead during the peak season from July to September. To help preserve the environment, the Department of Parks and Wildlife has set strict limits on accommodation capacities inside the park. This means that bookings, especially for Guthega, Perisher-Smiggins, as well as the popular Victorian resorts, must be arranged prior to the opening of the season, which is in the first week of June. Many skiers

A good season brings large amounts of snow and sometimes powder skiing

MARK STEVEN

find accommodation outside the park, below the snowline around Jindabyne, which is within daytripping distance from all the New South Wales resorts and has become a popular and less costly alternative. This tiny town, which was once flooded by the Snowy Mountains Hydro-electric Scheme, is now receiving a facelift. Current developments include increased ski accommodation, shops, an ice skating rink and indoor swimming pool. Ansett Pioneer runs an hourly shuttle service from Jindabyne to the nearby slopes.

Both Victoria and New South Wales offer a similar range of skiing opportunities, with the former boasting Australia's largest resort, Mt Buller, which is suitable for advanced skiers. Victorians are also fortunate in that their slopes are close to Melbourne, allowing for easy day trips. It also has a greater variety of cross-country skiing than New South Wales, with the closest resort, Lake Mountain, being only 100 kilometres from Melbourne. While it does not have vast open plains, it provides pleasant skiing on wooded tracks and is ideal territory for beginners. Mt Baw Baw, only 180 kilometres from Melbourne, is a quiet resort for beginners and intermediate downhill skiers as well as for cross-country skiers.

In New South Wales, Perisher Valley is considered to be the most sophisticated resort. It has the greatest lift capacity, large luxurious lodges, long smooth intermediate to advanced ski runs, and many cross-country ski trails.

Mt Blue Cow (1,900 metres) provides Australia's highest downhill ski runs. The site of Australia's newest ski resort, its name came about when a local farmer lost some cattle, called Blueys because of their colour, on the mountain. After a harsh winter, one of the missing cows was found completely frozen and stiff as a board. The resort is situated between Guthega and Perisher and opened for the 1987 ski season. It appears to have some of the best 'black' ski runs in Australia. The steepest, aptly named the 'Kamikaze', is a 42% slope with the longest run being over three kilometres.

The completion of a 24-hour underground ski tube in 1987 marked the transformation of the New South Wales ski fields. This Swiss-style rail link carries people from Bullocks Terminal (between Jindabyne and Thredbo) to Guthega, Perisher and Mt Blue Cow and handles over 3,000 passengers per hour. The ride takes 15 minutes to reach its terminus at Mt Blue Cow and only ten minutes to reach Perisher. It costs the equivalent of a bus ticket and is a major step towards eliminating traffic delays, and cars generally, from the Alps.

Officially, the ski season runs between June and early October, but there is rarely adequate snow cover before late June or after late September. The ideal month to ski downhill is generally August, though conditions can be unpredictable with insufficient snow cover, late or early snow, and congestion during school holidays. If sufficient cover prevails, there is some fantastic spring skiing in September, which is blessed with brilliant sunny weather. The mountain temperature is in any case rarely below −6°C. Cross-country skiers can tour from June through to November (sometimes December) in the High Country alpine plains. However, September and October are ideal, with cross-country skiers taking advantage of the spring sun, whether or not there is a sufficient cover in the downhill resorts.

Lift tickets in Australia are relatively expensive compared with overseas prices, and costs vary considerably between the various resorts.

Ski equipment hire also varies in price at the different resorts, and it is generally more economical to hire from outside the resorts in Sydney, Cooma, Canberra or Melbourne or, in Tasmania, in Hobart and Launceston. These centres have many ski shops that provide a good range of clothing and equipment for both hire and purchase, and which cater for both cross-country and downhill skiers. Anyone considering buying skis, stocks and skiing clothing should consult the experts at these retail outlets.

Tasmania, the coldest state in Australia, also has beautiful snow-capped mountains suitable for downhill and Nordic skiing. The mountains are low and the weather conditions are unpredictable — consequently, the resorts are not well developed. Skiers are advised to check the seasonal conditions prior to booking in Tasmania.

Ski holidays can be booked through state tourism centres, or through any of the specialised ski-tour operators in Sydney, Melbourne or Hobart.

Further information on ski-fields instruction, equipment, insurance and publications can be obtained from the Australian Ski Federation or the State Ski Associations. These bodies cover aspects of both downhill and cross-country skiing, and are valuable sources of information.

Downhill skiers who wish to keep in touch with their skills during the off-season can avail themselves of several grass-skiing facilities in New South Wales and Victoria. *Yellow Pages* telephone directories should be consulted for locations.

The high point of the Australian alpine experience is its cross-country terrain with vast snowfields, as seen above in the Snowy Mountains

Locations

New South Wales

Downhill Skiing

Thredbo is situated on the Alpine Way, 20 minutes' drive south of Jindabyne. A European-style resort, in a good season it is considered to be Australia's most challenging, due to the number of advanced trails such as the Funnelweb, the face of Merritts, Crackenback, Ramshead and many hidden trails. As the village is situated on the snowline, in the past the lowest slopes suffered from lack of snow. However, a multi-million dollar snow-making system was installed in 1987, guaranteeing a full season of snow.

Thredbo has beginner, intermediate and advanced ski conditions. One of Australia's earliest and most developed resorts, it has four chairlifts, three beginners' T-bars, several tow ropes and four access T-bars situated high in the mountains opening onto advanced runs. The snow-making machinery will add new beginners' areas on the lower slopes and increase

has one of Australia's largest bed capacities, the lodges are close together. Consequently, all facilities are within walking distance along safe roads and paths.

Early bookings are essential. Alternative accommodation can be found at Jindabyne, which is linked by shuttle bus.

2 Originally, **Smiggin Holes** (one of Australia's earliest resorts) and **Perisher Valley** were two

ALLAN MOULT

₃ opportunities through unique

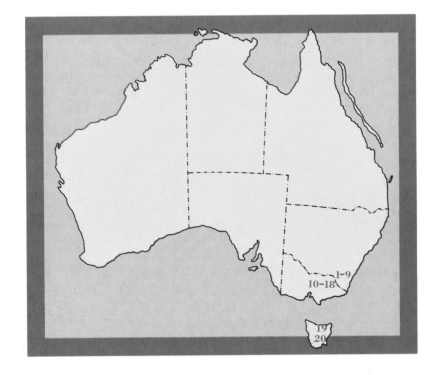

the length of runs used by more advanced skiers. Day tickets are expensive, reflecting the resort's improved mountain management and its technological developments.

A variety of accommodation is available through the Thredbo Alpine Resort Centre. Listings include private lodges, hotels, apartments, clubs and the Thredbo Alpine Hotel. The latter has the most luxurious facilities, including an outdoor heated swimming pool, gymnasium, conference facilities, bars and excellent views.

Traditionally, the resort has a very active nightlife. Many bars and restaurants are easily accessible given its small size and lack of snow and ice. And although it

separate resorts. Now, with the development of Australia's most extensive uphill lift system (30 lifts), Smiggins, a small resort for beginners, has been absorbed into the valley. Perisher Valley is a popular family spot. Luxurious and modern, it has over 120 kilometres of ski runs, 160 ski instructors and a lift capacity of over 29,000 skiers per hour. There are excellent wide-open intermediate to advanced runs which are well groomed to avoid excess moguls. Its lowest slopes are harnessed by many beginner T-bars. Over 15 hectares of snow-making system was recently installed to cater for the early period and tail-end of the season.

From 1987, a fast, efficient road/rail service will transport skiers into the heart of the resort. Jindabyne daytrippers and people visiting from Guthega and Thredbo will benefit most from the completion of the ski tube which will relieve traffic congestion from Jindabyne.

Accommodation at Perisher-Smiggins ranges from a large number of private clubs and large lodges to luxury hotels, some situated above the village.

Lift, lesson and hire prices are similar to those at Thredbo. Up-to-date prices, general information and booking procedures are available through the Perisher-Smiggins Information Centre.

Like the major Victorian resorts and Thredbo, Perisher-Smiggins has all the facilities of a small town, including a post office, bank, newsagent and shops.

3   **Mt Selwyn** is New South Wales' ideal beginners' resort. It offers the least expensive ski lessons, ski hire and lift facilities as well as few queues. Cross-country skiing lessons are also available.

An uncommercial style of resort, Mt Selwyn offers six beginners' rope tows and one poma, six T-bars, a takeaway restaurant and bar facilities, but there is no overnight accommodation. Transport to accommodation at Adaminaby and Cooma is available.

Mt Selwyn's top station has an elevation of 1,880 metres. This elevation allows for some intermediate skiing which will be increased by development in 1988, doubling the capacity of the resort by 1989. Mt Selwyn's lift tickets are among the most reasonably priced in New South Wales.

4   **Guthega** is extremely picturesque. It overlooks the famous Snowy River and is the only resort to face the Main Range. Mt Tate, Mt Townsend (Australia's second highest mountain) and Mt Kosciusko (the highest) are in direct view. The Snowy River runs past the village into Guthega Dam, which is part of the Hydro-electric Scheme. The dam is visible from the village.

Guthega was traditionally a private, secluded ski club area. It now has 250 beds in club lodges, but only 19 commercial beds in the village. A free shuttle-bus service, linked to accommodation, runs to and from Jindabyne. Car access is available throughout the season and a free sealed car park area is situated at the base of the lifts.

The height of the village is 1,640 metres. The lifts rise to 2,000 metres, offering gentle beginner slopes as well as intermediate and advanced skiing down sheltered trails. The resort has three T-bars, two J-bars and a double chairlift. A limit exists on the number of lift tickets sold daily. Consequently, no more than 1,800 people can ski in the area, which helps to retain the seclusion of the resort.

Guthega is becoming a popular snowboarding resort, with snowboards for hire and special learning areas set aside. Cross-country instruction is also available here from the ski school.

Compared with the other resorts, Guthega is an ideal family resort. It is small enough to be friendly and large enough to offer comprehensive ski facilities at a very reasonable cost. Up to 40 ski instructors are available for lessons. A family lift package, including lessons for each family member, is available.

5   **Mt Blue Cow**, Australia's highest and newest ski area, commenced operation during the winter of 1987. Accessible only by the 8.5-kilometre ski tube from Bullocks Flat Terminal or Perisher station, the resort is situated in the heart of the New South Wales snowfields. Both Guthega and Perisher can be spotted from high points at the resort.

Blue Cow has 80 hectares of ski terrain, with four quad lifts and one double chairlift. It has been independently assessed by an Austrian expert as 40% beginner, 40% intermediate and 20% advanced. Blue Cow claims to have the largest beginner run — off the Blue Calf Pass into Pleasant Valley through 1,400 metres of gentle wooded slopes. However, the advanced runs appear to be some of Australia's most challenging. The 'Kamikaze' has an incline of 45-50° for hundreds of metres. It is comparable to Perisher's Olympic run, but is much longer. Rumours abound that the trees growing at the back of the Blue Calf Mountain create a great natural slalom.

The slopes have been developed to maximise Blue Cow's aspect. As the majority of Australia's snow comes from the south, most of its slopes face in a southerly direction. They catch the sun from the early morning and are well positioned in a snow catchment basin to hold the snow longer into the season. Nearly all its runs are on the lee side of the harsh southerly winds that can plague other areas.

To ensure top skiing for everyone, Australia's biggest snow-making machine is being installed at Blue Cow. It has 70 snowguns up to 1.2 kilometres in length.

Perisher offers the closest accommodation, with Blue Cow linked to accommodation west of Jindabyne due to open in 1988.

Cross-country Skiing

6   The route between the two famous alpine points of **Kiandra and Kosciusko** has been called the quintessential Australian alpine excursion by experienced cross-country skiers, and it includes a variety of interesting scenery. In a nutshell, skiers start at Kiandra, then walk south, following the Great Dividing Range until they can go no higher. The trip of 100 kilometres can take up to ten days, depending on weather conditions, the skiers' skills and the time available. The required maps for this route are Khancoban 8525 — I and IV, and Mt Kosciusko 8525 — II and III. However, there are many variations on the exact route marked on these maps.

Starting at Kiandra and the goldfields, skiers follow Tabletops fire trail from Pollocks Gully near downtown Kiandra. Climbing Dunne's Hill, the trail takes skiers up and away from the treeless plains and along the crest of a broad ridge. Mt Tabletop remains hidden until skiers reach the top, as the tracks make a rising traverse along its eastern flank. The view from the top is spectacular, looking across to Bogong Peaks, and the Australian Capital Territory Alps to the north.

Diverging south, skiers descend to the prime

Young skiers wait their turn for the tow, above, and a group relax at their ski lodge after a day's activity

skiing country of the Happy Jack Plain and Happy Jack Creek, the lowest point of the trip. Skiers then move on to the Jagungal wilderness, Tibeaudo's Hut and the summit of Mt Jagungal, from where they can view the route in its entirety. Due south lies some of Australia's best ski-touring country. A succession of gentle up and gradual down slopes lead across to the lovely valleys of the Geehi River and Valentine Creek.

7 **Mt Jagungal** (an Aboriginal word meaning 'mother of the waters') is in the heart of New South Wales' best cross-country ski terrain. With good access, remote beautiful touring country and easy skiing, it provides the ideal opportunity for intermediate and advanced skiers to experience Australia's wilderness.

Access to the wilderness is available from Guthega Power Station, ten kilometres below Guthega resort. Skiers can make a comfortable base camp on the Jagungal Plateau, carrying daypacks to explore the region's rich variety of open valleys and mountains.

An alternative access is via Tibeaudo's Hut, which can also be included in the Kosciusko to Kiandra trip. This route follows a natural break in the terrain caused by the Doubtful River. Camp is pitched on the Geehi River, enabling a pleasant amble up the

south-eastern or southern faces. The run from the top of Jagungal is one of the best in the country. An interesting trip into Jagungal is across the Rolling Grounds from Guthega Ski Resort. But this is an area for experienced skiers only as it presents difficult navigation in bad weather. This route to Jagungal takes a leisurely three days and two nights.

Although there are some mountain huts in the Jagungal Wilderness, it is essential that all ski parties travel self-sufficiently with snow-camping equipment, as the mountain huts are often crowded and can be difficult to find.

8   The **Main Range** is the largest and highest alpine area. It is not unusual to ski in both early May and November if the season is good. The Main Range will have some beautiful ski conditions regardless of a poor season faced by the resorts. The ideal time for weather and snow quality is in spring from September to October.

The western side of the Main Range has varied and challenging cross-country downhill skiing. Long steep slopes of 30° and 700-metre descents are not uncommon, providing slopes as good as anywhere in Colorado or the Sierra Nevadas. The Main Range is very much the domain of the more experienced cross-country skier. Generally, metal-edged cross-country skis are advisable as conditions can become icy and dangerous. A feature of the area is the excellent views, south to Mt Bogong over 100 kilometres away, north over Cooma to the Brindabellas, and down into the green valleys of the Monaro sheep country.

There are a multitude of spots to ski. A day trip from Thredbo to Kosciusko is very popular with intermediate skiers, with the trip passing Lake Cootapatamba, along a pole line. A loop, from Guthega around Mt Tate and back to Guthega, is another enjoyable one-day trip. Many wooden refuge huts, once a common feature of the landscape, have now been demolished due to pollution problems. No hut accommodation is available on the Main Range and overnight snow camping is not encouraged near the glacial lakes due to the problems of pollution affecting their fragile ecology.

The Valentine to the Schlink Pass Run incorporates the Kerries Mountains, which is the classic route to the beginning of the Main Range. Schlink Pass marks the beginning of the final movement, with skiers climbing up the slopes that look across to stupendous views such as the precipitous Watsons Crags and the ice-gouged hollows of Blue Lake and Club Lake, and continuing up Mt Kosciusko.

9   **Perisher** attracts the majority of cross-country skiers, with most being interested in day trips or a few hours' cross-country skiing. Over 100 kilometres of marked and well-groomed trails spread out from the resort, ranging from a 2.5-kilometre loop to a ten-kilometre loop with trails up and around Rock Creek, routes through to Charlotte Pass, and access onto the Main Range.

Charlotte Pass, a small private resort above Perisher, provides the most direct route to the Main Range. In winter, it is accessible only by snowcat. In spring, skiers need a four-wheel drive or possibly a two-wheel drive in order to get to Charlotte Pass.

The length of time spent on the Main Range is as dependent on a group's knowledge of navigation and survival techniques as on basic experience in cross-country skiing and snow camping.

Victoria

Downhill Skiing

10   **Mt Buller,** situated three hours from Melbourne, is the biggest ski resort in the southern hemisphere and is Victoria's most popular place for downhill skiing. At peak season, busloads of daytrippers from Melbourne pack the already busy roads.

Buller is the last high country resort to the south. Steep and rugged, and rising to 1,800 metres, it stands alone, not overshadowed by any other mountains. All 360° of its slopes are skiable. Amongst its 400 hectares and 80 kilometres of designated runs, the faces have difficult black runs — the Bull Run, Federation and Fanny's Finish are renowned. The creeks, gullies and valleys running off the spurs offer some steep, tight trails and plenty of challenging intermediate skiing.

The village is close to the summit; at the end of the day, skiers catch the lifts back up to the top and ski

Cross-country skiers gain access to broad mountain faces and forests of snowgums

down small south-east facing runs back into the village. There are 23 lifts, with a capacity of 26,131 skiers per hour. Its accommodation capacity is 6,000. There are 80 full-time instructors.

Buller attracts a mix of families and individuals interested in weekend and week-long holidays. It has an excellent reputation for ski and après-ski fun. Typical of this après-ski atmosphere are restaurant bars such as The Alberg, which attracts the 14-20 year olds, and the Iva Whittaker (Ski Club of Victoria), which attracts a more sophisticated older clientele. The resort has all the facilities of a small town, including child-minding.

11 Falls Creek is an excellent family mountain resort and has the reputation of having the liveliest and best après-ski life. It has 52 ski runs and includes intermediate and advanced downhill ski runs on well-groomed slopes. Its 22 lifts, including the new quad chairlift, Haleys Comet, can carry a maximum of 2,799 people per hour. A snow-making machine has also been installed for the off-peak periods.

Nestled in a gully at 1,800 metres, the resort gives skiers the advantage of being able to ski in and out of the lodges during winter. Accommodation is similar in price and variety to Mt Buller, Thredbo and Perisher. Budget accommodation of all kinds is available at the sub-alpine village of Mt Beauty, 40 minutes away. Mt Beauty has restaurants, ski-hire facilities, a modern shopping centre and a regular bus service up to Falls.

Air, coach and car package tours, which include accommodation, hire, food and lessons, usually offer the very best value for new skiers and the skiing family.

12 Mt Hotham is the third largest Victorian ski resort (bed capacity, 1,707) and boasts some of the best and least crowded beginner slopes in Australia, as well as some of the most challenging, such as Snake Gully. The resort has three chairlifts, two T-bars and three pomas. It is an excellent base for cross-country skiing.

In 1987, the new Heavenly Valley ski area opened at the top end of Mt Hotham. This extension has increased Hotham's skiing area to 40 hectares, and the area boasts Australia's largest fixed-grip quad chairlift, with a capacity of 2,400 people per hour.

Rental, lift tickets and accommodation are marginally cheaper than in the larger resorts and Mt Hotham is also slightly less crowded.

At 1,840 metres, it is the highest resort in Victoria. Unlike the other resorts in the state, its lodges are romantically situated on the snowpeaks, with trails running down through the village to the lifts and slopes. At the end of the day, skiers catch the lifts back up to their lodges. A free shuttle service, consisting of vehicles called zoo carts, zips around the village to the beginner, intermediate and advanced ski runs as well as through the après-ski spots, the commercial centre and the ski clubs.

13 Mt Buffalo is the site of Australia's first ski lift and it remains an excellent beginners' resort. Day tickets are the cheapest anywhere in Australia, giving access to well-groomed slopes, one chairlift, one T-bar

A lone cross country skier in the Snowy Mountains

and two pomas. The highest lift point is 1,610 metres. The ski school offers lessons for intermediate as well as beginners.

Mt Buffalo is a much smaller resort than Hotham, Buller or Falls Creek. Accommodation exists for 80 people in bunk or motel-style rooms. The Tatra Inn complex at the resort includes bars, lounges, ski rental and retail outlets.

Cross-country Skiing

14 The most spectacular trip in Victoria may well be a tour on **The Bluff**, near Mansfield, and for many it is the heart of the High Country. The scenery is magnificent. *The Man from Snowy River* film was made in Mansfield and featured stunning scenes of the Bluff/Mt Howitt area. Since 1835, when horsemen ranged these remote Victorian Alps, it has had an ongoing association of history and romance. Their hardiness and courage have passed into folklore and maps today read of Mt Despair, The Terrible Hollow, Ratcamp, Mt Lovick, King Billy and Mt Eadley Stoney, paying tribute to some of the high country's sagas.

The Bluff, only two and a half hours from Melbourne and half an hour east of Mt Buller, is one of Australia's unexplored treasures. It is a plateau which on its north face is a 600-metre cliff. A walking track across the top provides views up to 100 kilometres away — virtually to Melbourne — across to Mt Bogong, down to Baw Baw, and right into the Mt Buller ski fields.

The summit of the Bluff is 1,737 metres. Access is difficult without the guidance of a tour company as it involves a four-wheel drive or a climb up the cliff face.

The Bluff Hut, nestled at 4,630 metres in a saddle overlooking the Howqua Valley and Mt Buller, was originally carried up the treacherous face of the Bluff on horses. It appears very rustic, but its facilities and bunk-style sleeping are quite adequate and very warm. It is sometimes occupied by ski-touring groups. Many exciting day trips, east along Mt Howitt or over the Bluff, can be made from this base.

Experienced cross-country skiers can seek valuable direction and advice from local residents, the Stoney family. They have been connected with the High Country for generations. Father and son rode in *The Man from Snowy River*, and provided advice and direction on the region's spectacular environment. For those with little or no experience of touring, they offer one of the most enjoyable introductions to cross-country skiing in the country. Utilising the old huts for overnight stays and supplies, skiers need only carry a daypack. Participants are divided into several groups, depending on ability, and they meet for picnics at spectacular spots. On longer tours, they are introduced to rudimentary snow camping.

15 Victoria's best-known area for cross-country skiing is the **Bogong High Plains**. It is now nearly 100 years since Bogong Jack roamed the region, but the legend of this well-to-do English horse thief, after whom the plains were named, lives on. He disappeared when he was discovered to be an expert thief, but some cross-country skiers and cattlemen believe his ghost lives on in the wilderness of these High Plains and beyond. Situated in the 40,000 hectares of Bogong National Park, the Bogong High Plains rise to 1,524 metres and encompass Falls Creek and Hotham.

Undulating rolling hills with untracked snow make for easy advanced and intermediate skiing. Beginners are advised to learn on the well-groomed ski trails around the villages of Falls Creek and Hotham.

Once in the High Plains, the Alpine Walking Track between Mt Hotham and Mt Bogong provides a popular trail. The trail begins near Mt Kosciusko at Tom Groggin and traverses the entire Victorian Alps.

Australia's skiing infrastructure has grown enormously in recent years, with many long-range chairlifts and expanded runs

The full trip takes several weeks. For those going part of the way, the track through East Gippsland, called the Walhalla, has marker poles and is quite popular.

The trip from Mt Bogong to Hotham is reserved for experienced skiers. One locally owned commercial operator in the area offers a leisurely seven-day tour along the trail. It takes many side trips, climbs Mt Bogong and skis lots of steep gullies.

Mt Bogong is very exposed, being Victoria's highest peak (1,986 metres). Its ascent has become a favourite and challenging route for experienced cross-country skiers. It includes a ten-kilometre ski along a ridge called the Bogong Massif, a 2,134-metre climb, followed by a 1,220-metre drop and another climb. To descend onto the High Plains again, skiers follow another part of the Alpine Walking Track and Dwane Spur.

The Tawanga huts are a great attraction. The earliest were built in the 1850s by cattlemen and

While downhill skiing has enjoyed a continued surge in popularity, cross country skiiers are especially blessed by Australia's gigantic snowfields and unique flora and fauna that make it a world class destination for the nordic skiing enthusiast.

drovers and have since been partly rebuilt. Perhaps the most famous, Wallace Hut, was built in 1869 and is now classified by the National Trust. It has an earth floor, a shingle roof and a rugged, old-style atmosphere. Nestled in the valleys surrounded by snowgums, cross-country skiers stay in the huts in emergencies or as an alternative to snow caves or tents. Some tour groups have access to particular huts. In winter, these huts cannot be relied on and must be viewed as emergency ski shelters only.

16 The small downhill ski resort of **Mt Buffalo** is now attracting as many cross-country as downhill skiers to its surrounding plateau. Some 60% of the Buffalo plateau has good cross-country ski trails marked on gentle and undulating slopes, making the area ideal for beginners.

Although it is four hours from Melbourne, Buffalo's attraction is greater than the closer beginner resorts as it is much higher and more beautiful. Its trails run through forests of snowgums, mountain ash and woolly butt — so named because its stringy bark peels and curls down to the treebase. One tour group runs a snowshoe tour through the forests and its neighbouring landscape of granite boulders. This area is spectacular but difficult terrain for cross-country skiers due to the bushes and trees underfoot.

17 **Mt Baw Baw** is a small downhill as well as cross-country ski resort, with a lift capacity of 6,000 skiers per hour and ski runs up to the plateau. The edge of Baw Baw resort is excellent for cross-country skiing. Situated two and a half hours from Melbourne, Baw Baw is the best beginners' area within day-tripping distance of the city. Skiing into the plateau, beginners will find many interesting marked trails.

Across the plateau is a well-marked trail to the neighbouring village of Mt St Gwinear, which is a very popular cross-country skiing destination. Ski-touring instruction and snow camping trips are provided by a well-established locally based company.

18 **Lake Mountain** is situated one and a half hours' drive from Melbourne. This is ideal beginners' territory and suitable for day trips. Recent developments have created extensive ski trails which are easy and enjoyable to follow — an energetic skier can cover its 25 kilometres of trails in one day.

The resort can become very busy at the weekend. It is advisable, therefore, to go further north to Baw Baw Plateau or Mt Sterling if skiers wish to ski unguided along marked resort trails.

The elevation is low. Lake Mountain has its best snow during the peak season of July and August.

Tasmania

Skiing in Tasmania is not a predictable activity, since snow cover cannot be guaranteed, and the anticipated July to September season can extend for as little as six weeks. However, visitors to Tasmania may like to take their chances during the season, as skiing here, when it is available, is excellent.

19 **Ben Lomond,** 60 kilometres east of Launceston, is Tasmania's largest resort which caters for beginners and intermediate skiers. Facilities at the ski village have recently been improved and the 1987 season saw the completion of six lodges, enabling skiers to stay at the resort rather than travel from Launceston each day. The slopes here have both poma and T-bar tows, and equipment hire is available at the resort. For those travelling from Launceston, special transportation can be arranged. Cross-country skiing is also possible in this area.

20 **Mount Field National Park,** situated just 70 kilometres west of Hobart, is the ski centre for the southern region. Also catering for beginners and intermediate skiers, the Mt Mawson area of the park offers three rope tows and one poma lift for beginners. Accommodation on the mountain itself is only available to lodge members, but huts, camping facilities and caravan parks are located nearby.

The Mt Mawson area is perhaps better equipped for cross-country skiing. When snow conditions are good, cross-country fans will enjoy the beautiful scenery and solitude of a day out on the ranges.

Equipment and clothing hire services are available both on the ski slopes and from outlets in Hobart. Accommodation at both Tasmanian resorts is limited, so bookings should be made in advance.

An exciting moment in one skier's day!

The Australian Adventure

Skiing Contacts

Operators

New South Wales

Two organisations that provide ski-holiday packages are:

Alpine Tours International
Suite 7, Wallaceway Shopping Centre
Cnr Orchard & Endeavour Streets
Chatswood
Sydney NSW 2067
Ph. (02) 411 1033

Sydney Snow Centre
4th Floor
74 Pitt Street
Sydney NSW 2000
Ph. (02) 231 1444

1 Thredbo

The Thredbo Centre
Level 2
49 Market Street
Sydney NSW 2000
Ph. (02) 268 2681 (Inquiries)

Thredbo Alpine Village
PO Box 92
Thredbo NSW 2627
Ph. (064) 57 6360 (Bookings)

Bookings for the Thredbo Alpine Hotel, the most luxurious accommodation in the Thredbo Valley, can be made with the above agency.

2 Perisher/Smiggin Holes

Perisher/Smiggins Resort Centre
Perisher Valley NSW 2630
Ph. (064) 57 5211 (Inquiries)

World Travel Headquarters (Bookings)
Sydney   Ph. (02) 237 0300
Melbourne Ph. (03) 602 2855
Adelaide   Ph. (08) 212 2655
Perth   Ph. (09) 322 2133
Brisbane   Ph. (07) 221 3744

The Wildhaus
This alpine chalet has established a reputation as one of the most luxurious chalets in the Perisher/Smiggins resort. Excellent cuisine, fine facilities and live entertainment make this a worthwhile place to stay. Bookings can be made through Alpine Tours International.

See above for details

3 Mt Selwyn

Mt Selwyn Ski Resort
PO Box 363
Tumut NSW 2720
Ph. (064) 54 9488 (Inquiries)
Ph. (069) 47 1849 or
    (064) 52 1108 (Bookings)

4 Guthega

Guthega Resort
Guthega NSW
Ph. (064) 57 5333

Jindabyne Reservation Centre
Ph. (064) 56 2457 (Bookings)

5 Mt Blue Cow

Blue Cow Ski Resort & Skitube
Bullock's Flat
Alpine Way
Jindabyne NSW 2627
Ph. (064) 56 2010 or 57 5444

6 Kiandra to Kosciusko

Wilderness Expeditions
Wilderness Expeditions, the Snowy Mountains specialist, offers a nine-day Kiandra to Kosciusko cross-country ski tour for experienced skiers only. Departing from Cooma, the trip takes you from Kiandra and allows time for side excursions to Mt Jagungal and Mt Townsend before reaching Mt Kosciusko and, finally, Thredbo. The package includes instruction and guiding and all snow camping equipment.

26 Sharp Street
Cooma NSW 2630
Ph. (064) 52 1587

100 Clarence Street
Sydney NSW 2000
Ph. (02) 29 1581

World Expeditions
Although their 'Historic Huts of the High Country' tour does not cover the entire Kiandra to Kosciusko route, the five-day itinerary explores the Mt Tabletop/Kiandra region and makes use of the huts along the way. The tour is for experienced skiers only.

3rd Floor
377 Sussex Street
Sydney NSW 2000
Ph. (02) 264 3366

7 Mt Jagungal

Kosciusko Expeditions
A five-day ski tour from Kosciusko Expeditions takes cross-country skiers of moderate ability into the Jagungal wilderness area on a snow camping trip. A base camp is set up below Mt Jagungal and day trips are made to various locations. Although previous experience is necessary, further instruction is given along the way.

PO Box 72
Jindabyne NSW 2627
Ph. (064) 56 2458

Peregrine Adventures
An eight-day Jagungal ski tour departs from Khancoban and utilises a base camp in the Jagungal area, from which day trips are made. The trip is graded as intermediate, and experienced instructors help to perfect your technique and style, as well as teach the basics of snow camping and survival.

1st Floor
117 York Street
Sydney NSW 2000
Ph. (02) 264 6033

Wilderness Expeditions
This Jagungal tour is of seven days' duration and also uses a base camp for day trip exploration of the region. Previous snow camping and ski touring experience is required, but further instruction is given on the tour.

See (6) above for details

8 Main Range

Kosciusko Expeditions
Kosciusko Expeditions offers a variety of trips that take in the main range. Lodge-based beginners' five-day courses, intermediate weekend courses and snowcraft courses all take place in this area.

See (7) above for details

Peregrine Adventures
Wildtrek/Peregrine offers a six-day ski tour, based at the Alpine Hideaway Lodge, which explores some remote areas of the range. The tour is aimed at beginners and intermediate-level skiers.

See (7) above for details

Wilderness Expeditions
One of Wilderness Expeditions' many trips into the mountains takes in touring of the main range. This is a three-day itinerary, for skiers of a moderate grade, which includes (weather permitting) visits to Mt Kosciusko and Mt Townsend. Instruction and all snow camping equipment are provided.

See (6) above for details

World Expeditions
Their 'Snowy Lakes and Summits' trip is a weekend tour of the main range. Using a base camp, extended tours are made into the region and there is an opportunity for some cross-country downhill skiing. Participants must have completed a beginners' course before joining this trip.

See (6) above for details

9   Perisher Area

Most of the operators listed in (6), (7) and (8) above visit this area.

Victoria

Two organisations that provide ski-holiday packages are:

Life. Be in it! Tours
12 Claremont Street
South Yarra
Melbourne VIC 3141
Ph. (03) 241 1066

Wanderers Ski Holidays & Travel
3rd Floor, Wales Corner
227 Collins Street
Melbourne VIC 3000
Ph. (03) 654 6144 or 654 6879

10   Mt Buller

Mt Buller Ski Resort
Mt Buller VIC 3723
Ph. (057) 77 6052

11   Falls Creek

Falls Creek Ski Resort
Falls Creek VIC 3699
Ph. (057) 58 3224 or 58 3280

12   Mt Hotham

Mt Hotham Ski Resort
Ski Tours
PO Box 140
Bright VIC 3741
Ph. (057) 59 3508 (Inquiries)
Chalet accommodation
Ph. (057) 59 3636 (Bookings)

Foard at Dinner Plain
This luxurious 40-bed lodge is a new development in the Mt Hotham area. Set in the Snowgum Village complex, the lodge has been well-designed and tastefully furnished to accommodate both downhill and cross-country skiers, and provides civilised living in the snow.

PO Box 61
Omeo VIC 3898
Ph. (051) 59 6455

13   Mt Buffalo

Mt Buffalo Ski Resort
Victour Travel Centre
230 Collins Street
Melbourne VIC 3000
Ph. (03) 619 9444

Mt Buffalo Chalet
This Edwardian building, with its magnificent views, provides the most colourful accommodation at Mt Buffalo. Log fires, hearty meals and evening entertainment are special features of a stay at the Chalet, which is owned by Victour.

PO Box 76
Porepunkah VIC 3740
Ph. (057) 55 1500

14   The Bluff

The Bluff is the special province of High Country Adventures, owned by the Stoney family. Ski tours to the area range from two to five days and are all hut-based. Beginners are welcome on all trips and special groups can be catered for. Sleeping bags and clothing are available for hire.

PO Box 287
Mansfield VIC 3722
Ph. (057) 75 2212

15 Bogong High Plains

Bogong Jack Adventures
Bogong Jack is a local organisation specialising in the Bogong High Plains region. They offer a large range of instructional and touring trips into the area that vary in length from weekends to seven days. Their six-day 'Grand Ski Tour' of the High Plains is the ultimate exploration of the area and is for experienced skiers only. Snowshoeing is also available on a day or weekend basis.

PO Box 209
Wangaratta VIC 3677
Ph. (057) 21 2564

Peregrine Adventures
Peregrine also offers a six-day Bogong High Plains Trip. This tour utilises a base camp and spends the first two days improving participants' skills. Tours are then made to Mt Cope, Mt Jim and other scenic spots around the area. The trip is suitable for both beginners and intermediates.

Suite 9A, 9th Floor
343 Little Collins Street
Melbourne VIC 3000
Ph. (03) 602 3066

Roadknights High Country Guides
This organisation is another local operator, based at Tawonga, just north of the Bogong area. Using their Mountain Creek Centre, a modern lodge/camp complex of pine log construction, day and half-day ski tours are made into the Bogong High Plains. Snowshoeing trips are also available, and downhill skiers can be catered for.

Mountain Creek Centre
Mountain Creek Road
Tawonga VIC 3697
Ph. (057) 57 2257

World Expeditions
Departing from Mt Beauty, their five-day Bogong tour is graded as 'difficult' and is for experienced skiers only. Both mountain huts and snow camps are used for accommodation and some of the most remote areas of the High Plains are explored. Participants must be able to carry a 15-20 kilogram pack.

Suite 602
Wellesley House
126 Wellington Parade
East Melbourne VIC 3002
Ph. (03) 419 2333 or 419 2920

16 Mt Buffalo

Bogong Jack Adventures
Bogong Jack also operates tours into the Mt Buffalo area, not far from their base at Wangaratta. The most interesting is a one-day snowshoeing tour that follows trails amongst forests of alpine ash and snowgums with beautiful views to the valleys below. The tour is suitable for novices.

See (15) above for details

17 Mt Baw Baw and Mt St Gwinear

Peregrine Adventures
The Mt St Gwinear area is the scene for a weekend ski touring course that is ideal for beginners. Lodge accommodation is provided and all the basic techniques of nordic skiing are taught. All accommodation and meals are included and ski gear can be hired at additional cost.

See (15) above for details

Smith's Skinny Skis
This organisation is the Mt St Gwinear and Baw Baw specialist, and offers a range of beginners' and more advanced courses as well as ski tours into the region. Snow camping and navigational skills courses are also available for the more experienced skier. Trips range from one to four days.

PO Box 196
Churchill VIC 3842
Ph. (051) 22 2430 or 22 1718

18 Lake Mountain

Cross Country Ski Schools are operated at the resort by the Management Committee.

Lake Mountain Committee of
 Management
46 Aitken Street
Alexandra VIC 3714
Ph. (057) 72 1633 or (059) 62 3242

Tasmania

19 Ben Lomond

Ben Lomond Alpine Village and
 Ben Lomond Creek Inn
Ben Lomond National Park TAS 7212
Ph. (003) 72 2444 (Inquiries)

Tasbureau
Cnr Paterson & St John Streets
Launceston TAS 7250
Ph. (003) 32 2101 (Bookings) or phone any Tasbureau Office.

20 Mt Field

Skigia and Sport
213 Elizabeth Street
Hobart TAS 7000
Ph. (002) 34 6503

Sitzmark Lodge (Accommodation and
 hire)
Mt Field National Park
Westerway TAS 7140
Ph. (002) 88 1166

Tasbureau
80 Elizabeth Street
Hobart TAS 7000
Ph. (002) 30 0211 (Bookings) or phone any Tasbureau Office.

Information Sources

Australian Ski Federation (ASF)
Olympic Park
Swan Street
Melbourne VIC 3000
Ph. (03) 429 8066
Ph. (03) 878 6333 (ASF Nordic Committee)

New South Wales

NSW Ski Association
Sports House
157 Gloucester Street
Sydney NSW 2000
Ph. (02) 241 1581

NSW Nordic Ski Club
PO Box A683
Sydney South NSW 2000

Victoria

Victorian Ski Association
PO Box 210
South Melbourne VIC 3205
Ph. (03) 699 3292 or 690 3537

Ski Touring Association of Victoria
GPO Box 20A
Melbourne VIC 3001
Ph. (03) 329 2262

Tasmania

Ben Lomond Ski Association
C/- 15 Brisbane Street
Launceston TAS 7250
Ph. (003) 31 1312

Southern Tasmanian Ski Association
GPO Box 1197M
Hobart TAS 7001

Ski Council of Tasmania (Cross-country
 Division)
C/- 1/3 Alroy Court
Rosetta
Hobart TAS 7010

The National Parks and Wildlife Services in New South Wales, Victoria and Tasmania can also provide valuable information for skiers. (See National Parks Contacts section for addresses and phone numbers.)

State Tourism Information Centres

Listed below are the contacts for the major offices of all State Tourism Information Centres. These offices can provide detailed information on the various regions within their states and territories, and also act as booking agents for many of the adventures.

New South Wales

New South Wales Travel Centres:

Cnr Pitt & Spring Streets
Sydney NSW 2000
Ph. (02) 231 4444

Wodonga Place
Hume Highway
Albury NSW 2640
Ph. (060) 21 2655

Pacific Highway
Tweed Heads NSW 2485
Ph. (075) 36 2634

353 Little Collins Street
Melbourne VIC 3000
Ph. (03) 67 7461

7th Floor, TAA Building
144 North Terrace
Adelaide SA 5000
Ph. (08) 51 3167
(Representatives for South
Australia and Western Australia)

Cnr Queen & Edward Streets
Brisbane QLD 4000
Ph. (07) 229 8833

Australian Capital Territory

Canberra Tourist Bureaux:

Jolimont Tourist Centre
Northbourne Avenue
Canberra City ACT 2601
Ph. (062) 45 6464

64 Castlereagh Street
Sydney NSW 2000
Ph. (02) 233 3666

247 Collins Street
Melbourne VIC 3000
Ph. (03) 654 5088

Ground Floor
Allendale Square
77 St George's Terrace
Perth WA 6000
Ph. (09) 325 1533

Victoria

Victour Offices:

230 Collins Street
Melbourne VIC 3000
Ph. (03) 619 9444

192 Pitt Street
Sydney NSW 2000
Ph. (02) 233 5499

Jolimont Centre
Northbourne Avenue
Canberra City ACT 2601
Ph. (062) 47 6355

Trafalgar Centre
126 Collins Street
Hobart TAS 7000
Ph. (002) 31 0499

16 Grenfell Street
Adelaide SA 5000
Ph. (08) 51 4129

56 William Street
Perth WA 6000
Ph. (09) 481 1484

221 Queen Street
Brisbane QLD 4000
Ph. (07) 221 4300

Tasmania

Tasbureau Offices:

80 Elizabeth Street
Hobart TAS 7000
Ph. (002) 30 0211

Cnr Paterson & St John Streets
Launceston TAS 7250
Ph. (003) 32 2101

129 King Street
Sydney NSW 2000
Ph. (02) 233 2500

5 Canberra Savings Centre
City Walk
Canberra ACT 2600
Ph. (062) 47 0070

256 Collins Street
Melbourne VIC 3000
Ph. (03) 653 7999

32 King William Street
Adelaide SA 5000
Ph. (08) 211 7411

100 William Street
Perth WA 6000
Ph. (09) 321 2633

217 Queen Street
Brisbane QLD 4000
Ph. (07) 221 2744

South Australia

South Australian Government
Travel Centres:

18 King William Street
Adelaide SA 5000
Ph. (08) 212 1644

143 King Street
Sydney NSW 2000
Ph. (02) 232 8388

25 Elizabeth Street
Melbourne VIC 3000
Ph. (03) 614 6522

C/- Vintage Holidays
13/14 Mezzanine Floor
Wesley Arcade
93 William Street
Perth WA 6000
Ph. (09) 481 1268

Western Australia

Holiday WA Centres:

772 Hay Street
Perth WA 6000
Ph. (09) 322 2999

92 Pitt Street
Sydney NSW 2000
Ph. (02) 233 4400

35 Elizabeth Street
Melbourne VIC 3000
Ph. (03) 614 6833

108 King William Street
Adelaide SA 5000
Ph. (08) 212 1344

2nd Level Capita Building
307 Queen Street
Brisbane QLD 4000
Ph. (07) 229 5794

Northern Territory

Northern Territory Government
Tourist Bureaux:

31 Smith Street Mall
Darwin NT 5790
Ph. (089) 81 7899

Ford Plaza
Todd Mall
Alice Springs NT 5750
Ph. (089) 52 4711

89 King Street
Sydney NSW 2000
Ph. (02) 235 2822

35 Ainslie Avenue
Canberra City ACT 2601
Ph. (062) 57 1177

415 Bourke Street
Melbourne VIC 3000
Ph. (03) 67 6948

93 Liverpool Street
Hobart TAS 7000
Ph. (002) 34 4199

9 Hindley Street
Adelaide SA 5000
Ph. (08) 212 1133

62 St George's Terrace
Perth WA 6000
Ph. (09) 322 4255

48 Queen Street
Brisbane QLD 4000
Ph. (07) 229 5799

Queensland

Queensland Government
Travel Centres:

196 Adelaide Street
Brisbane QLD 4000
Ph. (07) 833 5337

75 Castlereagh Street
Sydney NSW 2000
Ph. (02) 232 1788

25 Garema Place
Canberra City ACT 2601
Ph. (062) 48 8411

257 Collins Street
Melbourne VIC 3000
Ph. (03) 654 3866

10 Grenfell Street
Adelaide SA 5000
Ph. (08) 212 2399

55 St George's Terrace
Perth WA 6000
Ph. (09) 325 1600